THE CAMBRIDGE COMPANION TO

ANCIENT GREEK LAW

This companion volume provides a comprehensive overview of the major themes and topics pertinent to ancient Greek law. A substantial introduction establishes the recent historiography on this topic and its development over the past thirty years. Many of the twenty-two chapters, written by an international team of experts, deal with procedural and substantive law in classical Athens, but significant attention is also paid to legal practice in the archaic and Hellenistic eras; areas that offer substantial evidence for legal practice, such as Crete and Egypt; the intersection of law with religion, philosophy, political theory, rhetoric, and drama; as well as the unity of Greek law and the role of writing in law. The volume is intended to introduce nonspecialists to the field as well as to stimulate new thinking among specialists.

Michael Gagarin is James R. Dougherty, Jr. Centennial Professor of Classics at the University of Texas, Austin. He has been president of the American Philological Association and the Classical Association of the Middle West and South and has written widely in the areas of Greek law, rhetoric, literature, and philosophy. He is the author, most recently, of *Antiphon the Athenian: Oratory, Law and Justice in the Age of the Sophists*.

David Cohen is Professor of Classics and Rhetoric at the University of California, Berkeley. He is the Director of the UC Berkeley War Crimes Studies Center and an Adjunct Fellow at the East-West Center. Dr. Cohen has published widely in the areas of Greek law, comparative legal history, and contemporary international humanitarian law. He received the Historical Research Prize from the Historisches Kolleg, Munich.

The Cambridge Companion to
Ancient Greek Law

Edited by

Michael Gagarin
University of Texas, Austin

David Cohen
University of California, Berkeley

CAMBRIDGE UNIVERSITY PRESS
Cambridge, New York, Melbourne, Madrid, Cape Town, Singapore,
São Paulo, Delhi, Dubai, Tokyo, Mexico City

Cambridge University Press
The Edinburgh Building, Cambridge CB2 8RU, UK

Published in the United States of America by Cambridge University Press, New York

www.cambridge.org
Information on this title: www.cambridge.org/9780521521598

© Cambridge University Press 2005

This publication is in copyright. Subject to statutory exception
and to the provisions of relevant collective licensing agreements,
no reproduction of any part may take place without the written
permission of Cambridge University Press.

First published 2005

A catalogue record for this publication is available from the British Library

Library of Congress Cataloguing in Publication Data

The Cambridge companion to ancient greek law /
edited by Michael Gagarin, David Cohen.
p. cm.
Includes bibliographical references and index.
ISBN 0-521-81840-0 (hard cover) – ISBN 0-521-52159-9 (pbk.)
1. Law, Greek. I. Gagarin, Michael. II. Cohen, David (David J.) III. Title.
KL4106.5.C36 2005
340.5'38 – dc22   2004023792

ISBN 978-0-521-81840-7 Hardback
ISBN 978-0-521-52159-8 Paperback

Cambridge University Press has no responsibility for the persistence or
accuracy of URLs for external or third-party internet websites referred to in
this publication, and does not guarantee that any content on such websites is,
or will remain, accurate or appropriate. Information regarding prices, travel
timetables, and other factual information given in this work is correct at
the time of first printing but Cambridge University Press does not guarantee
the accuracy of such information thereafter.

Contents

List of Contributors		*page* ix
Preface		xiii
Introduction DAVID COHEN		1

PART 1: LAW IN GREECE

1	The Unity of Greek Law MICHAEL GAGARIN	29
2	Writing, Law, and Written Law ROSALIND THOMAS	41
3	Law and Religion ROBERT PARKER	61
4	Early Greek Law MICHAEL GAGARIN	82

PART 2: LAW IN ATHENS I: PROCEDURE

5	Law and Oratory at Athens S. C. TODD	97
6	Relevance in Athenian Courts ADRIAAN LANNI	112
7	Differentiated Rhetorical Strategies in the Athenian Courts LENE RUBINSTEIN	129
8	The Role of the Witness in Athenian Law GERHARD THÜR	146

9	Theories of Punishment DAVID COHEN	170
10	The Rhetoric of Law in Fourth-Century Athens HARVEY YUNIS	191

PART 3: LAW IN ATHENS II: SUBSTANTIVE LAW

11	Crime, Punishment, and the Rule of Law in Classical Athens DAVID COHEN	211
12	Gender, Sexuality, and Law EVA CANTARELLA	236
13	Family and Property Law ALBERTO MAFFI	254
14	Athenian Citizenship Law CYNTHIA PATTERSON	267
15	Commercial Law EDWARD E. COHEN	290

PART 4: LAW OUTSIDE ATHENS

16	The Gortyn Laws JOHN DAVIES	305
17	Greek Law in Foreign Surroundings: Continuity and Development HANS-ALBERT RUPPRECHT	328
18	Greek Law in the Hellenistic Period: Family and Marriage JOSEPH MÉLÈZE MODRZEJEWSKI	343

PART 5: OTHER APPROACHES TO GREEK LAW

19	Law, Attic Comedy, and the Regulation of Comic Speech ROBERT W. WALLACE	357
20	Greek Tragedy and Law DANIELLE ALLEN	374

Contents

21 Law and Political Theory   394
    JOSIAH OBER
22 Law and Nature in Greek Thought   412
    A. A. LONG

    Bibliography   431
    Index Locorum   457
    General Index   475

LIST OF CONTRIBUTORS

DANIELLE ALLEN is Dean of the Division of Humanities and Professor of Classics, Political Science, and the Committee on Social Thought at the University of Chicago. She is author of *The World of Prometheus: The Politics of Punishing in Democratic Athens* (2000) and *Talking to Strangers: Anxieties of Citizenship since Brown v. Board of Education* (2004) and is working on issues of leadership in late fifth- and early fourth-century Athens.

EVA CANTARELLA is Professor of Roman Law at the University of Milan Law School, where she also teaches ancient Greek law. Among her more than 100 publications are *Pandora's Daughters: The Role and Status of Women in Greek and Roman Antiquity* (1986), *Bisexuality in the Ancient World* (1993), and *Ithaque: De la vengeance d' Ulysse à la naissance du droit* (2002).

DAVID COHEN is Professor of Classics and Rhetoric at the University of California, Berkeley. He is the Director of the UC Berkeley War Crimes Studies Center and an Adjunct Fellow at the East-West Center. He has published widely in the areas of Greek law, comparative legal history, and contemporary international humanitarian law and received the Historical Research Prize of the Historisches Kolleg, Munich. His books include *Theft in Athenian Law* (1983), *Law, Sexuality and Society: The Enforcement of Morals in Classical Athens* (1992), *Law, Violence and Community in Classical Athens* (1995), and *Intended to Fail: Trials before the Jakarta Ad Hoc Human Rights Court* (2003).

EDWARD E. COHEN is Professor of Ancient History (adjunct) at the University of Pennsylvania and Chief Executive Officer of Atlas America, a leading U.S. producer and processor of natural gas. Among his books are *Ancient Athenian Maritime Courts* (1973), *Athenian Economy and Society: A Banking Perspective* (1992), and *The Athenian Nation* (2000).

LIST OF CONTRIBUTORS

JOHN DAVIES, FBA, is Emeritus Professor of Ancient History and Classical Archaeology at the University of Liverpool. Apart from his books *Athenian Propertied Families* (1971: 2nd edition in preparation) and *Democracy and Classical Greece* (1978: 2nd ed. 1993), his work has focused largely on the economic, social, cultic, and administrative history of classical and Hellenistic Greece.

MICHAEL GAGARIN is the James R. Dougherty, Jr. Centennial Professor of Classics at the University of Texas. He has written widely in the areas of Greek law, rhetoric, literature, and philosophy, including *Drakon and Early Athenian Homicide Law* (1981), *Early Greek Law* (1986), *The Murder of Herodes* (1989), and *Antiphon the Athenian: Oratory, Law and Justice in the Age of the Sophists* (Austin, TX 2002).

ADRIAAN LANNI is an Assistant Professor at the Harvard Law School.

A. A. LONG is Professor of Classics and Irving Stone Professor of Literature at the University of California, Berkeley. His most recent book is *Epictetus: A Stoic and Socratic Guide to Life* (2002), and he is the editor of *The Cambridge Companion to Early Greek Philosophy* (1999).

ALBERTO MAFFI is Professor of History of Roman Law at Milano-Bicocca State University. He has written numerous books and articles on Greek and Roman law, including *Studi di epigrafia giuridica greca* (1983). He is the founder and editor of *Dike*, a journal of Greek and Hellenistic legal history.

JOSEPH MÉLÈZE MODRZEJEWSKI is Professor Emeritus of Ancient History at the Sorbonne and Professor of Papyrology and Ancient Legal History at the École Pratique des Hautes Études. In 1971, along with H. J. Wolff and A. Biscardi, he founded the Society for the History of Greek and Hellenistic Law (Gesellschaft für griechische und hellenistische Rechtsgeschichte), which sponsors a series of Symposion meetings. He has written extensively on the history of the Hellenistic world, ancient legal history, Greek papyrology and Greco-Roman Egypt, and the history of Judaism in the Second Temple period. His next book (forthcoming, in French) is on Greek law after Alexander.

JOSIAH OBER is David Magie Professor of Classics at Princeton University and holds a joint appointment in the University Center for

Human Values. His books include *Fortress Attica* (1985), *Mass and Elite in Democratic Athens* (1989), *The Athenian Revolution* (1996), *Political Dissent in Democratic Athens* (1998), and most recently *A Company of Citizens* (2003). His current research focuses on the circulation of technical and social knowledge within democratic societies.

ROBERT PARKER is Wykeham Professor of Ancient History in the University of Oxford. He has written *Miasma: Pollution and Purification in Early Greek Religion* (1983), *Athenian Religion: A History* (1996), and *Polytheism and Society at Athens* (2005).

CYNTHIA PATTERSON is Associate Professor of History at Emory University in Atlanta, Georgia. She is the author of *Pericles' Citizenship Law of 451/0 B.C.* (1981), *The Family in Greek History* (1998), and articles on aspects of Greek family and social history.

LENE RUBINSTEIN is Reader in Ancient History in the Department of Classics, Royal Holloway, University of London. She is the author of *Adoption in IV Century Athens* (1993) and *Litigation and Cooperation: Supporting Speakers in the Courts of Classical Athens* (2000) and has contributed chapters on the city-states of Aiolis and Ionia to the Copenhagen Polis Project. She is currently working on the institution of the volunteer prosecutor in the Greek world outside Athens in the classical and early Hellenistic periods.

HANS-ALBERT RUPPRECHT is Professor of Papyrology on the Law Faculty at the University of Marburg. Among his many publications on law in the Greek papyri are *Studien zur Quittung im Recht der graeco-ägyptischen Papyri* (1969) and *Kleine Einführung in die Papyruskunde* (1994). In addition he is editor of the posthumous work of Hans Julius Wolff, *Das Recht der griechischen Papyri Agyptens in der Zeit der Ptolemaeer und des Prinzipats vol. I* (2002) and, since 1976, the *Sammelbuch griechischer Urkunden aus Agypten*.

ROSALIND THOMAS is Ancient History Fellow at Balliol College Oxford. Among her many works on literacy and orality in the Greek world are *Oral Tradition and Written Record in Classical Athens* (1989) and *Literacy and Orality in Ancient Greece* (1992). She has recently published *Herodotus in Context: Ethnography, Science and the Art of Persuasion* (2000) and is currently working on Greek historiography.

LIST OF CONTRIBUTORS

GERHARD THÜR is Professor of Roman Law and Ancient Legal History in Graz, Austria, and Chairman of the Kommission für Antike Rechtsgeschichte at the Austrian Academy of Science. He works mainly on Greek procedural law and (with Hans Taeuber) published *Prozessrechtliche Inschriften Arkadiens* in 1994. A second edition (in English) of his first book, *Beweisführung vor den Schwurgerichtshöfen Athens: Die Proklesis zur Basanos* (1977), is in preparation.

STEPHEN C. TODD is Reader in Classics at the University of Manchester. Among his many studies of Athenian law and oratory is *The Shape of Athenian Law* (1993). He is currently preparing a multivolume commentary on the speeches of Lysias.

ROBERT W. WALLACE, Professor of Classics at Northwestern University, is the author of *The Areopagos Council, to 307 B.C.* (1989) and numerous articles in the field of Greek law, chiefly on questions pertaining to the regulation of personal conduct. He has also published in the fields of Greek history and the politics of Greek music theory.

HARVEY YUNIS is Professor of Classics at Rice University. He is author of *Taming Democracy: Models of Political Rhetoric in Classical Athens* (1996) and editor of a commentary on Demosthenes' *On the Crown* (2001) and of *Written Texts and the Rise of Literate Culture in Ancient Greece* (2003).

Preface

When Beatrice Rehl at Cambridge University Press first approached me with the idea of editing a Companion to Ancient Greek Law, I thought it would be a large undertaking. Now, as I look back over the five years it has taken to bring the project to completion, I see that the work has far outgrown my initial idea, just as in recent years the study of Greek law itself has grown well beyond its traditional boundaries. My co-editor, David Cohen, and I have enlisted the help of eighteen other authors from different countries and different schools of thought, and yet, even with the very generous amount of space Cambridge has allowed us, there are many fine scholars and worthy subjects that we have had to omit. Nonetheless, we hope readers will find the ensuing chapters as rich and interesting as it has been a rewarding experience for us to assemble them.

After our initial work together on the conception and composition of the volume, David and I took on separate tasks. In addition to writing two chapters, David's main contribution was the Introduction to the volume – a fascinating and quite personal account of the changing nature of scholarship on Greek law during the last quarter century. My own contribution, in addition to my two chapters, has been the more mundane editorial work of compiling bibliographies, copyediting, and nagging contributors to meet deadlines. All important decisions, however, have been made by David and me together.

Through all of this Beatrice Rehl has provided exceptionally useful advice, unfailing encouragement, and strong support. Her firm but always reasonable hand has guided our work throughout. She and her entire staff at Cambridge have been a pleasure to work with. I would also like to thank Jess Miner for her help translating two chapters from German. Finally, I would like to acknowledge the help of research funds from the University of Texas at Austin that enabled me to hire Luis Salas to compile the Index Locorum.

Michael Gagarin, January 2005

INTRODUCTION

David Cohen

When Michael Gagarin and I first met in Berkeley in the mid-1970s, we were the only two scholars (both at the very beginning of our careers) in the United States who thought of their academic specialization as "Greek law." At that time Douglas MacDowell was the only British scholar with such an established specialization. In other words, the study of Greek legal history was a largely continental European enterprise, and it was traditionally dominated by German, and secondarily French and Italian scholars. The composition of the contributors to this volume testifies to the dramatic changes to this field of study in the last twenty-five years. This is due to a variety of factors, including the decline in interest in most areas of pre-modern legal history in countries such as Germany that were once the bedrock of the discipline, as well as the marked increase in interest among British and American scholars. The majority of the contributors to the volume are thus British and American because this is where in recent years there has been the greatest amount of scholarly interest. Although the most eminent and established senior figures in Greek legal studies include many Europeans (represented here by Cantarella, Maffi, Rupprecht, Modrzejeweski, and Thür), a younger group of Anglo-American scholars (not all of whom, of course, figure in this volume) are rapidly making their mark on this discipline. In selecting the contributors for this volume, Michael Gagarin and I tried to represent the wide variety of approaches and subject matter areas that characterize Greek law scholarship. We also deliberately included both the most senior and some of the newest and most promising researchers (such as Allen, Lanni, Rubenstein, Thomas, Todd, and Yunis), as well as distinguished individuals, such as A. A. Long and Robert Parker, whose areas of specialization lie outside of Greek law, but whose expertise can fruitfully be brought to bear on important topics of central concern in our field. Our aim was to provide the reader with not only a broad and intensive introduction to the field, but also a sense of where it is going, a sense of the exciting variety of intellectual and disciplinary perspectives that are increasingly being brought to bear in studying Athenian and other Greek legal systems. We have thus included essays representing a number of traditional approaches, as well as some that push the boundaries of the field.

Along with the shift in the center of gravity away from traditional centers such as Germany and toward the United States and England, there has been an even more important change in the presuppositions about what Greek law is and how one ought to study it. The advent of Anglo-American scholars has brought a variety of new perspectives and methodologies to the field. New questions are being asked, neglected sources used, and comparative and theoretical perspectives brought to bear on Greek legal institutions. This is in significant part because of the simultaneous intellectual growth of the disciplines of classics and legal, social, and cultural history. Scholars with a whole new set of questions, methods, and research agendas have turned their attention to Greek legal institutions. They have revolutionized and enriched the field through their efforts, and we hope that our selection of contributors provides the reader with a sense of the excitement and innovation that now characterize much of the work being done in this field. This expansion of scholarly activity has also, as one might expect, been accompanied by the growth of a much larger audience for scholarship in this area. Thirty years ago scholarship regarding Greek law, with the exception of handbooks like the one written by MacDowell,[1] was published in specialist journals and scarcely read outside of a fairly narrow circle of researchers. Today, no longer the province of a handful of specialists, Greek law has increasingly been recognized as vital for an understanding of a whole range of political and social institutions in ancient Greece. This can most clearly be seen, for example, in studies of gender and sexuality, ancient democracy, politics and political theory, social conflict, and so on. At the same time, sources such as the Athenian legal orations, which were once scarcely read except by Greek law specialists, have now been recognized as being of central importance for the study of Athenian social, political, and cultural history.

One of the most welcome developments, in my opinion, has been the demise of orthodox paradigms for the study of Greek law. In the 1970s the field appeared to be divided between two approaches: a

[1] MacDowell (1978).

INTRODUCTION

majority of continental European scholars, for the most part trained in law, who focused largely on technical doctrinal questions, following the model of civil (and Roman) law jurisprudence; and a much smaller group of British classicists, with little knowledge of legal theory or substantive law, who concentrated largely on procedural and institutional issues. In retrospect these differences now seem less important than they once did because both schools of thought now stand in far greater contrast to the variety of approaches that have exploded the boundaries of the study of Greek legal history in recent years. There is now no dominant paradigm, and the result is that questions previously neglected are now being explored and older issues once thought resolved are being reexamined by a wide range of perspectives, many of which draw on the methods and insights of other disciplines. Whereas disputes in Greek law once tended too often to focus on stale controversies and arid disputation of narrow doctrinal questions, now lively and multifaceted debate swirls around fundamental questions of Greek legal practice and institutions and their relation to broader political and social frameworks. Such controversies are only to be welcomed and encouraged, and the reader of this volume, the editors hope, will emerge with a sense of the way in which such discussions are expanding the contours of this field of inquiry.

As a way to explore further some of these issues of scope and method, as well as to provide the reader with a context for what is to follow, we now turn to an overview of some of the contributions to this volume and the questions the authors raise.

In the opening chapter, "The Unity of Greek Law," Michael Gagarin addresses one of the oldest controversies in Greek law, which involves some of the most basic questions defining our field of study, such as, "What is Greek law?" Continental scholars had once largely assumed a fundamental unity of Greek legal institutions across the Greek world. Challenged in the 1950s by Moses Finley to justify this assumption in light of a good deal of evidence that suggested the contrary, these scholars retreated from the notion of unity of institutions to a more limited view of an underlying unity of basic ideas.[2] Gagarin argues that Finley's view vis-à-vis continental scholars was correct: There was no "Greek law" in terms of common underlying legal ideas and basic principles of substantive law. Gagarin resumes Finley's critique, showing how in the area of marriage and inheritance there are fundamental differences among the laws of various Greek cities, differences significant enough to

[2] See Gagarin for references.

render the idea of any common underlying fundamental conceptions (*Grundvorstellungen*) meaningless.[3] More importantly Gagarin suggests the way in which the idea of this unity is largely the product of, or made possible by, our lack of evidence for other Greek legal systems: "The more detailed our knowledge, the more clearly the differences stand out." This underscores major methodological problems that remain to be explored; as the contributions of Rupprecht and Mordzejeweski in this volume show, there are still many influential adherents to the unity thesis. In the Anglo-American world, however, the overwhelming tendency is to speak of "Athenian law" or the law of particular *poleis* when referring to legal doctrines or institutions.

Gagarin also shows that what is ultimately at stake in such debates – and this is vitally important – is the desire to use what we do know to reconstruct what we do not.[4] Scholars have attempted to use the idea of Greek law to reconstruct the huge gaps in our knowledge about cities other than Athens. Using Greek evidence as well as analogies from modern American law, Gagarin shows the folly of attempting to do so.

Having properly indicated the way in which we can now regard this issue as settled, Gagarin then moves the discussion to a new level. He advances a provocative and interesting claim that places the question of Greek law in a new perspective. He suggests that although there is no *substantive* Greek law, there may well be underlying common ideas in the realm of procedure, understood in the broadest terms as legal process. He makes the highly original and important claim that one of these underlying procedural notions has to do with the way in which trials in Greece, in contrast with many other premodern legal systems, consisted of litigants freely presenting their cases "as they saw fit." Another claim focuses on the way in which Greek legislators readily acknowledged the notion of "gaps" in the laws because they saw the role of judges as "filling in" what was required to do justice in individual cases. This, he suggests, is in stark opposition to legal systems that believe that gaps must at all costs be avoided and seek to deny the "lawmaking" capacity of judges. These are very large claims that will require a lot of comparative research both inside and outside of ancient Greece to explore.[5] As always, Sparta, which did not have a system of written

---

[3] See also my analysis of *hierosulia*, which reaches the same conclusion based on an examination of all the evidence concerning the crime of "theft of sacred property" (1983: Chapter 4).

[4] See also D. Cohen (1989, 1991) on these methodological issues.

[5] The contrast with civil law systems oriented toward comprehensive codifications is useful, but these same issues have been hotly debated in many such jurisdictions. The Swiss Civil

laws, may prove an obstacle to acceptance of the universality of such ideas.

What is important here, however, is that Gagarin has refocused the debate in an extraordinarily useful way. Here we see, in strong contrast to the state of the discipline a few decades ago, the way in which contemporary scholarship has moved us beyond the aridity of earlier debates about the "unity of Greek law." What Gagarin suggests here is that we focus instead on the features of the "Greek" way of thinking about *how law functions and is practiced* in a polis. This suggests that the Greek attachment to what Gagarin calls "procedure broadly understood," and, to my mind, might be more aptly labeled as legal process, has to do with the distinctive forms of political organization that characterized Greece in the age of the polis. In the challenge that this bold thesis presents, and in the way in which it can be addressed only through comparative legal historical studies, Gagarin has opened the door to the "Greek law" debate of this century.

Rosalind Thomas's chapter, "Writing, Law, and Written Law," shows the way in which the contributions of social and cultural historians have enriched the study of Greek legal traditions. It also provides an example of how far the study of Greek law has come in the past few decades. Thomas is perhaps the leading expert on literacy and writing in ancient Greece. Building on her work on the role of written texts and literacy in the development of political institutions, she addresses here important questions about the nature of written law, its connection to political and social developments in archaic and classical Greek *poleis*, and the relationship between written and unwritten law.

Above all, Thomas shows how important it is to understand legal developments, such as the introduction of written laws, in the political and social context. This may seem evident to some, but to legal historians used to thinking of the legal system as having an autonomous life of its own, this point is anything but obvious. For this reason, and because of general advances in our understanding of the impact of the introduction of writing and literacy, Thomas's work goes well beyond earlier scholarship on the nature and importance of written law in archaic and classical Greece.

Thomas argues that, "the writing down of law was probably undertaken in a variety of ways by different city-states for rather varied

---

Code, enacted early in the twentieth century, for example, provides that a judge who refrains from deciding a case because of the silence or insufficiency of the law fails in his fundamental duty as a judge.

purposes; depending on politics and context, such written laws did not have identical implications everywhere." Examining the variety of evidence (much of it fragmentary) that we have for the legal traditions of different *poleis*, she demonstrates how the adoption of written legislation was connected to fundamental political and social changes that transformed the archaic polis. The innovation of written statues seems often to come at times of crisis or institutional reform. In such situations the device of writing down the law may, depending on the political setting, serve to limit or underscore the power of officials and rulers.

Even more important from a comparative legal historical standpoint is Thomas's discussion of the nature of early Greek legislation and its relation to unwritten laws or norms. Thomas points out that the introduction of written laws builds on preexisting traditions and norms. In deference to modern, positivistically oriented lawyers, she is hesitant to label such norms as "laws" even though the Greeks had a clear conception of "unwritten laws." We need not be so deferential to the quibbles of legal philosophers, however, because legal anthropology and comparative legal history have shown clearly enough that elaborate legal systems can function in the absence of written codes. In any event, one of Thomas's central insights is that written statutes appear often to have been introduced to solidify and make permanent innovations or resolutions or controversial points: "This brings us to the probability that for most communities the laws which went up in writing were particularly special: these were not the ones agreed by all, but the contentious ones, the rules which constantly caused trouble...." Although David Daube had made the same argument about early Roman and Biblical codifications, his contribution on this crucial issue has too often been ignored and has scarcely had any impact on historians of Greek legal institutions.[6] Thomas's analysis of particular cases of early codification reveals how crucial it is to look at the broader social and political context of legal innovation.

Thomas's chapter, then, is a vivid illustration of the way in which the flourishing of Greek social and cultural history has in turn produced nothing less than a minor revolution in the study of Greek legal history. Without the advances in our understanding of the introduction of writing and the nature and scope of ancient literacy, this nuanced and rich account of the introduction of written legislation would not have been possible. Likewise, it is Thomas's authoritative understanding of these issues that enables her to sketch the relation between written and

---

[6] See D. Daube (1947, 1973).

INTRODUCTION

unwritten law in a way that goes far beyond earlier discussions and to demonstrate how, from this perspective, "this new idea of written law may even have represented the first use of official writing by the early polis, and it is not surprising to find that these early groups attempt to set apart the law in as many special ways as possible in an attempt to give it an authority it might not otherwise have.... It was radical new laws which needed this kind of protection rather than the traditional customs and rules of a community."

In "Law and Religion" Robert Parker explores the different dimensions of the relation of law and religion in Greece. As the preeminent scholar of Athenian religion he is ideally suited for such a task. His study reflects the development in our understanding of the institutional framework of Greek religious practice and of its integral connection to the political institutions of the polis. It also shows, like Thomas's contribution, the way in which "nonspecialists" in Greek law have become increasingly sophisticated in dealing with legal issues and texts, as well as with the relation of legal issues to the broader social, cultural, and political context.

It is apt that Parker deals at length with the important contribution of the German philologist, Kurt Latte, to our understanding of the sacral element in legal process. Like Latte, Parker is not a specialist in Greek law, but also like Latte he has read widely in comparative legal history. His grounding in this subject and other relevant disciplines has also enabled him to go considerably beyond Latte in important respects, for example, by seeing the limitations of the evolutionary theories of law implicit in Latte's account of the development of oaths and the like. Both scholars show how classical scholars and ancient historians can, if they acquire a solid-enough understanding of legal institutions, use their own extraordinary specialist expertise, in this case in religion, to make a unique contribution to the understanding of aspects of Greek legal tradition and practice.

In Chapter 4, "Early Greek Law," Michael Gagarin takes on another large and fundamental issue. The history of early Greek law is an enormously fraught subject to which generations of scholars have devoted their learning and ingenuity. The same is true of early Roman, Germanic, and English law, for example, because the origins of most premodern legal systems are cloaked in the obscurity of historical eras for which little reliable evidence exists. The study of the early developments in legal systems thus raises serious substantive and methodological questions. In regard to the earliest period of Greek law (defined in this chapter as ca. 700–500 B.C.) these questions have to do with issues such as the literary nature of the sources; questions, in the case of Homer, as to what extent they refer to actual legal institutions and of what historical period; how to interpret and generalize from isolated and fragmentary evidence; how to counter the "evolutionist" tendency to use what we know of later periods to reconstruct what developments "must have" been like; and how to deal with the very large temporal gaps in our sources in this period and the implications they have for attempts to trace institutional "continuities" into later periods.

Traditionally, scholars of Greek law have been reluctant to confront these methodological problems, in significant part because such a methodological critique seems to threaten our ability to say anything about the legal institutions of this period of which we know so little. Scholars often admit that any conclusions must be "speculative" but then expend enormous energy arguing for and against such speculations. The history of the scholarship on topics such as the trial scene depicted on the shield fashioned by the god Hephaestus for Achilles (*Iliad*, 18.497–508) bears ample witness to this tendency. Although there is still a pressing need for many such methodological issues to be more fully addressed, some contemporary historians of early Greek institutions have made considerable advances in taking them into account.[7] In regard to early Greek law, the development of Michael Gagarin's work in this area demonstrates how much progress has been made.

Gagarin is the leading modern scholar of this difficult and arcane area of Greek legal history. His chapter on the topic demonstrates that awareness of methodological difficulties does not preclude drawing important conclusions from the evidence we have. Developing themes he also discusses in his chapter on the unity of Greek law, Gagarin shows how the Greek understandings of dispute resolution and legal process eschew formalistic legal ritual in favor of oral proceedings in which litigants and judges are relatively free to present and decide the case as they see fit. Gagarin sees the "two aspects of early Greek law – written legislation and oral procedure" – as "an unusual combination, unlikely to be the result of influence from some other legal system. Rather, I would suggest, both aspects exemplify the Greek tradition of open, public debate and discussion among a large segment of the community." In my view such conclusions are based on a sober assessment of what the limited evidence we have can and, more significantly, *cannot* tell us. Gagarin engages at some length Gerhard Thür's interpretation of the shield of Achilles. A comparison of their approaches reveals how vitally important

---

[7] On methodological issues in Greek law, see D. Cohen (1989).

Introduction

such methodological awareness is, for Thür's seemingly almost total lack of concern for methodology leads him to extreme and untenable conclusions that Gagarin has little difficulty demolishing. It is perhaps not unfair to generalize here by claiming that to a significant degree (though by no means completely) the greater concerns for methodological issues characterize contemporary Anglo-American scholarship on Greek law in comparison with its continental counterpart.

Another merit of Gagarin's approach raises a different serious methodological issue that has engaged not only legal historians but also the wider historical disciplines. This concerns the use of comparative evidence from other legal systems. Gagarin rightly rejects the so-called comparative method as employed by earlier major figures in Greek legal history such as Louis Gernet, Hans Julius Wolff, Kurt Latte, and, more recently, Gerhard Thür. This method, rooted in unexamined presuppositions ultimately derived from nineteenth-century social evolutionist theories, proceeded from the starting point that comparative evidence can be used to reconstruct the legal institutions of early Greece because, "that in matters legal the human mind is so constructed as to seek similar solutions for similar situations under analogous conditions, needs no justification" (Wolff 1946: 35). Modern scholarship in anthropology, social theory, historiography, and other disciplines has more than adequately revealed the glaring inadequacies of such approaches. In the rest of his chapter Gagarin provides an example of how comparative evidence from, for example, Near Eastern legal systems may fruitfully be employed, not as an evolutionary "model" on which to base "reconstructions" but rather as an analytical tool. Drawing on the important differences between early Greek and Near Eastern approaches to legal process, Gagarin arrives at the important hypothesis that

> From the beginning, Greek law conforms to this Greek tendency toward openness and public debate that some (e.g., Lloyd 1979) have seen as the root of Greek intellectual achievements. And as it grew during the archaic period, Greek law maintained this productive combination of fixed, stable, written legislation together with an oral, dynamic process for settling disputes that will persist in Athens right through the classical period.

In Chapter 5, "Law and Oratory at Athens," Stephen Todd lucidly emphasizes the participatory and oral nature of Athenian litigation. He explores the role of the orators in this system where litigants were, at least in principle, expected to prepare and present their own cases. This participatory, democratic characteristic, he points out, extends also to the lay judges who are expected to reach decisions without conferring and without any instruction in the law by legal experts. Todd largely confines himself to an elucidation of the differences among the orators, the tradition that led to the corpus we now possess, and the role of the logographer, or speechwriter, in Athenian litigation. Although earlier scholars like Wolff looked at legal advocacy, one of the distinguishing features of contemporary Anglo-American scholarship on Athenian law has been ever greater attention to the rhetorical and performative dimensions of Athenian trials, as well as to the crucial importance of rhetoric as an organizing category for both forensic oratory and legal thought.

In "Relevance in Athenian Courts" Adriaan Lanni, guided by a lawyer's understanding of the dynamics of ancient and modern litigation, uses the issue of relevance to raise some of the most important and most controversial questions in contemporary Greek law scholarship. Traditionally, scholars of Greek law had measured Athenian trials by the standards (frequently idealized) of contemporary legal systems and often found them wanting. Athenian orators too frequently "perverted" the legal process by rhetorical appeals to emotion or irrelevant facts and issues. The "better" advocates, in this view, stuck closer to the case at hand and thus displayed a commitment to the rule of law. This view has come under attack in recent years, provoking a wide range of responses from the community of Greek law scholars.[8] The main thrust of the critique was to suggest that before criticizing Athenian trials against some modern criterion, we ought to ask how the Athenians themselves understood the purposes, nature, and legitimate scope of the trial and of the kind of justice it sought to achieve. Seen from this perspective, Athenian trials may seem very different from their modern counterparts, but this is not because selfish demagogues or unscrupulous orators distorted the legal process but rather because the Athenian judges and litigants in this participatory system had very different expectations about what a trial was and how legal justice should be conceived. Such interpretations have roused the ire of scholars who want to defend Athenian courts as committed to the rule of law, which in their opinion apparently consists in confining the trial to the relevant legal and factual issues.[9] But

---

[8] For the critique, see Osborne (1985), Ober (1989), and D. Cohen (1991, 1995, 2003). For the response, see Lanni's lucid exposition of the various positions and her bibliography.

[9] See, e.g., Harris (1994), Rhodes (2004).

INTRODUCTION

what did Athenian judges, as opposed to modern classicists, think was relevant? Why should we assume that there is a universal standard of relevance in legal argumentation? This is the crucial question that such scholars have too often overlooked or sidestepped. Lanni's chapter ably addresses this crucial nexus of the issue.

Lanni advances a very powerful and well-documented argument in favor of an approach that accepts the idea that Athenian judges saw their role as arriving at context-specific decisions based on considerations that might seem irrelevant in modern Western adjudication. Apart from her incisive analysis of three major categories of "irrelevant" arguments that Athenian judges apparently did find relevant, she adduces another very compelling consideration in favor of her position: In the homicide and maritime courts Athenians did apparently adopt far more restrictive standards of relevance. This shows that such notions were by no means unknown to them, but that they did not find them appropriate for the kind of litigation conducted before the regular courts:

> ... [I]n the vast majority of cases Athenian jurors produced largely ad hoc decisions, as a wide variety of extra-legal material was considered relevant and important to reaching a just verdict tailored to the particular circumstances of the individual case. In this respect, the Athenian courts were both more and less removed from modern courts than is commonly believed: the legal system cannot be characterized as embodying a rule of law, but the participants nevertheless viewed the process as aiming for recognizably "legal" rather than social ends. The Athenians' distinctive approach to relevance in the popular courts reflects a highly individualized and contextualized notion of justice.

One might, however, go a step further here by inquiring what participants in the legal system of democratic Athens considered to be the "rule of law"? There is little question that they saw themselves as committed to and generally upholding the rule of law on which, in their opinion, their democracy depended. The crucial point here, however, is that unlike Lanni they did not conceptualize "legal" and "social ends" as standing in opposition to one another.[10] It is their understanding of the

---

[10] See Cohen (1995: Chapters 3 and 9) for an account of this "democratic" conception of the rule of law and its connection to judgment in particular cases and the perceived interests of the demos.

way in which the interests of the demos and the rule of law intersect that produces what Lanni rightly calls a "highly individualized and contextualized notion of justice." In response to Lanni's critics, who will rush to present examples of cases where there is considerable attention to the legal issues at hand, one must point out that of course not every case was treated in the same way. Orators and litigants exploited the rhetorical opportunities that each case, viewed in its particular social and institutional context, presented. In some cases this would dictate a strategy whereby a party (we normally only have one side of the case so we cannot know to what extent an opponent responded "in kind") would focus on legal and factual matters that seem relevant by modern standards. But, as Lanni aptly points out, in many trials they did not, and the vast majority of extant cases include some such material. One must take care here not to presuppose that all cases must be explained according to one paradigm or that we are dealing with an absolute opposition between the rule of law and social interests. As I have attempted to argue elsewhere, this is certainly not the case.

This debate, in which Lanni's chapter represents a major contribution, again shows the way in which Greek law as a discipline has developed in recent years. Rather than focusing on narrow doctrinal or procedural issues as in the dominant mode of scholarship prior to the 1980s, a vibrant debate here addresses the very nature of the Athenian legal system, seen from the standpoint of *legal process* rather than formal legal structures. This debate inevitably engages fundamental issues concerning our understanding of Athenian democracy and its conceptions of law and justice, as well as raising important questions of political philosophy and legal theory. One can only hope that debate on these unresolved issues continues, as it offers, as demonstrated in Lanni's chapter, rich opportunities for reexamining a variety of legal issues as well as basic questions of what it means to do justice before the law, whether in the world of classical Athens or our own.

The increased sensitivity to the rhetorical dimensions of Athenian litigation forms the basis of the contribution of Lene Rubinstein. Her chapter on differentiated rhetorical strategies in the Athenian courts examines the way in which rhetorical strategies depended to a significant degree on the type of procedural rubric under which a trial proceeded. Greek law scholars have paid considerable attention to the multiplicity of actions from which litigants might choose to prosecute certain kinds of wrongs they claimed to have suffered. Although earlier Greek law scholarship tended to view these categories rather rigidly, in recent years scholars have shifted to a less formalistic interpretation, which emphasizes the similarities in the way in which public and private actions were conducted. This has been a welcome change from previous approaches that tried to make sense of the basic Athenian distinction between public and private actions by matching them up against modern notions of criminal and civil actions. The increased recognition of the consequences of the fact that both kinds of actions depended completely on the initiative of private citizens, from the filing of a suit through the trial itself, has led to a far better understanding of the participatory and democratic nature of the Athenian legal system and of the role this multiplicity of actions played within it. Rubinstein adds to this understanding by showing how different kinds of legal rubrics in turn defined the rhetorical situation of the trial in varying ways and thus demanded appropriate rhetorical responses. Although this point may seem at first glance obvious, it has not always been sufficiently appreciated that particular kinds of rhetorical appeals were by their nature more appropriate in some legal settings than in others. Rubinstein looks at three such contexts in particular and shows that "the strategic deployment of the arguments on anger, punishment, and the educational role of the court was context sensitive and that the type of case that the litigant was fighting had a clear influence on his method of pleading." Again, thinking through the consequences of the centrality of rhetorical performance in Athenian trials results in a better understanding of the factors that shaped those trials as legal events and of legal practice itself.

The rhetorical turn in scholarship on Athenian law has also influenced scholars who follow more traditional approaches. Gerhard Thür, for example, a leading expert on the law of evidence in Athens, acknowledges to a much greater extent now than he did in his book on the subject some twenty-seven years ago the need for understanding the rhetorical context and techniques at work in particular cases.[11] His chapter in this volume on the role of witnesses in Athenian law shows how important such an increased awareness can be for considering the role of witnesses in particular cases. Thür's chapter provides a fine demonstration of the kind of traditional methodology in Greek law, also characteristic of a previous generation of scholars such as Harrison, Hansen, and MacDowell, which emphasizes detailed technical exposition of legal norms and, more particularly, procedures.[12] Anglo-American methodologies have largely evolved in the direction of looking at legal process in its social and cultural historical context, informed by comparative

---

[11] Thür (1977).
[12] See, e.g., Harrison (1968, 1971), Hansen (1975, 1976), and MacDowell (1963, 1978).

evidence drawn from social history, anthropology, and the practices of other historical and contemporary legal systems.

The contrast between such approaches and those of traditional Greek law scholarship appear quite vividly in the final part of Thür's chapter (Section III), where he briefly considers a few of the different kinds of treatments of witnesses produced by Anglo-American scholars in recent years.[13] One senses here the attempt to communicate across a methodological divide that cannot easily be bridged. One has the same sense when reading earlier treatments by the traditional scholars just mentioned against many of the essays on similar subjects in this volume. One can see quite clearly here the distance that Greek legal studies have traveled in the past twenty years or so. This is not to deny the value of the approaches of such traditional scholarship. They are still vitally important, and any student of Greek law has an enormous amount to learn from a careful reading of such texts. The important point is that thirty years ago such traditional approaches were overwhelmingly dominant, whereas today our field of study benefits from an extraordinarily wide variety of theoretical, methodological, historiographical, and intellectual orientations (whether explicit or implicit).

Harvey Yunis' chapter on "The Rhetoric of Law in Fourth-Century Athens," raises issues that would in all likelihood not have been addressed at all a few decades ago. To the extent that legal scholars of previous generations concerned themselves with the question of rhetoric, the focus would either have been on advocacy, understood in something like a Roman law sense, or on examining formal rhetorical techniques. Yunis represents an approach to Athenian law that has benefited greatly from the kind of recent scholarship, like that of Josiah Ober, that has taken a fresh look at Athenian democracy and emphasized the role of rhetoric and the practices of the law courts in the way that democracy worked.[14] Such treatments of Athenian democracy proceed from an orientation informed by political and social theory, sociology, and anthropology and have revitalized the study of this topic about which many scholars once believed that little new was left to say. Contemporary students of Athenian law were quick to adapt such orientations to the study of legal institutions by showing their embeddedness in a democratic political culture defined by participatory institutions on the one hand and the recognition of the power of persuasive speech

---

[13] Humphreys (1985), Todd (1990), D. Cohen (1995: Chapter 8), and Rubinstein (2004), to which one might add Osborne (1985, 1990) and Todd (1993).
[14] See Ober (1989) and Yunis (1996).

(rhetoric) on the other. Yunis here presents a view of fourth-century Athenian law that, in contrast to earlier approaches, emphasizes *practices* over institutional structures and formal norms and shows the way in which those practices are shaped by participatory democracy and the rhetorical political culture of which they were a part. For Yunis this involves, for example, examining trials as rhetorical contests and showing how the rhetorical construction of the twin goals of doing justice in the case at hand and serving the interests of the demos produced a distinctive notion of the democratic rule of law.

Eva Cantarella is one of the most important figures in modern Greek law scholarship. Her work spans the full range of approaches of the past three decades, always staying at the cutting edge of the discipline. Her oeuvre grows out of rigorous juristic, but nonetheless literarily refined, treatments of Homeric law and the law of homicide in the 1970s and proceeds to the thoroughly interdisciplinary studies of women, sexuality, and gender for which she is best known today. Surpassing previous Italian scholarship by figures like Paoli and Biscardi, Cantarella, together with her colleague and student Alberto Maffi, has made Milan the most important center in contemporary continental Europe for Greek law scholarship. Although Italian scholars of Athenian law once looked to Germany for inspiration, the direction of creative energy has in recent years been reversed as the traditional German interest in Greek (and for that matter Roman) legal history has waned.

As demonstrated by her magisterial survey in "Gender, Sexuality, and Law" from Homer to fourth-century Athens, Cantarella's approach is characterized by enormous erudition coupled with an intimate familiarity with the most recent developments in gender studies in a wide variety of disciplines. The study of gender and sexuality, apart from the pioneering work by Kenneth Dover,[15] was neglected even longer in the study of Greek law than in many other areas of historical research. Beginning in the 1980s, however, a substantial body of work, in which Cantarella was an important innovative force, turned to such questions and began to examine systematically the role and status of women and the legal regulation of sexuality in Athens and elsewhere in the Greek world. Building on insights from gender theory and anthropology, Cantarella situates her account within a framework defined by the application of social construction theory to the law: "In other words, the law is gendered, and at the same time engenders society: on

---

[15] Dover (1978).

the one hand it reflects the social construction of sexual roles, on the other it reinforces this construction."

Moving with ease through the wide range of sources from Homer onward, Cantarella shows how the earliest literary tradition defined women as "a different race, indeed: for the Greeks, women were the otherness which one could not comprehend. And like everything that is incomprehensible, women – unless tamed by marriage – were dangerous." From this starting point she develops a powerful argument to show how the earliest known Athenian legislation, the laws of Draco, incorporated such a conceptualization of women, "transforming the social stereotype into a legal classification which had fundamental legal consequences on women's life." In the remainder of the chapter she traces out how this classification shaped the way women were treated in the full range of legal contexts, ranging from adultery and rape to the law of property, marriage, and inheritance. Although her approach is deeply informed by feminist scholarship and perspectives, she avoids the extreme positions taken by some scholars by virtue of the balance, independence, and open-mindedness with which she approaches the sources and the secondary literature. For example, on the much discussed issue of the legal status of women, she rejects the widespread, but utterly mistaken, position that women's legal status was like that of slaves and children.[16] She recognizes that although Athenian women could not participate in political institutions, they were, in fact, citizens and that this status had important legal and political consequences. Making an important distinction, too often overlooked by some scholars, Cantarella concludes that, "In other words, they had the *status*, but not the functions of citizens.... After a decree passed in 450 by Perikles, their status of citizens (as *astai*) became a condition for the citizenship of their children."

In Cantarella's work on gender and sexuality, as is well-represented by her contribution to this volume, one can see how the study of Greek legal institutions has progressed from a marginal and esoteric subdiscipline of classical scholarship to being a powerful tool for examining basic questions of Greek society and politics. Law, of course, is a central societal institution, and legal history should address such questions rather than confine itself to the study of doctrinal and procedural questions as if they were independent of larger social and cultural contexts. Nowhere is this more true than at classical Athens, where there were no specialized legal institutions that, as at Rome, attempted to define

---

[16] For perhaps the most blatant example of this interpretation, see Sealey (1990).

for themselves an independent realm for the juristic imagination to develop.

Although closely associated with Cantarella in Milan, Alberto Maffi's scholarship has been, for the most part, more traditional in its approach. Over the past two decades Maffi has produced a wide range of detailed and rigorous studies of aspects of Athenian private law. Taken together, this oeuvre represents one of the most significant contributions to our understanding of the law of the family and property. It is a token of the changes in our discipline that in an earlier period such work would have found its place in the central core of Greek legal studies, whereas today Maffi is one of relatively few major scholars whose research concentrates in this area. This makes his unique expertise that much more valuable in reminding us of the importance of understanding the legal norms and practices that shaped Greek economic life. He has also made a fundamental contribution through his many methodological essays surveying the state of contemporary Greek law scholarship. In this volume, largely eschewing interdisciplinary methods or comparative analysis, Maffi's broad overview of family and property law, based on his mastery of the sources of Athenian law, concentrates on doctrinal analysis of major features of the laws of marriage, inheritance, ownership, and property. As such it provides an indispensable introduction and overview to these important areas of private law.

Cynthia Patterson is the leading expert on the Athenian law of citizenship. Thanks to many years of fruitful research on the family, marriage, and gender in classical Athens, she is also the person most able to put the study of citizenship law into the context of Athenian constitutional, political, and social developments from the sixth to the fourth centuries B.C. This is precisely what she does in her chapter on Athenian citizenship law, which provides the best available treatment to date of this complex topic. As an exemplar of recent interdisciplinary scholarship on Greek law, the chapter also shows how central the institution of citizenship is to an understanding of the development of Athenian democracy. But Patterson also shows that Pericles' famous "citizenship law" (excluding from citizenship those not born of two citizen parents) is only one part of the "law of citizenship" in Athens, and that it, and other legal provisions, can be understood only in relation to the way in which Athenian society reacted to the momentous changes of the fifth and fourth centuries.

Her lucid analysis proceeds from a consideration of the terminology of citizenship, which dispels many previous misconceptions and also to my mind, definitively demonstrates that Athenian women who met the requirements of the law were, as Cantarella also argues, citizens. It also shows how the development of norms relating to citizenship in the age of Cleisthenes and Pericles was a product of both the democratic reorganization of Athenian society and the increasingly imperial identity of the Athenian polis: "In sum, although Pericles' law of 451/0 is of clear importance as a statement of self-conscious Athenian identity as a democratic and imperial power, setting the *Athenaioi* apart from *xenoi* (foreigners), both Greek and barbarian, it is by no means the whole story of Athenian citizenship law – or the whole of Athenian citizenship law." Moving beyond Pericles to the impact of war and other demographic, social, and political developments on the ideology and practices related to citizenship over the next century, Patterson tacitly demonstrates the insufficiency of approaches centered on the analysis of legal statutes. She shows how only an interdisciplinary understanding of social institutions related to marriage, population, and the family can illuminate the complex pattern of norms that together define the "law of citizenship" in Athens. On the basis of this account, she rightly concludes that "Citizenship law, therefore, should be understood to include not just the minimum necessary criterion of citizen parentage, but also the nexus of laws governing inheritance, marriage, religious participation – and of course judicial and political privilege. Athens had not one citizenship law – but an interconnected set of laws that set forth the privilege and responsibilities of those who 'shared in the city.'"

Over the past three decades Edward Cohen's research on commercial and banking law in Athens, and, in particular, on the operation of the Athenian maritime courts, has established his preeminent expertise in these areas.[17] His scholarship has largely defined this field in recent years, and in this volume his account is informed by a deep understanding of modern commercial law and practice as well as of their counterparts in ancient Greece. His broad perspective helps to illuminate Athenian commercial and maritime law within the larger socioeconomic and political context of Athens' prominent role in the eastern Mediterranean. His chapter on commercial law makes clear the deep divide in Athenian law and practice between "ordinary" commercial transactions involving nonmaritime trade and those commercial transactions that did have a maritime element. The fact, for example, that written contracts were required in the latter and almost unknown in the former testifies to the fundamental nature of this division. It also illustrates the continuing importance in the fourth century of issues pertaining to writing and

[17] E. Cohen (1973, 1992).

INTRODUCTION

literacy as discussed by Thomas. Cohen's chapter provides a lucid account of Athenian commercial law in both of these contexts and also points to the important larger questions remaining to be explored involving the implications of such categorizations in Athenian law, society, and economy.

In Part IV we leave Athenian law. As discussed by Gagarin in his treatment of the "unity" of Greek law, the single greatest problem for generalizing beyond Athens is the lack of sources. Although in Athens we have a wide array of contemporary literary sources as well as evidence in the form of legal inscriptions of various kinds, for the rest of the archaic and classical Greek world the former are almost altogether missing and the latter are significant but random in terms of their dating and subject matter. The great exception to this state of affairs is represented by the Cretan city of Gortyn, where the largest single legal inscription (as well as the largest collection of legal inscriptions) from anywhere in the Greek world has been preserved. John Davies, a leading authority on Gortyn, explores in Chapter 16, "The Gortyn Laws," what these texts represent, who created them, and why they were inscribed in monumental fashion in the heart of the city. Gortyn presents one of the most difficult methodological problems for dealing with Greek cities other than Athens. In the absence of the kind of evidence needed to sketch a social and political context in which to locate such legal provisions, how do we use them and what kind of conclusions can we draw about the legal system of which they were a part?

Davies tackles these problems systematically and always with a meticulous awareness of the difficulty the methodological problems present for interpretation both of the whole corpus and of individual provisions. He considers the sources of this legislation, the constitutional and institutional framework it reveals, and a series of substantive topics encompassing procedure and evidence; citizenship and legal status (including gender), marriage and the family, property, contracts, and crime. His survey of these areas provides the reader with a clear account of what we can learn from these sources but also the limits of our knowledge. Here one confronts the most basic methodological problem of dealing with any ancient legal system where the sources are necessarily fragmentary and problematic: how to negotiate the boundary between what we cannot, but desperately need to, know and the legitimate inferences that can be drawn from the evidence that we do possess. This is also a problem in regard to Athenian law, but the relative plethora of sources makes it easier for scholars to sidestep its implications. In Gortyn, on the other hand, one must confront this problem head on to make any progress at all, and Davies provides an admirable example of how this should be done.

The great postclassical exception to the concentration of legal evidence in Athenian sources is represented by the law of Greco-Roman Egypt. Here thousands of legal papyri document a wide variety of transactions and regulations. They provide us with the kind of documentation for actual legal instruments and their use that is almost completely lacking for Athens, as well as with a great deal of information about the administrative and social context of which they were a part. This area of Greek legal history requires formidable technical skills and erudition to pursue, and Hans-Albert Rupprecht is the leading exponent of a line of German scholarship that over the past century has largely defined this field. Because from the Greek law perspective the case of Egypt represents a legal transplant, the starting point of Rupprecht's chapter, "Greek Law in Foreign Surroundings: Continuity and Development," is what happens to Greek legal institutions as they are brought into the hybrid cultural context of Egypt in the Hellenistic period. He shows the way in which some legal forms are abandoned, others preserved and often adapted to new circumstances, and new ones invented. Rupprecht concludes that Greek legal institutions preserved their "basic structure over the centuries into Roman times. This continuity did not stand in opposition to further development in response to the demands of changing economic and social life; rather, the newly developed legal institutions and forms fit smoothly into the previously founded legal system while the basic structure remained intact." Significantly, the innovations were not the work of jurists but rather the product of the efforts of practitioners in adapting legal forms to the needs of commercial and economic life. As mentioned, this field of Greco-Egyptian law is largely separated from the concerns of those scholars who work on other areas of Greek, and particularly Athenian, law. One of the great unanswered methodological questions of our discipline is in what way the study of this astonishingly rich evidence for the "life of the law" in the Egyptian context can help us to understand the legal culture of other times and places in the Greek world and elsewhere.

Joseph Mélèze-Modrzejewski's chapter, "Greek Law in the Hellenistic Period: Family and Marriage" raises some of the same issues touched on by Rupprecht. Modrzejewski deals with the development of Greek law after the expansion of the Greek world in the aftermath of Alexander's conquests. His central thesis is that "Hellenistic law" does not represent a mixing of Greek and non-Greek legal cultures in the eastern Mediterranean but rather that "Hellenistic law is nothing else but Greek law practiced by the Greek-speaking immigrants . . ." Further, this body of law, developed not through legislation but by "notary practice," "achieved the unity of Greek law." The result was that, "A Greek 'common law' prevailed in the Hellenistic world." Needless to say, such broad claims raise important methodological and substantive issues. Modrzejewki supports his claims by using examples drawn particularly from the law of marriage and the family. He also acknowledges that though Greek law was not "mixed" with local legal traditions, "the coexistence of diverse private laws could not help but lead to an interplay of mutual exchanges and borrowings between the rules and practices. Estimating their accurate extent is not easy. . . ." Modrzejewski's claims represent an opportunity for scholars of Greek law to deviate from the comparatively well-trodden paths of Athenian law into the complex legal culture and difficult source material of the Hellenistic world. To assess his larger thesis from the standpoint of comparative analysis of the extant evidence from the range of Hellenistic cities where significant legislative and transactional evidence is preserved would be a daunting but important and rewarding task. It is unfortunate that the study of Greek law has become so specialized that there is relatively little work that encompasses the classical and Hellenistic periods or even communicates effectively between them. One can hope that the next generation of Greek law scholars will take up this challenge.

"Law and literature" is one of the most fruitful of current interdisciplinary aproaches to law. We offer two examples, beginning with Robert Wallace's chapter on law and Attic comedy. Wallace has produced an important study of the Areopagus and more recently focused his work on the realm of personal morality and the shifts in Athenian attitudes toward personal freedom through the fourth century B.C. His chapter in this volume takes as its starting point the extraordinary freedom of speech displayed in Attic Old Comedy, as best exemplified in the plays of Aristophanes. Wallace shows the relation of comic license to the larger values of freedom of expression that characterized Athenian radical democracy. He also explores the legal limits on this freedom, and particularly the law of slander and the way it was reflected in and affected comic satire of contemporary Athens, its problems, and its politicians. Moving beyond Aristophanes and the fifth century, Wallace insightfully explores the way in which New Comedy, as reflected in Menander's plays, adopted a very different stance toward the law and the wild freedom displayed in some of the plays of Aristophanes. More significantly, he again shows the way in which this shift in literary-cultural production is related to larger societal changes in regard to law, democracy, and the regulation of morality:

> In the second half of the fourth century, the Athenians came to think it right that people's lives should be more carefully guided by legal regulation. That perspective was repeated and reinforced on the comic stage, as dramatic characters seek to resolve the difficulties they confront through legal recourse. Aristophanes' rebellious and irreverent license has given way to a more structured and orderly world. Both developments were historically contingent. Military defeat, legal experience, and broader cultural shifts took Athens away from the liberating freedoms of its young, fifth-century democracy, toward the greater regulation that characterized bourgeois fourth-century society and Macedonian control.

In *The World of Prometheus: The Politics of Punishing in Democratic Athens* (2000b), Danielle Allen demonstrated the importance of a methodology that builds on her dual expertise in literature as well as in legal and political theory. In her chapter on Greek tragedy and law, Allen explores the major methodological issue of how law and tragedy can be read against one another in the context of democratic Athens. Many previous scholars have used tragedy as evidence for legal institutions[18] or legal thought.[19] Others, particularly in regard to Aeschylus' *Oresteia*, have explored the connection between the depiction of legal institutions in tragedy with Athenian political developments and the very notions of politics and political theory.[20] Few scholars, however, have addressed the methodological issues raised by such an approach, and in this regard Allen's contribution here is vitally important. Building on developments in contemporary literary theory, Allen emphasizes that we cannot merely look at tragedy as a repository for information about legal institutions. Using two examples involving the treatment of anger and of law in tragedy, she shows how one must look to the way in which tragedy and law mutually inform one another, for only then

---

[18] B. Daube (1939).
[19] E.g., E. Wolf (1952).
[20] Meier (1988, 1990).

can we construct a methodology adequate to understanding what law can tell us about tragic drama and tragedy can tell us about law:

> Tragedy becomes useful for studying Athenian law only after scholars have already taken the time to work out not merely the procedures of Athenian law but also its conceptual foundation and implications. The tragedians responded profoundly and robustly to the content of their contemporaries' political, legal, and ethical aspirations, that is, to their *ideas*, regardless of what they thought about current events.

In this sense, Allen's chapter demonstrates what such an approach has to offer but also offers another example of the way in which innovative interdisciplinary approaches are changing the way in which we think about the study of Greek law.

Like Danielle Allen, Josiah Ober approaches Greek law from the perspective of political theory. Ober demonstrated in his pathbreaking account of Athenian democratic politics how such an approach can illuminate the role of legal institutions in the broader political context.[21] As Allen has usefully drawn on tragedy and other literary genres in much of her work, Ober, far more than previous students of Greek political theory and Athenian democracy, turned to the orators as a key source for his reinterpretation of Athenian democratic institutions. In "Law and Political Theory," he draws on a wide variety of sources to explore the different kinds of issues that Athenian political theorists raised involving the nature of law and legal institutions. These problems include the very conception of law itself; the positivist orientation of most Athenian theorizing about law, legislation, and legal interpretation; and the institution of punishment. In a final and very interesting section, he considers the way in which figures such as Demosthenes were also engaged in the enterprise of political theorizing. This implies, for Ober, that the Athenian courts were also a place where legal practice and legal theory came together:

> Athenians were not unique among Greeks in their conjoined concern for law and political theory. But democracy in the distinctive Athenian style provided an especially fertile ground for that conjunction. In his career as democratic

[21] Ober (1989).

politician, Demosthenes served as legislator (proposing important new laws) and as a "consumer" of law (frequent legal prosecutor and defendant). But he also served as a "public political theorist of law," concerned with law's operative authority, the relationship between amendment procedure and legal substance, and the relationship between the regime and the effects of legal judgment.... Although all Greek states had laws of one sort or another, and we find political theorizing in the earliest works of Greek literature, it was in classical Athens that the recursive relationship between self-conscious political theorizing and current legal practice was most fully realized.

Ober's comments here open fruitful avenues for future exploration of the way in which the Athenian orations can be read as reflecting a theoretical discourse on the nature of legal institutions, the rule of law, and so on. Ober's interdisciplinary approach, deeply informed by contemporary political and legal theory, is well-suited for such an enterprise and shows the way in which we would do well to consider figures like Demosthenes as original thinkers about theoretical legal issues, engaged in an enterprise connected to that of Aristotle, Plato, and the other Greek philosophers who pondered the nature of law and justice.

The Greek words for law (*nomos*) and nature (*physis*), and particularly their use in the antithesis of law (as convention or custom) as opposed to nature (what is universal not contingent), have attracted an enormous amount of scholarly attention. The word *nomos* itself has been the subject of book-length treatments as has its antithetical opposition to *physis*.[22] Such accounts have typically focused on political perspectives involving the role of the idea of *nomos* in the development of Athenian democracy, the nature of justice in Greek political thought, or the concept of law and legality. In his chapter on law and nature in Greek thought, A. A. Long, one of the preeminent scholars of Hellenistic philosophy, turns to the connection between the two terms evoked in the conceptions of "natural law" and "laws of nature" (which he rightly points out are often confused). Long asks why, given the preoccupation of earlier Greek thought with the concepts of law (*nomos*) and nature (*physis*), they were not conjoined in ideas of natural law or laws of nature until much later in antiquity, particularly by the Stoics. Long's

---

[22] See Ostwald (1969) and Quass (1971).

answer to this question is as interesting and important as his survey of the way in which these terms were used in legal and other contexts from Hesiod and the Pre-Socratics to the political philosophies of Plato and Aristotle:

> The principal reason, I suggest, for early Greek philosophy's reticence about associating law with nature was not an inherent disparity between the terms, *nomos* having normative and strictly human connotations and *physis* construed as value-neutral and purely mechanical; if that had been so, we would never hear, as we do, of natural law or laws of nature or divine law or personification of nature. The deeper explanation must be the strongly human and specifically legislative and local connotations that *nomos* acquired in fifth-century political life.

Turning from the political and legal speculation encapsulated within the world of the classical polis, Long explores the new life taken on by these terms in the broader context of the Hellenistic and Roman worlds. His depiction of the development of ideas of natural law among Stoic thinkers is interesting in its own right but also because it shows how the political theory of the classical polis was in important ways shaped by the narrowness of vision implicit in the constrained context within which it chose to limit itself. In the aftermath of Alexander's political reorientation of the Greek world this all changed:

> With the extension of Hellenism, accompanied by the decline in autonomy of the numerous city-states, the idea of law fully transcended local boundaries, as we observe in the early Stoic concept of natural law. When Greek philosophy infiltrated Rome, it encountered a tradition of law that was far more systematic and articulated than local Greek experience had at hand. Untrammelled by the *nomos/physis* controversy, Roman thinkers found it easier than their Greek forbears to construe nature in terms of law and quasi-legal regulation.

In this enormously stimulating essay Long also demonstrates how much ancient philosophers can contribute to broadening our understanding of even the most basic concepts in Greek legal thought.

This introduction has been a highly personal reflection on the development of Greek law studies over the past few decades. Although it clearly reflects my own perspective on the discipline, and not necessarily always that of my coeditor, I hope that it has also given a sense of the extraordinary intellectual range of contemporary contributions to the study of Greek legal ideas and institutions. Where I think I can indeed speak for both myself and Michael Gagarin is in the hope that this volume of essays will not only introduce readers to this field but will also provoke them to join in the ongoing enterprise that the contributors collectively represent.

Part I

LAW IN GREECE

1: THE UNITY OF GREEK LAW

Michael Gagarin

It may surprise those who are new to the field to learn that the very expression *Greek law* is a point of contention for scholars in the field. For the most part, those in the United States and the United Kingdom avoid the expression, and only two books with "Greek law" in their title have been published in English since Pringsheim's *Greek Law of Sale* in 1950.[1] Even Sealey, who accepts Greek law as a valid concept, entitled his book on the subject *The Justice* [not *Law*] *of the Greeks* (Sealey 1994; see Gagarin 1996). This situation contrasts sharply with the case of Roman law, which is unproblematic in this regard: histories of, textbooks on, and introductions to Roman law appear regularly. Continental scholars tend to be more sympathetic to the notion of Greek law, though they too tend to avoid the expression in titles (Biscardi 1982a is a notable exception).

Although nineteenth-century scholars were aware that the existence of dozens of politically independent Greek *poleis* (or "city-states") made the concept of Greek law problematic, they generally agreed that the laws of different cities, in the words of Ludwig Mitteis, "rested on the same juristic conceptions."[2] Mitteis' position dominated the first half of the twentieth century, until it was strongly attacked by Moses Finley, first in a review of Pringsheim's book mentioned above and later in a more comprehensive essay entitled "The Problem of the Unity of Greek Law."[3] After noting that (unlike Rome) Greece before the conquests of Alexander was never politically united, Finley observes that however much some Greek *poleis* may have copied provisions from, or

---

[1] Gagarin (1986), Foxhall-Lewis (1996a). I do not count Stoddart (1990), a dissertation published without revision, or (of course) works on modern Greek law.
[2] "Auf den gleichen juristischen Anschauungen ruhten" (Mitteis 1891: 62).
[3] Finley (1951); Finley (1966) (which I quote from the 1975 reprint).

been influenced by, the laws of other *poleis*, significant substantive differences are clearly evident even in those few places for which we have a reasonable amount of evidence. Regarding marriage, for instance, Finley writes (140):

> If we take as nodal points the Homeric poems, Gortyn, Athens and the earliest Greek papyri from Ptolemaic Egypt, I am unable to discover a single common "basic conception" or "principle" except for the notion, familiar from societies of the most diverse kinds all over the world, that marriage is an arrangement involving families past, present and future, and the transmission of property.

In other words, common features exist only at a level of such generality that Greek law becomes a useless concept; whenever we have evidence for specific rules, significant substantive differences appear.

Although Finley's challenge has been largely accepted by Anglo-American scholars (but cf. Sealey 1990, 1994) continental scholars generally rejected it. In Germany, the most eminent scholar of Greek law at the time, Hans Julius Wolff, repeatedly reaffirmed his commitment to the concept of Greek law, as did Biscardi, the leading Italian scholar in the field, with his book explicitly entitled *Diritto greco antico*. For Wolff[4] (like Mitteis), Greek law was the realization of an abstract spiritual unity (*geistige Gemeinsamkeit*) that bound together the legal systems of the different Greek *poleis* and that differed from the spirit underlying the laws of other peoples. Certain basic concepts (*Grundvorstellungen*) are thus evident, however much the positive laws may differ. Among these are basic forms of political organization (*Organisationsprinzipien*) and common ideas like *dikē* ("law, justice"), *blabē* ("harm, injury"), *hybris* ("insolence"), *homologein* ("to agree"), and *kyrios* ("master, in control of"). Wolff also stressed the mere existence in different *poleis* of laws governing "heiresses,"[5] regardless of the substantive differences among these laws. Biscardi defended the concept in similar fashion, noting that the Greeks themselves recognized a common cultural basis (*questo fondo culturale comune*) for their laws in their language, religion, and customs (1982a: 9).

---

[4] I cite from Wolff (1975: 20–2); see also Wolff (1965).
[5] "Heiress" is the closest English term to designate a woman whose father dies leaving no living male descendants. The heiress was expected to marry a male relative on her father's side to keep his estate within his family.

The kinds of basic concepts or principles to which both Wolff and Biscardi appeal in defending the concept of Greek law are dismissed by Finley, who concludes (137) with regard to the so-called basic principles of property law – private ownership, inheritance by blood heirs, and being different from Roman law – "if that is all that is meant by the unity of Greek law, there can be no argument, but there is equally nothing worth discussing." Few scholars have attempted to defend the unity of substantive law in specific areas, but Sealey, a British scholar teaching in the United States but heavily influenced by continental scholars, has argued directly against Finley, especially in *The Justice of the Greeks*.[6] Sealey's first case in point is marriage, where he disputes Finley's assertion (see above) that the only common features of marriage law in different cities are too general to be of any use.

If we restate Finley's case to remove a few minor errors or overstatements noted by Sealey,[7] it is as follows: In fourth-century Athens a citizen had to marry another citizen for the marriage and the offspring to be legitimate. In most cases, betrothal was accompanied by a dowry, though an "heiress" brought her father's entire estate with her and thus naturally received no additional dowry. A woman did not inherit, had no right to administer or control more than a very small amount of property, and depended on a "guardian" (*kyrios*), normally a father or brother, to attend to her interests in legal matters or significant financial transactions. At Gortyn there is no sign of a "guardian" and no sign of formal betrothal or a dowry. Instead, women inherited property directly, in their own right, just as men did (but only half as much); they controlled their property themselves, took it with them if they were divorced, and passed it on to their children or blood relatives just as men did. Even allowing for the general nature of these descriptions, there are

---

[6] Sealey (1994: 59–89, esp. 67–83) expands and broadens Sealey (1990: 151–60).
[7] Sealey (1994: 68–9) has a few misstatements of his own. First, in the normal sense of "inherit" a woman in Athens did not inherit property. Property could pass to an "heiress" or other female relative, but she would only be a conduit, so to speak, for the property, which would be controlled by her husband and inherited by her male descendants. The woman herself did not control the money, and in all cases we know of involving such inheritance (e.g., Isaeus 3) a male relative contends against another male for control of the property. Second, the relation between a woman and her *kyrios* was not that of a modern litigant to his/her attorney. A woman had no choice in selecting her *kyrios* or in whether to have one at all, and a *kyrios* did not need a woman's permission (or even knowledge) to act in matters such as investing her dowry. Third, the fact that a provision at Gortyn mentions the possibility that a woman was given in marriage by her father or brother, does not mean that the institution of betrothal (*engyēsis*) existed there, as in Athens. In many cultures a male relative gives away a woman in marriage.

real and substantial differences between the two cities, and no amount of ingenious special pleading can turn them into "a mere difference in wording."[8]

Even in the area of women and family law, moreover, one could point to other significant differences not mentioned by Finley. For example, in contrast to the restrictions on citizen marriages at Athens, at Gortyn a free woman[9] could marry a slave, and if she bore children to him, these would be not only legitimate but also free. In light of differences such as these, we must conclude that family and property law in these two cities are not the same in any significant way, and we cannot in any useful way say that a single set of principles underlie Greek marriage and family law.

In short, although we can find certain general features of substantive law that are common to Athens and Gortyn, and thus may perhaps have been widespread in Greece, the more detailed our knowledge becomes, the more clearly the differences stand out. Finley's claims thus have a large degree of validity. But this does not necessarily mean we should ignore points of similarity or dismiss entirely the argument of Wolff, Biscardi, and others that a common cultural heritage would necessarily manifest itself in some way in the legal systems of the different *poleis*.

Must we then conclude that the question of unity is simply a matter of definition where those who see unity in broad terms accept it but those who look for a more detailed unity deny it? I think we can move beyond this point if we return to a question asked by Finley (136), "What is really the point at issue?" Foxhall and Lewis indicate one possible approach when they write (1996a: 2–3), "the structural consistency of legal behaviour within the wide range of Greek times and places covered in the papers here suggests that a notion of 'Greek law,' or perhaps

---

[8] "At Gortyn, as at Athens, a woman brings property with her into her marriage. This property is called dowry in Athens and the woman's property in Gortyn. That is a mere difference of wording" (Sealey 1994: 80). This ignores the real difference between a male relative's property handed over (after negotiation) along with the bride to another man, who will control both the bride and the property and property that belongs to and is controlled by the woman herself whether or not she marries.

[9] There is very little indication that the Gortynians had any concept of citizenship other than the status of being free. Treaties may refer to "Gortynians," but there is no evidence that anyone in Gortyn ever explored the ramifications of this word. Willetts (1967: 10–11) understands *dromeus* (lit. "runner") as a citizen, but the term seems to mean nothing more than "adult" or "of age" (it is contrasted with *apodromos*, or "minor"). Another term, *apetairos* (lit. "excluded from the *hetaireia* or clan") may imply a class of free persons with restricted rights. See further Davies' chapter, below.

rather 'Greek legal behaviour,' as variations on a theme does remain analytically useful." But they do not pursue the idea of "analytically useful" any further. Perhaps a better approach is to ask why scholars of Greek law are so concerned about this issue of unity when, for example, American legal historians can write books about "American law" that draw evidence from statute laws, court decisions, and legal writings of many different states without apparently being bothered by the fact that each U.S. state has its own law in addition to the federal law of the U.S. government.[10] What's different about Greek law?

The answer, as Finley well understood, lies in the use scholars make of the concept, and this arises directly out of the fact that our evidence for Greek law (in contrast to our evidence for the history of law in the United States) is so sparse. No American legal historian would look to the laws of, say, California to reconstruct those of Texas, because we have direct evidence from the state in question. But historians of Greek law do not have this luxury. Scholars like Wolff may appear to treat the issue of unity as a purely theoretical issue, but many defenders of unity use this concept, often only implicitly, to elucidate the laws of a polis for which we have inadequate direct evidence. Biscardi (1982a: 9) is perhaps the most explicit on this issue:

> the study of Attic law can be considered not only an end in itself, but also, if properly understood, as a means of recovering other Greek laws; laws, let us repeat, that are indisputably diverse among themselves but among which, nevertheless, can be found the existence of a common substratum, which – with the reservation just expressed – makes it legitimate, if only for didactic purposes, to continue to talk about Greek law pure and simple.[11]

The dangers of such an undertaking are evident, and many of Finley's complaints about Pringsheim's work amount to observing that

---

[10] For example, nowhere in his very influential book *The Transformation of American Law 1780–1860* (1977) does Morton Horwitz raise the question whether there is such a thing as American law.

[11] "Lo studio del diritto attico può essere considerato non solo come fine a se stesso, ma anche, a ben vedere, come mezzo di recupero degli altri diritti greci: diritti, ripetiamo, indiscutibilmente diversi fra loro, ma fra i quali tuttavia è riscontrabile l'esistenza di un sostrato comune, che rende tuttora legittimo – sia pure con le riserve ora esposte – che, non foss'altro a scopi didattici, si possa continuare a parlare di diritto greco 'tout-court'" (Biscardi 1982a: 9).

a particular conclusion about, say, Athenian law cannot be supported by evidence from Ptolemaic Egypt. But in view of the scarcity of evidence, if one sets out to write a book on a topic like "the Greek law of sale," one will be forced to draw conclusions from one system to another. A better way to deal with the problem is to describe, for the laws on a given subject, characteristic features that are found in several different *poleis* without insisting that the same features must have existed everywhere. This is the method of Modrzejewski in his influential paper on marriage (Modrzejewski 1983), in which he largely confines himself to the evidence from classical Athens and various Hellenistic cities. He says almost nothing about Gortyn, which in important respects (such as the absence of dowries) does not fit his general schema. Modrzejewski's approach proves useful, even though it does not satisfy Finley's insistence that any work utilizing the concept of Greek law should identify significant features that are common to all times and places for which we have evidence (as well as being different from most other legal systems).

To my knowledge, no work on any substantive aspect of Greek law has yet met Finley's demanding criteria, and (as noted above) Anglo-American scholars have thus largely abandoned the concept.[12] But there is another aspect of law that has been generally overlooked in this debate, namely procedure,[13] broadly understood as the process of litigation and the organization of justice (legislation, courts, judges/jurors, magistrates, etc.). In this general area, I think, we can find features that are similar, if not for all *poleis*, at least for most of those for which we have evidence, and (just as important) that are not found in most comparable legal systems outside of Greece.

As with substantive law, of course, evidence for Greek legal procedure is limited, and conclusions must remain tentative. Nonetheless, as I have argued elsewhere (Gagarin 2001: esp. 42), Greek legal procedure seems to be characterized by several features not found in other premodern legal systems. Greek laws, for example, at least those found at Athens and at Gortyn, devote considerable attention to procedure and show less interest in setting precise penalties for offenses. Most cases, moreover, are freely decided by judges or juries after hearing the pleadings of the litigants, and the use of automatic procedures such as oaths is relatively rare. In other words, open forensic debate and free judicial

---

[12] Many would agree with Todd's preference (1993: 16) for speaking of "the Greek family of legal systems."

[13] Here too, Sealey (1994) is an exception; see below.

decisions are central to the legal process at Gortyn and Athens but are relatively rare in the legal systems portrayed in the non-Greek law codes.

Most of the evidence for these conclusions comes from Athens and Gortyn, but the relatively scarce evidence from other cities is not inconsistent with it. We do occasionally hear of automatic processes for resolving cases,[14] and of course many laws set penalties for offenses. But inscriptions also provide abundant evidence of concern for procedure (Gagarin 1986: esp. 72–7), and for oral argument and debate, which characterize procedure at Gortyn and Athens. It thus appears that Greek *poleis* largely shared the same general approach to the judicial process, with the litigants themselves pleading their case as they saw fit before the judge or judges, who were free to reach a decision as they saw fit within the established rules (i.e., in accordance with the laws, etc.). The formalism that is well known from Roman or early English law seems never to have had a significant place in Greek legal procedure.

Several other features of Greek legal procedure can best be understood if we begin with an aspect noted by Sealey and others, namely the presence of gaps in legislation. Because no legislator, no matter how diligent, can enact laws covering every conceivable situation, there are always some "gaps" in the laws and cases arise that are not directly covered by existing legislation.[15] Greek legislation is unusual, however, not because gaps are present, but because the Greeks explicitly recognize gaps and are willing to tolerate them. Instead of striving to find rules to fill the gaps in this legislation, laws in several *poleis* specify that judges or jurors should judge cases not covered by the laws "according to the view that is most just (γνώμῃ τῇ δικαιοτάτῃ)," or some variation of this Athenian expression. In addition to Athens, Sealey (1994: 51–2) cites legislation from Eresus and Naupactus showing that this approach was widespread in Greece. He also mistakenly cites legislation from Gortyn (11.26–31) that distinguishes between cases where the law requires the judge to decide according to a witness or an oath and cases where he is to "decide under oath according to the pleas." This rule does not apply to gaps in legislation, but it probably stems from the same general desire not to exercise excessive legislative control over judicial decisions, but

---

[14] For example, Aristotle (*Politics* 1269a1–3) states that at Cumae, "if the plaintiff provides a certain number of his own relatives as witnesses to the killing, the defendant is guilty of homicide."

[15] *Pace* Sealey, who writes (1994: 55), "The law in Rome and in modern systems has no gaps." What he means, I think, is that where gaps are found to exist, the law requires that they be filled by either juristic interpretation or judicial decision. But no system ever fills every possible gap.

to allow a judge or jury discretion in their rulings. And it is certainly possible that the Gortynians also had, if not a law, at least a customary practice, that dealt with gaps in the same way as other *poleis* for which we have evidence.[16]

Like modern legal systems, both civil and common, Roman law treats gaps differently – not as an opportunity for a judge or juror in an individual case to decide as best he can but as a legal shortcoming that needs to be remedied by the use of legal reasoning, which will create a new rule to cover the unlegislated situation (see Sealey 1994: 53–4). The new rule is reached through interpretation (often by analogy), and indeed much of the work of the Roman jurists consisted in proposing rules to cover unanticipated situations. Similarly, in both civil and common law systems today, gaps in legislation are filled by professional legal scholars or judges using similar legal reasoning, and the rules they develop are often formally adopted in legislation at some later time. The Greek approach to gaps is significantly different: the Greeks were perfectly capable of reasoning by analogy,[17] but they apparently felt no need to fill gaps but were content to leave it to a judge or jury to decide in each case.[18] Nor is the Near Eastern approach to gaps quite the same as that of the Greeks. For although there are many obvious gaps in the collections of laws of Hammurabi and others and there is no indication that anyone felt that these gaps needed to be filled, there is also no hint in the Near Eastern laws of how individual cases not covered by the inscribed laws should be handled. The same is true of early medieval collections of laws, though these seem to make more of an effort to be complete.[19]

One of the reasons Near Eastern law collections apparently show no concern for the need to fill gaps is because, in the view of most scholars, these laws were not truly legislation, because they were not intended to serve as a guide for actual judicial activity. Instead, they were meant to display to contemporaries the king's fairness and commitment

---

[16] There are obvious gaps in legislation at Gortyn, as, for example, in the regulations of sexual assaults in the Great Code (2.2–45).

[17] For example, the plaintiff in Hyperides 3 can cite no law directly applicable to his situation, so he argues that his complaint is just because of a principle derived by analogy with laws that regulate certain other commercial transactions (cf. Sealey 1994: 54, with n. 68).

[18] Some people criticized Solon's laws (*Ath. Pol.* 9.2) not for their gaps but for not being simple and clear. The reform/reorganization of Athenian laws at the end of the fifth century sought to eliminate conflicts and delete obsolete laws but not to fill existing gaps.

[19] Conclusions about medieval law codes are based on two of the most important of these, those of the Salian Franks, including the *Lex Salica* (Drew 1991) and of the Lombards (Drew 1973). See further, Gagarin 2001.

to justice and to preserve for posterity this image of him as a just king.[20] It has also been argued that the intent of Anglo-Saxon collections of laws was similar (Wormald 1999). Greek laws, however, were true legislation, intended to guide litigants and judges/jurors in actual cases. One clear indication of this is that both Draco's homicide law and several sections of the Gortyn Law Code include a provision specifying that a particular law is or is not retroactive (Westbrook 1989). Such a provision is only needed when the law is intended to be used in actual cases.

A related feature of law in Greece is that from a very early period laws were not only written but also inscribed on stone or other relatively durable materials and conspicuously displayed in a public place, usually either a sacred area or in the agora or community gathering place.[21] Careful study of the surviving early inscriptions shows that some care was taken, within the limitations of early writing abilities, to make these laws clear and accessible to those who might need to use them. And the people apparently did use them, for the public inscription of laws rapidly proliferated all over Greece.[22]

Despite their fondness for writing down and publicly displaying legislation, however, the Greeks appear to have been much less inclined than other people to use writing for other legal matters. The use of writs as the major tool for initiating litigation was well established in England by the thirteenth century, if not earlier (Clanchy 1993), and almost 10 percent of the provisions in Hammurabi's laws include references to written documents such as contracts or property transfers; probably none of these refers to a written law.[23] But in the Gortyn Code, by contrast, the only mentions of writing refer to written laws, either laws in other parts of the Code itself or laws inscribed elsewhere, and this is generally true of all Greek archaic legal inscriptions. Indeed, in many parts of Greece during this period the word for a law is some form of a word for writing – *to graphos* ("writing"), *ta gegrammena* ("what has been written"), and so on. This highly restricted use of writing, for laws and for almost nothing else legal, persisted into classical Athenian law, well after the use of writing for documents such as contracts and wills became established practice in the early fourth century. Written documents such

---

[20] See, e.g., Roth (2000), and, for a dissenting view, Lafont (2000).
[21] The following remarks on writing in Greek law are based on my current work, which will appear in a forthcoming book. For preliminary studies of the material, see Gagarin (2003, 2004).
[22] As in other matters, Sparta is an exception.
[23] In Roth's translation (Roth 1995), there are two references to "royal ordinances," which are probably decrees (LH 51, frag. M).

as these could be brought into court, but even then they were read out loud to the jurors, who thus received all their information about the case orally. The scarcity of detailed evidence about legal procedure in other *poleis* in the classical period prevents us from generalizing with confidence, but it is possible that a tendency to avoid using writing in the heart of the legal process, combined with a fondness for writing and displaying legislation, characterized other Greek *poleis* in addition to Athens and Gortyn.

A related feature that clearly characterizes Athenian law and may also have characterized Greek law in general is the lack of professionalization. The history of legal systems such as those in Rome and early England shows clearly that the increase in the use of writing goes hand in hand with the growth of a legal profession and the increasing importance of professionals in the legal system. No matter how widespread the ability to write is among ordinary members of these communities, the technical demands of most legal writing generally require the help of scribes, who were common in Hammurabi's time, or other professionals such as the English notary or the Roman jurist. But the little evidence we have for scribes in Greece before the Hellenistic period indicates that their primary function was writing texts, such as laws, for public display. Slaves may have written documents for the use of their masters, but Athenian forensic speeches generally speak of litigants and others writing (and reading) their own documents. And the absence of legal professionals in Athenian law is well-known.[24]

In these respects, the legal system of Ptolemaic Egypt shows significant differences from earlier practice. Despite the quantity of surviving papyrus texts from this period, our knowledge of Ptolemaic court procedure is still very incomplete, but it appears that not only do scribes and notaries play a prominent role in legal matters, but other professional magistrates also have a large degree of control over the legal system. Sometimes these officials are not local but traveling groups of judicial officials. In other cases nonjudicial magistrates settle disputes in their areas of specialization. Jury trials seem to be relatively rare. In addition, the use of writing for judicial matters appears to increase considerably.[25]

---

[24] See, e.g., Todd (1993: 77–8). Among the semiprofessional personnel of Athenian law one might include logographers, who for a fee would write a speech for a litigant, and *exēgētai* ("interpreters"), who gave (nonbinding) advice on religious matters that occasionally overlapped with legal issues.

[25] This is suggested, to begin with, by the large number of papyrus documents that survive from the period, though the disparate nature of our evidence makes any comparison with earlier periods insecure.

There is much we do not know about Ptolemaic law, and some features of earlier law undoubtedly persisted, at least for a time. But despite certain continuities, the whole concept of law as an open, public institution that is in the hands of the community seems to have changed.

The change may be related to the fundamental political changes that occurred after Alexander. It can be argued there is a connection between the type of political organizations found in archaic and classical Greece and some of the procedural features noted earlier – the relatively large role of oral argument in the judicial process and the correspondingly minimal role of formalism and automatic proofs, the proliferation of publicly displayed written laws, the concern for procedure expressed in these laws, the relative absence of writing during the legal process itself, and finally the lack of professionalization. Whether the governments of Greek cities were primarily democratic or oligarchic, they always seem to have allowed for open, public discussion of important issues by a relatively large segment of the community. Even as early as Homer, kings (*basileis*) are regularly presented as discussing important public matters in a large forum that is representative of the community and may even include its least desirable elements (such as Thersites in Book 2 of the *Iliad*). The passion for open discussion and debate has been seen as influencing many aspects of Greek thought (Lloyd 1979), and the openness of the Greek legal process may be a further manifestation of it.

If there is, in fact, a connection between the open nature of archaic and classical Greek law and the relatively nonauthoritarian political systems of this period, then we would expect Greek law to undergo significant change when it was imported into a country that was ruled at the time – and had been ruled for centuries – by a single, all-powerful monarch. In Ptolemaic Egypt, much of the law no longer came from the community but devolved from the king and the royal administration in Alexandria, and as a result law was no longer the open, public process of the archaic and classical periods but more of a private affair between the litigants and a magistrate with the help of scribes and notaries. In this respect, however much the substantive law retained elements of classical Greek law, the legal system changed fundamentally.

Similar changes may have occurred when Greek law was introduced into parts of Asia where it had not previously been known, that is to say into all of Asia except for the Greek cities along the Aegean coast of Asia Minor. But these long-established Greek cities, like the cities of mainland Greece, appear to have retained a degree of autonomy in their internal affairs, at least, despite the overall imposition of monarchic rule. Smyrna and Ephesus, like Athens, Corinth, and other cities, were indeed ruled by Hellenistic monarchs, but they seem to have retained considerable autonomy in their private law. The evidence for law during this period is widely scattered and mostly indirect, and much more work needs to be done before we can draw certain conclusions about Hellenistic law with regard to the issues raised above.[26] But if we confine ourselves to the law of Ptolemaic Egypt, then we can be fairly certain that at least some of the common features of archaic and classical law discussed above were no longer part of the legal system in this later period.

This conclusion is something of a paradox. The concept of the unity of Greek law originated in the nineteenth century in the work of scholars like Mitteis who were trained as papyrologists, grounded in Roman law, and specialized primarily in Greek law of Ptolemaic and Roman Egypt. Even after Finley's challenge, the majority of defenders of the unity thesis have continued to be scholars trained in Roman law and (often) papyrology who do significant work on Hellenistic law. Those (primarily Anglo-American) scholars who object to the traditional views of the unity of Greek law, on the other hand, work mostly on classical Athenian law and tend to consider this a unique system. The conclusion I have proposed, however, suggests that although Athenian law may be different in its substantive details, in the realm of procedure (broadly understood) it shares significant features with other legal systems of archaic and classical Greece. These allow us to speak of an essential unity of Greek law – or at least of Greek legal procedure – which is somewhat different from what Finley had in mind, but which would, I think, satisfy his criteria for unity. There appears to be a substantial division, however, between the legal systems of archaic and classical Greece and that of Ptolemaic Egypt. The unity I find in Greek law, therefore, is a general procedural unity, grounded in the archaic and classical periods, not the substantive unity, grounded in Hellenistic law, in which Mitteis and his followers believed. Even in the archaic and classical periods, this general procedural unity is not strong enough to allow us to draw conclusions about the law of one polis on the basis of the law of others. But the concept of a unified Greek law can be an aid in understanding the nature of the different legal systems of archaic and classical Greece, including Athenian law, and in appreciating the differences between law in Greece and elsewhere.

---

[26] See Mélèze-Modrzejewski's and Rupprecht's chapters in this volume.

2: Writing, Law, and Written Law

Rosalind Thomas

Athenians of the classical period so venerated their ancient lawgiver, Solon, that the laws of Solon still formed the basis of Athenian law in the radical democracy. Even after they revised the law code in the late fifth century, Athenians still referred to Athenian laws as "the laws of Solon," confusingly mingling new and old laws under this one description. Yet we are told, even these laws were flawed. Some critics are mentioned by the Aristotelian *Constitution of Athens* (*Ath. Pol.* 9.2): Solon's laws, they claimed, suffered from lack of clarity, which created disputes, and "some think this was deliberately to put the demos in charge (*kyrios*) of the trials."[1] This example brings out several of the themes of this chapter: the role of early Greek laws and lawgivers like Solon, the perceived and actual importance of writing down the law, the problems that arose even when the laws were recorded in writing, and the intimate connection between written laws and the bodies which put them into action.

At least some of those critics were oligarchic, for the *Ath. Pol.* later tells us that the oligarchy of the Thirty, in its anxiety to remove all power from the people, "removed the laws of Ephialtes and Archestratos about the Areopagus, and annulled the laws of Solon which had ambiguities (*diamphisbētēseis*) and abolished the authority of the jurors" (35.2). One law that laid itself open to malicious prosecution was, they thought, the law about inheritance and the authority of the testator's will. This gave the testator full power to determine the contents of his will, "except when he is insane, senile or under the influence of a woman." This gave an excellent excuse for questioning wills, and therefore opportunities for

---

[1] Cf. Plut. *Solon* 18.

sycophants, or at least so the the Thirty claimed, and they abolished this exception. The author of the *Ath. Pol.* defended Solon on the grounds that the legislator had to draw up his laws in general terms (9.2), but we can see instantly here that the nature and scope of written laws could be a point of contention between oligarchs and democrats. Democrats were content to leave the jury scope for interpretation in individual cases, and oligarchs were keener to iron out ambiguities. This emphasizes how closely the force of law is bound to its institutional context – there is no point in having democratic laws if there are not democratic juries to support them – and also how written laws need supplementing by interpretation because they cannot cover everything, as Aristotle puts it in the *Politics* (1282b2). This illustrates a further theme – that the writing down of law was probably undertaken in a variety of ways by different city-states for rather varied purposes; depending on politics and context, such written laws did not have identical implications everywhere.

Greeks in the classical period identified the Greek polis with the rule of law and looked askance at imaginary or real communities of non-Greeks who lacked law. By the latter part of the fifth century, written law was increasingly identified as a necessary factor in providing justice for all. The high-minded words of Theseus, portrayed as the democraticaly inclined king of Athens in Euripides' *Suppliants* declared, "When the laws are written down, then both the weak and the rich have equal justice" (430–4).[2] They voiced the conception common in classical Greece that written laws were necessary to bring justice to all, for the laws to transcend the interests of one or other social group and be applied impartially. They also hint at the common identification of the Greek polis with the rule of law. But it is increasingly recognized that the coming of written law in archaic society was not necessarily equivalent to the emergence of greater justice or equality, let alone of democracy.[3] Besides, ideal and practice are not always a close match, and the significance of written law in Greek society and the development of the Greek city-states is fascinatingly complex. What people thought they were trying to do by creating written laws may not have been borne out in practice, and one suspects that written laws sometimes had unforeseen implications.

Written laws are attested first in our evidence around the mid seventh century, and they increase at precisely the period when the Greek city-states were developing more formal political systems in a

---

[2] See also Gorgias, DK 82, 11a 30: "written laws are the guardians of justice."
[3] See Gagarin (1986), Ch. 6; Thomas (1995); Eder (1986); Hölkeskamp (1992).

process of state formation. The role of written law can be seen within this larger development, the more so because so many early written laws were imposing checks on polis officials in *poleis* which were regularly prone to civil strife. Our firmest evidence for Greek law in the archaic and early classical period remains the inscriptions recording laws; thus we know far more about those laws which were inscribed on stone (as opposed to wood or bronze) and survived to this day. A further point is that the bare texts of these laws do not easily reveal the complexities which are likely to have existed in, say, a legal dispute about inheritance or office holding, let alone the social and political dramas that may have brought added pressure to the attempted enforcement of a new law. Later Greek traditions attributed numerous laws and extensive reforms to early Greek lawgivers, and because the traditions seem to become elaborated in the telling, these lawgivers remain misty, uncertain characters. Only for Solon of Athens do we have the early evidence of his own poems, and later records of his laws, as well as idealizing or propagandizing later traditions.[4]

What remains clear, however, is that by the classical period written law was widely regarded as *in itself* conducive to fairness, justice, and equality – not only democracy – and that the gradual development of written law in the archaic period touches not only on the role of writing but also on some of the central developments of the archaic period. Solon may stand as a symbolic figure here who presented his reforms in his poetry as saving the polis from civil strife, creating "good order" or *eunomia*, preventing either faction from gaining unjustly and – part and parcel of this – he "wrote down the laws for rich and poor alike, fitting straight justice to each."[5] We concentrate here on the character and significance of written laws in archaic Greece, the relation of these written laws to earlier forms of rules and the maintenance of order, and finally the ideals surrounding written law in classical Athens.

Writing appeared in Greece in the early eighth century and was harnessed rapidly for private and personal messages, labels, and dedications. It is not until the mid- to late seventh century that we have the earliest concrete evidence of its use for official public inscriptions of laws. The earliest written law found so far is from Dreros on Crete (ca. 650 B.C.), a place with enough civic self-consciousness already to have built an agora. The cities of Crete remained major creators of

---

[4] See Szegedy-Maszak (1978); and for the idea of the great lawgiver as an essentially fourth-century construct, Hölkeskamp (1999), with Robinson (2003).
[5] Fragment 36W, from *Ath. Pol.* 12.4; cf. Gagarin's chapter on early Greek law in this volume.

inscribed stone laws throughout the sixth century and down into the fifth, culminating in the "Gortyn Code," and the fact that as many as eleven Cretan cities have left us stone laws from the archaic period leaves the evidence overwhelmingly weighted toward Crete.[6] This cannot be merely an accident of evidence: Crete was evidently keen on written laws (on stone) from the earliest times onwards. The literary sources add traditions about early lawgivers who might belong to the seventh century, for example, Charondas of Catana, Zaleucus of Locri, Philolaos of Corinth, lawgiver for Thebes, Lycurgus of Sparta, and a few others, though there are well-known difficulties in accepting the traditions as they stand.[7] More secure is the late-seventh-century Drakon of Athens, whose homicide law was reinscribed in the late fifth century, and Solon in the early sixth century. By around the early sixth century, then, written law is becoming familiar. Epigraphic evidence for laws becomes more common by the mid and late sixth century. Why, then, do these communities resort to written law? Are these laws the refuge (or weapons) merely of certain groups within these communities? To what extent did these new written laws replicate or "codify" previous practices or produce radical new rules? And what about the apparently larger scale production of laws attributed to lawgivers?

Not only are the traditions about the laws of the earliest lawgivers often unreliable but there is a certain contrast between the literary traditions about lawgivers and the inscriptions. Our evidence provides large numbers of laws on stone from Crete, quite a few on bronze from Olympia/Elis and the Argolid, especially Argos, but none or only the scantiest fragments from Thebes, Catana, Sparta, Athens, and Locri, which were famed for their lawgivers. Spartan tradition said that their lawgiver, Lycurgus of Sparta, actually forbade written law (Plutarch, *Lycurgus* 13.3). For the others, there have been a few fragments from Leontini (Monte San Mauro) and Ephesus, both of which had a tradition of a lawgiver.[8] Solon's extensive laws were written on the *axones* and *kyrbeis*, which have not survived and archaic Athens has left us no archaic laws on stone.[9] This leaves the possibility (unless we disbelieve the traditions of these lawgivers altogether) that certain cities had

---

[6] See the important collection of political and legal inscriptions in van Effenterre and Ruzé (1994–1995) – henceforth, *Nomima*; Whitley (1997) usefully collects the Cretan evidence. See also Davies in this volume.
[7] See Szegedy-Maszak (1978) and Hölkeskamp (1999).
[8] Hölkeskamp (1999), 109–14; Sokolowski: *LSAM* (1955), no. 30, 30A, 30B.
[9] For Solon's *axones* and *kyrbeis*, the fundamental study is Stroud (1979); for Solon's laws, Ruschenbusch (1966).

bodies of laws that were written on material other than stone or perhaps not publically written down at all. The literary tradition records that Charondas's laws were sometimes sung or chanted, in particular after the paeans, "so that the ordinances should become ingrained."[10] Not all scholars have been happy to take this literally, but it raises the possibility that some of these early lawgivers did not always promulgate or preserve their laws in the manner that later became standard, that is, in a public place and on an imperishable material.

To understand why communities increasingly resort to written law, we need to consider the subjects and form of these early laws. Many of the earliest extant laws show an overwhelming preoccupation with setting penalties, with specifying the officials responsible for dealing with misdemeanors, and with checking up on those officials. A recently published law from Tiryns, for instance, possibly a sacred law, dated to the late seventh or early sixth centuries, is still highly obscure, but we can make out clauses about fines and various officials collecting and enforcing penalties, and the "community" or people.[11] Argos had written laws on stone and bronze at least by 575–550, among them a penal law engraved on a bronze plaque listing major crimes against the city that would invite penalties of cursing, death, and exile; it begins with penalties for defacing the plaque itself.[12] A particularly good example of a series of sanctions and a hierarchy of responsible officials occurs in a law from Elis (Olympia), inscribed on a bronze plaque, which sets out meticulous sanctions and fines: its primary subject is Patrias, secretary of the Eleans, and one clause appears to declare that he and his family should be immune if he is accused – an attempt to diminish collective responsibility and protect Patrias.[13] Such emphasis on penalties and officials means that it is sometimes hard, especially from fragmentary texts, to determine what the basic misdemeanor was.

Such inscribed laws are not, on the whole, setting up political institutions (and many are in any case concerned with procedure – to which we return). Yet various lawgivers are attributed in the literary tradition with reforming or changing the social and political structures of their cities, and we must believe something of this, particularly for

---

[10] Stob. IV 2.24, p. 154–5 Hense; cf. also Athen. 619b=Hermippus fr. 88 Wehrli; on oral or sung laws, see above all, Camassa (1988); Piccirilli (1981); Thomas (1995; 62–4).
[11] Jeffery (1990), 443, no. 9a. For the obscure *platiwoinoi* and *platiwoinarchoi*, cf. *Nomima* I 78; cf. Osborne (1997), 75.
[12] Jeffery (1990), 158, 168 no. 9 (ca. 575–550).
[13] *IvO* no. 2; Jeffery (1990), 220 no. 15, 218 and n. 5; *Nomima* I 23.

Solon of Athens and probably Sparta. The famous law from Chios of the early sixth century (ML 8) might come under this category, for on one side of the stone [Back (C)] it talks about appeals to the "council of the people" and appears to set out the time of meeting and some of its business, but the front (A) appears to be protecting the property of the sanctuary of Hestia and mentions the people's decrees (rhetras), demarchs, and the basileus.[14] Such laws about constitutional matters are relatively rare in our epigraphic evidence. Yet the early law from Dreros is another well-known constitutional law that declares first that the polis has decided that the highest official, the Kosmos, should not be Kosmos again for ten years and then proceeds to list punishments and penalties if this rule is broken. It is striking that the earliest extant law on stone is one limiting the chief official's tenure of office. In formal terms it is a mixture of prescriptive and procedural law, first setting out what is forbidden. This implies that written law might often have been turned to in times of political and social upheaval and represented an attempt in some places (like Dreros) to limit or regularize the power of the politically active elite, perhaps by their very peers.[15]

The impetus toward written law was probably not uniform in these widely diverse places, but the very written form was surely supposed to be significant. For Solon's laws, we have his own words, and his expression "I wrote down laws (*thesmoi*) for rich and poor alike" (36W) fits well with the stress elsewhere in his poetry on social justice and the unreasonable demands of both sides in the civil strife: for Solon, a written version of the laws would hold firm for all classes; they would be equal for all. This alone is enough to show that the idea of written law as an equalizer was not anachronistic in the archaic period. Although other binding laws might not be written, we do not need to follow Whitley's suggestion that writing down a law did not necessarily confer a special status on the law in relation to laws that were primarily transmitted orally (1997: 640). It might be an unintended result that written laws merge in importance with oral ones, but it is hard in this case to see why the cities would write down laws at all if they were not intended to be any different from what went on before. Why, otherwise, is there such stress in many archaic laws on keeping to "what is written" and not defacing "the writing"? Solon's poetic claim reinforces the sense that *written* law was supposed to be significant.

---

[14] On early democracy at Chios, see Robinson (1997), 90 ff. and Robinson 2003.
[15] Cf. Eder (1986) for the theory of written codification as a conservative act. For the Dreros law see ML 2 = Jeffery (1990), plate 59, 1a.

Another aim might be stability. In Athens the written form of Solon's laws might have been intended to confer stability. In time of revolution, there was little point in agreeing on reforms and other measures if they could be easily forgotten or "mislaid" by opponents. Hence the importance of the publicly visible *axones* and *kyrbeis*. There was also surely the fear that laws, once agreed, would be ignored or countermanded by the very officials or other members of the ruling elite who were supposedly bound by them: the publically written versions were accessible and visible, and even if few of the citizens could actually read them, there were perhaps enough who could and more who could point to the public inscription as a reminder of the law. Thus there are sometimes severe penalties for tampering with the inscription. Some recently published Tean curses have a clause cursing certain officials who do not read out the writing on the stele "to the best of their memory and power" (a reference to the fact that they also recited them by heart?).[16] Anyone who spoils the stone was probably also cursed, and in the other Tean Curses, there was certainly the extreme penalty for anyone who broke the stelai or cut out or obliterated the letters (ML 30). All this implies, of course, an anxiety for the stability and preservation of the public stone law.

Here we may turn to Crete. The paradox of the extensive legislation by Cretan cities is that there was a well-established tradition of written laws on stone, yet so little evidence for other kinds of writing exists that these impressive stone inscriptions seem to be virtually the only manifestations of literacy in Crete.[17] The virtual absence of any informal writing such as we find in Athens strongly suggests that ordinary Cretan citizens were not reading these laws. Yet perhaps it is not so much a paradox as an awkward reminder that the progressive model of law does not always hold good. Crete cannot provide a model of the way written law *may* promote equality or even democracy, and there is sometimes a slightly apologetic note in modern discussions of Cretan laws. But we cannot explain away the Cretan evidence as an accident of discovery – despite recent finds elsewhere, Crete has still produced by far the most inscribed written laws. So we are left to seek other explanations. The inscribed laws may have been a form of intimidation meant to impress the population with the authority of the law. But this still seems somewhat unsatisfying, as does a recent suggestion that the Gortyn Code was primarily meant as an imposing text, "first a

---

[16] *SEG* 31.985 D, and Herrmann (1981).
[17] See Whitley (1997) for a useful list, and also *Nomima* I and II.

monument then a text," representing "in symbolic form that for which the community as a whole stood" (Whitley 1997: 660). The "Code" is remarkable for its immense detail and the complexity of its laws covering many possible (and some improbable) eventualities in areas of life such as inheritance, adoption, and heiresses; amendments are added and there are indications of attempts at systematization – all of which point to more than a gigantic symbolic statement. Moreover, the Gortyn Code is only the longest among a very great number of legal inscriptions at Gortyn, clearly part of a tradition and context of legal rules on stone.[18]

The massive inscribed wall at Gortyn holding the Code emphasizes the authority of the laws, the grandeur of the Code, and the power of its creators. But is that all? If Crete is so different from the rest of Greece, why precisely is it different, and what is the context that could make it so different? There are hints that in archaic Crete the role of the scribe could be very extensive indeed, as the Spensithios decree shows[19]: scribes would then be one type of official whose power might need watching, also the *mnēmones* and judges who feature prominently in the Gortyn Code. If scribes had power, then further written laws may have seemed useful to control their actions.[20] The actual content of the laws also needs to be considered. There is much in the Code about the behavior and powers of the officials involved in administering justice, as well as injunctions to act "as is written." For example, there are instructions on procedures for judge and *mnēmōn* in a particular complex situation (IX 24–40); the judge is to give judgment "as is written" on whatever is specified "in the writing" (XI 26–31); the regulations are to be valid from the time they were written (XI 19–23). This implies that the Code laid down its extensive laws about inheritance, property, and heiresses in part to control and stabilize the judges' treatment of such matters and to cover problems that subsequently arose, something that might be especially likely when there was already an established tradition of written law.

It is interesting to note that despite the details of the written laws here, the *mnēmones* have a great deal of authority in the code, for they seem to be closely attached to the judge and share with the judge the potential power of being a witness to the results of past cases; hence

---

[18] Willetts 1967 remains the most comprehensive edition. See further, Gagarin (1982), Gagarin (1986: esp. 109–11), Davies (1996), and his chapter in this volume.
[19] The *editio princeps* is Jeffrey and Morpurgo-Davies (1970).
[20] See Ruzé (1988) on the potential power of early Greek scribes and secretaries.

both officials have authoritative knowledge.[21] Because presumably they could read even if the mass of the population could not, the written version of the laws could be aimed partly at enabling such officials to check up on each other.[22] Aristotle remarks (*Politics* 1272a36–9) that for Cretan officials in the late fourth century, "Their arbitrary power of acting on their own judgement and dispensing with written law is dangerous," but this may show a failure to *enforce* the laws rather than that the laws were not meant to have teeth in the first place.

Although the prominence of legal inscriptions in Crete was surely exceptional, it is worth considering whether the role of written law in Crete might be typical or indicative of the place of law in other archaic communities – a body of law not upheld by egalitarian or proto-democratic organs, enforced and administered by a powerful group of officials and accompanied by *mnēmones* and their (inherently unstable) "memory." Cretan laws were, after all, admired and emulated by the rest of Greece, to judge from the literary tradition. It is significant that for once the inscriptions and the literary tradition reinforce each other, for later Greek writers, including Herodotus, Plato, and Aristotle, were convinced of the importance of the Cretan legal tradition. Admittedly the traditions stressed mythical lawgivers of Crete going back to Minos, but as early as Herodotus, the Spartan Lycurgus is recorded as getting his laws from Crete (1.65.4), and this is more elaborately expressed in Plato's *Laws* and Arisotle's *Politics*.[23] The presence of written law in *poleis* that were not democratic in character or intention may have been more common in Greece than the Athenian (and Solonian) model.

Writing seemed, then, to offer permanence, stability, and security for the laws. This brings us to further questions about what precisely gets written down in an archaic law and what is done with the inscription when it is written. But first we should stand aside and consider more closely what happened in these communities before they wrote down laws in large or small quantities.

The impact of early written law must have been at least partially affected by the earlier customs, systems of maintaining order and settling disputes, and indeed the officials and political structures already there.

---

[21] IX 31 ff.; cf. Willetts (1967), on IX 32; cf. Ruzé (1988); Thomas (1995), 66ff. on the *mnēmones* in general in Greece as potentially powerful figures.

[22] Though see provisos by Davies (1996: 54–5) on the difficulties of cross reference in the code.

[23] For illuminating discussion of Plato's attitude to law and written law, see Bertrand (1999) and Nightingale (1999).

This raises the question of whether we can talk of preexisting nonwritten or oral laws, a body of fairly firm rules that might deserve the name *law* or binding rule. It is often held, particularly by modern lawyers, that laws must, by definition, be written down; otherwise they would lack the definition, autonomy, special marking, and (perhaps) precision that makes a law a statute or a law. It is certainly hard to think of statute law as nonwritten, and it is tempting to agree that once one or other rule has been written down, it gains an independent and special status that perhaps raises it above other binding rules. But if we regard law as effectively written law in archaic Greece, then to chart the increase of written laws is to chart the invention of law itself,[24] and this may risk simplifying the picture too far. It makes it harder to understand why only certain kinds of laws get written down and not others, and it is possible to find pretty rigid rules/standards in Greece that were not written down. It also leaves unanswered the question why the Greek terms used to denote rules or regulations that we would like to call law are often so very indeterminate.

Often references to law are really only references to their mode of preservation. Early laws often refer to themselves simply as "the writing": for instance, the Gortyn Code refers repeatedly to itself as "the writing" (*to graphos*).[25] A late-sixth-century law at Olympia (*IvO* no. 7) against improper behavior in temples adds the dire warning that "If anyone pronounces judgment against the writing (πὰρ τὸ γράφος), his judgment shall be void," obviously referring to the law itself – an interesting hint that they fear some official may well ignore the law completely (to which we return). The sentence then declares that "the *rhētra* of the people shall be final in deciding." Here *rhētra* seems to refer to a one-off decree of the people about dealing with some wrongdoer, but elsewhere (*IvO* no. 2) *rhētra* is used in a sense that denotes law, that is, a binding rule for the foreseeable future, rather than a circumstantial decision, and the word *rhētra* itself denotes by its root an oral pronouncement. Quite apart from this interesting mixture of written and oral in maintaining community order, we may also wonder if the reference to the law as "the writing" does indeed imply, first, that the only or main writing around is this law and, second, that written law has not yet been conceptualized as separate from unwritten.

---

[24] See Gagarin (2003); Thomas (1995) for more detailed arguments concerning "oral law" and articles in note 10 above.

[25] For example, XI 19–23; see also Hölkeskamp (1994: esp. 137–8), (2000).

Writing down the laws may well have been an important step *toward* conceptualizing law as written law, even if the final step was not yet taken.

The word used for law (written) outside the Peloponnese is often *thesmos*,[26] which implies something specially laid down for the future, established, and thus set aside from traditional and customary rules. Another term, *nomos*, is notoriously wide,[27] denoting custom, binding rule, and written and unwritten law. By the mid fifth century *nomos* can refer to written law (e.g., at Erythrae and Halicarnassus), and after a period of uncertainty in Athens, it was eventually pinned down as denoting written law by the post–403 constitution, which banned the use of "unwritten laws."[28] Thus *nomos* was acquiring a more specific and defined meaning, perhaps in response to political manipulation and the perceived problems in the definition of "the law/*nomos*," which sophists discussed in the late fifth century (see Long's chapter below). Hippias, for instance, asked whether justice can be defined as keeping to the law, because law can be altered, but unwritten laws, such as the law that everyone must look after their parents, are divine and observed everywhere (Xenophon, *Memorabilia* 4.4.13 ff.). The Spartans were notorious for their rigid adherence to their laws (*nomoi*), and Herodotus signaled it as their great strength (using *nomos*, 7.104.4), yet such laws must have been oral.[29] Herodotus also describes very specific and binding customs to be found in non-Greek areas of the world that one might equally call custom or law and for which the word is *nomos*. He praises the *nomos* of Amasis king of Egypt that forces everyone each year to show the governor that he earns an honest living – and, if not, condemns him to execution (2.177.2). Herodotus adds that it is borrowed by Solon of Athens, presumably to become the *nomos argias*/law against laziness that (if genuine) was certainly written, but whether Amasis' *nomos* was written is not clear and perhaps did not matter so long as political pressure and custom upheld it.

---

[26] For example, Solon 36W, line 18; cf. ML 13 and ML 20 (twice), where the form is *tethmos*.

[27] See now especially Hölkeskamp (2000: 74–81), stressing the inherent ambiguities of *nomos*; also Humphreys (1988); Ostwald (1969); Thomas (1995: 64–5).

[28] Andocides 1.85, 87 gives the text of the decree; unwritten laws may have been manipulated unscrupulously by the oligarchy.

[29] Gagarin (1986: 57–8); an obvious exception is the Great Rhetra, recorded in Plutarch, which got written down somehow: it seems likely that the embargo on written laws was a later development, while seventh-century Sparta was experimenting with written law like other Greek communities. For *nomos* in Herodotus, see Thomas (2000: Ch. 4).

Greek writers mention unwritten laws explicitly. Later sources also talk of the chanting of laws, which shows that later Greeks were not uneasy about the idea of making the laws ingrained by chanting them, even if their testimony is not necessarily a reliable source for the archaic period they concern. The term *unwritten law* starts to appear in the late fifth century: the first surviving reference occurs in Sophocles' *Antigone* 454–5 (*agrapta nomima*) of around 442 and then in Aristophanes' *Acharnians* 532 in 425 and in the Periclean Funeral Speech (Thucydides 2.37). Although we must agree that it could be a dangerously slippery concept, its appearance seems also to imply a development in the nature of Greek law, probably a growing assumption that most laws were written, and perhaps, too, growing contemporary debates in late-fifth-century Athens about the nature of *written* law.[30] But in any case certain Athenian remarks about writing down the laws as a move toward greater justice imply strongly that there already existed some concept of binding rules on which to base judgment. In Euripides, as we noted, Theseus declares that there is equal justice for all, "when the laws are written down" and the antecedent of this was that under a tyrant, "there are no public laws (*nomoi koinoi*), but one man has control by owning the law himself, for himself" (*Suppliants* 429–34; cf. Solon frag. 36W). The obvious implication is that it was possible for a single tyrant to have control of the laws before they were written, but that once written down, they were more accessible, in the public domain, and thus able to afford justice for all.

This reminds us that there is an inherent danger in unwritten laws – sleights of hand in applying them, omission of awkward laws, a dangerous openness to the vagaries of social and political bias in a traditional political system – but written law by itself does not necessarily achieve just, fair, and consistent treatment for all alike either. Much depends on the judges and judicial system that administers them, and even if the texts of the laws are minutely examined, there will inevitably be problems of interpretation and gaps in the provision of the law, if the system of judicial process even allows for discussion. Written laws can, of course, be deliberately partial, as the apartheid regime in South Africa well illustrated. Archaic Greek cities seem to have been aware that the officials themselves might be the problem, hence the clauses in so many archaic laws that seek to control the officials and force them to obey the new law.

---

[30] See Thomas (1995: 64 ff.), Ostwald (1973), Ostwald (1969), Hölkeskamp (2000).

What emerges here is that there were some sort of binding rules before written laws, whether you call them unwritten laws, *nomoi*, or oral laws, and therefore there was a dynamic and changing relationship between the use of written laws and unwritten, and in the perception of their significance, as political and social circumstances changed over the centuries. Yet although cities attempted to penalize arbirtrary judgment and prevent political chaos in the archaic period by erecting written laws, some writers in the late fifth and fourth centuries go back to the idea that unwritten laws were intrinsically fairer and more fundamental: we mentioned Hippias above, and Aristotle in the later fourth century spoke about the greater fairness of customary (i.e., unwritten) laws (*Politics* 1287b). But we may be seeing here a later stage of anxiety about written laws once they have become normal, numerous, clearly changeable, and potentially motivated by particular groups, a product of lost innocence about the immutability of law.

Sometimes early written laws presuppose what is not written. Many early written laws concern procedure rather than substance; that is, they detail procedures to follow in the case of a misdemeanor rather than set out what one might call "commandments" or prohibitions. This can have the effect of creating (to our minds) rather ill-balanced laws. For instance, the Drakonian homicide law (ML 86), copied in the late fifth century from "the first axon" as it states, seems to start in midstride, "Even if someone commits homicide unwillingly...," and goes on to the procedures for prosecution, the emphasis being on who is responsible for bringing the homicide to justice rather than on declaring the wrongs of homicide. It takes for granted that homicide, even unwitting homicide, needs punishing, but does not state this explicitly. In other words, it seems to presuppose a certain tradition of dealing with homicide, and the writing either sets out the current procedure or (more likely) what it is to be from now on. Other laws concentrate on listing penalties rather than stating the substance of the law (i.e., the crime). Even the Dreros law is laconic and leaves much unexplained. The early law of Sparta called the Great Rhetra (Plutarch *Lycurgus* 6) does not explain its main clauses and confusingly contains verbs merely formed from the nouns they govern (thus, "obing the obe" – but what is an obe?).

That much was taken for granted has interesting implications for the role of writing. First, it implies that in this relatively early stage of creating binding written rules, it was not always recognized how much to spell out. This could create problems later when the meaning once so obvious was forgotten. Second, it implies that there was a large body of assumptions and traditional customs that lay behind these laws and that did not seem to need spelling out in writing. There were institutions and officials that did not need defining in the laws – from the *kosmos* in Crete to the *boulē* in Chios – unless they sorted them out elsewhere (in a period of rapid political development this too could lead to problems). A crucial unknown for the modern historian is the perceived role and duties of each official mentioned, for there must have been some continuity with the officials who resolved disputes or ran the city before written law, and their powers, arbitrary or traditional, would often continue and might distort the workings of the new written laws.[31] In other words there was a preexisting body of customs, traditions, and assumptions onto which the written laws were grafted. We can see what this means particularly clearly in later funerary legislation, which implies at every turn that there are current customs and habits at funerals that need to be limited or stopped. For instance, when the late-fifth-century law regulating funerals from Keos states, "the deceased is to be carried covered and in silence to the tomb," it implies that current custom insists on precisely the opposite.[32] For any of these early laws, there may be many current customs that are being swept away by their laconic and often enigmatic clauses.

This brings us to the probability that for most communities the laws that went up in writing were particularly special: these were not the ones agreed by all, but the contentious ones, the rules that constantly caused trouble, like the laws on heiresses, perhaps, listed at such length in the Gortyn Code. Or they might be the particularly fraught political ones where – we may speculate – rival aristocrats had perhaps been taking it in turns to seize power or twist the top office to their own ends and where their peers got together to try a permanent settlement. Perhaps this was what lay behind the Dreros law (ML 2), which attempted to limit the highest official's access to high office.

Could we envisage any of these laws being agreed in an entirely oral context? And, if so, what does the written text add? We might, after all, envisage an oral agreement in the seventh-century assembly of Dreros (or some smaller group) stipulating that no one should be *kosmos* twice in ten years. In fifth-century Teos, the curse they engraved, which in essence had the force of law, could well have been in oral form only: "Whoever makes poisonous medicines against the Teians as

---

[31] Thomas (1995), for instance, stresses the traditional and continuing powers of the *mnēmōn*; cf. Osborne (1997) for some thoughts about the "background structures."
[32] Sokolowski (1969) no. 97, A, line 10–12.

a community or against an individual that man shall die, himself and his family." After listing other nefarious actions, from preventing the import of grain to plotting, the inscription ends, "Whoever takes the stelai on which the curse is written, and breaks them or chisels out the letters and makes them invisible, that man shall die, both himself and his family" (ML 30, side A, lines 1–5; side B, 35–41). This could have had force as an oral pronouncement – oral curses are powerful in themselves. But it *is* written, and this was perhaps in the hope that the written version conferred extra authority and weight, as well as permanence, for a written curse is even better than an oral one. The Dreros law was engraved on the temple wall, with an invocation to the gods at the start and the officials (the *damioi*) who are to be "the swearers" to the law mentioned at the end. This seems, then, to be an attempt to bind those implicated even more firmly than a simple oral oath would. Its presence on the temple wall meant it was not only in a public place, but also that divine authority might be brought to bear on the enforcement of the law.[33] Other early laws mention explicitly that a certain god is to be the protector or guarantor. An early Locrian law of ca. 525–500 B.C. declares itself to be "sacred to Pythian Apollo and the gods who dwell with him," and it hopes or, rather, decrees, "may the god be kind to him who observes it [the law]" (ML 13, lines 14–16). Zeus and Apollo are called on to be guarantors of a treaty between Sybaris and the Serdaioi, in ca. 550–525, along with "other gods and the city of Poseidonia," and the bronze plaque was erected symbolically at the panhellenic sanctuary at Olympia where other Greeks could see it.[34]

The monumental written form, then, is only one among several means by which these early communities attempted to make their laws binding. We may suggest that the written law not only crystallized and made permanent a decision that might have been contentious – or at least not meekly accepted – but it also enabled the city to place the written law, now in physical form, in a prominent public place and declare the protection of the god. The curses from Teos roll all this into one. They neatly invoke divine aid, through the curses, in upholding the law, present themselves in written and permanent form that magnifies the force of a curse, and mention – in the form of a threat – the oral pronouncement of the curse at the festival of the Anthesteria (ML 30, B 29 ff.) while also threatening anihilation to anyone who defaces the

---

[33] H. and M. van Effenterre (1994) suggest the god is speaking through the writing, though this is not well supported by the evidence.

[34] ML 10; note that the treaty is "for ever."

writing on the stele. The Tean curses date to the early fifth century, the same period in which Athens formed her radical democracy. This reminds us that not all city-states were as developed politically or legally as Athens.[35]

Many of these early laws were being created in periods of rapid political and social change or in times of revolution. It is precisely in periods not marked by placid stability and political complacency that the status of new agreements and new laws might be expected to be most fragile. Lawgivers were called in by archaic cities in times of civil unrest – Solon at Athens, Demonax at Cyrene (Hdt. IV 161–2) – and it is a fair supposition that for single enactments, too, there might be serious questions as to whether these laws could be kept at all. It is most likely, then, that communities in tense circumstances would be trying to give the new laws as much authority as they possibly could; and if such laws were effectively agreements reached by the ruling elite, as was surely true in Dreros and most archaic cities, in an attempt to limit the ambitions of one's peers, then the same pressures might exist. For many cities, this new idea of written law may even have represented the first use of official writing by the early polis, and it is not surprising to find that these early groups attempt to set apart the law in as many special ways as possible in an attempt to give it an authority it might not otherwise have: preservation in writing, particularly in stone (or bronze); preservation in a sacred space; invocation to the gods at the beginning; and oaths and invocation of a god as guarantor at the end. It was radical new laws that needed this kind of protection rather than the traditional customs and rules of a community.[36]

Before written law there were "unwritten rules" or norms and customs, and even after some laws were written, others remained unwritten. Certainly the idea of "general unwritten rules" (such as the law about honoring one's parents) which could have any binding force before the piecemeal coming of written law is rather vague,[37] but without precise evidence about previous "rules" we can only speculate. Before Drakon's homicide law, there were presumably accepted rules about responsibility and recompense, penalties for the killer (probably exile), and actions allowed by the deceased's relatives. Perhaps it left too

---

[35] See also *SEG* 31.985 D and Herrmann (1981). An inscription from Chios (*GDI* 5653, C lines 5–10) mentions in passing "when the *basileus* utters the customary curses," which reminds one that the habit may have been relatively frequent.

[36] As argued in Thomas (1995), with further detailed examples; see also Hölkeskamp (1994).

[37] Gagarin (2003), Osborne (1997).

much ambiguity or was unclear about *accidental* homicide, the subject of the preserved law, and this prompted clarification and further details of procedure in writing.[38] Tradition and custom might also begin to seem intolerable in the area of officials' power: in an emerging political system, these might have been understood vaguely at first and then began to seem dangerously wide, hence attempts in written law to limit officials' powers.

It is unwise to abandon a concept of oral or unwritten law, for it is difficult to do entirely without some idea of binding rules before writing. It is hard to know what else to call the set of customs and norms and procedures that evidently lie behind the scene of arbitration on Achilles' shield in *Iliad* 18 (497–508).[39] There we see a combination of elders or judges, an arbiter, people, and a dispute about the blood price for a homicide, but no written law. It presupposes basic agreement in the community about penalties for homicide and procedures to use when there is a dispute. One problem with unwritten law must be precisely this, that it ends up often being dependent on social memory and on the officials or elders who have the responsibility of settling disputes. If disputes arise even when there is extensive written law, we can presume they arose equally or even more when only unwritten law was in place.

We see, then, individual laws for many parts of Greece that do not form part of a long set of laws: they appear to be isolated enactments, and their very phraseology, when they refer to "the writing," implies that as well. This begs the question what the city did about the rest of its public or religious life. It is also the case that many early laws concern religious activity, usually called "sacred laws," and several early fragments have mention of oaths. Early written law was closely bound up with religious sanctions, and indeed much early polis law may actually have been concerned with the gods.[40] This meshes with the previous suggestions about the preexistence of unwritten law, for very often these might be regarded as maintained and protected by the gods, like Antigone's "unwritten laws of the gods." To this picture we can add a number of lawgivers for certain cities who created a larger body of laws that were probably written as well as propagated orally.

---

[38] On the law, see esp. Gagarin (1981). Gagarin suggests (1986: 89 n. 23) that homicide laws were not common in the archaic period perhaps because homicide was dealt with by the respective families: this points again to an area where there must have been unwritten rules commonly accepted.

[39] See, for example, Gagarin (1986: Ch. 2); also Gagarin on early Greek law above.

[40] See Parker's chapter in this volume.

Much of this legislation is part of the development of the polis as a self-conscious, self-governing body that could actively create new rules for the community. Most of these archaic communities, to be sure, were run by a privileged elite or aristocracy, and phrases such as "it has been decided by the polis" (as at Dreros) may not indicate widely based popular decision making. Rather than a broad popular movement, many archaic rules may indeed have been attempts by this elite to ensure their peers would behave. Yet even so, the creation of a public inscription declaring that it was a polis decision (Dreros), or the rhetra of the Eleans, or that "It appears good to the Lyttians" to forbid the acceptance of strangers into the polis must be significant on some level of an awareness of the possibility of the community making new laws. Perhaps low literacy rates mattered less, so long as someone could read the laws who was in a position to object if they were ignored: we do not need to see them as merely or exclusively symbolic.[41] These early laws were an early and significant manifestation of the polis as self-governing and self-conscious community. The insistent emphasis on keeping to the writing in so many of these laws seems to imply a pious hope that the written rules will somehow straighten matters out. Similarly, Solon was supposed to have left Athens for ten years, while the Athenians lived with his laws and could not alter them. If the written laws were regarded – correctly or not – as being set up forever when they were first created, they were a major step in the crystalization of the polis as self-governing community.

The status of written and unwritten law emerged into open debate in Athens in the late fifth century and Athens pledged itself to use only written law in law courts from 403 onward. This may be read as an attempt to set her house in order after oligarchy and defeat; it is interesting that amid so many political changes, written law was clung to as a talisman for good order. Similarly, the revision of the Athenian laws, begun in 410, dragged on for six years and resulted in a revised law code on the wall of the Stoa Basileos and a court case against Nicomachus (Lysias 30), who was thought to have "erased some laws and inscribed others." Much of this is still not completely understood.[42] But the revision was, first, probably attempting to bring order to the Athenian laws and decrees that allowed mutually contradictory rules

---

[41] *Contra* Whitley's suggestion that they represented "in a symbolic form that for which the community as a whole stood" (1997: 660).

[42] Clinton (1982), Robertson (1990), Todd (1996), esp. for Nicomachus; most recently, Carawan (2002).

to coexist – another example of an attempt to stabilize the polis after political upheaval by organizing the laws, symbol and bulwark of political order. Second, the attempt to codify (if that is what it was) was either dropped or had little effect, because there are no references in oratory after 399 to the supposedly newly inscribed wall of laws.[43] This may have been because the revision brought Athenians face to face with a fact they did not like to confront: that laws could change and that the much revered "ancestral laws" might actually be no longer valid.[44]

This returns us again to the deep reverence for "the laws" and in particular for written laws. Aristotle makes numerous remarks on the question of whether written laws should be changed, the danger of weakening respect for written laws by changing them needlessly, and the importance of *epieikeia*, fairness, or, as often translated, "equity," alongside written law (esp. *Nicomachean Ethics* 1137b), for "customary laws have more weight and relate to more important matters than written" (*Politics* 1287b). This reminds us that the argument about written law went on well into the fourth century:[45] were written laws better than unwritten? Could a wise man be wiser than the laws (a useful argument for monarchy, as Aristotle lets on, *Politics* 1286a10)? How precise should the written laws be? And when does a jury or magistrate have to consider questions not covered by the law? The degree to which *epieikeia* was used in Athenian courts, as opposed to the written law, has been much debated.[46] It certainly seems that extralegal considerations not strictly convered by a directly relevant law had some influence in Athenian courts. But the force of rhetorical appeals to the law are such that Athenian juries are never openly invited to disregard the *nomoi* (i.e., the written *nomoi*) altogether – all juries are there to uphold the *nomoi* (Carey 1996). Athenians continued to call their laws the "laws of Solon" despite later additions (e.g., Demosthenes 20.92) and their revision, and appeals to the intentions of the ancestral lawgiver evidently had great rhetorical appeal in the fourth century (Thomas 1994), surely indicating considerable unease about departing from the ancient and ancestral laws and a deep nostalgia for the single authority of their great lawgiver Solon.

---

[43] Hansen (1990a: 70–1).
[44] Suggested by Todd (1996: 130).
[45] See *Rhetoric* I 1.7, 1354a–b; I 13.13, 1373–1374; *Politics* 1268b 39, 1269a 8ff, 1282b 2, 1286a10.
[46] For example, Todd (1993: 58–63), Harris (1994). See also Lanni in this volume.

Demosthenes (24.139 ff) actually cites as a cautionary and admirable law a Lokrian law that is elsewhere attributed to the ancient lawgiver Zaleukos (Polybius 12.16): anyone who wished to propose a new law had to do so with a halter around his neck. No surprise, then, that the Locrians had gained only one new law in the past two hundred years. This exemplifies both the strength and the weakness of written law in Greece: it gave permanence, stability, and importance, even divine sanction, to the law and yet for that very reason inhibited change even when there was obvious need for it. Much of the ambivalence in Greece to written law in relation to unwritten law may have arisen because written law often promised so much more than it really provided in practice.

3: LAW AND RELIGION

Robert Parker

THE REGULATION OF CULT: "SACRED LAWS"

Within the rubric "law and religion," a bundle of issues are united. One of the most important emerges from a fragmentary decree passed by the Athenian assembly either in the 440s or the 420s:

> (name lost) proposed. A priestess for Athena Nike ... shall be appointed from all Athenian women, and a door shall be built for the shrine in accord with the specification of Kallikrates. The leasing officials shall contract out the work in the prytany of Leontis. The priestess shall receive 50 drachmai and the legs and skins of public victims. And a temple and a stone altar shall be built in accord with the specification of Kallikrates. (ML[1] 44)

We see here how legislation concerning "the gods" or "the things of the gods" (these being the nearest Greek equivalents for the untranslatable "religion") was passed in Athens: it went through the people's assembly like legislation on any other topic. (The distinction between "decrees" and "laws" is not, for these purposes, of any importance.) As far as we know, the principle that decisions on religious matters were made by the same body or bodies that made secular decisions applied in all Greek communities and at all periods of Greek history. The character of the decision-making body and the process would be very different in a tight oligarchy from what they were in Athens, but nowhere do we

---

[1] Abbreviations in this chapter are taken from *The Oxford Classical Dictionary*, 3rd ed.

find a separate council or procedure for "the things of the gods" and them alone.

The fundamental structures of Greek religious life were regulated and, if necessary, adjusted in this way. At a certain point, for instance, many east Greek cities decided, probably for financial reasons, to alter the mode of appointment to the priesthoods of public cults: henceforth many if not all were to be sold at auction to the highest bidder. It will have been the citizen assembly that decided in each case on this very radical disruption of ancestral traditions. Greek religion is often nowadays characterized as "polis religion,"[2] religion of the city. The point of that description is not to deny, which would be absurd, that individuals sacrificed and made dedications on their own account. It is rather to bring out the implications in terms of authority and decision making of the cliché that there was no church in ancient Greece. The city and its subdivisions aside,[3] no human body had power to regulate religious affairs.

"Human" was added in that last phrase to prepare for an important qualification.[4] The gods themselves were often consulted, through their oracles, about major and indeed minor alterations to traditional practice. To remain with the topics just mentioned, in the fifth century the Athenians consulted an oracle, perhaps that of Dodona, about the terms of eligibility for a second newly established priesthood (that of Bendis) (*IG* I^3 136), and early in the first century B.C. the city of Herakleia under Latmos similarly asked whether the priesthood of Athena Latmia should be filled by annual election or offered for sale and held for life (*SEG* xl 956 IIa). In Plato's *Republic* all decisions of this type were to be entrusted to Apollo of Delphi (427b–c). Once the advice of the gods had been sought on such a matter, it was always followed. But the decision whether to consult an oracle and what precise question to put to it was made by the citizen assembly. The god merely chose between the options put to him, both of which must have been tolerable, if not equally pleasing, to the citizens. There was no opportunity here for a priestly class to promote an agenda of its own. This was theocracy of the most controlled and moderate kind.

Modern scholarship is familiar with a class of inscriptions known as "sacred laws."[5] The term has ancient authority insofar as Greeks

---

[2] Under the influence of a seminal study by Sourvinou-Inwood (1990).
[3] Or, for the regions of Greece organized by *ethnos* ("tribe"), "the *ethnos* and its sub-divisions aside."
[4] Cf. Garland (1984: 80–1).
[5] See Parker (2004). These texts are collected in Sokolowski (1955, 1962, 1969).

sometimes spoke of "sacred laws" and sometimes even so described some texts found in the modern collections. But the modern category is an ill-defined one, and it does not look as if the ancient usage was any more precise. Many "sacred laws" are indeed true laws, in the sense of regulations emanating from the citizen assembly or other legislative body of the city concerned, and backed by its authority. And this is exactly what the argument thus far would lead one to expect. The city legislated about the perquisites owed to priests, protection of sanctuaries, good order at festivals, the sacrifices to be made at public expense, and so on. But other "sacred laws" are rather what one might call recommendations for best ritual practice. They seem to be designed not as a check on potential lawbreakers but as a source of guidance to those who wish to be pious, to respect local ritual tradition in all its pernickety particularity. They explain, above all, how to sacrifice in a given sanctuary and what conditions of purity are required for access to it: wait a day after sexual intercourse, three days after contact with a woman in childbed, five days after contact with a corpse.... Such texts normally do not contain sanctions against infraction and probably derive from local convention rather than specific decisions of the assembly. Some "sacred laws" combine characteristics of both types. A remarkable inscription from Iulis on Keos that begins "These are the laws/customs about the dead" blends measures of social control (restrictions on the scale of expenditure on funerals, for instance) with rules such as "do not put a cup under the bier or pour out the water or take the sweepings to the tomb" (Sokolowski 1969: no. 97).

"Impiety": Laws against Religious Offences

We turn now to look more specifically at the sanctions that threatened religious offenders. The discussion relates almost exclusively to Athens[6]; it is clear from inscriptions that "temple robbing" and "impiety" were recognized as categories of offence in many Greek cities, but it is only in Athens that we can observe the laws in action.

There were at least four religious counts on which one could be indicted at Athens. "Wrongdoing concerning a festival" as a specific offence would be all but completely unknown to us but for the chance that it is the ground of action underlying one of Demosthenes' finest

---

[6] Cf. MacDowell (1978: 192–202), Todd (1993: 307–15).

invectives, the *Against Meidias* (Dem. 21); the rich Meidias hit Demosthenes while he was serving as sponsor (*chorēgos*) for his tribe's chorus at the Dionysia, and the blow inflicted in such circumstances struck not just Demosthenes but religion itself, the orator pathetically explains (126). Such charges had normally to be brought before the council and people by the special procedure known as *probolē* on the day after the festival (cf. Andoc. 1.111–2). Demosthenes' speech contains (175–80) a useful little catalogue of instances, from which it emerges that "wrongdoing concerning a festival" typically[7] involved physical violence (perhaps in the form of distraint in pursuit of a debt) perpetrated during a festival and could at the limit be punished by a death sentence. The procedure was designed, therefore, to protect the character of the festival as a special time of peace, when even debtors could roam in public without fear of creditors.

"Theft of sacred money" is an ill-known charge, supposedly brought in one attested case (Dem. 19.293) against an individual who was three days late in making a payment to a sacred fund.[8] There remain "impiety," "temple robbing," and offences concerning sacred olive trees (unless this last counted as a subclass of one of the others, despite being tried in a different court from them). The Athenian attitude to their sacred olive trees can seem like a gnarled old relic of primeval piety: cases were heard in the venerable court of the Areopagus, and offenders were originally liable to severe penalties (death, according to Aristotle, though the attested case mentions only a fine[9]). But the need to protect the sacred olives arose only at an identifiable date in the sixth century when it was decided to offer huge numbers of amphorae full of the sacred oil as prizes at the *Panathenaea*, and when in the fourth century a new system of levying the oil was instituted (not by individual tree but by estate), such trials ceased to take place (Arist. *Ath. Pol.* 60.2). A resource was being protected, as well as a myth.

Of the other charges, impiety, associated as it is with some of the most famous incidents in Athenian history, has been of much greater interest to scholars than the little-known temple-robbing.[10] But it was against temple robbers that the greater ferocity of law was directed. Like the actions for impiety and for harm to sacred olives, the *graphē* for

---

[7] For a different possibility (a failure, for reasons unclear, to provide sacred crowns) see Dem. 21.218.

[8] The only other reference is in Antiphon 2.1.6, which establishes only that the action was a *graphē atimētos*.

[9] Arist. *Ath. Pol.* 60.2; Lysias 7.

[10] For the three attested cases see Todd (1993), 307 n. 19.

temple robbing could be set in motion by information laid by slaves, who in the event of a conviction could hope to secure their freedom. It was perhaps only in relation to religious offences that such power over their masters was granted to slaves.[11] And temple robbers shared with traitors (alone) the severest penalty that the ancient city could inflict, death or exile aggravated by confiscation of property and denial of the right of burial in Attica (Xen. *Hell.* 1.7.22). Unlike impiety, the offence admitted apparently of no degrees. It is a great lack that we have no case law to show just what might count as temple robbing and how fiercely the Athenians acted against minor instances.

Impiety is likely to have had no defined content[12]: the law will have been of the form "if any individual commits impiety, let anyone who wishes indict him . . .", and the prosecutor will then have mentioned in the indictment particular forms of impious behavior:

> X does wrong [even in relation to impiety this verb often occurs, as for instance in the charges against Socrates] because he has mutilated divine images/ because he has revealed the Mysteries/ because he has violated this or that sacred law/ because he has associated with a parricide/ because he does not worship the same gods as the rest of the Athenians but other, new gods.[13]

Certain forms of behavior were doubtless commonly recognized as symptoms of impiety, but it will have been open to prosecutors to try to bring others too under the rubric; as there was no fixed penalty, offences of very different degrees of gravity could all be treated as impiety. When the Athenian "Amphictyons" on Delos, a resented foreign presence, were driven out of the temple with blows by a group of Delians in 376/5, the charge on which the Delians were condemned was one of impiety.[14] There was a variety of procedures too by which impiety charges could be introduced (Dem. 22.27). If this line of argument is

---

[11] See Harrison (1968), 171, n. 1, with the important restriction proposed by Osborne (2000a). Slave denunciation in ordinary impiety cases (as opposed to the quite exceptional events of the year 415) is attested by Dem. 25.79.

[12] See Cohen (1991: 203–17).

[13] The last item in this list refers to the trial of Socrates in 399, the first two to the great scandal of 415 B.C. (Thuc. 6.27–9, 60–1; Andoc. 1 *passim*); for the others see Dem. 59.116 (with the verb "do wrong"), Dem. 22.2. Dem. 59.116 shows that a case brought for violation of a specific sacred law counted generically as "impiety"; for another such case see Andoc. 1.113–16.

[14] *IG* II² 1635 (Tod, 2, no. 125), 134–42.

correct, the question whether, say, to "introduce new gods" to Athens was illegal turns out to be unanswerable in the form in which it is put: there was no specific law against "introducing new gods," but to have introduced the wrong ones in the wrong circumstances might form an item in an indictment for impiety.

With introducing new gods there comes into view the issue about which modern observers of Athens care most, that (to speak anachronistically) of religious toleration and freedom of thought. The stakes are high, the evidence is open to challenge and debate on many points: this is a paradigm case where even honest enquirers are liable to depict the Athens of their wishes or their fears. We are told by ancient sources that at Athens in the late fifth century a string of intellectuals – Anaxagoras, Protagoras, Prodikos, even Pericles' mistress Aspasia – were prosecuted, and in most cases condemned, for impiety and that one other, Diogenes of Apollonia, "came close to danger"; the impiety in question is normally said to have consisted in outrageous claims about the gods contained in their writings. But the evidence for these attacks on philosophers is never contemporary and is often demonstrably unreliable.[15] The least ill-attested case is that of Anaxagoras (who thought the sun was not a god but a stone), and here the sources present the prosecution as a mode of oblique and politically motivated attack on his patron Pericles (not that this, given Pericles' popularity, could explain the attitude of the jurors who voted to condemn him – if they did). It is fairly certain that, late in the fourth century, politically motivated accusations of impiety were brought against the philosophers Theophrastus and Aristotle; their pro-Macedonian political stance was widely resented, and the formal charge is likely to have been just a pretext for all concerned, including jurors. We are also told that shortly before the Peloponnesian war a seer, Diopeithes, proposed a decree whereby "those who do not acknowledge the divine" or who "teach about the things in the air" were to be liable to prosecution by the special procedure of *eisangelia*, presumably on a charge of impiety. That information is owed to a single passage in Plutarch (*Per.* 32.2), but is not otherwise exposed to serious doubt. And it is certain that the philosopher Socrates was executed for impiety in 399. Political resentments almost certainly contributed to his

---

[15] The very sceptical study of Dover (1988) is fundamental; for further references on all the issues here treated see Parker (1996), Ch. 10 and (Theophrastus and Aristotle) 276–7. The case of the poet Diagoras of Melos is different: he was certainly condemned, but according to the earliest evidence (Ar. *Av.* 1071–3 and the ancient commentaries thereto; Lys. 6.17–18) for mockery and profanation of the Mysteries, not for writings. (See, however, Janko 2001.)

condemnation, but the formal indictment ran "Socrates does wrong by not acknowledging the gods the city acknowledges, and introducing other, new powers. He also does wrong by corrupting the young."

To pick a path through this boggy landscape, one needs to distinguish two questions. If one asks how tolerant of unorthodox teachings (and cults) Athenian society was in practice, the answer will fluctuate depending on how one judges doubtful cases, but nothing would justify talk of systematic repression. If one asks whether the Athenians recognized an ideal of freedom of thought or of religious tolerance, the answer is unequivocally no: no text suggests that they did, and the decree of Diopeithes (if historical) and the successful charge against Socrates show them untroubled by such ideals. Freedom of speech à l'Athénienne meant the right of the poor man to make his voice heard alongside that of the rich, not a licence for impious talk.[16]

One was also supposed to worship the gods "in accord with tradition" ("as modified by decrees of the assembly" we must add, to make the formula fit known facts), not in one's own way. There were many private religious groups in Athens, and doubtless the majority of them went about their business unmolested. But, if they came to be perceived as being socially undesirable, the undesirable behavior they encouraged could be rolled up along with "innovation in religion" in a charge of impiety against their leader. We know of three such prosecutions in the fourth century, all brought against women, two of which resulted in condemnation and execution. (In one "impiety" is not identified as the charge, but may be confidently inferred.) The prosecutor in one declared (L. Spengel, *Rhetores Graeci*, I, 455.8–11): "I have demonstrated that Phryne is impious; she has led most shameless revels, she is the introducer of a new god, she has assembled illicit *thiasoi* of men and women." In the other cases, accusations of dealing in magical potions and inciting slaves against masters also appear. The precise weight of each individual item in these composite accusations cannot be determined: would magic-working on its own, for instance, have constituted ground for an impiety prosecution?[17] One notes that all these impious women were leaders of groups, not isolated individuals. The uncertainties are

---

[16] Todd (1993: 311–12).
[17] For an excellent agnostic discussion see Dickie (2001: 49–54); he stresses the potential relevance to fourth-century Athens of an Aesopian fable (56 Hausrath) in which a woman is condemned for magic. See too Jameson (1997), who studies the implications for female roles in the fourth century, and Collins (2001), who doubts the actionability of spells and incantations per se.

frustrating. But it is likely that uncertainty about the possible scope of impiety was also part of the lived reality of Athens.

Moderns often explain that the reason why the Athenians had no choice but to strike hard against impiety was that otherwise the wrath of the angered gods would fall on themselves. The idea finds support (of course) in Plato, who in his old age had a religious explanation for everything.[18] It is otherwise less often expressed in Athenian sources than one might have expected; perhaps it was just taken for granted. A similar explanation, the need to protect the city from pollution, has often been offered for the enactment of homicide legislation at Athens in the seventh century and for its continuing form. It is true that the "involuntary" killer who returned to Athena after a period of exile was required to undergo purification (Dem. 23.72); to this limited extent the law gave expression to religious concerns. It is also true that poetic texts constantly, and prose texts sometimes, speak of the danger posed by the polluted killer; the singularity and almost scholasticism, however, of the one prose text (Antiphon's *Tetralogies*) that harps on the theme obsessively has been well recognised of late.[19] Athenians also often explained the aims and workings of their homicide laws in terms that are not those of pollution avoidance,[20] and there is no feature of them except the requirement of purification just mentioned that is best explained in those terms alone.[21]

RELIGIOUS FORMS OF LEGAL ACTION: *HEILIGES RECHT*

I turn to a different kind of "sacred law," one translated from the German this time and in which *Law* stands not for specific statutes but for legal order and process. A short book so entitled (*Heiliges Recht*) published in 1920 remains the fundamental point of reference on the subject indicated by its subtitle, "Investigations on the history of sacral legal forms in Greece." Here are studied the religious forms of action, preeminently the oath, embedded within Greek legal process. The author, Kurt Latte, understood the phenomenon in several different ways.

---

[18] For example, *Laws* 910b1–6, cited by Dickie (2001: 329, n. 13) to illustrate ordinary Athenian attitudes.
[19] Williams (1993: 189 n. 28): "casuistry, not religion"; Carawan (1998: 192–8).
[20] MacDowell (1963: 1–7).
[21] See Carawan (1998: 1–167; on pollution especially 17–19).

At times he sees religion as a chrysalis from which, by a rather mysterious process, law emerged. Study of the surviving remains of sacral legal forms gives us, he writes,[22] a "glimpse of the times when 'religion gave men the strength to create for themselves law and state'" (the embedded quotation is from a chapter contributed by the great hellenist Wilamowitz to the study of "the most ancient criminal law" by his father-in-law, the Roman historian Mommsen). In this mood he emphasizes the unshaken, unquestioning piety of primeval times: men feared the gods, it seems, before they learnt to fear the law. This approach bespeaks its origin in nineteenth-century evolutionism and has been duly criticized. But it is only one element and not the most prominent in Latte's understanding. More important to Latte was the problematic status of law in societies lacking strong central authority and power of enforcement. In such conditions, the challenge for legal forms was to win recognition of their legitimacy by all parties to a dispute; and an oath might have an authority that a judge's simple fiat lacked. Sacral forms are not an inevitable expression of the piety of the age, but a kind of default option where more compelling modes of proof and enforcement are lacking. Latte would, for instance, have been very happy to see the role of the ordeal in the European Middle Ages explained through the absence of strong central political authority, not through superstition.[23]

The point of this argument is not to bleed the religious content out of the sacral forms, but to stress that their greater or lesser prominence in different ages is not a simple function of the piety or impiety of the times. It must always have been obvious to everybody that, as the philosopher Xenophanes was to note, an "oath challenge between an impious and a pious man is not on equal terms, but just as if a strong man were to challenge a weak one to strike or be struck" (Arist. *Rhet.* 1377a 18–21); the art of "cheating by oaths" was already known to Homer.[24] The oath was never supposed to be a perfect instrument, but it might be the best available. Men had recourse to oaths not in blind faith but after canny and cautious negotiation; we might reapply to the early Greeks

---

[22] Latte (1920: 4).
[23] See Brown (1982). But contrast Murray (1978: 10). Strubbe (1991: 40–1) notes that curses gain in prominence "in circumstances or places or periods in which human law is vitiated by its powerlessness, unsteadiness, partiality, or even absence" and gives references from several cultures.
[24] *Od.* 19.395f. In Ptolemaic Egypt, oaths had a substantial role in arbitration procedures: the writer of a papyrus petition (*SB* 4638.16) complains that his opponent planned to "drench [i.e., swindle] him by oath" (ὅρκῳ ἐπικλύζειν) before arbitrators.

Peter Brown's identification of "the vast bedrock of cunning with which mediaeval men actually faced and manipulated the supernatural in their affairs."[25]

Yet one handled the supernatural with immense care because it was powerful. Few swore false oaths lightly, whether in the eighth century or the fourth. Let us hear the speech put into the mouth of a client's wife by Lysias, that master in the depiction of character and, we must suppose, of credible speech. At a family council she supposedly arraigned her own father "When (Diodotos, her husband) sailed out, you received five talents as a deposit for safe keeping from him. About this I am willing to bring both my children by Diodotos and those borne to me later wherever you say and to swear. But I am not so desperate or so mad for money as to commit perjury by my children before I die" (Lysias 32.13). Like so many oaths alluded to in Attic forensic oratory, this one was never in fact sworn (because of "the vast bedrock of cunning," oaths were usually offered only in circumstance where it would have been disadvantageous for opponents to accept), but had it been, the whole company would have gone to a temple, and the woman would have taken in her hands, or stood on, portions of the flesh of a sacrificial animal in order to invoke "evil destruction" on herself and the children who stood at her side should she swear false, all this before the eyes of many people, some of whom knew the true facts.[26] Perjury was both very easy and very hard.

Generalized talk of this kind about oaths and perjury, however, may mislead. One of the strengths of Latte was the precision with which he distinguished situation from situation and oath from oath. The Gortyn Code is (along with related texts from the same city) the most important single source, and several possibilities appear. A procedural passage of central importance runs, "Whatever it has been prescribed that the judge shall judge in accord with witnesses or on the basis of an oath of denial, he shall judge as has been prescribed; about other matters he shall judge by oath with reference to the pleas" (xi. 26–31). Three possibilities are envisaged, settlement by witnesses, by oath of denial, and by judgment. The character of "witnessing" at Gortyn is discussed in John Davies' chapter in this volume.[27] In the majority of certain cases, witnesses at Gortyn were the precursors to our witnesses to a signature, not to our witnesses to a street accident or crime: they attested not events that they

---

[25] Brown (1982: 315).
[26] On oath procedures see in brief Burkert (1985: 250–4); also Casabona (1966: 220–5).
[27] See also Gagarin (1989).

chanced to have been present at, but the due performance of procedures which they were specifically summoned to observe. Or neighbors might be called to attest matters of general knowledge in a vicinity. But a few instances of chance witnessing have, it seems, to be accepted; and once some are accepted, the door is open. An example of a case to be settled "in accord with witnesses" is a dispute over ownership of a slave. If one party and one only has the support of a witness (to the act of purchase?), that party prevails (i.18–21). We note that in such instances the witness is not said to be on oath; in a society where such things mattered hugely, it surely follows[28] that he was not.

Judgment "in accord with an oath of denial" refers to an oath by one party to the case that is granted probatory force. The party with the right to swear is identified through the expression "more entitled to the oath"[29]; usually it is the defendant (the Greek word ἀπόμνυμι often used in this context contains the separatory prefix ἀπό, giving the sense "to swear away"), and such oaths are often called "purgatory oaths" from the name of a similar practice known from early Germanic law, *Reinigungseid*.[30] If, for instance, a slave disappears who has been pledged by A as security for money lent to him by B, A must swear that he was not responsible for the disappearance himself or in association with another and has no knowledge of the slave's whereabouts; otherwise he must pay the value of the slave[31] (the common "swear or pay" option). This example also shows that the form of the oath was not left to the swearer to choose, but prescribed in each instance. As far as the court was concerned, an oath of this type settled the case. In the example chosen the oath was in fact one of denial[32] ("I had nothing to do with it"), but other oaths occur that are not of this form (e.g., "we offered this woman's separated husband the opportunity to rear this child, and he refused it," Code iii.49–52, cf. iv.6–8) and yet have the same crucial function of settling a disputed point once and for all. The section on rape ends by saying that if raped the indoor slave-girl is "more entitled to the oath"

---

[28] Gagarin (1989: 49) disputes this.

[29] For a slightly different view of this formula see John Davies' article in this volume. Headlam (1892–1893) in a classic article attempted to dissociate the oaths indicated by this expression from true purgatory oaths, and his distinction is taken over by Willetts (1967: 33). But oaths of this type too have probatory force, as for instance in iii. 49–51, iv. 6–8.

[30] For Egypt cf. the supposed code of king Bokchoris in Diod. 1.79.1, with Seidl (1929: 65, 72).

[31] IC iv. 47 = van Effenterre/Ruzé (1995–1996), II, no. 26. For "swear or pay" see Latte (1920: 18).

[32] So also very clearly, in the Gortyn Code, iii.5–9, xi.48.

(ii.15–16). The provision is difficult because no similar right has been assigned to the raped free woman, but whatever precisely one supposes the slave girl to have been entitled to swear (that she had been raped? that she was a virgin when raped? that the attack occurred by night?) this is certainly a case of a decisive oath sworn on the side of the plaintiff, not the defendant. And this concept, that of the "action-deciding" oath, seems to be the crucial one; the purgatory oath is just one especially frequent form.

Witnesses, as we have noted, normally testified unsworn; but they sometimes joined with a party to the case in an oath. Dramatically, if a man was seized in adultery and claimed to have been entrapped, the captor was required "in a case of fifty staters and more [there were differential ransoms according to the status of the adulterer] to swear along with four others, each one invoking curses on himself, that they had caught him committing adultery and had not lured him" (ii.36–45).[33] The text does not use the word *witnesses* here of the "four others," but what is envisaged must surely be persons brought along by the suspicious husband to capture the adulterer in the act, as in Lysias 1.23–24. Witnesses had to swear in this case because this was in effect a reinforced action-deciding oath. According to the most widely accepted view,[34] a difficult passage runs as follows: "let the relevant witnesses give testimony. Once they have testified, let the judge rule that the plaintiff and his witnesses shall swear, and so gain the sum without multiplication" (ix.36–40). That is to say, a certain group of witnesses are required to swear an action-deciding oath along with the party they supported not before but after giving their testimony. If this is correct, the point of the oath was not to confirm the truth of the testimony as a guide to judgment, but visibly to expose the witnesses to religious danger if it was false.

The third of the three forms of procedure at Gortyn was that where the judge was required to "judge by oath in accord with the pleas." The judge's role was not then simply to supervise automatic, action-deciding procedures: he sometimes also had to judge. And the responsibility was terrible. Its nature emerges from a passage treating the division of household goods after marital breakdown. "If a third party

---

[33] Two oaths mentioned in the previous paragraph (iii.49–52, iv.6–8) were also joint sworn.
[34] That of Latte (1920: 10–11); cf. van Effenterre/Ruzé (1995–1996: II, no. 45). An alternative translation, which substitutes "but if they refuse" for "once they have testified," was generally accepted before Latte and is still championed by Maffi (1983: 157–61). The verb can bear either meaning; Gortynian usage of the conjunction ἒ favors "once" (Willetts 1967: 67).

joins (with the wife) in removing (goods), he shall pay ten staters and twice the value of what the judge *swears he joined in removing*" (iii.12–16). Swearing and judging are not, therefore, two processes but one. The judge does not swear to judge justly and then opine that the third party joined in removing goods worth, as it might be, three staters; he swears that the third party removed goods worth three staters. If he has been misled by false testimony, the religious guilt is none the less his.

Latte explained the sum of these procedures by the need to make the intrusion of the court into the litigants' affairs acceptable. The judge may reach an automatic verdict in accord with the formal testimony of witnesses; a fixed rule may transfer the moral burden of swearing an action-deciding oath onto one of the plaintiffs (and his witnesses); where neither of these automatic procedures applies, the judge engages himself by the most powerful pledge available to him not just for his good intentions but also for the literal truth of his verdict. The situation becomes a little more complicated if we allow (against Latte) that witnessing at Gortyn was not always of a formal and uncontroversial character. If a verdict was issued "in accord with witnesses" who claimed to speak as observers of controversial facts, it was surely needful, according to Latte's rationale, either for these witnesses to incur religious risk through swearing an oath to the truth of their testimony or for the judge who chose to trust them to back his judgment with an oath. Our evidence fails us here; no detail of procedure in just these circumstances survives. But very probably such an oath was indeed required.

The developed formalism of Gortynian law is unparalleled elsewhere in Greece. Purgatory oaths are found quite often, but nowhere else are they a prescribed part of state legal procedure. An obscure fragment of Solon suggests that they may once have been at Athens, but by the time we have reliable evidence we find only "oath-challenges" issued by one party to a dispute. Because it was normally in a spirit of rhetorical jousting that such challenges were made, they were seldom to our knowledge taken up; voluntary challenges are anyway a different thing from the fixed procedures of Gortyn.[35] In other states we hear of purgatory oaths in private or semiprivate contexts, within a phratry at Delphi (in the form "swear or pay") or quite often in connection with

---

[35] See Harrison (1971: 130–3); Mirhady (1991b), who thinks purgatory oaths may have had a real role in arbitration procedures, and Gagarin (1997), who stresses the elements of rhetoric. On the fragment of Solon (F42 Ruschenbusch ap. Bekker, *Anecdota Graeca* I. 242, 20–2), see Latte (1920: 24–5) and Gagarin (1997: 127). On the various forms of oath see further Gagarin on early Greek law in this volume.

private deposits or loans.[36] For conclusive oaths by prosecutors (for oaths are surely what is at issue, though this is not explicitly said) we have only Aristotle's account of what he judges an absurd archaic survival in homicide procedures at Kyme (*Pol.* 1269a 1–3): "if the prosecutor provides a certain number of his own kinsmen as witnesses, then the defendant is found guilty of the killing." These Kymaean kinsmen are, incidentally, the closest available parallel for the "Oath-helpers" (*Eideshelfer*) of early Germanic law; for in other instances of group swearing, such as some from Gortyn mentioned earlier, the co-jurors, though their mere number was undeniably important, were certainly or probably not mere supporters of the principal but also witnesses to relevant facts.[37]

The main form of prescribed oath-swearing at Athens was quite different.[38] Both parties to every case swore, whereas at Gortyn the "more entitled to the oath" system seems to have been designed to avoid the clash of conflicting oaths, and they swore as a way of introducing the case, not of resolving it. In homicide cases the oaths were of famed solemnity – they were taken "standing over the cut pieces of a boar, a ram and a bull, slaughtered by the proper persons on the proper days" (Dem. 23.67), and the oath was to the fact: "he killed" countered by "I did not kill" (e.g., Ant. 6.16). In homicide cases alone witnesses too swore, again to their "sure knowledge" that the defendant had, or had not, killed (Ant. 1.8, 28). In other cases only the parties swore, again to the fact (Pollux 8.55). (Jurors, however, had only to swear to judge in accord with the laws.) Here, too, we are dealing with formalism (a formalism that perhaps turned into a formality), but one different from the Gortynian. Latte called these preliminary oaths "trial-grounding": neither party could be expected, he argued, to allow the validity of the other's challenge to a trial (or rejection of that challenge) unless validated by oath; the oaths permitted a trial in lieu of a brawl. (The logical consequence that every trial entailed perjury by one party or the other was noted disapprovingly by Plato, *Laws* 948d.) After the

---

[36] Buck (1955), no. 52, C 25–9, D 22–5, and, for example, Hdt. 6.86.5. For their role in arbitration in Ptolemaic Egypt (a continuation of earlier practice) see Seidl (1969: 62–74). For their role in popular justice in the Roman period see Chaniotis (1997: 371 n. 100), who cites inter alia Babrius, *Fable* 2; Petzl (1994: no. 34); note too Diodorus 11.89.5–6.

[37] So Latte (1920: 29 n. 2 and 31 n. 9), modifying Meister (1908). The context of the important provision for oath-swearing by a family group in *IC* iv 51 = van Effenterre/Ruzé (1995–1996), II, no. 13 is lost. The precise role even of Germanic *Eideshelfer* appears to be controversial (Scheyhing 1971).

[38] See Harrison (1971: 99–100); MacDowell (1963: 90–100); Carawan (1988: 138–43).

verdict in a murder case, the victor was required to "touch the cut pieces and swear that those who cast their vote for him voted for what was true and just, and that he had spoken no falsehood; he should invoke destruction on himself and his household if this were not so, but pray for many blessings for the jurors" (Aeschines 2.87). This is a most intriguing form, a squaring of the circle. At Gortyn, if the judge judged "in accord with the pleas" and not by formal criteria, he had to take the full responsibility for the verdict on himself. The Athenian juror exercised freedom of judgment while passing the religious danger back onto one of the contending parties.

We turn from procedure to penalties. If *Heiliges Recht* was necessary because of the weakness of secular tribunals, it is not surprising if sacral forms appear in the penalties that they sought to inflict; for the courts' power of enforcement was very slight. (All tribunals were secular, although let us note in passing a famous inscription of the fifth century from Mantinea that records, obscurely, a verdict passed by "the judges and the goddess" (Athena Alea) against a list of men: the charge was of committing murder within the goddess' temple, and the consequent recourse to an oracle to discover the goddess' verdict was quite exceptional.[39]) In archaic Rome, outlawry could take the form, through the so-called *leges sacratae*, of declaring the offender "sacred" (in no good sense) to a god whom he had offended. Latte detected traces of a similar penal consecration in certain archaic texts from Elis. We follow him into this difficult territory only in a footnote[40]; for, even if some form of penal consecration did exist in the holy land of Elis, in Greece as a whole a declaration of outlawry normally took a simple secular form

---

[39] Thür Taeuber (1994: no. 8) (with a full discussion).

[40] Latte so interpreted (1) a sixth-century inscription that specified that anyone who performed seizure against a particular favored friend of the Eleans was to "go away to Zeus" (van Effenterre/Ruzé 1995–1996: I no. 21); (2) a fourth-century text (Buck 1955: no. 65) that he takes to permit the "consecration" of a class of offenders, whereas a sixth- or fifth-century text (van Effenterre/Ruzé 1995–1996: I no. 23, Buck 1955: no. 61) forbids the "consecration" (same verb) of a particular favored individual (or category). For other views see Buck (1955: 260) and Casabona (1966: 26–8), who gives the verb a different basic sense ("sacrifice against" rather than "consecrate"). A further remarkable text from Elis is a treaty of the early fifth century (?): "The covenant for the Anaitoi and the Metapioi (two unknown communities, probably from the neighborhood of Elis). Friendship for fifty years. Whichever side fails to keep it firm, let the proxenoi and the seers drive them from the altar, should they break the oath. The priests of Olympia are to decide" [van Effenterre/Ruzé 1995–1996: I no. 51 (with a change in the sentence division)]. The power here accorded to the priests and other religious officials to intervene in the disputes of two communities is most singular.

such as "let him die without recompense."[41] Two better attested forms of sacralized sanction are the sacred fine and the curse. The sacred fine payable to a named deity was the normal form for a fine in archaic and even classical Greece. Where the whole property of an exiled or executed person was forfeit, it too went to a god. Sacred fines appear to have been irrevocable, but a more crucial factor may have been that archaic Greek cities lacked, as it seems, even the concept of a "public" as opposed to a sacred treasury. Windfall profits were disposed of immediately, either by use on a public project or by simple distribution among the citizens[42]; if they were to be kept, it had to be through consecration.

A sacral form of pervasive occurrence is the curse. We have already encountered its importance in judicial procedure; for what gave force to every oath sworn in a court was the conditional self-cursing (usually in fact "self and offspring") that it contained. Communities too had their curses. The most vivid comes from Teos on the coast of Asia Minor early in the fifth century. It begins as follows:

> Anyone who should make destructive drugs (or "spells") against the Teians as a community or against an individual, may that man and his family perish. Anyone who should by any craft or device prevent the bringing in of corn to Teian territory by sea or by land or should send it away once imported, may that man and his family perish.

There follow curses against anyone who establishes or exercises a form of monarchic rule in Teos, who betrays Teian territory, who engages in brigandage or piracy or supports brigands or pirates, who plots any ill against Teos; also against any magistrate who fails to pronounce these curses on three stated occasions during the year and against any individual who damages the inscription on which the curses are recorded.

A new version was published in 1981 that reflects the close ties between Teos and her settlement Abdera in Thrace and gives a new curse formula: "may that man and his family perish out of Teos and Abdera and Teian territory."[43]

---

[41] See Youni (2001).

[42] The verb used for "confiscate" in a Locrian inscription of the early fifth century (ML 20 = van Effenterre/Ruzé 1995–1996: I no. 43, line 44) means literally "eat property." Cf. Latte (1948), and on fines Latte (1920: 48–61).

[43] See van Effenterre/Ruzé [1995–1996]: I no. 104 (=ML 30) and (new version) no. 105].

Similar public curses are known in many Greek cities, persisting well down into the Hellenistic period. Always they were directed against offences held to be particularly threatening to the general well-being.[44] Individual decrees could be reinforced in the same way. What relation exists between such curses and secular justice? Sometimes one finds a decree that threatens offenders both with a specified penalty and with a curse.[45] Latte saw such a combination as indicating a loss of faith in the unaided power of the curse; the curse sanctions attached to public decrees in the Hellenistic period were for him meaningless formulae. But it is inconceivable that the Teians would simply have left traitors, for instance, to be punished by the gods. Those guilty of such offences often incurred permanent exile, confiscation of property, even a symbolic annihilation of their whole place in the community through destruction of their house.[46] There is no incompatibility, no tension, between threatening the same offender with both punishments and curses. There may well have been Teian decrees that specified that traitors were both to be outlawed and to be made targets in the annual ritual of public cursing. But the curse is the more comprehensive instrument, because it reaches out to the offender even prior to detection. And the ritual of public cursing conveyed a powerful statement about collective values.

The general tenor of Latte's presentation was evolutionary. The story of the Greeks' dealings with *Heiliges Recht* is the story of how they ceased to need it; and this was progress. Yet he ended with a remarkable example of the use of sacral forms that, unknown in the archaic period, emerged in the fifth or fourth century, became very common in the following centuries, and persisted until late in the Roman empire. This was sacral manumission.[47] There were two broad ways to release a slave in Greece, the civic and the sacral. The choice between the two (there were also mixed forms) was roughly one by region. Civic manumission

---

[44] See Latte (1920: 68–77); Parker (1983: 193–6).
[45] E.g., *Syll.*³ 364.30–32 (Ephesus, early third century); Latte (1920: 76).
[46] See Connor (1985). The expression "may that man and his family perish out of Teos and Abdera and Teian territory" in the second copy of the Teian curses may in fact be thought to presuppose exile, though one must agree with Latte (1920: 69 n. 21) that a curse is not a piece of secular legislation in disguised form; any human punishment threatening the target of a curse will have had to be imposed by separate legislation.
[47] There is no up-to-date synthesis, but valuable partial studies include Hopkins and Roscoe (1978) for Delphi, Ricl (1995) for Phrygia, Darmezin (1999) for central Greece, and Youni (2000: 54–120), for Macedonia. Particularly important is the study of a large new dossier from Macedonia in Petsas et al. (2000). For a different postclassical phenomenon touched on by Latte see Chaniotis (1995).

was performed (normally against payment by the ex-slave to his master) by proclamation and registration. Sacral manumission in turn had two subforms, again normally divided by region and sometimes occurring in a mixture. One is illustrated, for instance, by the following inscription of the beginning of the second century B.C. from Lebadeia in Boeotia[48]:

> God. Good luck. In the archonship of Astias among the Boeotians and of Dorkon at Lebadeia, Doilos son of Iraneos consecrates his own servant Andrikos to Zeus Basileus and to Trophonios to be sacred, remaining with his (Dorkon's) mother Athanodora for ten years, as his father left instructions. If Athanodora is still alive, Andrikos shall pay the sum written in the will. If anything happens to Athanodora, Andrikos shall remain for the rest of the term with Doilos, and thereafter let him be sacred, not belonging to anybody in any respect. It shall not be permitted to anybody to enslave Andrikos. Andrikos shall serve at the sacrifices of these gods.

Doilos consecrates his slave to Zeus Basileus and Trophonios. The consecration is not to take effect immediately; Andrikos must perform slave services for another ten years to identified owners. Such "staying with" or postponed freedom clauses are an extremely frequent, though not a necessary, feature of these documents; they remind us, as does the reference to a payment by Andrikos, not to mistake these usually prudential transactions on the part of owners for acts of charity. Thereafter the dedication becomes real, and Andrikos is to be "sacred, not belonging to anybody in any respect." What the individual document does not reveal, but is quite clear from study of the ensemble of such texts, is that Andrikos has not exchanged a human master for a divine one. He is not to become in any significant sense a sacred slave, but a free man, and the point of declaring him "sacred" is precisely to discourage all efforts to reenslave him. Several comparable texts specify that anyone who makes the attempt is to be liable to a charge of "theft of sacred objects."[49] It is true that he is bound to render assistance at sacrifices to

---

[48] *IG* VII 3083 = Darmezin (1999: no. 13).
[49] Darmezin (1999: 190). The situation is not altered by the fact that the term *sacred slave* (*hierodoulos*) is in fact sometimes used of the status acquired by persons liberated by consecration.

his two divine patrons, but that requirement is almost unique in texts of this date; in texts of the imperial period from Macedonia and Phrygia a similar obligation to help "on the customary days" is often imposed,[50] but such occasional service at festivals that the ex-slave would probably have attended anyway was no serious derogation from his or her freedom (except freedom of residence). Shorter texts that seem to imply the same institution of "manumission by consecration" first appear in Laconia in the late fifth century.

The other subform of sacred manumission is first attested later and is known above all from an enormous dossier of texts from Delphi. The essential principles are the same, except that here the ex-owner does not consecrate but "sells" the slave to the god; the purchase price is in fact provided not by the god but by the slave, who here too is buying his freedom. Religious obligations to the new divine master are never mentioned. In these contexts, consecration and sale amount to almost the same thing. In both cases we are dealing with a legal fiction whereby the ex-slave becomes "sacred" not primarily to serve the god, but as a form of protection. Individuals from whom property had been stolen sometimes consecrated what they had lost to a god for a somewhat similar reason, to turn the thief's offence into a form of sacrilege.[51]

It is interesting that at Athens in the fourth century slaves secured freedom by a process that is not perfectly understood but that again involved a legal fiction (their victory in a sham *dikē apostasiou*) and had a religious element, the requirement to dedicate a phiale worth 100 drachmai to Athena as a kind of registration.[52] What this proliferation of legal fictions underlines is the extreme precariousness of the ex-slave's position, the constant threat of reinslavement, and the need to improvise whatever protection could be devised. The rise of sacral manumission refutes the evolutionary and progressivist strand in Latte's interpretation of *Heiliges Recht*, but provides powerful support for the other strand, that which saw sacral forms as discharging functions that at the date in question could be discharged in no other way.

---

[50] Occasional cases exist of free children being dedicated by their parents to similar service. Where sacral manumission does have religious obligations attached to it, it is plausible, with Hatzopoulos (1994: 116–22), to detect the influence of a preexisting custom of this character.

[51] But there are many interesting complications: see Ogden (1999: 37–44).

[52] Lewis (1959: 237–8), with references. For compulsory dedications by the manumitted in Macedonia see Hatzopoulos (1994: 103, 110–11).

CODA

How important then was the relation between religion and law in archaic Greece? The question is too broadly formulated to admit of an answer; one aim of this chapter has in fact been to show how it divides into a series of subquestions that are largely separate. But let us, in conclusion, evoke the spectre that always haunts discussions of this topic, that of the great Victorian legal historian Sir Henry Maine. For Maine, the spheres of law, religion, and morality in what he called "early" legal systems were intricately intertwined. (He did not, however, argue, as has often been supposed, for the historical priority of religion over law.[53]) "There is no system of recorded law," he writes, "literally from China to Peru, which when it first emerges into notice, is not seen to be entangled with religious ritual and observance" and "the severance of law from morality, and of religion from law" belongs "very distinctly to the later stages of mental progress."[54]

Some of the phenomena that we have studied conflict with important arguments used by Maine in support of that case. Where, for instance, Maine supposed the first lawyers to have been priests, we have seen that in Greece most "sacred laws," including those relating to priesthoods, were in fact ratified by citizen assemblies; an interconnection of sacred and civic is indeed observable, but not of the type postulated by Maine. The role of a sacral form of procedure, the oath, in the Gortyn code does not reinforce Maine's case either (or only in a different sense), for the substantive rules of that code are not religious in character. A full set of the "laws of Solon" would certainly have contained many that related to festivals and sacrifices and sacred property, because these were matters of public concern and public expenditure; but we have seen reason to think that many areas of "ritual best practice" were regulated not by the laws of Solon or by their equivalent elsewhere, but by unenforced local tradition.

Thus far then the blurring of spheres postulated by Maine is not to be detected in Greece. As for the complicated issue of the relation of law to "morality" (i.e., social rules), we can note in brief that some, but not all, of the strongest social obligations were legally enforced: to neglect one's aged parents while still alive was actually illegal, whereas

---

[53] On this error see Hoebel (1954: 258); Diamond (1935), which is very critical of Maine; also Daube (1947: 62 n. 2).
[54] Maine (1883: 5) and (1861: 14); Maine (1861: Ch. 1) and (1883: Chs. 1 and 2) are the main relevant discussions.

to deny them cult after death was, it seems, merely disgraceful. Yet a Mainean perspective is genuinely enlightening in at least one area, that of the funerary legislation of archaic Greek states. The remarkable "laws about the dead" of Iulis on Keos mentioned above might almost have been drafted to illustrate Maine's "entanglement" of law with "religious ritual and observance."

4: EARLY GREEK LAW[1]

Michael Gagarin

If we take law to be a society's established means of settling disputes among its members peacefully, then law exists to some degree in most communities, and early Greece is no exception. Well-established procedures for dispute settlement are evident in our earliest literary texts, the poems of Homer and Hesiod, which were probably put in writing around 700 B.C.E., and several other works composed during the next two centuries support the epic description of dispute settlement. In addition, the earliest surviving legal inscriptions – texts of laws inscribed mostly on stone – have been dated to ca. 650, a date that coincides roughly with the dates given by later Greek authors for the earliest Greek lawgivers. By the fifth century individual Greek cities had well-established legal systems of their own, and from at least two of these, Athens and Gortyn (on the island of Crete), enough evidence survives from the fifth and fourth centuries that we can study them in some detail,[2] but in this chapter I will confine myself to the period from 700 to ca. 450.[3]

LEGAL PROCEDURE

I begin with procedure, for which our evidence is fullest. Homer and Hesiod show that settling disputes (judging) was a common activity

---

[1] This chapter covers some of the same ground as Gagarin (1986), where the reader may find more extensive discussion of much of the evidence. However, the present essay has a rather different focus; it treats only selected pieces of evidence and raises issues not considered in that work.
[2] Some would include Sparta in this group; see MacDowell (1986).
[3] In this volume the laws of Gortyn are also discussed by Davies, and some of the procedural issues I discuss are also treated by Parker.

around 700.[4] For example, Sarpedon is described as "he who protected Lycia with his dispute-settling (*dikai*) and his strength" (*Iliad* 16.542), and when Odysseus waits for the whirlpool Charybdis to regurgitate the remnants of his makeshift raft, the pieces finally appear "late, at the time when a man gets up from the *agora* [the public gathering place] to return home for dinner after deciding (*krinein*) many disputes brought by young men seeking settlements (*dikazomenōn*)" (*Odyssey* 12.440). Settling disputes is evidently a primary task of a Homeric king, and when the god Hephaestus creates a panorama of the universe on the new shield he makes for Achilles, he represents human activity in three places – a city at peace, a city at war, and a rural scene – and he gives the peaceful city only two scenes, a wedding and a trial.

This famous trial scene (*Iliad* 18.497–508) shows two disputants seeking a settlement before a group of elders assembled in a public space on a solemn occasion:

> Meanwhile a crowd gathered in the *agora* where a dispute
> had arisen: two men contended over the blood price
> for a man who had died. One swore he had paid everything,
> and made a public declaration. The other refused to accept
>   anything.   500
> Both were eager to put an end to their dispute at the hands of an
>   umpire (*istōr*).
> People were speaking on both sides, and both had supporters;
> but the heralds restrained them. The old men
> took seats on hewn stones in a sacred circle;
> they held in their hands the scepters of heralds who raise their
>   voices.   505
> Then the two men rushed before them, and the elders in turn
>   gave their judgments (*dikazein*).
> In the middle there lay two talents of gold
> as a gift for the one among them who would speak his judgment
>   (*dikē*) most straightly (*ithuntata*).

Whatever the precise issue at stake here,[5] it is clear that the two disputants are both seeking a settlement and have thus initiated the

---

[4] The Homeric poems are set in the time of the Trojan War (ca. 1200), but the social institutions portrayed in them must represent those of a later period.

[5] The main possibilities are (a) the amount of the blood price, (b) whether it has been paid (or paid in full), or (c) whether the victim's relatives are required to accept it. There is a vast quantity of scholarly literature on this scene; for several different approaches, see Wolff

process (501). The fact that the killer speaks first does not mean that he is the "plaintiff" in the sense that he alone requested the trial;[6] rather, when both disputants seek a settlement, then either one may speak first.[7] Here both disputants are eagerly seeking a settlement and are clearly acting voluntarily (though undoubtedly under pressure from family, friends, and others). Each has his crowd of supporters (502), who vocally make their views known. There are elements of ritual in the scene, including the circle of stones where the elders sit and the scepter each takes as he rises in turn to speak (505–6). The amount of gold (507–8) is probably not large enough to be the blood price; most scholars take it as a prize for the elder whose judgment is accepted as best. We are not told how and by whom it is decided which elder speaks the straightest judgment, but in my view the most likely method is a general consensus of the community.[8]

Two other epic scenes show a similar procedure at work. First, Hesiod describes how the gift of the Muses, which is the ability to speak eloquently, can cause a king (*basileus*) to be highly honored by the people (*Theogony* 84–92):

> All the people
> behold him, sorting out (*diakrinein*) the rules (*themistes*)
> in straight settlements (*itheiai dikai*). And he, speaking surely,
> quickly and skillfully puts an end to even a great dispute.
> Therefore there are intelligent kings, in order that
> in the *agora* they may restore matters for people who have suffered
>   harm,

(1946: 34–49), Gagarin (1986: 26–33), Thür (1996a: 66–9), and Cantarella (2002b). I try to focus here on points not in dispute.

[6] This is the theory of Wolff (*loc. cit.*), who argues (despite the acknowledged implication of verse 501) that the first speaker, the killer, brings the case because he is seeking the community's protection against the relatives of the victim, who are employing the traditional method of self-help; if the relatives had refused to accept a trial, the community would have protected the killer indefinitely. But Wolff fails to appreciate the force of ἱέσθην ("were eager to," 501), which indicates that both not only agreed to the trial but wanted it. Another difficulty is that his interpretation requires a "public authority" (1946: 49), which would have extended or withdrawn its protection over a disputant if one of them refused to participate in the trial. There is no sign of such an authority in Homer or elsewhere in early Greece.

[7] In the *Hymn to Hermes*, Hermes and Apollo together bring their dispute to Zeus; Hermes is the first to suggest they go to Zeus but Apollo speaks first. In *Eumenides*, both Orestes and the Furies ask Athena to decide their dispute (*Eu.* 235–43, 431–5, 467–9); Orestes is the first to request a trial but the Furies speak first (583).

[8] Larsen (1947).

easily, persuading them with gentle words.
And as he comes to the hearing, the people honor him as a god
with gentle reverence, and he is conspicuous among those
    assembled.

   Here the king's ability to speak, specifically in the context of settling disputes, is of utmost importance if he is to persuade the disputants — and also the members of the community who are present — to accept his settlement. For this reason a king needs the gift of the Muses as much as a poet does (*Theogony* 94–103)

   A similar process is evident in the story of Deioces, the first king of the Medes (Herodotus 1.96–100). There is little, if any, historical truth in the story, but it illustrates Herodotus' and his contemporaries' understanding of the early (sixth-century) procedure for dispute settlement. Before Deioces, Herodotus says, the Medes lived scattered in small villages, in one of which Deioces judged disputes brought to him by the villagers. He was so good at this that he gained a wide reputation for justice (*dikaiosynē*), and soon everyone from the whole region would only bring their disputes to him. In this way he gained a monopoly over dispute settlement. One day, however, he abruptly stopped hearing disputes. As a result, violence and lawlessness broke out everywhere. In desperation the Medes decided they needed a king, and naturally they chose Deioces. He promptly restored law and order — but of a very different kind: he received complaints from litigants in writing, decided them in private, and returned his judgments in writing.

   The story makes it clear that in the beginning, the settlement process was initiated by the disputants themselves, who apparently could take their disputes to anyone they wished for settlement. A judge's success in this system depended on his ability to satisfy his customers by producing settlements that were perceived as just, that is, that were acceptable to both sides and probably also were seen as fair by other members of the community. To gain his monopoly, Deioces must have excelled at this, and he must, therefore, have had the ability not just to devise acceptable settlements but to persuade both litigants to accept them.

   Each of the three scenes just discussed has a different focus and purpose and conveys only selected details appropriate to that purpose, but they all provide evidence of the same general judicial process, and other scenes that I shall not consider here confirm many of these details.[9] The

---

[9] Gagarin (1986: 19–50).

process begins with the disputants themselves seeking a settlement; when a third party proposes a settlement without the disputants requesting it, he is more likely to fail, as when Nestor tries unsuccessfully to end the dispute between Achilles and Agamemnon (*Iliad* 1.245–84). Other features of the process reflected in these scenes and others are that it is a public process, regularly attended by many other members of the community. It takes place in a public place, often the *agora*, and involves a considerable amount of speaking on the part of everyone, disputants, judges, and the community. There may be a single judge or several; these may be kings or elders or other respected members of the community, but they are apparently not professional judges. And, as the Greeks appear to have been a fairly contentious people, the process is a relatively common one. Even the legendary king Minos in the underworld is portrayed as settling disputes for the dead souls who crowd around him (*Odyssey* 11.568–71).

The Judicial Decision

There is no indication in any of the scenes described above that a judge or judges were restricted in the kinds of settlements they could propose, but some scholars have argued nonetheless that such restrictions existed. The strongest proponent of restrictions on the judicial decision is Thür,[10] who argues that the settlement (*dikē*) each elder proposed had to take the form of an oath to be sworn by one of the disputants, which would then decide the issue conclusively. Thür argues that even if the original issue was a simple question of fact (whether A paid B), it must have grown more complex (e.g., whether some of the animals that formed the payment were sick). In such disputes it would be possible to propose a wide variety of complex oaths, and thus, Thür argues, first the disputants each proposed an oath as part of their plea, and then each elder proposed an oath in turn. The crowd then decided which proposed oath was the fairest and the disputant on whom the winning oath was imposed either swore the oath and won the case or declined to swear it and lost. The outcome was guaranteed by a divine "witness" (*istōr*), the deity or deities by whom the oath was sworn. "Neither voluntary arbitration nor control of self-help by police power was the principle of

---

[10] Most fully in Thür (1996a: see esp. 66–9) for the shield scene. I present some counter arguments in Gagarin (1997).

early Greek dispute settlement, rather control by supernatural means, by the imposition of decisive oaths" (Thür 1996a: 69).

More likely, in my view, is that early Greek procedure resembled the process we find in some preliterate societies, such as the Tiv in northern Nigeria (Bohannan 1957), where debate and dialogue gradually lead to sorting out and resolving the issue, to the satisfaction, or at least the acquiescence, of all concerned. In such cases, even simple questions of fact (for example, whether A took something from B) generally turn out to be just one part of a more complex set of issues (e.g., whether B previously took something from A or injured A or a member of A's family in some other matter, etc.). Thus even if Homer's disputants initially argued over a simple question of fact,[11] it is likely that other issues soon entered into the debate and that a considerable variety of proposals for settlements were thus possible.

This dispute about the judicial decision ultimately concerns the nature of early Greek law as a whole: did it depend on "control by supernatural means" (Thür) or on more rational, human procedures?[12] As Thür is aware, in the shield scene Homer says nothing about the content of the elders' proposals, never mentions oaths, and in his brief report on the content of the disputants' pleas he gives no hint that either mentioned an oath. Oaths can be introduced into the shield scene only by analogy with other scenes, and for this Thür relies on the dispute between Menelaus and Antilochus after the chariot race in *Iliad* 23.[13]

During this race, Antilochus had used a bold but risky maneuver to pass Menelaus on the turn and had come in second, with Menelaus third. When Antilochus steps up to receive the prize for second place (a mare), Menelaus objects: he claims that his own horses were much

---

[11] In my view Homer does not provide enough information for us to determine the precise issue. For one possibility, see Gagarin (1986: 31–3).

[12] For another perspective, see Parker in this volume.

[13] Thür also draws on fifth-century laws from Gortyn (see Davies in this volume), where *dikazein* is used four times (twice in the Great Code) when the judgment involves a decisive oath imposed on one of the litigants (Gagarin 1997: 126–7). But in these laws *dikazein* is in fact used of any judgment specified by law, including those that involve no automatic proof. For instance, at the beginning of the Code (1.2–7), if someone has seized someone before a trial, the judge must condemn him (*kata-dikazein*) to a specified fine and must give judgment (*dikazein*) that he release the person within three days. Thus *dikazein* by itself means only "pronounce judgment"; it specifies no particular means by which that judgment was reached. Maffi (2003) argues (unconvincingly, in my view) for an even larger role for oaths in determining verdicts at Gortyn.

faster and appeals to his colleagues for help: "Come then, Argive leaders and men of counsel: judge (*dikazein*) between the two of us now, and without favor" (23.573–4). But he then changes course: "Or rather, I myself will give judgment (*dikazein*), and I think no other man of the Danaans can call it in question, for it will be straight (*ithys*)" (579–80). He then asks Antilochus to take his whip, lay his hand on his horses, and swear by Poseidon that "you did not intentionally hinder my chariot by a trick (*dolos*)" (585). In an eloquent response (586–95) Antilochus ignores the proposed oath, indirectly admits to unspecified failings, and so as not to lose favor with Menelaus or the gods, offers him the mare and anything else he might want. Menelaus relents, gives the mare back to Antilochus, and the two are reconciled (though each continues to speak of the mare as his own).

In this scene, the Argive leaders never speak, so we do not know what judgments they would have proposed. But because Menelaus's proposed judgment asks Antilochus to swear an oath, Thür argues (1996a: 66) that the other leaders would have formulated oaths too. But this is mere speculation, and I see no reason to conclude that because *dikazein* once (and only once) in Homer designates a judgment that consists of an oath, in other passages it must always, or even sometimes, designate a similar judgment. In some disputes, an oath might provide a good means for resolving the issue but surely in some cases it would not. It is far more likely, then, that *dikazein* means "propose a judgment," which may or may not take the form of an oath.[14]

Thür also fails to distinguish clearly between imposed oaths and oath-challenges, which are common in classical Athenian law (Mirhady 1991b).[15] An oath may be imposed by a judge on one of the litigants, often the accused (the so-called exculpatory oath). If he swears the oath, he is automatically absolved of the crime. In the Gortyn code (3.5–9), for example, a woman accused of taking her ex-husband's possessions during a divorce must swear an oath of denial, and then she can keep the property. An oath-challenge, on the other hand, is proposed by one litigant, who either asks his opponent to swear a specific oath or offers to swear one himself. It is implied that if the opponent agrees to the proposed oath, the oath will be sworn, and this will settle the case, or at least some issue in the case. If, however, the opponent refuses to accept

---

[14] See Talamanca (1979).

[15] For our purposes we may ignore the widespread use of oaths of confirmation, with which a litigant, witness, judge, or juror confirms that his statement or judgment is true or just.

the proposed oath (as he almost always does), the proposer may cite this refusal as evidence of his opponent's guilt.

Thür treats Menelaus' proposal to Antilochus in *Iliad* 23 as an imposed oath because Menelaus is acting as a judge and refers to his own proposal as a judgment (*dikazein*). But Menelaus has no special authority to judge his own case and cannot impose a decisive oath on his opponent, though to the extent that his proposal is considered fair by others, Antilochus would be under pressure to accept it. His proposed judgment is in fact an oath-challenge, and Antilochus responds to it only indirectly. Other examples of oath-challenges in early literature include Hermes in the *Hymn to Hermes* (274–5) and the Furies in Aeschylus' *Eumenides* (429–32), who complain that Orestes will not swear the oath they request (that he did not kill his mother). All these literary oath-challenges form part of verbal exchanges between the disputants, just like the oath-challenges in Athenian forensic discourse. By contrast, early literature provides no example of an imposed oath. And even at Gortyn imposed oaths are rare and are used only for relatively minor issues.[16] Authority may at times be said to rest with the gods, but the authority of the Homeric gods is often questionable, and when the Homeric Greeks did wish to put something in their hands, they typically did so by drawing lots. Even when the gods themselves judge a dispute, they do not impose an oath.[17]

In support of his view, Thür cites evidence from early Babylonia, where imposed oaths were common (Thür 1996a: 70). This raises the possibility, he suggests, either of Oriental influence on Greek law or (because there is no evidence of such influence) that Greek law, like early Germanic law, was an "independent parallel development." In this approach Thür follows Wolff (see also Gernet 1951) in seeking to elucidate early Greek law by means of the so-called comparative method. "The comparative method, which rests on the *established fact* that in matters legal the human mind is so constructed as to seek similar solutions for

---

[16] Gagarin (1997: 126–7). Note that at Gortyn whenever no means of judgment is specified, the judge can decide freely: "Whenever it is written that the judge shall judge either according to witnesses or by an oath of denial, he is to judge as is written; but in other matters he shall swear an oath himself and then decide according to the pleas" (11.26–31).

[17] Hera accuses Zeus of judging in secret by favoring Thetis and her son Achilles (*Il.* 1.542). She later tells Athena they should let Zeus judge between the Greeks and Trojans however he wishes (*Il.* 8.431). And Odysseus tells how he won the arms of Achilles in a contest that the children of Troy and Athena judged (*Od.* 11.547). In every case the verb is *dikazein*, and nowhere is an imposed oath even remotely likely.

similar situations under analogous conditions, needs no justification" (Wolff 1946: 35, my italics). This assertion may have occasioned little dissent in Wolff's day, but since then, belief in universal patterns of human social development has largely vanished.[18]

Medieval European laws do make frequent use of automatic proofs – oaths, ordeals, and trial by combat – that are imposed on one or both litigants, and Near Eastern laws make similar use of oaths and ordeals. In these processes a separate test that has no direct connection with the facts of the case produces a clear decision, when one party either passes the test (often by surviving), thereby winning the case, or fails it and loses. The justification for these proofs (sometimes called "irrational") is that the "hand of God" is at work so that the test will truly separate the guilty from the innocent.[19] In Greek law, however, ordeals and combat are unknown[20] and decisive oaths are rare.[21] At Athens no oath is mentioned in the surviving text of Draco's law, no decisive oath is found in the remnants of Solon's laws,[22] and imposed oaths have no place in classical Athenian law. The Greeks could use decisive judicial oaths if they wished, but they rarely did. We may conclude that from the beginning early Greek legal procedure made less use of automatic proofs and relied more on rational argument and free decision making on the part of judges than did other comparable legal systems.

---

[18] For those who like comparison, I would still suggest that dispute settlement in African societies is more enlightening for early Greek law than ancient Near Eastern or early Germanic law (Gagarin 1986: 4–5 and *passim* – see index s.v. "preliterate societies").

[19] The context and use of these proofs in medieval law is more complex than my simple description may imply; see Brown (1982), van Caenegem (1991: 71–114).

[20] Latte (1920: 5) cites the messenger in Antigone (264–7) as evidence for early ordeals ("We were ready to take molten lead in our hands and walk through fire and swear oaths to the gods that we did not do the deed, etc."). This may refer to means by which a master tested a slave, but there is no hint of them in any Greek legal procedure. For combat, the duel between Paris and Menelaus in *Iliad* 3 is sometimes cited, but this too is outside of any legal context.

[21] An example outside Gortyn is an early-fifth-century law on property at Halicarnassus (Meiggs and Lewis (1969) 32, 22–28 = van Effenterre and Ruzé (1995–1996) I.19, Koerner (1993) 84), which says that if after a certain time someone lays claim to a property, the person in possession of the property has only to swear an oath and the claim will be rejected.

[22] Oaths are mentioned in F15b (= Lysias 10.17) and F42 (= Bekker, *Anecdota Graeca* I.242, 20–2). The first of these may mean "let him swear by Apollo and give surety," but the archaic language is subject to different interpretations (Hillgruber 1988: 71). The second reports that Solon told both litigants to swear an oath if they had no contract or witnesses; even if this oath was imposed, it cannot be decisive if both litigants swore (see Gagarin 1997: 127–8).

Substantive Law, Written Legislation

Early judicial procedure was an entirely oral process. Even after writing was introduced into Greece, perhaps around 800,[23] it played no significant role in legal procedure until the fourth century, when witness testimony, along with other documents, began to be introduced in court in written form. Substantive law (such as it was) also remained unwritten for more than a century after the introduction of writing. Homer and Hesiod speak of kings and others knowing *themistes* – traditional rules and customs – that came from the gods and were the basis for judicial settlements, and these rules are invoked in various contexts. For example, in trying to persuade Achilles to soften his anger against Agamemnon, Ajax says (*Iliad* 9.632–36): "a person accepts the blood-price from the killer of his brother or his dead son, and the killer pays a large compensation and remains in his land, and the person's heart and anger are curbed, when he has received the blood-price." Similarly, Hesiod's advice in *Works and Days* includes such rules as "wealth is not to be seized" (320). Judges and litigants certainly were familiar with these traditional norms and could rely on them explicitly or implicitly in a trial, but I would classify these rules as customs or norms, not laws.[24]

The Greeks began to write laws around 650. The earliest surviving legal inscription is from Dreros in Crete (see Gagarin 1986: 81–2), and during the next century, laws were inscribed all over Crete (especially at Gortyn) and the rest of Greece. These inscriptions confirm the tradition that the first lawgivers in different cities began their work in the mid seventh century, although it seems that the large-scale legislation attributed to some of these lawgivers was relatively rare.[25] Despite the fragmentary state of many of these inscriptions, we can see that early legislation covered many areas of law, including (to use modern classifications) constitutional law, family, inheritance, property, criminal law, religious law, and others. These laws were inscribed, mostly on stone though less durable materials like bronze and wood were also used, and were displayed prominently in public areas, often in or near a temple or sanctuary. This location may have conveyed the sense that the laws

---

[23] Greeks in the late Bronze Age (ca. 1400–1200) wrote using a syllabic script, Linear B, unrelated to the later alphabet. This script then died out, and the alphabet was a separate invention.

[24] I leave aside here the difficult questions of what law is and whether or to what extent law depends on writing; see Gagarin (1986: esp. 9–12), and Thomas's chapter in this volume.

[25] Solon of Athens may have been the earliest to enact an extensive set of laws (early sixth century); see Gagarin (1986: 51–80), Hölkeskamp (1999).

had divine authority but they were not "religious" laws such as, say, the collections of laws in the *Old Testament* (see Parker in this volume). Unlike many Near Eastern law codes, Greek legislation was meant to be used in actual litigation.[26] Even the earliest inscriptions make some effort to organize provisions in ways that are useful to users (e.g., by grouping together provisions on the same subject) and to incorporate other physical and stylistic features that make the laws easier to read. Probably few people could read easily at the time, but in my view, those who were likely to find themselves involved in litigation probably could read these texts.[27] In addition, the monumental nature especially of large collections like the Gortyn Code and their location in a public (sometimes religious) place would have conveyed the impression of authority and communal power that would be crucial to the enforcement of legislation at a time when other enforcement measures were weak or nonexistent.

Writing down laws on relatively permanent materials and displaying them in public had several important effects. First, it marked certain rules as separate from the community's traditional rules and customs, so that they could be identified as a separate class – laws. Second, it conveyed a sense of the stability and permanence of these rules, including those small details (especially of procedure) that could easily be lost or altered in oral transmission. Third, it assured that the laws were available to the members of the community – not to all members, given the fairly low degree of literacy at the time, but probably to most of those who regularly participated in public affairs and would be likely to be involved in litigation. Fourth, it conveyed the idea that these rules were a single body ("what was written") with special authority, and the stories about one original lawgiver, even if distorted or false, reinforced the sense that a community's laws were a unified body of authoritative rules. Fifth, it implied or affirmed that these rules were backed by the authoritative political body that caused them to be enacted and written.[28] In essence, then, writing created the idea of law – henceforth a law would be any rule that belonged to this special body of written rules backed by the authority of the *polis*.

---

[26] See Roth (2000), Gagarin on unity in this volume.
[27] W. Harris's (1989) minimalist conclusions about early literacy are often accepted, but even his view, which is probably too restrictive, does not exclude the possibility that the laws were intended to be read.
[28] The law from Dreros mentioned above begins, "the following was pleasing to the *polis*" (i.e., "the *polis* approved the following").

The sheer quantity of inscribed legislation in Greece is striking. The inscriptions discovered to date probably constitute only a small fraction of all archaic legislation,[29] but even they show that the Greeks devoted considerable time and resources to this activity. It is also striking that the vast majority of public inscriptions during the period 650–500 are laws. Indeed, legislation so dominates the inscriptional output of this period that expressions for writing, such as *to graphos* ("the written") or *ta gegrammena* ("the things written"), are regularly used together with other special names (*thesmos* and *rhētra*) to designate laws.[30] And almost no judicial texts other than laws were inscribed during this period. Archaic Greece was thus unusual, if not unique, among premodern legal systems in both the large amount of legislation it wrote and the virtual absence of writing for other legal matters.[31] The Greeks, in other words, were very concerned to provide written rules for bringing cases to court and to make these rules clear and accessible to those members of the community who would be likely to use them, but the litigation that arose from these written rule in fact required little or no ability to read or write.

Conclusion

In my chapter on unity (in this volume) I argue that Greek judicial procedure during the archaic period possessed certain general characteristics that distinguish it from procedure in most other early legal systems. Litigants in Greece presented their disputes to a judge or judges in an open, public space. The process was to a certain extent a ritual performance but it had little of the formalism that characterizes many other early legal systems. Verdicts were generally reached freely by the judge(s) rather than by formal procedures or automatic proofs, such as oath-swearing. And the large quantity of written legislation in archaic

---

[29] Almost none of the early legislation of Zaleucus, Solon, et al., reported in the literary tradition survives. We do not know whether the exceptionally large number of laws from Gortyn reflects a fondness for legislation (or for inscribing legislation on stone) or is the result of chance discovery or other factors.

[30] Thus, when the Gortyn Code says to do something "as is written," it means "according to the law" (e.g., 12.1–4).

[31] The one other community that may be similar is early Rome, around the time of the Twelve Tables. Unfortunately, despite this fascinating (mostly fragmentary) document, we know little about law at this time. Later, written legislation appears to be less important in Rome than in Greece, but other kinds of legal texts (*responsa, formulae, legis actiones*) soon begin to be put in writing.

Greece was intended to be accessible to and used by those engaged in (or potentially engaged in) disputes. At the same time, writing was almost entirely absent from procedure, which remained an oral process.

Taken together, these two aspects of early Greek law – written legislation and oral procedure – form an unusual combination, unlikely to be the result of influence from some other legal system. Rather, I would suggest, both aspects exemplify the Greek tradition of open, public debate and discussion among a large segment of the community. Even a "king" in Homer or Hesiod does not have the absolute power of monarchs in other ancient societies. Both authors, in fact, regularly speak of a plurality of kings, and these kings often meet with councils that comprise a larger segment of the community. From the beginning, Greek law shows this Greek tendency toward openness and public debate that some (e.g., Lloyd 1979) have seen as the root of Greek intellectual achievements. And as it developed during the archaic period, Greek law maintained this productive combination of fixed, stable, written legislation together with an oral, dynamic process for settling disputes that will persist in Athens right through the classical period.

Part 2

Law in Athens I: Procedure

5: LAW AND ORATORY AT ATHENS

S. C. Todd

INTRODUCTION

The late fifth century at Athens marks an important change in the nature of the historical record. It is not so much that earlier forms of evidence disappear – indeed, the rise of what is often called "radical" democracy after ca. 460 B.C. sees an exponential increase in the number of surviving inscriptions, though these are often of less significance as legal sources than might have been anticipated[1] – but that they are joined from ca. 420 by a new type of literary text, which has come to dominate modern study of the Athenian legal system: lawcourt speeches, which purport to present a record of what was said by one (or occasionally both) of the parties performing at a trial.[2]

My brief in this chapter is to use the medium of the speeches to introduce the study of fourth-century Athenian law, which forms the subject of the next two sections of the volume. But to focus simply

---

[1] This is partly because a significant proportion of public inscriptions deal with issues of administration such as public accounts, rather than issues of law. (For the paradoxical rôle played by written law at Athens, see n. 5 below.) In addition, one of the commonest forms of legislative inscription comprises honorary decrees, which are collectively interesting as evidence both for the process of legislation and for the workings of Athenian politics, but individually tell us little about the law itself. Contrast, for instance, Gortyn (Davies in this volume), where by far the largest surviving inscription is a major compilation of legal statutes.

[2] The balance between prosecution and defence speeches is roughly equal: of ca. 110 surviving lawcourt orations in total (see below), Rubinstein below, p. 133 with n. 10, lists twenty-nine public and thirty-one private prosecution speeches, but there is in some cases room for debate as to the appropriate classification. Only twice do we have the leading speech delivered on both sides: see n. 32 below. The question of how far the speeches may have been revised after the trial is discussed at n. 38 below.

on the status of these texts as historical evidence may be too narrow a perspective. Athenian lawcourt speeches reflect a system of procedural law in which the respective rôles played by performers and by hearers within a trial are very different from those found in modern jurisdictions, whether in common-law countries such as England and the United States or in civil-law systems such as those of Continental Europe. In this respect the Athenian system is different also, it would appear, from what we see reflected in earlier texts such as the Shield of Achilles in *Iliad* 18, where most scholars agree that even though the initiative may come from the litigants who plead their cases, nevertheless it is the elders of the community sitting as judges who seem to be responsible for arguing out a solution for which they need to secure popular consent.[3] In Athens by contrast, as we shall see, it is the litigants who are represented not simply as initiators but as the primary speakers and who present the court with their own (often tendentious) interpretations of the law. There is no independent judge to offer legal rulings, and the jury's verdict is rendered by majority vote with no formal opportunity to discuss the case: this is presumably because (unlike Homeric elders) an Athenian court possesses a level of institutional authority which means that it does not need to seek the consent of the community by giving reasons for its judgment.

Speeches therefore are significant not only because they are our primary source of historical evidence, but more importantly because of the central rôle that they will have played in the Athenians' own experience of litigation: hence the priority given to legal procedure over substantive law in the organization of this volume.[4] In addition, the fact that the speeches are themselves in some sense literary representations of what were originally oral performances raises a wide range of further questions: for instance, about the continuing rôle of orality within the law;[5] about the function of rhetoric, performance and

---

[3] Thus, e.g., Gagarin, above, pp. 83–84. The procedural system at Gortyn is not entirely clear, but judicial officials in the papyri from Greco-Roman Egypt seem to play a much more interventionist rôle than at Athens.

[4] The idea that procedure is the key to substantive law is argued more broadly by, e.g., Todd (1993). Cf. also Rubinstein in this volume, who sees choice of procedure as a significant factor in determining the nature of a speaker's arguments.

[5] It is something of a paradox that a society such as classical Athens, which could in certain contexts regard written law as the basis of democracy (Euripides, *Suppliants*, 430–4, quoted and discussed by Thomas, above, p. 42), nevertheless operated a system in which legal statutes played a relatively minor rôle as sources of law (thus Yunis, below, pp. 194–7). It is worth noting here the fact that ancient rhetorical theorists classified laws as a form of evidence, cf. n. 34 below.

narrative; and more generally about the relationship between law and literature.[6]

The speeches that survive today are those attributed in antiquity to a group of ten writers known as the Attic Orators.[7] The canonization of ten such writers is not firmly attested until the first and second centuries A.D.,[8] but may have been the work of earlier scholars in the Hellenistic period,[9] selecting their favored authors on the basis presumably of perceived literary quality. The authors that comprise the canon fall into two chronological groups: the earlier orators, Antiphon, Andocides, Lysias, Isocrates, and Isaeus (active from ca. 420 to ca. 360, though Isocrates survived until 338); and the later orators, Aeschines, Lycurgus, Demosthenes, Hyperides, and Dinarchus (the first four of them broadly contemporaries, whereas Dinarchus alone survived the Macedonian abolition of the democracy in 322).[10] To describe them as Attic (i.e., Athenian) Orators is perhaps something of a misnomer, because only seven of them were Athenian citizens (the exceptions being Lysias, Isaeus, and Dinarchus): what unites them is that all were based at Athens and that only one of their surviving speeches (Isocrates 19) was composed for a trial outside Athenian jurisdiction.

LOGOGRAPHY

It is worth pausing here to reflect on the significance of the fact that three of the ten canonical orators were metics (noncitizens resident at

---

[6] See the chapters in this voume by Yunis on rhetoric and by Wallace and Allen on comedy and tragedy respectively.

[7] The question of survival, and the way in which this may distort the historical record, is discussed further below, pp. 102–6.

[8] Caecilius of Calacte (first century A.D.) wrote a lost treatise *On the Distinctive Style* (*charaktēr*) *of the Ten Orators* which at first sight implies that ten was already the canonical number, but it has been suggested that Caecilius was himself the inventor of the canon for polemical reasons (thus Worthington 1994, with full refs.). Certainly his contemporary Dionysius of Halicarnassus (*On the Ancient Orators*, §4) proclaims an intention to write essays about six leading orators and justifies his failure to discuss other orators by mentioning not just our ten but various other writers now lost (*Isaeus*, §§19–20). From a slightly later period, however, there survives a *Lexicon to the Ten Orators* by Harpocration, itself a valuable source for the content of lost speeches, and a set of *Lives of the Ten Orators*, wrongly attributed to the second-century biographer Plutarch, which combines useful information with significant error and confusion.

[9] The case for this earlier date is set out most fully by Smith (1995: e.g., 76–7).

[10] The order given here is that of Pseudo-Plutarch (see n. 8 above) and is broadly though not entirely chronological. For the numbers of surviving speeches, see below, pp. 102–6.

Athens), and as such were unable to take any direct part in Athenian public life. Only citizen adult males were members of the Athenian Assembly, so a metic orator had no right to speak there. The legal capacity of metics in a lawcourt is admittedly less certain: they could apparently serve as witnesses and could certainly sue and be sued in private cases and probably also in certain public ones. We do know, however, that a metic was legally obliged to register the name of a citizen as his *prostatēs* ("patron" or "guardian"),[11] and many scholars believe that in at least some categories of case a metic litigant would normally be represented by the *prostatēs* speaking on his behalf.[12]

At first sight it is paradoxical that metic speechwriters could attain prominence within the context of a system that blocked them from the most prominent avenues of public speaking, but the key to this paradox is the custom of logography or unofficial ghostwriting. Athenian lawcourts frowned on professionalism at all levels, as can be seen for instance in the way that the majority of cases were judged by a large body of *dikastai*.[13] This term is often translated "jurors," but the point is that Athens had no judges in our sense. Instead, the *dikastai* gave their verdict, and where appropriate passed sentence, on the basis of a simple majority vote: this took place, as has already been noted, without judicial direction and with no formal opportunity for discussion.

An underlying assumption of the Athenian legal system was that just as the *dikastai* are collectively competent to decide the law, so an individual litigant ought to be competent to plead his case in person, whether as defendant or as plaintiff. (It is worth emphasizing here that the vast majority of prosecutions even in public cases were brought by individual citizens in their own name rather than by public officials.)[14] It was not illegal to invite others to speak on your behalf, and one of the contributors to this volume has rightly emphasized in another context the extent of coordination and teamwork between litigants and their

---

[11] A small number of metics were granted special privileges (e.g., the right to own land or to be exempt from the metic tax), and the obligation to have a *prostatēs* may have been suspended in such circumstances.

[12] The two leading cases here are Lys. 12 and Lys. frag. *Hippotherses*, which are both discussed in Todd (1993: 198 with n. 46). Also relevant is the phrasing of the indictment at the start of Dinarchus' lost speech *Against Proxenos*, which may suggest that Dinarchus himself delivered the speech.

[13] Numbers were large (in private cases 200–400; in public cases normally 500 but occasionally multiples of that number): they were made up of volunteers aged over 30, selected at random in the early morning for a single day's hearing.

[14] On the significance of this point, see Rubinstein, below, pp. 130–1.

sunēgoroi (lit. "fellow speakers"),[15] but there does seem to have been a sense that a *sunēgoros* ought not to be a paid advocate. What went on behind the scenes, however, was harder to monitor, and this is the context in which men like Lysias or Dinarchus made it their task to ghostwrite speeches for the benefit of clients who would then deliver them in their own person.[16]

By no means all ten of the canonical orators operated primarily as logographers. One of the most frequently noted features of Athenian politics in the second half of the fourth century is a growing tendency toward specialization between military leaders on the one hand and public speakers on the other, and the later orators in particular tended to take full advantage of this. Both Demosthenes and Aeschines, for instance, were members of the embassy to Macedon which negotiated the Peace of Philokrates in 346, and the resulting combination of personal rivalry and policy disagreement dominated Athens' policy toward Macedon for the following decade, as reflected in a string of lawcourt cases in which they sought personally to destroy each other's careers. Hyperides similarly served on a number of embassies and played a leading part in the diplomatic buildup to Athens' failed attempt to secure independence from Macedon following Alexander's death (the Lamian War of 323/2). Lycurgus was effectively in charge of Athenian finances for much of the decade around 330, and is indeed primarily responsible for transforming Athens' system of public finance into that of a Hellenistic *polis*: as a political prosecutor, his readiness to seek the death penalty became notorious.

None of the early orators had such a distinguished public career, though this may not have been for want of trying in the case of Andocides, who spent much of his life attempting to live down the part that he seems to have played as a young man in the politico-religious scandals of 415. But for two of them at least a reluctance to speak in public appears to have been a matter of personal choice: Antiphon was notoriously a backroom fixer, whose earliest active participation in politics (at the age of about 70) led to his execution as one of the leaders of the oligarchic

---

[15] See Rubinstein (2000). Note the care taken by litigants to explain that their relationship with prominent *sunēgoroi* is personal rather than financial (e.g., Dem. 59.14–15), or by the *sunēgoroi* to explain why it is that the litigant cannot reasonably be expected to deliver the main speech on his own behalf (e.g., Dem. 36.1).

[16] There is dispute among scholars as to how far such a speech would be written entirely by the logographer (the majority position, for which see Usher 1976, with which I broadly concur) and how far there may have been collaboration on the part of at least some litigants (the view of Dover 1968b, supported most recently by Lambert 2002).

coup of 411; Isocrates, who had a reputation as a poor speaker, devoted himself to pamphleteering, pedagogy, and political theory.[17]

Logography, however, was clearly a professional business, although we know virtually nothing about the level of fees that it commanded. As befits its nonformal status, it had something of a shady reputation, at least in certain circles. A number of the surviving orators, including for instance Andocides, Aeschines, and possibly Lycurgus, were rhetorical amateurs in the sense that they are not known to have written speeches for anybody else to deliver, and Aeschines in particular takes great delight in attacking Demosthenes as a logographer; correspondingly, Demosthenes as a would-be political leader, and perhaps also Isocrates as an educationalist, were evidently keen to live down their earlier career as logographic orators.[18] But there is no trace of any shame being felt by those who did not aspire to a public career (including of course the three metic orators, Lysias, Isaeus, and Dinarchus) – nor indeed in the surviving portions of Hyperides, though the loss of much of his work renders the inference here less than secure.[19]

Patterns of Survival

The Attic Orators, or more specifically those among this group who worked professionally as logographers, were prolific writers. Pseudo-Plutarch gives figures for the numbers of speeches attributed to all except Andocides (who, like the other amateurs, seems to have written only a few); and he often adds further details, such as the number of these that were regarded as genuine works of an orator in the opinion either of Caecilius or of Dionysius.[20] In total, his numbers add up to more than

---

[17] Thuc., 8.68.1–2 (Antiphon); for Isocrates, see Dion.Hal., *Isoc.*, §1, and Pseudo-Plutarch, *Life of Isocrates*, 837a5–10 (though the latter is clearly wrong in believing that Isoc. 15 was delivered in court).

[18] Dem. 19.246–250, responding to Aesch. 1.94 (a criticism repeated at Aesch. 2.180 and 3.173). In Isocrates' case it is the orator's family (in the person of his son Aphareus) who is said to have denied his father's authorship of the early forensic speeches attributed to him (Dion. Hal., *Isoc.* §18).

[19] Antiphon does defend his having written speeches for other people, possibly against criticisms that he did so for financial motives (*On the Revolution*, frag. 1, lines 14–22: this is suggested by the standard reading καὶ ὡς ἐκέρδαινον "that I benefited" at lines 19–20, though Maidment's καὶ τὸ ε'ἐκέρδαινον "that the Four Hundred benefited" would suggest that the alleged motives were political), but it was not until the end of his career that he came out as a public figure.

[20] For Pseudo-Plutarch, Caecilius, and Dionysius, see n. 8 above. The question of whether particular speeches were written by the orator to whom they are attributed is one that

770, including just under 550 that were held to be genuine. Of these, only about 150 survive today, with roughly 110 of these relating directly to lawcourt trials.[21] But the quantities ascribed to individual authors and the rates of survival vary considerably. To Lysias, for instance, he attributes no fewer than 425, while noting that Dionysius and Caecilius agreed that the genuine number was either 230 or 233: but only 31 of these 425 survive in medieval manuscripts, plus three others that are included in modern editions on the basis of substantial but partial quotation by Dionysius himself, though we do possess the titles and sometimes some fragments of about 140 others.

The question arises, why particular speeches have or have not survived. As a general rule, it is safe to say that the really famous orators stood in one sense the best but in another sense the worst chances. In the case of Demosthenes, for instance, the number of surviving speeches very nearly matches the total number attributed by Pseudo-Plutarch (59 of 65). But there is clear evidence that the prestige of Demosthenes' name (and possibly also therefore that of other orators) has attracted at least some work written by other people. Any process of canonization encourages misattribution, and there is general consensus among scholars that seven speeches attributed to Demosthenes but dealing with litigation that involves his lesser-known contemporary Apollodorus, son of the ex-slave banker Pasion, are mostly if not all the work of Apollodorus himself.[22]

Chance, however, is likely to have played a significant rôle in the survival of other texts. Hyperides, for instance, seems to have been

---

attracted a lot of attention from scholars particularly in the late nineteenth and early twentieth centuries. More recent scholars, however, have tended to focus more on the value of the speeches for the historian, for whom authenticity in the sense of authorship is usually less important than authenticity of occasion (i.e. how far the speech that we possess represents what was actually said in court). There is, as we shall see at n. 38 below, room for dispute about the extent of post-trial revision, but very few of the speeches are contested in the sense that there is serious doubt as to whether they derive from a real trial.

[21] These are the so-called "forensic" speeches. The bulk of the remainder comprise seventeen speeches in the corpus of Demosthenes, which are "symbouleutic" or "demegoric" (i.e., written for a deliberative body, usually the Assembly), and fifteen speeches of Isocrates, which later rhetorical theorists classified as "epideictic" ("written for display," a rather heterogeneous group that includes some substantial political pamphlets in the form of speeches).

[22] See now the extensive treatment by Trevett (1992). The speeches in question are Dem. 45, 46, 49, 50, 52, 53, and 59. This is a rather different question from that of collaborative authorship, for which see n. 16 above.

among the more highly regarded of the Ten Orators in antiquity,[23] and yet none of his speeches survived in medieval manuscripts, though substantial chunks of six have been identified on papyri since 1800. But perhaps most interesting in this regard are the cases of Antiphon and Isaeus on the one hand, and of Lysias on the other. Antiphon and Isaeus both seem to have had a reputation in antiquity as specialists in particular branches of the law (homicide in the case of the former, and inheritance in the latter case),[24] and it is unlikely to be coincidence that in each case what we possess is precisely those sections of what appears from the surviving fragments to have been a much more wide-ranging body of work. Our manuscipts of Lysias, on the other hand, can be traced back to the chance survival of a single archetype: the speeches it contains are by no means the most famous or the most likely to be genuine, but they do seem to have been organized on a thematic basis that to some extent overlaps with legal procedures.[25]

This pattern of survival has implications for the use of the speeches as historical evidence for Athenian law, precisely because they are our dominant source of knowledge. We know a great deal about inheritance and certain aspects of family law, for instance, primarily because of Isaeus' reputation as a specialist in this area.[26] Our knowledge of regulations surrounding homicide, on the other hand, though relying

---

[23] Longinus, *On the Sublime*, 34.1–2.

[24] This is directly attested in Antiphon's case (Hermogenes, *Peri Ideōn*, 2.11), though not to my knowledge in that of Isaeus. However, ancient collections of speeches tend to be organized on a thematic or procedural basis, and it is a plausible suggestion that where an orator had a reputation as a specialist, the collection would most naturally be headed by the largest or most famous group of speeches: thus Jebb (1893: ii.314), who notes that in the manuscripts of both these authors, the final speech seems to break off incomplete, which would serve to explain the survival of only this part of the corpus.

[25] Dover (1968b: 9–11), using *P.Oxy.* 2537 to support a suggestion originally proposed by the nineteenth-century scholar Blass. This type of thematic organization may account also for the order in which Demosthenes' private speeches appear in our manuscripts.

[26] Though there are a couple of relevant speeches elsewhere (e.g., Dem. 43–44 on inheritance, and Dem. 27–31 and Lys. 32 on guardianship). I use the term "family law" here in a broad sense: Isaeus provides a great deal of evidence e.g. for the rôle played by the phratry and the *genos* as well as that of the deme in verifying the citizen status of family members and the legitimacy of their marriages, and also for the ways in which aspects of religious cult within the family could be manipulated so as to represent favorably one's own relationship to the deceased. The property holdings of some of his litigants are also reported in considerable detail, though such evidence is both partial and unrepresentative.

heavily on Antiphon, is supplemented by one or two other speeches,[27] including one (Dem. 23) in which Demosthenes seeks to attack a proposal for an honorary decree on the somewhat far-fetched grounds that it contains a clause to the effect that anybody who killed the honorand would be liable to summary punishment: this gives him the opportunity for an extended tirade about the antiquity and sanctity of the various Athenian homicide courts. But the regulations for attempted homicide are from a legal perspective equally interesting, and we know about those only from the chance survival of a group of speeches in the corpus of Lysias (Lys. 3–4).

The crucial point here is the distorting prism created by what can sometimes be shown to be unrepresentative survival: in the cases mentioned in the previous paragraph, there is good reason to believe that a process of deliberate or accidental selection has preserved groups of speeches together in ways that do not fully reflect the balance of their author's activity. In circumstances where no such process of selection can be hypothesized, however, the pattern of survival may merit deeper investigation.

Take, for example, the process of *dokimasia* (the judicial scrutiny of newly appointed public officials before taking up office). Our manuscripts of Lysias contain probably four such speeches, and there is a further example preserved on a papyrus.[28] The fact that the four are scattered throughout the Lysian corpus rather than clustered together suggests that they have not been preserved as a thematic group, and the absence of *dokimasia* speeches by other orators suggests that there may be something significant going on here: my own explanation would be that this reflects the unusual circumstances of the generation after the Civil War of 403, when the presence of a general amnesty inhibited certain forms of prosecution against those who had backed the wrong side, but thereby encouraged their opponents creatively to develop the concept of what constituted ineligibility for public office.

---

[27] E.g. most famously Lys. 1 (a plea of justifiable homicide based on the claim to have found the deceased in bed with the speaker's wife).

[28] The three which are certainly *dokimasiai* are Lys. 16, Lys. 26, and Lys. 31. The procedure in Lys. 25 and Lys. frag. *Eryximakhos* cannot be identified with certainty, but it is generally agreed that *dokimasia* is the most likely. At first sight it would be tempting to see Lys. 25–26 as a thematic group like Lys. 3–4 (above), but in fact there is evidence that they were separated in the archetype of our manuscripts by a now lost non-*dokimasia* speech (*Against Nikides on Idleness*).

But even distorting survival can raise its own significant questions. We have noted, for instance, the survival of a group of Apollodorus's speeches within the corpus of Demosthenes. One of the effects of these speeches is that they have turned banking into an area of commercial activity and of commercial law about which we are disproportionately well-informed.[29] How far such knowledge is representative, however, and how widely Apollodorus can be used as proxy for a hypothetical class of commercially successful outsiders, is less clear – and this is a question that lies at the heart of much of the recent controversy over the relationship between law, commerce, and social status in fourth-century Athens.[30]

GENERIC DISTORTION

Patterns of survival are only one aspect of other more systematic distortions. It has to be remembered at all times that our texts represent the formal litigation of the élite, and we should forget neither the level of literacy that would be required for a client to benefit from a written speech, nor the financial investment that is likely to have been involved in commissioning it. Some scholars have suggested, for instance, that summary justice in dealing with the petty offences of the poor may have been more prevalent than our sources imply.[31]

What we possess is in most instances a single text of a speech in continuous prose. This has various implications, chief among which is that we normally hear only one side of the case. For only a tiny minority of trials do we have the speeches of both litigants, and only slightly more often do we know the result of the dispute, which normally requires evidence external to the speech itself.[32] Indeed, where we do know the result – or even occasionally the voting figures – the interpretation

---

[29] Contrast, for instance, the law of sale, which is represented by one fragmentary speech (Hyperides, *Against Athenogenes*).

[30] My fellow contributor Ed Cohen would, I think, see Apollodoros as a much more representative figure – thus, e.g., Cohen (1992) and (2000a: 130–54) – whereas I would tend to see Apollodoros as exceptional.

[31] Hansen (1976: 54).

[32] E.g., in the so-called Embassy trial of 343 B.C., Aesch. 2 is a defence against a charge brought by Demosthenes in Dem. 19 (which incidentally provides evidence at Dem. 19.284 for the result of the trial in Aesch. 1); in the Crown trial of 330, Dem. 18 is similarly a defence against Aesch. 3. In both cases, however, there is independent evidence for the existence of traditions about the result (e.g., Plut., *Dem.*, 15.3 and 24.2; Pseudo-Plutarch, *Life of Aeschines*, 840c-d).

of this data is itself ambiguous because Athenian dicastic juries (as we have seen) voted without formal discussion and without direction. To that extent, they were from the historian's perspective (and perhaps also that of the community) more like an English than an American jury,[33] and certainly unlike a modern appeal court, in that we do not hear their reasons for their decision; and indeed there is no reason to believe that the issues that swayed each individual *dikastēs* were ones which influenced his neighbor.

Another aspect of the speech format is that we normally hear the voice only of the orator and/or his client. Ancient rhetorical theorists group together a number of categories of supporting evidence, including the testimony of witnesses and the texts of legal statutes.[34] The assimilation here is an interesting one – a modern lawyer would be most unlikely to speak of laws as a category of evidence, preferring to see them as the rules by which the court makes its decisions – but one reason for the assimilation may have been that these two categories of information seem to have been presented similarly both in court and in our speeches. Unlike a modern Anglo-American court where the cross-examination of witnesses is a major weapon in the advocate's armory, an Athenian witness seems normally to have presented his testimony in the form of an uninterrupted statement, and from the 380s onwards the witness's appearance in court seems to have been confined to the affirmation of a written statement drafted in advance. It is not clear how far the drafting was done by the witness himself or by the litigant (or in our cases presumably by his logographer), but the fact that it is the litigant's privilege to call witnesses may suggest the latter; and it was certainly the litigants or their logographers who provided the texts of any other written documents, including laws, which would be read out at their invitation by the clerk of the court.[35]

The patterns of relationship between logographers, litigants, and their witnesses have far-reaching implications for the structure of the legal system, some of which will be touched on in the final section of the chapter. But the relationship between the surviving speeches and what is said at the trial deserves attention also. It is worth noting, for

---

[33] In English law it is contempt of court for a juror to reveal any of the deliberations within the jury room.

[34] Aristotle, *Rhetoric*, 1.15.1–2 = 1375a 22–25 has a fivefold classification (laws, witnesses, contracts, torture [of slaves], oaths), whereas Anaximenes, *Rhetoric to Alexander*, 14–17, speaks only of four categories (speaker's opinion [sic], witness-testimony, torture, oaths).

[35] We are told that death was the penalty for citing a nonexistent law (Dem. 26.24), which may indicate an awareness of the possibilities. On witnesses, see Thür in this volume.

instance, that our manuscripts generally omit the documents that were read out in court, substituting instead the lemma "law" or "testimony" to indicate that a legal statute or the evidence of a witness was to be read out at this stage. The reason for this omission seems to be that the speeches were preserved later in antiquity primarily as models of rhetorical style to be studied at school, and it was the words of the orator rather than the facts of the case that interested the scholars who copied the manuscripts. There are some exceptions to the pattern of nonpreservation, mainly in the corpus of Demosthenes, but this itself gives cause for suspicion: it is because Demosthenes was the most famous of the orators that documents involving him are precisely the sort of thing which conscientious schoolteachers would wish to reconstruct for the edification of their pupils. The authenticity of the documents in our speeches is a matter of considerable controversy, but the consensus of recent scholars is that rather than accepting or rejecting them *en bloc*, we need instead to consider each one on its own merits, looking, for instance, at such questions as whether the wording of the document accurately reflects normal patterns of legal drafting, or whether the witnesses are correctly located (we sometimes have independent epigraphic evidence for their demes). The extent to which the purported document is accurately summarized in the surrounding passages of the speech is another criterion, though it can be two-edged, because divergence could represent an orator's rhetorical manipulation of the statute, while similarity could denote a later scholar's forgery based on a reading of the speech.[36]

Even in its own terms, of course, a speech by an Attic Orator represents only a version of what the litigant said in court. This applies at several levels. Allusions to what happened before the trial, for instance, are largely incidental, which may lead us to underestimate the importance of such pretrial procedures as arbitration. This is important not simply in the positivistic sense that it is a gap in our knowledge, but more significantly because of the risk that we may therefore be overemphasizing those stages of litigation which are confrontational and performative, at the expense of those which might have been more likely to lead to compromise and consensus.[37]

At a more fundamental level, at least to the historian concerned about the status of historical evidence, is the question of how far the

---

[36] There are good discussions in Carey (1992: 20) and more fully in MacDowell (1990: 43–7).

[37] On the rôle played by arbitration and reconciliation, see Scafuro (1997: 31–42, 117–41, and 383–96).

speech that was published is the same as the speech that was delivered. This has been heavily contested by modern scholars, who have noted, for instance, that in the two instances where we do have the leading speech on each side of the same trial, the two litigants both attribute to each other statements that do not appear in our versions of the corresponding speeches.[38]

(RE-)PRESENTATION

One of the strongest impressions created by our texts is that Athenian litigation took the form of continuous though relatively short speeches, rather than the cut-and-thrust of extended cross-examination and debate that is the pattern of modern Anglo-American jury trials. Once again, there is the possibility of distortion here: although there was no right to cross-question witnesses, litigants did have the power to insist that their opponents respond to direct questions, and I have suggested elsewhere that this may have been more prevalent than is reflected in our texts.[39] There may also have been a greater degree of audience participation than might at first appear: indeed, in one of his attacks on his stepfather Phormion, Apollodorus claims that at a previous hearing the latter had used the legal subterfuge of *paragraphē* in order to speak first, and had so misrepresented Apollodorus himself that the jury refused to listen to his defence.[40] Having said that, however, we have a lot of independent evidence for the timing of speeches by means of a *klepsydra* (water-clock), from which it is clear that

---

[38] The two cases in question are the Embassy and Crown trials (for which see n. 32 above). Dover (1968b: 168–9) cites six passages in the two defence speeches (four in Aesch. 2 and two in Dem. 18), each of which allege that the opponent has said something that is not found in our texts of the prosecution speech. Several of these passages, however, are capable of other explanations (Harris 1995: 10 n. 6 rightly notes that jurors without access to the text of the speech might not have spotted the discrepancy in Aesch. 2.124 and 2.156, though this may not so easily explain Dover's other examples). Subsequent discussion can be found in Carey (2000: 93–4), and in greater detail in MacDowell (2000a: 22–7). For the related but separable question of how far the logographic speeches that we possess are the work entirely of the orator or how far there may have been coauthorship, see n. 16 above: for the historian, as is suggested at n. 20 above, the question of authorship is usually less significant than other forms of authenticity.

[39] Todd (2002: 164).

[40] We have of course no independent evidence to support this possibly exaggerated claim (made at Dem. 45.6, and referring back to the trial which forms the subject of Dem. 36). The broader evidence for verbal involvement on the part of the *dikastai* is collected and discussed in Bers (1985).

litigants were given a relatively short period of time in which to make their case. Athenian justice was rapid: so far as we know, dicastic trials never overran the day, and many private cases were considerably shorter than this.[41]

The principle[42] that individuals were expected to plead their own case has wide implications for the rôle of the litigant as both orator and narrator, who is expected to tell the story of the dispute in the course of his speech. This is significantly but subtly different from the relationships in a modern criminal trial, at least in common-law systems, where the prosecution case will normally be pleaded by an advocate, rather than by the victim of the offence; but where the victim may well appear as primary narrator, in the form of the chief witness for the prosecution. It is not simply the absence of professional advocacy that is important here, but the assumption that the proper person to take legal action is the aggrieved party. In a *dikē* (private case) this was indeed a statutory requirement, but even though a public prosecution (*graphē*) could be brought by a third party on the victim's behalf, nevertheless the norm at least in our cases seems to be that prosecutors even in *graphai* claim to have been personally wronged.[43]

Such personal involvement on the part of litigants is presumably a contributory reason for the frequent (and to us rather surprising) protestations of enmity toward one's opponent in public as well as private cases.[44] But it may also help explain some of the features of Athenian law to which attention has been drawn in this chapter. We have seen, for instance, that witnesses in Athenian courts play a relatively restricted rôle. They are not required to tell the story as primary narrators, but instead appear normally to confirm details of the narrative after it has been presented by the litigant. It is striking that although Athenian law did have an action for false witness (the *dikē pseudomarturiōn*), nevertheless we rarely find litigants during the original trial seeking to undermine the character of the opponent's witnesses: the reason for this, as also

---

[41] *Ath.Pol.* 67.1–2 (four private trials in a day). Worthington (1989) is right to point out that there is no direct evidence that public cases could not overrun into a second day, but the only clear example of this happening relates to an occasion when the Assembly sat as a court, and to reconvene a dicastic trial would fatally undermine the fourth-century principle that random selection prevented jury-nobbling. For a detailed rebuttal of Worthington's arguments, see MacDowell (2000b).

[42] Discussed above, p. 100.

[43] On the frequency with which public cases known to us are brought by the alleged victims rather than by third parties, see Osborne (1985).

[44] On this phenomenon, see Rubinstein below, p. 131.

for the absence of cross-examination, is presumably that the primary narrator on the other side is the opposing litigant himself.[45]

More broadly, the personal involvement of litigants is likely also to have affected the very nature of forensic rhetoric. It is notable that narrative, for instance, plays a far more important part in our speeches than it would be given in the training of a modern advocate. This may be worth bearing in mind when considering the parallels between lawcourt rhetoric and tragic drama. In her contribution to this volume, Allen notes that modern explanations of the phenomenon tend to concentrate heavily on the influence of the former on the latter, but some albeit speculative suggestions in the other direction may be worth making here. Whereas a modern advocate is a professional performer, at Athens the relationship between logographer and client will presumably have been closer to that between author and (amateur) actor, and this raises questions about the extent to which the former will have been expected to provide the latter with training in delivery. And it is possible, of course, that the perception of the logographic client as actor (in the dramatic sense) may have been accentuated by Greek tragedy's unusual emphasis on reported narrative (e.g., messenger speeches).

The conflation of orator and narrator, however, is linked as we saw at the start of this chapter to the silence (or at least the formal silence) of the dicastic jury. So it is perhaps appropriate to end this chapter, before I trespass too much on the topics allocated to my fellow contributors, by voicing the vexed question of how Athenians (including Athenian *dikastai*) viewed their legal system. How far did they see their rôle as being to apply rules (either individually or as a system)? Or as negotiators within a discourse? Or as interpreters of a set of stories (including perhaps the one that they were deciding or narrating)? And how far were these perceptions determined by the fact that their experience of law was in large part mediated not through judicial interpretation but through speeches?

---

[45] The absence of cross-examination is discussed above, p. 107. On the absence of character assassination, see Todd (1990: 24). For technical reasons, the *dikē pseudomarturiōn* was used with some frequency in disputes involving inheritance, where this was the only way of blocking a claim to be a son adopted by the deceased during his lifetime.

6: Relevance in Athenian Courts

Adriaan Lanni

One of the most striking features of speeches intended for delivery in the Athenian popular courts is the presence of material that would be considered irrelevant or inadmissible in a modern courtroom. The interpretation of this tendency to include information that does not bear on the legal issue in dispute is central to our understanding of the aims and ideals of the Athenian legal system. In recent years, it has been argued that the courts did not attempt to resolve disputes according to established rules and principles equally and impartially applied, but rather served primarily a social or political role.[1] According to this approach, litigation was not aimed chiefly at the final resolution of the dispute or the discovery of truth; rather, the courts provided an arena for the parties to publicly define, contest, and evaluate their social relations to one another and the hierarchies of their society. On this view, the extralegal arguments in surviving court speeches provide evidence that litigants were engaged in a competition for honor and prestige largely unrelated to the statute under which the suit was brought or the incident that ostensibly gave rise to the dispute. This approach to the Athenian legal system has been challenged by scholars who contend that the Athenian courts attempted to implement a rule of law.[2] They argue that jurors took seriously their oath to vote

---

[1] Cohen (1995), Osborne (1985).
[2] See Ostwald (1986: 497–525), and Sealey (1987:146–8), for an institutional approach; Meyer-Laurin (1965), Meinecke (1971), and Harris (2000) for interpretation of lawcourt speeches. Meyer-Laurin and Meinecke argue that Athenian litigants and jurors applied the law strictly, whereas Harris suggests that the open texture of Athenian law left room for creative statutory interpretation. All three share the view that litigants and jurors considered themselves bound by the law and that the goal of the system approximated modern notions of a rule of law.

according to the laws and tend to dismiss the extralegal arguments in the surviving speeches as stray comments reflecting only the amateurism and informality of the system.

This chapter examines Athenian notions of relevance, focusing primarily on popular court cases, which accounted for the vast majority of trials in the Athenian system. I argue that the nonlegal arguments we meet in the surviving speeches were vital components of making a case in an Athenian popular court rather than aberrations in an essentially modern legal system. However, the seemingly irrelevant material does not suggest a disregard for the factual and legal issues in dispute in favor of an unrelated social purpose; rather, extralegal arguments provided information about the context of the dispute to assist the popular court jury in reaching a just verdict that took into account the particular circumstances of the individual case.[3] By contrast, a much narrower notion of relevance prevailed in two special types of suit: cases heard in the homicide courts and maritime cases. The Athenians could imagine a judicial process involving the regular application of abstract, standardized rules, but apparently favored highly contextualized and individualized assessments in the popular courts.

Relevance in the Popular Courts

There appears to have been no rule setting forth the range and types of information and argument appropriate for popular court speeches. The *Athenaion Politeia* states that litigants in private cases took an oath to speak to the point, but this oath is never mentioned in our surviving popular court speeches and if in fact it existed, it appears to have had no effect.[4] Speakers were limited only by the time limit and their own sense of which arguments were likely to persuade the jury. Although anything was fair game in the popular courts – Lycurgus's extended quotations from Euripides, Homer, and Tyrtaeus on the honor and

---

[3] My view of the Athenian juror's task is in accord with those of Humphreys (1983: 248), Scafuro (1997: 50–66), and Christ (1998: 195–6).

[4] *Ath. Pol.* 67.1. Whereas speeches made before the homicide courts or referring to them make frequent mention of the relevancy rule that applied in those courts, speeches delivered in the popular courts never mention such a legal requirement. In the few allusions to speaking to the issue, most of which are found in a single speech (Demosthenes 57), nothing in the phraseology suggests a duty imposed by law to avoid straying from the issue at hand. Compare Dem. 57.59 and Lys. 9.1 with references to the homicide court rule in Lys. 3.46, Ant. 5.11 and 6.9.

glory of battle in his prosecution of a citizen who left Athens when the city was threatened with attack[5] is perhaps the most creative use of speaking time in our surviving speeches – there are discernible categories of nonlegal evidence that appear repeatedly in the corpus.[6] Experienced speechwriters undoubtedly had a good feel for the types of arguments and information that were likely to appeal to the jury and constructed their speeches accordingly.

It is therefore possible to speak about Athenian notions of the types of information and arguments that were particularly relevant to popular court decisions in the absence of a stricture on the presentation of evidence in these courts. Because we rarely know the outcome of an ancient case and generally do not have the opposing litigant's speech that would allow a comparison, it is impossible to know which strategies were most persuasive to an Athenian jury, and, as we will see, the categories of relevant evidence were fluid and contestable. Nevertheless, the surviving speeches clearly show the popular court juries' receptivity to three sorts of argument: (1) the expansion of the litigant's plea beyond the strict limits of the event in question to encompass the broader background of the dispute, (2) defense appeals for the jury's pity based on the potential harmful effects of an adverse verdict, and (3) arguments based on the character of the parties. Before we examine in detail each of the three classes of nonlegal information, a few general comments may help to clarify my approach. I discuss types of information and argument that are common enough in our surviving speeches to indicate that logographers and jurors thought them relevant to popular court decision making. In any individual case, however, litigants might dispute the relevance and relative importance of different types of argument. The corpus of forensic speeches contains, for example, impassioned arguments both for and against the relevance of character evidence.[7] Indeed, speakers sometimes contend that the jury should ignore nonlegal evidence and focus solely on the legal arguments made in the case.[8]

---

[5] Lyc. 1.100, 103, 107.

[6] Rhodes (2004) argues that court speeches focus mostly on the issue in dispute. My own view is that most popular court speeches contain a mixture of legal and nonlegal information, and it was left to the jury to determine which sort of evidence was most important in any individual suit. In any case, the repeated use of a particular type of nonlegal argument in our surviving speeches suggests that this sort of evidence was considered relevant to the jury's verdict, even if it accounts for only a small portion of litigants' arguments.

[7] Compare, for example, Dem. 36.55 and Dem. 52.1.

[8] E.g., Isoc. 18.34–5; Dem. 52.1–2; Hyp. 4.32.

Such arguments were themselves part of the remarkably individualized and case-specific approach to justice employed in the popular courts: most speeches included a mixture of nonlegal and legal argument, and it was left to the jurors to decide which sorts of evidence were most important given the particular circumstances of the case.

Background Information and Fairness in Light of the Particular Circumstances of the Case

Modern lawyers translate a client's story into legal form in large part by winnowing down the client's experience to a limited set of facts that correspond to claims and arguments recognized by the applicable law. Athenian litigants, by contrast, provide a "wide-angle" view of the case, one that includes not only a complete account of the event in question, but also information regarding the social context of the dispute, including discussion of the long-term relationship and interactions of the parties. In cases that are part of a series of suits between the parties, for example, speakers do not confine their argument to the immediate issue in question but rather recount the past litigation in some detail.[9] This practice is particularly prominent in speeches for suits charging false testimony, which generally include an attempt to reargue the previous case as well as evidence that a statement made by one of the opponent's witnesses was false. For instance, the speaker in Demosthenes 47 says to the jury, "I now present to you a just request, that you both determine whether the testimony is false or true, and, at the same time, examine the entire matter from the beginning."[10]

Litigants also commonly discuss the manner in which each of the parties has conducted themselves in the course of litigation. They emphasize their own reasonableness and willingness to settle or arbitrate the claim and portray their opponents as querulous, dishonest, and even violent.[11] To cite one example, the speaker in Demosthenes 44.31–2 states, "I think it is necessary to speak also of the things they have done in the time since the case regarding the estate was brought, and the way they have dealt with us, for I think that no one else has been as

---

[9] E.g., Dem. 21.78ff; 29.9, 27; 43.1–2; 47.46; 53.14–5; And. 1.117ff; Is. 2.27–37; 5.5ff.
[10] Dem. 47.46; see also Dem. 29.9, 27; 45.1–2; Is. 2.27–37. For discussion, see Bonner 1905: 18.
[11] Dem. 21.78ff; 27.1; 29.58; 30.2; 41.1–2; 42.11–12; 44.31–2; 47.81; 48.2, 40; Is. 5.28–30. For discussion of the importance of appearing eager to settle, see Hunter (1994: 57).

unlawfully treated in connection with an inheritance lawsuit as we have been."

When relatives or friends face each other in court, speakers describe the long-term relationship and interaction of the parties and seek to represent themselves as honoring the obligations traditionally associated with bonds of *philia* ("friendship") and to portray their opponents as having violated these norms.[12] As Christ points out, litigants at times exaggerate the intimacy of their past relationship in order to present their cases in terms of a breach of *philia*.[13] Lawcourt speakers do not discuss why information about the relationship between the parties was considered relevant to the jury's decision, but a passage from Aristotle's *Nicomachean Ethics* suggests one possibility.[14] Aristotle explains that just as the duties and obligations one owes to family, friends, fellow citizens, and other types of relations differ, "Wrongs are also of a different quality in the case of each of these [relationships], and are more serious the more intimate the friendship." He continues, "For example, it is more serious to defraud a comrade than a fellow-citizen, and to refuse help to a brother than to a stranger, and to strike your father than anybody else" (Ar. *NE* 1160a3ff). It may be that information about the relationship between the parties helped the jury evaluate the severity of the allegations and the extent of moral blame borne by each side.

In addition to presenting evidence about relationships and interactions prior to and after the event at issue, litigants at times provide a highly contextualized account of the dispute itself, often including arguments that are not explicitly recognized by law but that contribute to the jury's overall sense of the fair result of the dispute. For example, speakers at times discuss the extenuating (and, less commonly, aggravating) circumstances surrounding the incident – such as the absence of intent or the offender's youth – even though the laws enforced by the popular courts did not formally recognize such defenses and did not provide for degrees of offenses based on their severity.[15]

---

[12] Christ (1998: 167–80). Christ discusses the emphasis on the breach of *philia* in cases involving relatives, friends, neighbors, and demesmen.

[13] Christ (1998: 167).

[14] Aristotle's theoretical works must be used with great care as a source for the ideals or practice of the Athenian lawcourts; see Carey (1996: 42). However, the *Ethics* does seem to be a reliable source of Athenian popular values; Aristotle sets out to examine beliefs that are "prevalent and have some basis," Ar. *NE* 1095a28; cf. Millett (1991: 112).

[15] These topoi have been catalogued and discussed in detail in Saunders (1991: 109–18), Dorjahn (1930: 162–72), and Scafuro (1997: 246–50). This practice did not go entirely unchallenged: see Dem. 54.21–22; Aesch. 3.198.

Discussion of the circumstances and context of the contested event is most prominent in suits involving a challenge to a will.[16] As Hardcastle has shown, litigants often appeal to a variety of arguments rooted in notions of fairness and justice unrelated to the issue of the formal validity of the will. Speakers compare their relationship to the deceased with that of their opponents in an effort to argue that they have the better claim to the estate: they present evidence that they were closer in affection to the deceased, performed his burial rites, or nursed him when he was ill, and suggest that their opponents were detested by the dead man and took no interest in his affairs until it was time to claim his estate.[17] One such litigant concludes with a summary of his arguments that places equitable considerations on an equal footing with the will and the law: "First, my friendship with the men who have bequeathed the estate...then the many good deeds I did for them when they were down on their luck...in addition the will,...further, the law..." (Isoc. 19.50).

The frequency and centrality of discussion of the background and interaction of the parties in our surviving popular court speeches indicate that this type of information was considered relevant to the jury's decision. It has been suggested that the prevalence of such nonlegal arguments indicates that Athenian litigants and jurors regarded the court process as serving primarily a social role – the assertion of competitive advantage in a narrow stratum of society – rather than a "legal" function. One scholar, for example, explains the tendency to discuss the broader conflict between the parties as evidence that litigants were engaged in a competition for prestige unrelated to the "ostensible subject of the dispute": "rather than thinking in terms of a 'just resolution' of the dispute one should think instead of how the game of honor is being played."[18]

There may be a simpler explanation, however, one rooted in the pervasive amateurism of the Athenian courts. Human beings naturally tend to think about social interaction in story form.[19] The restrictive evidence regimes of contemporary jury-based legal systems are, from

[16] Other recent discussions of the use of arguments from "fairness" or "equity" include Scafuro (1997: 50–66), Christ (1998: 194ff), Biscardi (1970: 219–32). For a contrary view, see Harris (2000).

[17] E.g., Is. 1.4, 17, 19, 20, 30, 33, 37, 42; 4.19; 6.51; 7.8, 11, 12, 33–37; 9.4, 27–32. For discussion, see Hardcastle (1980), Avramovic (1997: 54–8). For an argument that equity argumentation in Isaeus is a response to obscurities and gaps in the inheritance laws rather than an attempt to appeal to fairness, see Lawless (1991: 110–35).

[18] Cohen (1995: 90).

[19] E.g., Lopez (1984: 3), Lempert (1991), Bennet and Feldman (1981: 7), Hastie et al. (1983: 22–3).

a layperson's perspective, counterintuitive; amateurs left to their own devices in contemporary small claims courts, for example, often set their dispute in a broader context and use a variety of everyday storytelling techniques forbidden in formal court settings.[20] It is perhaps not surprising that amateur Athenian litigants would consider evidence concerning the background of the dispute, the parties' conduct in the course of litigation, and arguments from fairness relevant in reaching a just outcome to the issue at hand; there is no need to resort to a theory of the Athenian court system as a forum primarily concerned with social competition to explain this contextual information included in our surviving popular court speeches. This explanation for the prevalence of nonlegal material becomes even more attractive when we consider that Athenian lawcourt speeches generally include what a modern observer would consider legally relevant argument as well as such nonlegal argumentation.

Defense Appeals Based on the Harsh Effects of an Adverse Verdict

One of the most striking topoi of Athenian lawcourt speeches is appeals for the jurors' pity based on the misfortune that will befall the defendant and his family if he is found guilty. From a modern perspective, this information is relevant, if at all, to sentencing rather than the determination of guilt. The frequency of this topos in Athenian defense speeches and its anticipation by prosecutors suggest that appeals to pity were for the most part considered appropriate in the popular courts.[21] Johnstone has demonstrated that prosecutors are more likely to argue that their particular opponent's character or actions have rendered him undeserving of pity rather than to challenge the legitimacy of the practice itself.[22]

The surviving Athenian verbal appeals to "pity" (*eleos*) and "pardon" (*syngnōmē*) in the courts did not take the same form as their modern counterparts, perhaps because they appear in speeches at the guilt rather than the sentencing phase. As Konstan points out, Athenian litigants who appeal to the juror's pity do not concede guilt and therefore express no remorse; rather, they provide information about the severe

---

[20] O'Barr and Conley (1985).
[21] E.g., Lys. 9.22; 18.27; 19.33, 53; 20.34–5; 21.25; Hyp. 1.19–20; Isoc. 16.47; Dem. 27.66–69; 45.85; 55.35; 57.70; Johnstone (1999: 111) shows that nearly half of defense speeches include a verbal appeal to the jurors' pity.
[22] Johnstone (1999: 113).

effects an adverse verdict will have on themselves and their families.[23] In Konstan's view, speakers who appeal to pity proceed on the assumption that they are innocent of the charge and use the topos "as another means by which a defendant insisted on his innocence" and as "a way of charging the jury to take seriously the power at their disposal, and be certain that they do not do grave harm, as they can, on the basis of insufficient evidence."[24] Certainly appeals to pity are always made in a manner consistent with innocence, and litigants do at times complain that if convicted their suffering will be all the worse for being undeserved.[25] Nevertheless, discussion of the effects a serious penalty will have on the defendant likely served the additional purpose of assisting the jury in determining whether a conviction was a fair result given all of the circumstances, including the severity of the likely penalty. Thus, the effects of an adverse verdict were thought relevant to the jury's highly particularized and contextualized calculation of moral desert at the guilt phase.

As a practical matter, Athenian jurors had little control over the specific penalty imposed after a conviction. For some offenses (*atimētoi*), the penalty was fixed by statute. For others (*timētoi*), the jury chose between the penalties proposed by the opposing parties during a second round of speeches. Even in these cases, however, it seems that juries were not always given a choice at the penalty phase: once a verdict of guilty was entered, the litigants could reach an agreement on the proposed penalty.[26] Moreover, jurors would often have a fair idea during trial of the range of penalties likely to be proposed. Prosecutors at times discussed their proposed penalty during the guilt phase,[27] and in some suits — particularly those which called for restitution, such as theft or breach of contract — the prosecutor included the value of his claim in the indictment.[28] A juror who believed that the defendant was guilty of the charge but did not deserve to suffer the fixed or probable penalty was more likely to vote to acquit than (in the case of an *agōn timētos*) to assume in the absence of deliberation that his fellow jurors shared

---

[23] Konstan (2000: 133ff).
[24] Konstan (2000: 136, 138).
[25] E.g., Dem. 28.18–19; Lys. 19.45.
[26] Is. 5.18; Dem. 47.42–43. Scafuro (1997: 393–4) suggests that there may have been a regular procedure for compromise on the penalty in trials without fixed penalties.
[27] Isoc. 20.19; Dem. 56.43–4; 24.19; 58.19.
[28] E.g., Dem. 45.46; Aristoph. *Wasps*, 897; Dion. Hal. *Dein.* 3. Although a defendant could submit a lower proposal at the penalty phase, it would be risky for a convicted defendant to propose a sum that was vastly lower than the value of the contract or the goods in question.

his desire for a lenient sentence and that the defendant would propose a more acceptable penalty. The vigorous attempt of the prosecutor in Lysias 15 to dissuade jurors from considering the severity of the penalty in their determination of guilt suggests that this practice may have been frequent in Athens:

> And so, gentlemen of the jury, if it seems to you that the penalty is too great and the law excessively harsh, you must remember that you are here not to make laws regarding these matters, but to cast your ballot according to the laws as they exist, and not to show pity for the wrongdoers, but rather to express your anger at them and to help the entire city. (Lys. 15.9)

It is important to note that appeals to pity in the Athenian courts were firmly rooted in the defendant's particular circumstances; litigants generally do not criticize the penalty itself as disproportionate to the charges, but rather bemoan the tragic effects that penalty will have on them given their specific situation.[29] Particularly common are appeals that an adverse verdict will leave the defendant's family without support or the means to dower its unmarried women[30] and that failure to pay the penalty will lead to the defendant's loss of citizen rights.[31] Alcibiades the Younger, for example, explains that the five-talent penalty carries more serious consequences for him than for other defendants: "For even though the same legal punishments apply to all, the risk is not the same for everyone: rather, those who have money suffer a fine, but those who are impoverished, as I am, are in danger of losing their civic rights [i.e., *atimia*].... Therefore I beg you to help me..." (Isoc. 16.47). Although Athenian defendants do not explicitly discuss what role their appeals to pity should play in the jury's decision, it seems

---

[29] These arguments are thus examples of the weakest form of "jury nullification." Green 1985: xviii distinguishes three meanings of this term, from strongest to weakest: (1) acquittal contrary to law because the jury believes that the defendant's act should not be proscribed; (2) acquittal because the jury believes that the act, though criminal, does not deserve the punishment prescribed for it; and (3) acquittal because the jury believes not that the law or its punishment is unjust in the abstract, but that such punishment is inappropriate given the particular circumstances of the case. In Athens, the particular circumstances that could render punishment inappropriate included not only the circumstances surrounding the act itself, but also the tragic effects the penalty would have on the defendant and his family.

[30] Lys. 19.33; 21.24–25; Dem. 28.19.

[31] Lys. 18.1; 9.21; 20.34; Isoc. 16.45–46.

likely that these arguments were thought not only to remind the jury of the seriousness of their task but also to assist in its determination of whether a conviction was a just result in the particular circumstances of the case.

Character

The most common type of nonlegal argumentation in our surviving speeches is the liberal use of character evidence. Some form of discussion of character occurs in seventy of eighty-seven popular court speeches.[32] Despite the frequency of arguments from character, there was clearly some ambivalence about the wisdom of this practice: litigants sometimes charge that they have resorted to a discussion of character only because their opponents' slander has forced them to respond,[33] and speakers sometimes urge the jury to ignore questions of reputation and character when reaching their decision.[34] Perhaps because of the contestability of character evidence and a worry that its use might lead to verdicts based solely on the prejudices of the jury,[35] litigants in several cases preface their character evidence with an explanation of why it is relevant to the jury's decision. These passages, along with other aspects of the way in which character evidence is used in our surviving speeches, suggest that discussions of character for the most part served a contextualizing function that assisted the jury in reaching a legal verdict. Of course, it is difficult to pinpoint the intended effect of any particular piece of evidence; discussions of character likely operated on more than one level of meaning.[36] Nevertheless, the liberal use of character evidence in our surviving speeches is more plausibly explained as part of the attempt to reach a just resolution of the case, rather than as part of a competition for elite prestige and honor in which the jury aimed to pick a favorite.

The first justification for character evidence we meet in the speeches is that it assists the jury in finding facts through an argument

---

[32] Speeches in maritime suits and homicide cases are not included in this calculation.
[33] E.g., Lys. 9.3; 30.15; Hyp. 1.8–9; Dem. 52.1. Litigants also at times apologize and suggest that they recognize discussion of character as a digression. E.g., Dem. 57.63; Is. 5.12.
[34] E.g. Dem. 52.1–2; Hyp. 4.32.
[35] The defendant in Hyp. 4.32, for example, expresses the fear that his opponent has emphasized the speaker's wealth in the hope that the jury will convict him out of spite.
[36] Carey (1996: 42–3).

from *eikos* or probability.[37] The Athenians tended to view character as stable and unchanging.[38] That a defendant had committed crimes in the past or otherwise exhibited bad morals or character was considered highly probative of whether he was guilty of the offense charged and whether he was telling the truth in his present speech.[39] Thus, for example, one speaker states, "If you knew the shamelessness of Diocles and what sort of man he was in relation to other matters, you would not doubt any of the things I have said" (Is. 8.40). Another explains his decision to discuss the prosecutor's history of bringing false accusations and the defendant's good character at some length:

> Now I think, men of Athens, that presenting witnesses on these matters is more to the point than anything. For if a man is always acting as a sycophant, what must you think he is doing in this case? And by Zeus, men of Athens, I think it is also to the point to present to you all signs of Phormio's character and his righteousness and generosity.... He who has never done wrong to anyone, but rather has voluntarily done good deeds for many people, on what basis would he, in any probability, have done wrong to this man alone? (Dem. 36.55)

Character was all the more relevant to factfinding in a world without modern techniques of forensic investigation and evidence gathering: in the absence of hard evidence, character was a proxy for guilt or innocence. Another speaker cites his clean record and meritorious service to the city before arguing, "You ought to take these things as proof for the purpose of this case that the charges against me are false" (Hyp. 1.18).

The second reason given for the citation of character evidence is that it is relevant to the jury's assessment of whether the defendant deserves the penalty for the charge or should be given pardon.[40] To cite just one example, a prosecutor engages in an extended character attack on Aristogeiton, noting that he failed to support or properly bury his father, had been convicted on several charges in the past and was even so base that his fellow criminals in prison voted to shun him (Din. 2.8–13). The speaker then asserts that Aritogeiton has forfeited any right to

---

[37] See Saunders (1991: 113), Johnstone (1999: 96).
[38] For discussion, see Dover (1974: 88–95).
[39] E.g., Dem. 58.28; 20.141–142; 25.15; 36.55; Hyp. 1.14; Is. 8.40.
[40] On the use of the defendant's record for this purpose, see Saunders (1991: 113–18).

a lenient penalty, arguing that he would justly suffer capital punishment "on the basis of both his whole life and the things that he has done now."[41]

Johnstone and Rubinstein have pointed out that character evidence focuses most commonly on the defendant rather than the prosecutor.[42] The emphasis on the defendant supports the view that the frequent citations to character in the surviving speeches are designed to assist the jury in reaching their verdict rather than to provide ammunition in a contest for honor[43]: the defendant's reputation and record is part of the contextual information considered by the jury in determining whether a conviction is warranted.[44] Although there are a handful of passages that suggest a nonlegal purpose for the citation of character evidence — most notably, statements that the jury should acquit a defendant because he has performed expensive public services in the past and, if victorious, will continue to do so in the future[45] — the bulk of the evidence suggests that the liberal use of arguments from character reflect the Athenian popular court's highly individualized and contextualized mode of decision making.

Relevance in Homicide and Maritime Cases

In contrast to the broad notion of relevance found in popular court cases, the Athenians followed a perceptibly more formal, legal approach in two special types of case: suits brought before the homicide courts and

---

[41] Din. 2.11. Other examples: Isoc. 18.47; 20.13; Lys. 20.34; 30.6; Din. 3.5, Dem. 45.63ff.
[42] Johnstone (1999: 94), Rubinstein (2000: 195).
[43] Johnstone (1999: 96) expresses this idea in terms of the defendant using character evidence to attack the plausibility of the prosecutor's narrative, whereas Rubinstein (2000: 218) states "the measurement of the defendant's *timē* was not relative to the personal record of his prosecutor(s), but, rather, relative to the accusations leveled against him."
[44] In fact, the instances where prosecutors do cite their public services tend to be cases involving inheritance and cases where the prosecutor argues that his honor has been violated, for example, assault prosecutions; see Johnstone (1999: 98–100). The prosecutor's character is relevant to the resolution of the dispute in these types of suit because in inheritance cases it is pertinent to whether the prosecutor deserves to own the property under the circumstances, and in assault cases it is relevant to the seriousness of the crime.
[45] Is. 6.61; 7.38–42; Lys.18.20–21; 19.61; 21.25; Dem. 28.24. Generalized requests for *charis* (gratitude or favor) on the basis of prior service and good character seem to be part of the calculation of moral desert. Cf. Johnstone (1999: 100–8).

maritime suits.[46] Space permits only a partial summary of the evidence for the distinctive approaches to relevance in homicide and maritime cases.

Homicide Courts

The homicide courts had a relevancy rule limiting the use of irrelevant statements.[47] None of our sources gives an exhaustive list of items that were considered "outside the issue" (ἔξω τοῦ πράγματος) but the context of Lysias 3, Lycurgus 1, and Antiphon 5 makes it clear that lists of services and attacks on an opponent's character were, at least formally, forbidden. Pollux, writing in the second century C.E., adds that litigants before the Areopagus (the most prominent of the homicide courts) were not permitted to include a *proem* or emotional appeals in their speeches, and Lucian includes a similar formulation.[48] Regardless of whether a formal mechanism for enforcing the relevancy rule existed or whether the experienced Areopagites judging cases in the homicide courts would simply make their displeasure known to a litigant who strayed from the point, our sources reveal that it was widely believed that irrelevant material had no place in the court of the Areopagus.[49]

Examination of the four surviving speeches written for delivery in the Areopagus (Ant. 1, Lys. 3, 4, 7) and the two written for the other homicide courts (Ant. 6; Lys.1) gives some indication of the extent to which the homicide courts employed a different standard of relevance from the popular courts. Speakers in the homicide courts are more skittish about citing their services to the state or slandering their opponents than popular court speakers, but irrelevancy (in modern terms) was by no means absent from litigation in these courts. Although the relevancy rule was not adhered to in all respects, there are significant differences between the surviving homicide and popular court speeches, and litigants seem to be aware that the homicide courts enjoyed a reputation for having higher expectations than the popular courts.

Litigants before the homicide courts were reluctant to adduce evidence of their good deeds or to criticize their opponent's character.

---

[46] Scholars differ on whether the special maritime procedure was heard in separate courts before specialist judges. Compare Cohen 1973: 93–5 with Todd (1993: 336).
[47] Lys. 3.46; Lyc. 1.11–13; Poll. 8.117; Ant. 5.11; 6.9.
[48] Poll. 8.117; Lucian *Anach.* 19.
[49] E.g., Aristotle *Rhet.* 1354a; Aesch. 1.92.

Although such references occur frequently in the popular courts, litigants in our surviving six homicide speeches employ this strategy in only three passages.[50] In two of the three instances,[51] the speaker does not mention character without citing the relevancy rule and immediately checking himself, not unlike the modern trial lawyer who deliberately refers to inadmissible evidence in the hope that it will have an effect on the jurors despite the inevitable admonition from the bench that they disregard it. The speaker's unease is clear in Lysias 3, where he squeezes in a quick attack on his opponent's conduct as a soldier but stops short with a *praeteritio*. He begins by stating, "I wish I were permitted to prove to you the baseness of this man with evidence of other things [i.e., acts or events outside the charge].... I will exclude all the other evidence, but I will mention one thing which I think it is fitting that you hear about, and that will be a proof of this man's rashness and boldness." After briefly recounting how his opponent assaulted his military commander and was the only Athenian publicly censured for insubordination by the generals, the speaker stops himself: "I could say many other things about this man, but since it is not lawful to speak outside the issue before your court...." (Lys. 3.44–6). In a survey of our entire corpus of court speeches, Johnstone has shown that defendants were much more likely than prosecutors to cite their liturgies and discuss issues of character.[52] The small number of references to character in the homicide courts becomes even more significant when we consider that all but one of our surviving homicide speeches were delivered by defendants.

The one consistent exception to the relevancy rule we find in the homicide speeches is the appeal for pity.[53] It is possible that this stricture was not as carefully observed as the limitation on character evidence. There is, however, another possible explanation. We have seen that only nonclassical sources include appeals to pity in the list of material considered outside the issue. It may be that, just as in the popular courts, discussion of the effect of a conviction on the defendant was considered

---

[50] Lys. 3.44–6; Lys. 7.31, 41.

[51] The exception is Lysias 7.31. This speech concerns the removal of a sacred olive stump, a religious offense within the Areopagus's jurisdiction unrelated to homicide and the other violent offenses associated with the homicide courts. The speaker indicates that the relevancy rule did apply in this type of case. Lys. 7.41–2.

[52] Johnstone (1999: 93–100). He shows that in private cases, defendants cite their liturgies 50% of the time, whereas prosecutors do so only 23% of the time.

[53] Lys. 3.48; 4.20; 7.41; Ant. 1.3, 21, 25.

relevant to the verdict. If this is the case, it is possible that later writers were aware of the Areopagites' reputation (perhaps borne of their age and experience) for not being misled by rhetoric, emotional appeals, or the speaking ability of litigants and mistakenly included appeals to pity as one type of argument considered outside the issue under the relevancy rule.

Maritime Cases

As Edward Cohen's contribution to this volume details, maritime suits (*dikai emporikai*) were exceptional in a number of respects, most notably in the frequency of noncitizen participation as litigants and witnesses and in the rule that only disputes over a written contract could be heard through this procedure. It is impossible to draw firm conclusions on the basis of the five maritime cases that survive, but these speeches tend to be more narrowly focused on the contractual claim at issue and to include fewer appeals to nonlegal argumentation than similar popular court cases. Lawcourt speakers appear to have had a notion of a distinct standard of relevance in maritime suits, though this "standard" was entirely informal, customary, and fluid, unlike the relevancy rule of the homicide courts.

One would expect that the requirement of written proof would focus the dispute on the terms of the written agreement. Our surviving maritime cases bear out this prediction: one of the most distinctive features of these speeches is the importance of the terms of the agreement to the speakers' arguments.[54] In stark contrast to the importance of the contractual terms in maritime suits, speakers in other suits involving written contracts or wills rarely dwell on the specifics of the legal instrument or suggest that the jurors should look only within the four corners of the contract.[55] One might also expect that the presence of foreigners, metics, and perhaps even slaves in maritime litigation would lead to a plethora of arguments in which the litigant of more favored status exploits his superior social standing. With few exceptions, however, the social standing, character, and services of the litigants play no

---

[54] Carey and Reid (1985: 200 n. 50), Christ (1998: 220–1), Cohen (2003: 94–5).

[55] Compare, for example, the focus on the written contract in maritime suits such as Demosthenes 33, 35, and 56 to nonmaritime contract cases such as Hyperides 3 or Demosthenes 48. Christ (1998: 180–91) has pointed out a similar difference between cases involving banking transactions and the *dikai emporikai*: whereas litigants in banking suits present their cases in terms of a breach of *philia*, parties in maritime cases emphasize a breach of contract.

role in arguments in the maritime suits.[56] Indeed, in several cases we are unsure of the legal status of the individuals involved in the transaction. A narrowed sense of relevance is also suggested by the complete absence of appeals to the jurors' pity, which we have seen is a well-known *topos* in our nonmaritime popular court cases. The only references to larger policy considerations in these speeches involve the importance of ensuring Athens' grain supply and the necessity of enforcing contracts as written to facilitate trade.[57]

The distinctive mode of argumentation in maritime cases can be usefully compared to two nonmaritime commercial cases that also date from sometime in the middle of the fourth century, Demosthenes 36 and 37.[58] Although the subject matter of these two suits — the leasing arrangement of a banking business and a series of transactions involving mining property — is similar to that of maritime suits, the speeches are not as narrowly focused on the business transactions at issue. Both speakers make extensive use of extralegal arguments such as character evidence and appeals to pity.[59] Most striking is the use in these two speeches of witnesses to testify solely to the good character of the speaker or the villainy of his opponent.[60]

In sum, Athenian attitudes toward legal relevance were considerably more complex than one might expect. In homicide and maritime cases, the Athenians could imagine (and, to a lesser extent, implement) a system that excluded social context in favor of generalized rules.[61] However, in the vast majority of cases Athenian jurors produced largely ad hoc decisions, as a wide variety of extralegal material was considered

---

[56] The one notable exception is Demosthenes 35, in which the speaker, a citizen, slanders his opponents as Phaselites and sophists. However, even in this speech the bulk of the oration is devoted to a close reading of the contract, which is twice read out in full.

[57] Although in a few cases speakers charge their opponents with having violated the Athens' grain laws, they do not argue that the jurors should vote in their favor for this reason. This evidence is presented as part of an argument for ensuring the grain supply and encouraging trade by strictly enforcing written contracts (Dem. 34.51; 35.54; 56.48).

[58] Like four of our five *dikai emporikai*, these two cases are also *paragraphai* actions.

[59] Dem. 36.42, 45, 52, 55–57, 59; 37.48, 52, 54.

[60] Dem. 36.55–56; 37.54.

[61] A discussion of why the Athenians treated homicide and maritime cases differently is beyond the scope of this piece. In brief, I believe that the peculiar development of homicide law in the archaic period, rather than a sense that homicide was more serious or in some way different from other charges, accounts for the unusual character of the homicide courts in the classical period. The narrower notion of relevance in maritime cases stems from the need to facilitate trade and attract foreign merchants by offering a predictable procedure based on a transparent and non-culturally specific standard: the terms of the written contract agreed to by the parties.

relevant and important to reaching a just verdict tailored to the particular circumstances of the individual case. In this respect, the Athenian courts were both more and less removed from modern courts than is commonly believed: the legal system cannot be characterized as embodying a rule of law, but the participants nevertheless viewed the process as aiming for recognizably "legal" rather than social ends. The Athenians' distinctive approach to relevance in the popular courts reflects a highly individualized and contextualized notion of justice.

7: Differentiated Rhetorical Strategies in the Athenian Courts[1]

Lene Rubinstein

It is widely recognized that the procedural complexity of the Athenian administration of justice provides us with an important key to understanding how the legal system worked in practice. The way in which individual statutes were framed meant that a citizen who wished to bring a complaint before a court would often have a range of different procedures to choose from, each of which would have different consequences for the defendant if he was found guilty as charged.[2] What has not attracted similar attention from modern scholars is the extent to which the choice of procedure affected the rhetorical strategies employed by the litigants involved in the action. Nor has there been much discussion of the question whether the nature of the dispute itself affected the way in which the litigants were expected to present their cases before the courts. We habitually talk about Athenian litigation and Athenian forensic rhetoric on the assumption that once an Athenian appeared as a speaker in the formal setting of a *dikastērion*, he would be expected to resort to a relatively well-defined and undifferentiated set of strategies and arguments, regardless of whether he was

---

[1] I am grateful to Prof. M. Gagarin, Prof. J. G. F. Powell and Prof. P. J. Rhodes for their comments on this contribution.
[2] The procedural flexibility that afforded prosecutors a choice between different types of legal action was well recognized also by the Athenians themselves. The complaint voiced by defendants that they ought to have been tried under a different procedure from the one presently employed by their opponent is found in several defence speeches (Ant. 5.9–10, Hyp. 1.12, 4.5–6, Isaios 11.32–5, Dem. 37.33–8). The most famous anticipation of this type of defence argument is the passage Dem. 22.25–28, which is paralleled in Isoc. 20.2 and in Dem. 21.25–26.

engaged in a high-profile public action for treason or a low-profile private action concerning, for example, the recovery of a dowry or a claim to an inheritance.

There are probably two important reasons why the issue of differentiated court strategies has not received much attention in modern scholarship. The first is that neither of our two surviving fourth-century treatises on rhetoric, Aristotle's *Rhetoric* and the *Rhetorica ad Alexandrum*, discusses the question. Both distinguish between techniques and arguments appropriate for defence and prosecution speeches respectively,[3] but neither suggests that different types of procedure and different types of case may call for different rhetorical strategies.

The second reason is that to a modern observer the similarities between Athenian public and private litigation appear far more striking than the differences, especially when we consider the position of the individual who had initiated the legal action. Although the Athenians did to some extent differentiate terminologically between the initiators of public and private actions,[4] the differences between the two were indeed far less pronounced than those that distinguish a modern plaintiff in a civil action from a modern impersonal (and ideally objective) public prosecution agency. In most Athenian public actions, including those that involved matters that might ultimately threaten the internal and external stability of the community as a whole, the volunteer who undertook to launch the prosecution had to assume full personal responsibility for the case at all stages of the legal process, from the gathering of evidence and the drafting of the writ to the formal presentation of the case in the courtroom. In that respect, his position differed only marginally from that of a plaintiff involved in even the most trivial private dispute launched under the heading of a *dikē*. The fact that most public prosecutions were launched at the initiative of individual citizens, who were expected to state the reasons why they had chosen

---

[3] For a modern discussion of the differences between prosecution and defence strategies see above all the seminal study by S. Johnstone (1999).

[4] The Athenians did make some terminological distinctions between the persons who pleaded in public actions and those who had initiated private suits. Although the expression *ho diōkōn* (literally "the one who pursues") was applied to the initiators of both public and private actions, the designations *katēgoros* ("accuser") and the participle with the definite article, *ho katēgorōn*, were used only of prosecutors in public actions and in the actions for homicide heard by the Areiopagos and other homicide courts. There is not a single attestation of the designation being applied in the context of a normal *dikē*. I shall use the terms prosecutor and plaintiff as approximate renderings of the Athenian distinction, but with the *caveat* that the Athenian categories of public and private actions do not correspond exactly to the modern distinction between criminal and civil actions.

to take action, gave rise to frequent professions by prosecutors involved in public actions of their direct personal involvement in the case against the defendant.[5] In stark contrast to a modern state prosecutor, an Athenian litigant pursuing a public action would not be expected to disguise his personal feelings of hostility against the defendant. Furthermore, the prosecutor's own desire for revenge (often for alleged wrongs entirely unrelated to the charge now brought against the defendant) was perceived as an entirely legitimate motive for launching a public action.

Although a modern observer may not be surprised to find personal enmity and desire for revenge displayed openly in the context of a private action (such displays of hostility are, after all, pretty standard fare in modern divorce and inheritance cases), the practice seems utterly alien to us when it is found in the context of a public prosecution, in which the prosecutors are at the same time claiming to be acting on behalf of the *polis* as a whole. The readiness with which prosecutors in public actions combined the themes of personal enmity and revenge with professions of public-spiritedness is often interpreted as an indication that the Athenians did not distinguish clearly between "public" and "private" or between the "personal" and the "political." On this interpretation it has been argued that an Athenian public action is best understood as an advanced stage of a conflict between two individual citizens, which differed from a private action only insofar as the stakes were higher for the defendant, for whom the consequences of a conviction would be far more serious in a public action than in an ordinary *dikē*.

It is also frequently argued that once it had reached the courts despite attempts to reach an out-of-court settlement, almost any dispute that formed the basis of private litigation could potentially be talked up by the litigants into a matter that would ultimately affect the entire *polis*. In recent scholarship much attention has been devoted to the Athenian courts as a forum in which positive and negative behavior was on display, through the litigants' descriptions of their own positive conduct in opposition to the negative conduct of their opponents. Through their decision, the judges would, in turn, signal to the rest of the community what constituted acceptable and unacceptable behavior.[6] According to this line of argument, *any* dispute had a clear political dimension. Indeed, it could be argued that the plaintiff's decision to transform a

---

[5] Although such professions occur in about half of our surviving public prosecution speeches, they were by no means a strategic requirement. See Rubinstein (2000: 179–180).
[6] E.g., Hunter (1994: 110), Christ (1998: 190–1).

private dispute into a lawsuit conducted in public was in itself political, for the consequence of that decision was that the *polis*, as represented by the *dikastai*, was invited to intervene directly in the social drama that was played out in the narratives of the two opposing parties. Thus, it would be entirely reasonable to expect that the public spectacle of dysfunctional *oikoi*, of trading relations gone wrong, and of relationships between friends and neighbors disintegrating into hostility would provide an opportunity to pronounce on the perceived limits of acceptable behavior between individual members of the community as well as between individuals and the community as a whole.

This suggests, in turn, that the line drawn by the Athenians between public and private was blurred, not only because a prosecutor could choose to represent a personal injury as a threat to the stability of the *polis* as a whole but also because he could in some circumstances choose between a private and a public procedural heading under which the case would be brought before the courts. Even so, the procedural choice made by a prospective prosecutor did nonetheless have some very real implications for his courtroom strategy, as did the nature of the dispute itself. In a private action, even of the heaviest kind, each party was granted only one-third of the speaking time allocated to litigants in public actions.[7] What is more, by making the length of the litigant's address in a *dikē* as well as the size of the dicastic panel depend entirely on the amount of property under dispute, the Athenians did apparently try to distinguish on objective grounds between disputes that were regarded as more or less deserving of the community's attention and resources.

The limited time available in private suits may account for, among other things, the widespread practice of reducing the formal *prooimia* in speeches delivered in *dikai* and *diadikasiai* to a minimum, or even dispensing with them altogether.[8] Conversely, the longer pleading time available to litigants involved in public actions, whether as prosecutors or as defendants, provides at least part of the explanation of the more widespread use of supporting speakers (*synēgoroi*) in this type of litigation.[9] A further regulation that differentiated public actions from private

---

[7] *Ath. Pol.* 67.2.
[8] Twenty-six of the private orations of which the beginnings are preserved contain *prooimia* of three paragraphs or fewer (Lys. 10, 17, 23; Isoc. 17, 21; Isaios 2, 4, 5, 6, 10; Dem. 27, 32, 33, 36, 37, 38, 39, 41, 43, 45, 48, 50, 52, 54, 55) while a further four contain no *prooimia* at all (Isaios 3, 9; Dem. 49, 56).
[9] For a broader discussion of the use of *synēgoroi* in public and private actions respectively and their role in the overall strategies of the litigants see Rubinstein (2000).

ones was that, in private actions, the water clock would be stopped while witness statements were presented to the court, whereas in public actions testimony would count against the speaker's time allocation (*Ath. Pol.* 67.3). The statistical data produced by Todd (1990) strongly suggest that this procedural rule had a direct influence on the use of evidence in different types of legal action, because the frequency with which such testimony is introduced by the litigants is much higher in the private orations.

These differences are well recognized and relatively straightforward, as are their implications for the rhetorical strategies of the litigants. In what follows it will be argued that there are at least three other areas in which the choice of procedure and the nature of the dispute appear to have affected the litigants' method of pleading and their choice of arguments:

1. the litigants' appeals to the judges to display anger at the defendant's behavior and their professions of their own feelings of anger and desire for revenge
2. the representation of the outcome of the case as an act of punishment inflicted on the defendant by the court and the use of penal terminology to describe the effect of a verdict against the defendant
3. the representation of the role of the court as educational, in the sense that the verdict passed in the current case will instruct other citizens as to what constitutes acceptable and unacceptable behavior.

The evidence for what we may call differentiated court strategies in these areas is, first and foremost, our sixty extant prosecution speeches delivered in the ordinary *dikastēria*. The distribution of speeches in the categories of private and public actions is sufficiently even to make a comparison possible: twenty-nine speeches were delivered in public actions; the other thirty-one were delivered by plaintiffs in private suits.[10] Although caution will have to be exercised in any attempt to generalize from such relatively few examples, the material is sufficiently large and sufficiently representative in chronological terms to warrant

---

[10] The extant prosecution speeches delivered in public actions are the following: Lys. 6, 12, 13, 14, 15, 22, 27, 29, 30; Dem. 19, 20, 21, 22, 23, 24, 25, 26, 53, 58, 59; Aisch. 1, 2, 3; Lyk. 1, Hyp. 2 *Phil.*, 5 *Dem.*; Dein. 1, 2, 3. The private prosecution speeches are: Lys. 10, 32; Isokr. 17, 18, 20, 21; Isaios 3, 5, 6, Dem. 27, 28, 30, 31, 32, 33, 36, 37, 38, 39, 40, 41, 44, 45, 46, 47, 48, 49, 50, 54, 56; Hyp. 3 *Ath.*

some conclusions on the basis of the distribution of arguments across speeches of different types.

What contributes further to the validity of such generalizations is that the corpus of forensic oratory also provides us with an interesting control group with which to compare the speeches delivered by prosecutors and plaintiffs, namely the seven surviving speeches that were delivered in inheritance suits (*diadikasia klērou*).[11] The procedure of *diadikasia* differed from all other Athenian legal actions by not operating with "prosecution" and "defence": all participants in such actions were defined as being on the same footing as rival claimants to the property under dispute.

Another feature peculiar to these *diadikasiai* was that the process of litigation was by no means a last resort to be engaged in only when all possibilities for reaching an out-of-court settlement had been exhausted. When an Athenian man died leaving no sons either natural or adopted *inter vivos*, any claim to his estate (and his daughters, if he had any) *had to* go through the courts. Any potential claimants were directly invited to come forward through a public announcement made by the herald during a meeting of the Assembly (*Ath. Pol.* 43.4). The heirs' taking possession of and sharing an inheritance without a prior court hearing was not only discouraged but actually illegal (Dem. 46.22), except when the claimants were legitimate male descendants, whether natural or by adoption *inter vivos*. Thus, the decision to litigate in inheritance cases did not presuppose a deep-seated personal conflict between the opposing claimants. This may be one important reason why litigants involved in disputes of this type tend to avoid overt displays of personal aggression and why they refrain from using the language of punishment and revenge. In regard to the three areas of differentiated court strategies identified above, the seven speeches delivered in *diadikasiai klērou* all share the following characteristics:

1. The speakers never tell the judges explicitly that they should feel anger or hatred at the behavior of the rival claimants, although the speakers' graphic descriptions of their opponents' antisocial or even unlawful conduct are of course designed to generate precisely those feelings in the audience. Nor do the speakers state openly that they are harboring feelings of anger or hatred against their opponents.
2. The judges' decision to award the disputed property to one of the contesting claimants is never represented as a way of

[11] Isaios 1, 4, 7, 8, 9, 10; Dem. 43.

punishing simultaneously the other contestants who will have to leave the court empty-handed. No speech in this category employs the terminology of penalty or punishment to describe the decision reached by the court.[12]

3. The litigants never claim that the outcome of the current dispute has the potential to shape future community behavior. Although the judges are sometimes told that the litigant's own model behavior as a citizen ought to constitute an additional reason for them to award him the disputed inheritance (e.g. Isaios 4.27–29), they are not told that their public recognition of his personal qualities will turn him into an example for other citizens to emulate. Nor are they told that their rejection of the speaker's rival claimants will serve as an example to other citizens of how *not* to behave.

What makes the *diadikasia* speeches so valuable as a control group is that they represent one extreme on a scale that has as its other extreme the speeches delivered by prosecutors in public actions. The three types of argument avoided by litigants in *diadikasiai* are employed, often in close proximity to each other, in the vast majority of public prosecution speeches. This suggests very strongly that the strategic deployment of the arguments on anger, punishment, and the educational role of the court was context sensitive and that the type of case that the litigant was fighting had a clear influence on his method of pleading.

When discussing the factors that may have influenced and constrained litigants in their choice of rhetorical strategies, it is of course important to be aware that almost any restrictions on the litigants' tactics would have been self-imposed rather than imposed by any formal rules regulating the litigants' rhetorical performance. It is true that before the trial the opposing parties, at least in private actions and in cases heard by the homicide courts, had to commit themselves by oath to addressing only the issue that had given rise to their legal dispute, a commitment that itself was open to rhetorical negotiation and manipulation.[13] But this, as far as we know, was the only *formal* restriction on the litigant's

---

[12] The three most important Athenian terms for punishment and the act of punishing are: *timōria/timōreisthai*, *kolasis/kolazein*, and *zēmia/zēmioun*. "To incur punishment" is frequently expressed more loosely with the words *dikēn dounai*, literally "to render justice." All of these are entirely absent from *diadikasia* speeches, and, as we shall see, are used only sparingly in speeches delivered by litigants involved in *dikai*.

[13] The requirement that litigants should address the case directly is best documented in the context of the homicide courts (see the references in MacDowell 1963: 90–93). Our most important source for the requirement in trials heard by the ordinary *dikastēria* is

argumentation, although he was of course also bound by the laws that limited freedom of speech outside the courtroom.[14] On the whole, it is fair to say that, although the Athenians operated with strict rules concerning the way in which witness statements and law texts should be presented in the courtroom, a litigant would be free, at least in theory, to present his case and interpret its significance for the *polis* as a whole in almost whatever way he wished.

In practice, however, a litigant would have to adjust his pleading to conform to the expectations of his audience. A litigant who failed to gauge accurately what the judges would consider as acceptable and appropriate argumentation ran the risk of alienating his audience to the point where they might actually shout him down and prevent him from continuing his pleading.[15] What we may describe as Athenian "court etiquette" was created and perpetuated by continuous interaction between litigants and their audiences, including both judges and bystanders.[16]

The corpus of forensic oratory offers us at least two means by which we may form an impression of the limitations that court etiquette imposed on the litigants' strategies in different types of litigation. One is to look for passages where speakers attempt to anticipate and counter a hostile response from their audiences to a particular line of argument, presumably because they fear that they may be breaching conventional limits of acceptability. The other is to map out the occurrence

---

Ath. Pol. 67.1, which mentions it only in connection with private actions. Rhodes (2004) argues that litigants appear to have taken this part of the oath more seriously when pleading their cases than they have been given credit for by modern scholars. Still, the Athenian perception of "relevance" was a good deal broader than the corresponding modern notion, and the lawcourt speeches often include material that would be regarded as irrelevant by a modern court. See also Lanni's chapter, above.

[14] The law on *kakēgoria* defined certain types of defamation as unlawful, including accusations of throwing away one's shield in battle, murder, and mistreatment of parents (Lys. 10.6–8). Lysias 10 provides an example of a *dikē kakēgorias* launched by the speaker in response to an allegation of parricide that his opponent had made during a previous trial.

[15] On the informal control exercised by the *dikastai* over the litigants' performance through *thorybos*, see Bers (1985), still the most comprehensive treatment of this phenomenon.

[16] Lanni (1997: 187–8) has drawn attention to a number of passages that indicate that litigants often drew on their experience as bystanders in other people's trials when devising their own court strategies. Most modern discussions on the development of Attic forensic oratory have tended to focus on the matter of formal rhetorical instruction as offered by famous teachers such as Isokrates and by written manuals such as the *Rhetorica ad Alexandrum*; less attention has been paid to the more informal ways in which rhetorical techniques could be acquired through the watching and imitation of other litigants in action.

and, equally important, the *non*occurrence of particular rhetorical *topoi* ("commonplaces") in the surviving speeches in order to reconstruct what the Athenians themselves would have perceived as appropriate arguments in various procedural contexts.

The two methods may, to a certain extent, complement each other. Consider, for example, the apparent unease with which the speaker of Isocrates 18, a speech delivered in a private blocking action (*paragraphē*), justifies his lengthy admonition to the judges that their decision in the current case will have serious consequences for the community as a whole. The speaker claims that the original lawsuit brought by his opponent was in breach of the amnesty agreed after the bloody civil war between the supporters of the regime of the Thirty and their democratic opponents in 403/2 and probably renewed in 401. If his opponent is allowed to proceed with his original action, he argues, then this will mean that the ban on lawsuits pertaining to acts committed during the rule of the Thirty is rendered null and void (18.27–32). In 18.33–34 he justifies this line of argument as follows:

> And let no-one think that I exaggerate or am speaking out of proportion (*meizō legein*), because I, who am a defendant in a private action (*dikē idia*), have adduced these arguments. For this lawsuit is not just about the sum of money specified in the writ: that is the issue for me, while for you the issue is what I have just described. No-one would be able to do justice to this matter in his argumentation, nor could he adduce an adequate compensation to the writ. For this lawsuit differs so much from other *dikai* that while they are of concern only to the litigants involved in them, the common interest of the *polis* is at stake in this one.

At first glance, this may seem just a tactical device on the part of the speaker to stress the seriousness of his case. There can be no doubt that his attempt to describe his own lawsuit as exceptionally important for the entire community serves this purpose. However, his awareness that some members of the audience might find his argumentation too heavy in the context of the current legal dispute should not be dismissed as mere coyness. By describing the verdict in his own case as one that is likely to shape the future conduct of other members of the community and to set a precedent for the way in which the terms of the amnesty are to be upheld, the speaker is in fact employing a *topos* that is a standard feature in public prosecution speeches (twenty-three of twenty-nine),[17] whereas it is far less frequently used in speeches delivered by plaintiffs in private actions (eight of thirty-one).[18] The speaker's concern that he may be bending the rules of normal court etiquette thus seems to be well-founded.

If we return to the first of the three areas of differentiated court strategies defined above, namely the litigants' declaration of their own anger and desire for revenge and their admonition to the judges that they, too, should display their anger in the form of punishment inflicted on the defendant, we find a similar pattern. Plaintiffs involved in ordinary *dikai* may sometimes vent their feelings of intense annoyance (expressed by the verb *aganakteō*),[19] but in only three speeches do we find the plaintiffs referring directly to their own anger (*orgē*) at the defendant's behavior (Lys. 10.28, Dem. 45.7, 54.42). Two plaintiffs (Lys. 10.3, Dem. 50.65) openly state their wish to avenge themselves (*timōreisthai*) with the assistance of the court, whereas revenge as a personal motive for litigation occurs in nine of the public prosecution speeches.[20] These differences in themselves do not allow us to talk about a pattern. But when we consider them in relation to the passages in which the litigants urge the judges to display their anger against the defendant, it is clear that the distribution of the *topoi* is not random. Direct appeals to dicastic anger are employed in twenty-four of twenty-nine public prosecution speeches, suggesting that prosecutors who adopted that tactic were on safe ground and that such appeals were unlikely to meet with disapproval from the audience. By contrast, plaintiffs in private actions were far less likely to instruct their audiences explicitly that a display of *orgē* towards their opponents was part of the duty of the court, or that a rejection of their opponent's case would serve to articulate the community's collective anger at a particular pattern of antisocial behavior as exemplified by the opponent's conduct. Only eight of the speeches delivered by plaintiffs in private actions contain that *topos*, namely Isoc. 18 and 20, Lys. 10 and 32, and Dem. 40, 45, 47, and 54. What is equally significant is that most of these private speeches also share another

---

[17] Lys. [6].54, 12.35, 85, 14.4, 12, 45, 15.9, 22.17–20, 21, 27.6–7, 29.13, 30.23; Dem. 19.232, 20 *passim*, 21.98, 183, 220–225, 227, 22.7, 68, 23.94, 24.101, 218, 25.10, 53, 26.1–2, [53].29, [59].111–113; Aisch. 1.90–91, 176–7, 192–3, 3.246; Dein. 1.27, 46, 67, 88, 107, 113, 2.21–23, 3.19.

[18] The *topos* is found also in Isoc. 20.12–14, 21.18; Dem. 36.58, 45.87, 50.66, 54.43, 56.48–50.

[19] Isaios 3.30, 6.56, Lys. 32.12, Dem. 27.63, 28.1, 54.15.

[20] Lys. 13.1, 3, 41, 42, 83–84, 14.1, 15.12; Dem. 21. 207, 22.29, 24.8, 53.1–2, 58.1, 58, 59.1, 12, 15, 126.

characteristic, namely that the speakers use the Athenian vocabulary of punishment to characterize the possible outcome of their case against the defendant.

Athenian penal terminology is not used indiscriminately to describe the consequences of an adverse verdict for the defendant. Although all but two of the speeches delivered by prosecutors in public actions employ this terminology when referring to the outcome of the case in hand, the vocabulary of punishment is found only in the following private speeches: Isoc. 18 and 20, Lys. 10, Dem. 45+46, 47, 50, 54, 56, and Hyp. 3 *Against Athenogenes*. There is thus a conspicuous overlap between the speeches that contain the *topos* on dicastic anger and those that refer to the judges' decision as an act of punishment inflicted on the speaker's opponent. Isoc. 18 and 20, Lys. 10, and Dem. 45, 47, and 54 display both features, suggesting that the two themes are normally closely linked to each other in terms of the plaintiffs' court strategies.

The *dikai* in which these speeches were delivered share some important characteristics. The plaintiffs in Isoc. 20 and Dem. 54 were both engaged in private actions for violent assault (*dikē aikeias*), the speaker of Lys. 10 was pursuing an action for slander (*dikē kakēgorias*), and Dem. 45+46 and 47 were delivered in private actions for false testimony (*dikē pseudomartyriōn*). Each of these three procedures required the court to "translate" a specific act of injustice that had not inflicted direct financial loss on the plaintiff into a sum of money intended to compensate him for what he had suffered,[21] rather than simply restoring or awarding to the plaintiff the money or property that he claimed was rightfully his. Moreover, the *dikē kakēgorias* carried a fine payable to the public treasury, and the *dikē pseudomartyriōn* could result in *atimia* if the defendant was facing a third conviction in this type of action. The issue of an additional penalty over and above simple restitution of property or money to the winning party is also at stake in Isoc. 18 and Dem. 56. Both actions carried the penalty of *epōbelia*, calculated as a sixth part of the property or money under dispute. Although the *epōbelia* appears to have been payable to the winning party rather than to the *polis*, the

---

[21] Although it might be argued that the loss of a court case as a result of the opponent's use of false testimony might be regarded as a form of financial loss, the issue is not so simple. A plaintiff did *not* have to claim direct financial loss to bring a *dikē pseudomartyriōn*: we know of at least two *dikai pseudomartyriōn* that were brought by a litigant who had won his original action despite his opponent's use of allegedly false evidence (Isaios 3 following up another successful *dikē pseudomartyriōn* attested in Isaios 3.2–4) and who therefore would not have been able to maintain that he was bringing the action to recover his losses from the witness.

person who incurred it faced *atimia* (Dem. 29.50) or even imprisonment (Dem. 35.47, 56.4) if he failed to pay this extra sum.

By contrast, where the case was a private action that turned primarily on the question of who had the better claim to a piece of disputed property or a sum of money, there appears to have been less scope for the litigants to represent the outcome of the action as an act of punishment inflicted by the court on the unsuccessful party. A litigant who demands from the judges that they should simply restore to him what is "rightfully his" implies that, in fact, the defendant will incur no real loss, except insofar as he will have to give up property to which he is not entitled. One example of this line of argument is found in Dem. 27.67, a speech in which Demosthenes tries to recover what he claims is part of his inheritance from one of his former guardians. He asserts that the defendant, if he loses the action, "will make payment, not out of his own funds, but out of mine" and thus incur no personal loss whatsoever, a *topos* that is found also in other speeches delivered by plaintiffs (e.g., Dem. 40.56). Disputes of this type are the ones that come closest to *diadikasiai* in the sense that the opposing parties are, in effect, making competing claims to a defined sum of money or a particular piece of property, and the judges' role is defined as establishing which of the two contestants has the better claim rather than to punish. This goes some way toward explaining the absence from the majority of private speeches not only of penal terminology as such, but also of appeals to the judges to display their anger at the defendant's behavior by inflicting a form of punishment upon him.

To the modern observer it may not seem particularly strange that the Athenians appear to have distinguished between "restitution" on the one hand and "penalty" or "punishment" on the other. Even so, the fact that the Athenians did make that distinction is important for our assessment of how the Athenians themselves perceived the role of the courts in different contexts. Most of the speeches that contain *topoi* on dicastic anger and on the representation of the outcome of the case as a collective act of punishment administered by the judges on behalf of the *polis* also share a third characteristic that concerns the very role of the court itself as an institution that contributes to the creation and perpetuation of community values through its decisions in individual cases.

Let us return to the passage from Isoc. 18, which I quoted earlier. I argued that the speaker displays a certain unease when making his claim that the case was not only of concern to him and his opponent, but that it also had far-reaching implications for the *polis* as a whole, because the judges' verdict was bound to shape the future behavior of the rest of the Athenian population, for better or for worse. The speaker may have been conscious of bending the unwritten rules of Athenian court etiquette, because he was employing a *topos* that was mostly used in the context of public actions. He was not the only litigant in a private action to do so; what is interesting is that the educational *topos* tends to occur in speeches that refer to the verdict as an act of punishment to be inflicted on the defendant (Isoc. 18, 20; Dem. 45, 50, 54 and 56). The match is not a perfect one – in addition to these six speeches both Dem. 36 and Isoc. 21 contain the educational *topos* but neither penal terminology nor the *topos* on dicastic anger. Even so its concentration in the speeches that by now have become a group of "usual suspects" is significant.

The role of the courts in instructing the citizen body at large as to what constituted acceptable and unacceptable behavior is represented as absolutely essential by most prosecutors in public actions. In their rhetoric the verdicts passed by the courts are important both as a means of restraining the conduct of adult citizens who might otherwise be tempted to break the law and as a means of passing the *polis'* values on to the next generation. Just as the *polis* was constantly engaged in the creation of positive role models of civic virtue by rewarding outstanding individuals for their services, normally through honorific decrees passed by the Assembly, a very important role of the court was to create examples (*paradeigmata*) of vice by punishing individuals who had violated the *polis'* norms of acceptable behavior. A typical example of this *topos* is found in Aischines' speech *Against Ktesiphon*, in which he stresses the educational and political dimension of the court's decision (3.245–7):

> And most important of all, the young men will ask you on what model (*paradeigma*) they should live their lives. For be well aware, Athenians, that it is not the palaistra or the schools or training in the arts which alone educate the young, but far more the public proclamations. It is proclaimed in the theatre that a disgusting man, who leads a disgraceful life, is crowned because of his noble behaviour, his upright character, and his loyalty. A younger man is corrupted by watching this. A person who is wicked and a pimp, such as Ktesiphon, is punished. The others will have received instruction. A person who returns home after having voted against morality and justice educates his son. His son, as is reasonable, does not obey, but is now justified in referring to

admonition as a nuisance. So now you must cast your vote not only as men who are sitting as judges but also as men who are being watched, to be called to account by those of the citizens who are not now present but who will ask you what your judgment was.

Aischines is considering the serious educational consequences of public reward and punishment: if the Assembly crowns a villain for his good qualities it will have created a destructive role model, which the young citizens will attempt to imitate. If the court punishes a villain, other citizens will receive the correct message on vice and shun his example out of fear of the punishment laid down by the laws and enforced by the courts. In that way the democratic institutions can contribute to the perpetuation of established definitions of *aretē* through correct choices of positive and negative *paradeigmata*, and, conversely, they have the power to redefine civic *aretē* in a destructive way by commending individual negative behavior by a public endorsement. In that respect the verdict is invested with a political dimension that goes far beyond the current legal dispute itself.

As noted earlier, many recent contributions to the debate on Athenian law have focused on the close connection between the courts and the political life of the *polis* in general, as articulated for example by Aischines in the passage just quoted. Current discussions of the so-called "politicization" of the Athenian courts are not confined to the types of action that were "political" in the narrow sense, i.e. limited to the citizens' behavior in the public sphere, for, as Todd puts it (1993: 155):

> At Athens, indeed, a case necessarily takes on political overtones the moment that it involves a confrontation between litigants who are politically active; or even only one such litigant, whose personal credibility will be dependent upon the outcome of the hearing. In effect, therefore, any trial for which we have evidence is likely to have at least potentially a political significance: for all our speeches concern disputes among the social élite, and political and social prestige were at Athens closely related.

Likewise, Christ (1998: 160–192) has drawn attention to the litigants' adherence to the *polis*' co-operative values, which is exhibited particularly in the context of private disputes, and concludes that such displays had a wider significance for the community as a whole. By finding in favor of a litigant who had convincingly demonstrated his allegiance to the cooperative values of the community, the judges were also contributing to shaping the behavioral norms of the community as a whole:

> Athenians serving on juries were not merely passive observers of the construction of social ideals in the courts but active participants in the process. Every verdict issued was, among other things, a verdict on the competing visions of community that litigants offered. In this way Athens's courts provided a venue not only for the adjudication of individual disputes but also for the articulation and confirmation of collective ideals. (Christ 1998: 190–1)

But if that is the case, what do we make of those speeches that lack the educational *topos* altogether? As noted previously, in cases that turned on competing claims to property (including *diadikasiai* concerning inheritance) and other strictly *oikos*-related matters and in which penal terminology is avoided the judges are normally *not* told that their function as *dikastai* involves the shaping of community behavior or that their decision will have an effect on how the laws will be enforced in the future. Isoc. 21.18, concerning the reclaim of a deposit, is the only obvious deviation from that pattern. Generally, however, the judges' role in disputes of this type was defined primarily as that of deciding which of the two litigants had the better case, an assessment based in part on an assessment of the general conduct of the two opposing parties. What is important is that the scope of their decision is normally defined in narrow terms as one that should serve to restore the balance between the opposing contestants and which will have no immediate wider implications for the *polis* as a collectivity.

Given that the educational *topos* is found predominantly in private actions that carried a penalty over and above simple restitution, this suggests that the Athenians perceived neither the rhetorical confrontations in court nor the litigants' creation of competing positive and negative *paradeigmata* as educational in themselves. It was the judges' decision to *punish* by inflicting a genuine loss on the defendant that created the *paradeigma* with a wider educational value and that invested the verdict with a potential political dimension. Sending a litigant away empty-handed because his opponent was believed to have a better claim to a piece of disputed property, or forcing a litigant to return property that was not believed to be 'his' did not apparently offer the same opportunities for rhetorical amplification. And it is significant that not all legal disputes fought out in the courts, in the full view of the community as a whole, appear to have offered the litigants an occasion to represent their own plight as one that ought to be of concern to the *polis* as a whole.

In the private speeches, in contexts where the dicasts are told to display their anger, to punish, and to create a deterrent to others, the issues being discussed normally relate to very specific kinds of antisocial behavior, which did not require amplification or further elaboration in order to be represented as potential problems that might threaten the stability of the entire community. The kinds of misbehavior that seem to have called for appeals to dicastic anger combined with instructions to punish are as follows: violent behavior in the form of *hybris* in Dem. 54 and Isoc. 20, the excessive use of force in connection with self-help in [Dem.] 47, the general undermining of the legal process through false evidence in Dem. 45+46, violation of the amnesty in Isoc. 18, the lack of respect for trierarchical duties in [Dem.] 50, the breaking of the laws designed to protect the shipping of grain to Athens in Dem. 56, the defamation of a dead man and unfounded accusations of parricide in Lys. 10, and, finally, the maltreatment of orphans in Lys. 32, a matter that was by definition of public interest until the orphans reached the age of majority. These ten speeches are also the only ones in which the plaintiffs seek to involve the *polis* collectively as a party to the dispute with the claim that the community as a whole has suffered directly from the defendant's actions and that the judges, as the representatives of the *polis*, are therefore now obliged to exact vengeance (*timōreisthai*) from the defendant.

There are of course many factors that might have influenced the court strategies of individual litigants in private disputes, not all of which are related to the nature of the legal procedure or the level of potential communal interest that a particular legal case could command. Thus, the absence of appeals to dicastic anger as well as of the terminology of punishment in disputes concerning dowries, inheritance, or other *oikos*-related matters may be due not just to the private nature of the dispute *per se* but also to the fact that such disputes nearly always pitted kin against kin. In disputes of that kind, a speaker who appealed too strongly and too openly to negative dicastic emotions against his relatives, and who was too vehement in expressing his desire to see the defendant incur a heavy penalty, would very likely have met with precisely the type of resentment that he wanted to stir up against his opponent. This may seem a straightforward, even trivial, observation: yet it is very important for our general interpretation of the workings of the Athenian courts and the strategies of Athenian litigants. Private actions of that type were likely to have constituted a considerable part of the courts' business. It would therefore be difficult to maintain that the imposition of penalties and the display of collective anger in order to teach other citizens a lesson in civic behavior were invariably a central part of the function of the Athenian courts in general.

In private actions that did not set members of the same family against each other, different strategic considerations were likely to have applied. What held speakers in such cases back from employing a combination of the educational *topoi*, penal terminology, and appeals to dicastic anger in *dikai* or *diadikasiai* may have been first and foremost their fear that such appeals might backfire, because their claim that their case was of common concern simply would not have seemed plausible to their audience. If that is the case, the absence of such arguments from certain categories of private actions provides important information about where the Athenians themselves would have drawn a line between public and private. To some extent that line coincided with the admittedly fuzzy line drawn between public and private actions, and although the litigants were certainly left a good deal of room for improvisation, the evidence does suggest that they had to adjust their rhetorical performance to suit the type of legal dispute in which they were engaged.

That, in turn, suggests a need for us to distinguish between different kinds of Athenian litigation and different types of court strategies. It warns us against generalizing too freely about "Athenian litigation," "Athenian forensic rhetoric," and indeed about the character of the Athenian courts as a legal and political institution. Litigants could choose to appeal to the judges either as a third party whose main duty it was to decide on a particular question that affected the two opposing parties and them alone, or as the true injured party whose duty it was to exact revenge and to make a politically important decision to punish that would affect the community as a whole. And that choice does not seem to have been an arbitrary one, but rather a highly informed strategic decision.

8: THE ROLE OF THE WITNESS IN ATHENIAN LAW

Gerhard Thür

I

The authority of the great philosopher Aristotle and the suggestive power of his systematic mind misled the compilers of older handbooks on the law in Athens and clouded their view of Athenian legal procedure. In their chapters on evidentiary procedure, they accept the five "nonartistic proofs" (*atechnoi pisteis*) canonized by Aristotle in his *Rhetoric* (1375a24): *nomoi, martyres, synthēkai, basanoi*, and *horkos* (laws, witnesses, contracts, confessions under torture, and oath).[1] More recent studies have recognized that only one form of evidence, witnesses, had legal significance in the practice of the Athenian jury courts.[2] Aside from a few regulations governing witness testimony, Athenian law had no legally specified rules of evidence. We cannot take the various methods of finding truth in modern law as a natural given, nor can we uncritically apply those standards to the large Athenian courts (*dikastēria*). In Athenian law, the principle of determining the truth is not primary, but rather the principle of equal opportunity:[3] both prosecutors and defendants should have a fair opportunity to present their positions to a body of fellow citizens selected objectively and not influenced by bribery or pressure. This assembly of jurors decides the case immediately after the speeches, rendering their first and final decision without deliberating or giving reasons. Their verdict is a simple yes or

---

[1] Lipsius (1905–1915: 866–900), Harrison (1971: 133–54), MacDowell (1978: 242–7). Following the modern legal categories more closely, Bonner (1905), Bonner and Smith (1938, 117–44).
[2] Thür (1977: 316–9), Todd (1990: 33) and (1996: 96f.).
[3] Thür (2000: 49).

no (guilty or not guilty). In Athens, legal conflict was a part of direct democracy. The Athenians thought that if the democratic principles of fairness were obeyed in court, then the broader goals of legal procedure, such as truth and justice, would best be assured.

The democratic regulations include: the most equitable allotment possible of jurors from all ten tribes (*phylai*) of the citizens on the day of the trial and their distribution among the *dikastēria*; allotting each juror's seat within the courtroom he already had been allotted to; and the double allotment that assigns the available court magistrates to preside over of the *dikastēria* in session that day. Before the moment of the hearing neither the litigants nor the court official know which citizens will be deciding the case. By mixing up the jurors (*dikastai*) from all ten tribes and then further mixing up their placement, supporters of the prosecutor or defendant are prevented from forming groups within the juries (that numbered from 201 to 1501) and disturbing the delivery of the speeches. Through this procedure and through a perfectly organized system of voting by secret ballot, an objective decision – at least as seen from an external perspective – is best guaranteed. The entire process is described in the *Athenaion Politeia* (Chapters 63–69; composed sometime after 335) with great attention to detail and has been confirmed by archaeological evidence.[4] A further, very simple mechanism also contributed to the principle of equal opportunity: exactly the same amount of time for speaking was measured out for the prosecutor and defendant by a waterclock (*klepsydra*). The times ranged from approximately fifteen minutes (five *choes* of water) for the simplest private case to exactly one-third of the day for the most important political cases. The length of the day was calculated according to the daylight of the shortest day in December (*Ath. Pol.* 67.2–5, unfortunately only fragmentarily preserved; cf. Harpokration *diametrēmenē hēmera*).

The list of nonartistic proofs I mentioned at the beginning is also related to the time allowed for speaking and the litigants' method of pleading. In contrast to the speech, which was composed by a logographer according to the art (*technē*) of rhetoric and delivered by the litigant himself and his supporting speakers (*sunēgoroi*), these nonartistic proofs were written documents[5] that the court secretary (*grammateus*) read aloud at the request of the speaker. In court, no speaker ever held a document in his hand and read it aloud to the jurors. While the secretary read, the waterclock stopped, unless the time allotted to the speaker was

---

[4] Rhodes (1981: 697–735), Boegehold (1995).
[5] Gagarin (1990: 24), "Evidentiary material."

calculated according to the length of the day, because the day cannot be lengthened. Among the examples of the written documents that the secretary read aloud outside of the allotted speech time, *Ath. Pol.* (67.3) names law (*nomos*) and witness testimony (*martyria*), but two other types of documents, which may have been located in the gaps that precede and follow in the text, can perhaps be added.[6] The documents used by the litigants in the main trial before the jurors are collected during arbitration and then placed in two containers called *echinoi* (we now know that these were clay jars),[7] which were then sealed and brought into court so that the documents could be read aloud. In a well-preserved section of the *Ath. Pol.* (53.2) discussing the preliminary hearing before the official arbitrators (*diaitētai*), three types of documents are listed (again as examples): witness testimonies (*martyriai*), formal challenges (*proklēseis*), and laws (*nomoi*). Neither in practice within or outside of Athens[8] nor in rhetorical theory[9] was there agreement on a firm number or typology of documents that were read out before the court; a litigant was free to decide what he wished to have read aloud. By interrupting the coherence of his speech he did run the risk that the jurors would lose interest or become impatient and begin to protest. But according to the court speeches and the more general sources cited above, witness testimonies in moderate numbers[10] were a standard part of the trial process in the Athenian courts as well as in similarly organized court procedures elsewhere.

The litigants' and their supporters' entire performance in court basically served to provide proof (*pistis*) of their own side of the case. The litigants' presentations became credible and convincing both through the narration of the facts, strengthened by additional arguments from probability (that is by "artistic proofs," *entechnoi pisteis*), and also by reading aloud written documents ("nonartistic proofs," *atechnoi pisteis*) whose precise wording was objectively determined ahead of time, thus removing them from the art of rhetoric. But the rhetorical handbooks naturally show how to include these documents in the argument. Seen

---

[6] The text probably enumerates: [*psēphisma*], *nomos, mar*[*tyria, symbolon*]; see Rhodes (1981: 722).

[7] Boegehold (1995: 79–81), E 1 (T 305), fourth to third centuries B.C.; Wallace (2001).

[8] *Ath. Pol.* 53.2: *martyriai, proklēseis, nomoi* (also 53.3); 67.3: see above, note 6; IPArk 17.42–6 (Stymphalos, 303–300 B.C.): *martyriai, syngraphai; IvKnidos*, I (*IK* 41) 221 (*Syll.*[3] 953) 43–5 (Kalymna, circa 300 B.C.): *psēphismata, proklēseis, grapha tas dikas, allo eg damosiou, martyria*.

[9] Aristot. *Rhet.* 1.2 (1355b36): *martyres, basanoi, syngraphai*; 1.15 (1375a24): *nomoi, martyres, synthēkai, basanoi, horkos*; Anaxim. *Rhet.* 7.2: *martyres, basanoi, horkos*. See Mirhady (1991a), Carey (1994).

[10] See the statistics by Todd (1990: 29) and Rubinstein (2004) (appendices).

in this way, it is only logical that rhetorical theory includes "laws" among the nonartistic proofs as objectively preexisting texts that are read aloud by the secretary, even though legal statutes, now just as then, have a status completely different from facts that are affirmed but (in the modern sense) remain to be proved.

Like laws, all other nonartistic proofs except witness testimony should also be excluded from the law of evidence as we understand it today. To prove the authenticity of a contract or other document read aloud by the secretary, the speaker relied entirely on witnesses. In the short time of the trial, the popular courts had no chance to examine the authenticity of a document. Certainly litigants could settle the matter ahead of time in a preliminary hearing – in the *anakrisis* before the court magistrate or in the official arbitration (*diaita*, see below) – or also in a private meeting. If someone wished to refer to a document such as a will during the trial in front of the jurors (Dem. 36.7; 46.8), he summoned witnesses and challenged his opponent beforehand either to concede that the copy was true or to open the sealed original that was deposited with a third party for safekeeping. If the opponent granted that the copy was true and the original document was authentic, then "proof" of the document was unnecessary. If he refused the formal challenge (*proklēsis*), however, those present as witnesses at the time would confirm this in the trial, and following the rules of rhetorical art, the speaker would draw his own more or less detailed conclusion about the accuracy of the copy and the authenticity of the original.

The challenge (*proklēsis*) issued before witnesses also is important for the rhetorical argument about the two remaining nonartistic proofs, slave testimony under torture (*basanos*) and oath (*horkos*). Both of these could be described as evidence in today's sense, but Athens was peculiar in that these types of evidence took place outside of court, not before the jurors. These procedures, interrogation under torture and oath, became relevant to the trial only if both parties agreed. Because slaves were not normally allowed in court as witnesses, a litigant could interrogate his opponent's slaves under torture about a particular topic only if his opponent agreed.[11] In the same way, the parties could agree that one would accept an oath sworn by the other on a particular subject. In such challenges it is often suggested that the decision for the entire case should depend on the outcome of these procedures taking place outside of court.[12] But in most cases it remains merely the suggestion of one

---

[11] Thür (1977).
[12] Thür (1977: 214–32), cf. Mirhady (1996) and Thür (1996b).

party, because the opponent does not, as a rule, accept the challenge. But even in these cases, the speaker can have the written text of the challenge read to the jurors and confirmed by the witnesses present at the time, and can draw his own conclusions, as Aristotle recommends (*Rhetoric* 1.15). Then, the nonartistic proof as a document is not the exact text of a testimony under torture or a sworn oath, but rather the text of the challenge, where the contents of the interrogation or of the oath to be sworn are recorded precisely. Thus only the fact that the challenge happened is proven, not the contents of the challenge that was proposed to no effect.[13] For Athenian procedure, then, more precise than Aristotle's textbook on rhetoric is *Ath. Pol.* 53.2, where he gives the documents typically sent by the public arbitrator to be read aloud to the jury courts as "laws, witness testimonies, and challenges," without worrying about the broader application of the challenge.

When describing the law of evidence in classical Athens, necessarily in the terminology of modern law, we should not make the mistake of seeing the list of nonartistic proofs, which merely groups together a few types of documents coming from outside the court speech, as a systematic account of evidence in our sense. Evidence (*pistis*) in the rhetorical sense is a general means of persuasion, not of legal proof.

II

From the considerations put forth thus far, one can conclude that – contrary to rhetorical theory and against the expectations of a modern observer – only one type of evidence, witnesses, was used directly in the procedure before the jury courts. The narrow time frame alone in which the trial took place suggests that the process of presenting witnesses' testimony in Athens was essentially different from modern evidentiary procedures. In the following sections the few rules governing the testimony of witnesses will be discussed: (1) witness qualifications, (2) witness formulas and types of testimony, (3) arbitration and witness obligation, (4) the witness in the main trial, and (5) the false witness. In Section III, we will consider the function of witnesses in the overall structure of litigation at Athens.

(1) The first question, who is allowed to be a witness in the *dikastēria*, already shows that Athenian law was far from exhausting all possibilities of determining material truth. Only free adult males were

---

[13] Thür (1996b: 132) against Mirhady (1996).

allowed to be witnesses. Slaves of either gender, as previously mentioned, were normally subjected to interrogation under torture carried out jointly by both parties outside of court. In the court speeches, the parties often mention having challenged each other, but no evidence of this kind is ever used in a trial, or even mentioned as being used. Likewise, the knowledge women held, which was often decisive in inheritance speeches, could be introduced only indirectly. Either the woman affirmed her knowledge outside of the court through an oath – in Dem. 29.33, and 55.27, for example, the speakers challenge their opponents to agree to it but no oaths are sworn – or the woman's male authority (*kyrios*) testified for her (Dem. 57.67) with her consent (Isai. 12.5). A woman did not appear in court on her own behalf, either as a litigant or witness, nor could she be held legally responsible for perjury or for the false testimony of her *kyrios*. Foreigners, however, could be witnesses, perhaps by special regulations or agreements between states.

Whether slaves and women could testify in private homicide cases is disputed.[14] Anyhow, the sacred foundations of homicide law resulted in several peculiarities, above all solemn oaths. Aside from homicide cases, slaves managing their businesses independently could apparently litigate and testify about their own affairs.[15] From these regulations we see that the ability to testify did not depend on a person's mental capacity but was seen as the privilege of appearing in public on one's own, before citizens assembled as jurors in court.

Litigants and their *sunēgoroi* undoubtedly had the right to speak in court, but were they also authorized or obligated to appear as witnesses? A litigant could not be a witness in court in his own case in order to increase the credibility of his plea (Dem. 46.9). Only in a *diamartyria* could someone be a witness in his own case (Dem. 44.42; Isai. 7.3), but such cases did not involve a witness testifying in court but rather a formal deposition before the archon that he must not hand out the inheritance to more distant relatives because legitimate sons exist.[16] After a *diamartyria*, the archon's hands are tied unless formally effective, extrajudicial testimony is eliminated by a successful suit for false witness (see Section II.5).

Just as a litigant cannot force his own testimony on the court, he also cannot force his opponent to be a witness: "The two litigants must

[14] Harrison (1971: 136).
[15] E. Cohen (1992: 96–8).
[16] Wolff (1966: 122), Harrison (1971: 124–31); for other forms of *diamartyria*, see Wallace (2001).

answer each other's questions, but are not obligated to be witnesses" (law cited in Dem. 46.10). This rule refers primarily to pretrial procedure. In the *anakrisis* (preliminary examination) before the magistrate or in the public arbitration, each litigant prepares step by step the case he will present in a continuous speech at the trial in court. We can call this the "dialectical" stage of procedure, in contrast to the "rhetorical" stage, when his timed pleading is cohesively presented in court.[17] In pretrial proceedings a litigant questioned and challenged his opponent before witnesses, and, as we will see, the litigant had to show to his opponent all the documents that would be read aloud in court, which could provoke more questions and challenges. At every step, either litigant must cooperate to ensure a fair preparation for the main trial. This obligation, however, does not extend to compelling one party to testify for the other.

What is forbidden for the litigants for obvious reasons, however, is permitted for their supporting speakers (*sunēgoroi*), who argue alongside them in court. As a result, a paradigmatic trial strategy developed of presenting the *sunēgoros* as a witness immediately before he gave his supporting speech (Isai. 12.1, 4; Aisch. 2.170, 184), thus emphasizing that, like a witness, the *sunēgoros* himself risks a suit for false testimony.[18] The extant speeches from witness trials show that their testimonies were in fact attacked under every conceivable pretext, whereas the only risk that the *sunēgoros* faced – that he would be prosecuted for "paid legal assistance" – was negligible: the acceptance of money was difficult to prove, but it was quite easy to twist the wording of a deposition and present it as false. It is easy to delineate the boundaries between *sunēgoria* and witness testimony, when a witness said nothing but merely confirmed a written document that was read aloud in court, but the difference may seem problematic during the period when testimony was presented orally – ostensibly in one's own words.[19] This problem is only apparent. As I will soon show, even oral testimony in fact adhered to a fixed formula that clearly distinguished it from the unconstrained speech of the *sunēgoros*.

(2) Particularly informative are the witness formulas, which, unlike the issue of oral versus written testimony, have received too little attention until now. The witness accepts responsibility that a statement, carefully formulated ahead of time, corresponds to the truth. Beyond

---

[17] Thür (1977: 156).
[18] Rubinstein (2000: 71).
[19] Rubinstein (2000: 72–5).

that, he gives no further information of any kind to the court. In the fourth century this statement was commonly prepared before the preliminary hearing by the litigant who wanted to present the testimony in court and was written on a whitened wooden tablet (Dem. 47.11). Almost throughout, the wording adheres to a set formula. After the name of the witness or witnesses come, for example, the words "testifies to knowing that Neaira was a slave of Nikarete and..." (Dem. 59.23) or "testify to knowing that Phylomache, Euboulides' mother, was considered the sister of Polemon..." (Dem. 43.35). The formulaic verb "know" (*eidenai*) introduces a subordinate clause that precisely expresses the fact to be proven. The same formula, "to know" something, is used to specify the subject about which a slave will be interrogated under torture in a private *basanos* procedure: "I requested from him [Onetor] three slaves who knew that the woman lived with him in marriage..." (Dem. 30.35; reporting a challenge).[20]

In witness testimonies, the verb "be present" (*pareinai, paragenesthai*), is also used in a similar way as "know": "...testify to having been present before the arbitrator when Philomache defeated all other claimants to the estate" (Dem. 43.31). "Having been present" is normally included in the testimony of witnesses who were summoned to business transactions or important procedural transactions. By contrast, most persons who testify that they "know" are accidental witnesses to an event. A third formulaic verb for expressing the subject of witness testimony is "hear" (*akouein*): "...testify to having heard from their father that Polemon had no brother but a sister, Philomache" (Dem. 43.36). Such hearsay evidence was only allowed if the informant, the bearer of "knowledge," was already dead. Sometimes the witness's relationship to the litigant is recorded in the deposition just before the subject of the testimony, particularly to point out kinship and therefore the competence of the witness ("...testifies to being a relative and to having heard..." Dem. 43.42; cf. 35–46). The three different formulaic words that introduce the subject of the testimony are also found in the legal regulations underlying the speaker's argument in Dem. 46.6–7: "The laws prescribe that a person should testify to what he knows or to events at which he was present, and that this should be recorded in a document so that no one could delete something from, or add something to, the written text. They do not allow testimony from hearsay while someone is still alive, but only after his death."

---

[20] Thür (1977: 128f.).

This passage could give the impression that a fixed formula was only introduced with the written form of testimony. Scholars dispute not only the date when the Athenians changed from oral to written testimony but also the reason for this change.[21] The innovation is probably connected with the reform of pretrial procedure, when the circle of those responsible was expanded to include all sixty-year-old citizens who, as "arbitrators by lot," performed a similar function to the archons in the *anakrisis*, preparatory to trial.[22] In fact, the clay jars (*echinoi*) in which documents for trial are stored (*Ath. Pol.* 53.2, see above, Section II.1) are mentioned in connection with public arbitration.[23] Presumably public arbitration, which was established soon after the restoration of the democracy in 403/2, needed more stringent public control than the preliminary hearing before the archons. When witness testimony was submitted in written form, a litigant could be confident that in the main trial his opponent would not change the wording of the testimonies announced at the arbitration. For trials in which the same archon presided over both the preliminary hearing and the main trial, this risk was minimal. These conclusions, however, are not directly provable from the sources. The only certainty is that from the 370s, at the latest, speakers in court asked the clerk to read out the witness testimonies, whereas in the fifth century, they asked the witnesses "to speak."[24]

Giving oral testimony is typically understood as if the witness described relevant facts to the court in his own words,[25] whereas a fixed formula was only introduced along with written testimony. Two passages in particular are cited as evidence that witnesses recounted events in their own words: Andok. 1.69, "They will mount the speaker's platform and speak to you as long as you want to listen..."; and Lys. 17.2, "...they will recount to you... and testify."[26] Upon closer examination, however, both speeches contain clear hints that oral testimony was already couched in the above-stated formula. For instance, Andokides (1.69) asserts that the relatives he saved from the death penalty "knew" the information best; we can therefore assume that as witnesses, they described their rescue with similar statements using *eidenai*

---

[21] Rubinstein (2000: 72–4), with references to earlier works.
[22] See Scafuro (1997: 126f. and 383–92) (opposed in part by Thür 2002: 408f.).
[23] However, the only known example of an *echinos* (above, n. 7) comes from an *anakrisis*.
[24] Leisi (1908: 85f.), Rubinstein (2000: 72, n. 143).
[25] Bonner (1905: 46f.), Leisi (1908: 86f.), Rubinstein (2000: 72), Gagarin (2002: 138), *contra* Thür (1995: 329).
[26] Rubinstein (2000: 73).

("know"). And the restriction that follows – "as long as you (the judges) want to listen" – refers grammatically not to the content of the witnesses' statements or their speaking, but rather to the number of witnesses who, pronouncing identical formulas, would be coming up to the speaker's platform (*bēma*). For good reason (cf. 1.47) Andokides has not called all eleven relatives mentioned in 1.68 but already stopped the process earlier. The alleged desire of the jurors to listen (or not) is a rhetorical trope, like the challenge to the jurors in 1.70 to request the completion of an argument that just ended. In the second passage (Lys. 17.2) both verbs known from the formula are in fact used: "those who 'know' more than I and 'were present' when that man concluded the deal will recount to you and testify." Here too, obviously, the witnesses' narratives consist in the recital of formally introduced statements that were agreed on with the litigant ahead of time.

From these passages, one can conclude that in the change from oral to written testimony only the medium, not the formula, changed; what was previously stored only in memory was now documented. Further evidence that oral testimony follows a fixed formula is the *diōmosia*, the statement that a witness in a homicide case must give under oath, which is also introduced with the verb "know" before the introduction of written testimony (Ant. 1.8, 28). In the same way the subjects about which slaves are to be tortured, in the fifth and into the fourth centuries, are formulated consistently as what the slave "knows."[27]

We may conclude that the boundary between witnesses and *sunēgoroi* was always clear. The witness used formulaic words and was responsible for each and every word of his formulaic statement under *dikē pseudomartyriōn* (suit for false testimony – Section II.5). In the period of oral testimony, the memory of the participants was obviously sufficient to ensure the wording, but in accordance with the bureaucratic regulations of the restored democracy, testimony proceeded from the pretrial stage to the main hearing and, if necessary, to the suit for false testimony in the form of an unalterable document.

(3) If we follow the course of a trial, the witness testimony (that, as we have seen, in each case was prepared and formulated by the parties in private) first appears publicly during the pretrial proceedings. In the scholarship, both the purpose of the different types of pretrial proceedings and the function of the witnesses in the whole trial are disputed. The first issue can be considered only briefly here, the second will be

[27] Thür (1977: 128, n. 155; 131).

treated more fully later (III), after the overall legal framework of the evidence from witness testimony is clarified.

During pretrial proceedings, the witness first had to state his view of the prepared testimony. If he refused to appear, he exposed himself to compliance by force. Cases that fell under the jurisdiction of one of the nine archons went through a preliminary hearing called the *anakrisis*.[28] Presumably, at this time the archon would have checked on his authority to administer the case and any other formal requirements before conducting the trial in a court session under his control. It is thought that the other trials, which fell under the jurisdiction of the Forty (*Ath. Pol.* 53.1–3), would have been prepared totally differently: these trials would have to go through arbitration before a public arbitrator (*diaitētēs*), a sixty-year-old citizen chosen by lot; but each party could "appeal" the arbitrator's decision, and a "higher court" presided over by one of the Forty made the decision.

Steinwenter[29] has already shown that the arbitrator's verdict was at most the basis for a free and amicable agreement between parties, but otherwise was not legally binding. If the parties did not come to an amicable agreement, the trial took its normal path toward the sole binding decision of the court. As mentioned above, the legal consequence of public arbitration rested only in the fact that the parties "could use no documents other than those placed in the *echinos* before the arbitrator" (*Ath. Pol.* 53.3). We can thus see the procedural purpose of public arbitration as (in addition to attempting to end the conflict amicably) fairly preparing for the main trial. Following dialectical rules, the parties were supposed to clarify their opposing positions. As its name ("examination") suggests, the *anakrisis* before the archons also had this dialectic nature, though the archon did not question the litigants (at least not about formal requirements) but rather the litigants examined each other.[30] Because *echinoi* are never mentioned in the literary sources in connection with the *anakrisis*, Lämmli[31] concluded that the rule of fairness was not in force there and new documents, even witness testimonies, could be introduced until the beginning of the main trial. The discovery of a lid with an inscription showing that the *echinos* held documents from an *anakrisis*[32] proved the opposite. Accordingly, the litigants had to let each other see all their evidence

---

[28] For details, see Harrison (1971: 94–105).
[29] Steinwenter (1925: 68–73), Lämmli (1938: 92).
[30] Thür (1977: 76).
[31] Lämmli (1938: 117) still generally followed, see Wallace (2001: 98).
[32] See above, n. 7. The literary sources examined by Lämmli (1938) need further discussion.

in every procedure before the main trial.³³ This does not mean, however, that witnesses gave testimonies in the *anakrisis* or in the public arbitration.

Because the witness did not give testimony in either pretrial proceeding, he was not liable under *dikē pseudomartyriōn* for his appearance there. However, he was responsible for appearing at the pretrial proceedings before either the archon or the arbitrator chosen by lot. Each litigant had the opportunity to summon (*kalein, proskalein*) privately a person he would present as a witness. In pretrial proceedings, the witness had to declare if he would confirm the formulaic testimony presented to him in court, or would at once "swear himself exempt" by an oath called *exōmosia* (Pollux 8.37): "He must either confirm or swear himself exempt that he does not know or was not present." From the words used by the lexicographer, clearly taken from the formula for witness testimony, it is easy to see that in the *exōmosia* the witness does not excuse himself by "not knowing"; rather, he takes an oath that the statement devised by the litigant and formulated as the witness's knowledge is not true. A witness swears "not to have been present" if he denies that he was summoned for an act of legal significance. Denial under oath, however, has no legal consequences; a witness can be prosecuted under *dikē pseudomartyriōn* only if he confirms a stated fact during the trial before the jurors. From Dem. 45.58, we learn that the *exōmosia* normally took place before the trial, in this case at the public arbitration, and that the oath ceremony claimed a considerable amount of time. Moreover, *Ath. Pol.* mentions (55.5; cf. 7.1) that, as a particularly celebrated oath, the *exōmosia* was sworn on the stone before the Stoa of the archon basileus.³⁴

Instead of swearing oneself exempt, an unwilling witness could also decide to stay away from the proceeding altogether; however, he thereby exposed himself to legal force by the litigant who summoned him. One source (Dem. 49.19–21) gives information about this, during arbitration, but much of this account remains unclear.³⁵ The witness Antiphanes did not appear at the last session of the public arbitration in which his testimony should have been placed in the *echinos*. The passage states clearly that testifying before the public arbitrator meant nothing more than introducing the formulaic testimony in the presence

---

[33] IPArk 17.43–46 (Stymphalos, 303–300 B.C.) has the same regulation; cf. the commentary on p. 236.
[34] The *lithos* has been excavated in front of the Stoa, Rhodes 1981, 136; 620. *Ath. Pol.* 55.5 is speaking about the *exōmosia* generally (*contra* Carey 1995b: 115); cf. Lyk. 1.20 (see below, Section II.4 and Appendix).
[35] Harrison (1971: 141f.).

of the witness. Out of fairness, the identity of the witness and the wording of his testimony had to be revealed to the opposing litigant. The arbitrator could only accept a deposition in the presence of those who would confirm them in court. Because Antiphanes did not appear, Apollodoros, who had summoned the witness in vain, paid "a drachma for the refusal of a witness to appear" before the close of the arbitration (49.19).

Apollodoros then brought a suit for avoiding testimony (*dikē lipomartyriou*) against Antiphanes to prosecute him for the damage (*blabē*) he had caused (49.20). Of course, Apollodorus incurred damages only if he were to lose the main trial.[36] Nevertheless, if he mentioned in court that the arbitrator did not consider the defendant, Timotheus, guilty after he waited until night for the witness to appear, but instead ruled in his favor, he is still not making an argument for damages but is rather accusing the absent witness. Oddly enough, in the main trial Apollodoros still tries to get Antiphanes to confirm two statements under oath (49.20). From this passage, we can conclude that Antiphanes was actually present in court, but most likely as a witness for the opponent. Apollodoros' irrelevant challenge to Antiphanes to swear an oath on the spot is meant to disguise his failure at the arbitration to get Antiphanes to show up as witness for his side. Dem. 49.19 has been wrongly understood to mean that a witness can be sentenced to pay the amount of damage caused by a "broken promise" to appear.[37] By comparison with a parallel regulation from Stymphalos, however, it is clear that to avoid becoming liable to a penalty the witness had to comply with a private summons, even without consenting.[38]

In the remaining sources from Athens, it is not from arbitration that the witness is absent, but rather from the main trial. This topic will be discussed in the next section. There are no sources dealing with the absence of a witness from the *anakrisis*, but at least for political trials we can speculate (Section II.4). Naturally, no force could be used against individuals who had already been convicted twice for false testimony, because a third conviction threatened them with disenfranchisement (*atimia*) (Hyp. 2.12). As a consequence, they were also exempted from swearing an *exōmosia*. This regulation explicitly protected

---

[36] If Apollodoros won his case against Timotheus, the same problem would have arisen as in a *dikē pseudomartyriōn* by a winning party (see below, Section II.5); in both instances, the loss is not financial, but rather one of reputation.

[37] Lipsius (1905–1915: 659); *contra* Harrison (1971: 142f.).

[38] *IPArk* 17.10–14 (303–300 B.C.): "to not be present" after being summoned could result in being penalized for the entire amount of the claim.

even those witnesses who "had been present," when summoned at business transactions – a stipulation that could have caused trouble for some parties involved in a contract case. Nevertheless, these individuals could still appear as witnesses of their own free will.

(4) At the conclusion of the arbitration process, which could extend over several sessions, the *thesmothetēs* determined a time for the trial (*Ath. Pol.* 59.1). A court had to be available with adequate capacity for the size of the jury. For private suits, 201 or 401 jurors were needed (*Ath. Pol.* 53.3), and 501 for most public cases. The trial had to be conducted according to a strict schedule because of the costs associated with jury payment. A court could decide several cases on the same day. Because of the pressure of time and the large number of jurors, only rudimentary means were developed for presenting one's evidence. The most important tool for persuading the court were the speeches of the two litigants, each forming a cohesive unit. The length of their speeches was determined exactly by the time measured out by the waterclock (*klepsydra*). The trial was the domain of rhetoric. A litigant could lengthen the time of his presentation as much as he wanted by having documents read aloud because then the waterclock was stopped, but this tactic ran into psychological limitations; the audience, fellow citizens serving one day as jurors, preferred to hear exciting stories rather than dry accounts of deeds.

Evidence from witnesses also had to fit into these limits. The most important features have already been mentioned: at the trial the witness had to appear before the court in person and had to go up to, or onto, the speaker's platform (*bēma*). There, he had to either recite the formulaic testimony himself or, later, confirm it silently by nodding after the secretary read the text aloud. He never had to answer any questions.[39] Only the fact that he was there in person, that he was either praised or insulted by the litigants in their speeches, and that by testifying he risked a suit for false witness gave the jurors an idea whether he was telling the truth in the testimony created for him by the litigant. The jurors had an important criterion for assessing the testimony in the rule that before the jurors voted, the litigants had to announce by *episkēpsis* if they wished to bring a *dikē pseudomartyriōn* against a witness (*Ath. Pol.* 68.4). No further measures for evaluating the truth of a testimony were available to the court. Because the verdict in the *dikastērion* occurred simply by

---

[39] The unique "questioning" of a witness in Andok. 1.14 is nothing other than the deposition pronounced by the party himself and the witness answering "I know." An *anakrisis* of a witness is mentioned only in *IvKnidos* 221.67–72 (see above, n. 8).

a vote without deliberation (*Ath. Pol.* 69.1) and no reasons were given, no one could know what influence a particular witness had exerted on the outcome of a trial.

Under these circumstances, it is evident that the litigants were given the means to compel a witness to appear for the main trial too. At the trial in court, unlike the preliminary proceedings, the witness took personal responsibility for the truth of the facts asserted by the litigant. Forcing a witness to appear was not conceivable in Athens. Compulsion could only be applied indirectly through fines or penalties. We must keep in mind that by swearing the *exōmosia* a witness could avoid all responsibility for the content of the statement. For practical reasons, the *exōmosia* was already sworn during arbitration.[40]

One simple means of indirectly forcing a witness to appear before the court was to have him officially summoned (*klēteuein*) by the court secretary (Aisch. 2.68). In view of the harsh sanctions that accompany this official summons, we must assume that *klēteuein* is allowed only against absent witnesses (*mē elthein*, Lyk. 1.20) who had already been summoned by the litigant and appeared during the preliminary hearing. Only someone who is prepared for his appearance before the court, or who is present but not willing to go to the speaker's platform, can fairly be put under pressure by being officially summoned.

Klēteuein has different consequences in private and public cases.[41] Although we do not know what means of compulsion could be used against a witness who failed to appear for the *anakrisis* in a public trial, we are well-informed about the next stage and the compulsion used to get witnesses to appear in court and approach the speaker's platform. It is certain that a reluctant witness in political trials had to pay a fine of a thousand drachmas (Aisch. 1.46). According to the general view, the witness had to pay this fine only if he did not approach the speaker's platform when summoned. The thousand drachma fine is exactly the same penalty a prosecutor had to pay if he abandoned his case or received less than one-fifth of the votes (Dem. 21.47). Just like the prosecutor, the witness in political trials should not yield to threats or bribery, after he has already taken a position during the preliminary hearing. For the most part, a witness in a public trial could not be held accountable for material damages (*blabē*) as a witness in a private suit could. Therefore, a fixed fine, paid to the state, seems appropriate.[42]

---

[40] See Appendix and above, n. 34.
[41] First seen by Rubinstein (2004).
[42] Rubinstein (2004: 109–11).

Only in the *anakrisis* of a public trial was someone who summoned a witness uncertain whether he would confirm the testimony in the main trial or take the *exōmosia* at once. This situation is best suited for the almost formulaic expression used in connection with *klēteuein*, "the witness may (in the future) confirm the testimony or (immediately) swear the *exōmosia*." Perhaps one can conclude from this that *klēteuein* was also permissible in preliminary hearings along with the fine of one thousand drachmas, of course only against witnesses privately summoned according to the rules.

In private cases the expression "*klēteuein*" is used only once in a comparable sense (Dem. 32.30). Because a witness who has already failed to appear at the public arbitration – as shown above – is prosecuted with *dikē lipomartyriou* for *blabē* (Dem. 49.20), it is unlikely that the penalty of 1,000 drachmas would also be imposed on him for failing to appear in court. Perhaps *klēteuein* in private cases was a procedure like *episkēpsis*, undertaken before the vote as a condition for bringing a *dikē lipomartyriou*,[43] to take revenge for sustained damages or an injured reputation. Dem. 32.30 deals with none of these questions. Failure to appear as a witness in court was clearly not a common problem in private suits.

In sum, we can assume that a litigant was able to compel witnesses to appear both in preliminary hearings and in the main trial. Although the *exōmosia* was sworn only in preliminary trials, the witnesses who exempted themselves under oath still had to go before the jurors in the main trial and stand by their oath in person. This is indicated by those passages we have thus far examined – and refuted – as arguments that an *exōmosia* could also still be sworn before the court. These passages, however, can best be explained by the rhetorical device of feigned uncertainty.

The texts cited thus far deal with reluctant witnesses, but Athenian law also solved the problem of witnesses who were unable to appear at the main trial because of illness or travel. Before the trial, these individuals, in the presence of other witnesses, confirmed the testimony formulated by the litigant in a procedure called the *ekmartyria* (Dem. 46.7).[44] The original testimony of the absent witnesses and the testimony of the present witnesses that they were properly transmitting the original

---

[43] Rubinstein (2004: n. 22) understands *klēteuein* here as the "formal summons to a legal action"; but the international political affair in Dem. 18.150 is not comparable to the private one of the poor metic Protos in Dem. 32.

[44] Harrison (1971: 146f.); similarly, IvKnidos 221.47–65 (above, n. 8); Pap. Hal. 1.70–73.

testimony were combined into a single document, in which the testimonies of the witnesses who were present in court were added at the end of the original deposition that the absent witness had given before the trial (Dem. 35.20, 34). An *ekmartyria* could be attacked at the end of the trial in a single *episkēpsis* for false content as well as for false transmission.

(5) Only after the verdict was it possible to test the truth of testimony taken during the trial. If a party had promptly protested through *episkēpsis* against one of his opponent's witnesses,[45] he could bring a suit for false testimony (*dikē pseudomartyriōn*). We do not know what happened if the litigant did not bring suit after his *episkēpsis*; perhaps the simple attack was considered *hybris*. Deposition suits were mostly directed against false statements, but in the case of *diamartyria*, they were also brought against false legal claims (e.g., one's status as the legitimate son of the deceased was disputed in the deposition suit). Finally, suit could be brought against filing an inadmissible deposition, one based on hearsay from a person still alive. It is generally accepted that the prosecutor's goal in this type of suit is to receive payment of a fine in the amount of the damage (*blabē*) that resulted from the testimony.[46] This sanction is meaningless, however, if the winner in the main trial brings a deposition suit (Lys. 10.22; Isokr. 18.54–56) or if a witness who testified in a public trial is prosecuted. In these cases, it is not a matter of material damage, but only of one's injured reputation, which to be sure always played a role along with *blabē*. Because a witness who had been convicted three times lost his civil rights, it might have been enough for the prosecutor to bring the witness one step closer to *atimia*. It is unclear if, and under what conditions, the trial could be reopened after the conviction of a witness (*anadikia*).[47] We can assume that, as a rule, the conviction of the witness did not set aside the verdict of the main trial.

III

The present study tries to understand witness testimony strictly from the procedural rules in effect in Athenian jury courts. Here at the end, I will first summarize the most significant conclusions, which deviate

---

[45] *IG* II² 1258 (324/2 B.C.), honoring the prosecutors for entering an *episkēpsis* in time.
[46] Harrison (1971: 144), Thür (1987: 406–12), as against Bonner (1905: 92), Berneker (1959: 1370).
[47] Harrison (1971: 192–7), Behrend (1975).

in part from the general opinion. Then finally, I will give my view of the purpose of witness testimony in the overall concept of litigation in Athens.

The fact that the five "nonartistic proofs" are given from a rhetorical, not a judicial, perspective yields the important conclusion that in the legal process witness testimony is the only enforceable means of discovering the truth in court – and even this only to a modest extent. It is undisputed that restricting the capacity to bear witness to free males restricted the search for truth. There is also agreement that written testimony – a statement formulated by the litigant that the witness only silently confirmed – did not promote the discovery of truth in court. It is a new realization that a fixed formula was also used in the period of oral testimony; in my opinion, the witness never recounted events in his own words – thus, he was always clearly distinct from a *sunēgoros* – and was never questioned or cross-examined in court.

Both types of preliminary hearings, the *anakrisis* and the public arbitration, serve as preparations for the main trial. The most important tool in this "dialectic stage" of the procedure is question and answer between the litigants. The witness is obliged to appear there and must decide if he will at once swear an oath that the statement prepared by the litigant is false (*exōmosia*) or if he will confirm it in the main trial. The *exōmosia* should not be understood as an excuse of not knowing, but rather as a negative assertion, denying the content of the testimony. If the witness did not appear at the preliminary hearing, then in a private suit, after receiving a private summons, he had to pay a penalty to the litigant for damages, and it is possible that in a public trial, after being officially summoned (*klēteuein*), he had to pay a fine of one thousand drachmas to the state. Because public arbitration, as we have known for a long time, did not end with a definitive verdict, but rather with the arbitrator's decision that was not binding at all, we cannot speak of giving evidence at this stage. In both types of preliminary hearings, the wording of the entire deposition and the identity of the witness or witnesses were to be made known to the opposing litigant on the principle of fairness (though this is disputed for the *anakrisis*).

The main trial can be characterized as a battle of speeches – the "rhetorical stage" of the judicial process. Speaking or reading aloud the short, formulaic testimony, even one denied by *exōmosia*, carried little weight, at best, in the overall speech. Contrary to the claims of previous scholarship, an *exōmosia* sworn before the jurors in the main trial is not attested. It is also a new finding that in each case the witness, whether he confirmed the testimony or already swore the *exōmosia* in the preliminary hearing, must approach the speaker's platform and show himself in person to the jurors. In public trials, a witness who did not go before the jurors after being summoned both by the litigant and officially was fined 1,000 drachmas. In private cases, he was perhaps penalized with a fine in the amount of the damage or simply with a guilty verdict. A perjured *exōmosia* thus had the serious social consequence of public stigma, but only the testimony positively affirmed by a witness (*martyria*) had legal consequences. The witness exposed himself to a suit for false testimony (*dikē pseudomartyriōn*) and could be convicted and fined the amount of the damage; in each case, he risked the loss of civic rights (*atimia*), which occurred after a third conviction. The extant speeches from these trials show that attacks on witnesses consist of hair-splitting quibbles (see, e.g., Thür 1997: 252–5 on Dem. 47); the main weapons are the emotions aroused in the previous trial where the deposition originally was given.

Thus far I have attempted to reconstruct the legal principles of witness testimony in the Athenian jury courts. Now we can finally turn to the identity of the witness. Who were the people who approached the speaker's platform alongside the litigants and their *sunēgoroi*? What function did they have in the interaction between the litigants and their fellow citizens selected as judges? In the past twenty years this issue has prompted profound and continually refined analyses of the entire corpus of court speeches. The results must be placed in the legal framework of witness evidence. Humphreys (1985: 322 and 353) very rightly denies the thesis – which, in any case, was never proposed in this form – that witnesses in classical Athens acted as oath-helpers. The institutional prerequisites for this, in fact, are entirely lacking. In the time of the orators, the verdict in an Athenian trial never depended on an oath that, as in Gortyn, a court magistrate could impose on one of the litigants or his supporters. Nevertheless, Humphreys understood witnesses as supporters and followers of the litigants and grouped these into types of inner and more distant circles. She explained this as resulting from a court system that presumed the rural mentality of a face-to-face society that, however, found itself becoming an urbanized society by the end of the fifth century. The primitive system of the Athenian *dikastēria* has conserved that mentality. Comparing Athenian law suits with those of other Mediterranean agonistic societies D. Cohen (1995: 107–12), without going into legal details, holds that giving testimony, also a false one, was a noble act of family and kinship solidarity.

Todd (1990: 31f.) created distinctions based on the statistical frequency of witness testimony in the speeches; witnesses are much more often found in private cases than public ones, where the *sunēgoroi* more often appear.[48] Rubinstein (2004) combines the statistically supported difference between private and public trials with the substantive criterion of how close in every single case the personal connections were between the witness and the litigant. In this way, she reveals the different means of compelling testimony; she assigns the fine of 1,000 drachmas after an official summons (*klēteuein*) only to public trials. In these she also finds the long overlooked figure of the neutral witness.

As already emphasized, the legal structure excludes the possibility of oath-helpers in classical Athens. Already in Draco's law (621/0) the verdict in a homicide case occurs not by an exculpatory oath but by the vote of a panel of judges, the Ephetai (*IG* I³ 104.13). Nevertheless, the formulaic language of classical witnesses is reminiscent of the formulas of oaths. Witnesses in a homicide case, like oath-helpers, had to swear an oath that was formulated in terms of "knowing" either the guilt or innocence of the defendant (Ant. 5.12; 1.8, 28), and "know" is one of the words that introduce the content of the testimony, that is, the assertion in the formula of the deposition that requires confirmation. Because the formula, which is similarly used in oral and written testimony, was too little noticed until now, the archaic character of witness testimony at Athens was also unrecognized. Here we cannot investigate the origins of archaic witnesses in the practice of oath-helpers. But the fact that the fourth-century formula reaches back to earlier times allows the conclusion that the view of the witness as primarily a helper and friend of the litigant did not originate in the fourth century. Along with the formula, the peculiarity of Athenian witness testimony, that the witness, without being questioned, merely confirmed a statement formulated by one of the two litigants, can also be dated to the time of oral testimony. Therefore, the strict polarization of witnesses between one party and the other also cannot be an innovation of the fourth century. All this confirms the assumption that the witness in an Athenian trial was – from a legal perspective – a helper of one of the litigants more than an instrument for judicial truth finding.

Not to be overlooked, however, are the tendencies in the opposite direction.[49] The risk of being prosecuted by the opponent for false witness after the trial bound even the closest supporter to the truth. By

---

[48] For reservations about the use of statistical methods see Mirhady (2002: 262–4), who stresses the function of witnesses as a means for finding the truth.
[49] These are stressed by Mirhady (2002) and especially for citizenship and inheritance trials by Scafuro (1994: 157, 182), who calls witnesses in these cases a "living communal archive."

analyzing the court speeches, however, we see that testimony was very often employed that is legally irrelevant or slightly beyond the truth. On the other hand, even testimony that was by all appearances completely truthful was attacked with flimsy arguments by a *dikē pseudomartyriōn*. Statistics about the extant testimonies cannot take all these imponderables into consideration. In view of the residual risk that even truthful testimony before the Athenian *dikastēria* brought, the conjecture seems justified that neutral witnesses too were asked for their support by the litigants ahead of time. To sum up, each trial had its own individual agenda depending on the subject of the conflict and the litigants' strategies of argumentation, and this determined the witnesses to be selected and the formulation of appropriate statements to be confirmed by them.

General considerations so far support the conclusion that litigants chose their witnesses according to the subject of the testimony from the circle of their closest supporters or at least from those who were well intentioned toward them. Nevertheless, the legal sanctions that could affect a reluctant witness may tell us something different: the indirect compulsion of a fine for not appearing as a witness in the preliminary hearing or the main trial could – in theory – serve best to determine the truth objectively. But the means of coercion lay in the hands of the litigants who also formulated the testimony. The first stage, summoning a witness to the preliminary hearing, compelled him to take a stand either for or against the litigant who had summoned him. Either the witness agreed to put the previously formulated statement on the record and to have it used in the main trial or he swore at once a solemn oath that the statement was false. With the latter, the *exōmosia*, he declared himself a supporter of the opposing litigant. At a second stage, the litigant could compel a witness who had appeared in the preliminary hearing to go before the jurors in the main trial. The compulsion to testify was, therefore, not so much a tool for finding the truth; rather, it served most of all to align the witness as the supporter of one litigant or the other. Nevertheless, clever logographers succeeded in finding arguments for the truth of a statement denied by the witness even when an *exōmosia* was delivered; they branded witnesses who were present in court and supporting their opponents as perjurers (Aisch. 1.47; Dem. 45.60; similarly, Isai. 9.18).

The identity of the witness and the content of his previously formulated testimony are inseparable. For every single testimony, the legal information in the sources reveals a strict polarization of the witnesses in favor of one party or the other. Through cleverly formulated testimony, litigants – if not their logographers – succeeded time and again in getting supporters of an opponent, who shied away from obvious perjury, to testify for their side.[50] The superficial impression that the witness was an unconditional supporter of one litigant was qualified by the masterful manipulation of a witness's duty to testify.

APPENDIX: *EXŌMOSIA* AND *KLĒTEUEIN*

Most scholars agree that the *exōmosia* (oath of disclaimer) was sometimes sworn directly before the jurors during the main trial (Rubinstein 2004, n. 15 with further references), but the direct sources, including two passages from private suits connected with compulsory testimony and four from public trials, speak convincingly against an *exōmosia* taking place in court.

In the prosecution of Stephanos for false witness (Dem. 45), Apollodoros accuses Stephanos of stealing a document with witness testimony and adds that people present at the time can testify to this (45.58). He then has the testimony he wishes these witnesses (who are Stephanos' friends) read out (45.60) and directs them either to confirm or deny it under oath. The caption *Exōmosia* follows and directly afterwards Apollodoros tries to convict the witnesses of perjury, implying that they swore the *exōmosia* (45.61). But the charge that Stephanos stole the document is insignificant, and it is out of the question that Apollodoros and the witnesses went to swear this *exōmosia* at the stone by the Stoa of the basileus during the trial, leaving the jurors with nothing to do. Even if the oath ceremony could have taken place in court, it would have interrupted and thereby destroyed the logical progress of the well-constructed story (45.57–62). Thus, Apollodoros's uncertainty (45.58) is fabricated. He presents his evidence for the supposed theft as concisely as possible with two documents and the single word *Exōmosia*, referring in all probability to an *exōmosia* that had already taken place during the public arbitration and was not repeated in court.

The speaker in Isaios 9.18–19 proceeds along the same lines, but is not so creative. He summons Hierocles, who has testified for his opponent, as a witness for his side. This time the *exōmosia* is read aloud. The speaker then attempts to show that Hierocles' *exōmosia* is perjury (9.19). But it is most unlikely that in this rather short speech there is a break in the speaker's description of mutual hostility between the two families just as it is reaching its peak. Here too, then, the document

---

[50] For examples, see Harrison (1971: 140 n. 1) (add Dem. 29.20).

read aloud was presumably only an *exōmosia* that had taken place in a preliminary stage. We can conclude that in both cases the witnesses appeared during the main hearing even though in all probability they had already sworn the *exōmosia* in the preliminary hearing. There is no mention of any kind of compulsion.

In four public cases, the speakers threaten their witnesses with *klēteuein* (an official summons).[51] In Aisch. 2.68, the speaker successfully ensures the appearance of his witness at the speaker's platform; the possibility of swearing the *exōmosia* is not even mentioned. In Dem. 59.28, the witness is formally given the choice either to confirm the deposition or exempt himself under oath. When he does neither, the speaker threatens him with *klēteuein*. Here too the testimony is obtained. In the same way, only in more words, Lykurgus (1.20) proceeds against three groups of witnesses. Even though the last two passages mention the possibility of witnesses exempting themselves under oath, nothing in the actual depositions indicates that witnesses did or would make use of this possibility. Also in these passages, the speakers only put rhetorical pressure on their witnesses to confirm the prepared statements at the speaker's platform. To encourage the witnesses to confirm their testimony, Lykourgos uses the analogy of military obligation and warns against desertion from the battle lines (*lipotaxia*), which is easily associated with *lipomartyria*, the failure of witnesses to appear. For rhetorical balance, he also explains the possibility of *exōmosia* in detail, although his reference to the solemnity of the oath that (as we know from *Ath. Pol.* 55.5) was sworn at the Stoa of the basileus, must have made it obvious that it was technically impossible to swear the oath during the main trial. But the speaker's actual argument gives no indication of the different time frames. Perhaps the formulaic alternative in the last two passages, "testify or swear oneself exempt," originates from the formula for *klēteuein* that developed for the preliminary hearing (see above, Section II.4).

An entirely different situation presents itself in Aisch. 1.44–50 in the affair of Misgolas. Here too the three possibilities are first described at length: Misgolas could confirm the testimony that he had sexual relations with Timarchos, not appear and pay the 1,000-drachma fine for ignoring the summons, or swear the *exōmosia* as a perjurer (1.46f.). Aischines has already prepared for the last possibility by filing other depositions affirming the acts (1.47), but he presents his evidence in reverse order, first calling other witnesses and only at the end calling

---

[51] For *klēteuein* in private cases see above Section II.4.

on Misgolas. Thus, he has already expressed doubt that Misgolas will confirm the statement (1.50). The rhetorical tactic is obvious: Aischines first leaves the jury uncertain whether Misgolas had already exempted himself from the testimony during the *anakrisis*. Then, under the threat of *klēteuein* and the penalty of 1,000 drachmas, Aischines forces his witness before the jury to stand by his oath that has already been rhetorically branded as perjury by the depositions previously read aloud. Just as in the case discussed above about the supposed theft of a document in Dem. 45.60, here also the evidence about sexual relations is creatively provided through a deposition that was never confirmed. Because the jurors do not get to see the documents before the trial, the speakers are able to enhance the suspense of their speeches by presenting an already sworn *exōmosia* as if the witness at that moment had not yet decided on it. The stylistic device of feigned uncertainty is particularly suitable for the themes of *martyria*, *exōmosia*, and *klēteuein*, a fact that must always be considered when interpreting such passages.

9: THEORIES OF PUNISHMENT
David Cohen

Legal punishment typically involves the deliberate infliction of pain, harm, or loss on an individual by the state or community in the form of a judicial response to the violation of a legal norm. Legal punishment is what gives the criminal law its coercive force and distinguishes, in modern legal systems, criminal law norms from the norms of contract, property, and the like. In different legal systems punishment may take different forms: loss of life, liberty, or property; deprivations of civic rights or social status; banishment; dishonor; torture, branding, or mutilation; outlawry/prescription; or the infliction of such penalties on family or relatives of the convicted person. All of these forms of punishment are found in some manner in Athenian law, though not all of them could be inflicted on citizens, as opposed to foreigners or slaves. As Demosthenes puts it in *Against Androtion* (22.55–56), what distinguishes the slave from the free man is that the latter is sacrosanct in his person/body, which is respected even when he is convicted of wrongdoing. The slave, on the other hand pays the penalty with his body. Indeed, punishment in most premodern legal systems was linked to civic and social status.[1] It is beyond the scope of this chapter to address the practices and modalities of punishment at Athens, though there is much room for further research in this area.[2] Instead, the focus

---

[1] For Roman law, see Garnsey (1970). In the Athenian context, the orator Dinarchus addresses the importance of considerations of status in criminal prosecutions in his speech, *Against Demosthenes* (1.26–27). He claims that there is one way and only one way to make people better: to convict the prominent and punish them as their crimes deserve. In the case of ordinary persons no one knows or is eager to find out what sentence has been passed. But in regarded to prominent men everyone hears and praises the judges if they have not sacrificed the interests of justice to the reputation of the defendants.

[2] On methods of punishment, see, for example, Eva Cantarella's definitive study of capital punishment (Cantarella 1991b) that supersedes Barkan (1935). On corporal punishment and the torture of slaves, see Hunter (1994), Chapters 3 and 6 (with bibliography).

here is on the variety of ways in which Greek thinkers conceptualized punishment as an institution and its relation to the goals and purposes of the criminal law.[3]

In Western legal theory, and particularly since the eighteenth-/nineteenth-century reform movement associated with figures such as Cesare Beccaria and Jeremy Bentham, punishment has been seen as posing a question that the state must answer: What is the justification for depriving this citizen of his or her life, liberty, property or rights? Debates about the appropriate answer to this question have preoccupied modern philosophers from Kant to H. L. A. Hart and Michel Foucault, as well as sociologists, psychologists, behavioral scientists, and politicians.[4] The debates have largely turned around what has become the clichéd trinity of retribution, deterrence, and rehabilitation or, from a Foucauldian perspective, the exercise of the ever-increasing disciplinary power of the modern state. The nature of these debates need not preoccupy us here. The salient point is that political thinkers, orators, and philosophers in classical Athens explicitly confronted the problem of the justification of punishment and debated largely the same theories in their responses to it. The ways in which they did so, as we will see, were inevitably a product of their larger attitudes and preoccupations toward fundamental issues of law, politics, and justice.

Protagoras: Revenge and Retribution

The participatory system of criminal prosecution at Athens invited aggrieved or feuding parties to seek redress and/or revenge through the courts. A series of rhetorical topoi found in forensic orations deals with the role of revenge as a motivation for prosecution. One type of argument advances the respectability of seeking revenge, casting it as a familial or religious duty or as an imperative of honor.[5] From the rhetorical perspective, of course, every argument requires a counterargument, and Athenian orators were ready to answer such claims by saying that individuals seeking vengeance were using public institutions for private gain. What is important here from the standpoint of theories of punishment, however, is the question of whether Athenians also distinguished

---

[3] For the most important recent work on theories of punishment in ancient Greece, see Allen (2000b).
[4] See, e.g., Hart (1968) and Foucault (1977).
[5] See, e.g., Lysias, *Against Agoratus* (13.3, 48) and Aristotle, *Rhetoric* 1370b–1371a, 1378a–b). On this topic generally, see Cohen (1995: Chapter 4).

the *private* motives (revenge) of the prosecuting party from a *public* interest in punishing an individual who had violated the laws of the city. As my chapter on crime and criminal law in Athens (below) will make clear, they did make such a distinction, and it was for this reason that prosecuting parties typically claimed that punishment would not only provide them with redress but also uphold justice and the laws of the city. In Lysias's oration, *Against Agoratus*, the combination of private and public motivations in punishment is articulated. The speaker emphasizes his own duty to avenge the wrongs perpetrated by the defendant (13.3, 42, 48–49, 92, 97). His argument is basically that the criminal law is the vehicle by which individuals *and* the community take vengeance on those who have harmed them through punishment. In so doing they will avenge those who have been wronged as well as acting justly and piously.

What this claim leaves open, however, are the precise features of punishment that serve justice and the interests of the demos. In modern discussions of punishment since at least Kant, discussion has often turned on whether "retributive justice" should be counted as such a feature or whether retribution is just a euphemism for the primitive desire for revenge. Kant, of course, argued that retributive justice was the very foundation of a just legal order and warned against the "serpent-windings" of utilitarian thinking that sought to justify the infliction of punishment not as the "righting" of a past wrong, but rather for the future good which the societally sanctioned infliction of pain might produce. In the Western, and particularly the Anglo-American, traditions the forward-looking approach won the day and succeeded in identifying retribution with a backward-looking, blind desire for revenge for its own sake. It is only in the past few decades that some legal philosophers have again seriously explored the merits of retributive thinking and sparked reconsideration of its legitimate role in the justification of punishment.[6]

As we will see, although an agonistic society like classical Athens by no means denigrated the private desire for revenge in response to intentional insult or injury, those thinkers who pondered the nature of legal institutions raised the same kinds of questions about the legitimacy of retribution as an appropriate *public* response by the institutions of the *polis*. As in our own society, judging by the rhetoric of the law courts ordinary Athenians appear not to have been troubled much by such concerns and were readily prepared to hear arguments that wrongdoers

---

[6] See Morris (1968, 1981), Feinberg (1970, 1984), Moore (1997), Fletcher (1998).

should by "paid back" for what they had done and punished for their allegedly heinous behavior because they "deserved" it. This is the language of retribution, and in the prosecutorial speeches of the orators it blends easily with claims that punishment of such wrongdoers will thus serve justice and inhibit others from engaging in such conduct in the future. We turn now, however, to the attempts of intellectuals and philosophers to explore these issues in the context of legal and political theory.

In the dialogue *Protagoras*, Plato portrays an encounter between Socrates and the eminent intellectual figure Protagoras, in which the latter provides an example of his eloquence on the theme of whether virtue can be taught. In the course of this rhetorical display he offers what is perhaps the most famous account of theories of punishment in ancient literature. We are not concerned here with the much-debated larger philosophical and methodological issues raised by this dialogue, nor with the extent to which the views advanced in fact represent those of the historical Protagoras. The passage is remarkable because it sets out the problem of punishment and its justification with remarkable lucidity and in much the same terms in which it has been debated in Europe and America since the late eighteenth century.

Protagoras raises the issue of punishment in connection with his contention that the civic virtues can be taught through instruction so as to prevent vice and injustice: "Just consider the function of punishment, Socrates, in relation to the wrongdoer. That will be enough to show you that men believe it possible to impart goodness" (324a).[7] This formulation suggests that punishment needs to be assessed in regard to its impact on the person who is the object of the penalty. That such a perspective inevitably raises the issue of justifying the pain or deprivation inflicted on the wrongdoer appears from the argument that Protagoras develops immediately afterwards: "In punishing wrongdoers, no one concentrates on the fact that a man has done wrong in the past, or punishes him on that account, unless taking blind vengeance like a beast [*hōsper thērion alogistōs*]" (324a–b). Here Protagoras conflates revenge and retribution, arguing that any backward looking rational for punishment is primitive or bestial. This is the central thrust of the critique of punishment by reformers from Beccaria and Bentham onward: that punishment as the mere infliction of pain in response to a past event cannot be justified.

In other words, Protagoras denies the force of the argument that wrongdoers or criminals should be punished simply because justice

---

[7] Translations of *Protagoras* are from Guthrie, Penguin edition, 1956.

"requires" it, because they "deserve" it, or because honor or the suffering of the victims demands it. Given the widespread notion in Greek culture from Homer onward, that revenge is "sweeter than honey dripping down the throat"[8] and that avenging homicide, for example, is a sacred religious duty,[9] Protagoras's view distances itself from contemporary values concerning the proper role of desert, retribution, and private revenge in criminal prosecutions. But it also does much more than this. It asserts the primacy of the policies of the state as the only legitimate rationales by which punishment can be justified. We will see in Chapter Eleven how private vengeance and public interest can easily be conflated in contemporary understandings of the operation of the criminal law. Protagoras here draws a strict line between the two spheres and argues that only public policies can justify punishment and, further, that such policies must look only to the future consequences of punishment: "No, punishment is not inflicted by a rational man for the sake of the crime that has been committed (after all one cannot undo the past), but for the sake of the future..." (324b).

On this account neither the suffering of the victims or their families nor the heinousness of the crime itself is relevant to the institution of punishment. Like all antiretributivists, Protagoras argues that the past cannot be undone and that punishment is not "for the sake of the crime" but for the sake of the future. The rejection of the notion that "the crime itself" demands a societal response implies a complete denial of the force of the notion of "moral desert" as the basis of justice or, as that notion of desert is variously expressed in different legal and cultural contexts, that "the balance must be restored," that "blood demands blood," or, in the vernacular of the *lex talionis*, an "eye for an eye." This rejection of conflated notions of revenge and retribution under the rubric of "blood demands blood" would have been familiar to Athenians from Aeschylus's portrayal of the demise of "blind" retributivism in the *Oresteia*.[10] At the end of the *Eumenides*, the final play of that trilogy, Orestes, a confessed matricide is acquitted at the first trial conducted by Athens's homicide court, and the angry spirits of retribution, the Erinyes, are domesticated in the service of the future political interests of the Athenian state. This trial is a literary fiction, of course, but in terms of its conceptualization of

---

[8] Homer, *Iliad*, 18.109, and cf. Aristotle, *Rhetoric*, 1378a.
[9] See, e.g., Plato, *Euthyphro*.
[10] "He who has wrought shall pay; that is the law. Then who shall tear the curse from their blood? The seed is stiffened to ruin" (*Agamemnon* 1564–66).

vengeance, retribution, and punishment it represents the same conflict explored by Protagoras between retrospective and prospective justifications of punishment. It also amply illustrates how forward-looking rationales of punishment, in emphasizing the interests of the polity as the only justification for punishment, blur the line between the issue of doing justice in the particular case at hand and the larger political context in which the judicial system as a whole operates.

Discussions of the goals of punishment in the Athenian orators confirm this view. Such discussions typically blend arguments about both justice and the interests of the demos being served by inflicting punishment on the accused. That is, they employ both backward- and forward-looking motivations. Lysias, for example, develops such a strategy in *Against Alcibiades*. He begins the oration with the language of private revenge and public retribution: "Since our fathers were previously at feud, and since my long-standing sense of his bad character has now been increased by mistreatment at his hands, I will try with your aid to make him pay the penalty for what he has done" (14.3). He later builds on his argument about the necessity of punishing the defendant by expounding on the future benefits to the *polis*. Punishment, he argues, aims not only at the offender but at the reform of other potential offenders as well. This is especially true if prominent offenders are punished, and the "citizens, with this example (*paradeigma*) before them, will be improved" (14.12–13; see also 45).[11] Demosthenes, in *Against Meidias* (21), deploys a similar argument about the benefits of punishment for the *polis*. The reason that hubris is committed so frequently, he claims, is the failure to punish offenders; to prevent hubris they must in the future always be punished (37). In his peroration he combines retributive and forward-looking perspectives in making an accumulative argument about the manifold nature of the positive consequences of punishment. If the judges vote to convict, he says, they will be coming to his aid, providing satisfaction for the demos, teaching others moderation, enabling themselves to lead their lives safely, and making an example of the defendant for the benefit of others (227).

---

[11] Lysias also makes this argument in *Against Nicomachus* (30.23–24): Severe punishment of criminals reforms others and does justice to the accused. This use of the idea of making an example (*paradeigma*) of the defendant, so familiar in modern discussions of punishment, is typical of Athenian thinking on the matter. Demosthenes asks the judges to punish Androtion for the sake of the victims [retribution] and to make him an example (*paradeigma*) to others so that they will act with moderation [deterrence]. (22.68 and cf. 88)

To return to Protagoras' view that punishment should only be inflicted "for the sake of the future," we must next ask precisely how he defines those future goods that the imposition of punishment provides. Protagoras, like most modern commentators on punishment, gives two answers to this question. The first answer is that punishment has as its aim, "to prevent either the same man or, by the spectacle of his punishment, someone else, from doing wrong again. But to hold such a view amounts to holding that punishment is inflicted as a deterrent [*apotropēs goun heneka kolazei*]." To use the vocabulary of modern criminal law, Protagoras here distinguishes between two kinds of deterrence: "general deterrence," which aims at using the punishment of an offender as an example to educate the populace as to the consequences of crime and to strike fear into the hearts of other potential criminals. Public torture, executions, or the display of the bodies of executed criminals, have been widely used as such "educational" devices by many legal systems from antiquity to the spectacular dismemberment of the French regicide, Damiens, in 1757, so indelibly commemorated by Foucault in the opening passages of *Discipline and Punish*.[12] The second kind of deterrence, "specific deterrence," aims at preventing the same wrongdoer from committing other offenses, whether through some kind of incapacitation, in the form of incarceration, banishment, or mutilation or through education by the pain of the punishment as an educational or motivational device to teach the offender that "crime does not pay." Although thinkers such as Protagoras typically have great faith in the educational and deterrent effect of punishment, as we will see, some Athenian intellectuals, like their modern counterparts, were skeptical about the actual deterrent effect of punishment on other would-be criminals. As in our own day, however, it was a commonplace in Athenian public discourse, at least as represented by the orators, that punishment served the purpose of setting an example for others. Protagoras's second answer to the question of the future goods advanced by punishment brings him back to the theme of education with which he began.

In modern debates about punishment, another rationale advanced to justify the institution also rejects backward-looking retribution but takes the argument about specific deterrence and the educational impact of punishment a step further. Proponents of rehabilitation argue that the "punishment" must be tailored so as to reform and educate the offender from within so that he or she may later prove to be a useful and

[12] (1977: 3–6).

law-abiding member of society.[13] In contemporary discussions these three positions are not necessarily mutually exclusive, and many commentators advance some combination of them as a multistranded justification. Protagoras also turns his account of punishment to its connection to education and inner reform. Having identified moral virtue (*aretē*, combining justice, moderation, and respect for the sacred) as the preeminent foundation for an orderly society (324e–325a), Protagoras considers what must be done with those who do not possess such virtues. Such an individual must, he maintains, be "instructed and corrected until by punishment he is reformed." This may seem very much in line with contemporary advocates of rehabilitation, who argue that it is the only humane and civilized reason to impose punishment, but the last part of Protagoras' remark provides a distinctively Greek qualification: "And whoever does not respond to punishment and instruction must be banished from the *polis* or put to death as incurable" (325a–b[14]).

Modern proponents of "scientific" rehabilitation tend to prefer permanent incarceration until the person is "cured," but two aspects of Protagoras's point bear examination. The first is the conceptualization, even if only metaphorically, of criminal disposition as a kind of disease, a medical problem. Education in the form of instruction *and* punishment is like a kind of medicine for the character. Because human beings can be educated in virtue, most will respond to the proper course of "treatment." Some, however, will not, and they are deemed incurable (325a *aniaton*). The second aspect has to do with the response to the "medical" dilemma of incurability. Even though the individual in question is in some sense "sick," if even only in a moral sense, this condition does not give rise to sympathetic treatment. Their "disease" of moral incurability is dangerous and demands a "social" treatment in the form of permanent expulsion or death. This treatment, or punishment, is not meted out because they "deserve" it according to some retributive logic, but rather simply to protect the state. This follows naturally from the forward-looking, utilitarian rationale adopted by Protagoras in the first place. Specific deterrence must be accomplished one way or the other. The best method is through education and the educational force of punishment. If this fails, however, the "diseased" member of

---

[13] For critiques of the rehabilitative ideal and an exploration of its implications, see Morris (1968) and the Hart–Wooten debate. For a devastating critique of the whole notion of penal reformation, see Foucault (1977: 135–56) and D. Garland (1985).

[14] See also the mythological account of the distribution of civic virtues to men by Zeus, ending with the admonition that, "if anyone is incapable of acquiring his share of these two virtues he shall be put to death as a *disease* to the city" (323d; my emphasis).

society must be permanently removed in the interests of protecting the community. This position is, as we will see, developed and explored at length in other Platonic dialogues. Before turning to these, we will first examine a text that expresses a robust skepticism for the kinds of deterrent arguments advanced by Protagoras.

THUCYDIDES: PUNISHMENT AND THE PROBLEM OF HUMAN NATURE[15]

In Book 3 of his *History of the Peloponnesian War,* Thucydides describes the revolt of the city of Mytilene, led by the oligarchic, pro-Spartan faction, against the hegemony of Athens. After capturing the city, the Athenians debated the fate of its citizens and decided to put all the men to death and sell the women and children into slavery. The next day, however, they began to feel that their decision was "cruel and unprecedented" because it encompassed the innocent and guilty alike (3.36). Thucydides' account of the debate uses two speeches to crystallize the opposing viewpoints not only on the fate of Mytilene, but also the process of political deliberation by which the Athenians should respond to such events. The debate on this issue, in turn, leads to a lengthy consideration of the question of the usefulness of punishment as a mechanism for guiding human behavior.

Thucydides represents the arguments in favor of killing the Mytilenians through a speech by the leading demagogue of the day, Cleon, a man "remarkable.... for the violence of his character" (3.36). That violence, as Thucydides shows, manifests itself in his approach to political decision making, where Cleon tells the Athenian Assembly that they should act like judges and punish the Mytilenians as criminals guilty of "calculated aggression" (3.39). His argument about punishment emphasizes retributive notions of desert: "Let them now therefore have the punishment which their crime deserves... Pay them back in their own coin.... Pay them back for it...." (3.39–40). But he also claims that such punishment will be in the interests of the Athenians because of its deterrent effect on other cities: "Make an example [*paradeigma*] of them to your other allies" (3.40). In summation he concludes that by punishing the Mytilenians in the way he suggests, Athens will both be doing what is just and acting in her own interests (3.40).[16]

---
[15] Translations are from Rex Warner, the Penguin edition of Thucydides (1954).
[16] See also 3.39: "Now think of your allies. If you are going to give the same punishment to those who are forced to revolt by your enemies as those who do so of their own accord,

What is also noteworthy about his rationale is that he conflates the distinction between private vengeance and public retribution by casting the Assembly as both judges and the injured party. As such, he urges them not to deliberate objectively but rather to act in anger, as if in the heat of the moment: "...[D]elay...is to the advantage of the guilty party. After a lapse of time the injured party will lose the edge of his anger when he comes to act against those who have wronged him; whereas the best punishment and the one most suited to the crime is when retaliation follows immediately" (3.38). In his peroration he returns to this theme, telling the Athenians to imagine how they felt when they first learned of their injury and to "remember how then you would have given anything to have them in your power. Now pay them back..." (3.40).

It is perhaps worth noting that in the Athenian orators one also finds such arguments about the role of anger in forensic judgments.[17] In *Against Aristogiton* (2), for example, Dinarchus tells the judges that they should hate such wrongdoers as the defendant, recall their anger at what he has done in the past, and kill him. The confusion of judicial retribution and private revenge is emphasized by the fact that he does not ask them to *punish* the accused, but simply to *kill* him. In the Demosthenic oration, *Against Conon* (54.42–43), the speaker also asks the judges to share in the anger he feels toward Conon and claims they should not regard this as a private matter but as something that might happen to any man. Like Cleon, he then appeals to the personal interests of the judges by invoking the deterrent affect of punishment: "Will it be in the interests of each of you to let off a man who beats people up and commits hubris? I think not. But if you let him go there will be many, if you punish him, fewer." Such appeals to interest might easily lead into the political realm, as in *Against Philocles*, where, in language reminiscent of post–9/11 America, Dinarchus tells the Athenian judges that they must respond differently to threats to the *polis* than to other cases. He says that although in the case of other crimes they must first carefully and meticulously establish the truth and only then decide on the punishment for the offender; in the case of open treason on which everyone agrees, they should *give sway to anger* and the desire for revenge or punishment [*timōria*] that goes with it (3.8).[18]

---

can you not see that they will all revolt upon the slightest pretext, when success means freedom and failure brings no very dreadful consequences."

[17] For a comprehensive treatment of anger, see the magisterial account of W. Harris (2001).

[18] Note how this passage plays on the wide meaning of *timōria*, encompassing both private revenge and legal penalties. He later sums up what he considers to be the appropriate

From a philosophical perspective Cleon's version of retributive justice is not justice at all, because he calls on the Assembly to put to death the entire population and not just the oligarchic leaders who instigated the revolt. He explicitly claims that they, "rightly or wrongly must be punished" if Athens is to maintain her imperial power. This is not retributive justice, but a combination of revenge exacted in anger and the instrumental use of punishment, including of the innocent, to further political goals. These are precisely the "serpent-windings" of utilitarian thinking about punishment that Kant inveighed against, but whatever their philosophical shortcomings their rhetorical appeal to the emotions of an angered citizenry are obvious. It is precisely this quality that makes Thucydides' account of Cleon's speech such a great example of demagogic oratory. Because, as Plato tirelessly pointed out, the demos is not likely to listen to philosophical discourse, what rhetorical strategy can counter the power of this emotional appeal to the desire for vengeance? This is the challenge that faces Diodotus, the speaker whom Thucydides portrays as successfully answering the claims made by Cleon.

To meet this challenge, Diodotus must offer an alternative account of political deliberation, which he does by, among other things, reminding the Assembly that wise decisions are not made in anger and that "this is not a law court, where we have come to consider what is fit and just; it is a political assembly, and the question is how Mytilene can be most useful to Athens" (3.44). Having said this, he goes on to meet at length Cleon's argument for the deterrent affect of punishment. He does this primarily by denying that the fear of future punishment can have sufficient motivational force to alter an individual's (or city's) intent once they have embarked on a course of action:

> Cities and individuals alike all are by nature disposed to do wrong, and there is no law that will prevent it, as is shown by the fact that men have tried every kind of punishment, constantly adding to the list, in the attempt to find greater security from criminals.... Either, therefore, we must discover some fear more potent than death, or we must admit that here certainly we have not got an adequate deterrent.

emotional disposition of the judges: "You must hate the wicked and eradicate such monsters from the city, and show the world that the demos has not been corrupted by the orators and generals, nor enslaved on account of their reputations..." (3.19).

Why is it, on Diodotus's view, that the fear of future punishment is ineffective? He first argues that despite the death penalty, individuals and states typically feel confident that if they take the risk they will probably get away with it (3.45). Building on this feeling of false confidence, he suggests a variety of sociological, psychological, and cultural factors and dispositions that lead to criminal behavior:

> So long as poverty forces men to be bold, so long as the insolence and pride of wealth nourish their ambitions, and in other accidents of life they are continually dominated by some master passion or another, so long will their impulses drive them into danger. Hope and desire persist throughout and cause the greatest calamities... Then too, the idea that fortune will be on one's side plays as big a part as anything else in creating a mood of over-confidence....

Against such motivating factors, he argues, law is powerless, for it is simply part of human nature to act on the basis of such motivations no matter how much they fly in the face of prudential considerations. As he sums it up, "In a word it is impossible.... for human nature, when once seriously set upon a course, to be prevented from following that course *by the force of law or by any other means of intimidation whatever*" (3.45; my emphasis).

This is a rather bleak assessment, not only of human nature, but also of the possibility for law as a mechanism for maintaining social order through the institution of punishment. Deterrence, Diodotus claims, is simply wishful thinking. He does not claim that it works imperfectly, but rather that it is "impossible," that it, whether operating through law or any other threat, cannot stand up against the force of human nature once set on fulfilling a desire. It is not merely that desire is so strong, but that human beings will use their rationalizing capacity to imagine that hope or fortune will enable them to succeed. How then can civic order be maintained? Is law utterly useless?[19]

Diodotus does not answer this question directly, for he turns from his examination of the shortcomings of deterrence to an account of how

---

[19] In *Against Aristogeiton* I (25), Demosthenes offers a similarly negative assessment of human nature, but a very different account of its relation to law. Law, he explains, is universal, whereas human nature is unpredictable and individual and inclines men to injustice. It is only the law that restrains them. Thus, the two goals of all laws are to deter men from wrongdoing and, by punishing the transgressor, to make the rest better (15–17). Without legal punishment, he concludes, chaos would reign (25–27).

the Athenian empire and its allies can best be managed, This, of course, is in keeping with his admonition that the decision before them is one to be made by a political assembly and not a court of law. His answer, however, may be extrapolated from the international to the domestic context. He says that true security for Athens lies in moderation, not in inflicting severe punishment, and in "good administration rather than in the fear of legal penalties" (46). Fairness, moderation, and good administration will prevent cities "from even contemplating the idea of revolt" (46). The civic analog to this would involve a legal system that relies on a social order that inhibits the formation of the poverty, desire, arrogance, and envy that Diodotus identifies as the causes of criminal behavior, a legal order that operates through motivational factors other than the fear of punishment. The negative exemplar of the ideal legal system is described by Thucydides later in Book 3, when he analyzes the nature and causes of civil strife in the city of Corcyra. There, the preemption and abuse of legal institutions by rival political factions sets in motion a downward spiral of self-destruction in which both human and divine laws are powerless to prevent or discourage even the most horrific forms of violence. Thucydides appears convinced that a system of laws can succeed in preserving order only where the laws are fairly and impartially applied and the citizens understand that the preservation of civic institutions is more important than their own individual short-term self-interest.

It is beyond the purview of Thucydides' concerns to describe how such a legal order might come into being or what it would be like. All Greek political thinkers, however, were well aware of the fragility of legal institutions in their world. In many ways Greek political thought is fundamentally a response to the potential for civil strife and instability within the *polis*.[20] All other Greek political theorists also shared Thucydides' conviction that a legal system based primarily on the fear of punishment was unlikely to prove effective in maintaining the social order, particularly in times of need or crisis. Accordingly, thinkers such as Isocrates, Aristotle, and, above all, Plato turned their speculative abilities to incorporating legal punishment into a larger framework of education and socialization that would inculcate the kinds of moral dispositions that might make law an effective guide for human behavior. In the remainder of this chapter we will briefly assess two such philosophical attempts to provide a fuller and potentially more successful theory of punishment.

---

[20] See D. Cohen (1995: Chapter 2) and Gehrke 1985.

ISOCRATES: EDUCATION, NOT PUNISHMENT, MAKES GOOD CITIZENS

Isocrates' sketch, in *Areopagiticus* (7), of how Athenian institutions might be reformed for the better proceeds from assumptions about law and punishment very similar to those articulated by Diodotus. The forefathers of the present day Athenians realized, he states, that "where there is a multitude of specific laws, it is a sign that the state is badly governed; for it is in the attempt to build up dikes against the spread of crime that men in such a state feel constrained to multiply the laws." "Being of this mind," he continues, "our forefathers did not seek to discover first how they should penalize men who were lawless, but how they should produce citizens who would refrain from any punishable act. They thought this was their duty, for it was proper for private enemies alone to be zealous in the avenging of crimes" (40–41).

Isocrates' remarks reveal a skepticism, similar to that of Diodotus, about the deterrent force of punishment. A badly governed state will vainly attempt to prevent crime by passing ever more laws, but laws in themselves are not sufficient for this task. Officials may seek to enforce these laws with great energy, but such attempts will also fail. What this implies for Isocrates is a clear recognition of the limited value of either deterrent or retributive thinking. His analysis reinforces a strong divide between revenge, to be associated only with private enmity, and the administration of justice by those who enjoy a public trust. Those who are responsible for the administration of justice should not be eager (unlike Cleon) to inflict punishments for their own sake, but should be thinking about how to improve the virtue of the citizenry so as to prevent the commission of crime in the first place (much like the logic of Diodotus). These efforts must be directed beyond the simplistic notion of "education" through the example of punishment (41–42). This forward-looking perspective on preventing criminal behavior by addressing the *source* of the dispositions that produce it vitiates the need either for exacting strict punishment on the basis of desert or for using punishment as an deterrent to others. Isocrates does not reject the role of law altogether, but rather simply the notion that the *polis* will benefit from making ever more specific laws for every possible criminal act and punishing violations of the laws with zeal. "Men who are badly reared," he maintains, "will venture to transgress even laws which are drawn up with minute exactness." It is not that law cannot ever be effective, but only when it is combined with proper moral dispositions, for "Those who are well brought up will be willing to respect even a simple code" (41–42). How then is such a legal system to be constructed and what role in it is there for punishment to play?

In keeping with his nostalgic reconstruction of a golden age of moral order, Isocrates looks to the powers once enjoyed by the Areopagus and to the more "balanced" (i.e., less radically democratic) ancestral constitution as sources of inspiration for present reform. In regard to the role of law, he emphasizes that only proper socialization from the earliest age can produce the kinds of citizens who are naturally disposed to obey the law and act with moderation and self-restraint. He imagines the members of the ancient Areopagus as having understood the falsehood of the belief that "the best citizens are produced in a state where the laws are prescribed with the greatest exactness" (7.39). Instead, they realized that "virtue is not established through written laws but by the habits of daily life, for most men tend to assimilate the manners and morals in which they have been reared" (40). This socialization must begin at a very early age and should be exercised with greatest diligence over the young, who are filled with desires and disposed to be unruly (43). Such supervision should continue when they are adults, for they are not "watched over in their boyhood only to be allowed to do what they like upon reaching manhood" (37). This previous regime covered all aspects of life and assigned young men work and activities befitting their social station to make sure that they were not idle (44–45). The Areopagus was the nodal point of this disciplinary (in the Foucauldian sense) fantasy, rebuking, warning, and punishing wayward citizens as was appropriate (46). For they understood that, "where it is not easy for wrongdoers to escape detection, or, when detected, to obtain indulgence, there the impulse to do wrong disappears. Understanding this, they restrained the people from wrongdoing in both ways – both by punishment and by watchfulness" (47).

One might well ask here whether Isocrates has not arrived back at the very deterrent theory he earlier rejected. Doesn't this evocation of the salutary effects of punishment and discipline contradict his denial that the example of punishment had a deterrent effect? The answer to this question is no, because Isocrates saw a fundamental distinction between the notion that lots of laws and zealous enforcement would produce orderly citizens and the regime of the Areopagus he advocated. The socializing effect of the latter came not from laws and their sporadic enforcement when a wrongdoer was detected, but rather through the ongoing *regime* of supervision and discipline that lasted from childhood to maturity. The presence of the Areopagus was always to be felt, so as to inculcate proper dispositions of self-restraint, moderation, and obedience to the principles of virtue one had been taught.[21] The Areopagus intervened whenever and however necessary, warning, admonishing, rebuking, and punishing as it saw fit. That this is a disciplinary model, and not a judicial framework of the enforcement of laws through the mechanism of trials, is made absolutely clear by the continuation of passage cited at the end of last paragraph: "For so far from failing to detect those who had gone astray, they actually saw in advance those who were likely to commit some offense. Therefore the young men did not waste their time in the gambling-dens or with flute girls ... but remained steadfastly in the pursuits to which they had been assigned" (7.47–8). In other words (and in keeping with Aristotle's description of its discretionary power to punish, *Ath. Pol.*), the Areopagus exercised a kind of censorial power over the conduct of the citizens that did not depend on the transgression of those many "specific" laws whose usefulness Isocrates rejected.

Of course from this perspective such specific laws are always a hindrance to censorial discretion, because on the Athenian democratic understanding of the rule of law they are meant to define the *limits* of, as well as the legitimate instances of, the state's intervention in the lives of its citizens. This is part of Isocrates' hostility to such laws, for he wants public officials to be able to call citizens to account and, if they see fit, to "punish" them, even when no specific law has been broken. For the deterrent effect of punishment based on violations of legal statutes, Isocrates substitutes the internalized awareness that the watchful eye of the Council will detect any deviations from prescribed norms of daily conduct.[22] From this perspective, one can understand why Isocrates so readily discards not only retributive rationales, but also the kind of forward-looking policies advocated by Protagoras. From

---

[21] The importance of socialization is also acknowledged in the orators, but without going to the extremes recommended by Isocrates. Rather it is seen as working together with the deterrent effect of legal punishment. Thus, Lycurgus (*Against Leocrates*) develops an argument about punishment that blends deterrence with socialization. Punishment serves as one of the two key forces in shaping the character and dispositions of the young: In punishing wrongdoers the judges provide an incentive to the young to right conduct. There are two influences on the young: the punishments suffered by wrongdoers and the rewards to the virtuous. Fear is the basis of one, and the desire for honor of the other (1.9–10, 14–15).

[22] In *Politics*, Aristotle adopts much the same view of broad and discretionary magisterial powers as the appropriate solution to the problem of maintaining social order, though he connects it to a far more elaborate theory of constitutional reform designed to produce a virtuous and stable polity.

this perspective one can also appreciate the force of the claim somewhat paradoxically advanced by contemporary scholars that individuals have a right to punishment, because punishment respects them as autonomous citizens rather than objects of manipulation by the apparatus of the state.[23] Such concerns about respecting the autonomy of citizens have also been voiced in regard to the most highly developed theory of punishment in antiquity, or indeed anywhere in the Western tradition until the eighteenth century, and it is to that that theory that we now turn.[24]

Plato and the Philosophy of Punishment

Given the space limitations and scope of this volume it is impossible here to discuss Plato's theory of punishment in any detail. Plato develops his thinking about punishment over the entire span of his oeuvre, encompassing major dialogues such as *Gorgias*, *Protagoras*, *Republic*, and *Laws*, to name only those where it most prominently appears. His account of punishment has also been the subject of book-length scholarly treatments.[25] More significantly, to do justice to the complexity of his position, one must also locate it within his treatment of law and justice in general, which in turn cannot be done without discussing his political philosophy as a whole, the immortality of soul, the nature of virtue, and a host of other related topics. What follows then will be merely a brief reference to a number of passages where Plato provides his own unique interpretation of some of the themes discussed above. At the most, such a discussion may serve to stimulate readers to investigate this rich and rewarding topic that has by no means been fully explored.

Plato first explores the issue of punishment at some length in *Gorgias*, where it grows out of a discussion of the educational and political benefits of philosophy as opposed to rhetoric. Simplifying a good deal, a discussion of the nature of happiness and the good life leads Plato's Socrates to posit that the person who is punished for his wrongdoing will be happier and better off than someone who escapes any legal penalties (472–3). This apparently simple proposition appears so paradoxical to

---

[23] See particularly Morris (1968) and (1981) working creatively from a contemporary reinterpretation of a Kantian view of retributivism.
[24] Apart from the more infamous version of such concerns advanced by Popper (1966), see the still unsurpassed account by Adkins (1961).
[25] See Mackenzie (1981) and Saunders (1991), with extensive bibliography.

his interlocutors that one of them remarks that if it were true it would "turn human life completely upside down" (481). Plato's position proceeds from a similar starting point to that invoked by Protagoras, namely that punishment can serve an important educational purpose in curing the moral "disease" of wrongdoing. In *Gorgias*, Plato, rather than focusing on the educational/deterrent effect on others, concentrates on the "moral physician" of justice, which represents the sole cure for the soul of the wrongdoer of the "excesses" that dispose it to wrongdoing (478). The instrument of that "cure" is punishment, which alone can deliver an individual from the worst of all fates, which is the incurable state of being a person disposed to evil rather than to moral virtue (478–9).

If this position seems strange to modern ears, it was virtually incomprehensible within the system of traditional Greek values.[26] Plato was well aware of the revolutionary nature of his views and takes great care in *Gorgias* to emphasize the paradoxical nature of this theory of punishment by carrying it to its most extreme formulation. Thus the person who commits wrong and wants to achieve happiness and wellbeing must seek punishment, "whether it be flogging, or imprisonment, or a fine, or banishment, or death. He must be the first to accuse himself and members of his family...." It follows from the same principles, Socrates continues, that if one really wanted to harm an enemy, instead of denouncing or prosecuting him, one would do one's utmost to ensure that he was *not* punished, for this would mean that he would suffer the ultimate harm (470–81).

At the end of the dialogue Plato presents a myth of the judgment of souls in the netherworld, where the true cost of unredeemed wrongdoing is made apparent. In commenting on this myth he returns to a somewhat more conventional sounding assessment of punishment and its purposes (525):

> The object of all punishment which is rightly inflicted should be either to improve and benefit its subject or else to make an example to him of others, who will be deterred at the sight of his sufferings and reform their own conduct. The men who are helped by undergoing punishment, whether by god or by man, are those whose faults are remediable; yet both in this world and the next this benefit is procurable only at the cost of pain and anguish. Those who have committed the deadliest wrongs.... being incurable... do good

[26] See Adkins (1961).

to others, who see them suffering an eternity of the most severe and terrible torments... They are literally hung up as object lessons in the prison-house of Hades, in order that every newly arrived wrongdoer may contemplate them and take the warning to heart.

In this passage Plato uses the language of deterrence and education/rehabilitation, but in a context far removed from the debates discussed in previous sections of this chapter. The metaphysical theory of punishment here rests not on considerations of political policy, but on notions of moral virtue that are rooted in a certain conception of the nature of the soul and of the human capacity for reason. The mythological portrayal of the souls in Hades serves as an explanatory device for the proposition that Socrates' interlocutors, Polus and Callicles, find so perplexing. This is, of course, the proposition that the happiest and best life is not that of the tyrant, who can satisfy all of his desires with impunity, unrestrained by law or morality, but rather that of the truly virtuous man, who, even if he is an impoverished philosopher unjustly condemned to death, leads the life most to be envied. The tyrant, on the other hand, is most to be pitied, because he suffers the punishment his crimes deserve; that of being who he is, a man irredeemably devoid of reason and virtue.

In his last dialogue, *Laws*, Plato must move beyond the metaphysics of punishment to its institutional manifestations. In this last dialogue, Plato imagines and legislates for the foundation of an ideal community that will achieve social harmony and political stability. His solution of how to do so is to retreat from the rule of philosopher-kings as developed in the *Republic* and substitute in its place the rule of law.[27] The entire social and political system of this ideal community emphasizes the crucial role of an educational system that is designed to inculcate moral virtue, based on a proper balance of the rational and irrational parts of the soul, from the earliest age. The law statutes themselves are adapted to this purpose, for rather than merely threatening a punishment for transgressions (and thus treating free citizens like slaves, according to Plato), they are preceded by preambles that persuade the citizens of the wisdom and rightness of the provisions. Plato's conception of the rule of law demands that citizens avoid wrongdoing through the exercise of their rational capacities, as taught through education and

---

[27] See D. Cohen (1993) for an analysis of Plato's concept of the rule of law in this dialogue. For different views see Morrow (1960) and Saunders (1991).

socialization, rather than merely blindly obeying the law in response to its threats of punishment.[28] To the extent such an educational system succeeds, punishment will scarcely be necessary, but Plato proceeds from the assumption that some individuals will nonetheless always be disposed toward wrongdoing. What then is to be done with them?

The penal provisions of the laws are designed to deter those few citizens whose bad character is too resistant to have been properly formed by the educational system (853). When someone has violated one of the laws, the response will "combine instruction and constraint" so as to prevent the criminal from committing such violations in the future. The modes of instruction are to be flexible and matched to the needs of the offender and situation: "We may take action or simply talk to the criminal. We may grant him pleasures or make him suffer. We may honor him; we may disgrace him. We can fine him, or give him gifts. We may use absolutely *any* means to make him hate injustice and embrace true justice..."[29] (862). The variety of these negative and positive incentives, as well as the lack of limits on them, indicates the totality of the rejection of a retributive notion that wrongdoing necessarily demands the infliction of a legal penalty. Like Protagoras, Plato's concern is to cure a diseased part of the body politic. But what if the disease resists cure? Again like the views of Protagoras as he portrays them, Plato is ruthless in his response. He claims, in a manner reminiscent of the theories of punishment in *Gorgias*, that even the wrongdoer himself "will recognize that the best thing for all such people is to cease to live – best even for themselves. By passing on they will help others too: first, they will constitute a warning against injustice, and secondly they will leave the state free of scoundrels. That is why the legislator should prescribe the death penalty in such cases... but in no other case whatever" (862–3).

Plato seems to believe that no matter how good a system of education one provides, there will always be citizens who resist the moral socialization that inculcates the disposition to follow the law of one's own volition. When such a person is convicted of a crime, all means of education and persuasion are to be used to bring them around to virtue. If, however, they resist this "cure," they are simply to be excised from the state. Punishment in its most severe form thus remains the fallback position for protecting the social order when other, "gentler" means fail.

---

[28] See D. Cohen (1993) for a detailed account of this position and of the centrality of the notion of moral autonomy in Plato's conception of the rule of law.

[29] Translations are taken from T. Saunders's (1970) Penguin edition.

The lengths to which Plato appears prepared to go to defend the health of the political community against those who threaten to contaminate it appears most clearly in his treatment of the crime of impiety. As in classical Athens, impiety in Plato's city can ultimately be punished by death. Unlike Athens, however, the first commission of such a crime by a person who "has fallen victim to foolishness" is punished by a five-year term in a "reform center," where the prisoner will be restored to "health." Should this "treatment" fail and he is reconvicted of the same offense, he should be punished with death. On the other hand, those who commit impiety out of a fixed disposition that leads them to believe that the gods do not exist or that they can be bribed, and so on, are to be treated differently. Because they represent a much greater threat to a state in which civic religion is a foundational element of moral socialization, they are treated as incurable. Such offenders are to be cut off from all social contact and imprisoned until they die. Their bodies are then to be cast beyond the boundaries of the state (908–09).

Here one sees the moral limits of Plato's "therapeutic" approach to punishment. The interests of the "health" of the political community are weighted so heavily that the individual who is an atheist out of conviction is treated as a source of infection that must be prevented at all costs from spreading. Although not put to death like the repeat offender, he is isolated for the rest of his life in conditions of confinement. As with any theory of punishment that focuses on the larger societal interests that punishment may serve rather than on the moral responsibility of the individual offender, the result will always tend to be that the interests of society prevail. This is the danger of making the decision to punish in individual cases the product of a social and, inevitably, political calculus. This was a danger largely unrecognized by Greek theories of punishment because, as indicated above and in Chapter 11, it was so natural in their political discourse to identify justice with the interests of the demos or *polis*. It is ironic (and one can only wonder if Plato did not acutely appreciate this irony) that this common feature unites Plato's condemnation of the individual impious by conviction with the Athenian judges' condemnation of Socrates on the same charge.

10: THE RHETORIC OF LAW IN FOURTH-CENTURY ATHENS

Harvey Yunis

Following a brief exposition of the rise of rhetoric in Athenian democracy, the first task of this chapter is to explain how rhetoric became a primary instrument of the judicial process in fourth-century Athens even though rhetoric had no intrinsic interest in the law. The second task of this chapter is to demonstrate how rhetoricians spoke about the law and used it for rhetorical purposes in speeches delivered by them or others before the law courts of Athens.

ATHENIAN DEMOCRACY AND THE RISE OF RHETORIC

The Athenian democracy of the fifth and fourth centuries B.C.E had no executive office or executive council. Rather, official, binding decisions were made in two public, democratic institutions, the Assembly and the courts. The purpose of both institutions was to express the will of the *demos* – that is, the mass of ordinary citizens who made up the vast bulk of the citizen body and wielded power in the state – in a fair, open, institutionally stable way. The *demos* delegated tasks and decisions to lesser institutions or colleges of magistrates in the name of efficiency. Initiatives in the Assembly and courts were in the hands of individuals, who competed for political leadership. And the *demos* often reconsidered or revised its own decisions. But there were no institutional mechanisms to limit the *demos'* sphere of activity, and there was no doctrine of rights restricting the will of the *demos*. The power of the *demos* within the state was absolute, its decisions in the Assembly and courts were final and not subject to appeal.[1]

There were differences in the procedures that governed the organization and conduct of the Assembly and the courts, but the same underlying process operated in both institutions and gave them both democratic integrity. A large audience of ordinary, anonymous citizens, effectively representing the *demos* as a whole, listened to a debate among individual citizens on whatever question was to be decided. At the conclusion of the debate the audience voted and the question was decided. (In the Assembly the debate was open-ended; in the courts the debate pitted prosecutor against defendant.) Hence, the state's decisions in the Assembly and courts depended on the debate that preceded and led to the vote. Individual citizens acquired power in the community, or lost it, precisely to the extent that they could persuade the audiences in the Assembly and courts to vote in their favor and against their opponents.[2]

With such an enormous premium on the ability to manipulate popular audiences and defeat opponents by means of the spoken word, persuasive speaking naturally became the focus of considerable energy and intelligence. Throughout Greece at this time, the empirical and theoretical sciences were mushrooming. The tendency to theorize and systematize experience led in the realm of public speaking to the development of rhetoric (from *rhētorikē technē*, literally "art of speaking") as a formal discipline. By the early fourth century, rhetoric was producing teachers, students, schools, and handbooks. It developed its own theories, principles, practices, and controversies. One crucial consequence of the formation of a discipline is the ability to articulate and pursue goals that pertain strictly to that discipline and are independent of all other concerns. So in the case of rhetoric, the only goal that it considers is how to win the audience over to the speaker's view; in court that means victory over the opponent. Because from the point of view of rhetoric victory is the only objective, everything else – justice,

---

[1] The key statements on the nature of Athenian democracy are Finley (1973, 1983). On the evolution of Athenian democracy, its institutions, and its procedures, see Hansen (1991), Bleicken (1994). Proper description of Athenian democracy remains controversial in certain points; for an account, with review of the bibliography, see Millett (2000).

[2] On the Assembly and courts as parallel venues for the will of the *demos*, see Ober (1989: 141–7), Bleicken (1994: 224–8). On the problems of mass discourse and decision-making in democratic Athens, see Ober (1989), Yunis (1996).

law, statutes, communal welfare – is reduced to merely instrumental interest.[3]

The growth of the discipline of rhetoric gave forensic speeches a use beyond the circumstances in which they were originally delivered: written copies were produced, circulated, and preserved as examples of rhetorical art. Some preserved speeches were both composed and delivered by the litigant for a trial that he was involved in. In other cases, a citizen involved in a legal dispute could buy a speech composed specifically for his case from a professional speechwriter (*logographos*). This was an important, if expensive, service for a citizen untrained in rhetoric or inexperienced in public speaking; he would memorize the speech and recite it in court.[4] For present purposes the two kinds of speeches can be treated alike. All the extant material stems from the most experienced and highly skilled rhetoricians of fourth-century Athens.[5] They all use the same terminology and approach their task in the same basic way: seeking to compose a winning speech, they subordinate everything to that purpose.

ATHENIAN TRIALS AS RHETORICAL CONTESTS

In many respects, a trial in fourth-century Athens was not unlike what goes on in a modern court in the Anglo-American world. The trial was conducted on the basis of a specific indictment that presented a legal basis for the court's decision. The court followed established procedures designed to insure fairness. Prosecution and defense faced off on equal terms before a jury of their peers. The court's decision followed the adversarial encounter between the contending parties. It was generally

---

[3] On the development of rhetoric as a discipline, see Cole (1991). On the influence of Athenian democracy on the development of rhetoric, see Yunis (1998). On the rhetorical schools and rhetoricians of fourth-century Athens, see Kennedy (1963). On the growth of science and disciplinary knowledge and the role of the sophists, see Lloyd (1979), Kerferd (1981).

[4] Reading from a text in hand would have breached the taboo against written texts in court (discussed below). Logographic speeches make up about two-thirds of the roughly 100 complete Athenian forensic speeches that survive; see Usher (1999) for a guide to this material. Quotations and fragments of other speeches also survive. Todd (this volume) discusses logographic speeches in the context of Athenian law. On professional speechwriting in Athens, see Lavency (1964), Dover (1968b: 148–74), Usher (1976).

[5] On the canon of ten Athenian orators, which comprises all the surviving historical material of Athenian oratory, see Worthington (1994).

accepted that trials contributed to the rule of law, which was essential for communal welfare. Insofar as Athenian litigants pursued victory in court while exploiting the rules of the justice system to the extent possible, they seem no different than modern trial lawyers.

But one crucial difference between an Athenian trial and its modern counterpart gave rhetoric a scope for operation in Athenian courts that is scarcely possible in a modern court of law. Athenian trials lacked any mechanism for considering *on the basis of norms derived from the law itself* what the law was and what the law required in the case at hand. That is, Athenian trials were not informed by the demands of jurisprudence, which might inhibit the litigants' naked pursuit of victory by enforcing adherence to independently established norms of law. As a result, Athenian litigants had free rein. They could, and did, dispute the law, but there was no third party to intervene and hold litigants to an independent, impartial, or scientific standard of legal argument.[6]

In an Athenian trial only three parties were involved: prosecutor, defendant, and a panel of citizens, known as *dikastai* (literally "judges"), who, combining the functions of judge and jury, determined the outcome. All three parties functioned without training, expertise, or supervision in the law. Prosecution and defense spoke in turn for an equal amount of time. When they were finished, the *dikastai* voted by secret ballot for either the prosecutor or the defendant; simple majority ruled. The *dikastai* had no opportunity to question the litigants or to discuss the case among themselves. There was no presiding legal officer to impose rules of evidence or relevance, to require litigants to address any matter of fact or law, or to question or limit the litigants in the presentation of their cases. Scrutiny of the statutes at stake never developed into an official part of the process that issued in the court's decision. A trial would take no more than several hours, even for cases that were crucial for the community as a whole. The court's decision was final, issued summarily, and not subject to appeal.[7] Thus, in an Athenian trial litigants had

---

[6] The critical legal studies movement has questioned whether there is, or can be, an independent, impartial, or scientific standard of legal argument. This chapter takes no view on that issue, but merely cites the traditional role of jurisprudence for the sake of comparison with the Athenian situation. Even if the traditional standards of jurisprudence prove to be untenable, the dynamic of modern courts, in which a judge guides the proceedings, differs fundamentally from the unguided proceedings of an Athenian court. For a history of Anglo-American jurisprudence that includes critical legal studies, see Coquillette (1999). On the beginnings of jurisprudence in Greek thought, which had little influence on the conduct of Athenian trials, see Jones (1956), Romilly (1971).

[7] On the procedures of Athenian trials, see Hansen (1991: 178–224).

no institutionally imposed constraints on what they could say during their allotted time. The only effective constraint was rhetorical; that is, litigants would constrain themselves from saying anything that might alienate their audience, the *dikastai*.

Other factors minimized the legal expertise that was brought to bear in an Athenian trial. First, trials functioned largely without the use of written documents. Although literacy was expanding rapidly in fourth-century Greece, only the pretrial stage of Athenian legal adjudication was affected.[8] Full literacy was still restricted to the upper class (and to slave functionaries of the state and upper class families). A large portion of the citizen body, if not the bulk of it, was either barely literate or functionally illiterate. Because average citizens had to maintain access to the legal system and also had to represent themselves in court, a high degree of literacy could not be required just to participate in a trial and address a court. Further, in spite of an attempt to organize the body of statutes into a written, publicly accessible form, in fact the statutes were neither well organized nor easily accessible. A public archive existed but was neither systematic nor comprehensive.[9] Court proceedings were not recorded in writing. Briefs formed no part of the legal process. To preserve the power of the ordinary citizens en masse, Athens' courts, like the Assembly, continued to rely on oral procedures and confined literacy to areas where it would not hinder the participation of the masses. Thus, the possibilities of legal examination that writing and legal texts might have provided were never exploited in Athenian courts.[10]

Second, whereas Athenian democracy hastened the development of a discipline devoted to persuasive speaking, it hindered a similar development with regard to law. The introduction of a trained, independent judiciary or trained legal advocates into court proceedings would have been perceived as an intrusion on the direct democratic rule of

---

[8] The Athenian legal procedure known as *graphē* (literally "writing"), used for disputes of public import, required the indictment to be submitted in writing when the case was initiated and vetted; in 403 the Athenians decided that henceforth only written laws would be recognized as valid; and witnesses no longer testified in court, but depositions taken down in writing were read out to the court. On the importance of writing in the development of Greek law, see Gagarin (2003). On writing and law in fourth-century Athens, see Sealey (1987: 35–41). On literacy in classical Athens, see W. V. Harris (1989: 65–115), Thomas (1989).

[9] On the attempt at organization of the laws at the end of the fifth century, see Todd (1996). On the public archives in Athens, see Sickinger (1999).

[10] On the persistence of oral practices in preference to written documents in the Athenian courts, see Cohen (2003).

the masses.[11] As ordinary citizens in good standing, the *dikastai* were deemed to have no need of special training to decide legal disputes. Like the great questions of state policy that were debated and decided in the Assembly, so too legal disputes were considered to fall within the natural and proper competence of every ordinary citizen. Any suggestion to the contrary would give offense and meet with resistance.

Issues of law in an Athenian court were further muddied by the fact that, far from attempting to insulate legal decisions from political ones, the Athenians consciously mixed the two together. The courts considered explicitly political charges such as treason, misconduct in office, and public fraud. But charges that were not explicitly political, such as embezzlement, impiety, homosexual prostitution, and many others, were also used to bring disputes among politicians into court. In such cases the litigants' political motives were patent, the political arguments were explicit, and the court's decision was recognized as bearing on public policy. This meant that arguments on the law would complement and compete with arguments on the integrity, loyalty, communal service, and political and military record of both prosecutor and defendant. But the range of nonlegal concerns that were introduced to an Athenian court went well beyond politics. It was normal for an Athenian litigant to refer to his or his opponent's social and economic status, family background, education, and moral character. Outright vituperation and character assassination were customary in court. Such pleas, clearly intended to bias the *dikastai* in favor of the speaker and against the opponent, would normally be excluded in a modern court of law as defamatory and prejudicial. The Athenians, who had no notion of modern jurisprudence, entertained such pleas in court on the view that a litigant's social standing, character, and family background could well affect communal welfare, which it was the court's duty to protect. In an Athenian trial it was impossible to separate law, politics, ideology, and the litigants' style and personality. All were on trial simultaneously.[12]

In these circumstances, the Greek word for a trial in court, *agōn* (literally "competition"), was entirely apt: an Athenian trial was an all-out

---

[11] Advocates (*synēgoroi*) were used on the basis of political or family ties, but unlike speechwriters, who worked only behind the scenes, they were not professionals and not available for hire. On advocacy in Athenian trials, see Wolff (1968a), Rubinstein (2000).

[12] On Athenian litigation as social process, see Cartledge, Millett, and Todd (1990), Cohen (1995), Christ (1998). On popular Athenian ideology and its role in the democracy, see Ober (1989). On the political role of the courts, see Hansen (1990b). On the mix of legal and political argument, see Yunis (1988).

verbal contest between two litigants vying to persuade a large audience of average, anonymous citizens to vote in their favor and against the opponent. Yet, paradoxical as it may seem, from the perspective of the democratic system, it constituted no harm to the law if the court had no mechanism to examine the statutory basis of the dispute that was being contested and the litigants discussed statutes purely at their convenience. Rather, the most significant fact with regard to the law was simply that the dispute was being heard in a popular court under the aegis of the democratic regime. This meant that due process was being followed, that the law was taking its proper course, and that the *demos* was exercising its exclusive privilege to adjudicate disputes among citizens in the best interests of the *demos*. The law was an instrument of democratic rule. Athenian litigants faced the *dikastai* as petitioners and by doing so they reaffirmed the *demos*' exclusive privilege to provide binding adjudication in the state. Insofar as litigants availed themselves of any and all means of persuasion in the verbal onslaught that constituted the trial, not only were they within their rights but they were also providing the *demos* with every consideration that could be deemed relevant in the Athenian system.[13]

Because an Athenian trial was a rhetorical contest and included no independent norm to regulate what litigants said, a litigant seeking only his own advantage could use rhetorical skill unimpeded to manipulate the *dikastai* into deciding a case contrary to their true wishes or best judgment. Thus, while adhering to due process in every formal respect, such a litigant could theoretically pervert the law and thwart the *demos*

---

[13] See Gernet (1955a), followed by Todd (1993: 54–60). Todd responds to Meyer-Laurin (1965), who argued that Athenian litigants made their cases and Athenian courts decided them primarily on the basis of the statutes. Meyer-Laurin's position has been revived with adjustments by E. M. Harris (1994, 2000). Harris' argument is interesting but untenable: it requires us to believe that the arguments about the law included in law court speeches were the only passages relevant to the courts' decisions. Likewise, it strains credulity when Harris (1994: 133–4) stresses the dikastic oath, sworn by all *dikastai* to qualify them for service, as evidence of the courts' adherence to the law in rendering their decisions. Among other clauses, the oath obliged the *dikastai* to render their decision according to the law and where there was no law according to justice. (On the oath, see Bonner and Smith (1938: 152–5).) But there was no mechanism for the court to be apprised of relevant law. The *dikastai* were entirely dependent on the litigants for being informed of whatever law, if any, the *litigants* deemed relevant, and that, naturally, was not only biased but, given the lack of safeguards, also potentially inaccurate and deceptive. There was also no mechanism for enforcing the oath's principles, which were left entirely to individual *dikastai* to interpret as they wished. In one passage where Demosthenes mentions the oath (24.148–52), he does so expressly to affirm the court's unlimited authority to decide however it pleases. See also Lanni's chapter in this volume.

by preventing the *dikastai* from deciding in the interests of the *demos*. It is impossible for us to judge today to what extent or how often Athenian courts were actually duped by clever, rhetorically skilled litigants.[14] But just as concerns with the ability of modern trial lawyers to manipulate the courts are periodically voiced today, so a concern with the possibility of outright deception by rhetoric is plentiful in Athenian popular sources and political theorists.

Aristophanes' *Clouds* (produced in 423) is one of the earliest texts to reflect this anxiety. An Athenian citizen, saddled with debt because of his profligate son, is due to face his creditors in court. He attempts to learn rhetoric in order to deceive the *dikastai* and escape the punishment that he knows he deserves and that the court would otherwise likely impose. Aristophanes sharpens the problem further. Having proved incapable of learning the new skill himself, the father sends the son to the school of rhetoric and science, where a debate between "Right Argument" and "Wrong Argument" demonstrates that rhetoric can put all conventional social values in question. Declaring his conversion to new unconventional values, the newly educated son beats his father up and the father then burns down the school. As satire, the *Clouds* functions through exaggeration; but the connection it makes between rhetoric, sophistic education, and public upheaval is typical. Law-court speeches of the fourth century are less spectacular, but litigants often warn the *dikastai* that the opponent is trained in rhetoric and will use his skill to deceive them.[15]

Plato's opposition to rhetoric, inseparable from his opposition to democracy and his views on human nature generally, is too large a topic to consider here;[16] a couple of points relevant to the law must suffice. The account of Socrates' trial in the *Gorgias* (521c–522e) illustrates Plato's view that rhetoric was a form of flattery supremely effective, and destructive, in a democratic court of law. Socrates, the defendant, is likened to a physician; the rhetorically skilled prosecutor is likened to a pastry cook; the *dikastai* are likened to children. On trial for the harsh

---

[14] For instance, Cawkwell (1969) argues that in 330 Demosthenes used his rhetorical skill in court to dupe the Athenians into confirming his leadership against their better judgment and best interests. On that case, a famous one, see also Yunis (2000). Assessments of the judicial savvy of Athenian courts range from one extreme to the other; for discussion and bibliography, see Bleicken (1994: 517–20).

[15] E.g., Isocrates 18.21, Isaeus 9.35, 10.1, Aeschines 3.16, 137, 200. On the mistrust of sophists and rhetorical training in Athenian public discourse, see Ober (1989: 165–82).

[16] See Yunis (1996: 117–71).

measures he imposed on the children in the name of health, what chance does Socrates stand when the cook offers the children sweets and cakes? Callicles, Socrates' interlocutor in the *Gorgias* and an avid proponent of rhetoric as a means of acquiring power in the democratic state, considers Socrates a fool for depriving himself of an effective weapon in the democratic courts. Plato's point, however, is that by encouraging litigants to use rhetoric to advance their own interests at the expense of the community, the democratic courts undermine both justice and communal welfare. Thus whereas the Athenian *demos*, for whom democracy was sacrosanct, were wary of rhetorical expertise but tolerated rhetoric for the sake of maintaining democratic rule, Plato rejected both rhetoric and the democratic institutions that fostered it.

The deliberative and judicial institutions of the ideal state described in the *Laws*, Plato's last dialogue, are democratic, but the freedom of the *demos* to act without constraint is limited by mechanisms borrowed from oligarchy, aristocracy, and Plato's own brand of intellectualized social engineering. Most of the courts in this ideal state are, like those in Athens, popular courts.[17] But to prevent the kind of abuse that in Plato's view regularly takes place in Athenian courts, Plato outlaws schools of rhetoric, the learning of rhetoric, and the use of rhetoric by litigants pleading their cases in court (937d–938c). The underlying idea is that popular courts can deliver justice and can enforce the laws if litigants are prevented from using rhetoric and compelled to declare their arguments openly. The idea was already anticipated in the opening words of the *Apology of Socrates*, one of Plato's earliest works. Socrates contrasts his own plain, truthful discourse – which would be useful to a court actually concerned with deciding justly and enforcing the law – with the elaborate, deceptive discourse of the rhetorically skilled prosecutors (17a–18a).

At the beginning of his treatise on the *Art of Rhetoric*, the most incisive theoretical account of rhetoric from the ancient world, Aristotle espouses a modified version of Plato's view that rhetoric perverts the true purpose of law courts. Criticizing unnamed rhetoricians, Aristotle argues that trials would be better conducted if litigants avoided the emotional appeals that aim to sway the *dikastai* but are extraneous to the case itself; rhetorical legal discourse is "like making a rule crooked before using it" (*Rhet.* 1.1.3–5). Then, in the spirit of the *Laws* and the Socrates of the *Apology*, Aristotle endorses a plain forensic discourse

---

[17] See Morrow (1960: 251–73).

that would be restricted to demonstrating facts and would allow *dikastai* to decide justice on their own without the litigants' distorting input (*Rhet.* 1.1.6).[18] But following these introductory remarks, the rest of the treatise is written not from the point of view of the political philosopher, who evaluates rhetoric in the light of its benefit and harm to society at large, but from the point of view of the rhetorician, concerned strictly with the demands of the discipline. Not only does Aristotle show no further concern about rhetoric's power to deceive, but he explains in detail how that power can best be realized.

It is precisely in its implementation of disciplinary standards that Aristotle's *Rhetoric* exploits the lack of statutory scrutiny in Athenian trials. Aristotle devotes the bulk of the treatise to what he terms artistic proofs, namely the three kinds of discourse whose persuasive appeal can be controlled by the rhetorically skilled speaker and that therefore constitute the intrinsic part of the art of rhetoric. The artistic proofs are arguments concerning the subject matter at stake, assertions of the speaker's trustworthiness, and appeals to the audience's emotions (*Rhet.* 1.2.2–5). Along with oaths, contracts, witness testimony, and oracles, statutes fall in the category of nonartistic proof; these are things that exist independently of the speech. As a nonartistic proof, statutes can be introduced by the speaker or not, according to their availability and suitability to the case. Aristotle accords statutes brief treatment (*Rhet.* 1.15.1–12), merely advising the speaker to emphasize equity if the statutes tend to weaken his case and to emphasize law if the statutes tend to bolster his case.[19] Thus for the rhetorically trained speaker, statutes are of no intrinsic interest. Whatever probative value statutes may have in court, it concerns the rhetorically trained speaker only insofar as they can be arrayed to support one's own case or to weaken the opponent's.

---

[18] Earlier in this passage (1.1.5), Aristotle says that in the Areopagus it was forbidden to speak outside the subject. The Areopagus Council, a relic from Athens's predemocratic period, still functioned as a court for certain kinds of cases. This limitation on legal discourse in the Areopagus is mentioned elsewhere too, but, as in Aristotle, with no details (Lysias 3.46, Lycurgus 1.12–13). The three surviving forensic speeches delivered before the Areopagus, all by Lysias (3, 4, 7), are no different from any of Lysias' other speeches in their inclusion of emotional and ethical material. It is not easy to imagine a formal procedure whereby such a limitation could have been enforced. Perhaps the members of the Areopagus, who were all former magistrates and permanently ensconced, could simply exert authority by verbally restraining litigants when they chose to. See further Lanni in this volume.

[19] On Aristotle's account of rhetoric and law, see Mirhady (1990), Carey (1996).

The Intent of the Lawgiver and the Defense of Democracy

Athens' extensive apparatus of laws and legal procedures, greater than anything else known in Greece, was built up over two centuries into an essential tool for maintaining social stability and the democratic regime. The rule of law was a fundamental tenet of Athenian democracy and, as affirmed by the oath taken by all *dikastai*, trials in court were recognized as essential for enforcing the law and preserving the democracy. Penalties existed for abusing the legal process in pursuit of private ends. The mere fact that deciding the law, like making it, was a democratic prerogative that the *demos* refused to delegate reveals the seriousness with which the *dikastai* approached their judicial task. Thus, given the importance of the rule of law to Athenian democracy generally, it was common for litigants to wrap themselves, so to speak, in the law and assert their commitment to the law against the lawlessness of the opponent.[20]

When arguing about the law, Athenian litigants frequently cite and quote specific statutes to suggest to the *dikastai* a clear, palpable adherence to the law.[21] This section will focus on a group of arguments that use statute law to create a motive for action beyond the statutes themselves. The arguments turn on the role played by the courts in protecting the democracy and they provide the *dikastai* with an incentive to act in that capacity. The speaker identifies what he contends is the lawgiver's intent in a particular statute and uses that intent to imply or to explicitly claim that voting in his favor is essential for the democracy. Of course, given the lack of independent statutory examination during trial, the lawgiver's intent enjoyed no official status in interpreting or deciding the law. Such intent could at best only be inferred anyway because there was no information about the intent of the original legislation and Athenian statutes seldom provided any information about the meaning of key terms.[22] But on the level of ideology, the lawgiver's

---

[20] E.g., Aeschines 3.37, Demosthenes 18.2, 21.188, Demosthenes 59.115, Lycurgus 1.3–6. On the orators' use of law to denigrate the opponent's character or to extol their own, see De Brauw (2001). On the ideology of the rule of law and its contribution to democratic stability, see Finley (1983: 122–41), Ober (1989: 299–304). On the rule of law in fourth-century Athens, see Sealey (1987), Cohen (1995). On penalties for abusing the legal process, see E. M. Harris (1999b). On the dikastic oath, see note 13 above.

[21] See Wolff (1962, 1970b) and Meinecke (1971).

[22] On the vagueness of Athenian statutes, see Todd (1993: 61–2). On the manner in which fourth-century orators use the lawgiver's intent to interpret the law, see Hillgruber (1988: 105–20).

intent invariably suggested the support and advancement of the democratic regime. Both the body of law as a whole and individual statutes were considered to be expressions of the will of the *demos* just as much as the actions of the courts and the Assembly. In the fifth century legislation (*nomothesia*) took place in the Assembly; in the fourth century it involved popular participation on a scale comparable to the courts. Statutes that were considered "traditional" (*patrios*) and attributed to the archaic lawgivers (*nomothetai*) Draco (seventh century) and Solon (early sixth century) were equally thought to embody the *demos*' interests, both because those lawgivers were by popular conception faithful servants of the *demos* and because the *demos* demonstrated their acceptance of those statutes by continued usage over time.[23] The arguments to be discussed here illustrate the distinctively Athenian rhetoric of law because, although they depend on a statute, their purpose is to introduce considerations that go beyond the statute and depend on the democratic and social utility of the law in general.

Consider Lysias' speech *On the Death of Eratosthenes* (Lysias 1), where the defendant, Euphiletus, is on trial for murder. Admitting that he killed Eratosthenes, Euphiletus argues that the deed was legally justified: he caught Eratosthenes in bed with his wife, and Athenian law permits — nay, commands (34) — a husband to kill an adulterer on the spot if he is caught in the act. At the climax of the narrative, as Euphiletus recalls the fatal blow, he addresses the seducer and identifies his private revenge with the laws of the *polis*: "It is not I who will kill you but the law of the city. You have broken the law and have less regard for it than for your own pleasure. You have preferred to commit this crime against my wife and my children rather than behaving responsibly and obeying the laws" (26, trans. Todd). Having portrayed himself, the admitted killer, as the defender of the law and the murdered seducer as the enemy of the city and its laws, Euphiletus substantiates these claims by introducing three statutes (28–30). The texts of the statutes were not preserved with the speech, and though Athenian laws on homicide are known from other sources, it remains unclear what kind of statutory support Euphiletus had for his action.[24] The prosecution will hardly

---

[23] On laws and legislation in fifth- and fourth-century Athens, see Hansen (1991: 161–77). On the democratic status of the fourth-century *nomothetai* ("lawgivers"), see Ober (1989: 96–97, 101–2) and Bleicken (1994: 187–90). On the fourth-century view of Solon as democratic lawgiver, see Hansen (1989) and Thomas (1994). On the statutes attributed to Solon, see Ruschenbusch (1966). On Draco, see Gagarin (1981) and Carawan (1998).

[24] From Euphiletus's paraphrase (30), it is likely that the third of his three statutes is the one recorded at Dem. 23.53: "if somebody kills a man...lying with his wife or mother or

have conceded that the statutes cited by Euphiletus exonerated him; and the prosecution probably argued that other statutes properly cover Euphiletus' behavior and should be enforced against him. But where a statutory examination in the manner of modern jurisprudence was lacking and both prosecution and defense could each introduce their own statutes to justify their cause, the case was unlikely to be decided by the disposition of statute law alone. Euphiletus introduces his statutes to also argue that a decision in his favor is necessary for the welfare of the democracy.

After the first statute is read out to the court, Euphiletus says: "I exacted from him [the seducer] the penalty [i.e., death] that you yourselves, believing it to be just, have established for people who behave like that" (29, trans. Todd). Banking on the democratic nature of Athenian legislation, Euphiletus identifies the *dikastai* in court — "you yourselves" — with the legislators of the particular statute that (supposedly) condemns seducers of married Athenian women to death. By means of this identification Euphiletus implies a more extensive message: first, that the *dikastai* should take offense at the prosecutors (the dead man's relatives) who, merely by prosecuting Euphiletus, are brazenly repudiating the *demos*' express directive on seduction and death (i.e., the statute); and further, that the *dikastai* should defend their statute by quashing the prosecution's attempt to nullify it. As Euphiletus has it, if the *dikastai* fail to enforce the statute that justified (nay, commanded) his action, they would be allowing their own rules to be flouted, which would be intolerable.

The message that was implied by Euphiletus is spelled out by Aeschines in a speech against Demosthenes (Aeschines 3). Aeschines says to the *dikastai*, "You legislated [the statute] with the intention of ruling out the excuses [of the defendants, Ctesiphon and Demosthenes]" (14); thus like Euphiletus, Aeschines identifies the *dikastai* with the legislators of the statute. But after the statute is read out, Aeschines explicitly warns the *dikastai* of the defendants' insolence in seeking to violate it with impunity: "It is your job to remember the law and confront their insolent claims with it; and you must reply to them that you refuse to tolerate an unprincipled sophist [i.e., Demosthenes] who thinks he can nullify the laws with his words.... When the law says one thing and a politician another, your verdict should go to the just claim of

sister or daughter or a concubine he keeps for free children, he shall not for that reason be exiled as a murderer."

the law, not the insolence of the politician" (16, trans. adapted from Carey).

In the speech *On the Mysteries* Andocides defends himself against the charge of having illegally participated in the rites of the Eleusinian mysteries (Andocides 1). The prosecutor alleged that Andocides, who had returned from exile under the amnesty of 403, was barred from participating in the rites by the decree of Isotimides, which stemmed from before the amnesty. Andocides argues that the decree of Isotimides was no longer valid after the amnesty, hence it could not bar him from the rites. In fact, the decree was never specifically rescinded, and when the amnesty was enacted it was not given a precise scope. Cases were settled by the courts as they arose.[25] To make his case, Andocides introduces to the court a whole series of official democratic measures – decrees, statutes, the oaths of amnesty – that in its totality is meant to establish the *demos*' intention to exclude virtually all prosecutions based on the laws valid before the amnesty, including, of course, the decree of Isotimides (71–91). Throughout this section of the speech, Andocides repeatedly addresses the *dikastai* as if they themselves were the authors of the decrees, statutes, and oaths, thereby making the *demos*' intention into the intention of the *dikastai* before him. His rhetorical goal is the same as that of Euphiletus and Aeschines in the speeches discussed above. But he concludes the argument with restraint: "You must consider these facts, to see whether you think I'm right when I tell you that I'm speaking in support of yourselves and the laws" (91, trans. MacDowell).

A second argument that connects statutes to the welfare of the democracy through the lawgiver's intent also occurs in Lysias 1. Euphiletus has two more statutes read out to the court (29–30), which, like the first one, (supposedly) justify his taking of Eratosthenes' life. He infers that the lawgiver legislated the statutes because he placed the highest value on protecting Athens' married women and because he wanted to protect the paternity of the children and the integrity of the families (31–33). Euphiletus then exhorts the *dikastai* to rise in defense of these same priorities by enforcing the statutes in his favor. If the *dikastai* fail to do so, the predicted consequences for the *polis* are dire indeed (34–36):

> It is for you to decide whether the law is to be powerful or worthless. In my opinion, every city enacts its laws in order

[25] On the amnesty of 403, which followed the Peloponnesian War, civil war, and the restoration of democracy, see Wolpert (2002).

that when we are uncertain in a situation, we can go to them to see what to do, and in such cases the law commands the victims to exact this penalty. So I ask you now to reach the same verdict as the law does. If not, you will be giving adulterers such immunity that you will encourage burglars to call themselves adulterers too. They will realize that if they describe adultery as their object and claim that they have entered somebody else's house for this purpose, nobody will dare touch them. Everyone will know that we must say good-bye to the laws on adultery and take notice only of your verdict – which is the sovereign authority over all the city's affairs. (trans. Todd)

Beyond his interpretation of the lawgiver's intent, Euphiletus portrays the action of the *dikastai* in the present case as decisive for the welfare of the *polis* as a whole. The *dikastai* are not only judges of justice and the law and they are not only asked to identify with the *demos* as the beneficiaries of the law. Rather, because their present decision, like that of the original legislators, will have the effect of determining social behavior, they are also *de facto* legislators themselves. As such, they must be aware of the consequences of their decision and act firmly in the interests of the *polis*.[26]

The decisions rendered by Athenian courts did not create law or set legal precedent that was binding or even advisory for future cases. As discussed above, court decisions were not recorded and there was no body of case law. *Dikastai* always consulted only their consciences when rendering decisions in the cases before them.[27] So the argument in Lysias 1 on the legislative impact of the *dikastai* and the consequences of their decision is purely rhetorical; that is, the argument's effectiveness hinges entirely on the speaker's ability to rouse in the audience the belief – or just the vague feeling – that their decision will have the impact that he attributes to it. The key to creating that belief or feeling lay in the speaker's forthright assertion of the power that belongs to the *dikastai* – "your verdict – which is the sovereign authority over all the city's affairs" – and in the speaker's palpable suggestion that the safety and virtue of Athens' (citizen) women were at stake. That was a potent combination in Athens, though we do not know how the *dikastai*

---

[26] The argument is briefly reiterated at the end of the speech, 47–49.
[27] On the lack of precedent in Athenian law, see Todd (1993: 60–1).

decided the case.[28] So although the legal foundation for summoning the *dikastai* to act as the equivalent of legislators in protecting Athens' best interests was tenuous, the rhetorical effectiveness of this approach was considerable. In another speech, Lysias used the same plea with less drama but greater explicitness (14.4): "It is appropriate that you should be not simply *dikastai* but lawgivers (*nomothetai*). You are fully aware that in the future the city will treat such matters in whatever way you decide today. The task of a responsible citizen and of a just-minded *dikastēs*, it seems to me, is to interpret the laws the way that will benefit the city in future" (trans. adapted from Todd).

Perhaps the most effective use of this argument occurs in Demosthenes' speech *Against Meidias* (Demosthenes 21), where it makes a stirring conclusion. The speech, which constituted but one round in a long-running battle between Demosthenes and Meidias, was composed to prosecute Meidias by a procedure known as *probolē* (literally "putting forward," i.e., to the Assembly), applicable to violations of the sanctity of religious festivals.[29] Meidias had (apparently) punched Demosthenes while Demosthenes was executing his duties as producer of a chorus during the festival of Dionysus. When Demosthenes displays the statutes governing *probolē*, he includes the first type of argument discussed above; that is, he identifies the *dikastai* in court with the original legislators of the statute and implies that they should actively defend their own rules (8–12). But it is a crucial part of Demosthenes' overall strategy to portray Meidias as not just his own personal enemy, but an enemy of the *polis* as a whole. To that end Demosthenes argues that Meidias also committed *hybris* (aggravated assault) and impiety (*asebeia*) and could well have been prosecuted under those statutes as well (42–61).[30] From the statute on *hybris*, which as a crime of public import (*graphē*) was prosecutable by any citizen, Demosthenes infers that the lawgiver viewed *hybris* as a crime not only against the victim but also against society as a whole (45–46). As for impiety, that was by definition a crime against the entire community. But Demosthenes also cites two oracles and, in a manner parallel to inferring the intent of the lawgiver, he here infers the intent of the gods, namely that those who wear

---

[28] On the Athenians' concern with the safety and virtue of the women of citizen status, see Just (1989).
[29] On the procedure, background, and other features of this speech, see MacDowell (1990).
[30] On the actions available under Athenian law and the reasons for proceeding in one way rather than another, see Osborne (1985).

crowns at a festival (as Demosthenes was doing) wear them not just for themselves but for all of Athens (54–55).

Because Meidias was not charged with *hybris* or impiety, the argument that includes those statutes was purely rhetorical. The payoff comes at the end of the speech when Demosthenes returns to the law, urging the *dikastai* to defend Athenian society by securing the civic safety intended by the lawgivers. After claiming that Meidias' attack on him has put at risk the personal security of all citizens, indeed the security of the *dikastai* themselves when they walk home after the trial (219–222), Demosthenes appeals to the power that the *dikastai* wield as a result of their stewardship of the laws (223–224):

> Your power [as *dikastai*] is derived from the laws. And what is the power of the laws? Is it that, if any of you is attacked and gives a shout, they'll come running to your aid? No; they're written documents, and they couldn't do that. What is their strength then? You are, if you guarantee them and make them effective on each occasion for anyone who asks. So the laws through you are powerful, and you through the laws. (trans. adapted from MacDowell)

The view of judicial activism and responsibility presented in this passage accords with the demands of the Athenian system of law, justice, and politics. But the effectiveness of the passage in context has little to do with its accuracy as a report about Athenian society. Rather, the passage is an urgent appeal for action.

Demosthenes has established that Meidias – who just happens to be Demosthenes' personal enemy – has not merely punched Demosthenes and violated the statute on festivals, but has committed serious crimes against the entire community and represents a threat to all of Athens' citizens. Demosthenes has also established the lawgiver's intent in making laws to safeguard the security and welfare of all citizens. Something then is seriously amiss. How can things be repaired and the laws' purpose be realized? Demosthenes takes his audience through the following steps. First, the laws are personified: will they come running to the aid of a citizen who is attacked? The personification is rejected: of course the laws will not do that; they are merely written documents, and written documents cannot actually do anything. But the laws do have the purpose (as intended by the lawgiver) of securing civic order; how then is that to be achieved? If you *dikastai* convict Meidias and enforce the laws in court, you and the laws together will bring about the laws' purpose and all will be well with Athens. The passage has emotional impact because these steps are conveyed so quickly and vividly that the *dikastai* spontaneously sense the urgent need for action and grasp where their duty lies.

The last sentence puts a seal, so to speak, on this message. It contains the rhetorical figure of speech known as *chiasmus*, in which the two main components of a thought are arranged in the order ABBA – "the laws through you are powerful, and you through the laws." Here the components "the laws" and "you" (i.e., the *dikastai*) surround the central idea of "power." The *chiasmus*, a purely artificial arrangement of words, communicates surreptitiously the power and fundamental propriety of the social compact of the *dikastai* and the city's laws. Having articulated this compact so effectively, Demosthenes seems to belong to it. Meidias, naturally, is excluded. The entire passage is an appeal that cannot have been easy for a good, patriotic citizen to resist.

The examples from Lysias, Aeschines, Andocides, and Demosthenes demonstrate a rhetorical approach to the law. They introduce the law not to make an argument about the legal or statutory basis of the case, but to create in the *dikastai* a feeling that will move them to decide in the speaker's favor for the sake of the community as a whole.

PART 3

LAW IN ATHENS II: SUBSTANTIVE LAW

11: Crime, Punishment, and the Rule of Law in Classical Athens

David Cohen

Introduction

The past two decades have seen a dramatic increase in scholarly research on aspects of the prosecution of crime in ancient Greece, and in particular in Athens. Scholarship has focused on the process of prosecution, the history and workings of courts such as the Areopagus, as well as specific crimes like homicide, adultery, theft, sycophancy, and hubris.[1] Such research has enhanced our understanding of the procedures used in criminal prosecution and the substantive law of particular crimes. What has received far less attention, however, is the way in which Athenians conceptualized the category of "crime" and the laws enacted to deal with it. Did the Athenians in fact have conceptions of something like our notions of "crime" and "criminal," as distinct from other types of wrongs and wrongdoers? Did they think of the methods of prosecuting and punishing criminal offenses as a separate legal category from other sorts of proceedings? Did they have a distinctive conception of punishment as opposed to other kinds of legal remedies? What did they believe were the distinguishing features of this area of the law and its relation to the larger framework of Athenian litigation and government? These are large and complex questions that could only be comprehensively answered in a book-length study. This

---

[1] See, for example, Gagarin (1981, 1986, 2002), MacDowell (1963), Hansen (1975, 1976), D. Cohen (1983, 1991, 1995), Cantarella (1976, 1979, 1987, 1991b), Saunders (1991), Wallace (1989).

chapter will suggest some answers to them that may furnish a starting point for further reflection and debate.

In discussing a particular problem in Athenian law many experts begin by looking at procedural aspects as a starting point. In the case of Athenian criminal law this tendency has naturally focused on a fundamental distinction in procedural law between two means of initiating a legal action: *dikē* and *graphē*. The former, usually taken as denoting a private suit, is an older term and has a very broad range of legal meanings embracing a case at law, justice as an abstraction, a legal remedy or penalty, and so on. The latter term is much narrower and refers to a specific form of legal action that proceeds on the basis of this particular kind of written indictment. The chief distinguishing characteristic is that a *dikē* may only be brought by the aggrieved party or, in the case of homicide, by relatives of the victim, whereas any citizen could prosecute a wrong for which the law provided a *graphē*.

Scholars have attempted to classify the types of substantive legal actions under these two categories, but this expedient involves some difficulties because of the uncertainty regarding the attribution of particular kinds of cases.[2] A further problem is indicated by Douglas MacDowell's well-founded admonition that scholars have often interpreted these categories too rigidly as constituting a "comprehensive set of 'actions' " on the model of Roman law.[3] Despite all of these difficulties today there is fairly broad agreement that *graphai* generally involve public wrongs. The case with *dikai* is a bit more problematic because although in general they involve legal actions that seem like private matters, there are important qualification to be made regarding the law concerning cases of homicide and intentional wounding. So although the view has been held that *graphai* were criminal prosecutions[4], most contemporary scholars, especially in the Anglo-American world, are more cautious. In the two most recent English handbooks on Athenian law no clear position is taken on the matter.[5]

One has to be clear, of course, about what questions need to be asked in regard to crime, punishment, or criminal law in a particular legal system. It does not follow, for example, that because the way a legal system categorizes or treats public offenses differs from our own that it does not embody a conception of crime or a system of criminal law.

---

[2] See most recently Todd (1993: 99–112).
[3] MacDowell (1978: 59).
[4] Calhoun (1927).
[5] MacDowell (1978) and Todd (1993: 109–10).

It may just have one that proceeds from different values and embodies different assumptions about society, the public sphere, the relationship of the family to society, the nature of punishment, and so on.

For example, mistreatment of parents and offenses against religious ritual were clearly considered among the very serious forms of wrongdoing in Athens, were both prosecutable by *graphai*, and might involve the most severe penalties. This, of course, tells us a good deal about the way in which Athenian values differed from our own. Likewise, the criminal law of Nazi Germany provided that any act that harmed the interests of the German people was a crime punishable by death. This points not only to different values but also to an understanding of the criminal law as a naked instrument of state power. Different societies conceptualize the power of the state or community to deprive individuals of their life, liberty, or property in different ways and vary in their opinions as to what sorts of acts justify such deprivations. This was well recognized by Greek political theorists such as Aristotle and Plato, for whom it was a commonplace that different constitutional forms of the state would adopt different kinds of laws suitable to the values and interests enshrined in a particular constitution.

A further difficulty arises from the fact that at Athens there was no Office of Public Prosecution charged with investigating and prosecuting criminal conduct. It is easy from the modern perspective to imagine that such an institution is essential for a system of criminal law to function properly. This says more, however, about how we imagine the authority of the state and its role in maintaining public order than it does about the nature of crime and punishment. It is sobering to recall that public prosecution is actually a rather late development in most Western legal systems. In England, for example, private prosecution was the primary method for pursuing most criminal acts until late in the eighteenth century. Legal systems that rely on private initiative for the prosecution of acts considered to impact the public sphere may do so for a variety of reasons, including the simple lack of centralized governmental institutions equal to the task. One of the goals of this chapter is to arrive at a clearer understanding of what the private initiation of prosecution meant in the Athenian context.

In pursuing this inquiry we will first examine the conceptualization of certain kinds of wrongdoing, with particular attention to the way in which the public/private dichotomy was used to construct distinctions in the courtroom. We will then turn to an examination of citizen prosecution, arguing that it must be understood in Athens in its relationship to the form of participatory government associated with the radical democracy. This inquiry into private initiative in prosecutions will inevitably involve discussions of the role of private enmity in public litigation as well as the reliance on self-help in the apprehension and punishment of wrongdoers. Finally we will take up the Athenian understanding of the political force of criminal justice and the way in which this understanding informs conceptions of the functions and nature of the popular courts, of the Athenians who sat in judgment, and of the law which they applied.

The overarching argument of the chapter will be that regardless of what label we attach to it, the notion of certain kinds of wrongs as harming or threatening not just the immediate victim but the community as a whole and therefore requiring not merely compensation to the victim but punishment of the offender in the name of the *polis*, was central to Athenian thinking about law and justice. This, of course, is the core idea of "criminal law" as an analytical category in historical jurisprudence. We may do well to recall that the German term for criminal law is *Strafrecht*, literally, "the law of penalties/punishments." The same is true in French: *Droit Penal*. At its core, criminal law is the judicial expression of the authority of the state to punish through legal process in the name of the public interest, by depriving citizens of their lives, status, liberty, or property. It is these features that distinguish it from the redress, usually in the form of compensation for loss or harm, provided in private cases (however the substantive content of "public" and "private" may be defined in a particular legal system). Such analytical conceptions of public harms and punishment were well-known in Athens, but although they may seem very familiar to us, their contours in the Athenian legal system were, in important ways, quite distinct from our own and they were enmeshed within a political and legal system that strongly identified the unity of the law, the judges, the *demos*, and the *polis*. This identification, it will be seen, shaped criminal trials in ways that produced a tension with notions of the rule of law, both Athenian and our own.

Private Interests and Public Wrongs

In his history of the Athenian constitution, Aristotle devotes considerable time to the development of the Athenian system of courts. The way in which the system developed over time and the interplay of a variety of other factors (in an historical process largely obscure to us) resulted in a system where different kinds of prosecutions were brought to different officials and were heard by different courts or other bodies. The central theme in Aristotle's account, however, is the development of the jurisdiction of the Areopagus and its subsequent limitation in favor of the popular courts associated with democratic reforms, where the lay judges were selected by lot from among the male citizens over 30 and served in large panels (101, 201, 501) assembled for a particular trial. The political and legal implications of this development will be discussed later, but immediately relevant is Aristotle's description of the tasks of the Areopagus.

In speaking of its historical importance, he says that although the Areopagus had the position of guarding the laws, "actually it administered the greatest number and the most important of the affairs of state, punishing and fining those who offended public order without appeal" (*Ath. Pol.* 6.3). Later in his discussion he explains that under Solon the Areopagus continued in its function of guarding the laws and watching over the most important affairs of state, "and it had sovereign power to scrutinize offenders and to punish and to fine" (8.4). In these passages Aristotle makes clear that the function of punishing those who transgressed public order is of vital interest to the *polis* as a whole, one of the most important political functions. On this view, maintaining order by punishing wrongdoers is the state's business not a private matter. Because homicide and intentional wounding were closely associated with the Areopagus, this would presumably apply as well to them, despite their formal procedural status as *dikai*, or private prosecutions.

With the emergence of the popular mass courts as part of the development of democratic institutions from Solon onward this conviction that the punishment of public wrongdoing was of vital importance to the state did not diminish. But what constituted public wrongdoing? What lent particular kinds of harms their public quality and made them of interest to the *polis* as a whole instead of merely to the aggrieved party? For the category of offenses that deal with acts directly harmful to the institutions of the state, such as treason, bribery of public officials, or attempting to overthrow the democracy, the answer to these questions is fairly obvious. But what of other kinds of wrongdoing that were inflicted on an individual citizen?

We may take as our starting point an oration by Isocrates, *Against Lochites* (20), involving an accusation of assault. The action for assault (*aikeias*) was classified as a *dikē*, and judgment for the plaintiff resulted in compensation in an amount determined by the judges. This was the least serious category of wrongdoing involving physical assault and appears typically to involve cases where there has been an altercation that escalated into blows being exchanged rather than a premeditated attack. Although the action may be classified as a *dikē*, the speaker nonetheless makes the argument that the case involves public wrongs. He claims, for example, that cheating someone of money is a far less serious offense than a wrong committed against the person, because the latter is a matter of public concern (1). To increase the persuasiveness of this argument about the public nature of assaults on the person, the speaker employs a strategy found in other orations involving assault as well, asserting that the defendant is actually guilty of a far more serious form of physical violence, *hubris*. Hubris can take the form of violent assault or sexual violence, but its distinguishing characteristic was the intentional infliction of humiliating treatment that dishonored the victim, in addition to the physical violence and harm.[6] Hubris was prosecuted by a *graphē* and did not result in compensation to the victim, but punishment; the penalty as severe as the judges thought appropriate. The perceived advantage in using the rhetoric of *hubris* in an action that was actually based on only simple assault (*aikeias*) is that the public quality of the former will make the judges see that this sort of conduct represents a public harm and a threat to the public interest. This indicates, of course, the centrality of this distinction and the greater emotional weight attached to public as opposed to private harms.

Thus, the speaker in *Against Lochites* claims, because hubris is a matter of public concern the law provides that any citizen, and not just the victim, can lodge a prosecution before the appropriate officials (20.2). He later explains that he is seeking revenge not because of the harm caused by the blows, but because of the humiliation and dishonor (characteristics of *hubris*). He supports this argument by saying that the punishment for private theft (*klopē*) or theft of sacred property (*hierosulia*) is not measured according to the value of the stolen goods, but rather all such offenders are punished by death. That is, the judicial response is not redress but punishment, the severity of which is based on the public harm represented by these acts, not the economic loss to the individual or to the *polis*. Likewise, he argues, the punishment for assault should not depend on the amount of physical injury inflicted (5). In concluding his plea, rather than asking for damages in compensation for his injury, he accordingly reminds the judges that severe penalties/punishments in such cases will be in the interest of all and will both cause others to restrain themselves from such acts and make the lives of all citizens

---

[6] See Aristotle, *Rhetoric* 1374a13–15, 1378b23–5, and D. Cohen (1995), Chapter 7. On the general concept of hubris, see Fisher (1992).

(he addresses the judges here as representatives of the demos) more secure (15–18).

Another oration that employs the same strategy of using the rhetoric of hubris to inflate the severity of what the defendant will try to pass off as a minor assault is Demosthenes' *Against Meidias* (21).[7] This case arose out of Meidias' insult to Demosthenes by slapping him in the face at a public festival. Though the actual charge on which the oration is based involves a violation of the festival regulations, Demosthenes' central strategy is to use hubris to argue that violent men such as Meidias represent a threat to the security of the *polis*. He does this by emphasizing the public quality of hubris and the way it harms and threatens all ordinary citizens, arguing at length throughout the oration that he is not bringing the prosecution from private motives but in the public interest (7–8). What is important, he argues, is not just rendering justice to individuals wronged, but to the Laws, which Meidias violated, and to all of the citizens, for they were also wronged (20–1). Punishment, he claims, is thus not carried out in the interest of the accuser, but strengthens the law in the interests of the demos (again addressing the judges in the second person as representatives of the demos). This argument articulates the fundamental distinction between punishment inflicted by the state on certain classes of wrongdoers as opposed to remedies designed to compensate those who suffer other kinds of losses or harms.

Building on this point about the difference between public punishment and private remedies, he develops this argument in an interesting way by inquiring into what makes a particular kind of wrongdoing public. Why, he asks, is it the case that the laws provide that when a man withholds even a very large sum of money from someone who has deposited it with him the state has no concern with this matter? But if someone takes even a very small amount by force, the laws provide for a fine to be paid to the treasury equal to that paid to the private party. The reason, he claims (21.44–5),

> is that the lawgiver considered all violent acts as public offences (*koin' adikēmata*) committed also against those who stand outside the deed.... The man who agreed to the transaction can care for his interests privately, but the victim of violence needs public assistance. On this account the law allows anyone to bring a public indictment for hubris, but

---

[7] For a different approach, see MacDowell's edition (1990).

the penalty is paid entirely to the *polis*. The legislator considered that the *polis* was wronged as well as the victim and his punishment was sufficient satisfaction for the victim.

This argument sets out a basic theory of public offences and characterizes them in much the way that we would define acts of violence as a crime against the community as well as the victim. Alleged wrongdoing in voluntary contractual or other financial transactions is posited as fundamentally distinct from crimes of violence because of the nature of the threat the latter poses to public order. The distinction between the wrongs is also manifested in the notion of the response appropriate to each. Public offenses require punishment, which is exacted by the *polis* on its own behalf. We are dealing, then, with the notion of a body of law that deals with such offences, distinguishes them from private wrongs, and punishes them in the name of the *polis* as opposed to merely providing compensation to the victims for the harm or loss they have suffered.[8] Of course, the pattern of what is included within each of these categories will vary from legal system to legal system, as will the capacity to control or influence which path is adopted in a particular case, and other factors.

In the closing passages of the oration Demosthenes returns yet again to the theme of the hubristic rich as a danger to the *polis* as a whole. In doing so he identifies a conceptual nexus between the integrity of the rule of law, the judges as the embodiment of that rule, and the interests of ordinary citizens in preserving their equality by punishing such wrongdoers. He argues that the physical victim of hubris is not the only victim but all of the citizens as well, because the failure to punish such an offender only produces more such acts against citizens and thus creates a situation where all ordinary citizens are in danger. The reason why citizens do not walk around in constant fear, he maintains, is that they trust in the laws/constitution (*politeia*) to protect them from violence. Thus he asks the judges, "Do not betray *me or yourselves or the laws*" (my emphasis). This willingness to enforce the law regardless of the wealth or status of the defendant is the basis of the rule of law. To drive this point home he asks the judges, "What is the strength of the law? If one of you is the victim of a wrongful act and cries out, will the laws come to his assistance? No, they are only letters and incapable

---

[8] Demosthenes, in *Against Meidias* (21.19), says that in bringing a public action he is foregoing the financial gain damages would have given him and instead is entrusting his punishment (*timōria*) to the state.

of this. Wherein then resides their power? In you, if you support them and enforce them for those in need. So the laws are strong through you and you through the laws" (224–5; and cf. 20–1).

The punishment of all wrongdoers through legal process is, on this view, the bedrock of legal order. Such men, who commit these kinds of crimes against individuals, must meet with an appropriate response from the political community that they have wronged. Thus he tells the judges that they must consider that wrongful acts in violation of the laws are public (*koina*), regardless of who has committed them, and that no excuse such as public service, pity, or influence, should enable the man who has violated the law to escape punishment (219–25). Combining all of these themes together, he concludes that in voting to convict, the judges will be coming to his aid, providing redress for the demos, teaching others moderation, enabling themselves to lead their lives safely, and making an example of the defendant for the benefit of others (227). We find here a clearly articulated, though rhetorically hyperbolic, rationale for the way in which crimes such as hubris are public in nature and demand a public response in the form of criminal penalties rather than private remedies. All of this reflects an understanding of criminal law and the rule of law as the bulwark of society by which impunity for any person because of their status undermines the law which is the protection of everyone. Only punishment of those who act with impunity can preserve that order.

CITIZEN PROSECUTORS AND LEGAL PUNISHMENT

The functioning of the system Demosthenes describes depends on the willingness of individuals to seek redress through the courts. This means, of course, foregoing seeking revenge on their own. The most famous rationale in the Athenian context for refraining from private vengeance is in Aeschylus' *Eumenides*, where only the establishment of the first Athenian homicide court can end the cycle of murderous retaliation.[9] In an agonistic society where personal honor was a highly prized commodity, there might be considerable social and psychological pressure to avenge oneself directly.[10] In *Against Meidias*, for example, Demosthenes explains at some length why he chose the better course of action by restraining himself and leaving it to the courts to punish

---
[9] See Allen (2000b) and Meier (1988).
[10] See D. Cohen (1995: Chapters 4–5). On *Against Meidias*, see Wilson (1992).

Meidias (21.74–6). Similarly, in *Against Aristocrates*, he develops an argument (however self-serving in the context) that those who are the victims of violence should not take revenge themselves but should leave it to the courts to punish the wrongdoer. It is the role of the judges, not the victim, to enforce the protection against violence provided by the laws (23.75–6). The fact that he felt compelled to make this argument in these orations indicates that there were countervailing values to the rule of law at Athens, values that dictated that men should answer certain kinds of violence against their persons or families in like terms. Such values existed in tension with the recognition that the purpose of the laws providing punishment for violence, hubris, and the like is to take such conduct outside of the realm of private vendetta and make it the business of the state and its courts. As Demosthenes repeatedly puts it, this involves prohibiting revenge and providing public penalties for the punishment of wrongdoers.

A legal system in which prosecution remains in the hands of citizens naturally implies that the individual bringing the action must decide which remedy to pursue. In another oration of Demosthenes we see the way in which this choice involves a strategic dimension that differs significantly from our notion of how the law should, at least ideally, operate. The oration *Against Conon* (54) arises from another lawsuit for simple assault, brought by a young man who claims to have been humiliated, stripped naked, rolled in the mud, and badly beaten by Conon and his sons and their friends. In this suit (*dikē*) for assault (*aikeias*) the plaintiff, as in the orations just considered, acts as if it were an action (*graphē*) for hubris because of the far greater emotional weight that public offense carries with it. The evocation of hubris is particularly appropriate here because his allegations of Conon's conduct read like a textbook case of that offense.[11] Moreover, this will clearly be on the minds of the judges, because the word "*hubristheis*" ("I have suffered hubris") is the first word of the oration. Why then did he not bring an action for hubris and seek the judicial revenge that it would have provided?

The speaker explains that he is young and inexperienced and that after he recovered from his injuries he consulted friends and relatives as to what to do. They said that the defendant was in principle liable for the procedure of summary arrest (*apagōgē*) as a cloaksnatcher

---

[11] In addition to the violent and humiliating acts mentioned above, the victim claims that after doing all of this to him Conon stood over his bloody, muddied, naked body and flapped his arms in a kind of victory dance like a crowing rooster. This is paradigmatic of the conception of hubris articulated by Aristotle, above.

(i.e., because Conon allegedly stripped his cloak from him he committed this crime, *lōpodusia*) or for an indictment (*graphē*) for hubris. But they advised him not to pursue such actions and to content himself with a private suit. The grounds he gives for this is that they said that the other kinds of prosecutions would appear as too ambitious for one his age and he would not be able to bear the burden of conducting them. What does this suggest about the Athenian legal system? It indicates the way in which in any system that relies on popular prosecution the choice of remedy will depend on the identity and status of the parties, not just when it comes to judgment, but even in initiating such a case. This is, of course, part of the rationale for state prosecution, for the state is less likely to be intimidated by powerful defendants (though in practice in many states this is not the case).

Further, what does the speaker mean when he says that his advisors counseled him that he would not be able to bear the burden of prosecuting for hubris? This indicates the way that the gravity of the redress sought would determine the response by the defendant. The higher the stakes, as reflected in the status and connections of the defendant and the seriousness of the charge, the more that litigation may come to resemble feud, or a kind of private war, and the greater the capital (symbolic, social, economic, political) someone must have to enter into this struggle, which will continue long after the case at hand is over.

At the same time, however, it is important for a plaintiff like the young man in *Against Conon* not to appear too timid. For if his injuries are as great as he claims he must demonstrate to the judges an appropriate desire for revenge or risk being suspected of having exaggerated the charges. So he says that he decided to follow the advice of his elders (demonstrating his good character) though it would have pleased him to have pressed a capital charge (54.1). Having detailed the horrific nature of his humiliation and injuries, in his peroration he argues that the judges should share in the anger he feels toward Conon and should not regard this as a private matter that might happen to any man. Again taking the language of criminal wrong from hubris and the like he asks the judges, "Will it be in the interests of each of you to let off a man who beats people up and commits hubris? I think not. But if you let him go there will be many, if you punish him, fewer" (42–3).

We see in these orations the way in which speakers utilize the rhetoric of public wrongs, harm to the public interests of the *polis* as a whole, and punishment (as opposed to compensation to the victim) to press their case, even when in a technical sense it is a kind of action involving only a private matter. The rationale of punishment is expressed as advancing the public interest in deterring others from committing such wrongs. The pervasiveness of this strategy in the corpus of legal orations reveals the power of such appeals and, hence, the centrality of such thinking in Athenian conceptions of wrongdoing and legal process. Athenian law may provide a series of remedies for many kinds of wrongs, but regardless of what procedural rubric they fall under orators expect the mass courts of citizen-judges to respond to characterizations of private violence as a threat to public interests.

The cases reviewed thus far all involve nonlethal bodily violence, but such arguments were also thought appropriate where the object of the wrongdoing was property. Thus, in *Against Timocrates* Demosthenes applies a similar argument to the variety of actions by which individuals might pursue different kinds of thieves. The speaker notes how the various kinds of theft may be punished summarily or through a trial, depending on the circumstances. These are clearly conceptualized as public offenses and involve capital penalties rather than compensation (24.113). But even private suits for theft might be so regarded. The speaker discusses the various options and says that if someone is convicted in a private (*idian*) suit for theft (*klopē*) the normal penalty is to pay double the amount of the value of the stolen property. But, he continues, the judges can also assess an additional punishment of confinement in the stocks for five days and nights "so that everyone can see him bound." He says that the purpose of this law was to deter other potential thieves, because in addition to paying double, the humiliation of this public confinement would cause them to live in shame for the rest of their lives (115). This again shows the way in which certain kinds of conduct that represent a forcible violation of protected private spheres could formally fall under the procedure of private lawsuits (*dikai*) but might nonetheless be regarded as an offense against the public.

PRIVATE ENMITY AND PUBLIC PROSECUTION

If the prosecution of crime depended on the actions of private citizens, what did Athenians think of these citizen prosecutors and their role in the *polis*? Our principle knowledge on such matters comes from the persuasive efforts of such prosecutors to characterize themselves to the judges. These rhetorical constructions, in turn, reflect the speakers' expectations of how judges will view them and what kinds of criticisms they might expect. Aeschines' oration *Against Timarchus* (1) offers valuable insight into what anticipated responses guide such rhetorical constructions. This oration involves the prosecution of Timarchus for speaking to the Assembly when the laws prohibit him from doing so because he allegedly prostituted himself as a young man. The real motive behind the prosecution appears to have been Aeschines' enmity toward Demosthenes, with whom Timarchus was closely associated. This points up one of the dangers of popular prosecution, which is its potential misuse in the service of private enmity. Indeed, the Athenians considered malicious prosecution a serious offense that endangered the integrity of the administration of justice.

The seriousness with which such matters were taken is indicated by the very first words of Against Timarchus: "I have never indicted (*graphēn grapsamenos*) any citizen nor assailed any man when he was giving an account of his office . . ." (1.1). The role of the citizen-prosecutors can thus cut either way. On the one hand they may be seen as doing their civic duty to protect the city from wrongdoers who commit crimes against the public interest, or, on the other hand, they may be viewed as abusing the ability to initiate criminal actions for gain or revenge. Accordingly, in these very first sentences Aeschines makes clear that his prosecution is in response to a public wrong: "When I saw that the city was being greatly harmed. . . . I decided that it would be most shameful if I did not come to the aid of the *whole city, and its laws and you and myself*" (my emphasis). He concludes this opening section by arguing that his conduct proves the truth of the adage which maintains in regard to public prosecutions (*dēmosiois agōsin*) that "private enmities (*idiai echthrai*) very often rectify public wrongs" (1–2). Here the private citizen, though he may be motivated by enmity against the defendant, appears as the defender of the interests of the *polis* and its laws and institutions. In the absence of magistrates entrusted with public prosecutions the system relies on individuals acting in such a manner. In the following passage Aeschines offers a rationale for this way of organizing the city's affairs.

For Aechines this is a central feature of Athenian democracy. He begins by contrasting the role of law in democracy with other forms of constitution. In democracies, he claims, "the laws guard the person of the citizens and the constitution of the city," whereas oligarchies and tyrannies are preserved by force (1.5). The democratic idea of the rule of law thus rests on the notion that it is the law that protects citizens in their persons from harm. This is because in a democracy the law is enforced through the citizens themselves, as judges and as prosecutors. It is this democratic unity of interest that underlies the identification of the prosecutor, judges, law, and the interests of the demos/polis embodied in formulations such as that quoted in the preceding paragraph: "the whole city, and its laws, and you and me." We saw the same sentiment voiced by Demosthenes in *Against Meidias*, and it appears throughout the corpus of forensic orations. This position, as Aeschines makes explicit, rests on a notion of law as a support not just of public order, but of the democratic political order. Thus, he argues, when legislating, the demos (as represented by the judges) must consider how to make laws that are in the interests of their democratic constitution. Further, once the laws are enacted, if the state is to fare well they must punish those who do not obey the laws (6, and cf. 36 and Aeschines, *Against Ctesiphon*, 3.6–7). Punishing crime thus appears as the necessary foundation for upholding the rule of law and the democracy on which it is based. Citizen prosecutors and judges are the instruments by which the democracy is preserved. As Demosthenes sums it up in another oration (18.123), "Our ancestors established the law courts (*dikastēria*) not so that speakers would air their private grievances against one another but so that those guilty of offenses against the *polis* might be convicted."

This view is made even more explicit in an oration by Lycurgus that in parts reads like a kind of "civics lesson" in Athenian democracy. In *Against Leocrates* (1) Lycurgus portrays himself as prosecuting Leocrates for his crimes for the benefit of the demos and the *polis*. He justifies this stance by setting out a democratic conception of criminal law and public prosecution. He begins by saying that those who prosecute should be regarded with gratitude by the city. Instead, though they are acting for the common good, the reverse is true, which does not result in either justice or advantage for the *polis*. He supports this claim by explaining how, on his view, the system of popular prosecution works.

There are three main factors, he maintains, that preserve the democracy and the prosperity of the *polis*: the system of laws, the vote of the judges in the popular courts, and the system of prosecution by which crimes are brought to court. He then explains in detail how this schema works. The laws, he says, proscribe what must not be done. The prosecutor (*katēgoros*) accuses those who are liable to the penalties prescribed by the laws. The judges punish those whom the other two elements have brought into court. On the basis of this conceptual diagram of how a system of popular prosecution for crime works, he concludes that the whole system depends on someone who will bring the criminals into court. This is, of course, his role, which he has just elaborated and defended (1.3–5). Thus, though driven by private initiative, the system works in the public interest and expresses and preserves the Athenian democracy.

Articulating the same concern about the role of private enmity as Aeschines, Leocrates gives it a different rhetorical spin, but one that reflects similar concerns about how the relation of enmity to public prosecution will be perceived. He thus claims that he brought the case forward not out of enmity or vexatiousness, but rather to prevent harm to the city. Elaborating the principles behind this, he says that the just citizen will not bring public (*koinas*) prosecutions against one who has committed no crime on account of his private enmity (*dia tas idias echthras*). Rather, he will regard as his private enemies those who violate the laws of the *polis*. The public quality of the crimes (*ta koina tōn adikēmatōn*) provides public grounds (*koinas kai tas prophaseis*) for enmity toward such men. Here the central thrust of the passage is that when the system operates properly, prosecutions, though initiated by private citizens, respond to public wrongs and serve the public interests of the *polis*, not the private interests of the prosecuting party (1.5–6).

For Aeschines and Lycurgus, then, the role of the good citizen is to prosecute crimes on behalf of the demos or, when sitting as a judge, to punish such crimes in the name of the democratic order that they are sworn to defend. What of those who defend wrongdoers? Lycurgus indicates that it is to be expected that friends and relatives will speak in their defense, but he attacks individuals who otherwise defend those who betray the democracy. Such rhetorical skill, he says, should be used "on behalf of you, the laws, and the democracy" (138).[12] The identification of the interests of the judges, laws, and the democratic constitution is a natural one in Athens, but as one sees here, it has its dangers in providing a rhetoric for condemning or silencing opposition. These will be explored in more detail below, but one such problem appears in a later section of *Against Leocrates*, when Lycurgus argues that the judges should take vengeance on Leocrates for his crime (141–6). Conceiving of the judges in this way threatens to collapse the distinction between vengeance and punishment that the rule of law and the public trial of offenders is designed to preserve. This collapse is, however, already implicit in claiming that in meting out punishment the judges are at once serving the laws and their own interests as citizens and members of the demos. The rhetoric of Demosthenes and Lycurgus at times verges on that of a kind of public and institutional self-help, not the impartial application of judicial judgment.[13] This was perhaps at Athens

---

[12] See also Dinarchus (*Against Demosthenes*, 1.113).

[13] There would have been a natural tendency in this direction in political offenses against the *polis*. See Dinarchus, *Against Philocles*, 3.8 and cf. 19.

a natural tendency, given the centrality of participatory government and the elements of self-help and summary action that played an important role in the Athenian treatment of crime.

Permitting Self-Help, Limiting Revenge

We have seen the way in which Athenians were well aware that the private desire for revenge or the pursuit of enmity might well be the fuel that impelled individuals to initiate prosecutions. The idea here is that if the defendant is convicted the *polis* will substitute its punishment for the vengeance of the aggrieved party. Athenian law, as in many other legal systems, permitted even more direct forms of self-help. For example, certain kinds of serious offenders might be dealt with by summary procedures if apprehended in the act. In such cases they might be executed on the spot by private citizens or detained and brought before officials known as The Eleven (by the procedure of *apagōgē*), who could execute them immediately or bring them to trial if they plausibly denied their guilt.[14] Despite scholarly disagreement about the details of these summary procedures, what is important for our purposes is that they legitimized summary execution without trial, whether carried out by private citizens or public officials. How did the Athenians conceive of this exercise in self-help and extrajudicial execution and how did they reconcile it with their commitment to judicial punishment and the rule of law?

The case is more straightforward when the execution is carried out by the Eleven, for the law permits them to do so only where the offender does not deny his guilt. This may sound strange at first glance, but as in most other legal systems that adopted such provisions, essential to this manner of proceeding is the public apprehension of the criminal in the act. A thief caught in the act and dragged off by witnesses to the Eleven with the stolen property will be hard put to deny his guilt to the satisfaction of the Eleven. If he does so, perhaps claiming that he was only recovering his own property, he will be tried before a popular court. The more difficult case arises where the victim takes matters into his own hands.

Lysias' oration *On the Murder of Eratosthenes* (1) represents such a case.[15] A cuckolded husband takes the adulterer Eratosthenes in the act, having summoned many witnesses before he enters the bedroom that is

---

[14] See Aeschines, *Against Timarchus*, 1.90–1, and Aristotle, *Ath. Pol.* 52.1. For different interpretations see D. Cohen (1983: Chapter 3), Hansen (1976), and Todd (1993: 117–8, 228).

[15] For detailed accounts of this case see D. Cohen (1991: Chapter 5) and Cantarella 1991a.

the scene of the crime (23–8; 37). As he admits, he killed the man on the spot and is later prosecuted for homicide. This would be part of the considerable risk that those engaging in direct self-help would have to bear. What is of interest for our purposes is the rhetorical strategy by which he defends and justifies his actions. What he does is to portray his exercise in self-help as the legal punishment for a public offense as ordained by the laws of the *polis*. His argument is a classic statement of criminal punishment as opposed to private vendetta. When Eratosthenes begs for mercy, the husband replies. "It is not I who am going to kill you but our city's laws, which you have transgressed..." (26). He presents his self-help as an instrument for the execution of the laws of the *polis* and repeats this theme over and over as his central argument (29, 34). In his peroration he sums up the point in the clearest terms: "Therefore I do not regard this penalty to be on behalf of my own private interest, but rather on behalf of the whole city" (47). Whatever the actual merits of this case, the salient point is that Lysias believed that the most persuasive strategy lay in constructing self-help as a means by which citizens acted for the laws and the demos in punishing wrongdoers. In a participatory system for the prosecution of crime that depended on a citizen's initiative he might well expect such a plea to be persuasive.

As noted earlier, it might seem that the area of prosecution of homicide, of which *On the Murder of Eratosthenes* is an example, does not fit in with the notion of public offenses, crime, and punishment because it was pursued through a category of action (*dikē phonou*) open only to the kin of the victim. We have seen, however, that this procedural classification did not necessarily imply that the prohibited act was seen as merely a private wrong that did not affect the *polis*. That this is in any event unlikely is indicated not only by the prohibition against the polluted perpetrator entering the public spaces of the city but also by the fact that those accused of intentional homicide (like those accused of intentional wounding, also a *dikē*) were not brought before the courts that heard ordinary *dikai*, but before the court of the Areopagus that in classical times only heard these kinds of cases and was regarded with particular awe.[16] The literary portrayal of the foundation of this court in Aechylus' *Eumenides* amply reveals the way in which the stability of the *polis* was regarded as depending on the establishment of a public court to punish homicide and prevent vendetta. As will appear, it is quite clear from our sources that homicide was not regarded as a purely private

---

[16] See Demosthenes 23.66: "The Areopagus is the only tribunal which no democracy, oligarchy, or tyrant has dared to deprive of its jurisdiction over homicide."

wrong affecting only the family of the deceased, and it is important to understand why from the Athenian perspective there may have appeared to be no contradiction between murder being seen as one of the most serious offenses and not including it in the category of crimes which any citizen might prosecute.

Demosthenes' oration *Against Aristocrates* (23) deals at some length with the law of homicide. The portrayal of homicide law here insists on its public quality. Thus, the speaker says that when someone is accused of homicide it is the city that punishes him only after it has satisfied itself by a trial whether the accusation is true – and not before. He expounds on this by indicating how the law of homicide substitutes public legal process for private revenge. This is because, he explains, the lawgiver thought that because "we avenge the victim" we must first know if the defendant is guilty. In homicide cases, regardless of the fact that they are brought by a *dikē*, the city is portrayed as the avenger of the victim and trial, rather than vendetta by the kin, is the mechanism (25–6). The speaker goes on to explain the difference between punishment and vengeance, using as an example the summary arrest of a convicted murderer who has come back from exile and is apprehended and taken to the Archons. He explains that taking a man to the Archons is fundamentally different than leaving him to the mercy of the prosecutor. In the former case, he says, "the man is punished as the law commands, in the latter case as the prosecutor pleases. And there is the greatest difference whether the law has sovereign authority over punishment/retribution (*timōrias*) or the man's enemy" (31–2).

He continues by adducing the many prohibitions on mistreatment of those who have gone into exile after a homicide. As an example he cites how killing the murderer who has fulfilled the requirements of the law in fleeing into exile is treated the same as ordinary homicide against any Athenian citizen (38). These measures, he explains, are designed to prevent an endless chain of revenge killings (39), that is, blood feud. The conception of homicide as an offense that in a direct way involves the public interest is clear. This whole battery of laws is designed to limit revenge, curtail the role of the kin, remove the violence of feud from the city, protect the man who goes into exile, and vest the sole authority for punishment for homicide in the *polis*.[17] In a later section (69) he concludes by arguing that even when the prosecutor has proved the

---

[17] Of course the distinctions that go back to Draco between intentional, unintentional, and accidental homicide are also a limitation on the process of seeking vengeance by classifying homicide according to public standards of justice. On the development of early homicide law see Gagarin (1981) and Cantarella (1976).

charge and the murderer is convicted, the laws (*nomoi*) alone have the authority to punish him. Significantly he adds that it is only permitted the prosecutor to see the penalty that the law prescribed being inflicted and that is all. The interest of the family in prosecuting homicide is apparent here, but so are the limitations that the *polis* places on the family's role in recasting private vengeance as public punishment. All that remains of the duty of kin to avenge blood with blood is that they are permitted to observe the execution being carried out.[18] This, he says, is the right of the prosecutor (69); no less, but also no more.[19]

As we have seen thus far, Athenian sources discuss a notion of the rule of law that requires that the power to punish be vested in judges who pronounce judgment in the name of the *polis*. It was also seen, however, that although Athenians might "condemn as uninhabitable those states where citizens are sometimes put to death without trial" (Isocrates, *Antidosis*, 15.22), the Athenian legal system's ways of dealing with crime incorporated a significant measure of summary procedures and self-help. This was, of course, the result of the way in which the system developed over time, the general participatory nature of Athenian democracy, and the persistent respect for the right, within carefully demarcated limits, of the *oikos* (household, family) to protect its domain against violation and dishonor. It is also important to recognize, however, that summary procedures might also be institutionalized in other forms where they seem to conflict clearly with the requirements of the rule of law. This involves extrajudicial execution by public bodies.

THE POWER TO PUNISH AND THE DEMOCRATIC RULE OF LAW

Aristotle, in his history of the Athenian constitution (*Ath. Pol.* 44.1), explains how

> The Boule formerly had the power to fine, imprison, and execute. But once when it had brought Lysimachus to the public executioner and he was waiting, about to die, Eumelides

---

[18] For the authoritative treatment of capital punishment see Cantarella (1991b).
[19] Of course the other role assigned to the family is to seek vengeance through legal process through their role as initiators of the prosecution. Though in actuality blood money may well have been paid not to do so, in terms of social norms and ideals it was unthinkable for a family not to seek to avenge the deceased and it was considered an act of impiety (*asebeia*) not to do so.

of the deme Alopece rescued him, saying that no citizen ought to die without being convicted by a court.... And the demos deprived the Boule of the right to fine, imprison, and kill, and made a law that all convictions and penalties passed by the Boule must be brought ... before a court, and that the judgment of the dikasts should prevail.

Little is known of the way in which such discretionary power to punish citizens without trial was exercised.[20] Aristotle's discussion indicates that the limitation of this power represented a shift in power to the popular courts by giving them the exclusive right to punish (see below). It also demonstrates a commitment (however imperfectly it may at times have been implemented) to a model of the rule of law where the power of the state to punish wrongdoers is conceived as operating exclusively within and through the law. This indicates the recognition of the kind of principles of legality that we today see as intrinsic to a legitimate system of criminal justice that protects citizens from arbitrary punishments through application of the principle that punishment can only proceed from conviction after a fair trial.

The grave public interests at stake in such circumstances are further indicated by another event recounted by Aristotle in the same text. After having discussed the oligarchic coup of the Thirty Tyrants and the excesses of their extralegal executions, banishments, and confiscations, Aristotle turns to the reconciliation of 403 B.C. and the amnesty which prohibited seeking legal redress for wrongs suffered. In this context, he describes the three great statesmanlike acts of one of the leaders, Archinus. One of these takes place when an individual began to provoke grudges against the returnees. Archinus takes him off by summary arrest to the Boule and persuades them to put him to death without trial (*akriton apokteinai*) on the grounds that this is the moment to make an example and show they are committed to saving the democracy. Aristotle, who has just condemned the illegal execution of the generals from Arginusae, has only praise for this measure. What accounts for the difference in his reaction to these two instances of extrajudicial execution?

On my view, such judgments arise from the widespread conviction in Athens that that the criminal law is ultimately an instrument to preserve the political order, an exercise of political power. When

---

[20] See Lysias 22.2–4, Todd (1993: 316 n.2), and MacDowell (1978: 189–90).

swift action is required to save the state, then it is legitimate for a political body other than the courts to exercise that power extrajudicially, that is, to use their political authority to deprive someone of his life without resort to trial. The willingness to do so and the way in which it is viewed as unproblematic, statesmanlike, and praiseworthy by Aristotle tells us a lot about the way in which Athenians may have viewed the criminal law and its power of life and death over citizens – not just as impartial justice dispassionately meted out but as the bedrock of the political order in the use of which the ends may justify the means. This is buttressed and justified by the identification of the laws, the judges, the demos, and the democracy frequently cited above. Athenian judges took the Heliastic oath, which requires impartiality, and acknowledged principles of legality and the rule of law, but these values existed in tension with others that identified the laws with the interests of the *polis*.

This is what for Aristotle distinguishes the democratic excess of the response to Arginusae from the statesmanlike act of Archinus and the Council. As Isocrates asserts in his *Areopagiticus* (7.46–7), when Athens was well-governed the Boule enforced discipline by summoning the disorderly and threatening or punishing them. They understood that order is maintained only through both punishment and watchfulness (*epimeleia*). They thus could see in advance who were likely to commit an offense. Such disciplinary (in the Foucauldian sense) fantasies are typical of Athenian political theorists skeptical of radical democracy, but more democratically minded thinkers were also not immune to this logic. In such a context Lycurgus (*Against Leocrates*, 1.124–7) refers to a law adopted after the overthrow of the Thirty, which provided that anyone who killed a person trying to overthrow the democracy or aspiring to tyranny should be guiltless. Commenting on the wisdom of this provision, he says that for normal crimes the punishment follows the crime, but in the case of treason or overthrowing the democracy it should precede it. This comment again demonstrates the participatory nature of the system of criminal law, its intermingling with the political goals of protecting the democratic constitution from its enemies, and the way in which self-help can be put to use in such a system. In a political context where the interests of the prosecutors, judges, law, and *polis* might be so closely identified, such attitudes could naturally arise. In the remaining part of the chapter we explore other tensions this might produce within a system that viewed itself as embodying the rule of law.

In his account of the development of the Athenian judicial system from the time of Solon to the fourth century, one of Aristotle's overarching themes is the steady growth of the power of the demos through legal reform. This begins with the extension of the power to prosecute to "any citizen who wished to do so" (*Ath. Pol.* 9.1–2) and culminates with measures like the introduction of pay for serving on the popular courts (27.4–5). What Aristotle understands by this is judicial reform as a principal means by which the power of the demos was enhanced at the expense of the "better" classes. That is, the courts become dominated by those who associate their political interests with the radical democracy. In his review of eleven stages of the development of the Athenian constitution (*politeia*), he concludes his account of the final stage by emphasizing how it has given ultimate power to the demos: "For the demos has made itself sovereign over everything and administers everything by decrees and by popular courts in which the demos is the ruling power, for even the cases tried by the Council have come to the demos" (41.2).

In his discussion of the radical democracy in his *Politics*, Aristotle argues that these courts have even put themselves above the law and in doing so have made this form of democracy like a tyranny in its lawlessness. Athenian democrats did not share Aristotle's conception of the rule of law,[21] but what was clear to all who viewed Athenian legal institutions was that they represented a major source of political power. Tyrants from Peisistratus to the Thirty Tyrants, tried to control or eliminate the authority of the Athenian *dikastērion* (*Ath. Pol.* 35.2). Plato advances a theoretical account of this view in his *laws*, where he sees all existing states as merely having institutionalized the results of social conflict in their constitutions, whereby the wealthy in an oligarchy or the many in a democracy write the constitution in such a way so as to use the laws and judicial institutions of the state to advance their own interests at the expense of the group that is out of power (713–15). On Plato's view, under such conditions there can be no rule of law for the law is subordinated to the political interests of the ruling party.

Athenians of all political perspectives recognized what our belief in the ideology of the neutrality of the administration of justice and the rule of law tends to blind us to (unless we belong to the groups who feel that the legal system discriminates against them on account of race or poverty). That is, they understood that the power to punish violations of the law in the name of the state is central to the authority

---

[21] See D. Cohen (1995: Chapter 3),

of those who (on the Greek view of constitutions) wield the power in the state, whether the many (democracy), the few (oligarchy), or a tyrant or monarch.[22] That is, they recognized that laws and courts did not just establish that offences against the public weal must be defined and punished according to the law so as to maintain the social *and* political order, but also that this function is an instrument of political power. In the orations discussed above speakers often identified the interests of the democracy with "its" laws and courts. As Demosthenes put it in one oration (24.154), reducing the authority of the courts is a sure way to facilitate the overthrowing of the democracy. It was in this light that they, democrats and their critics alike, saw the historic shift of power to democratic courts and citizen prosecutors. The impact of this recognition is felt throughout the corpus of legal oratory, for it underlies the constant fear that the rule of law, and particularly its component principle of equality before the law, will be undermined in particular cases by considerations of the interests of the demos.

The fear, depending on one's point of view, was that the wealth, status, and influence of a person would weigh for or against the arguments in the case at hand. Demosthenes (51.11–12) employs widely used rhetorical topoi in commenting on the ideology of equality before the law and the problem of different punishments for rich and poor. He asks the judges, "If a poor man commits a crime because of his poverty he will be punished with the most severe penalties, but if a rich man does the same thing on account of shameful love of gain he will be pardoned. Where then is equality for all and democratic government if you manage things in this way?" In *Against Meidias* and other orations Demosthenes also inveighed against the way in which the hubristic rich used their influence to harm other citizens with impunity and to deny equality before the law (21.112, 123–5, 169–70).

The real problem here is not just that wealth and status might help a citizen avoid punishment for wrongdoing (as it also does in our own legal system through a variety of means). What underlies the fear that such factors (e.g., hostility or deference to the wealthy) will play a role in reaching judgment is the realization that in an Athenian prosecution a person's life is on trial as well as the act for which he is accused. This results in the attacks on character that are such a striking feature of Athenian forensic oratory. Equally striking is that they are leveled not just at the defendant, but also at his accuser. In a sense, both parties' lives

---

[22] See Allen (2000b).

are on trial in many cases. This seems wildly at odds with our notion of criminal prosecution, where *the accused* is to be judged for what he or she did or did not do, not for what he or she *is* or might have done in the past. But given the tendency of Athenians to identify the interests of the laws, the judges, the demos, and the *polis*, it was natural to view a prosecution in a different light.

This is the danger represented by this notion of the unity of the demos with its laws and courts. In Athens the idea that a criminal trial is not about what a man is but about what he has done is also present in forensic rhetoric, but it exists in tension with the ideas advanced by orators such as Aeschines, Demosthenes, or Lycurgus that the laws and courts are mechanisms for the demos to protect itself from those who may harm it. This notion can result in the criminal conviction of a Timarchus, but also of a Socrates. In *Against Ctesiphon*, Aeschines tells the judges that they will protect their democracy if they punish those whose policies are opposed to "the laws and to your [i.e., the judges'] interests" (3.8). On Aeschines' formulations, or Lycurgus's admonition that in cases of treason punishment can precede the crime, it is not clear that the interests of the demos are not enough to convict, regardless of the niceties of legal guilt. The point here is that the nature of Athenian democratic institutions, and the manner in which thinkers such as Aeschines and Demosthenes conceptualize them rhetorically, blend legality and interest together in a way that makes them largely indistinguishable and tends to convert some criminal trials, at least of those engaged in public life, into a trial of their social standing and usefulness to the *polis* in relation to that of their opponent. In this sense it is an *agōn* about who they are as much as it is a trial about whether a particular violation of the law occurred. Of course, this would have been different for the average thief or cutpurse who comes before a *dikastērion* to stand trial, but it is itself telling that such individuals largely fall below the horizon of our sources except in occasional anecdotes. It is equally telling that they are the types of criminal who are subjected to summary procedures and may have only infrequently come before a court.

As we have seen, on the one hand, prosecutions for public offenses in Athens were informed by ideas about crime, punishment, and the rule of law that are clearly familiar to modern readers in their adherence to notions of impartial judgments dispensed in the name of the law to vindicate and prevent harms to the community as a whole. On the other hand, the incorporation of elements of self-help, summary procedures, execution without trial, and judgments based on the character, wealth, political clout, and public benefactions of the parties challenges us to understand why the understanding of crime and punishment in democratic Athens could differ so sharply from that of today. And differ not because their legal system was corrupt, primitive, or incompetent, but because the Athenian understanding of concepts of justice, democracy, and the rule of law in important ways differed fundamentally from our own.

12: GENDER, SEXUALITY, AND LAW

Eva Cantarella

Until the 1970s, more or less, the history of women and sexuality did not interest the academic community. When it was even considered, such history was limited to a few references within research dedicated to more traditional subjects, regarded as scientifically more interesting. In the past thirty years, however, the horizons of classicists have expanded to include these issues and to dedicate ever more attention to the problem of social construction of gender as a political organizing principle.

The opening up of these new horizons is part of a more general transformation of ancient and modern historiography, tied to the French school that followed Fernand Braudel, who criticized the history that concentrated on the great events and major figures ("l'histoire evenementielle," as Francois Simiand defined it), neglecting the underlying social reality and ignoring the existence of millions and millions of anonymous individuals. In this light new historiographic subjects were born, the different and marginal from every epoch: the sick, the old and young, homosexuals, women – subjects, all of them, whose history is not determined by events, but rather by mental attitudes, ideologies, practicalities of everyday life and their position in a socioeconomic context. The history of women and sexuality and the reconstruction of gender problems have thus established themselves inside this new history, no longer only "evenementielle." They have begun conquering ever larger spaces thanks to the effort and the forward push of feminist research. Inevitably, then, approaches and perspectives of the imposing historiography produced in recent years vary greatly, according to the differing viewpoints of various disciplines. Communication and exchange between disciplines, however, even though initially scarce, have intensified through the years, leading to new and important results.[1]

The Construction of Gender: Interaction between Law and Society

Today, scholars facing questions related to gender construction and sexuality can use heterogeneous but complementary sources, ranging from medical texts to philosophical treatises, from literature to legal texts, from funerary inscriptions to archaeological reconstruction of public and private spaces. Among these sources, although all of them are relevant, those that refer to legal rules merit particular attention.

These rules, which show what was allowed and what was forbidden to men and women, obviously do not always reflect social reality. Between law and society there is a distance, which can vary over space and time. Depending on the time and individual situations, this distance sometimes favors the law, which is more advanced than society; at other times it may be on the side of society, which is more advanced than the law. Often, in the same place and in the same moment, some branches of the law are more advanced than society, while others remain behind (family law, for example, can be more advanced than criminal law or the other way around). But this does not alter the fact that the rules of law, general and abstract as they are, indicate clearly what a society wants (or would like) from those to whom the rules are addressed. They define the limits of individual freedom and the behaviors considered intolerable. Thus they reflect a model of behavior that society (or the ruler, in a nondemocratic regime) wishes to impose on men and women.

However, legal rules are not always the same for both sexes. In other words, the law is gendered, and at the same time engenders society: on the one hand it reflects the social construction of sexual roles, and on the other it reinforces this construction. This does not mean, naturally, that the law is the only source of gender construction. In the Greek world – but not only there – poetry and literature in general play an analogous role; and they do this since an epoch in which laws did not yet exist. In other words, poetry (in particular epic poetry, whose pedagogical role in oral societies is well-known)[2] was the means that

---

[1] See, for example, I. Morris (1999: 305–17).
[2] Bibliography in Cantarella (2002c: 20–30; 204–7).

proposed to the Greeks, for centuries, a series of female stereotyped images, which paved the way for the earliest legal regulation of women's condition.

The Homeric Epics and the Division of Women into the Seduced and the Seductresses

From poetic performances, the Greeks learned that there were two categories of women: the "honest" ones and "the others." They also learned the criteria – objective, not subjective – that placed women into one or the other: honest women lived in an *oikos*, that is to say, in a household, governed by a man (*anax oikoio*, in Homer: the sovereign of the house). The others lived alone. Their different style of life determined the way their sexual behavior was perceived: if an "honest" woman protected by the *oikos*' walls and by bonds of family affection had illicit sexual relations, she was either seduced by a man or induced by a force that she could not resist.[3] "The others," instead, had sexual relations by seducing their partners, often overcoming their resistance.

Let us start with the honest ones and consider Helen's case. In the *Iliad*, she repents her behavior and calls herself a "she-dog," but the Trojans do not despise her. As Priam says (3.162–65), she cannot be held responsible for her action, because she was driven by Aphrodite. Even the prototype of the adulteress, the infamous Clytemnestra, who betrayed her husband and slaughtered him, even Clytemnestra was brought to commit adultery against her nature, driven by a decision of the Moira (*Odyssey* 3.266–72).

As far as "the others," independent, different, and disquieting, how their behavior was dangerous was taught by characters such as Calypso or Circe. Calypso, says Homer, had kept Odysseus with her (for seven years) "with enchanting words" (*logoisi haimylioisi*, *Odyssey* 1.56), an irresistible feminine weapon, as Hesiod says speaking of Pandora, the first women sent as a punishment among men to make their life miserable. Calypso then, thanks to her "enchanting words," has sexually seduced Odysseus, whose story with the nymph was perceived as a relationship by ancient commentators, who attribute children to the couple – although they do not agree on their number.[4] He had a similar relationship with Circe, the witch. Like Calypso, Circe lives alone: no husband, no father,

---

[3] On this homeric stereotyping of women see Cantarella (2002c: 129–42).
[4] One in Apollodorus's *Epitome*; two in Hesiod, *Theog.* 1017-18 and Eustathius, *ad Homeri Od.*, 16.118.

no brothers. Like Calypso she sings when Odysseus meets her. Women such as Penelope, the honest women, never sing. It is perhaps not chance that the voice of the housewife is silenced through the centuries of the *polis*. Silence is a sign of respectability. The Homeric stereotyping of women is clear: honest women live in a house governed by a man; "the others" live alone. As a corollary, honest women obey, keeping silent; the others, the dangerous ones, sing and seduce.

The First Athenian Law

The first Athenian law was enacted by Draco in 621/0 B.C. and was reinscribed by the *anagrapheis* in the late fifth century (409/8 B.C.).[5] It stated that a person accused of homicide had to undergo a judicial trial. It established different courts and different degrees of punishment for voluntary and involuntary homicide. The aim of the law was to regulate and limit private revenge, which until that moment had been the habitual and unquestioned response to every wrong that a person claimed to have suffered. But although it prohibited revenge in a general way, the law established some exceptions. Among these, one is especially illuminating as far as gender ideology is concerned: in contrast to the new principles that signaled the birth of a true penal law, Draco guaranteed impunity to the man who had killed another man caught "next to" (*epi* + dative) his wife, mother, daughter, sister, or the concubine (*pallakē*) he kept for the purpose of having free children, that is, his free concubine.[6]

In so doing, the law divided women into two categories: those whose sexual good behavior was protected by the impunity granted to the killer of the man caught "next to" them, and those not falling under the law, "the others" with whom sex was allowed. To a careful analysis, it appears that the law, for all intents and purposes, codified the Homeric division of women as "seduced" and "seductresses," transforming the social stereotype into a legal classification that had fundamental legal consequences on women's life.

The derivation of the Draconian category of the "protected" women from the epic stereotyping appears when we consider the criteria that induced the law to protect them. What had these women in

---

[5] The text of the law, currently at the Athenian Epigraphical Museum, has been published by Stroud (1968). On its controversial interpretation see Gagarin (1981) and Cantarella (2002b), with updated bibliography.

[6] This part of the law, not visible on the marble stele, is quoted in Demosthenes 23.53.

common? On reflection, they had in common two things. The first was that they all lived in the house of an Athenian citizen, the man entitled by the law to kill with impunity. They shared a *de facto* situation, which was given legal consequences by Draco in recognition of the right of the head of a household to be certain that all the free women living under his roof were respected, that is, sexually protected. The rationale (or one of the rationales) that induced Draco to "protect" these women was the presumption that they were always "seduced" or "induced" – as we will see – if they had illicit sexual relations. To this rationale, however, a second rationale induced Draco to allow the lawful killing of the lover, a rationale tied to the birth of the *polis*: these women shared a further common characteristic, they all gave birth to Athenian citizens.[7] The second, but not secondary, aim of Draco's law, then, was to protect the purity of the civic lineage.

SEXUAL CRIMES AND WOMEN'S CONSENT

Archaic Age

Draco's law, in perfect adherence to the social stereotypes that had inspired it, did not take into account women's consent. When dealing with a "protected" woman, the law presumed that this consent had been extorted. Therefore the law made no distinction between the lover and the rapist, granting immunity to the person who killed either.[8]

This is proved first by the myth of the trial of Ares, who had slaughtered Halirrothius, the son of Poseidon, after surprising him in the act of raping his daughter and was acquitted by the Areopagus.[9] Second, the law stated that a man could be killed only if caught in the house where the woman lived. This is explicitly stated in Lysias's speech in defense of Euphiletus, based on Draco's law. Accused of having killed his wife's lover, Eratosthenes, Euphiletus insists on the fact that he found Eratosthenes in his house, a circumstance that outraged (*hybrisen*) him. But this was a necessary, yet not a sufficient condition to make a

---

[7] As I suggested in Cantarella (1997). This is, however, a controversial issue, closely tied to the debate on the public status of illegitimate children, depending on the interpretation of Perikles' citizenship law (Aristotle, *Ath. Pol.* 42.1) On the topic see Ogden (1996: 15ff.) and Patterson, this volume.

[8] Among others, Harrison (1968: I, 34), D. Cohen (1984), Ogden (1997: 28).

[9] Apollodorus 3.14.2. See also Pausanias 1.21.1, cf. Hellanicus *FGH* 323 a F22 and Dinarchus 1.89.

homicide "lawful." The man had to be caught "next to,"[10] meaning during the moment of sexual intercourse, as the reading of Lysias's defense of Euphiletus shows very clearly,[11] and as confirmed by later sources.[12]

The necessity of catching the culprit in flagrante, then, confirms the hypothesis that rapists too could be killed with impunity. Otherwise the "lawful" killers, to be considered as such, would have to demonstrate in court that the woman had consented – a problematic task under the circumstances.[13] The text of Draco's law shows that when the law was promulgated in the seventh century, consensual relations with a "protected" woman and rape were indistinguishable. Exactly as in the Homeric poems, because sexual relations with these women was an offense to the man who had the power and responsibility to control them, their real consent or the lack thereof was simply irrelevant.

The Age of the Orators

As the centuries passed, the Greeks' mentality and law changed. Let us jump ahead a few centuries, to Athens of the fourth century B.C., where Lysias writes the already-quoted oration in defense of Euphiletus. Accused of having killed Eratosthenes, his wife's lover, Euphiletus maintains that he killed him to uphold the city's laws, which required him to punish a man who, as he says, "committed *moicheia* (adultery) *on* my wife (the emphasis on *on* will be explained later) and corrupted (*diephtheire*) her and outraged (*hybrisen*) my offspring and myself, entering my house."[14]

---

[10] The translation of the Greek "*epi* + the dative" with "next to" is controversial. In fact, in Greek it means also "on top" and some scholars prefer this translation (Harris 1990). On this issue see also Carey (1995a: 409–10 and n. 8 and 9) and Omitowoju (2002: 75 n. 9).

[11] For reasons in favor of this interpretation, see Cantarella 1976.

[12] See Lucian, *Eunuchus* 19 and a passage of the Roman jurist Ulpian, in Justinian's *Digest*, 48.5.24 (23) 4, quoting Draco's law.

[13] See Harrison (1968: I,35) and E. Harris (1990: 372).

[14] I do not enter the controversial question of the meaning of *moicheia*. According to the traditional scholarship the word has a broader sense, including all the sexual relations that, according to Draco's law, under certain circumstances allowed the killing of the man caught "next to" one of the "protected" women. Other scholars maintain that *moicheia* indicates adultery in the modern, more limited, sense of the word (D. Cohen 1984 and 1991 followed by Todd 1993: 277), G. Hoffmann (1990: 12). For the traditional broader meaning of the term see Cantarella (1991a: 289–96), Carey (1995a: 407), Ogden (1996: Chapter 3) and (1997: esp. p. 27), Omitowoju (1997: esp. pp. 14–16).

The illicit sexual act (in this case, adultery) was still perceived as an act that offended primarily the man who possessed the right to control the woman's sexual life. Furthermore, although Euphiletus's wife had carefully orchestrated the encounter with her lover (such that her consent was beyond question), Euphiletus considers his wife seduced ("Eratosthenes committed adultery *on* my wife and *corrupted* her"). The subject of the action is Eratosthenes; Euphiletus's wife is a passive object, if not a victim. The role of the adulteress and that of a raped woman are not neatly differentiated, even at the lexical level.

However, Euphiletus, after citing Draco's law, to convince the judges of the magnitude of Eratostenes' crime, says that adultery is such a hideous behavior that is punished with death, whereas rape is punished only with a monetary fine. He introduces, then, a difference that did not exist in Draco's law. He distinguishes two crimes that were originally indistinguishable and quotes a law stating that "if a man outraged with force (*aischynē biai*) a free man or a boy (*pais*) he has to pay a fine amounting to double the damage: the same if he (outraged with force) one of the women 'next to whom' it is allowed to kill" (Lysias 1.32).

Can we trust this quotation? May this distinction be considered the effect of an increasing interest of the postdraconian legislation in the problem of women's consent?[15] In this case, according to modern concepts, we would expect rape to be considered a more hideous crime than adultery. Lysias instead suggests that in Athens it was the other way around. Of course, this could reflect a different cultural evaluation. Before going to the possible cultural changes, however, it is necessary to check the credibility of Lysias's quotation of the law, as well as his explanation of its rationale:

> those who act with force are hated by those to whom they have done violence, while those who have used persuasion corrupt the soul of the victim, making the wives of others more attached to themselves than to their husbands, become masters of the *oikos*, and make it uncertain whether the children are the husband's or the adulter's. (Lysias 1.32–33)

---

[15] According to Plutarch, *Solon*, 23, the first law on rape goes back to Solon. This law, however, would have punished rape with a fixed penalty (100 drachmas). For attempts to explain the contradiction with the law quoted by Lysias, see S. Cole (1984: 97–113) and E. Harris (1990). Updated literature on rape in Omitowoju (2002).

Though considered by some scholars to make sense,[16] Lysias's reasoning appears an ingenious but totally inconsistent attempt to convince the jury to acquit his client. Among other things, I should point out that the distinction between "adulteress" and "raped woman" has been made only in the past few decades in Mediterranean cultures, where until a few years ago a raped woman found it nearly impossible to find a husband and still today has great difficulty in some areas and cultural groups. Moreover, when Lysias quotes the penalties for rape and *moicheia* he lies: he says that these penalties were a fine for rape, death for adultery. None of these statements correspond to reality.

To start with, it is controversial whether the Greeks had a concept and a crime corresponding to what we call rape. Greek language lacked a single name for it and used different verbs, at times "shame" (*aischynein*) or "to shame with the use of force" (*aischynein biai*: Lysias 1.32), at times "to force" (*biazomai*: Plutarch, *Solon* 23), and at times "outrage" (*hybrizein*: Aeschines 1.15–17). Furthermore, the verb "seize" (*harpazein*), *per se* meaning "abduction," was often used in context of sexual assault. Equally indeterminate in Athens was the number of legal actions available to punish rape. A specific lawsuit for such a crime did not exist. However, some lawsuits not specifically designed for it could be used. They were the *dikē biaiōn* and (perhaps) the *dikē blabēs*, private lawsuits for assault and damages, ending with a fine (Harrison 1968: 35), and the *graphē hybreōs*, a public lawsuit that ended with a penalty left to the decision of the jury that in some cases could be death. Although the meaning of *hybris* was much broader than rape,[17] there were nonetheless cases where sexual violence was *hybris*: some cases of rape, thus, could end with a death penalty. But Lysias avoids recalling this fact. And he lies when he says that the penalty for *moicheia* was death. The law of Draco authorizing the killing of the adulterer caught in the act did not deal with adultery. In addition to the fact that it also authorized the killing of the rapist, this law dealt with the possibility of killing with impunity in some exceptional case, listed by the law (among them some that had no connection with sexual behavior). The penalty for adultery was stated by another law that unfortunately does not survive. We know nonetheless that the punishment for this crime was assessed by the court at the

---

[16] Namely Carey (1995a: 416–17).

[17] *Hybris* is generally considered behavior that is excessive, insulting, and designed to diminish the honor of another person. Because of its central position in Athenian criminal law, it is the object of ongoing discussions. See, among others, MacDowell (1976a), Gagarin (1979), Fisher (1976, 1979, 1990, 1992, 1995), D. Cohen (1991).

end of a public action (*graphē moicheias*) heard by the *Thesmothetai* (*Ath. Pol.*, 59.3). Because many public actions left the penalty to the decision of the jury, it could also be that this trial ended, but not necessarily, with a death sentence.

Furthermore, as far as we know, the punishment for adultery in other Greek *poleis* was not death: in Locri Epizephirii the lawgiver Zaleucus stated that the *moichos* had to be blinded (Aelian *Var. Hist.* 13.24), whereas the law in Lepreum and Cumae wanted him to be strictly tied in ropes, walked enchained along the streets of the *polis* for three days, and deprived of his civic rights (*atimos*).[18]

Finally, we must recall that according to some authors the Athenian law on adultery authorized some so-called minor punishments that included depilation of the genitals, *raphanismos* (or *raphanidōsis*) which consisted of anally raping an adulterer with a radish, and an analogous action performed with a mullet, a particularly spiny fish. However these practices (beyond any discussion about their real application) were not legal penalties.[19] They were typical modes of revenge, presumably of very ancient origin, that weakened the masculine image of the person undergoing them, opening him to ridicule. There is no evidence to support the notion that Athenian law legalized them and transformed them into punishments. The only revenge that the law cared to regulate in the realm of sex crimes was, as we know, the killing of the adulterer and the rapist caught in flagrante. Other forms of revenge, the so-called minor penalties, were left to the realm of common practice and probably practiced also on the rapists.

The punishment for adultery, thus, was the nonfixed penalty assessed at the end of a *graphē moicheias*. Both rape and adultery, then, were punished with a variety of penalties that ranged from a fine to death. When adultery and rape came to be differentiated, neither of these crimes was more hideous *per se*. They were both differently evaluated according to subjective and objective circumstances, to the status of both the victim and the offender, and to the legal action chosen to pursue the criminal. Women's consent was not an issue taken into account *per se* by the Athenian legislators. Even if Athenian law may not be representative of Greece, and in spite of the many differences between the two cities,[20] it is worth considering that the consent of the woman

---

[18] For Lepreum see Heracleides Ponticus in Muller, *FHG* 2, p. 217 ff; for Cumae see Plutarch *Quaest. Gr.*, 2.

[19] See D. Cohen (1985: 385–7), Roy (1991), Carey (1993).

[20] See in this volume Gagarin on Unity and Davies.

was irrelevant also in the Gortynian law. According to that law if a free man raped a free woman the penalty was 100 staters and double this if the offender was a slave (col. II, 2–7); the same penalty, 100 staters, for the free man who committed adultery with a free woman in the house of her father, brother, or husband, and double if the offender was a slave (col. II, 20–23). But if a free man was caught committing adultery with a free woman in a house not belonging to her father, brother, or husband the penalty was only fifty staters (col. II, 23–4). In Gortyn as well as in Athens the penalty for rape and adultery depended on the status of the involved persons, and the involved persons were not only the man-offender and the woman, but also the male relatives and the husband of the woman. If committed in their house, it required a major penalty. Clearly, the women's consent *per se* had no relevance.

Finally, going back to Athens, it is important to consider that the rape law quoted by Lysias did not punish sexual violence committed against *all* women, but only against *some* women: those taken into consideration by Draco's law. The women born and raised in the house of an Athenian citizen or living in it as free concubines. The others apparently could be raped with no penalty.

Legal and Social Status

Athenian women were considered citizens and indicated as such by the words *astē* and *politis* (feminine forms of *astos* and *politēs*), two words indicating two different levels of participation in civic life. As in every ancient culture, however, they were barred from taking part in political life. In other words, they had the *status*, but not the functions, of citizens. After a decree passed in 450 by Perikles, their status as citizens (as *astai*) became a condition for the citizenship of their children (*Ath. Pol.* 42.1). Until this time citizenship descended only in the male line (see Patterson in this volume).

In the field of private law, Athenian women were not considered capable of deciding their own affairs with competence, and they were subjected all their life long to a *kyrios*, a man with power and authority over them. In the first instance, the *kyrios* of a girl was her father. If the father was dead, the *kyrios* would be her homopatric brother. If she had no brothers, it would be her paternal grandfather or uncle. When she married, her husband assumed the responsibilities of the *kyrios*, but he did not have the power to give her in marriage to another man in his lifetime. He could instead choose her future husband in his will. If the husband died, the *kyrios* of the widow was her son. In case of dissolution of the marriage the rights of the former *kyrios* revived.[21]

Marriage

Among the powers of a *kyrios* was the right to decide the woman's marriage. Marriage had to be preceded by a ceremony called *eggyē* (or *eggyēsis*), a term usually translated "betrothal."[22] The *eggyē* consisted in the promise of the *kyrios* to give the woman to a man as his bride and was often made when the bride-to-be was extremely young. Demosthenes' sister, for example, was betrothed when she was five (Dem. 27.4ff). But *eggyē* was not really or not only a betrothal. It did not bind the *kyrios* to fulfill his promise, and no sanctions were provided for breaking it. However, it was a condition legally necessary to give the woman the *status* of wife and her children the *status* of legitimate (*gnēsioi*), if and when the "betrothed" woman was taken to the groom's house and given to him, with an act called *ekdosis*. The beginning of the conjugal life was accompanied by rituals more or less solemn and rich according to the economic and social status of the spouses. In its canonical form a marriage ritual lasted three days. The marriage ceremonies, however, were only social indicators of the existence of the marriage, as well as the dowry (*proix*), which was nonetheless customary, not to say socially compulsory (Schaps 1979: 74–88). What made the difference between the cohabitation of a man and a concubine (usually indicated by the verb *suneinai*: "to be together") and the cohabitation of two married persons (indicated as *sunoikein*, "to share the participation in the household") was the sequence *eggyē-ekdosis*. A woman was a wife (*gynē, damar*) and not a concubine (*pallakē*) only if the beginning of her cohabitation with a man (celebrated by an *ekdosis*) had been preceded, no matter when, by an *eggyē*.[23]

How long an average marriage lasted in Athens we cannot tell. In addition to the death of one of the spouses a marriage could be dissolved by three different acts. The first and more diffused was repudiation by the husband (*apopempsis* or *ekpempsis*). Repudiation was possible at the will of the husband, without need of justification. The husband who wanted to divorce his wife simply had to give back the dowry. The second way

---

[21] On the economic authority of the *kyrios*, see Schaps (1979: 48–60).
[22] On the meaning of the word *eggyē*, see Patterson (1991: 48–53).
[23] Even if ignored by recent scholarship, this was the hypothesis formulated by Paoli ([1930] 1974: 264–5).

to dissolve a marriage was the abandonment of the conjugal roof by the wife (*apoleipsis*). This had to be recorded by the *archōn*, and the woman had to be represented by her *kyrios*.[24] How often the decision of divorcing was taken by the woman and how often by the *kyrios* is up to speculation. Anyhow divorce *really* initiated by women was a rare occurrence. As Medea says in her famous speech denouncing the many injustices experienced by women, if a woman divorces her husband she gets a bad reputation (Eur. *Medea* 226 ff); this did not happen, of course, to men who divorced their wives.

The dissolution of a marriage could also be the consequence of the decision of a third person, the father of the bride, who could call back his daughter, usually to give her to another husband. This act was called *aphairesis* and was possible only if the daughter had not yet borne a child. It was the birth of a child then, not marriage, that tied the bride to the husband's family.

These are the legal rules. As for love and sexuality, scholars debate their presence, quality, and intensity in marriages. Even if certainly some married couples could feel a strong reciprocal sexual desire, as a rule marriage – decided and often interrupted by persons other than the spouses – can hardly be considered the most appropriate venue for Eros. It was, instead, the institution that Athenian society and law had designed for the ordered procreation of citizens.

Economic Rights and Inheritance

In Athens, at their father's death, women did not participate in the division of their father's estate if there was an equally close male relative. A woman's share of inheritance was the dowry received at the moment of marriage (Schaps 1979: 74–88). The value of the dowry depended on the economic status of the family, ranging from 5 to 25 percent of the father's property (Leduc 1991: 302 ff).

The dowry was usually composed of money, furniture, and other mobile goods, but it could, if rarely, include also land. In any case, women could not administer their dowries. The full and totally free management of the dowry belonged to their husbands. When the marriage ended, the husbands had to pay back the dowry to the original *kyrios* of their former wife. If they failed to do this, they were bound to pay interest up to 18 percent per year (Blundell 1995: 114–16).

---

[24] Examples in Dem. 30.15, 17, 26, 31. Reference to this procedure also in Isaeus 3.8, 78.

As we have already noted, Athenian law may be different from other cities' laws. Specifically, as far as women's economic rights are concerned, it is very different from Gortynian law, which gave women a better status. Anyway, even in Athens women had some property of their own (Foxhall 1989: 22–44). Even if excluded from the division of their father's estate, they could inherit as sisters, cousins, and aunts,[25] even if only in the absence of brothers, male cousins, and uncles. They could inherit under a will;[26] they could receive gifts, and they owned personally the goods distinct from the dowry that they were given at marriage, known as *paraphernalia* usually indicated as *himatia kai chrysia* "clothes and gold jewelry," but including also other movable goods.[27] However, even if they could hold property, they could not manage it, and they could not make a will. In one of his speeches, Isaius says that "the law explicitly forbids a child or a woman from contracting for the disposal of anything of a value above one *medimnos* of barley" (Isaeus 10.10), a limit that prevented women from engaging in major transactions. We know, however, of cases when this happened, and even if this is open to speculation, it is probable that the transactions violating the law were not invalid *per se*, but could be declared void if the *kyrios* challenged them in court (Schaps 1979: 52–6). In addition to this, it seems that, although a woman needed her *kyrios*' assent to make any really valuable act of disposition, her *kyrios* did not need her consent (Foxhall 1989: 37). How women felt about the limitation of their decisional powers can perhaps be inferred from some lines of Aristophanes' *Women at the Assembly* (1024–5), where women, having gained political power, passed a law that imposed on men the limit of one *medimnos*.

A most interesting institution, showing clearly the reality of the Greek gendered organization of property and inheritance laws is the so-called "epiklerate," a word coming from the Greek *epiklēros* (literally "upon, with the estate"), usually mistranslated as "heiress." Although in general it is important to remember that Athens might not be typical of Greece (especially the Dorian cities such as Gortyn; see Davies in this volume), it is very interesting to note that the heiress is a character existing widespread in the Greek cities, both Ionic and Doric, where the heiress was called *patroukos or patrōiōkos*.[28] These terms indicated a woman who happened to be the only descendant at the moment of

---

[25] Cf. Isaeus 11.1–3; Dem. 43.51; Isaeus 7.20–22.
[26] Cf. Isaeus 5.7–9.
[27] The distinction is made in Isaeus 2.9; 8.8
[28] Schaps (1979: 25–47). On the Spartan "heiress," see Pomeroy (2002: 84–6).

her father's death. To transmit the patrimony in the masculine line, the ironically so-called heiress was bound to marry her nearest relative in the masculine lineage, usually her father's brother. If this man was not interested in marrying her, she had to marry his son, and so on, along the line of relatives. If more than one person claimed to be her nearest relative (which could happen, given the lack of public registers of citizens in Athens) she was adjudicated by the magistrate (*archōn*) at the end of a legal action called *epidikasia*, an application of the *diadikasia*, the action designed to resolve the dispute among persons claiming the right of ownership over the same good. The *epidikasia* had the same legal effects as an *eggyē* (Isaeus 6.14).

The Question of Seclusion

Up to some decades ago scholars used to say that Athenian women were secluded in their houses, scarcely allowed to cross the threshold, and before marriage were even prevented from leaving the boundaries of the inner apartments (*gynaikōnitis*). More recent works, however, are skeptical about the existence of quarters of the house where women and children would have been physically segregated. The archaeologists have debated this issue at length, reconstructing a space map of houses that from the late eighth to the fourth century include a male space (a public room, the *andrōn*), where visitors were allowed, and a private, inner part of the house, where women lived, but that was not barred to the men of the family.[29] However, the inner part of the house, symbolically feminine, was accessible only through male space and through a door guarded by the *kyrios*. Thus, despite the absence of a secluded women's space, Greek house design suggests the existence of a strong gender distinction.

The recent reading of the archaeological evidence is confirmed by a new interpretation of the literary sources that lead some scholars to maintain that traditional scholarship has too often mistaken separation of spheres and roles for seclusion and isolation (D. Cohen 1996: 135–45). In fact, the careful reading of the sources shows that, even if only with the permission of the head of the household, women used to go out in the streets for different purposes and on different occasions, according to their social and economical status. Recent scholarship tends to believe

---

[29] The space, thus, was "asymmetrically gendered": women could not enter the male space, but men could enter the so-called female space. This is the conclusion of Nevett (1994: 98–112) and (1999).

that they even attended the theatrical performance, and finally, women of every class participated in religious festivals (Goldhill 1994).

To conclude, women were not secluded in their houses and denied any kind of social relations. But at least if they belonged to the upper classes, they were strictly controlled by men. If they possessed slaves they were accompanied by them in the streets. In short, they were not physically secluded, but were certainly socially controlled.[30] Moreover, Athenian women were not required to be cultivated. Once they had born a child, their function was accomplished. The education of the sons, which in Rome was shared by the parents, in Athens was a masculine matter. If this was a consequence of the fact that women did not receive an education, or if women did not receive an education because they were not in charge of their children's education is an old and debated question, whose answer is connected with the equally controversial question of the cultural and pedagogical role of pederasty. As is well known, young Athenians of the elite class were not taught to become good citizens by their father, but by a "lover," a choice resulting, perhaps, from the overwhelmingly public nature of Athenian men's lives, which demanded that an educator be identified with the public, not the private, realm. Of course we cannot face these problems here (Cantarella 2002a: XI–XII). What matters, here, is the fact that the maternal role of Athenian women was purely biological.

"THE OTHERS": *HETAIRAI* AND *PORNAI*

Although a woman was bound to have sex only with her husband, men were allowed to have relations with more than one woman (not to speak of the possibility of having a relation with a boy; Cantarella 2002a: 54–78). Each of these women had a different function, as stated in a famous passage of a speech attributed to Demosthenes (59.122). Athenian men may have three women: a wife (*damar*) "for the production of legitimate children"; a concubine (*pallakē*) "for the care of the body," that is to say, to have with her regular sexual relations, and a "companion" (*hetaira*) "for pleasure." To give a full account of the possible heterosexual encounters of Athenian men, we must add to the aforementioned women the prostitutes, called *pornai*, who were only occasional partners in an act that did not involve any kind of relationship.

---

[30] For an overview of these problems, see Just (1989: 105–25).

Having already described the condition of the wives we have now to focus on the "others," that is to say, the women who got paid for accompanying a man and having sexual intercourse with him. These women, the *hetairai* and the *pornai*, played different roles and had different social statuses.

The *hetairai* (companions), as their name indicates, were not occasional partners of a one-night or one-hour stand. They had a more stable, even if not exclusive, relationship with their partners. They responded to the social and psychological need for a feminine presence in situations where wives, sisters, and daughters were not allowed, namely the banquets. To exercise this function, they needed to be in some way cultivated. At times, but not always, coming from abroad, they received some education, including the art of singing, playing musical instruments, and dancing, and possessed the basic social knowledge that allowed them to take part in the men's conversation. This has often led scholars to compare them to the Japanese *geishai*, an incorrect comparison in the sense that *geishai* are not professional prostitutes, yet correct insofar as their role in male social life is concerned.

The *hetairai* were at times hired by a man and at times by a group of friends who paid to have exclusive use for a certain period. Some of them could earn a good amount of money and be celebrated for their beauty and elegance. Some of them could become the concubine (very rarely a wife) of a former client. In any case, they exercised their profession at a special level that gave them a very different status from the *pornai*.

The *pornai* belonged to a different level of the profession. Some of them worked in the brothels that, according to the tradition had been set up by Solon, who had assigned their profits to the temple of Aphrodite.[31] At a slightly higher level were the *pornai* who worked in the streets or in their houses. Some of the *pornai* were slaves, forced to work. Others were freeborn girls, abandoned at birth by their father and rescued for the purpose of putting them to work as prostitutes. Others were free Athenian citizens, who became prostitutes out of hunger or personal choice.[32]

It is uncertain if Athenian law regulated the fees of the prostitutes and imposed taxes on them. Aeschines, in the speech *Against Timarchus*

---

[31] Harpocration s. v. *pandēmos Aphroditē*.
[32] This is the point made by E. Cohen (2000b: 114–47), who disputes the idea of foreign predominance in the world of prostitution. Prostitutes, in his opinion, were often Athenian citizens who worked in a free market, where individual persons were free to conclude contracts, without regard to the parties' personal status.

(1.119), mentions a special tax called the *pornikon telos*, which was imposed on male prostitutes, hence the deduction that a similar tax was imposed on women. With regard to prices, Aristotle reports that the *astynomoi* established a maximum fee of three drachmas for women to play reed-pipes, harps, and lyres during banquets.[33] However, it is uncertain if the limit was related to their activity as musicians or as prostitutes; even if *hetairai* were often musicians, complete overlap between the two categories would be a mistake. The only certain public intervention regulated possible quarrels among two or more men concerning the "lease" of the same woman (*Ath. Pol.* 50.2): in that case the *astynomoi* decided the person to be preferred.

GENDER AND PHILOSOPHY

Poetry and law are not the only agents of the social construction of gender sterotypes. In Greece, an important role was also played by the "intellectuals," who debated for centuries a surprising question: What is the woman's role in reproduction? (Cantarella 1987: 52–3)

The major contribution to this debate was offered by Aristotle, whose theory about the female contribution to reproduction became a landmark for theorists of female biological and intellectual inferiority through the centuries. According to Aristotle, when the embryo is formed, next to the sperm flows the menstrual blood. The sperm is itself blood, but it is more complex than the menstrual blood. Both sperm and menstrual blood are food retained by the organism and transformed into a new and different substance by heat. Women, however, being less warm than men, cannot complete the final conversion, which produces sperm. In the reproductive process, then, the male seed "cooks" the female residue, transforming it into a new being. This means that female blood has a merely passive role. The male contribution is instead active and creative. In essence, in the reproductive process men with their sperm "convert" female matter into a human being (Aristotle *Gen. An.*, 728a).

The consequences of such biological theorizing on the formation of gender roles is easy to imagine. As Aristotle writes, the *oikos* (the central element of his political theory) is arranged around a head, and "although there may be exceptions to the order of nature, the male is

---

[33] *Ath. Pol.* 50.2; Hyperides 4 (*Euxenippus*) 3.

by nature fitter for command than the female."[34] Hence the man is the head of the *oikos*, and to him falls command over his wife, slaves, and children (*Politics* 1.13, 1260a). Aristotle's theory of passivity in reproduction was the final moment of a long process that, through the words of the poets, the statements of legal rules and the speculations of the intellectuals, gave strength and stability to the Greek social construction of gender stereotypes, reinforcing the discriminatory legal rules that governed women's lives (Cantarella 1987: 2–7).

[34] Aristotle *Politics* 1.5, 1254b, translation Jowett.

13: FAMILY AND PROPERTY LAW
Alberto Maffi

FAMILY
Marriage and Children

Although there are other corporate groups within the *polis*, for Aristotle the basic constituting element of the *polis* is the *oikia*, the family group. By *oikia*, Aristotle means the nuclear family, within which the relations between husband and wife, father and children, master and slaves assume legal significance (Arist. *Polit.* 1253b). Aristotle's approach is basically confirmed by the legal measures regarding family organization in Athens and these are not contradicted by fragmentary information on the law of persons in other *poleis* (even though the Spartan tradition gives a very different view of the family group, albeit one that is virtually impossible to verify).

The *oikia* is constituted by marriage (*gamos*). Marriage is virilocal: the woman proceeds from her father's house to her husband's. The marriage ceremony, which is undoubtedly of great social and religious importance, is not significant from a legal point of view. What is important, instead, is the agreement between the woman's father (or, after his death, her brother) and the future husband, according to which the woman will be "given" and "received." In Athens this agreement is given the name *engyē* or *engyēsis*; in legal speeches it is used as proof that a marriage exists. In the case of an heiress (*epiklēros*), *engyē* did not exist: the woman was assigned, according to *epidikasia*, to the male relative who demonstrated his right over other relatives to succeed the dead man (see further Cantarella in this volume).

The marriage is accompanied by an economic transaction. By virtue of a custom, which is certainly of ancient origins, the father (or the brother, after the father's death) gives the husband a certain quantity of movable goods or real estate that constitute the woman's dowry (in

Attic Greek *proix*). The dowry is administered by the husband, who is generally bound to provide real security for the return of the dowry, if the marriage should be dissolved.

Marriage determines the status of the offspring. Only children born of a legitimate marriage are considered legitimate offspring (*gnēsioi*). Children born to an unmarried woman (*nothoi*) have no right of inheritance from the father and, according to most experts, are not even considered citizens. To be considered citizens, the children must, in fact, be included as legitimate offspring in their father's phratry. Nonetheless, *nothoi* were not completely excluded from the Athenian community; we know, for example, that they were entitled to attend a city gymnasium, the Kinosarges.[1]

The marriage can be dissolved on the initiative of one of the two partners; but it is uncertain whether the bride's father has a legally recognized right to end the marriage by taking his daughter away from the husband (paternal *aphairesis*).[2]

Following divorce, the woman returns to the father's home with her dowry. Specific legal action, known as *dikē proikos*, may be taken against the husband who fails to return the dowry.

Marriage is also dissolved as a consequence of the death of one of the partners. In the case of the husband's death, if there are offspring, the widow may decide to remain in her late husband's house (thus showing that she is not available for a new marriage) or to return to her father's home. If there are no children, she normally returns to the paternal home. Subsequently, the father or brother may decide whether to offer her in marriage again.

The father exercises the power of *patria potestas* (which is not, however, denoted by a specific term in Greek legal terminology) over the offspring. Unlike the case in Roman law, when the son comes of age, he automatically acquires the right to become the recognized owner of his own estate and to dispose of it. Children were under an obligation to honor their parents and to support them if they were without means: a specific public procedure (*graphē goneōn kakōseōs*: Arist. *Ath. Pol.* 56.6) was provided to enforce respect for these obligations. In addition, after the parents' death, their offspring were obliged to arrange for suitable burial and to carry out regular memorial rites in their honor. Proof of the importance of these obligations were the questions put to citizens designated as archons during their *dokimasia*: "if they possess family

---

[1] Ogden (1996).
[2] See Lewis (1982).

tombs and where these are located, and if they behave correctly towards their parents" (Arist. *AP* 55.3).

Inheritance

The nuclear family is also the seat of inheritance. Ever since ancient times, at the death of the head of the family, the family's estate was shared among his sons. As regards the daughters, their inheritance coincides with their dowry, the size of which varies according to family traditions and the demands of the future husband. Again since ancient times, the inheritance can be divided up among brothers, in particular the real estate. The progressive decrease in the area of lands due to their being divided up on inheritance was a potential cause of social instability, which the ancient legislators endeavored to remedy.[3] In Athens there are no records of measures restricting the right to sell land.

In the absence of legitimate heirs, the patrimony of the head of the *oikos* devolved to his closest male relatives, thus to his brothers and their descendants. In the absence of brothers, his sisters and their descendants inherited it and after them the more distant relatives, up to the limits set by *anchisteia*, that is, the legally recognized family ties, which in Athens included the offspring of cousins (*anepsiōn paides*). In the absence of relatives included in the *anchisteia*, we do not know what happened. It is possible that the inheritance went to the city itself. In no case did the marriage partner have the right to inheritance according to legitimate succession. The mother's goods also went to her children. If the marriage was childless, the woman's dowry returned to her family of origin at her death.

An inheritance measure unique to the Greek world, and probably applied throughout Greece, regarded the case in which, at the death of the head of the family, only daughters were left. In this case, the heiress was obliged to marry the father's closest relative (in practice her paternal uncle or cousin). The objective of this measure is to keep the father's possessions within the family group and to prevent the patrimony being transferred to another *oikos* through the heiress's children. This principle was applied with particular severity in Athens, where the heiress, unlike the case in Gortyn, could not refuse to marry. The relative who considered he had the right to marry the heiress was obliged to claim her by means of a procedure called *epidikasia*. If there was more than

---

[3] In particular Phalea of Calcedone and Philolaos of Thebes: see Arist. *Polit.* 1267a–b and 1274a–b.

one claimant, the law courts would have to decide to whom the heiress was to be awarded.

The vast majority of researchers on Greek law think the relative had the right to marry the heiress even if she was already married at the time of her father's death (some say only if she was childless). This means that someone might declare that he was the nearest relative and make a claim for the *epiklēros* and, if the court of law recognized his right to marry the heiress, her own marriage would automatically cease (*aphairesis* of the *epiklēros*). It should be said, though, that the sources do not wholly confirm the existence of *aphairesis* of the *epiklēros*. It should also be considered that by giving the woman as bride to a stranger, the father (or brother) had chosen to make ties with another family rather than conserve his estate within his own, extended family group.

As regards the regulation of the Athenian *epiklēros*, it should further be observed that, two years after coming of age, the woman's sons became the rightful owners of the maternal grandfather's estate.

Alongside intestate succession, Athens was also precocious in recognizing succession by will, as early as the sixth century B.C. It appears that it was a law by Solon that introduced the will (*diathēkē*) into Attic law, according to which only those without legitimate male heirs could make one. The will therefore fulfilled the function of providing an heir for those without blood descendants, thus avoiding intestate succession by relatives. If, instead, the head of the family had a daughter only, he could appoint a husband for her by will; by marrying her, the designated husband became the heir to the maker of the will. Otherwise, the nearest relative would have had the right to claim her as his wife by *epidikasia*.

In the sixth century, a type of will started to appear by which a man could bequeath his property to nonrelatives. This form of will was admitted even where the maker of the will had legitimate heirs.

Because the will aimed to provide an heir to the head of a family who did not already have one, its function was similar to that of adoption (*eispoiēsis*), which was probably known and admitted in Athens and in other *poleis* even before the introduction of the will. Adoption by living persons provided for a male child to pass from his original *oikos* to the *oikos* of the adopter, with two important consequences: (a) the adoptee acquired the status of son to the same extent as a legitimate son and lost his ties to the family of origin, including his right of inheritance there; (b) after the death of the adopter, the adoptee could not abandon the adopter's *oikos* to return to his own (e.g., to recover his right of inheritance there), unless he left a legitimate son in the adopter's *oikos*.

Indeed, if the adoptee died without leaving legitimate offspring, the adopter's estate would go to the relatives of the adopter himself.

Guardianship

To complete the picture of the institutions of family law, some mention should be made of guardianship. Male children who are not yet of age and whose father is deceased, as well as women, are placed under the authority of a guardian (*epitropos*).

The woman's guardian, her *kyrios*, was her father or, after his death, her brother or, in any case, the nearest male relative. The married woman's *kyrios* was her husband and, after his death, her eldest son. The presence of the *kyrios* was required for any act of legal significance that the woman wished to undertake.

The guardian of children not yet of age may be designated by will or, if no one is so designated, by law: in the latter case he will generally be the nearest male relative. In the absence of a suitable relative, the guardian will be appointed by the archon (eponymous archon).

When the children come of age, the guardian must give an account of his actions and is liable to prosecution for poor administration, known as *dikē epitropēs* in Athens (in relation to this, there are the celebrated three speeches by Demosthenes against his guardians, Dem. 27–29). The guardian was authorized to lease out the whole of the minor's estate (*misthōsis oikou orphanikou*): an auction was called under the control of the eponymous archon and the court of law to assign the lease to the best offer. Mistreatment of a minor under guardianship was prosecuted in a particularly severe manner through public cases (Arist. *Ath. Pol.* 56.6).

Slaves

In addition to the wife and children, slaves were also to be found in the *oikos* and were subject to the authority (*despotikē*, to use the Aristotelian term) of the head of the family. Slaves were considered objects; they could therefore be hired out or sold, for example. Nonetheless, any offence to another man's slaves allowed their owner to take legal action for serious offence to him (*graphē hubreōs*); the killing of a slave also gave rise to prosecution for murder, which was dealt with by the court of the Palladion (Arist. *Ath. Pol.* 57.2). The master was responsible for any offence or damage caused by his own slave to others.

Slaves could be set free in ways that are not documented for Athens: however, a private deed by the master was almost certainly involved. The liberated slave (*apeleutheros*) gained his freedom but not citizenship (unlike the process in Rome). If he chose to remain in his ex-master's city he was placed in the category of the metics or resident foreigners. It is probable that the liberation deeds contained clauses obliging the *apeleutheros* to perform certain tasks for his former owner: the sum total of these obligations is known during the Hellenistic Age as *paramonē*. As regards Athens, we know of a legal procedure (*dikē apostasiou*), by which the ex-master could take legal action against the *apeleutheros* who failed to meet these duties.[4]

Property

The Object of Ownership

In Attic sources we come across many classifications of things. From a legal point of view, what is of greatest importance is the distinction between movable and immovable objects. Ownership of immovable objects – land and houses – is reserved for citizens. Foreigners, and in particular metics, can only acquire real estate if they receive the privilege known as *enktēsis gēs kai oikias* (i.e., the right to acquire ownership of land and buildings); on the other hand, they can freely buy and sell movable objects (as long as customs duty is paid and, if necessary, the fee for selling at the market).

Alongside privately owned houses and lands in Athens we also find publicly owned and sacred real estate. The owner of public real estate may be the *polis* or a minor body, such as a tribe, a deme, or a phratry. Sacred estate acquires this status after a consecration ceremony carried out by a public or private body. Public and sacred lands are generally leased to private tenants[5]; other public real estate, such as quarries or mines, were also leased to private persons. Of particular importance to Athens was the mining carried out at the Laurion silver mines, where the lease of the mines was bought from the *polis* according to rather complex regulations that are not easy to reconstruct.[6] Public property is also the result of confiscation of property, usually as a form of punishment, particularly in the case of political revolt, but also for those

---

[4] Todd (1993: 190–2).
[5] Osborne (1988).
[6] See Faraguna (2003).

unable to pay debts. The property confiscated was sold by magistrates known as *Pōlētai* (or heads of sales).[7] Private creditors did, however, have priority over the city to collect their debts.

The ownership of private property could be registered to an individual or to a group of people, in particular the joint heirs to an estate or a private association. It is debated whether each of the joint-owners considered himself owner of the entire property or only of a share of it. In the case of property belonging to associations, the deeds relating to the joint property (for sales, rent, etc.) are drawn up by "magistrates," who represent the partners.

The right to ownership of property was guaranteed by the *polis*. Each year, when the eponymous archon started his term of office, he ordered the herald to proclaim that every man would remain in full possession of his property and the right to enjoy it.[8] Nevertheless there were restrictions of landowners' rights. Since the age of Solon (beginning of the sixth century B.C.), those who built on their own land had to leave a certain distance between the building and the boundary with their neighbor's land; in addition, those who did not have water on their land had the right to draw it from the neighbor's land.[9] Another, equally long-established measure was that relating to the cultivation of olive trees: it was forbidden to cut down trees growing on private land, as they were considered sacred. Thus, in the public interest, the city could impose limits on things that were the object of the right to property.

Rights of the Owner: Transfer of Ownership and Securities

According to Aristotle,[10] being the owner of something meant being able to use it and dispose of it. "Dispose of it" means sell it: in this case ownership of the object passes to the buyer. It is also possible to transfer only the partial enjoyment of the object in question. The object may thus be given on lease (*misthōsis*) and in this case the enjoyment of it passes to the leaseholder. However, it may be transferred without the recipient having the right to use it: in this case we have a contract of deposit (*parakatathēkē*), well documented in Greece since archaic times.

From a legal point of view, a sale (*prasis/ōnē*) was the exchange of an object for cash – a cash sale. The buyer did not become owner of the

---

[7] See documents collected by Langdon (1991).
[8] Arist. *Ath. Pol.* 56.2.
[9] Plutarch, *Solon* 23.
[10] Arist. *Politics* 1257a; *Rhetoric* 1361a.

object until he had paid the price to the seller.[11] In theory, therefore, a seller who had delivered the object before receiving the price agreed on could not take legal action to obtain payment. All he could do was perhaps claim damages (through bringing a case for damages, known as *dikē blabēs*). A long fragment from Theophrastos' *Nomoi* informs us of the procedure by which publicity for real estate was guaranteed: in this way anyone who wished to buy real estate could check that the seller was effectively the owner of it. Theophrastos lists the proclamation of the coming sale by public announcements, the conclusion of the contract in the presence of a magistrate, the participation of neighbors as witnesses, and, above all, the obligation to record the sale in a property register. We do not know which of these systems was used in Athens. Nevertheless, there are signs that the *demes* kept registers of the property in their territory.[12] Bans on sales are documented only for real estate situated in the colonies and these exceptions to the principle of the freedom to sell are due to the necessity of ensuring the survival of the colony.

As well as being entitled to sell property he owns, the owner is also entitled to offer it as security. Ever since ancient times, Greece recognized both personal security (the person pledging himself) and real security (the object offered as security). Person as surety (*engyē*) does appear when a third person, known in Athens as *engyētēs*, guarantees payment of a debt and, consequently, if the debtor does not pay on time, the creditor may take legal action against the guarantor. Real security exists when the debtor offers something he owns as a guarantee to the creditor; in this way, if the debtor fails to pay in due time, the creditor can claim this object through procedures that vary according to the type of guarantee. In this way the creditor is protected both against the risk of the debtor no longer possessing goods to seize and against the risk that other creditors may compete with claims on an estate that is inadequate to satisfy them all. The oldest form of real security in Greece was certainly pawning, known in Athens as *enechyron*. However, from the earliest times it was customary to make the sale with the right to recovery by the debtor (*prasis epi lysei*): the ownership of the property (worth more than the credit) passed to the creditor but the debtor, who nevertheless generally remained in possession of it, so he could obtain the revenue it yielded to pay his debt, was entitled to have the property returned to him by the satisfied creditor. If, instead, the debtor failed to pay, the creditor retained the ownership and had the right to take

---

[11] Pringsheim (1950).
[12] Faraguna (1999).

possession of the thing. To inform third parties that the ownership of the property had been formally transferred to the creditor, it was customary to place an inscribed stone, called *horos*, on the land or on the wall of the house, witnessing the fact that the sale had taken place and indicating the name of the creditor and the sum owed. In this way people who might be interested in buying the debtor's property were warned that it had already been sold as security.

The *horoi* dating from the sixth century in Athens and the area under its influence inform us of two other forms of real security: *apotimēma* and mortgage. The characteristic of *apotimēma* is its socio-economic function. Both husbands and those who leased an estate belonging to an orphan (*misthōsis oikou orphanikou*) had to place part of their property as *apotimēma* – the former as security against the return of a dowry when the marriage was dissolved and the latter as security against the return of it at the end of the lease or on termination of guardianship.

In some *horoi* the estate is subject to a condition indicated by the verb *hypokeimai* (to be subject to): the debtor thus binds over a part of his estate (the verb used is *hypotithēmi*) for (future) possession by the creditor, giving us the noun *hypothēkē*. At least in theory, this type of security does not therefore involve the immediate transfer of property to the creditor. However, if the debtor does not pay in due time, the creditor may enter into possession of the estate and sell it, drawing the amount of his credit from the price, including any interest; the remainder must be returned to the debtor.

At least in theory there is nothing to exclude the same property being offered as security to different creditors,[13] unless the contract stipulates that the object constituting the security must be *anepaphos*.

Legal Protection for the Right to Ownership

Protection for the right to ownership meets two complementary demands. On the one hand, there is the question of protecting one's property against attempts by others to take possession of it or, in any case, to use it without the consensus of the owner; on the other hand, there is the question of gathering the means for obtaining possession of the thing one claims to be one's own, if it should be in the possession of another person who, in turn, claims to be the owner.

---

[13] See the case documented by the inscribed stone published in "Hesperia" X (1941: 14), in which the estate belonging to a public debtor appears to be the object of a mortgage but was also the object of two sales with an agreement on redemption.

It is probable that, originally, those who claimed as their own something that was in the possession of others were allowed to take possession of it: in the case of real estate, the owner could enter the estate or the building (*embateuein*), chasing away the person occupying it; in the case of movable goods, he could physically take the thing from its possessor (*agein*). If the possessor resisted, there was the risk of a physical conflict, where the winner was simply the stronger person. The law thus intervened to avoid fights and prevented the claimant from carrying out the self-help necessary for him to gain possession of the thing in question. However, there are some exceptions, i.e., cases in which resorting to self-help to affirm the right of ownership to a thing is allowed without first obtaining a sentence from the court of law ascertaining the existence of the right.

As far as real estate is concerned, it can be seen from Attic sources dating from the classical age that the power to take possession of land or buildings was recognized in the following cases: (a) when the right of ownership was recognized by a sentence of the law courts; (b) when possession was taken by a creditor of the estate belonging to a debtor who had designated it as security; (c) when the heir in direct line of descent of a dead person took possession of the inheritance that was in the possession of others who had no claim to it (and in this case the rule applies to movable goods, too); and (d) when a person had stipulated with the *polis* a lease contract or sale of public estate that was in the possession of others who had no claim to it. In all these cases, as real estate was involved, the holder of the right to ownership who had been prevented by the occupant from taking possession of the object in question could take action against the occupant, by means of a *dikē exoulēs* (or action related to a case for ejectment) so that the occupant found to be in the wrong had to pay damages to the rightful owner and the same sum to the public coffers (probably to emphasize the fact that respect for the right to ownership was important in the public interest: see the declaration of the eponymous archon mentioned above).

As regards movable objects, the claim to ownership of an apparently free person or a slave belonging to someone else is of particular interest, because this is a case in which the right to ownership could be brought to bear without requiring a preliminary sentence of confirmation. In the case of a free man, the claimant was permitted to catch the person (*agein*), maintaining that the latter was his slave. The free man subjected to *agōgē* could not object; a third person would have to intervene, ending the *agōgē* by removing (*aphairesis eis eleutherian*) the presumed slave from the hands of the claimant. At this point the claimant was permitted to take legal action by means of the *dikē aphaireseōs* (for illegitimate removal): if the court of law recognized that *aphairesis* had been illegally exercised, because the person who was the object of the *agōgē* really was a slave of the claimant, the party who had carried out the *agōgē* was obliged to pay a sum of money as a penalty, and the victorious claimant could take possession of the person recognized as his slave. The same mechanism applied in cases where the claim to ownership concerned someone else's slave: in this case it was the person actually in possession who would oppose the *agōgē* of the claimant by means of *aphairesis*.

Apart from these cases, in which the claimant was permitted to take possession of the object of which he claimed to be the owner and a trial was only held if there was resistance or opposition, what measures were foreseen by Attic law? Let us first consider real estate.

If one of the four cases mentioned previously did not exist, the claimant could not take possession directly of the property he claimed as his own: first of all a court of law had to recognize his rights. However, there is some debate about the legal measures available to him. On the one hand, we know of the existence in Attic law of a legal procedure through which *diadikasia* was attained, i.e., the recognition of the prevalent claim among two or more that had been brought to court. Recourse was made to this procedure both in public and in private law. In the field of private law, the best known application of it is the *epidikasia*: it was used when, in the absence of legitimate descendents of a deceased person, several people proclaimed themselves his only heir. In the field of public law, *diadikasia* obtains when it is necessary to ascertain who, of two or more contestants, has the right to a certain privilege or is bound to offer a certain service to the *polis*.

A particular case of *diadikasia* in the field of public law is *antidosis* (exchange): the citizen called to perform a liturgy, i.e., to pay for a service of use to the public, such as the training of a choir (*chorēgia*) or the maintenance of a warship (trierarchy), could indicate a fellow citizen whom he thought to be richer and therefore better suited to bear the cost of the liturgy: at this stage a trial was opened to decide which of the two contestants was really best suited to perform the liturgy.[14]

In the past it was thought that *diadikasia* was also used to enforce the right of ownership against the possessor of the object. However, the use of *diadikasia* to claim ownership of an object is not clearly

---

[14] See Gabrielsen (1987).

documented in Attic legal speeches or by other sources. Instead there is an alternative tradition, passed on to us by lexicographers, according to which the person claiming ownership of real estate in the possession of others followed the legal procedure available to a landowner against the lessee of an estate (*dikē karpou*) or an urban building (*dikē enoikiou*). By means of *dikē karpou* a claim was made for the equivalent of the revenue illegally gained by the tenant in arrears and, if the case was won, the owner was entitled to take possession of the revenue itself; through *dikē enoikiou* the owner claimed a sum corresponding to the unpaid house rent. The same procedures would enable the owner to proceed against an unlawful occupant. Indeed, the latter illegally received revenue (if an estate was involved) or enjoyed the use of the real estate (if an urban building was involved) without paying corresponding rent. However, to have his right to revenue or rent recognized, the claimant would first have to demonstrate that he was the owner of the real estate. In this way, by reason of the indirect confirmation of his right to ownership, the victorious claimant would be able to proceed to *embateia*, and, if the owner put up opposition, he could take action by means of *dikē exoulēs*. The problem is that this indirect procedure for ascertaining ownership is not clearly documented in Attic sources of the classical age but almost exclusively by lexicographers of the late Hellenistic and Roman Ages.

Scholars therefore disagree. Kaser, to whom we owe the still fundamental study on this issue, considered that *diadikasia* on the one hand and *dikai karpou* and *enoikiou* on the other were complementary procedures. G. Thür, in his latest study of this topic,[15] arrived at the conclusion that there was no single pattern of procedure for laying claim to property (like the *rei vindicatio* in Rome, for example) but that, according to the type of property claimed, legal action assumed different forms.

As regards claims relating to movable objects, the person intending to recover possession of the object brought a case against the person in possession of it, by which he demanded that the object be produced in court. If the possessor complied with this demand, the claimant could take possession of the object before the magistrate. To justify his possession, the person actually in possession had to prove that he had legitimately purchased the object; in particular, if he maintained that he had purchased it, he could call on the seller (by *anagōgē*) and the claimant would have to assert his claim against the latter.[16] If the seller refused

---

[15] Thür (2003).
[16] In Plato's *Laws* (914c–d) there is provision for recording bills of sale in a special register, to be referred to in the case of controversy over property.

to appear or if he lost the case and the possessor was obliged to return the object to the claimant, it was possible to proceed against the seller by means of *dikē bebaiōseōs*. If, instead, the person actually in possession of the object refused to produce it in court, he was summoned to pay a sum of money as a penalty, unless advantage was taken of the possibility to proceed against him for theft (by means of *dikē klopēs*).[17]

---

[17] Kaser (1944: 148 ff.); on theft, see Cohen (1983).

14: ATHENIAN CITIZENSHIP LAW

Cynthia Patterson

From Aristotle's perspective in the late fourth century, the question "who is a citizen (*politēs*)?" is one of the first questions that arise when thinking about the nature of the state. "The state," he says at the opening of Book 3 of the *Politics*,

> is composite, like any other whole made up of many parts – these are the citizens, who compose it. It is evident, therefore, that we must begin by asking, who is the citizen [*politēs*], and what is the meaning of the term? (1274b40–42)

After considering and then rejecting various options, such as those who "live in a certain place" or those who have the "legal right to sue or be sued," as too broad, Aristotle arrives at the conclusion: "he who has the power to take part in the deliberative or judicial administration of any state is said by us to be a citizen of that state" (1275b19–21). He then dismisses the "practical" definition that a citizen is the child of citizen parents as not in fact much of a definition – e.g., what about the founder of a new state – is he not a citizen (1275b23–33)?

Given Aristotle's authority and the clarity of the definition he proposes, modern discussions of ancient citizenship law have generally followed his lead *both* in taking political and judicial participation as the essential and necessary feature of what citizenship is *and* in positing the identification of the citizen as necessary first-order business for any polis. Citizenship and the polis are frequently taken as entering the Greek world at the same time; the "citizen estate" is the "essence of the polis" asserts the author of a book claiming to find the beginnings of both in the archaeological record of the eighth century.[1] From this

---

[1] I. Morris (1987: 7).

perspective, citizenship has a certain timeless content, so that Aristotle's considerably later philosophical view, rooted in his understanding of the experience of the classical polis, can be taken as normative for the eighth century as well: "in the polis only the citizens themselves belonged to the corporation; those within the residential group but without a political role – women, resident aliens, slaves – were excluded from the *politeia*."[2] But should Aristotle's account be authoritative in this way? Is his account historically accurate or even historically motivated? In this chapter I put forth an alternative account of Athenian citizenship law that emphasizes the gradual and historical development of both the idea of citizenship and citizenship law in Athens over time from the sixth through the fourth centuries. Aristotle's discussion and definition stand at the end of and reflect this history; his definition is not an historical given but rather an historical product.

Similarly, the "practical" law proposed by Pericles in 451/0 – that "whoever is not born from two *astoi* should not share in the polis" (*Ath. Pol.* 26.4) or "Athenians are only those who are born from two Athenians" (Plutarch, *Pericles* 37.3) – is only one important piece of the larger development of Athenian citizenship law and can be understood only within the context of the intertwined history of law and politics, family and society from Solon to Demosthenes. Many accounts of Athenian citizenship law from the Aristotelian perspective and centering on Pericles' law already exist; I hope that this chapter can provide Aristotle's account and Pericles' law with a critical and useful historical context.[3]

The Language of Athenian Citizenship

As is immediately apparent from the different ways of expressing membership in the Athenian polis used in the previous paragraph, the first question for this essay is one of translation and terminology. What are we calling citizenship? How does the term translate into Athenian Greek and how do the Athenian Greek terms translate into modern English? The answer to these questions is not simple, and attempts to force Athenian usage into systematic legal formulae, Roman or modern European, have compounded the problem. Given the limitations of space, I

---

[2] Morris (1987: 5). Note that Morris appears to consider (with Aristotle) citizenship a male privilege, yet the formal burial he posits as an indication of citizen status clearly is not limited to males.

[3] For a useful and concise discussion of Athenian citizenship law (with relevant bibliography) see Todd (1993: 170–84). For discussion of Pericles' law in particular, see Patterson (1981).

will offer here a summary of basic Athenian usage. Essentially, there were three ways of expressing membership or insider status in the Athenian community, which I take to be the most basic meaning of citizenship. All three formulations therefore are expressions of citizen status in Athens.

Nouns: Astos/Astē *and* Politēs/Politis

Athenians used two different nouns, each with both a masculine and feminine form, to express an "insider" connected with a community center: *astos/astē* (pl. *astoi* and *astai*) and *politēs/politis* (pl. *politai* and *politides*). The *astos* or *astē* belongs to the *astu* (settlement) and likewise the *politēs* (or *politis*) to the polis (citadel or city).[4] Further, *astos/astē* was implicitly and often explicitly used in contrast with *xenos/xenē* (foreigner) to indicate a native member of the community, whereas *politēs* tended to be used in a more strictly internal political sense for a privileged participant in the polis. The difference, however, cannot be equated with "civil" versus "political" rights, a distinction not made in classical Athenian law.[5] The two terms could refer to the same person or in the plural the same group of persons; the difference is one of perspective or connotation not denotation. The development in Athens of active political participation for male citizens seems in fact to have prompted the coining in the later fifth century of the new feminine form *"politis"* for the female member of the polis. As male Athenians gained more specific political rights and responsibilities, the difference between male and female citizenship (share in the polis) became more pronounced – and a *politēs* was understood to be a man. Nonetheless, both the terms *astē* and *politis* indicate citizen or "insider" status for the woman so described.

Proper Adjectives/Nouns: Attikos *and* Athēnaios

Athenians could also refer to themselves with proper adjectives derived from the land of Attika or the urban center of Athens – *Attikos* or *Athēnaios*. These words have an interesting relation to one another and

---

[4] For discussion of the relation of *astos* and *politēs* in early Greek, see D. Cole (1976). As noted in the text, the feminine form *"politis"* seems to have been coined in Athens in the later fifth century.

[5] Liddell and Scott use these terms to distinguish *astos* from *politēs* (s.v. *astos*); unfortunately E. Cohen (2000a) has returned to that unsubstantiated and misleading distinction in his recent book, which argues unconvincingly that some resident aliens in Athens (*metoikoi xenoi*) were *astoi*.

to the terms *astos* and *politēs*[6]; for present purposes, it may be enough to note that the term *Attikos* (fem. *Attikē*) connotes a strong sense of physical belonging to the land of Attica, whereas *Athēnaios* (rare fem. *Athēnaia*) suggests a member of the political community of *hoi Athēnaioi* ("the Athenians") – a common term for the polis of Athens itself.

Verbs and Verb Phrases

Although the previous terms can be translated "citizen" and "Athenian citizen," in the sense of "member of the community of Athens," the idea of citizenship is often conveyed by the verbal phrase "*metechein tēs poleōs*" or "*metechein tēs politeias*" – to have a share in the community.[7] The phrase is both precise in describing active participation and also vague in not specifying one particular sort of share or participation. Thus, "sharing in the city" describes a kind of community membership or citizenship that can have different modes and manners. On this point as so often in Greek history, Homer provides a paradigm in the image of the polis and its participants depicted on the shield of Achilles. Hephaistos's creation of two *poleis*, one at peace and one at war, illustrates citizen participation in war, law, religion, agriculture, and family life, according to age and gender (*Iliad* 18.478–616).

In sum, Pericles' proposal in 451/0 B.C. that "anyone who was not born from two *astoi* should not share in the polis" is a "citizenship law" if and only if we understand citizen and citizenship as translating the words and phrases just described. In Plutarch's much later paraphrase, this was a law about who was an *Athēnaios*; it did not necessarily imply any specific or strictly legal categories of citizen "rights" but simply the recognition of membership and insider status within the Athenian community. The development and articulation of Athenian citizen rights and responsibilities over time is the historical story to which I now turn.

SOLON AND CITIZENSHIP

The history of Athenian citizenship begins with Solon. Although in legend the mythical hero Theseus was imagined to have brought all of the communities of Attica together into one polis and the semimythical lawgiver Drakon was given credit for Athens' first code of law, Solon

---

[6] Patterson (1986).
[7] See Ostwald (1996).

is the first historical Athenian.[8] Solon's poems and laws, as quoted by later authors, open the story of Athenian citizenship and citizenship law, i.e., the rules about who shares in the polis and about what a share is or means for the shareholder. When the "curtain goes up" then at the beginning of the sixth century, Athens is a large but apparently loosely organized community extending through Attica, the ca. 1000-square-mile peninsula of southeast Greece, including the "eponymous" settlement marked by its prominent limestone acropolis as well as other communities of substantial age and size, such as Eleusis or Marathon.

Despite its clear potential, Athens was at the time something of an underachiever in the larger Greek world, and a defeat at the hands of neighboring Megara inspired Solon to come forth and, using elegiac verse, exhort his fellow Athenians to take stock and pull themselves together.[9] The weakness of the Athenian polis at this time was rooted in the economic and social distress of a significant part of the population. According to *Ath. Pol.* 5.1, the "many were the slaves of the few," an Aristotelian synopsis of the situation lamented by Solon in a poem beginning "Grief lies deep in my heart when I see the oldest of the Ionian [states] being murdered." Solon appears to hold the rich or the few responsible for he rebukes them with the words "Restrain in your breasts your mighty hearts; you have taken too much of the good things of life."[10]

In this situation, the "the wisest of the Athenians" (Plutarch, *Solon* 14) chose Solon as arbitrator and *archōn* ("ruler") to set things aright, and Solon responded by setting up not only basic judicial and political institutions but also rules of inheritance, family and social relations, as well as economic and agricultural production. The laws of Solon articulate a new self-consciousness about the privileges of being a member of the Athenian polis.[11]

Solon confronted the crisis of personal status by putting an end to the enslavement of Athenians by Athenians; no longer could loans be made on the security of the person – and no longer could an Athenian be

---

[8] Drakon's law code does not survive apart from the law on homicide, which was reinscribed at the end of the fifth century. The law (as set forth at that time) clearly recognizes a privileged group of insiders, *hoi Athēnaioi*, whose murders are to be avenged according to the procedures outlined in the law.

[9] Plutarch, *Solon* 8.2.

[10] The political poems of Solon are found primarily in Plutarch's *Solon* and in the Aristotelian "Constitution of Athens" or *Athenaion Politeia*. I refer to the latter in abbreviated form as *Ath. Pol.*; although it shows Aristotle's influence, I am convinced by the arguments of P. J. Rhodes that Aristotle is not its author.

[11] For a collection of Solon's laws, insofar as they are known, see Ruschenbusch (1966).

enslaved on account of debt (*Ath. Pol.* 6; Plutarch, *Solon* 15). This "lifting of burdens" (*seisachtheia*) was again personified by Solon as the freeing of the land itself: "my witness ... will be the great mother of the Olympian gods, dark Earth ... previously she was enslaved, but now is free." Then, in the same poem, quoted by both the *Ath. Pol.* and Plutarch, he goes on to explain more specifically that "Many I brought back to Athens, their divinely founded city, who had been sold abroad, one unjustly, another justly, and others who had fled under compulsion of debt, men who no longer spoke the Attic tongue, so wide had their wanderings been. Those at home, suffering here the outrages of slavery and trembling at the whims of their masters, I freed" (*Ath. Pol* 12.4; cf. Plutarch, *Solon* 5). Not all details of Solon's *seisachtheia* are clear, but the *Ath. Pol.* cites the principle that "nobody might borrow money on the security of anyone's freedom" as the first of the three "most popular" features of his constitution or *politeia* (9). "Nobody" and "anyone" here denote "no Athenian" and "any Athenian," and the protection of the person of the citizen enunciated by Solon remained a central and inclusive feature of citizenship in Athens – regardless of age, economic status or gender. The principle was populist or *dēmotikos* in the broadest Athenian sense – i.e., it promoted the interests of the Athenian demos (the people). Athens remained (and became increasingly) a slave-owning society, but now slaves were necessarily foreigners.

The other two of the three "most populist" features of Solon's new order further articulate the privilege of Athenian citizenship for the Athenian insider. The second, according to the *Ath. Pol.*, was that "anyone might seek redress on behalf of those who were wronged" and the third was the "right of appeal to the *dikastērion*," for, explains the author, "when the demos is *kyrios* (master) of the vote in court, it becomes *kyrios* of the politeia" (9.1). Here again, Solon's concern is the protection of the person and privilege of the Athenian citizen as member of the Athenian community. The community itself is not defined or delimited – nor is the legal protection given only to adult males. Only adult males could take direct legal action, but the protection of the law extends to the larger Athenian family as a whole. Although modern commentators often emphasize the ability to speak publicly in court as a key element of citizenship, the purpose and consequence of that public act for the larger Athenian family is what makes it a citizen privilege or responsibility. Citizen privilege lay in the protection from enslavement or other harm; it was a consequence of a status that included both men and women, but would necessarily be exercised according to the social and gender code of the community.

So far, we have seen that Solon's laws delineated the legal protections entailed by the status of Athenian citizen – i.e., member of the Athenian community – rather than the status itself. Although it may seem odd to a resident or citizen of a modern state, the first order of business was not the definition of the community but rather its protection. Generally, it seems, Solon considered Athenians to be those free or once-free families living in Attica and "sharing in" the "divinely founded polis" of Athens (Solon in *Ath. Pol.* 12.4). Two additional *nomoi*, however, were attributed to Solon that more directly raised the issue of who could "share in" the polis – or rather who could not. The first is a law stating, as cited in the *Ath. Pol*, that whoever "did not choose one side or the other" in times of civic dispute should be *atimos* (literally "without honor") and no longer "share in the polis" (8.5). Plutarch considered that rule "peculiar and surprising" (*idios* and *paradoxos*; *Solon*, 20); he also reported to his own puzzlement a law requiring the Athenians *not* to give citizenship *except* to *xenoi* in permanent exile from their homes or those who had moved with their whole household for the purpose of establishing a trade (*Solon*, 24.4). The authenticity of both laws has been disputed, but perhaps their very oddity is an argument for archaic genuineness. In any case, the negative formulation of both laws is important, as is the active character of the participation required. Neither law sets forth the conditions or requirements for citizen status, but both identify active participating behavior as essential to that status. If someone does not take part, he (she) should not have a part; and a part should not be given to a foreigner if he does not establish an active household in Athens. Early – indeed the earliest – Athenian citizenship law thus focuses not on who the citizen is but rather what the citizen does and how he or she should be treated. Citizenship – or "sharing in the polis" – is now an active and protected status that is exercised and enjoyed in accordance with rules of age and gender. From this perspective, Solon and his laws did create Athenian citizenship.[12]

PISISTRATEAN INTERLUDE

Although Solon himself had rejected the name and power of tyranny (*Ath. Pol.* 12.3) – and left town after setting up his laws – neither his laws nor his departure solved the problem of Athenian civil strife. In the 560s Pisistratus began a series of attempts on Athenian rule that resulted finally, in the 540s, in his establishing himself as tyrant – not a formal title

[12] Cf. Manville (1990); Todd (1993: 172–3).

but a descriptive label applied by Greek authors to a person who took power by force rather than by birth or other legitimate claim. Pisistratus was one of the last of the early line of Greek tyrants (or irregular rulers) who transformed the archaic Greek political landscape in the seventh and sixth centuries. His career is better known than some of the other earlier tyrants (it is both later and Athenian), but he shares with many of them a certain populist character as "friend of the demos." For the development of Athenian citizenship, the tyranny of Pisistratus and his sons is notable for both what they did and did not do. First, the Athenian tyrants were civic builders and added significantly to the physical stature and well-being of the urban center, with fountain houses and palaces as well as temples and altars.[13] They also seem to have fostered public festivals such as the Dionysia and Panathenaia, which would also have given Athenians a chance to actively participate or "take part" in their city and – through the public sacrifices and meals that were an important part of those festivals – a very immediate taste of a notably enhanced share. Second, Pisistratus is said not to have "disturbed the *nomoi*" of the city, even to the point of permitting a legal complaint on the charge of homicide to be lodged against him – the plaintiff, however, had second thoughts and did not show up in court.[14] His sons were less popular, but not apparently less law-abiding. Thus, although the evidence is somewhat limited, we could say that the rule of Pisistratus and his sons in the sixth century enhanced the value of Athenian citizenship without for the most part limiting the privilege protected by Solonian law. Tyranny itself, however, began a steep decline in the public mind – as is clear in the law against tyranny quoted (although misunderstood) by the *Ath. Pol.* at the end of the account of the career of Pisistratus (16.10): "any man who attempts to establish, or aids in the establishment of, a tyranny shall be *atimos*, both himself and his family."[15] To be *atimos* is again to be without honor – and without citizenship.

CLEISTHENES, *DĒMOKRATIA*, AND CITIZENSHIP

There were some Athenians, however, who by their own lights were without sufficient honor and privilege under Pisistratus, including some

---

[13] On the Pisistratean building program see Boersma (1970).
[14] *Ath. Pol.*16.8. Cf. Herodotus 1.59.6 and Thucydides 6.54.5–6.
[15] On this chapter of the *Ath. Pol.* and on the general topic of *atimia*, see Rhodes (1981: 220–2).

members of formerly highly privileged Athenian families. The next chapter in the story of citizenship law in Athens centers on one such figure, Cleisthenes son of Megacles. Despite being credited by Herodotus with "establishing the democracy" and also being a member of the prominent Alcmeonid family, Cleisthenes himself remains something of an enigma. Herodotus and the *Ath. Pol.* offer details of his career, but Plutarch wrote no biography of this democratic leader and reformer. Nonetheless, it is clear that Cleisthenes was a well-connected and ambitious Athenian willing to gamble on his own and his fellow Athenians' political skills in the face of both internal elite rivals and external Spartan preeminence. His career had a significant impact on the way in which citizen identity in Athens was marked, registered, and also utilized.

If Plutarch *had* written a *Life* for Cleisthenes, it would at least have included the following chapters:

Family Background

Cleisthenes was the product of a celebrated Hellenic marriage between Megacles of Athens and Agariste, the daughter of Cleisthenes, the tyrant of Sicyon. Herodotus tells some entertaining stories about both the courtship "contest" and also the peculiar reorganization or renaming of Sicyonian tribes carried out by the elder Cleisthenes. But although the maternal inheritance of tyranny is suggestive, the paternal inheritance of Alcmeonid ambition eventually set Megacles' son in opposition to Pisistratid rule in Athens. It seems that the younger Cleisthenes served as archon in 524, but within the next decade he appears as one of the leaders of the antityranny movement – most notably in the "bribing" of the Delphic oracle for the purpose of inciting the Spartans to drive out the Pisistratids (Herodotus 5.63 (cf. 6.123) and *Ath. Pol.* 19.4). So far, Cleisthenes of Athens shows himself as a man willing to flout tradition and *nomos* to get what he wanted, but not yet a democrat by any means.

From Foe of the Tyrant to Friend of the Demos

The Delphic trick worked; the Spartans marched into Attica and expelled the sons of Pisistratus. But Cleisthenes was not successful in the scramble for power that followed the tyrants' ouster. When it looked as if he had lost out "in the political clubs" to a certain Isagoras, Cleisthenes took the bold step of, in Herodotus' words, "taking the demos into his club" (5.66) or according to the *Ath. Pol.* of "promising them the control of the state" (20). With his new supporters behind him, Cleisthenes succeeded in driving out both Isagoras and also the Spartans, who, realizing that they had been duped, had returned to restore order. So Cleisthenes became a democrat.

Organizing the Demos: Demes, Trittyes, and Tribes

So far, the story of Cleisthenes seems to have little to do with either citizenship or citizenship law, but the enlarged political "club" now required organization, and Cleisthenes undertook that task with a flair that revealed his heritage and a result that dramatically affected the way in which Athenians were organized and recognized as Athenians. The details are provided by Herodotus and the *Ath. Pol.*; in essence, the new system built (or rebuilt) the Athenian community from the ground up, using local units called demes, grouped into thirty "trittyes" or "thirds" – ten each from the three major areas of Attica, town, plain, and coast – and then into ten "phylai" or "tribes," each with a town, plain, and coast *trittys* and each named for an Athenian hero. According to the *Ath. Pol*, Cleisthenes' purpose was to "mix up" the Athenians so that "more might share in the politeia" (21); Herodotus simply sums up the events with his designation of Cleisthenes as the one who "founded the *dēmokratia*."

Politeia in Place, Its Author Fades from View

The rest of Cleisthenes' career is a mystery. Where did he go? Did he institute the distinctive Athenian practice of ostracism – and then suffer it himself?[16] For present purposes, however, the biography matters less than the politeia itself. Whatever his motives and purposes, Cleisthenes' new tribal order had a dramatic effect on the mechanics of Athenian citizenship – and thus on the way in which Athenians participated in their polis.

The ten tribes became the essential basis of organization for the distribution of rights and responsibilities in democratic Athens, and it is for this, as much as for his "partnership" with the *demos* that Cleisthenes can indeed be credited with "establishing the democracy." The new

---

[16] See Rhodes (1981: 262). Ostracism was the "negative popularity contest" in which Athenians voted on pottery shards (*ostraka*) for the public figure they thought should be excluded from the polis. The "winner" was expelled from the city for ten years but did not lose his citizenship or property.

system of demes, trittyes, and tribes organized the Athenians as a citizen body – whether for war, politics, religion, or athletic competition. Henceforth Athenians participated in – shared in – their polis through the demes and tribes as established by Cleisthenes. To what extent then did Cleisthenes' new order change the citizen identity or status?

One answer is that citizens were now more effectively identified and organized by the new system of enrollment, with the result that more Athenians participated in their polis. The notable military success in the years immediately following Cleisthenes' reforms, which Herodotus attributed to the positive influence of *isēgoria* ("freedom of speech"; 5.78), might suggest as well that Athenian soldiers were more effectively organized by the new tribal contingents than by the old. It is also possible that the citizen population was enlarged when some who had not been considered *Athēnaioi* were now included in the deme/trittys/tribe organization. As noted earlier, the author of the *Ath. Pol.* specifically says that Cleisthenes intended that "more should take part in the politeia," and in the *Politics*, Aristotle asserts that Cleisthenes "enrolled in the tribes many foreigners and slaves" (1275b34–9). I suspect that both responses are correct and that both sorts of "new" Athenians were enrolled by Cleisthenes into an enlarged and invigorated citizen community. A third response is to note the emphasis placed by the author of the *Ath. Pol* on the equalitarian effect of making the deme the entry point into the citizen body and the deme name part of the official citizen name. All demesmen are theoretically equal. This response might then provoke a further and final observation that Cleisthenes' tribal system specifically emphasized the roles of male citizens in that it carried particular significance for Athenian men as soldiers or jurors; Athenian women were not enrolled on deme lists – or called up for military or judicial service. Of course women had not been so enrolled or called up before, but the new tribal order very likely underlined and emphasized the difference between male and female citizenship in the public eye.

Citizenship law, however, does not appear to have been affected by Cleisthenes' new order. Any "enfranchisements" would have been a de facto result of the enrollment of noncitizens in the new citizen groups. This may indeed have happened, but it would not, however, have set an "open admission" policy or precedent. Whoever was counted was in; the new enrollment was a one-time occurrence – as indicated by the fact that deme membership was hereditary. Thus, overall, it can be said that Cleisthenes' reforms gave the citizen body a new shape and political/military emphasis, but not a new legal definition. This was the citizen body that successfully resisted two Persian invasions and undertook the creation of a pan-Hellenic league or empire. On the home front, through a series of reforms associated with the obscure politician Ephialtes and with the year 462/1, that same citizen demos took on major responsibilities for the day-to-day running of the democracy and its empire in the popular assembly, the tribal Council of 500, and the courts.[17]

PERICLES' PROPOSAL

So far, we have seen significant development in the protection, organization, and (for men) political power of the members of the Athenian community. But in the year 451/0, according to the *Ath. Pol.* 26.4, the Athenians decided on Pericles' proposal that "anyone who was not born from two *astoi* should not share in the polis," a straightforward articulation of the criterion for citizen identity by direct decree of the demos. The passing of this law, however, receives almost no comment in the contemporary record; there is no notice in Thucydides and only possible oblique references in contemporary drama.[18] Modern scholars have been left to puzzle over Aristotle's brief comment that Pericles' proposal was made and passed "on account of the number (or large number) of citizens" and to attempt to square that statement with Plutarch's quite different and differently motivated account. In Chapter 37 of Plutarch's *Pericles*, we find the hero in the last year of his life. He has lost his legitimate sons in the plague and thus is moved to ask the demos to rescind his own law "about bastards (*nothoi*)" so that his *nothos* son might take the name Pericles and a place in the legitimate citizen community. Plutarch then explains that "many years earlier" Pericles had written a law stating that "Athenians are only those born from two Athenians" and then goes on to comment further that when the Egyptian king gave the city a large gift of grain, it was necessary to examine the citizen lists and many "illegitimates" were discovered. Neither the law nor the gift are given a date by Plutarch, but the *Ath. Pol.* provides the archon date (451/0) for the former and a fragment of the fourth-century historian Philochorus mentions the latter under the archon year of 445/4.

---

[17] On the "reforms of Ephialtes" and their significance, see Rhodes (1981: 309–18).
[18] Possible echoes of the law and its effects can be heard, for example, in Euripides' *Ion* (the status of the title character).

There are problems both with the laconic *Ath. Pol.* explanation and also with the chronologically vague if more expansive account in Plutarch. Neither provides a fully satisfactory explanation of Pericles' law, and so modern debate continues, perhaps allowing this particular law to loom larger over the discussion of citizenship in Athens than it may rightfully deserve. It is important to recognize that Pericles' law provides not a legal definition of citizenship in Athens but rather a legal necessary condition for citizenship: whoever is *not* born of two *astoi* should *not* share in the polis. The place of such conditions in the organization of the polis was of interest to Aristotle (cf. *Politics* 3), and the personal/biographical impact of the law was of interest to Plutarch; but we should not overburden the law of 451/0 with the full weight and significance of Athenian citizenship. Perhaps the lack of notice in contemporary Athenian sources reflects the law's significance more realistically than has been generally thought.

Nonetheless, Pericles' law of 451/0 – its meaning, context, and consequences – has a central place in discussions of Athenian and Periclean democracy. Indeed, this is one of the very few specific decrees attributed to the Athenian leader, who hobnobbed with philosophers and philosophized about politics, yet left behind nothing in writing. I offer here a necessarily brief summary discussion of the law and its interpretation.

When Pericles proposed his law in 451, Athens was rapidly becoming an imperial power in the Aegean and a more democratic as well as cosmopolitan society at home; the articulation of "who has a share of the city" carried a significant message for both the domestic and the foreign audiences. To the extent that Cleisthenes' reorganization of Athens' citizens propelled the polis to victory in the Persian wars, to an equal extent Pericles' law was a consequence of that victory and the empire that followed. By 451, the Athenians had made it clear that they ruled and their "allies" obeyed or suffered the consequences. Further, Athens was now a ruling and imperial city – and would now hold the "allied" treasury (moved in 454 to Athens from Delos) and expect all allies to honor Athena and her city by bringing tribute and participating in Athenian festivals. Now in 451, by Pericles' proposal and the demos' decree, shareholding in the city – i.e., citizenship – was explicitly reserved for the native-born, for the children of *astoi*, a term implicitly and often explicitly set against its opposite, the *xenoi*. The expression of citizenship as "shareholding" is notable for its concrete yet unrestricted expression of an active citizenship not limited to any one area of polis life – religion, law, economy, and so on – or any one gender. The nature of the share might differ in different spheres of polis life, but the notion of citizenship as active participation according to age and gender is particularly appropriate to democratic and imperial Athens, where both critics and admirers noted the confidence with which Athenian society at large embraced both the privilege and material benefit of Athenian citizenship. Contrary to those who see Periclean Athens as the exclusive domain of the male citizen, I suggest that the language of Pericles' law expresses a sort of imperial citizenship that could be enjoyed by both male and female – over, against, or above the allies or other *xenoi*.

Yet, the law need not be seen solely as a selfish or aggrandizing move by the imperial city to protect its privileged access to Athenian power, prosperity, and goods. It was also part of a larger development of polis organization and institutions during the fifth century, including, for example, public burial of the war dead, popular courts (now a paid service), and expanded public festivals (with their boards of ten overseers). Further, articulation of citizenship identity accompanied (or was accompanied by) articulation of the status of resident alien (the metic) and greater sophistication in the way in which privileges of citizenship could be extended or withdrawn as reward or penalty – and in the understanding of citizenship itself.[19] Although the *atimos* in the sixth century was simply an "outlaw," the fifth and fourth centuries saw the development of *atimia* as a more limited and temporary withdrawal of citizen privilege as penalty for wrongdoing, e.g., the *atimia* placed upon the public debtor until he paid his debt.[20] And conversely, specific privileges of shareholding, such as legal protection, religious participation, and even landholding, could at times be given out piecemeal to deserving *xenoi*.

Landholding, however, and inheritance of land continued to be a key privilege of Athenian citizenship, and a brief examination of the interconnections of citizenship and inheritance will be a useful way to end this section. The topic requires that we revisit Plutarch's account of the law, and in particular his description of the law as "about *nothoi*."

Nothos (fem. *nothē*) is a word as old as Homer referring to a man's bastard or irregular offspring, typically the child of a slave or concubine as opposed to the *gnēsios* (legitimate) child of a wife. The status of *nothoi* in Athens is the subject of considerable debate, one source of which is in fact Plutarch's use of the term – ostensibly for those "not born from two *astoi*." As a result, we are confronted with a term used in two

---

[19] Whitehead (1977); M. J. Osborne (1981–1983).
[20] For *atimia*, see Todd (1993: 365 and *passim*).

ways and with two different sorts of bastardy or illegitimate birth, one within the family and the other in the larger family of citizens or polis.[21] Without going further into this debate than is necessary here, the basic "facts" about *nothoi* in Athens can be summarized as follows:

1. Athenians credited Solon with a law that excluded the *nothos* from inheriting more than at most a token "bastard's share" of 500 drachmas.
2. Before Clesithenes' reorganization of the Athenian citizen body, the phratries (or "brotherhoods") seem to have been responsible for overseeing entry into both family and city inheritance – and such entry was restricted to *gnēsioi*.
3. Cleisthenes allowed the phratries to continue their traditional role, but established the demes as formal "gate-keepers" of the citizenship rolls. No source says that either he did or did not require that the deme admit only *gnēsioi*, but later practice suggests that the demes modeled their admission procedures on the phratry and that a claim of legitimate birth was required.
4. By the midcentury – and Pericles' proposal of 451/0 – Athenians thought of their city as a public family, in which they all shared as heirs. Thus Plutarch's "law about *nothoi*" may reflect a popular view of the law as metaphorically about who could "inherit" the polis. Such usage ought to be an argument against those who think "bastards" were legally citizens in Athens, but for present purposes we ought to consider the implications of Athenian inheritance law for Athenian citizenship law – or what is the consequence of *nothoi* having or not having a share?[22]

The Athenians practiced a system of partible inheritance in which direct descent from the deceased was preferred; in the absence of direct heirs and of a will, the property devolved in sequence to a legally defined bilateral kindred, called the *anchisteia* ("closest"), with males preceding females in each degree of relationship, extending first to the "children of cousins" on the paternal side and then through the same order to "children of cousins" on the maternal side.[23] Although such a system may at first seem to raise problems of fragmentation of property holdings, demographic reality made the problem of "no direct heirs" more likely

---

[21] See Patterson (1990).
[22] For general discussion of bastardy in ancient Greece, see Ogden (1996).
[23] Summary in Todd (1993: 216–28).

than "too many direct heirs," and the *anchisteia* can be considered a sort of "safety net" for the prevention of "empty" households. Solon's exclusion of the *nothos* (typically the child of a slave or concubine) from inheritance and so from the *anchisteia* (see above) thus focused inheritance on the organized bilateral family in the sense of kindred, producing a system that seems to have been remarkably effective in achieving stability for Athenian families and property holding.

If then we consider Pericles' law in light of the traditional or at least Solonian system of bilateral inheritance, the requirement of birth from two *astoi* seems also quite traditional in that it would prevent the intrusion of foreign claims on Athenian property. The extent to which Athenians were in fact marrying foreigners in the mid-fifth century – and whether this was more a matter of Athenian men marrying foreign women while abroad or foreign men marrying Athenian women while in Athens or both – is perhaps unknowable, but certainly the opportunity for both sorts of relationships dramatically increased as Athens became an imperial power in the Aegean. Earlier generations of elite Athenians, such as indeed Cleisthenes' father Megacles, had married non-Athenians, and it has been suggested that Pericles' law was therefore an "anti-aristocratic" measure intended to keep the elite and their interests at home.[24] The problem with this idea, however, is that Megacles' marriage must have taken place roughly a century earlier, and the other known aristocratic foreign marriages (e.g., that of Cimon's parents) also belong to an earlier era. There are no known examples of such aristocratic foreign marriages from the mid-fifth century. In contrast, a general concern for keeping the Athenian *anchisteia Athenian* seems in keeping with Athenian interest and the concrete, participatory character of Athenian citizenship. From this perspective, viewing the law as "about *nothoi*" – i.e., about those who could not be Athenian shareholders and heirs – is in practical terms quite accurate and understandable.

Did then Pericles' law declare the marriage of an Athenian and a foreigner invalid or illegal? The law as we have it is phrased in terms of parentage not marriage. Nonetheless, given that Pericles' law cannot be considered a full definition or law of citizenship, but only one piece of the larger nexus of rules on privilege and status, it is probable that Pericles' restriction of "shareholding" to those born of two *astoi* would also have had legal implications for Athenian marriage. And, as will be seen in the last section of this chapter, by the mid-fourth

---

[24] Humphreys (1974).

century any marriage between *astos* and *xenos* was explicitly illegal and invalid.

Finally, although modern discussion has generally assumed that Pericles' law modified and narrowed a preexisting rule requiring only one citizen parent (i.e. the father), there is in fact no evidence that such a law was "on the books" in Athens before 451, and the language of the law itself will exclude "full-bred" *xenoi*, whose presence in Athens would have been increasingly significant, just as clearly as those born from a mixed marriage. It is at least possible that Pericles in 451 *began* the polis' supervision of the citizen rolls in Athens, i.e., that his law provided the first standard Athenian criterion for entry into the demes and phratries, who prior to this time had managed their membership on traditional but not necessarily uniform procedures.[25]

THE PRESSURES OF WAR: CITIZENSHIP GRANTS AND CITIZENSHIP RESTRICTIONS

The *plēthos* of citizens, which the *Ath. Pol.* asserts precipitated the law of 451/0, was significantly reduced during the long twenty-seven-year Peloponnesian War, but no formal change in the dual parentage criterion for citizenship seems to have been made or even proposed. Instead, we find proposals both to extend citizenship – or partial citizenship – to *xenoi* and also to limit full citizen privilege, participation, and protection to a part of the *Athēnaioi*, proposals that reveal both the pressures of war and the development of Athenian legal thinking about the nature and divisibility of citizenship. First, sometime after the dramatic siege of Plataea, the Athenians voted that "the Plataeans should be Athenians."[26] The details of the grant are unfortunately provided only by considerably later sources but include the interesting detail that the Plataeans should have a share of all things just as the Athenians did, except for any priesthood held by family descent and – for the first generation of Plataeans – the nine archonships. Once a Plataean-Athenian has been born from Athenian parents, it seems, his or her citizenship becomes complete. A similar recognition that partial or limited shares could be given to non-Athenians is evident in the grant of *epigamia* – or intermarriage – to the Euboeans.[27] Just how or how widely this grant affected the citizen

---

[25] So Patterson (1981).
[26] Demosthenes 59.104–106.
[27] Lysias 34.3. The date and circumstances of this grant are unclear. Lysias says that it happened at a time when Athens still had her "walls, ships, money, and allies."

community is unfortunately unclear; the episode remains obscure and little noted. Another poorly documented "rule-change" apparently instituted in the latter years of the war was that an Athenian could "marry one *astē*" and have [legitimate] children with another.[28] The rule of dual parentage (and legitimacy) has not been overturned; with a clear shortage of men in Athens (cf. Aristophanes, *Lysistrata* 591–3), an unmarried Athenian woman could now produce legitimate children and citizens with an Athenian man not her husband.

In less formal ways as well, it is likely that during the long years of war noncitizens (*xenoi* or *nothoi*) found their way – or were invited – into the deme rolls. If a man was willing to join in the tribal regiment of the citizen army, the deme (and tribe) might be quite happy to call him an *Athēnaios*. However, there is no evidence that the demos formally revoked the Periclean criterion of dual Athenian parentage or gave up their exclusive right to make citizenship rules. Both the Plataean and the Euboean grants, in fact, reveal a self-consciousness about citizenship as a kind of family membership, which could be extended by "adoption" but only by decision of the demos itself.

The defeat of the Athenian navy at Syracuse precipitated a crisis not only of manpower but also of political confidence, leading in 411 to the fall of the democracy and to the restriction of full citizenship privilege on the basis of wealth. Thucydides tells the dramatic story of the events leading up to the vote to abolish the democracy by a cowed and terrified assembly, and the *Ath. Pol.* provides details of what seem to be the oligarchic "platform," including entrusting the politeia to "those most capable in person and property" (29.5), i.e., those of hoplite status to the exclusion of the thetes, who at the time may have made up roughly half the adult male Athenian population. The oligarchic regime, however, lasted only a few months before negotiations between the fleet in Samos and democratic proponents in Athens brought about the restoration of full democracy. After the loss of the fleet at Aegospotami in 405 and the surrender of the city in the following year, the democracy fell yet again, replaced by a Spartan-backed oligarchy. Thucydides' history does not go this far, but other accounts (including Lysias' dramatic *Against Eratosthenes*, Lys. 12) make it clear that the narrow regime of the "Thirty" succeeded in blackening the name of oligarchy so thoroughly that when full democracy was restored again in 403 the idea of limiting political participation or judicial protection

---

[28] Reported by Diogenes Laertius (on the authority of Aristotle) in his "Life" of Socrates (2.26). For discussion see Patterson (1981: 142–3).

to the wealthier "few" was decisively rejected. Further, it is not clear from the historical account that the Athenians ever rejected the basic Solonian citizenship of all Athenians – as opposed to limiting active participation and control of office to a more narrowly defined class.[29] But the story of Athens under the "Thirty" is an instructive lesson in the vulnerability of a passive citizenry. Finally, there were some Athenians who wanted to reward with a grant of citizenship those foreigners and even slaves who had come to the aid of the democracy (*Ath. Pol.* 40), but this was surely proposed as a "onetime" grant that did not in the end win approval. In the end the basic Periclean criterion was rearticulated and the fourth-century Athenian community remained a family community. In the language of the Athenian assembly: "no one of those after the archonship of Eukleides (403) should 'have a share in the polis' if that person cannot show that both parents are *astoi*, but those before the archonship of Eukleides should be left unexamined."[30]

The post–403 citizenship law, however, was not simply a return to the prewar status quo. The war had tested severely the core principles of an active participatory democracy, but also stimulated creative thinking about the nature of citizenship and its privileges. As will be seen in the last section of this essay, fourth-century Athenian law revealed a resulting self-consciousness about citizenship, and about political and judicial participation as components of citizenship, that provided the basis and context for Aristotle's discussion in the *Politics*.

Athenian Citizenship Law in the Fourth Century: The Evidence of the Law Courts

The restored Athenian democracy rearticulated the rule that Athenians were those born from two Athenians. But it did more than that. It developed a system of public litigation through which Athenians could

---

[29] So I would dispute J. K. Davies' representation (Davies 1977–1978) of the restrictions on citizenship in the constitutions of 411 and 404 as "alternatives" to the Periclean rule of dual Athenian parentage. Rather it would seem that what was being suggested were ways to limit active citizenship within that traditional citizenship body.

[30] Eumelus fragment 2, from Scholiast to Aeschines 1.39. "Those after" and "those before the archonship of Eukleides" are generally thought to be those born after or before this date, but perhaps the demos intended that those *introduced to the deme* before 403 should remain unexamined, but all new citizens would be so scrutinized. Cf. Humphreys (1974: 91–2).

exercise, dispute, and claim citizenship privilege – and for which were written and delivered speeches arguing the case for either side. A number of these speeches survive, so making fourth-century legal history a quite different enterprise than fifth- and opening an illuminating window on the Athenian conception of citizenship. I will conclude this essay with a brief consideration of the legal issues and legal arguments of two orations from the mid fourth century: the speech of Euxitheus "Against Euboulides" written by Demosthenes and the speech of Apollodorus "Against Neaira," written most likely by Apollodorus himself.

Against Euboulides *(Demosthenes 57)*

The speaker Euxitheus is appealing his rejection from the citizen roll of his deme; he speaks to the Athenian jury against Euboulides, the demarch (the deme leader or "mayor"). His claim to be in great danger and at risk for shame and destruction is no rhetorical hyperbole, because a defeat would mean not only loss of Athenian status but possibly also sale into slavery. Euxitheus does not in fact mention this penalty, but it would seem that the legal situation is analogous to that described in the second ("present-day constitution") part of the *Ath. Pol.* (42.1):

> Full citizenship belongs to men both of whose parents were citizens, and they are inscribed on the list with their fellow demesmen when they are eighteen years old. When they are being registered, the members of the deme vote under oath first on whether they appear to have reached the legal age, and if they do not, they are returned to the status of children, and secondly on whether the man is free and born as the laws prescribe. If they decide that he is not free, he appeals to the dikasterion, while the demesmen select five of their number as accusers; if it is decided tht he has no right to be registered as a citizen, the city sells him into slavery, but if he wins his case, the demesmen are required to register him.

There are some problems with the interpretation of this passage (e.g., does the rejected candidate always appeal and is he always sold into slavery if the appeal is unsuccessful, even if he is a free *xenos?*),[31] but the basic principle that the deme admits/scrutinizes citizens only in accordance with polis law is clear. In this case, Euxitheus argues that a long history of hostility between his family and the demarch Euboulides, his

[31] See Rhodes (1981).

opponent before the *dikastērion*, has resulted in his being unfairly voted out of the deme, and he marshals all the testimony and evidence he can find, direct and indirect, to convince the Athenians to overrule the deme and recognize that he is of citizen birth. For present purposes, i.e., our discussion of the nature of Athenian citizenship and citizenship law, Euxitheus's use of the argument "we have acted as citizens therefore we are citizens" is particularly notable (see, e.g., 57.46). In a world without birth certificates, passports, social security cards, or the IRS, proof of status often lay in the *de facto* demonstration of public behavior appropriate to that status. Not only, says Euxitheus, has his father's Athenian birth been attested by relatives and other witnesses, in addition, "he was chosen to office by lot, and he passed the probationary test, and held office" (25). Similarly, he asserts of himself that "I was nominated among the noblest-born to draw lots for the priesthood of Heracles, and ... passed the scrutiny and held offices" (49). Euxitheus even turns around the charge that he and his mother "sold ribbons" in the agora into an argument in their favor by quoting the laws, first that "anyone who makes business in the market a reproach against any male or female citizen shall be liable to the penalties for evil-speaking" (30), and second that it is "not permitted to any *xenos* to do business in the agora" (31).[32]

Euxitheus's arguments demonstrating active citizen status also demonstrate the inadequacy or incompleteness of the Aristotelian definition of citizenship as sharing in polis offices of assemblyman and juryman. Not only are local, deme offices important to his case, but also religious office (the priesthood of Heracles) as well as family rights of inheritance and responsibilities of burial. In his dramatic final plea, Euxitheus asks the jury to restore him to citizenship so that he can bury his mother in the family plot. "Do not deny me this" he continues,

> do not make me a man without a country (*apolis*); do not cut me off from such a host of relatives, and bring me to utter ruin. Rather than abandon them, if it prove impossible for them to save me, I will kill myself, that at least I may be buried by them in my country. (70)

Against Neaira (*Demosthenes 59*)

Citizenship as active participation – whether in family, deme, or polis and in matters of religion, politics, or the marketplace – is similarly

---

[32] Presumably, a metic could legally do business in the agora.

evident in the speech "Against Neaira" delivered to an Athenian jury in the 340s. This speech is in fact the only surviving prosecution on the charge of fraudulent claim to citizenship (the *graphē xenia*).[33] It is a remarkable speech, written and delivered by Apollodorus, son of Pasion, the enfranchised ex-slave banker. Apollodorus prosecutes Neaira on the grounds that she has usurped Athenian status by acting as the Athenian wife of Stephanus, who then introduced her sons into the demes as citizens and married her daughter to citizen husbands. He prosecutes with the zeal of the newly enfranchised and he backs up his case with learned quotation of law and history. Indeed, it is to this speech that we owe most of our knowledge of Athenian laws on marriage and adultery, laws whose violation demonstrates that Neaira is guilty of a false claim to be an Athenian, an *astē* and *politis*, and rightfully have a share in the polis – in sum, that is, to Athenian citizenship. As inserted by an unknown editor but usually taken as genuine, the law states that

> If an alien shall live as husband with an Athenian woman in any way or manner whatsoever, he may be indicted before the Thesmothetae by anyone who chooses to do so from among the Athenians having the right to bring charges. And if he be convicted, he shall be sold, himself and his property, and the third part shall belong to the one securing his conviction. The same principle shall hold also if an alien woman shall live as wife with an Athenian man, and the Athenian who lives as husband with the alien woman so convicted shall be fined one thousand drachmas. (16)

Here, as in the procedures outlined in the *Ath. Pol.* and those by which Euxitheus was brought to court to plead for his freedom, the *xenos* or *xenē* who participated as an Athenian in Athenian marriage and so claimed Athenian status fraudulently was punished by being sold into slavery – a fate we can remember that an Athenian citizen, male or female, could not suffer at the hands of his city or fellow citizens. The speech against Neaira is an important reminder of the point emphasized throughout this chapter: Athenian citizenship was a status marked by active participation, according to age and gender, in activities and relationships, and by the enjoyment of goods, within the interconnected spheres of family, local deme, and larger polis community. Citizenship law, therefore, should be understood to include not just the rule on

---

[33] See Carey (1992), Patterson (1994), Kapparis (1999), Hamel (2003).

citizen parentage, but also the nexus of laws governing inheritance, marriage, religious participation – and of course judicial and political privilege. Athens had not one citizenship law – but an interconnected set of laws that set forth the privilege and responsibilities of those who "shared in the city."

EPILOGUE: CITIZENSHIP AND THE END OF ATHENIAN DEMOCRACY

Athenian citizenship law was the product of the distinctive history of the Athenian polis and the Athenian democracy. When that democracy finally succumbed to Macedonian military autocracy at the end of the fourth century, the active participatory expression of citizenship was lost as well. But it was not given up easily. In 336, the Athenians issued a remarkable decree proclaiming that "if anyone attacks the Athenian demos with the intent of establishing a tyranny or collaborates in establishing a tyranny or destroys the democracy at Athens or its assembly, anyone who slays the doer of such deeds will be sacrosanct" and that if any member of the Areopagus continues to serve in the event of such an overthrow of the democracy "he will be *atimos*, both himself and his posterity."[34] The 330s and 320s were in fact years of vigorous debate about public policy, but the participatory spirit was nonetheless fading, and the successors of Alexander after 322 faced a very different Athens than had Philip a generation earlier. The name of democracy and of citizenship still could be invoked, but by the end of the fourth century Athens was ruled by the Macedonians in partnership with the Athenian elite.[35]

[34] *Hesperia* XXI (1952: 355), trans. Wickersham and Verbrugghe (1973: 107).
[35] Cf. Davies (1984).

15: COMMERCIAL LAW

Edward E. Cohen

A defining characteristic of classical Greek civilization is its tendency to understand and to organize phenomena not (as we do) through definitional focus on a specific subject in isolation, but through contrast, preferably through complementary antithesis.[1] In no context, perhaps, is this trait more striking than in the area of commerce and commercial law. Although Anglo-American law easily contrasts "real property" and "personal property" but still allows for items sharing certain characteristics of both ("fixtures"), the Greek antithetical universe recognized only two contrasting divisions – "visible property" (*phanera ousia*) or "invisible property" (*aphanēs ousia*)[2] – and even the differentiation between realty and personalty tended to be expressed through this distinction.[3] Even the sale of sex was practiced through polarity: pragmatic business and conceptual legal distinctions flow from the binary contrast of the *pornē* ("whore") and the *hetaira* ("courtesan").

But the fundamental commercial differentiation is between land and sea, a pervasive opposition between the nonmaritime and maritime spheres. Thus, interest (*tokos*, literally "yield") is either "maritime" (*nautikos*) or "landed" (*eggeios*): there is no alternative.[4] All commercial activity is "sharply separated," conceptually and legally, into *kapēleia*,

---

[1] On this dualistic opposition so central to Hellenic culture that it has been said to have "dominated Greek thought" (Garner 1987: 76), see Lloyd (1966: 15–85), E. Cohen (1992: 46–52, 191–4), Davidson (1997: xxv–xxvi).

[2] See Gabrielsen (1994: 54–6, 1986), Bongenaar (1933: 234–9), Koutorga (1859: 6–11), Schodorf (1904: 90 ff.), Weiss (1923: 173, 464, 491), Schuhl (1953).

[3] Harp. *s.v.*: ἀφανὴς οὐσία καὶ φανερά; Lys. Fr. CXXXIV (79 Th.); Dem. 5.8.

[4] See E. Cohen (1990), Lipsius (1905–1915: 721), Harrison (1968: 228, n. 3), Korver (1934: 125 ff.).

landed retail trade, and *emporia*, exchange by sea[5] – a division recognized juridically by the explicit separation of "commercial maritime" laws (*emporikoi nomoi*) from those of the landed community (*astikoi nomoi*).[6] This segmentation corresponded to Hellenic reality. In the modern world, maritime transactions may still constitute an important part of total economic activity, but technological developments and multifaceted mechanisms of communication have reduced marine trade to one factor among many (and in some countries to virtual insignificance). In the Hellenic world, however – because of the pervasive pattern of Greek settlement along the coasts of the Mediterranean and Black Seas (rather than inland) and the primitive nature and high cost of the mechanisms available for transportation and communication over the harsh ground terrain – the maritime sphere was probably the dominant half of a commercial universe divided between land and sea.[7] In the very construction and placement of their communities, the Greeks manifested this basic dualistic dichotomy: the nonmaritime city-proper (*asty*) with its "landed" market (*agora*) and its "landed" trade (*kapēleia*), separated from the "maritime" commercial center (*emporion*), generally on the coast and away from the "landed" hub.[8] The ultimate embodiment of this complementary disjunction, of course, is Athens, with its elaborate *agora* city-center miles from the sea, and its incomparable Piraeus harbor and maritime center directly on the water and constituting the *emporion par excellence*.[9] The important silver-testing legislation at Athens, for example, sets parallel but separate provisions for the *emporion* at Piraeus and for the *agora* in the city,[10] whereas Xenophon, in his proposals for increasing revenues at Athens, makes parallel provision for capital expenditures in the Piraeus and in the *asty* (*Poroi* 3.13). Five *agoranomoi*

[5] Gofas (1993: 167). For surveys of ancient references to these terms, see Finley (Finkelstein) (1935), Knorringa ([1926]1987).

[6] Hesykh. s.v. ἀστικοὶ νόμοι. Cf. Dem. 35.3.

[7] Cf. Biscardi (1982b: 28), Ste. Croix (1974: 42), Bleicken (1985: 73), Garland (1987: 85).

[8] Vélissaropoulos (1977: 61).

[9] The *emporion* was the physical, financial, and ideological sphere at Athens encompassing business people involved in maritime trade and finance. Physically the area encompassed the Western portion of the Piraeus harbor and centered on the *deigma*. (See Dem. 35.29 and 50.24; Xen., *Hell.* 5.1.21; Pollux 9.34; Suidas, s.v. δεῖγμα.) At some distance from the *emporion* was the Hippodameian Agora (west of Mounykhia Hill and north of Zea: Garland 1987: 141–2), where some retail activity presumably occurred (Panagos 1968: 223–4) although there is a dearth of positive evidence for consumer commerce here or in other areas outside the central Agora in Athens.

[10] See *SEG* 26.72 (Stroud 1974: esp. lines 37 ff.) for the text of this legislation. Cf. Stumpf (1986), Alessandri (1984).

("market controllers") were selected annually for Athens and five others for the Piraeus.[11] Yet the many analogous aspects of the two spheres are transcended by two seminal contrasts: *agora* transactions in their essence tend to be relatively simple — at retail, often undocumented and largely unwitnessed — and are almost entirely free of governmental intrusion; maritime commerce in its essence is complex — on a wholesale basis, almost invariably pursuant to witnessed, written documentation — and is fostered and fettered by governmental activism. Accordingly we will focus first on the Athenian Agora and then on the Athenian *emporion* during the fourth century B.C.E. (and the years immediately before and after the fourth century), an emphasis dictated by the fact that the overwhelming bulk of surviving evidence for Greek commercial law[12] relates to Athens during that relatively limited period.[13]

LEGAL CONSIDERATIONS AFFECTING THE LANDED MARKET (*AGORA*)

Athenian law in general was largely free of technical complexity or tortuous legalisms,[14] and this is especially true of the commercial law relating to retail transactions. Except for some limited protection against the making of patently false statements and the offering of adulterated or defective goods,[15] and against the charging of excessive prices for grain,[16] consumers were the beneficiaries of no legally imposed safeguards, such as warranties relating to the quality or usability of the products sold. Legal provisions directly affecting transactions in the Agora were effectively

---

[11] Arist. *Ath. Pol.* 51.1. For their duties, see n. 17 below and related text.
[12] Occasional reference to "Greek law" in this chapter should be understood as consonant with Foxhall and Lewis's conclusion that "as a coherent entity it does not exist ... but as variations on a theme (it) does remain analytically useful" (1996a: 2–3). See also Gagarin on unity, above.
[13] Pringsheim did collect masses of material (mainly scraps of papyrus) relating to "sale" in the Greek world over a 1,000-year period, but absence of context or interrelationship for these remnants forced him to acknowledge the impossibility of drawing conclusions from such disparate material (1950: 500).
[14] In large part, at Athens "the language of the street was itself the language of the law" (Todd and Millett 1990: 17). Cf. MacDowell (1978: 9), Todd (1993: 64–5) ("primitive").
[15] False Statements: Dem. 20.9; Harp. *s.v.* κατὰ τὴν ἀγοράν. ἀψευδῖν; Hyp. 3 *Ath.* 14. Cf. Marzi (1977: 221, n. 37), Ste. Croix (1972: 399). Goods: Arist. *Ath. Pol.* 51.1 (duties of the *agoranomoi*); Hyper. 3 *Athen.* 15 (defective slaves).
[16] Prices: Arist. *Ath. Pol.* 51.1; Lysias 22. Cf. Seager (1966), Figueira (1986). For the elements affecting the determination of prices in classical and Hellenistic Greece, see Grenier (1997).

confined to the areas of deceit or disorder.[17] This circumscribed juridical involvement appears to have grown out of a fundamental Greek belief – which "Greek law never abandoned" (Pringsheim 1950: "Thesis") – that a market transaction attains juridical significance (that is, gives rise to a legal action for claims relating to the transaction) only through simultaneous payment of the purchase price and delivery of the good being purchased.[18] This requirement rendered sale, for legal purposes, an instantaneous transaction: immediately prior to the exchange, neither party had any obligation or right relative to the other. Because a legal relationship, and hence a juridical basis for enforcement of an obligation between the parties, could thus arise only on actual delivery of goods against actual payment of the full purchase price, Athenians could not enter directly into legally enforceable "executory" (i.e., future) obligations, such as deferred delivery of merchandise or sellers' provision of credit to be secured by delayed transfer of unencumbered full title to the commodities being purchased. This rule would have sharply limited potential grounds for dispute or misunderstanding by effectively eliminating the judicial enforceability of unconsummated agreements. It is therefore not surprising that of the scores of extant law cases from Athens, only a single one (Hypereides, *Against Athenogenes*) deals with a transaction focused on sale of goods.

At least in theory, therefore, Athenian commercial law was juridically simple.[19] "The inflexibility of such a simple system and its inability to meet the sophisticated requirements of a more developed economy" (Millett 1990: 17) has confirmed for some commentators the essentially "primitive" nature of the Athenian economy.[20] But other scholars have

[17] The jurisdiction of the *agoranomoi* was restricted to maintaining order and preventing misrepresentations by buyers and sellers: Theophrastos, *Laws* (Szegedy-Maszak 1981: fr. 20).

[18] See Pringsheim (1950: 86–90, 179–219), Gernet (1954–1960: I. 261), Jones (1956: 227–32), MacDowell (1978: 138–40), Harris (1988: 360), Millett (1990: 174), von Reden (2001: 74). Cf. Theophr., *Laws* 21.4; Arist., *Rhetoric* 1361a21–22 (τοῦ δὲ οἰκεῖα εἶναι ἢ μὴ ὅταν ἐφ' αὑτῷ ᾖ ἀπαλλοτριῶσαι).

[19] In contrast to the Greek insistence on simultaneous payment and delivery, classical Roman law permitted legal relationships (*obligationes*) to arise from a multitude of sources, including oral consensual executory agreements (*stipulationes*). Greek philosophical writers did attempt to extend the concept of *blabē* ("damage") into a unifying and extended source for civil obligation (Vélissaropoulos 1993: 11), but this had little practical effect. Anglo-American law likewise has struggled in recent years, with limited success, to develop a unifying conceptualization of civil obligation (see Atiyah 1986: 42–3, 52; Cane 1991: 373).

[20] See Millett (1990: 180–2), Finley ([1973]1999: 141). Cf. Finley ([1951]1985: 298, n. 28). Gernet considers it a "paradoxe" that the system was able to function "dans un état économique déjà avancé" (1955b: 207). Cf. Gernet (1955b: 222, n. 1).

demonstrated the variety of sophisticated credit mechanisms that permitted Athenian commerce to function through the "legal fictions" of arrangements economically equivalent to sales with deferred delivery or sales on credit.[21] Purchasers did pay the full price, but often with funds lent by sellers. Financing by the seller allowed the buyer to take immediate possession of the good. In turn, if the buyer did not repay the loan on the terms agreed, the seller was able to bring legal action to recover the sums advanced. Such indirect mechanisms for sale on credit or delayed delivery were so commonplace in Athens that Plato – deeply opposed to artful business practices and the profit-seeking business people who engaged in them[22] – proposed (for the ideal state sketched in the *Laws*) the prohibition of all commercial exchange other than simultaneous "cash for goods and goods for cash" (*nomisma khrēmatōn, khrēmata nomismatos*). Plato's Magnesia, the state representing not the utopia of the earlier *Republic* but merely a "reformed" Athens,[23] would deny all right of legal action to a seller seeking repayment of monies lent to a buyer to "pay" for goods acquired from the seller. A vendor indulging in the legal fiction of an independent loan would have to "grin and bear it" (*stergetō*) if the purchaser did not repay the "loan." Similarly, a buyer would be denied court access to enforce arrangements permitting delayed delivery of goods.[24] But, in actual practice at Athens, surviving sources confirm that credit was widely available for consumer (and other) purchases, from both vendors and banks.[25] A producer of swords and sofas, for example, appears routinely to have offered consumer financing to expedite sales.[26] Seller financing for the purchase of slaves appears to have been so common that two separate surviving law court presentations highlight the practice. In one, Spoudias allegedly failed to repay to the seller, Polyeuktos, either the principal sum of 1,800 drachmas or the financing

---

[21] Demeyere (1952, 1953), Gernet (1953), Wolff (1957), Kränzlein (1963: 76–82).

[22] For Plato, "market people" (*agoraioi anthrōpoi*) were "defective men" (*phauloi*) who pursued monetary profit because they were incapable of more acceptable cultural and political pursuits (*Republic* 371c). Cf. Plato, *Protagoras* 347c; *Politikos* 289e.

[23] Kahn (1993: xviii–xxiii). Cf. Morrow ([1960]1993: 592). For Plato's recasting of the Athenian practice of publishing laws, for example, see Bertrand (1997, esp. 27–9).

[24] 849e: "Here they must exchange money for goods and goods for money, and never hand over anything without getting something in return; anyone who doesn't bother about this and trusts the other party must grin and bear it whether or not he gets what he's owed, because for such transactions there will be no legal remedy" (Translation: Saunders 1951). Cf. *Laws* 915d6–e2 (no legal action for delayed sale or purchase).

[25] In other parts of Greece, seller financing is also attested. For Ptolemaic Egypt, see von Reden (2001: 74); for Greco-Roman Egypt, Rupprecht (1994).

[26] Dem. 27.9 (see Gernet 1954–1960: vol. I 29 ff., 261).

charges (*tokos*) (Dem. 41.8). In the other, another vendor, Amyntas, is reported to have sold slaves for 3,500 drachmas to a buyer who lacked cash. Yet the sale was effectuated through the type of sophistication detested by Plato: a third party was entrusted with possession of a written contract providing for repayment to the seller of principal and financing charges (Lyk. *Leok.* 23). Sales of real estate on credit or for deferred delivery were legion. Athenian *horoi* ("mortgage") inscriptions disclose more than a dozen examples of parcels encumbered to mark a continuing financial obligation related to the purchase price (economically akin to a "purchase money mortgage") or to signal the possessor's obligation of delayed delivery.[27] Similarly, buyers could obtain an interest in goods by making a deposit (*arrabōn*) or an advance payment (*prodosis*), thereby creating a basis for legal action against a seller who conveyed the property to someone else or who failed to deliver an item on a timely basis despite timely tender of the full purchase price.[28] For their part, banks (*trapezai*) are known to have provided funding for the ongoing operations of retail fragrance businesses (Lysias, Frag. 38.1 Gernet) and to have been involved in the sale of perfume outlets (Hyp. 3 *Ath.* 5–9). Bankers provided loans to purchase mining concessions and processing mills (Dem. 37, 40.52), to establish a cloth-making operation (Xen., *Mem.* 2.7), to purchase land (*IG* II² 2762; *Arkh. Delt.* 17 [1961–62]: *Khronika* 35, no. 4), to finance the import of lumber (Dem. 49.35–36), and even guaranteed payment of overseas commercial obligations (Isok. 17.35–37; Dem. 50.28) – all arrangements that were enforceable in the Athenian courts.[29]

Although some scholars have extolled the sophisticated "legal fictions" created by Athenian ingenuity (see note 21 above), and others – committed to a "primitivistic" view of classical Athens – have sought

---

[27] Finley ([1951]1985: 63, 66c, 85c, 101, 112, 113, 114, 114B, 115 (all deferred delivery); 3, 18A, 114A (all deferred payment)). A further example of sale with deferred payment is *SEG* 34.167, published subsequent to Finley's study. For discussion of the legal significance of the earlier *horoi*, see Pringsheim 1953.

[28] *Prodosis*: Lysias Fr. I (38 Gernet): "Aren't the retailers – from whom he's taken advances and not made delivery – suing him?". *Arrabōn*: Isai. 8.23; Theophr., *Nomoi* Fr. 5–6 (Szegedy-Maszak); Menander, Fr. 459 (K–A); Plautus *Most.* 637–48, *Pseud.* 342–6, 373–4, *Rudens* 45–6, 860–2, 1281–3; Fine 1951 (No. 28). For delivery of a sample (*deigma*) to secure an interest in property prior to payment of the purchase price or transfer of the goods, see the discussion in Gofas (1989a) of Pollux 9.34, a fragment from Hypereides. Cf. Talamanca 1953.

[29] For the special significance accorded bankers' records as evidence in Athenian litigation, see Gernet (1955a: 176, n. 2); Harrison (1971: 22, n. 7); Bogaert (1968: 328 n. 46). For a full exegesis of Athenian legal accommodation to business practices, even in derogation of general rules otherwise prevailing, see E. Cohen (1992: 94–110).

to denigrate these transactions as "exceptional,"[30] in fact no elevated subtlety or advanced transformation underlay these practices. Athenian statutory law and Athenian courts simply (and uniformly) recognized as legally enforceable "whatever one party has agreed on with another."[31] As a result of this juridical acquiescence, the legality and enforceability of business arrangements was never dependent on mechanisms specifically sanctioned by statute or tradition. The simplicity of Athenian legal conceptualization was not incompatible with intricate business transactions, nor was it inappropriate for a retail market where, in the overwhelming majority of sales, there would be no "agreement" prior to the simultaneous exchange of cash for goods and hence no basis for a dispute actionable at law. The relatively small amounts involved in individual transactions would have further inhibited resort to litigation or demand for more expansive legislation.

The almost total absence of *polis* involvement in the "landed" economy is shown strikingly by the only domestic Athenian business transaction known in detail, a complex financial transaction in which a young citizen, Epikrates, was allegedly defrauded in connection with his purchase of a perfume business burdened by substantial (and allegedly undisclosed) debts (Hypereides, *Against Athenogenes*). Strikingly, Epikrates is left haplessly to seek redress for himself: no administrative body is available to protect his rights. He is forced to claim that the statute granting legal effect to "whatever one party has agreed on with another" (note 31 above) should apply only to "equitable arrangements" (*dikaia*), but for this proposition – despite his assiduous study "night and day" of potentially applicable laws (Hyp. 3 *Ath.* 13) – he is unable to present any confirmatory statute, precedent, custom, or administrative procedure.[32] But in sea trade, and in the maritime courts which heard its disputes, there was no lack of statutes, precedents, customs and administrative procedures, nor of intricate argumentations concerning their appropriate use.

---

[30] Finley ([1951]1985: 113–14); Millett (1990: 187) ("credit sales few and far between"). Because of the sparse quantity and fragmentary quality of surviving evidence – limitations compounded by the absence of ancient statistics – characterization of these numerous examples as "exceptional" (without the proffering of a multitude of "standard" examples) is necessarily a product of *a priori* assumptions.

[31] See Dem. 47.77. Similarly: Dein. 3.4; Dem. 56.2; Plato, *Symp.* 196c; Arist. *Rhet.* 1375b9–10.

[32] Whitehead 2000: 306 dismisses Epikrates' argument as merely "an appeal to the spirit, not the letter, of the law." On the role of "equity" in Attic procedure, see Meyer-Laurin (1965: 15–19, 24–5).

LEGAL CONSIDERATIONS AFFECTING THE MARITIME MARKET (*EMPORION*)

Hundreds of ship-cargoes were required annually to satisfy Attica's enormous need for grain[33] – and many other items were imported by sea in amounts at least equal to deliveries of grain.[34] Because of the primitive condition and high expense of overland transport (see note 7 and accompanying text), fourth-century Athens was entirely dependent on this maritime trade, and – in the perceptive words of an Athenian litigant – this commerce in turn was entirely dependent on the availability of financing.[35] As a result, discussion of the legal structure of Athenian maritime trade is perforce largely a consideration of the legal rules and procedures affecting Athenian sea finance.

These rules and procedures were much influenced by the central role of written agreements in maritime transactions. Although in other areas arrangements in writing were wholly unknown at Athens until well into the fourth century – and only very late in that century did unwitnessed written agreements cease to be unusual[36] – by the very beginning of the fourth century (and possibly earlier) maritime commerce was already functioning through written agreements.[37] In contrast to the relatively simple retail dealings of the landed Agora, sea trade in the fourth century was extraordinarily intricate, involving multiple contingencies and disparate complex circumstances and conditions. A single ship might carry many "traders" (*emporoi*), and each of these *emporoi* in turn might be transporting disparate cargo securing separate loans[38]: at least thirty merchants were on board the cargo ship whose sinking is the focus of the litigation at Demosthenes 34. The

---

[33] Despite wide variability in the assumptions, methodologies and conclusions of the large number of scholars who have studied the grain import requirements of Athens, virtually all agree on the need for extensive imports of grain: Whitby 1998 (with extensive reference to primary sources and prior scholarship). On a single occasion and in a single area, Philip of Macedon in 340 seized between 180 and 230 grain ships bound for Athens (Bresson 1994).

[34] Garland (1987: 85). For a summary list of imports other than cereals, see Hopper (1979: 92).

[35] Dem. 34.51: "Without lenders, not a ship, not a ship-owner, not a traveler could put to sea."

[36] See Pringsheim (1955), Thomas (1989: 41–5), Harvey (1966: 10).

[37] The earliest known written contract at Athens appears to be that reported at Isok. 17.20 (an agreement from the early fourth century between a banker and a customer deeply involved in overseas commerce).

[38] Cf. Dem. 32.5–8, 14; 35.31–32; 56.24.

vessel itself might be securing a separate loan from yet other lenders,[39] and the ship owner might have subjected part or all of his own cargo to further lien(s) from yet other financier(s). Each of these lenders would normally require the borrower to provide substantial equity subordinate to each borrowing. This capital might itself be borrowed, possibly against yet other collateral. The resulting complexity is illustrated by the transaction about which we know most, the voyage from Athens to the Crimea (Demosthenes 35), which is the subject of the only maritime loan agreement surviving from antiquity.[40] The vessel used for this transaction carried numerous merchants and agents pursuing their own separate undertakings: retainers of a certain Apollonides of Halikarnassos, a "partner in the ship," were on board (33); a loan had been made to the ship operator secured by the vessel and by goods being transported to the Pontos (32–3); freight was being carried from Pantikapaion to Theodosia (in the Crimea) under arrangements unrelated to the loan documented in Demosthenes 35 (34). So disparate were the transactions that in addition to crew members, eight other persons offer depositions (20, 34) concerning cargo transported from Mende to the Pontic area, relating to other goods on board when the vessel was sailing along the Crimean coastline, and mentioning various financing arrangements covering diverse freight. The preserved contract clearly anticipates multiple cargoes independently owned: decisions on jettison must be taken by majority vote of persons on board (11).[41] To keep track of these multitudinous obligations, Greek ship operators (*nauklēroi*) are known to have carried numerous written documents.[42]

Despite the simplicity inherent in Greek conceptualization of commercial legal obligations (note 19 above), these complex contracts were legally enforceable at Athens. In the conduct of maritime trade, as in domestic retail exchange, Athenian courts did accept as "legally binding" (*kyria*) "whatever arrangements either party willingly agreed upon with the other" (Dem. 56.2). In maritime matters, in fact, the parties (at least on occasion) envisioned that their agreements, often involving

---

[39] See Dem. 32.14 and 56.6. In the latter case the goods selected for transport to Piraeus were hypothecated to other creditors. Cf. Gernet (1954–1960: III.133, n. 4).

[40] This document is now generally accepted as genuine: see Purpura (1987: 203 ff.), Todd (1993: 338).

[41] A single individual, however, might perform multiple roles (see Gofas 1989b: 425–30, esp. n. 1). The *naukleros* Hyblesios of Dem. 35, for example, had an ownership interest in the vessel, personally sailed on the voyage, and was himself a borrower.

[42] Xen. *Anab.* 7.5.14. Cf. Isok. 17.20; Dem. 32.16; *IG* XII. Supp. 347 III.2. See Bresson (2000: 141–9).

individuals from widely disparate parts of Greece, might even negate the specific statutes of individual jurisdictions. The unique maritime loan document preserved in Demosthenes 35, the best evidence for actual Greek practice (above note 40), provides explicitly that concerning the matters covered in the agreement "nothing else be more legally binding than (this) contract."[43] A similar covenant was contained in the compact which is the subject of litigation in Demosthenes 56.[44] We have no way of knowing whether such provisions were merely hortatory (and without any expectation of actual enforceability in the courts of a *polis*) or whether the parties really anticipated that some Greek states might be willing to favor the parties' consensual arrangements over *polis* law. But we do know that the Athenians categorically rejected such attempts at absolute "contractual autonomy." To the contrary, the Athenians threatened capital punishment for residents of Attica who undertook to ship grain to any location other than Attica[45] and forebade residents to lend money for delivery of grain to sites outside Attica.[46] Athenian law further provided that once ships arrived in Athens – without regard to the parties' undertakings – no more than one-third of cereals on board could be reexported.[47] Athenian involvement in alimentary trade was so extensive that the grain supply was an obligatory subject for consideration on a recurring basis at meetings of the Athenian Assembly (*ekklēsia*),[48] and the provisions governing the taxation and delivery of grain from Lemnos, Imbros, and Skyros (contained in a law discovered in the American excavations in the Athenian Agora and published in 1998) offer striking examples of the detailed regulations that might be adopted at these sessions, extending even to provisions intended to avoid "shrinkage" in transit from the Piraeus to the city Agora.[49] Special officers (*sitophylakes*, "guardians of grain") were assigned to enforce the myriad rules pertaining to cereals: during the course of the fourth century their numbers more than tripled.[50] Other Athenians served as administrative officials of the harbor (*epimelētai emporiou*), charged with

---

[43] The speaker further interprets this clause as giving the contract priority even over laws and decrees (39). Cf. *IG* XII 7.67, 27, and 76.
[44] Although the actual text has not been preserved, section 26 of the court presentation confirms the presence of such a clause.
[45] Dem. 34.37, 35.50–51. Cf. Lyk. 1.27.
[46] Dem. 35.51. Cf. Dem. 56.11.
[47] Arist. *Ath. Pol.* 51.4. Cf. Harp. and Suidas, s.v. ἐπιμεληταὶ ἐμπορίου.
[48] Arist. *Ath. Pol.* 43.4. Cf. Mossé 1996: 37–8.
[49] Stroud (1998: esp. p. 26), cf. Harris (1999a), Faraguna (1999), Bresson (2000: 207–10), Osborne (2000b), Engels (2001).
[50] Arist. *Ath. Pol.* 51.3. Cf. Lysias 22.8. See Gauthier (1981).

enforcing a further broad variety of provisions.[51] And, perhaps most importantly, through their special maritime courts (*dikai emporikai*[52]), the Athenians managed both to offer an enticing jurisdiction for the adjudication of maritime disputes – to the advantage of merchants, shippers, ship owners, sailors, and financiers – and through these courts to exercise substantial influence over trade in the Eastern Mediterranean – to the Athenians' advantage.

The *dikai emporikai* provided an attractive and unique forum because of their supranationality of access, rapidity of process, rigor of procedure and enforcement of judgments.

In the absence of special bilateral treaty relationships (*symbola*),[53] the courts of the hundreds of independent Greek states were normally open only to litigants who were members ("citizens") of that state.[54] But the Athenian maritime tribunals accepted litigants without regard to personal status or place of origin or residence.[55] But not for all matters. Although these courts were clearly "well-used" (Todd 1993: 334), some maritime disputes did not qualify for consideration. (The exact configuration of the jurisdiction of these special courts has been much discussed in modern scholarship – as it was in the tribunals themselves in the fourth century: the bulk of surviving cases involve pleas against jurisdiction (*paragraphai*), claiming that the matter under adjudication was not appropriately brought before the emporic court.[56]) It seems clear, however, that at the very least these courts were available for commercial maritime cases involving a written contract providing for trade to or from the port of Athens. A key explanation of the courts' jurisdiction (Demosthenes 32.1), however, can be read expansively as granting the *dikai emporikai* jurisdiction over all maritime matters memorialized by

---

[51] Arist. *Ath. Pol.* 51.4; Dem. 35.51, 58.8, 9. Homonymous officials are also attested at Miletos, Delos and Rhodes: see Migeotte (2002: 121–2), Vélissaropoulos (1980: 33–4).

[52] The word "courts" seems to me the preferable rendering for *dikai* in the term *dikai emporikai* because their procedural and jurisdictional attributes differ markedly from those of other forms of legal action. See E. Cohen (1992: 125, n. 59).

[53] For these diplomatic arrangements through which a member of one state might obtain the right to litigate in another jurisdiction, see Gauthier (1972). Cf. Gernet (1938b: 14–15).

[54] Arist. *Pol.* 1275a (interpreted by Paoli [1930]1974: 283 ff.). For the vast number of separate communities in Hellenic antiquity, see Ruschenbusch (1978: 3–17, 1984: 55–7, 1985: 257). Cf. Hansen (1994: 14).

[55] Although open access to commercial courts may have been an Athenian innovation in the fourth century (see Vélissaropoulos 1980: 248), other states, including Syracuse (Dem. 32.18), Rhodes (Dem. 56.47) and Byzantion (Dem. 45.64), came to offer similar access to foreigners in maritime matters. Cf. Scholion to Dem. 21.176.

[56] Of the five emporic cases preserved in our sources, four revolve around issues of admissibility. See Wolff (1966), Paoli (1930: 75–174, 1935).

written contracts (*syngraphai*) – even those having no relationship with Athens – and in addition as bestowing jurisdiction over any emporic dispute involving trade to or from the Piraeus – even those lacking any written arrangements.[57] The more restrictive interpretation described above would link the availability of this legal procedure to the provision of imports and the taking of exports through the Piraeus – a boon for the Athenian economy, yet less domineering (and presumably less challenging for other states) than Athenian assertion of jurisdiction over a wider swath of sea trade.

In contrast to the protracted delays (*diatribai*) that seem to have been endemic in Athenian court processes, often extending the resolution of legal disputes for years and sometimes even for decades,[58] the *dikai emporikai* were summary in procedure, rendering rapid decisions on a monthly basis. But the exact nature of this swift justice is not entirely clear, and here too variant interpretations have been offered. Some scholars believe that expedited dispute resolution resulted from a requirement that in the *dikai emporikai* cases be adjudicated within a month after initiation[59]; others contend that expeditious disposal of litigation resulted from the introduction of new groups of cases each month and the exemption of this litigation from institutionalized sources of delay.[60]

Special measures were available to assure a defendant's appearance at trial and to enforce the judgments of the maritime tribunals. Despite the rarity of imprisonment as a procedural or punitive process at Athens,[61] in the *dikai emporikai* foreign defendants (*xenoi*) were required to post bail through sureties. A foreigner unable to provide this bail "would go to jail."[62] Because the maritime tribunal was effectively the only court in fourth-century Athens to admit "foreigners" (who constituted a large portion of the persons involved in sea trade and in maritime litigation[63]), this requirement of pretrial bail for *xenoi* meant that – in contrast to the procedures in other courts where defendants

---

[57] For this broader reading, see Gernet (1938b: esp. 22–4) and Vélissaropoulos (1980: 236–41).

[58] See, for example, Dem. 21, 30, 38, 39, 40, 43, 45. Cf. Aiskh. 3.219, 254; Lysias 17.5; Dem. 46.22, and the discussion of these cases at E. Cohen (1973: 10–12).

[59] Gauthier (1974), Vélissaropoulos (1980: 241–5), and Hansen (1983).

[60] E. Cohen (1973: 23–42), MacDowell (1976b, 1978: 232), Gofas (1978), Rhodes (1981: 583), Carey and Reid (1985: 223).

[61] See E. Cohen (1973: 74–83). MacDowell (1990: 268), Hunter (1997). For a variant interpretation, see Allen (1997).

[62] Dem. 32.29. Cf. Lysias 13.23, Isok. 17.12, Dem. 25.60.

[63] For estimates of aliens' importance in this trade, see Erxleben (1974: 462–82), Isager and Hansen (1975: 70–4), M. V. Hansen (1984: 71–921).

might freely depart after an adverse judgment – a substantial proportion of litigants here were required either to post bond prior to adjudication or to be imprisoned while awaiting their court hearing (which of course was imminent because of the courts' rapidity of procedure). Similarly, the *dikai emporikai* constituted the only courts in which, for "private" offenses (*dikai*), "imprisonment was the penalty until (defendants) should pay the judgment against them" (Dem. 33.1). Even for plaintiffs, possible imprisonment loomed: failure to capture a minimum share of the ballots carried liability for one-sixth the sum sought and jail for failure to pay.[64]

In all these ways, maritime litigation was an arena antithetical to the simplistically detached legalities of the landed sphere – both a continuing effect and a continuing cause of the fundamental commercial differentiation between land and sea pervasive in Greek society and in Athenian law.

[64] Dem. 56.4. Cf. Plut. *Solon* 15.2–3.

PART 4

LAW OUTSIDE ATHENS

16: THE GORTYN LAWS

John Davies

Gortyn, like the rest of classical Crete, presents a paradox. Though we know little of its history in the archaic and classical periods from literary sources, and though we know virtually nothing about individuals, the exceptional richness of its legal inscriptions has made the city a prime focus of attention for historians both of Greek law and of Greek society.[1] Yet, although no survey of Greek law can neglect these texts, they present intractable problems. Above all, there is no indigenous nonlegal material. Apart from the imaginary southern Cretan landscape and lawscape depicted in Plato's *Laws* (Morrow 1960), we have only a few pages' worth of literary descriptions, made mostly by non-Cretans. The virtual silence of the historians[2] is broken only by a long fragment of Ephoros (*FGrH* 70 F 149), an analytical passage of Aristotle's *Politics* (II 10, 1271^{b}20–1272^{b}23) and some excerpts of very uneven quality from later historians, Cretan and other.[3] This evidence has major weaknesses. It portrays Crete as a whole, whereas the epigraphic evidence shows significant diversity, and

---

[1] The main modern synoptic discussions are Willetts (1955), Willetts (1967), Metzger (1973), Gagarin (1982), Morris (1990), Gagarin (1991), Hölkeskamp (1992), Kristensen (1994), Davies (1996), Thür (1996a), Gehrke (1997), Lévy (1997), Maffi (1997a), Lévy (2000b), Perlman (2000), H. and M. van Effenterre (2000), Gagarin (2001), Link (2001), Perlman (2002). The principal editions of the Great Code are by Kohler and Ziebarth (1912), Guarducci (1950), Willetts (1967) (with Wolff 1968b and Meyer-Laurin 1969), and Calero Secall (1997). Koerner (1993) and van Effenterre and Ruzé (1994–1995), cited as *Nomima*, group sections by theme, not in epigraphic order. I thank Professor R. Westbrook for use of the subheadings used here, adapted from Westbrook 2003.
[2] Guarducci (1950: 18–20) collects the meagre evidence, including Hdt. 7.169–171 (Cretan neutrality in 480), Thuc. 2.85.5–6 (a strange episode in 429), and Xen. *Hell.* 4.2.16; 4.8.6; 7.5.10 (Cretan mercenaries employed by Sparta).
[3] Texts in *FGrH* 457–68, especially Dosiadas 458 F 2, Diodoros 5.64–80 (= 468 F 1), and Strabo 10.3.1 (= 468 F 2).

in major respects it appears to be simply wrong. The extant documentation has therefore simultaneously to document both the society and its law.

The available evidence comprises a series of inscriptions, dating from the end of the seventh century to the mid fourth century B.C.E.[4] All were written in local script, and all save one (**50**) were "legal" documents in the broad sense. As published in the authoritative edition of Guarducci (1950), they fall into four broad groups, defined and very approximately dated (there are no usable internal dates) by format, script, and location. The earliest group (**1–40**), from ca. 600 or earlier until ca. 525, inscribed on the walls and steps of the temple of Apollo Pythios (cf. Perlman 2002), comprises very fragmentary texts, few of which yield any continuous sense. From ca. 525 onward documents were cut, again for public display, on the walls of buildings in or near the Agora and can be put in a rough sequence that runs to the end of the fifth century (**62–64** ca. 525–500?, **41–61** and **65–71** ca. 500–450?, and **73–140** ca. 450–400?). Within this sequence comes the Great "Code" (**72**), usually dated ca. 450,[5] followed by laws (**141–159**) which use some Ionic letters and are therefore assigned to the fourth century. For reasons that are debated, the sequence of inscribed laws ceases after ca. 350, so that "the law of Gortyn" is universally viewed as the cumulative edifice evidenced by **1–159**, applying to the sixth and especially the fifth century B.C.E.

These documents are not uniform. Some comprise single ordinances, whereas others comprise a group that may or may not concern the same area of law. The tendency was to set such multiple documents

---

[4] All those published in *IC* IV (Guarducci 1950) are cited by **bold** numbers only. Documents from elsewhere are given full references to *IC*, *IG*, or *SEG*. Of relevant new documents published since 1950, one (*SEG* XXIII 585), a law of ca. 460, appears to echo an existing text (**42 B.**11–14), and others are uninformative scraps (*SEG* XLIX 1221–3). The dates given above largely follow Jeffery 1990: 309–16. The Great Code is cited throughout as **72** (for other editions see Bile 1994a, and for a French translation *Nomima* II 357–89, with II 2–18 for a guide): much of it is also translated in Arnaoutoglou 1998. For inscriptions other than **72**, cross-references to *Koerner* and to *Nomima* II are added. For sections of **72** I have modified Willetts' translations to preserve the word order and laconic style of the Greek. Translations of other material are my own. Square brackets in the translations reflect restorations of words and letters.

The Greek of the inscriptions is a form of Doric, similar to that used in most of Peloponnese but so different from Ionic-Attic that even good readers of Attic Greek have trouble in adjusting.

[5] Its single internal date ("when the Aithalian *startos*, Kyllos and his colleagues, formed the *kosmos*" [**72** V 5–6]) is quite useless for us. The date of 480–460 used in Arnaoutoglou 1998 is unorthodox but cannot be ruled out of court.

out in two or more columns – a format which may reflect how they were set out on the master copy. Twenty-two such documents survive, mostly of two columns, but two (**53** and **77**) have at least three, one (**75**) has four, one (**41**) has eight, and one (**72**) has no fewer than twelve. It is this last, enormous document that has been seen as *the* Gortyn Code ever since its first publications in 1884 and 1885, **41** being thought of as the Second or Little Code. Hardly surprisingly, as the only substantial corpus of law to survive from a single jurisdiction of ancient Greece apart from Athens, the material from Gortyn aroused much initial discussion.[6] However, it was only the complete re-edition of the material in Guarducci 1950 that allowed synoptic study on a reliable basis. Since then a full re-edition of **72** (Willetts 1967) and a new interpretative start (Metzger 1973) have intensified attention on both content and context among a small group of international scholars.

The available material is best surveyed by summarizing the contents of the Little and Great Codes before using them and the remaining inscriptions to focus, via the various subheadings, on salient aspects of Gortynian law and society. The extant columns of the Little Code **41**,[7] all of which lack a small number of lines at the top, start in midsentence with provisions about damage to or by animals (I), about the restitution of (stolen?) animals (II) and of recompense for hunting dogs (III 1–7), and about the return of animals pledged as security (III 7–17 and perhaps IV 1–5), continue with provisions about the sale of a fugitive *woikeus* (IV 5–17: for the term *woikeus* see §4 below), about whether persons given as security for debts are themselves liable for their actions (V), about their legal capabilities (VI), and finally about how the sale of a slave can be rescinded (VII) before breaking off. The Great Code **72** is a much more complex matter. It is virtually complete as originally set up apart from the first fourteen lines of col. X, and individual sections were flagged in various ways, but the absence of headings, and the huge variation in the length of sections have generated several, regrettably incompatible, schemes of division.[8] After the invocation "Gods" we have in col. I Seizure of persons (§1, 57 lines); in col. II Rape (§2, 8 lines), Forcible intercourse with a slave (§3, 5 lines), Attempted

---

[6] Maffi (1983: v–viii) traces its gradual emancipation from the terms first of Roman, then of Athenian law.

[7] **41** = *Koerner* 127 (I–IV 5) and 128 (IV 6–VII 19 only) = *Nomima* II 65.

[8] The most accessible are those of Willetts (1967: 34) and Gagarin (1982). *Nomima* II scatters the text through the volume (concordance at II p. 357), as does the selection in Arnaoutoglou 1998 (list p. 159), whereas *Koerner* presents a nearly continuous sequence as nos. 163–181. The divisions and titles given here follow those of Gagarin 1982: 131.

seduction (§4, 4 lines), and Adultery (§5, 25 lines); in col. III Divorce (§6, 26 lines), Separation of spouses (§7, 21 lines), Special payments to a spouse (§8, 3 lines), Separation of slaves (§9, 4 lines), and Children of divorced women (§10, 19 lines); in col. IV Exposure of children (§11, 9 lines), Unwed slave mothers (§12, 5 lines), and Distribution of property among children (§13, 32 lines); in col. V Nonretroactivity of law on gifts to women (§14, 8 lines) and Inheritance and division of the estate (§15, 45 lines); in col. VI Gifts to a daughter (§16, 1 line), Sale and mortgage of property (§17, 44 lines), and Ransom of prisoners (§18, 10 lines); in col. VII Marriage of slave men and free women (§19, 10 lines), Liability of a master for his slave (§20, 5 lines), and Marriage or remarriage of the heiress (§21, 70 lines, going into col. VIII); in the rest of col. VIII Further provisions concerning heiresses (§22, 26 lines); in col. IX Sale or mortgage of heiresses' property (§23, 23 lines), Liability of heirs (§24, 16 lines), The son as surety (§25, 3 lines), and Business contracts (§26, 11+ lines); and in col. X after the lacuna Gifts of males to females (§27, 10+ lines) and Adoption (§28, 43 lines, going into col. XI). The rest of col. XI and the short col. XII mostly provide amendments to earlier sections. Thus col. XI has an amendment to §1 Seizure of persons (§30, 1 line), a new item The duty of judges (§31, 5 lines), an amendment to §24 Liability of heirs (§32, 14 lines), an amendment to §6 Divorce (§33, 9 lines), an amendment to §27 Gifts of males to females (§34, 4 lines), and an amendment to §22 Further provisions concerning heiresses (§35, 13 lines).

The areas of particular preoccupation – procedures within the family in general, especially adoption and the management of heiresses, and other aspects of the due process of transfer of property – stand out at once, though it is unclear whether these were the concerns of a particular historical juncture within Gortynian society or reflected long-term anxieties. Nor can the direction of any innovation be easily discerned. Change there certainly was, driven in part by the need to reformulate penalties in terms not of tripods and cauldrons[9] but of coined staters and drachmai, but although there is a case for detecting a certain defensiveness about preserving the free/unfree boundary and about limiting accumulations of property, those need not be "new" elements. Likewise, though its own amendments show **72** to be reflecting ongoing processes of reformulation, and not to be in any sense a formal all-embracing enactment like a Code Napoleon, the directions of reformulation remain as obscure as their mechanisms.

---

[9] Cf. **I–II** *passim*, with Guarducci (1946).

1. Sources of Law

In the near-total absence of prescripts and preambles, the validating authority or process for most of the extant material is obscure. Analogy from elsewhere in Greece offers three possibilities. First, the lawgiver tradition (with or without a charter from a god) cannot be neglected, especially in a Cretan context,[10] and is represented in the archaic period by the semilegendary Thaletas of Gortyn.[11] However, his influence is portrayed as having been more musical than legal and focused principally on Sparta, and no known enactment at Gortyn can be attributed to him or any other appointed "lawgivers": indeed, the survival of so many singleton documents, sharing style and content with the "Codes," argues strongly against invoking lawgivers as the source of extant material. Second, the prescript of **78** ("Gods. The following were pleasing to the Gortynioi voting. . . . .") confirms that an enactment could emanate from a decree of a citizen assembly and encourages the assumption that the simple invocation "Gods" elsewhere (**43 Ba** and **Bb**; **51**; **64**; **65**) reflects other assembly decisions. Because the Great Code also begins thus (**72 I** 1), states its start date in public terms, and regulates the behavior of public officials, it too must have had some public validation. However, the process of codification that it reflects may have been a third form, on the lines of the Roman praetor's edict or of the activity of the *nomothetai* who recodified much of Athenian law in 410–399. The debate, revived in recent years,[12] has focused largely on **72**, which unquestionably reveals a strong disposition to organize, to systematize, and if need be to innovate, but that does not make choice from among the three alternatives any easier. Nor, finally, can we decide for certain whether our texts represented legal rhetoric, illustrative guidance, or enforceable statute.[13] Most scholars of Gortyn see the texts as genuine law, probably rightly in view of their particularity, but even so we have no idea whether they were actually applied and enforced in practice.

---

[10] Szegedy-Mazak (1978), Ruschenbusch (1983: 317–23), Gagarin (1986), *Nomima* I, pp. 1–8. For Minos cf. Arist. *Pol.* II 10, 1271^{b}31–40; Gehrke 1997: 60–2.

[11] Sources in Guarducci (1950: 18–19) and Gehrke (1997: 43 n. 86).

[12] Imprimis Roth (2000: 12), citing Rosen's four models of codification; Lemosse (1957), Gagarin (1991), Davies (1996), H. and M. van Effenterre (2000), Lévy (2000b).

[13] Debate has centred on the Mesopotamian "codes"; cf. Finkelstein (1961), Whitley (1997), and Gagarin (2001), and various papers in Gehrke (1994), Lévy (2000a), and Westbrook (2003).

2. CONSTITUTIONAL AND ADMINISTRATIVE LAW: LEGAL STRUCTURE OF THE STATE AND ITS MAIN INSTITUTIONS[14]

The two terms for the state as a collective were *polis* and *Gortynioi*. *Gortynioi* voted one extant decree (**78**; restored in **62** and **68**) and were party to an interstate agreement (**80**), and while "Gortyn as a whole" (*Gortyns epipansa*) voted another honorary decree (**64**.2). However, *polis* was the entity that received fines (**41** iii 17; **45B**; **78**.8; **79**.16 and [**21**]; **84**) and owned public land (**43 Ba**), and the use of *damos*, the old pan-Greek term for the community and its territory, is reflected in describing a public road as *damosia odos* (**46 B**.6–7).[15] In charge as principal magistracy was the *kosmos*, but the term is ambiguous. It can denote a collective "management group," as in the phrase "when the Aithalian *startos*, those with Kyllos, were the *kosmos*," which is used in **72** (V 5–6) as a date and in **142**. The Aithaleis were presumably a "*tribe*" (**19**; **72** VII 51 and VIII 32; **104**), one of the segmental divisions of the citizen population: for *startos* see below. Elsewhere, however, *kosmos* denotes the principal office holder as an individual (**29**; **62**). An early law prohibits his holding office again within three years (**14** *g–p*), and because other laws envisage him as having slaves (**41** IV 10) and enjoin that action over seizure of such slaves should be held over (**72** I 51 ff), he was clearly expected to be a man of substance and influence. That the need was felt to constrain his and other magistrates' discretion is clear from other rulings in **14** *g–p*, setting out that a convicted person "is to pay 50 cauldrons for each (offence?). The *kosmos* in charge, if he should not exact, is himself to owe, and the *titas*, if he should not exact, the double [- - -]." The specific provision that for a judge, "whether he gives judgment the same day or next day, it is to be without penalty" (**42** B 11–14), with its implication that judges might seek to avoid making decisions, likewise suggests that the civic community both could, and needed to, make clear what was expected of its officials. In addition to the main *kosmos* we have mention of "the *kosmos* for Rhitten" (**80**) and of "the *kosmos* of foreigners" (**30**; **72** XI 16–17; **78**.4; **79**.15; [**144**.15]), an office that carried a five-year prohibition on re-election (**14** *g–p*) and was supported by a remembrancer (*mnamon*)

---

[14] Conspectus of formal terms in Guarducci (1950: 31–2), with Bile (1981), Kristensen (1994), *Nomima* II, pp. 3–18, Ruzé (1997), and Gehrke (1997) for social organisation and Perlman (1992) for political and social diversity among Cretan cities. Willetts (1967: 3–34) merges information about Crete with specifically Gortynian material, using an unsafe anthropological model.

[15] The phrase *wastian dikan* (**13**) reflects the other pan-Greek word *astu*.

(**72** XI 16). The *kosmos* had his own remembrancer (**42 B** 3–9), who might be a noncitizen (**72** IX 32–3).[16] Whether the *gnomones* who appear once only, with a ten-year prohibition on reelection, are a separate magistracy or are the *mnamones* or the judges under an earlier name is not soluble on present evidence.[17]

That judge (*dikastas*) and *kosmos* were clearly distinct roles is usually assumed,[18] though Aristotle's report that magistrates rule "not in accordance with written ordinance but by their own judgement" (*Pol.* II 10, 1272ᵃ38–9) would be consistent with their roles being combined, as it is with the total absence from the Gortyn evidence of any evidence for juries. Hardly surprisingly, therefore, the judge is the most prominent official in the documentation. That the role was split among several men with differing responsibilities is implied by the provision that a litigant "is to bring suit where it belongs, before the judge where it is written for each" (**72** VI 25–31; similarly IX 23–4). The "judge of *hetaireiai*" and "whoever judges of pledges" (**42 B** 11–13, whence *SEG* XXIII 585) may be two such specialist roles, as too the "orphan-judges" who suddenly appear at **72** XII 7 and 11–12.

3. Litigation: Procedure and Evidence[19]

More importantly, the role of judge was also split procedurally. This is stated generically at **72** XI 26–31 ("The judge, whatever it is written to adjudge, according to witnesses or by oath of denial, is to give judgment (*dikadden*, Attic *dikazein*) as is written. Of the others he is to

---

[16] The parallel now quoted is with Spensithios, appointed as *poinikastas* (writer) by the central Cretan community of Dataleis ca. 500 on terms that suggest he had come from elsewhere (*SEG* XXVII 631 = *Nomima* I 22).

[17] **14** *g–p*, with Guarducci (1950: 71) and Bile (1988: 350) for the *mnamon*. Other officials, who appear in the documents but are not primarily concerned with law, are the produce distributors (*karpodaistai*, **77B** & **C**), the herald (**87**), two sorts of exactors of fines, *esprattai* (**75D**; **87**; **91**; **160B**, with their own remembrancer, **87**) and *titai* (**14** *g–p*; **15** *a–b*; **78**; **79**; **102**; **107**; **165**), the inspector (*epottas*, **84**, with Bile 1988: 331 n. 54), and the army leader (*startagetas*, **80**, with Guarducci 1950: 185).

[18] For their separation Willetts (1967: 78), following Wolff (1946: 63 ff.) and Guarducci (1950: 186).

[19] Cf. especially **72** I, with Rosén (1982), Gagarin (1988) and (1995). The focus of this section requires comment. Though the two verbs denoting "to contend in court" or "to assert" (*molen* and *ponen*) recur through **72**, and though litigants were active participants (Gagarin 2001, with 49 n. 16), extant procedural stipulations guide judge rather than litigant, and the kaleidoscopic array of distinct suits and writs available to an Athenian citizen litigant has no known correlate at Gortyn.

decide (*krinen*) under oath according to what are being contended") and exemplified at **72** I 18–24 ("If they dispute about a slave, each asserting him to be his, if a witness should testify, to give judgment (*dikadden*) according to the witness, but if they give witness for both or for neither, the judge is to decide (*krinen*) under oath."). The three roles – of judges, of witnesses, and of oaths – each need consideration. First, oaths, for in Gortyn much evidential weight was laid upon them, especially but not only when other evidence was unavailable (Gagarin 1997). The gods to be invoked by the judge were specified, as was the goddess by whom a woman was to swear an oath of denial and as were the men who were to swear on a particular (unidentified) matter and the oath they were to utter.[20] The system therefore had to accommodate competing oaths sworn by opposing litigants and witnesses, and left it to the judge in such cases to decide who was "more oathworthy," a stipulation which presumably meant in practice navigating among the silences of the various assertions made on oath.[21]

Second, the judge, for the difference between the verbs used to denote his role has aroused much discussion[22] and should reflect a real distinction of degree of judicial discretion. In part this has to do with the development of written law, displayed legibly in a public place. At Gortyn, as elsewhere in Greece, it increasingly defined, and thereby limited, the role of the judge[23] to the point where many of the sections of **72** either make no reference whatever to judge or court and envisage self-regulating social processes or stipulate that he is to *dikadden* "as is written." In part, however, it has to do with the debated role of witnesses. Earlier scholarship[24] saw their role as being purely formal, even as being comparable to the role, known from other early legal systems, of the oath-helper who supports a litigant even without direct

---

[20] Respectively **51**.1–5; **72** III 5–9; **51**.5–14. Similarly **75A** = **81**. An oath-guarantor appears once (**4**.3).

[21] E.g., **41** II 3–16; with other examples cited in n. 25 and Gagarin (1997) against Thür (1970; 1996a).

[22] Headlam (1892–1893), Talamanca (1979), Bile (1988: 348–50), Gagarin (1989: 47–52), Thür (1989, 1996a).

[23] Cf. **82** (= *Koerner* 156 = *Nomima* II 8), requiring in part that if the opposing parties are present an arbitrator is to give judgment within three days or be penalized. For other limitations cf. **42B**. Cf. also **22** B (= *Koerner* 104 = *Nomima* II 84, whence *SEG* XLV 1279), now best interpreted as a rule enforcing certain legal actions (Koerner ad loc.; *SEG* XLV 1276).

[24] Imprimis Headlam (1892–1893), followed by Latte (1930) and others listed by Gagarin (1989: 29 nn. 3–4); cf. Gagarin (1984, 1989).

knowledge of the circumstances. Thus, for example, he who apprehends another in an adulterous act "is to proclaim before three witnesses to the relatives of the one captured to ransom him within the five days: but of the slave, to the master before two witnesses" (**72** II 28–33). Here, as elsewhere, the specified minimum number of witnesses varies with the offence or with the status of the persons involved, and there can also be provision that a witness, in this case to a woman's oath of denial, must be "adult for fifteen years or more" (**72** XI 46–55). Though this particular provision envisages proceedings before a judge, it is clear that such formal witnessing was largely a matter of interpersonal procedures, not of court hearings. Only if matters did come to court would such witnesses become "real" witnesses, in which eventuality such witnesses were to be "more oath-worthy."[25]

However, renewed scrutiny of certain texts has established that provision is sometimes made for testimony from accidental witnesses of fact.[26] The most complex example concerns suits against a deceased person, the law stipulating

> to bring claim against him before the year. The judge is to give judgment (*dikadden*) towards the testimony. If one disputes won suits, the judge and the remembrancer, if he is alive and a citizen, and the witnesses the next-claimants (*epiballontes*); but of surety and of security-monies and of fraud and of promise, witnesses the claimants are to testify. If they *apoweiponti* (refuse to testify?), he is to give judgement that (plaintiff), having himself sworn and the witnesses, is to win the simple (amount).[27]

This is not the only case where evidence on oath overlaps with oath as evidence.[28]

---

[25] **41** II 12; **45B** 3–4; **72** II 15–16; III 49–50; IV 6–7. The provision that in case of dispute whether a man is free or slave "stronger are to be whoever claim free" (**72** I 16–18) uses different terminology (*kartonans emen*): for this phrase, and for the like expression "stronger witness" (**63**.4), see Gagarin (1989: 39–40).

[26] Decisive are **41** V 4–11 (cited below §7), **72** I 2–24, and **72** II 16–20, with discussion in Gagarin (1989: 35 ff.).

[27] **72** IX 24–40, with Metzger (1973: 106–7), Maffi (1983: 121–70), and Gagarin (1989: 44–5) for problems of translation.

[28] For oaths of exculpation cf. **28** (= *Nomima* II 12) and **72** III 5–9.

4. PERSONAL STATUS: CITIZENSHIP, CLASS, SEX, SLAVERY[29]

Though the many status-terms used in the documents give the impression of a complex, strongly layered society, much extant law is formulated irrespective of status, and the "semantic ambiguity" (Bile 1988: 342) of some terms created fluidity in practice. For example, although the term *poliatas* ("citizen") is used twice, in the same formula (**72** X 35–6; XI 13–14), and the verb *poliateuei* ("is an <active> citizen") once (**72** IX 33),[30] both *eleutheros* ("free," used to contrast with servile or bonded status) and *dromeus* (literally "runner," the widespread Cretan term for citizen) effectively denoted the same status. Specification of age was occasionally required by the subject matter. Thus, the term *pentekaidekadromeus* is used once to specify a witness "adult for fifteen years" (**72** XI 54–5), and the heiress law (**72** VII 15–IX 24 and XII 6–19) is drafted in terms of being or not being of age to marry, though the actual definition of marriageable age for heiresses as "twelve years old or more" is the very final afterthought of the Great Code (**72** XII 17–19).

With statuses other than that of citizen, problems multiply. *Apodromos*, which appears once only in the heiress law (**72** VII 35–6), must from the context denote "adult but not yet *dromeus*," Attic *ephēbos* (thus Lévy 1997: 27 n. 11), but the parallel formation *apetairos*, a term used only in the laws on rape and adultery (**72** II), is enigmatic.[31] Literally, it denotes one "not in a *hetaireia*," i.e., not a (full?) member of one of the "fellowships," which were both segments of the citizen body and military mess-groups. Of the two relevant passages, one runs as follows:

> If one copulates by force with the free man or the free woman, he shall pay one hundred staters; and if (with a dependant?) of an *apetairos*, ten; and if the slave with the free man or the free woman, he shall pay double; and if a free man with a *woikeus* or a *woikea*, five drachmas; and if a *woikeus* with a *woikeus* or a *woikea*, five staters. (**72** II 2–10: for *woikeus* and slave see below)

---

[29] Willetts (1967: 10–17), Link (1994b).
[30] For the qualification see Lévy (1997: 26).
[31] Willetts (1967: 12–13), Lavrencic (1988); other references in Lévy (1997: 27 n. 8). The isolated reference to *apetairoi* in **84**.6 does not help.

The other states:

> If one be taken in adultery with a free woman in (the house) of father, brother, or husband, he shall pay a hundred staters; but if in another's, fifty; and if with the wife of an *apetairos*, ten; but if a slave with the free woman, he shall pay double; and if a slave with a slave, five. He (i.e., the captor) is to proclaim before three witnesses to the relatives of the captive to ransom him within five days; and of the slave, to the master before two witnesses; but if he should not be ransomed himself, it is for the captors to deal with him as they wish; but if one claims to have been entrapped, the captor is to swear, for a fifty-stater case or more, himself the fifth, each invoking curses upon himself, and for an *apetairos* case himself the third, and for a *woikeus* case the master and one other, that he took him in adultery and did not entrap. (**72** II 20–45)

On this evidence the *apetairos* is neither 'free' (i.e., citizen), nor *woikeus*, nor slave. However, the status appears only in these laws on improper sexual behaviour, i.e., the only laws which prescribe so ferocious a differentiation of penalty (at the extreme, a 1:2400 ratio): the protection of legitimacy within lineages, and of sexual boundaries between statuses, was clearly felt to require the singling out of an inferior but nonservile status that was elsewhere assimilated to that of the *eleutheros*.

Much more debated[32] is the relationship between the statuses of *woikeus* and of "slave" (translating thus the general pan-Greek term *dolos*), a problem not eased by the use in other sources of many other terms for the subordinated populations of Crete.[33] The balance of argument favors the working assumption that for legal purposes the statuses were identical. The main arguments are that the provisions on rape and adultery quoted above are full and consistent if they are identical but illogically disjointed if they are distinct, that whatever distinction there may have been is not consistently maintained, that the capabilities and vulnerabilities of the two groups are identical, and that much of the Great Code (notably col. I, which concerns precisely relevant questions

---

[32] Favoring differentiation Willetts (1967: 13–17), Koerner (1993: 468 ff.); for identification or assimilation Lotze (1959: 14–20), Lévy (1997), Link (2001).

[33] *Perioikoi* (literally "dwellers-round") is the commonest, used by Arist. *Pol.* 1269a38–40 and 1272b16–19 and perhaps to be recognised for Gortyn itself in **65**.10. For others see Perlman (1996), Link (2001: 87–8 and 103 f).

of determining status) envisages only two statuses, free and "slave," not three. The counterarguments partly derive from the presumption that a *woikeus* cannot be sold as a slave (but the relevant passage, on fugitive *woikeis*,[34] prescribes delay in such a sale while implicitly envisaging it) whereas a *dolos* can (**72** VII 10–15), partly from the terminology of **72** II 11–13, which specifies penalties for forcible intercourse with a household slavewoman (*endothidian dolan*; but the adjective need not specify anything more than location), but mainly from the use of two terms. That undeniable fact must reflect some distinction, whether historical or current and whether of origin or location or occupation, but legally the convergence appears to be complete in practice, at least by the date of the Great Code.

On that assumption, what may now be called "serf" status at Gortyn can be sketched in some detail.[35] Such persons were "owned" by individual masters among the "perishable" property, could be inherited by the master's heirs and could be sold (see above). However, the law provided for some protection against violence even if the monetary compensation went to the master, not to the injured person, and did in certain circumstances recognize the "serf" as a juridical person (if a slavewoman is raped, she "is more oath-worthy," **72** II 15–16), though the capability of a serf to give witness is otherwise left unclear. That they could own property is to be inferred from the provision that "If someone dies, the houses in the *polis* and whatever there may be in the houses which a *woikeus* does not dwell in, living in the countryside, and the small and large cattle which are not of the *woikeus*, are to be towards the sons..." (**72** IV 31–37).[36] The implication is that a *woikeus* who dwelt in the countryside (as, it is thought, most did) had first call on use, and presumably possession, of house and beasts. In any case the possibility of being fined (e.g. **72** IV 13–14) and the admissibility of action if a divorced or widowed *woikea* takes away more than her own property (**72** III 40–44) clearly imply that "serfs" could own at least movable property. Moreover, as that last reference indicates, serfs could marry, divorce, and remarry under the same rules as free persons. Even more significantly, "[If the slave] going to the free woman marries her, free are to be the children. If the free woman goes to the slave, slaves are to be the children. If from the same mother free and slave children

---

[34] **41** IV 5–17 and V 1.

[35] This paragraph largely follows Lévy (1997: 32 ff., q.v. for detailed references).

[36] Adopting the normal interpretation of *epi korai* (34–5) as "in the countryside"; for rebuttal of objections see Lévy (1997: 36) and Maffi (1997b) against *Nomima* II p. 181 and H. and M. van Effenterre (1997).

are born, if the mother dies, if there is property, the free are to have (it), but if there be not free, those with a claim are to take it over" (**72** VI 56 – VII 10). It would be hard to find a more eloquent testimonial to the skill needed to manage the workings of a society split by status differences but united by language and culture and locked into the same tight-knit landscape.

Last, under this heading come aliens. One law[37] sets out the terms on which aliens were to work for the community, providing for their maintenance and placing them under the jurisdiction of the Kosmos for foreigners. That there was an "aliens' law," the correlate to the "citizens' law" attested in a sadly fragmentary early document (**13** *g–i* 2), is known from a second law discussed below,[38] whereas a third law appears (if the relevant restoration is correct) to be assimilating "freedmen," an otherwise unattested category, to the status of citizens of the dependent city Lato.[39]

5. FAMILY: MARRIAGE AND DIVORCE, CONCUBINAGE, CHILDREN, ADOPTION[40]

This and the next two sections cover topics with which extant laws were much concerned. Marriage as such is taken for granted, needing no definition and taking the normal Greek monogamous form. As **72** VI 56–VII 10 (quoted above) shows, it could be virilocal or uxorilocal and could cross the free/unfree boundary. Whether "twelve years of age or older," the specified minimum age of marriage for heiresses (**72** XII 18–19), was the norm is unknown. The end of a marriage, whether by divorce (**72** II 45–III 16 and XI 46–55), the death of the husband (**72** III 17–31), the death of the childless wife (**72** III 31–37), or the separation of serf from serf (**72** III 37–44), is readily envisaged and regulated at length, the concern of the law in each case being that the woman or her heirs should not take more than her specified share of the property. One case may be cited in full: "If husband should die leaving children, if the wife wishes she is to marry, holding her own property and whatever the husband gives according to what is written before three free *dromeis* witnesses; but if she purloins anything of the childrens', it is to be

---

[37] **79** = Koerner 154 = *Nomima* I 30. **144** seems to provide the same text.
[38] *ksenia dika* (**80.**8 = *Staatsverträge* II 216 = *Nomima* I 7). See §9 below.
[39] **78**, with §9 below and Chaniotis (1996: 162–3 n. 1039) for defence of the older restoration *ton apeleuth[eron]*: other references in *SEG* XLVI 1217.
[40] Willetts (1967: 28–31), Maffi (1997a).

judiciable" (**72** III 17–31). One is tempted to suspect that the lawmakers were attempting to protect male-to-male inheritance to minimize the numbers of free men unable to contribute adequately to their *syssition* (see §9 below).

The detailed provisions for dealing with adultery, cited above (**72** II 20–45), envisage purely monetary penalties and are framed in terms of self-help on the part of husband, brother, or father, and of arrest leading to ransom. Other forms of sexual union such as concubinage and homosexuality pass undocumented in our extant material, but illegitimacy, though not explicitly so called, lies behind various provisions, first to do with the child born to a separated (free) woman (**72** III 44–52), with penalties if she exposed it before her husband had the opportunity to receive it (IV 8–17), and second to do with the child born to a separated *woikea* (**72** III 52–IV 8). Interestingly, exposure is here neither envisaged nor penalized any more than in the contingency that "If an unmarried *woikea* should conceive and bear, the child is to be in the power of the master of her father; but if the father should not be living, to be in the power of the masters of the brothers" (**72** IV 18–23). Not that provisions for children end there,[41] for provision is separately made for the status of the children of a free woman by a "slave" and for disposal of property "if free and slave children should be born of the same mother" (**72** VI 56–VII 10), and the sudden appearance of the "orphan-judges" in **72** XII 7 and 11–12 implies that the system was being extended in a way not known in detail.

That these provisions all have in common a preoccupation with the proper continuation of lineages is obvious enough. It is therefore natural that thought was given to their artificial continuation via adoption. Though the details of earlier laws on the subject (**20** and **21**) are irrecoverable, the Code's own version deserves quotation in full:

> Adoption is to be whence one wishes. To adopt at the assembly-place when the citizens are gathered, from the stone from which they proclaim. The adopter is to give to his own *hetaireia* a sacrificial victim and a measure of wine. And if (the adoptee) should receive all the property and there should be no legitimate children besides, he is to meet the godly and human dues of the adopter and to receive as is written for legitimate children; but if he does not wish to

[41] Nothing can be made of the fragmentary and much earlier reference to "children" in **18**.3.

meet dues as is written, the next-claimants are to have the property. And if there are legitimate children of the adopter, the adopted son (is to) receive with the males just as females receive from their brothers; and if there are no males, but females, the adopted son is to be equal-sharer, and it is not compulsory to meet the dues of the adopter and accept the property which the adopter leaves; and the adoptee is not to take possession of more. If the adoptee dies without leaving legitimate children, the property is to revert to the next-claimants of the adopter. And if the adopter wishes, he is to renounce (the adopted son) at the assembly-place when the citizens are gathered, from the stone from which they proclaim; and he is to deposit ten staters with the court, and the *mnamon* of the *Kosmos* of foreigners is to pay it to the person renounced. A woman shall not adopt nor a person under puberty. To use these regulations from when he wrote these writings; but for earlier matters, however one holds (property), whether by adoption or from an adoptee, it is no longer judiciable.[42]

6. Property: Tenure of Land, State and Private Ownership, Special Types of Property, Inheritance and Transfer Inter Vivos[43]

Though there is evidence of ownership by the *polis* of some productive land (**43 Ba**), and though one strand of modern scholarship has seen all land as public, the stipulation in one document that "If anyone [of the househo]ld(?) wo[rk]s the immortal propertie[s or t]rees or [- -]" (**76 B** 7–9) is consistent with the list of "mortal items, farm produce, clothing, ornaments, and movables" (**72** V 39–41) in implying that land counted as an "immortal property" and was seen as the object of at least de facto private ownership; provision could hardly be made for pledging

---

[42] **72** X 33–XI 23, here and elsewhere translating *epiballontes* as "next-claimants" to beg no questions (for the problem Bile (1980, 1981), Rosén (1982), H. van Effenterre (1982)). For substantive matters cf. Maffi (1991), Avramovic (1991), and Gagarin forthcoming.

[43] For completeness' sake, regulations about easements (**43** Bb = *Koerner* 133 [irrigation water]; **46B** 6–14 = *Koerner* 137 [carriage of a corpse over others' land]; **52** = *Nomima* II 90 and 73A [water flow]) are noted here.

a threshing-floor (**43 A***a*) or a house (**81**.16 ff.), perhaps land itself (**30**), unless real property was alienable.[44] Certainly the prominence given in the Code to matters of inheritance (IV 23 to VI 46, one-fifth of the whole) is explicable only if land as well as movables could change hands thus. The two main relevant sections of the Code specify how to divide property among sons and daughters (**72** IV 23–48) and among the reversionary heirs (**72** V 9–28); other provisions regulate what is to happen "if some of the next-of-kin wish to divide the property while others do not" (**72** V 28 ff.). Much ink has been spilled on the provisions for the reversionary heirs,[45] which are indeed opaque, not least because they end by specifying that "if there should be no claimants, whoever of the house are the *klaros* are to have the property," and the nature of the collective denoted as *klaros* is unknown.[46] However, such contingencies are likely to have been remote. The lawmakers' preoccupations clearly lay elsewhere. One can detect, for example, repeated concern to ensure that, with gifts *inter vivos* as much as with inherited property, not too much should leach into female hands. Thus, the provision "A son may give to a mother or a husband to a wife one hundred staters or less, but not more. And if he should give more, the heirs are to keep the property if they wish, once they have handed over the money" (**72** X 14–20) is reinforced in the supplementary provisions as "If a son has given property to his mother or a husband to his wife in the way prescribed before these regulations, there shall be no liability; but henceforth gifts shall be made as here prescribed" (**72** XII 1–5). Likewise, a widow may not "take away anything belonging to the children" (**72** III 22–23), and if childless, "she is to have her own property and half of whatever she has woven, and is to take a share of the produce within together with the next-claimants, and whatever her husband gives as is written; but if she should take away anything else, that is justiciable" (**72** III 24–31: similarly for a *woikea*, III 40–44); similarly, "if the father, while living, wishes to give to the married daughter, let him give according to what is written, but not more" (**72** IV 48–51). It is therefore debatable whether women really stood to gain from the innovation that "Whatever woman has no property either by gift from father or brother or by pledge or by inheritance as (enacted) when the Aithalian *startos*, Kyllos and his colleagues, formed the *kosmos*, such women are to obtain their

---

[44] Link (1991: 114–16), Maffi (1997b), Martini (1998), Link (2001: 109).
[45] E.g., Avramovic (1990), Di Lello-Finuoli (1991); Koerner (1993); Avramovic (1994), Brixhe and Bile (1999).
[46] Cf. Mandalaki (2000).

portion; but there shall be no ground for action against previous female beneficiaries" (**72** V 1–9).[47]

Equally prominent is the emphasis given to inheritance via the heiress (**72** VII 15 to IX 24 and XII 6–19, again one-fifth of the whole), explicable only if heiresses formed a significant conduit for the transfer of property of all kinds.[48] The main section, exemplary in its lucidity, deserves to make its impact directly:

> The heiress is to be married to the brother of her father, the oldest of those living. And, if there be more heiresses and brothers of the father, to be married to the next oldest. And if there should be no brothers of the father, but sons of brothers, to be married to that of the oldest. And if there should be more heiresses and sons of brothers, to be married to the next after the son of the oldest. The next-claimant is to have one heiress and not more. If the next-claimant or the heiress is too young to marry, the heiress is to have the house, if there is one, and the next-claimant for marriage is to obtain half of the produce of everything; but if being *apodromos* the next-claimant wishes not to marry the heiress, though they are both of age, all the property and the produce shall be at the disposal of the heiress until he does marry her; but if the next-claimant being *dromeus* does not wish to marry her when of age and willing, the relatives of the heiress are to come to court and the judge is to adjudge to marry within two months. And if he should not marry her as written, she, holding all the property, if there is another next-claimant, (is to marry) him; but if there is no next-claimant, she is to be married to whomsoever she wishes of those who ask from the tribe. And if the heiress, being of age, should not wish to be married to the next-claimant, or the next-claimant be too young and she be unwilling to wait, the heiress is to have a house, if there be one in the city, and whatever may be in the house, and, receiving the half, she is to be married to another, whomsoever she may wish of those who ask from the tribe; but to give a share of the property to the former. And if there are no next-claimants for the heiress as is written, holding all the property she is to be married

---

[47] For the debate cf. Gagarin (1994), Link (1998).
[48] Cf. Maffi (1987), Bile (1994b), Link (1994a), Maffi (1995), Link (1997).

to whomsoever she may wish from the tribe. And if no one from the tribe wishes to marry her, the relatives of the heiress are to proclaim throughout the tribe: "Does no one wish to marry her?" And if anyone does marry her, within the thirty (days) from when they proclaimed; but if not, to be married to another, whomsoever she can. And if one becomes heiress after father or brother has given her, if she should not wish to remain married to one to whom they gave her, although he be willing, if she has borne children, she may be married to another of the tribe, dividing the property as is written. But if there should be no children, taking all the property she is to be married to the next-claimant, if there is one; and if there is not, as is written. (**72** VII 15–VIII 30)

Supplementary provisions are made for the heiress widow, allowing her a choice of husband only if she has children already (**72** VIII 30–35) and arranging how any debt obligations incurred by her husband are to be dealt with (IX 1–24), for the absence of the next-claimant (VIII 35–40), for administering her estate if a minor (VIII 42–53 and XII 6–19), and for legal action if the rules are infringed (VIII 53–IX 1). It all looks extraordinarily comprehensive. Yet there is an agenda. It is not just that, as at Athens, the heiress is seen first and foremost as the conveyor of property, not as a person, but also that every detail is directed toward maximizing the likelihood that she will marry the closest available paternal relative, thereby ensuring that property stays firmly within the paternal lineage, while minimizing the role of maternal relatives (explicitly only at VIII 52–3 and XII 13–14). Once again, it looks as if lawmakers are trying to minimize the leaching of property via women away from the direct chain of male-to-male inheritance.

7. Contracts, Debt, and Security[49]

The tone and direction of law at Gortyn on these matters is usefully set by the opening clauses of one of the major sections of the Code: "While the father lives, not to buy or take pledge on the properties of the father from a son; but whatever (the son) himself acquires or inherits, let him sell, if he wishes. Nor shall the father (sell or take pledge on) what is of the children, whatever they themselves acquire or inherit. Nor is

---

[49] In general Koerner (1993: 501–6).

the husband to sell or pledge those of the wife, nor son those of the mother." (**72** VI 2–12). The section continues with provisions against infraction (12–31) and for preventing sale or pledge of the property of a deceased mother (31–46).

The two processes, sale and pledge, are best treated separately. With sale, the approach throughout our documentation is one of restriction, while implicitly acknowledging that otherwise it would be permitted. Thus, a very early law has the (unfortunately fragmentary) provision "not to buy or to exchange(?),"[50] and publicly owned land cannot be sold by the lessee (**43 Ba**), whereas the purchase of a slave in the marketplace is explicitly envisaged.[51] Likewise, sale of a person in one's power was in principle permitted, but hedged about. Thus, "Not to buy a man while pledged until the mortgagor releases, nor one who is the subject of legal process, nor accept him (in payment) nor accept him (in pledge) nor take him in mortgage. And if anyone does any of these things, it shall be invalid, if two witnesses testify" (**72** X 25–32). Similarly, a fugitive *woikeus* is given some protection against being sold:

> Not to sell as slave the *woikeus* who has run away, not when he is in temple-refuge nor until a year should elapse. If the runaway is of a man in office as *Kosmos*, not to sell as slave while he is *Kosmos* nor until the year should elapse. If he should be sold before the time, (the seller) is to be convicted: as for the time, [the judge is to decide having taken] oath. (**41** IV 5–17)

However, the most prominent process in our extant documentation is that of pledge, offered or seized, as security for a debt. One might pledge property of most kinds, though **75B** appears to prohibit the taking of weapons and household basics. One could, for example, pledge the produce of a piece of land, even if it were rented and not owned outright,[52] and could pledge real property likewise, albeit with

---

[50] 4.1 (= *Koerner* 117 = *Nomima* II 61), with Guarducci ad loc. for the term *ameuwsasthai*.
[51] **72** VII 10–15, extending to sixty days the time limit for completion set at thirty days in an earlier document (**41** VII 7–19 = *Koerner* 128 = *Nomima* II 65, with Jakab 1989).
[52] I follow Guarducci's interpretation of **43 Ba**: "Gods. The *Polis* gave the plantation in Keskora and that in Pala to plant. If anyone should buy them or take them as pledge, the purchase is not to be valid nor the pledging. Nor is one to take a pledge if he does not measure the harvest." As *temene* the properties remained public land, so only the produce could be taken as pledge, not the actual land or the trees. Cf. also *Koerner* 132 = *Nomima* I 47, with *SEG* XXIX 825.

the limitations quoted above. However, most extant provisions deal with the acts of giving or seizing, as a pledge for return of a debt, a person, including and especially oneself, the latter procedure carrying consequences for status and capability with which pre-Code legislation (but not the Code itself) was much concerned. One law states: "If one should unjustly take a male or female slave as pledge or take their clothes or ornaments (?), he will pay in recompense the half of what is written for a free man, and the one-third of that for a free man for the clothes and the ornaments".[53] Here, as in **72** I, "slave" includes all unfree persons, including *woikeis*. However, "just" seizure, whether of free or unfree, was permitted: "But one who seizes a man condemned (for debt) or who has mortgaged his person shall be immune from punishment" (**72** I 56–II 2). Failure to repay the debt might eventually lead, perhaps via the kind of legal process "about free or slave" provided for in **72** I, to the type of sale of a slave illustrated above.

More prominent in law, and perhaps in life, was pledging oneself as security for a debt. The person thus pledged became *katakeimenos*[54] and the creditor became *katathemenos*. Explicit evidence about quittance from such self-pledging does not survive: what do are rules for apportioning between *katathemenos* and *katakeimenos* responsibility for acts committed by the latter. Thus, for example:

> But if at the bidding of the man with whom he is he should do or take something, he is not to be responsible. But if (his creditor) claims that it was not at his bidding, the judge is to decide having taken oath, unless a witness claims otherwise. If the *katakeimenos* wrongs another person in any way, he is to be held responsible. But if he does not have the wherewithal to pay, the victorious (plaintiff) and the *katathemenos* [- - -].
> (**41** V 4–17)

Consistently:

> If anyone should wrong the *katakeimenos*, the *katathemenos* shall go to law and shall exact the penalties as for a free man, and whatever he shall exact, the *katakeimenos* is to have the half, and the *katathemenos* the (other half). If the *katathemenos*

---

[53] **43Ab** = *Koerner* 131 = *Nomima* II 70, with Lévy (1997: 33 n. 25) (against Metzger 1973: 38–9 and others) for the words *ta tritra*, here translated as "one-third."

[54] Metzger (1973: 46–8), Maffi (1983: 90–4), Gagarin (1989: 35–7).

does not wish to go to law, the (*katakeimenos*) is himself to do so when he repays the debt. If the *katakei*[*menos* - - -]. (**41** VI 2–16).

Such provisions envisage a *katakeimenos* as being intrinsically free, but temporarily in legal eclipse, but there was a darker side to the relationship:

If the *katakeimenos* disappears, (the Judge) is to adjudge that the *katathemenos* is to swear that he is not guilty, himself or with another, nor that (the *katakeimenos*) is gone to someone else. If he (sc. *the katakeimenos*) dies, let him (sc. the *katathemenos*) show (the corpse) in front of two witnesses. If he should not swear as is written or does not show, he will pay as fine the simple value. If one accuses him of having sold or hidden (sc. the *katakeimenos*), if he is convicted he will pay as fine the simple value twice. If he takes refuge in a temple, (the *katathemenos*) is to show him visible. (**47**.16–33)

These and other texts show the kinds of rules that had to be put in place by a community that did not follow Solonian Athens in outlawing debt on the security of the body.

8. Crime and Delict[55]

Various provisions can be loosely grouped under this heading, without pretence that Gortyn, or indeed Greek legal systems in general, knew a specific category of "criminal law." That it amounts to a thin haul reveals yet again that lawmakers' preoccupations largely lay elsewhere and that custom and practice provided a necessary minimum. Apart from two fragmentary early laws on homicide,[56] the main extant provision on violence against the person concerns rape.[57] Theft of animals and violence against them, whether by humans or by other animals, generated various provisions that serve to remind us that animal husbandry

---

[55] H. van Effenterre (1991), Gagarin (1991), Perlman (2002).
[56] **8**, possibly protecting heiresses (on Comparetti's restoration [*epip*]*amatis* in fragment *k*); **9**. Cf. Perlman (2002: 201–3).
[57] **72** II 5–20, with S. Cole (1984: 108–10).

was a major component of economic life,[58] while failure to return in proper condition livestock taken in pledge also prompted stipulations (**41** III–IV 4). As for damage, the use of the word *ablobia* "harmlessness" (in an oath formulation, **81** 12–13) implies use of the concept *bloba* (Att. *blabē*, "damage") even though the two stipulations about possible water damage to property (**52B**; **73A**) do not attest the word.

9. Special Institutions

This final section reviews the remaining extant material. Two categories can be reported briefly, *leges sacrae* and documents about relations with external communities and individuals. For the first, there are some straightforward calendars of sacrifices (**3**, **27**(?), **65**, **66**, **142**, **143**, and **147**) and a handful of weird documents that have so far defied full explanation (**53B**, **76B**, **145**, and **146**), but the rarity of priests (only **65**.6) and the near-total absence of *res sacrae* from **72** (only III 7 ff., provision for an oath by Artemis) reflect choices about what to record on stone that differed sharply from those of Athens. Likewise, though the evidence for a *Kosmos* for foreigners, for a *kseneia dika*, and for a *ksenodo*[*qos*] ("foreigners' host')[59] implies the presence of at least some aliens, the two treaties extant from the period before ca. 350[60] are both made with dependent communities and illustrate Gortyn's expansionist tendencies rather than anything approaching "international law."

Two other institutions, however, are more informative. Though not itself the subject of an extant law, temple-refuge as sanctuary for an escaped *woikeus* or *katakeimenos* or "slave"[61] is accepted as a fact of life, gentling otherwise bleak statutory provisions. Last, ill-attested, but fundamental, is the provision that "If the Harvest-distributors should find harvest shut away or not distributed, to them taking the harvest it is to be without penalty, and to pay the simple value and the fines as is written. Of harvest, whatever they attest on oath, to [e]xac[t?] money [- -]."[62] This, plus the contextless words "in the Men's House"

---

[58] **41** I 12 – II = *Koerner* 127 = *Nomima* II 65, with Metzger (1973: 42–5), and perhaps **1** and **13** (on transhumance?), with Perlman (2002: 192–3 and 201 n. 77).
[59] Respectively **30**; **80**.8; **13**.*b*2. Cf. Chaniotis 1995; 1999b; Guizzi 1997.
[60] The treaty with Lebena (**63** = *Nomima* I 59), of the late sixth century, and the treaty with Rhitten (**80** = *Staatsverträge* II 216 = *Nomima* I 7), with Perlman (1996: 262–6, Chaniotis (1996: 160–8), and Capdeville (1997).
[61] Respectively **41** IV 8; **47**.31–3; **72** I 42–3.
[62] **77 B** = *Koerner* 152 = *Nomima* I 49, with Willetts (1961).

(**4.4**: *en andreioi*), the stipulation that "from *andreion* whatever the chief provides for *andreion*" is exempt from seizure in pledge (**75B.** 7–9), and *possibly* the stipulation that "The adopter is to give to his own *hetaireia* a sacrificial victim and a measure of wine" (**72** X 37–9) is the only even indirect reference in the epigraphic documentation from Gortyn to the system, described by the literary sources as general throughout Crete, of compulsory contributions of a proportion of produce from citizens' estates for the common messes (*syssitia*) within which male citizens largely lived and ate.[63]

It is ironic that what we have inscribed on stone from Gortyn, extensive and informative though it is, says so little about a basic component of the whole socioeconomic system that extant laws were designed to protect. Instead, the documentation takes the system for granted and directs its force elsewhere. Although it is more than a disjointed patchwork, it is not primarily "an agreement and guarantor to each other of rights" and still less is it "able to make the citizens good and just" (Ar. *Pol.* III 9, 1280^b 10–12): above all, to be blunt, it is a system of protecting privilege, of safeguarding the ownership and transmission of property (including "slaves"), and of ensuring the continuance of male lineages. How typical it was thereby is a matter of debate.

---

[63] Lavrencic (1988) assembles the literary evidence for the system; Gehrke (1997: 37–40). **184**.8–11 refers to tithes due at Gortyn and Kaudos, but payable to Apollo Pythios, not to the *andreia/syssitia*. **160** does not specify the powers of the *karpodaistai*: see Guarducci *ad loc.*

17: Greek Law in Foreign Surroundings: Continuity and Development

Hans-Albert Rupprecht

I

Egypt came under Greek rule after the conquest of Alexander the Great in 332 B.C.; the Ptolemaic dynasty ruled until the conquest by Octavian in 30 B.C. Egypt was then a province of the Roman Empire until the Arabs conquered it in 641 A.D.[1] After the Greek conquest, an important migration of Macedonians, Greeks, and other groups took place from Greece and the surrounding areas of the Mediterranean. These groups then settled either in Greek *poleis*, such as old Naucratis, or in the newly founded cities of Alexandria and Ptolemais, but by far the majority settled all over the flatland of the chora (countryside).

In keeping with their ancient customs, the immigrants brought their own law and lived according to it. The resulting questions about the continuity and development of law, the possibility of mutual influence between Greek and native Egyptian law, as well as questions about the practice of law, are of general legal-historical interest. In this chapter, these questions will be examined primarily for the Ptolemaic period. The problematic nature of the relationship of Roman law ("Reichsrecht") to native law, or better, to native laws ("Volksrechte") developed in different ways after the Roman conquest, and the question of provincial law will only be sketched here.

---

[1] In accordance with the nature of an introduction and preliminary overview of this topic, in the following article I cite only a little of the scholarly literature and, wherever possible, I refer to basic works of scholarship.

To begin with, we must emphasize that because of the particular nature of our sources, Greek law in Egypt means primarily private law. Public regulations essentially concern administration, taxes, the economy, and monopolies. In addition, regulations that concern the judicial system, trials, public security by means of criminal law and prosecution may be relevant. Questions concerning constitutional theory and the philosophy of law can be left aside. This article will therefore concentrate on private law restricted to the Ptolemaic period and the Principate.

Because the following discussion concerns Greek law, we can begin with the issue of the unity of Greek law, a topic which for the most part no longer constitutes a controversy among Greek legal historians. Despite the fragmentation of political and legal systems in ancient Greece, the existence of a number of basic juridical conceptions entitles us to take an affirmative stance on this question. The fact that there are differences in principles of family law and inheritance law as well as in the technical details (on which points the opposition, primarily coming from the areas of ancient history and philology, place particular weight) does not refute this assertion.[2]

The Egyptian papyri provide the most extensive group of extant sources for Greek law. From the more than 50,000 published texts, more than 7,000 come from the Ptolemaic period and more than 16,000 from the time of the Principate (Habermann 1998). The numerous administrative documents, private texts such as letters, receipts, and so on, can be left aside. For our purposes, we will rely on contractual documents, particular legal texts like wills, trial documents, petitions, and other documents of this kind.

II

Our interest, then, is in the development and shaping of the law imported by Greek immigrants into foreign surroundings.

To address this issue, we must first determine what was taken over from the traditional set of forms for legal activity and documents. With regard to the adoption of forms, we can say the most in the areas of the law of obligations, property law, and procedural law, at least with regard

---

[2] This view of Greek law (for which cf. Wolff 1975: 20 ff) is confirmed in this chapter (for the opposing view, see Finley (1966), and also Gagarin on unity in this volume). The formulation of juristic concepts – even of concepts not shaped by jurists – is properly the province of the modern jurist and entitles him also to form corresponding abstractions.

to the basics. Of course, this essentially excludes family law, for which the chapter by Modrzejewski in this volume should be consulted (cf. also Wolff 1973: 65–72). What follows here are only some brief remarks on the subject.

The *oikos* as an institution shaping the order of family and property in private and public law, which mediated membership in the citizenry via the phratry and the deme, was not taken over. This fact becomes clear also when we consider the differences among the individual original *poleis* of the immigrants. Along with the *oikos*, the institution of the *epiklēros* is inapplicable; the dowry in the form of *proix* was replaced by the form of *phernē*, which was more concerned with the interests of the woman during her lifetime, the *kyrieia* (paternal and domestic authority) was replaced by the guardianship of the *kyrios* (the guardian of the woman), which at one point later was laid down as law and which did not affect the wife's capacity to own property, but at best restricted her capacity to manage it. Likewise, prohibitions against *epigamia* (intermarriage) were not taken over (cf. Wolff 2002: 37–39).

As is well known, Greek law satisfied the requirements of everyday life in the area of economics with a number of simple judicial categories such as sale, loans, *misthōsis* (rent, lease, service contract, building contract, etc.), and transactions securing the lender, such as pledge, mortgage, the transfer of a title for the purpose of securing a debt, and guarantee. These categories were well known from the motherland (cf. Lipsius 1905–1915, Beauchet 1897, Pringsheim 1950, Harrison 1968, Behrend 1970) and remained unaltered in their basic structure. Moreover, sale is a cash transaction involving an immediate exchange of goods and money; the property goes over to the buyer simultaneously with the payment of the price. The other transactions, furthermore, involve furnishing an item for a fixed time for a fee – structured as real acts. Thus, a loan means the handing over of money or even produce for a time with the obligation of repayment, perhaps together with a specified interest rate. The *misthōsis* involves the handing over of something for a time and for a fee, particularly plots of land for cultivation, or of people for service, but also for professional training.

The *syngraphē* ("written contract") was taken over as a form for recording a transaction in an objective written form (cf. Dem. 35.10–13). The double certificate, which became the typical form for Egypt, could have come from the Eastern regions. Also in Egypt, the document was always only a document for proof; it had no constitutive or dispositive force and is therefore not a requirement for concluding a transaction.

Rather, a purely oral conclusion of a contract was also sufficient (see below; also Wolff 1978: 141–4).

In the light of new economic and social requirements, we must now discuss how far the adopted forms were further developed and which new formulas and types of transactions appeared.

Alongside the continuation of the traditional transactions, there are new forms, or at least they have been transmitted to us as new in the papyri. Thus, we can mention the formula for sale on delivery, or the development of the sale by credit, both of which transactions were necessary because commerce obviously required forms, which the cash purchase with its immediate exchange of goods and money as a hand-to-hand transaction could not satisfy, namely the crediting of payment and the later delivery of an item. The credit sale was composed in such a way that a sale contract with the (wrong) confirmation of the payment for the sale was combined with a loan contract, whereby the loan was confirmed as given at the amount of the sale price (fictitiously); these cases are only provable by exceptions (cf. for example, *BGU* I 189 = *MChr* 216 from the year 7 A.D.: *daneion kai prasis ōnou*). Regarding the sale for later delivery, a particular formula was developed after various tentative attempts, according to which the price was given as a loan, which was then to be repaid by the goods agreed on – a stipulation on repayment in conjunction with the exchange of objects which were to be given back (Rupprecht 1984). As a further combination of legal forms, we can also point to the sale of the harvest still in the field.

We can also mention the *antichrēsis*, according to which the services of a person, a plot of land for use, or a house or part of a house for inhabiting are handed over (therefore this is a case of *misthōsis*); the wages, lease, or rent is compensated either through the use of capital or through deductions from the interest or from the capital itself (therefore this is a case of *daneion*). The loan and *misthōsis* formulas were thus connected structurally and at the time were accordingly modified by the payment of wages or rent, the payment of interest, or the obligation of reimbursement (see, for example, *BGU* VI 1273 = *SP* I 65 from the year 221/0 B.C.).

Also new is the transfer of title to secure property in the form of *ōnē en pistei* as the successor to the *prasis epi lusei*, which came from the homeland; it was, at any rate, only mentioned as such in the documents until this point. In addition to this, we encounter still other forms of security that are based on particular forms of the actual execution of transactions (Pestman 1985b). Security in the form of *hypallagma*, the reservation of an item for compulsory execution without any specific pledge, is only solidly attested in Roman times.

Another form of document, the *cheirographon*, was newly developed as a document in the form of a letter – it seems possible that it was adopted from the eastern region after certain modifications (Wolff 2002: 62). In addition to this, we certainly encounter *agoranomoi* (notarial) documents already in the second century B.C. after the establishment of the state notary public offices (Wolff 1978: 81). Here we should note that the forms of documents are equal in value and exchangeable with each other, so that a transaction that was set up in public form, as for example in an *agoranomos* document, could be receipted by a private informal document like the *cheirographon*.

We find the bank notarized *diagraphē* used as documentary proof for the entry in a bank book already in the Ptolemaic period, parallel with developments outside of Egypt, and as an independent form of recording, but not until Roman times (Wolff 1978: 95–105). The *hypomnēma* is also a later development. Evidence for the Alexandrian *synchorēsis* as a legal document modeled on a judicial deed first appears in the time of the Principate (Wolff 1978: 91–95).

The existence of two legal systems developing historically alongside each other over centuries naturally brings up questions about reciprocal influence and the adoption of legal institutions from one system by the other, even if not the melting of the two into a unified system. To begin with, it should be pointed out that in Ptolemaic times, three legal systems existed alongside and contemporaneous with each other: native Egyptian law, Greek law practiced by the immigrants in the chora and – although in a separate form – in the *poleis*, and, last, the law established by the king which applied equally to the native people and the immigrants. As already mentioned, the latter primarily concerned public law, administration, taxes and also procedural law in the great judicial ordinance ("Justizdiagramma") from the third century B.C.

Greek law and Egyptian law existed, however, as systems that were separate, were deliberately kept separate alongside each other, and did not intermingle. Borrowing from each other was only occasional and in the end was limited to only minor assimilations of formulas. In the sphere of family law, it was in this way, probably, that the Egyptian institution of "women's property" as *parapherna* was adopted in the Greek documentary practice of the marriage contract (Wolff 2002: 88–91), and also possibly the institution of share cropping and the institution of the grain loan, which had to be reimbursed one and a half times. As a phrase used in documents like that which is usual for a promissory note, the expression *aneu heurēsilogas* and similar phrases were probably adopted (Wolff 2002: 93–95). These, however, are not substantial changes, nor did they influence the general character of the laws.

Egyptian law, which is recorded in Demotic documents, is found up to the end of the second century A.D., when these documents disappear. We can also refer to *POxy*. XLVI 2385 from the second century A.D. with Greek translations of passages from the Demotic law book of Hermopolis – recorded at least as early as the third century B.C. (Mattha-Hughes 1975) – apparently this law was still in use in the second century A.D. The question of the influence of Greek law on Egyptian law has not yet been sufficiently explored, but nothing at this time speaks of any great influence. We cannot, therefore, speak of Greco-Egyptian law; no osmosis between the two legal systems took place. A similar situation probably existed for Hellenistic Babylonia under the Seleucids (Oelsner 1995: 115–19).

If both legal traditions stood side by side and were kept separate, this does not mean, however, that there was also a separation in the use of legal institutions. Separation would mean that Greek law, according to a strict principle of personality, was used only by Greeks and those considered equal to the Greeks and that Egyptian law was used only by Egyptians. But the evidence is abundant for commercial transactions by Egyptians in Greek documents and therefore in the forms of Greek law. Less frequent are the cases in which Greeks appear in the Demotic documents. Just how much considerations of language played a role here is an open question. Marriage contracts between Greeks and Egyptians were even concluded sometimes in the Egyptian language, as were also sale contracts and contracts of guarantee (cf. Wolff 2002: 81–84). In the first century A.D. cases are mentioned in which there is a supplement in the Demotic documents next to the regulation of contract in Greek documents, as in the case of additional performances for a marriage, for example. In *P.Mich.* V 340 and 341 from the years 45 and 47 A.D. respectively, an additional gift of the father of the bride is mentioned in a Greek document, yet the marriage document had been drawn up in Demotic form. In *PVind. Sal.* 4, a Greek *arrha* sale (sale with earnest money) is agreed on between Egyptian priests for the sale of a plot of land, and then in *PSphinx* 1914, the final transaction is concluded in a Demotic document (the Greek copies and summaries are found in at least six examples, cf. *PLond.* II 262 p. 176). Another example we can mention is credit securing in the form of the so-called pledge-sale contract, when the loan is arranged in Greek form but the security follows through a (conditional) purchase of a plot of land in Demotic form (e.g., *PRyl.* II 160 d.).

Here we should note that the choice of Greek or Demotic documentary forms also, of course, includes the choice of Greek or Egyptian law. A fundamental problem then still is the competence of the court in the case of trials. This is true as long as special courts for Egyptians and Greeks existed in the form of the *Laokritai* as the national Egyptian board of judges – well into the first century B.C. – and the *dikastērion* for the non-Egyptian people until the end of the third century B.C. The *koinodikion*, the panel of judges that was probably of mixed nationality, is only dimly represented in the sources (cf. here anyhow Wolff 1970a: 37–56).

The philanthropy decree of Ptolemy Euergetes II from the year 118 B.C. (*PTebt.* I 5 l.207–220 = *SP* II 210) created a special rule that regulated the jurisdiction for conflicts between Greeks and Egyptians in accordance with the language of the document: for conflicts arising from Greek contracts, jurisdiction fell to the *Chrēmatistai*; for those arising from Egyptian documents, jurisdiction fell to the *Laokritai* (Wolff 1970a: 87–9). Judgment was passed according to the *lex fori* (i.e., according to the "national" law of the court).

Later the issue of competence was no longer a problem because by then the royal *Chrēmatistai* alone had jurisdiction in addition to the royal functionaries acting in judgelike capacity, as the coercive power inherent in their office allowed them to do. Here we can only note the recently documented administration of justice by a *politeuma* of the Jews in Herakleopolis from the second century B.C. (cf. Cowey-Maresch 2001).

We must also mention, of course, the difficulty (at least for us) of classifying individual people as Egyptians or Greeks; the name, in any case, is no longer a reliable criterion from the second century B.C. onward, because several cases are known in which, depending on the circumstances, individual people use either an Egyptian or a Greek name (Clarysse 1985).

We can now return to the issue of the sphere of documents, this time focusing on the question of state control and the registration of documents and transactions. The question does not arise about state-notarized documents as public documents because a copy of these always remained in the archive of the writer. It arises rather about the private six-witness documents and the *cheirographa*. At this time, we know of several pieces of evidence for the registration of six-witness documents in public registries, such as *CPR* XVIII, *PTebt.* III 1, 815, *BGU* VI 1258.

According to these, from the end of the third century B.C. an entry in the public registry becomes possible, although in very different ways. There was no necessity; the documents were usable in legal activity and in trial even without being registered. There is no evidence of registration of the *cheirographa*. Indications of a parallel process in other Hellenistic laws exists in *SEG* XXXIII 679 (Paros, 170–150 B.C.) and *SEG* XXXIII 1177 (Myra, 43 A.D.). Accordingly, a tendency toward the protection of private documents in public archives and registries from loss and falsification can be assumed.

We get a different picture of the situation regarding the Demotic documents. For these a state registration is probably required from 146 B.C. onward (*PPar* 5. = *UPZ* I p. 596 f. = *SP* II 410). In a complicated procedure, copies and Greek notes indicating the contents were to be made and archived (Pestman 1985a). The reason for this was certainly the state control of legal transactions. We have no knowledge of a corresponding treatment of local documents in the regions of the other Diadochi (Rupprecht 1995).

A new invention of the Principate was the so-called *bibliothēkē enktēseōn*, as the registry of property, i.e., plots of land, rights to plots of land, and slaves. Disposal, assignment, and cancellation of rights were registered. Therefore, a public control of legal activity was guaranteed in the form of a personal folio. The prerequisite for the registration of a sale was the execution of the transaction in a public document. In any case, it must be stressed that the registry did not have the character of a land register (which would be significant in private law). A special control on trafficking in slaves is the *anakrisis*, at the time of the first sale in Egypt. At that time, proof of the slave's status had to be furnished.

According to the findings of research on legal history since the first third of the twentieth century, it is certain that the dogmatic structures of Greek law clearly differ from those of Roman law and similarly also from modern laws. This can be illustrated quickly from foundational institutions like contract and debt.

We will first address the institution of contract as a basic legal institution. The first question is about how and in what form to conclude a contract. According to both the epigraphic and papyrological records alike, it has become clear that in Greek law the contract and its conclusion must be kept separate from the document. There is no special form of document for a type of contract or transaction, nor is there evidence of a corresponding form for compelling specific performance. The document should be kept separate from the transaction insofar as the transaction can take place even without being committed to writing, i.e., in the form of a purely verbal contract. The document is, therefore, always only a piece of evidence, not a prerequisite for the validity of the transaction; it is neither a dispositive or constitutive document.

In other matters Greek law developed no formal transactions, no oral formulas as in Roman law in the form of the *stipulatio*. Even the *homologia* is not a formula with particular force.

If, as mentioned above, in Roman times a public document or the public registry of a privately written document is required, then it is, however, only for compulsory execution and entry in the *bibliothēkē enktēseōn*. The reason for this can be found, on the one hand, in desired public control and, on the other, in the increased security which resulted from the collaboration of an official – or officially regulated – agency. The legal force of transactions recorded in privately written documents is not affected by these matters.

I will begin the discussion of the conclusion of a contract with a brief remark of a general sort: if (in accordance with the common opinion, at least among legal historians) one affirms the existence of the legal institution of the contract also for Greek law, then this does not mean that a theory of contracts, i.e., a deliberate, juridically outlined explanation of what constituted a contract, would have to be found in the Greek literary sources of the times, such as Plato, Aristotle, or Demosthenes. The existence of dogmatic, basic juridical conceptions does not presuppose the conscious juridical understanding and explanation of its constitutive elements by contemporary jurists who, as is well known, existed in antiquity only in Rome and not in the other ancient states.

How the binding force of the contract between the parties was produced can be explained, in the usual view, in juridical terminology with the Roman categories of consensual, real, or formal contracts. The contract in Greek law (A. Biscardi 1982a, 138–51) results from a real act that is determined by the consent of the parties – in the formulation of H. J. Wolff (1957: 62–6) by the disposition for a determined purpose ("Zweckverfügung"). Even if the consent of the parties is required, this by itself does not create a consensual contract, because obviously a real moment was always required in addition – even if, when necessary, it is only a fictitous moment, as can be seen in the papyrological sources. With regard to the process of the contract coming into being, we can talk about a kind of real contract because the thought of consideration is not its basis. For the typical format of a contract, a loan contract from the year 74 B.C. (*SB* V 7532) can be consulted in the Appendix as an example: it includes the date, the parties involved, the real act (in this case, the payment), and the conditions of payment (reimbursement and interest, penalty clause, execution clause). As a further example, we can cite a lease in a comparable format *SB* XII 11061 (218 B.C.), also in the Appendix.

Additionally, the consequences of concluding a contract in the area of liability law remain to be discussed. The dominant opinion (Rupprecht 1994: 113–15) today follows the view of H. J. Wolff (1957: 57–72), which was contested most of all by A. Biscardi (1982a: 144–6). In this view, in Greek law, there is no obligation that compels one to perform or fulfill the contract. Instead, the result is an indirect compulsion to fulfill the contract. The so-called penalty fee of the penalty clause (*timēma*) is, in the end, the sum for which the contract is forcibly executed. And this process serves to avoid the tortious liability of the debtor because he damaged the property of the creditor by not providing the performance that would empower the creditor to forcibly execute the contract. In sum, it is constructed as a delict.

The judgment in the trial accordingly does not lead to ordering the debtor to provide the performance, but rather to authorizing enforcement first by means of a controlled private initiative, then by compulsory enforcement through the official. The judgment only confirmed the prosecutor's right of compulsory enforcement; it did not bring about enforcement. The judgment was the "decision about authorizing a request for enforcement" ("Entscheidung über die Berechtigung eines Begehrens auf executives Vorgehen"; Wolff 1983: 446).

The discussion of the meaning of the *praxis* clause is not yet finished. It has now become clear, even if there is still dispute about the details, that the *praxis* clauses in the form of the *kathaper ek dikēs* clause (usual in both the Ptolemaic and Roman times) did not make the documents into executive deeds. Rather, an administrative procedure had to be opened of authorizing and carrying out compulsory execution.

The particular legal construction of a dogmatic foundation different from Roman law, however, meant no restriction on the practicability of this law (see above).

A brief remark on property law. Here too we see something similar. The concepts and structures of "property" and "possession" are foreign to Greek law. Here, we find *kratēsis*, namely the control of property that legitimizes seizure, and *kyrieia*, the authority to dispose, and therefore not the institutions of absolute rights. The same is true for the law on security; in probable contrast to Athens, the law on security in Egypt was not formulated as a restricted right *in rem*, but as a legal possibility to obtain possession of an item and to retain it permanently (Rupprecht 1997a, 1997b).

III

Thus, we can conclude that Greek law, in the sense mentioned at the beginning of the chapter, preserved its basic structure over the centuries into Roman times. This continuity did not stand in opposition to further development in response to the demands of changing economic and social life; rather, the newly developed legal institutions and forms fit smoothly into the previously founded legal system while the basic structure remained intact.

It can be further emphasized that these developments were not the works of jurists, but rather of those who drafted contracts who, in part by tentative attempts in the practice of writing the contents, developed new formulas and modifications of the existing transactions and types of transactions, cleverly adapting them to the needs of practice.

APPENDIX

A loan contract and a lease contract are offered here as examples of typical documents:
A. Loan (*SB* V 7532, Fayum, 74 B.C.):

Date: lines 1–5
Βασιλευόντων Πτολεμαίου καὶ Κλεοπάτρας ἐπικαλουμέ-
ν[η]ς Τρυφίνης τῆς ἀδελφῆς Θεῶν Φιλοπατόρων Φιλα-
δέλφων, ἔτους ἑβδόμου, ἐφ᾽ ἱερέως Ἀλεξάνδρου καὶ τῶν
ἄλλων τῶν γραφομένων ἐν Ἀλεξανδρείαι, μηνὸς Γορ-
5 πι[α]ίου πέμπτῃ, Ἐπεὶφ πέμπτῃ,
Place: lines 5–6
ἐν Νείλου πόλει τῆς
Ἡρακλείδου μερίδος τοῦ Ἀρσινοίτ[ο]υ νομ[οῦ].
Loan Parties: lines 6–12
ἐδάνεισεν Χ
Εἰρηναίωι τῶι καὶ Ἐργεῖ Εἰρεναίου τοῦ καὶ Ἐργέως Πέρ-
σῃ τῆς ἐπιγονῆς καὶ τῆι τούτου γυναικὶ Ἀπολλωναρί(ῳ)
10 τῆι καὶ Θαυῆτι Πτολεμαίου τοῦ καὶ Πετεσούχου Περσίνηι
με[τ]ὰ κυρίου τοῦ προγεγραμμένου ἀνδρ[ὸ]ς χαλκοῦ
νομίσματος τάλαντον ἓν καὶ δραχμὰς τετρακοσίας

ἐνενήκοντα
Interest: line 13
τόκων διδράχμων.
Repayment: lines 13–15
τὸ δὲ δάνειον
τοῦτο καὶ τοὺς τόκους ἀποδότωσαν οἱ δεδανεισ-
15 μένοι ἐν μηνὶ Θὼθ τοῦ ὀγδόου ἔτους.
Penalty Clause: lines 16–19
ἐὰν δὲ μὴ ἀποδῶσιν, καθὰ γέγραπται, ἀποτεισάτω[σ]αν [οἱ] δεδανεισμέ[νο]ι παρα-
χρῆμα, τὸ μὲν δάνειον ἡμιόλιον, τοὺς δὲ τόκους
ἁπλοῦς.
Joint Debtorship: lines 19–20
ἔγγοι ἀλλήλων εἰς ἔκτεισιν τοῦ δα-
20 νείου τούτου αὐτοὶ οἱ δεδανεισμένοι καὶ
Execution Clause and Witnesses: lines 20–23
ἡ πρᾶξις ἔστω ἔκ τε αὐτῶν τῶν δεδανεισ-
μ[έ]νων καὶ ἐκ τῶν ὑπαρχόντων αὐτοῖς πάντων
καὶ ἐξ ἑνὸς καὶ ἐξ ἀμφοτέρων καὶ ἐξ οὗ ἐὰν αὐτῶν
αἱρῆται. ἡ συγγ[ρα]φὴ κυρία. μάρτυρες.

Date: lines 1–5
   Under the rule of Ptolemaios and Kleopatra, called Tryphina, the sister-, father- and brother-loving gods, in the seventh year, in the priesthood of Alexander and of the others recorded in Alexandria, on the fifth day in the month of Gorpaiaios, on the fifth of Epeiph
Place: lines 5–6
   In Nilopolis, in the division of Herakleides, in the Arsinoite nome
Loan Parties: lines 6–12
   X has lent to Eirenaios, alias Ergeus, son of Eirenaios, alias Ergeus, a Persian, and to his wife Apollonarion, alias Thaues, daughter of Ptolemaios, alias Petesouchos, a Persian woman with her above-mentioned husband as *kyrios* 1 talent 590 drachmas of copper money
Interest: line 13
   On interest at the rate of 2 drachmas (per mina per month, = 24 percent)
Repayment: lines 13–15
   The loan recipients shall pay back the loan and interest in the month of Thoth in the eighth year.
Penalty Clause: lines 16–19

If they do not repay as written above, the loan recipients shall immediately forfeit one and a half times the amount of the loan and the interest as is.

Joint Debtorship: lines 19–20

Let the loan recipients be joint debtors for the payment of this loan and

Execution Clause and Witnesses: lines 20–23

the right of execution shall be upon the loan recipients and all of their possessions, either together or individually. Let the document be authoritative... Witnesses.

B. Lease (*SB* XII 11061 = *PHamb.* II 188, Tholthis, 218 B.C.):

Date: lines 1–4

[Βασιλεύον]το[ς] Πτολεμαίου τοῦ Πτολεμ[αίο]υ καὶ Βερενίκης θεῶν Εὐεργετῶν ἔτους τετάρτου
[ἐφ' ἱερέως Δ]ημητρίου τοῦ Ἀπελλ[ο]ῦ [τ]ὸ δεύτερον ἔτος Ἀλεξάνδρου καὶ θεῶν Ἀδελ-
[φῶν καὶ θεῶν] Εὐεργετῶν, κανηφό[ρ]ου Ἀρσινόης Φιλαδέλφου Νυμφαίδος τῆς
[Νυμφίωνος τὸ] δεύτερον ἔτος μην[ὸς Περ]ιτίου

Place: line 4

ἐν Θώλθει τ[οῦ] Ὀξυρυγχίτου νομοῦ.

Lease Parties: lines 5–11

5 [ἐμίσθωσεν εἰς ἐνιαυτὸν σπό]ρον [καὶ θερισ]μὸν [ἕνα ἀπὸ τοῦ σπόρου] τοῦ ἐν τῶι πέμ-
[π]τωι [ἔτει ὧν οἱ κα]ρ[ποὶ εἰς τὸ ἕκτον ἔτο]ς Θεόφιλ[ος Μακεδὼν τριακοντ]άρ[ο]υρο[ς] κλ[η]-
ροῦχος [τῶ]ν ἐν τῆι [c. 15] . . . . . . τ . . [c. 10 Ἀρι]στολόχωι τῶι Στρ[α]-
τίου Θρ[α]ικὶ τῆς ἐπι[γο]νῆς [τὸν ἑαυτοῦ] κλῆρον ὅλον ἄ[σ]περμον ἀκίνδυνον πλὴν ἀβρόχου ἐκφορίου πυρῶν ἀρταβῶν π[εντ]ήκοντα· ἐὰν δὲ ἡ γῆ ἄβροχος γένητα[ι], προσ-
10 δεχέσθω Θεόφιλος Ἀριστ[ο]λόχωι κατὰ λόγον τῶν ἐκφορίων τῆς ἀβρόχου γῆς γινο-
μένης.

Rent Payment: lines 11–14

τὰ δ' ἐκφόρια τὰ συγγεγραμμ[ένα] ἀποδότω Ἀριστόλοχος Θεοφίλωι ἐν μηνὶ Δύστρωι τοῦ ἕκτου ἔτου[ς πυρὸν] καθαρὸν καὶ ἄδο[λο]ν μέτρωι χοῒ δικαί-

ωι μετρήσει δικαίαι καὶ ἀπενε[γκάτω εἰς Θῶλ]θιν οὗ ἂν [Θεό]φ[ι]λ[ος συντά]ξη[ι]
ἰδίωι ἀνηλώματι·
Penalty Clause: lines 14–15
ἐὰν δὲ μὴ ἀπ[οδῶ κατὰ τὰ γεγραμμένα, ἀποτεισάτω Ἀριστό]-
15 λοχος Θεοφίλωι τιμὴν τῆς ἀρ[τ]άβης [ἑ]κά[στη]ς [τ]ῶ[ν πυρῶν δραχμὰς δέκα, καὶ]
Execution Clause: lines 16–17
ἡ πρᾶξις ἔστω Θεοφίλωι παρὰ Ἀριστολόχου πράσσ[οντι κατὰ τὸ διά]-
[γραμμα] . . . . . . [. . .]
Reservation of Grain: lines 17–18
κυριευέτω δὲ Θεόφιλος τῶν καρπῶν ἕω[ς ἂν τὰ ἑαυτοῦ κο]-
[μίσηται·
Guarantee Clause: lines 18–21
βε]βαιούτω δ[ὲ Θ]εόφιλος Ἀρ[ι]στολόχωι τὸν κλῆρον [καὶ τοὺς κατα]-
[σπαρέντ]ας ἐν αὐτῶι καρποὺς καθ' ἃ μεμίσθωκεν. ἐὰν δὲ [μὴ βεβαιώσηι]
20 [κατ]ὰ τὰ γεγραμμένα, ἀποτεισάτω Θεόφιλος Ἀριστολόχωι ἐπ[ίμον ἀρ]-
γυρίου δραχμὰς πεντακοσίας, ἐὰν μή τι βασιλικὸν κώλυμα γ[ένηται.]
ἡ δὲ συγγραφὴ ἥδε κυρία ἔστω οὗ ἂν ἐπιφέρηται.
Witnesses: lines 22 ss.

(Date-Place: lines 1–4)
Lease Parties: lines 5–11
Thirty *arourai* of land, his entire plot of land has been leased by Theophilos, Macedon, 30-Arouraiclerouch of the people of... (?), to Aristolochos, a Thracian of the *epigonē*, of the people of Stratios, for one year for the crops and harvest from the time of planting in the fifth year, whose grain will be harvested in the sixth year; without delivering seeds and endangered by no danger with the exception of draught, at a rent of 50 *artabai* of wheat. If the land remains dry, let Theophilos take this into account on behalf of Aristolochos in accordance with the perimeter of the dried up land.
Rent Payment: lines 11–14
Let Aristolochos hand over the rent to Theophilos in the month of Dystros in the sixth year in the form of pure and untainted wheat with

the dry measure in fair measurement and let him deliver it to Tholtis at his own expense, where Theophilos ordered it.
Penalty Clause: lines 14–15

If he does not deliver it in accordance with what is written, let Aristolochos pay Theophilos the price of 10 drachmas for every *artaba* of wheat as a fine and
Execution Clause: lines 16–17

Theophilos is entitled to the execution against Aristolochos in accordance with the ordinance.
Reservation of Grain: lines 17–18

Let Theophilos be entitled to the grain until the rent is delivered to him
Guarantee Clause: lines 18–21

Theophilos will guarantee to Aristolochos the plot of land and the planted grain, just as he leased it. If he does not guarantee accordingly, let Theophilos pay Aristolochos 500 drachmas of silver as a fine, except in the case of an obstacle by the king. Let the document be authoritative where it is submitted.
Witnesses. . . .

Bibliographic Note

For a list of the source editions, see Oates 2001.

A comprehensive account of private and public law is given by Taubenschlag 1955, though still entirely in Roman categories. The most recent treatment of the general principles of Greek law in Egypt and of the character of documents is found in Wolff 2002 (Wolff I) and Wolff 1978 (Wolff II). See also Wolff 1998 and 1973. For particular legal transactions and a general overview, see Rupprecht 1994. In addition, the detailed account in Montevecchi 1982 can be consulted. An introduction with texts is Pestman 1990. For an overview of demotic law see Manning 2003.

18: Greek Law in the Hellenistic Period: Family and Marriage[1]

Joseph Mélèze Modrzejewski

Hellenistic Law and Hellenistic Culture

"Mixed Law" and "Mixed Civilization"

What is Hellenistic law? When the adjective "Hellenistic" applies to law, it needs to be explained, just as when it stands next to the words "era" or "civilization." The idea of a "mixed civilization," advocated in the past by the historians of Antiquity, following Johann Gustav Droysen for whom the Hellenistic world was the result of a mixture of Greek Occident and Barbarian Orient, is presently abandoned. The meeting of local traditions with practices and ideas which the Greco-Macedonian immigrants imported to the provinces of the Achaemenid Empire conquered by Alexander the Great could surely not help but act on the evolution of the law. The Greek traditions henceforth act in a space larger than the narrow framework of the Greek state, *polis* or *ethnos*, and this necessarily entailed changes in the substance of law. For their part, the local legal cultures must have been influenced by the Greek element entrenched in an Egyptian or Oriental environment. Interplay of mutual influences starts and directs the lawgivers' action to solutions, which can combine a Greek form with a content determined by the local heritage. However,

---

[1] A first version of this chapter was presented as an opening lecture to the "Research Workshop on the Law in the Documents of the Judean Desert," at Bar Ilan University, Ramat Gan, Israel, on June 2, 1998, and published as Modrzejewski 2000. For more details, see Modrzejewski 1998b, 1999.

all this does not lead to a "mixture," and the idea of "Hellenistic law" can in no way refer to such a mixture.

Let us say it clearly: Hellenistic law is nothing else but Greek law practiced by the Greek-speaking immigrants within the kingdoms stemming from Alexander's conquests as we know it, thanks to the documents – papyri, parchments, ostraca, inscriptions – found mainly in Egypt, but also, though less often, in the Near East, at Dura-Europos or in the Judean Desert (Wolff 1973, Pestman 1974). Derived from the experience of ancient Greece, which was multisided by definition, it is characterized as for its substance by a high level of unity; as for its sources, it appears essentially as a customary law, which has its basis not in the legislation of a city or a sovereign, but in notary practice. Because it is not the law of a limited group, as were the *nomoi* of the classical Greek cities or of the *ethnē* it is within the reach of all who can fit the definition of a "Hellene," through adherence to Greek culture and an origin foreign to the conquered country; in this respect, the case of the Jews of Egypt is particularly significant. After the Hellenistic monarchies were reduced to the state of Roman provinces, Hellenistic law survived under the Principate in the practice of the provinces of the East.

Greek Contribution and Local Traditions

The Hellenistic era achieved the unity of Greek law. The differences that were characteristic of the traditions of various cities or regions, the immigrants' fatherlands, diminished in practice. This process, already underway in the fourth century B.C.E. as a result of intercity trade under the dominating influence of Athens, became stronger in the melting pot that was Alexander's army. A Greek "common law" prevailed in the Hellenistic world. The notion of legal *koine*, drawing a parallel between language and law, helps to explain this phenomenon (Gernet 1938a).

The new factor that ensured the success of this *koine* was not the kings' action, as one used to think, but the appearance of a new political structure: the Hellenistic monarchy, which is superimposed on the city. The city is no longer the only framework of legal life for the Greeks. The Hellenistic state released the Greeks from obeying the laws of the city, which were factors of diversity, and created a terrain favorable to the unity of legal practice in private law. Together with the decline of the autonomy of the city, the fetters that confined the Greeks' legal life in distinct systems for each independent *polis* disappear. Free of the individualism of the *polis*, Greek "common law" nevertheless kept a trace of its origin: in the judicial practice of Ptolemaic Egypt, it is called *nomoi politikoi*, "civic law" (discussion in Wolff 2002). The city remains an ideological reference point that allows us to contrast, as regards politics or anything else, the Greek contribution with the local heritage. The immigrants' "common law" stood facing the legal traditions of the conquered populations, which were maintained and protected by the state. Ptolemaic Egypt gives a most instructive example of this coexistence.

Ancient Egyptian local law survived the Macedonian conquest and continued to be used by the natives. During the late Egyptian period, the rules of this law were recorded in casebooks kept by the temples; the tradition, which attributes to Darius I the "codification" of Egypt's law prior to the Persian conquest, suggests the existence of quite extensive collections. As for the Ptolemaic era, this impression has been confirmed by extracts of a "demotic priestly casebook" that were found in different religious centers; the most famous ones come from Tuna el-Gebel, the ancient Hermopolis West, known under the widespread though misleading name "Hermopolis Legal Code" (Donker van Heel 1990). Actually, what we have here is a collection of practical instructions for judges and native lawyers, with models of deeds and sentences, or with solutions to hard cases. One could say it is a "handbook" ("prontuario legale" in Italian) created by the learned priests who produced and wrote down "holy books" – religious, scientific, or legal collections for the Egyptian clergy and their "customers" – in the "Houses of Life" of their temples. The priests who kept these books passed them on from one generation to the next, in different variants, according to the religious centers.

The Egyptian priestly casebook has to be connected with another "holy book" existing in Ptolemaic Egypt: the Jewish Torah. Both of them were translated into Greek in the reign of Ptolemy II Philadelphus (283–246 B.C.E.). The translation of the Jewish Law – the Alexandrian Septuagint – is well-known; its historicity has been confirmed by the fragments of the Pentateuch on rolls of papyrus anterior to the Christian era. A papyrus from Oxyrhynchus published in 1978 (*POxy.* XLVI 3285) informs us now that the demotic collection was also translated into Greek in the beginning of the third century B.C.E., in the reign of Ptolemy II. In both cases, the Ptolemaic monarchy will have underwritten the undertaking.

Numerous documents preserved by demotic papyri add the testimony of everyday legal practice to the data furnished by the demotic casebook in its various versions. For the Ptolemaic period, they represent about half of the documentary papyrus material found in Egypt. They attest an undeniable continuation of the Egyptian legal traditions under the Ptolemies that will be perpetuated under the Roman Empire and then appear again in the Coptic documents of the Byzantine and the Arabic eras. The Greeks call this *nomos* or *nomoi tēs chōras*, "the law of the land"; this expression should not be mistaken for "the laws of the Egyptians," *nomoi* (or *nomos*) *tōn Aigyptiōn*, mentioned by a few documents of the Roman period. We will come back to this point.

Coexistence and Interaction

Still without reaching an amalgam, the coexistence of diverse private laws could not help but lead to an interplay of mutual exchanges and borrowings between the rules and practices. Estimating their accurate extent is not easy: several significant facts will serve to illustrate the situation.

The influence of Greek law on the Jewish practice is a particular problem, which cannot be dealt with here (see Modrzejewski 1996). In respect to the interaction of Greek and Egyptian traditions, the main Greek influence on Egyptian law affects the form of legal deeds: this is the so-called *Doppelurkunde* ("double certificate"), duplication of written documents, which is thought to have been borrowed from the Greeks by the Egyptian notaries. It is however not certain that the *Doppelurkunde* was invented by the Greeks: its prototype is the Mesopotamian "envelope tablet," which was replaced in the neo-Babylonian era by the multiple original, of which a copy was kept by each of the contracting parties. Other presumed borrowings from Greek law by Egyptian law are still more uncertain.

Egyptian influences on Greek law seem to be more numerous. However, one has to be cautious. Thus, the changes characterizing Greek family law in Egypt in relation to its classical roots should not necessarily be attributed to the action of local models; at the very most, the surrounding environment will have stimulated or accelerated an evolution already begun within Greek life. In some cases the new historical context contributed to the institutionalization of tendencies characteristic of a Greek practice, which was, until then, secondary and marginal; this is notably the case, as we will see later, of women who give themselves in marriage or of endogamic unions. Elsewhere – like the eldest son's privileged situation in matters of inheritance or the institution of *parapherna* ("additional dowry") – the Egyptian influence seems to be more likely. But its effect is still limited.

One should be careful not to assume that all similarities in legal solutions are the result of mutual influences and borrowings. It is well known that distinct legal cultures, having reached the same stage of evolution, often elaborate similar solutions if the social and economic conditions are suitable: thus, what seems to be an influence or a foreign element may just be a coincidental convergence. From the comparative point of view, detecting such parallelisms would be a fascinating undertaking. A careful study of the bilingual documents, including not only the strictly speaking bilingual ones and the translations, but also the documents written in one language according to the patterns characteristic of the other, would be particularly useful in this respect.

All in all, the exchanges and borrowings between Greek and Egyptian law seem to be fewer than the supporters of the "mixed law" in the first half of the twentieth century would admit. Pluralism remains the dominant feature of legal life in the Hellenistic world. In Ptolemaic Egypt, it is supported by a system of judicial organization, which guarantees that Greek and Egyptian traditions will be protected by official sanction (Modrzejewski 1995). Furthermore, it is clear that the *nomoi politikoi*, on the one hand, and the *nomoi tēs chōras*, on the other hand, were the controlling law of the courts specific to each of the two main groups: the Greek dicasteries and the Egyptian *laocritai*. In this way, the Jewish Torah in Greek became the "civic law" (*nomos politikos*) of Egyptian Jews, who were an integral part of the community of the "Hellenes" (Modrzejewski 1997). That Jewish Law, especially in family matters, was actually followed by the Jews in Ptolemaic Egypt is now confirmed by the new material concerning the Jewish *politeuma* in Herakleopolis in the second century B.C.E. (Cowey and Maresch 2001).

The Roman conquest of Egypt did not change this situation as far as the substance of the law is concerned. The local laws continue to exist under the kindly eyes of the Roman authority. The provincial judges were ready to respect the peregrine law, even if it meant filling the gaps, resolving the contradictions or restraining extravagances by resorting to the scale of values that their own law, *ius Urbis Romae*, gave them. They failed to see the difference between the Greek and the Egyptian origin of a local rule. Both were for them no more than a local custom characteristic of the peregrines of the province of Egypt (Modrzejewski 1993).

The fact that a Greek version of the demotic collection of laws, which was made in the third century B.C.E., was copied in the Antonine era suggests that this translation could enlighten the provincial judge on the situation of the law actually practiced by native Egyptians and might influence his decision in case of disagreement. Nevertheless, this does not mean that the measures included in this book, "the law of the land," were considered legal rules by the Roman judge. Without a link that would connect them to a foreign city, they could not aspire to the authority of a peregrine *ius civile* according to the Roman categories. For the Roman authority, they were simply rules of local practice.

This "law of the land" (*nomos tēs chōras*) should not be mistaken for the "law of the Egyptians" (*nomos tōn Aigyptiōn*) that a few documents of the second century C.E. refer to. A careful analysis of these documents leads to the conclusion that the law known as "of the Egyptians" was Egyptian only in name; actually, it was Greek law. The Egyptians in question were the natives of Egypt who were not citizens of a Greek *polis*. As for their *nomos*, in some cases, it could appear to be private collections made by local practitioners, using material taken from the royal legislation and the laws of the Greek *poleis* in Egypt (Modrzejewski 1988). For the Roman judge, it did not make any difference for the validity of this law: whether they are Greek or Egyptian, the rules recorded in these books were for him only customs specific to the provincial populations – *mores provinciae, consuetudines loci*. After the generalization by Caracalla of Roman citizenship in 212 C.E. some of these rules, those in conflict with Roman law and order, will be left aside; others will survive as subsidiary provincial law, subordinate to the priority of the Roman "Reichsrecht."

From these general data, one would like to insist on a point that seems to be crucial for my purpose: the permanence of Hellenistic law within the monarchies of the successors of Alexander the Great and within the Oriental provinces, which replaced them after the Roman conquest. Let us limit ourselves to a few details concerning marriage, family structures, and transmission of property by means of succession.

Marriage and Family: The Permanence of Hellenistic Law

Marriage

The new conditions in which the Greek immigrants' family life organized itself modified matrimonial law. In the Hellenistic world, heads of families no longer settle by themselves the question of concluding a marriage, as in classical Athens; it becomes a matter for the married couple itself. In the oldest Greek matrimonial agreement found in Elephantine (*PEleph*. 1.310 B.C.E.), an anacoluthon lets us hear the couple's voice in the first-person plural, for the first time in the history of the Greek family. From now on, it is a purely personal bond that appears in the marriage contracts preserved on papyrus. The diversity of the forms and of the terms that those contracts reveal goes hand in hand with the unity of social fact: conjugal cohabitation (*synoikein*) with the intent of a durable common life (Modrzejewski 1983).

Nevertheless, the legal substance of marriage remains unchanged: it is based, as in the past, on the act of "giving" (*ekdosis*) the bride, which is accomplished by her father, or, in his absence, by a close male relative, and, failing that, by the woman herself. A patrimonial allowance – the handing over of the dowry – accompanies it; this is what gives the marriage its validity as a social institution. The classical *proix* gives place to the *phernē*; this term, which in the ancient Greek sources referred to the dowry in archaic or peripheral practice, applies in Egypt to a matrimonial system now generalized because it is in accord with the needs of a new type of family organization. On the other hand, some formalities disappear, like *engyēsis*, by which the father "placed" his daughter in the hands of the man who was about to become her husband. The written contract now assures the married woman that she is a lawful wife, *gynē gametē*. The contract replaces the solemn statements that accompanied the bride's passage from her father's power to that of her husband. The contractual clauses suffice to produce all the effects that conclusion of the marriage ensure concerning the legal status of the wife and that of the children (Yiftach 2003).

A set of documents found in Abusir el-Meleq, dated from the Augustan era but certainly representing the Alexandrian matrimonial law prior to the Roman conquest, shows that in Alexandria, after drafting a written agreement (*synchōrēsis*), a second act was performed to strengthen the matrimonial union by a ceremony (or an agreement), namely passing before the *hierothytai*, the magistrates of the city. There have been various attempts to explain this dual formality of Alexandrian marriage. The hypothesis of Egyptian influence was contemplated (Winand 1985) but it sounds frail. One can certainly notice a parallelism between the Alexandrian dual deed of marriage and the Egyptian practice in the *chōra*, in which a "support agreement" could be followed by a "payment document." Comparing the Alexandrian *hierothytai* with the homonymous magistrates in the epigraphic and literary sources would rather suggest the idea of a Greek continuity. The intervention of the *hierothytai* was probably no more than a formality, necessary to the handing down of the family estate, under the control of the city (Yiftach 1997).

The barriers the Greek cities used to erect against mixed marriages collapsed in Egypt and in Greek-speaking circles in the East. It could well be that Alexandrian law demanded dual civic ancestry to acquire the status of citizen, a principle whose panhellenic character is stressed by Aristotle (*Politics* 1275b21–22). Monimos, son of Kleandros, Alexandrian by his father, lives in the *chōra* with an Egyptian woman; Demetria, their daughter, in spite of her Greek name, is not an Alexandrian citizen (Clarysse 1988). On the other hand, a citizen of Ptolemais could certainly marry a foreign woman and, through this marriage, let her acquire the position of *astē* (citizen). Therefore, the road was opened to wider matrimonial exchanges than those that the *epigamia* clauses of the intercity treaties in the fourth century B.C.E. used to allow.

In the *chōra*, marriages between partners of different origins were possible and positively legitimate. In the middle of the third century B.C.E., Demetrios, a Cyrenean who came to Egypt following in the tracks of Princess Berenice II, daughter of Magas, who had married Ptolemy III Euergetes, himself married an Egyptian woman; the law of his original fatherland that allowed marriages outside the citizen body only with certain groups of the Libyan population did not matter much to him (*Inscr. Fay.* I 2). The case is not different for Antaios, an Athenian settled in Egypt, who married Olympias, a Macedonian, in the beginning of the second century B.C.E., unless one presumes that the Athenian law forbidding marriage with a foreigner was altered after the downfall of the democratic regime in 322 B.C.E. (*PGiss.* I 2, 173 B.C.E.).

Demetrios the Cyrenean's union with Thasis the Egyptian represents an exceptional case. Marriages between "Hellenes" and natives are extremely rare in Hellenistic Egypt. They were not formally forbidden, but a sort of "cultural *agamia*" made them impracticable (Modrzejewski 1984). We are far from the mixing of populations that the supporters of a Greco-Egyptian civilization used to imagine. Exceptionally, the barrier is overcome in some circles and at certain times. That is how, in Pathyris, in Upper Egypt, in the second century B.C.E., a certain mixture of Greek soldiers and the upper social class of the local population could take place. It was due to contingent reasons: a new form of military organization associating the Greek element with the Egyptian elites.

Family Structures

The Hellenistic era favored the endogamic tendencies of Greek matrimonial law. For the Greeks, legally, only marriage between full relatives was considered incest; unions between close collaterals, half-brother and half-sister, though morally disapproved of, were not illegal. Cimon, son of Miltiades, the Athenian, legally married Elpinice, his sister from the same father. Athenian law since Solon permitted marriage to a half-sister on one's father's side (*homopatrios*). One is less sure that Lacedaemonian law allowed marriage to a half-sister on one's mother's side (*homomētrios* or *homogastrios*). This information, resting on the sole testimony of Philo of Alexandria (*De spec. leg.* 3.22–4), might have simply been invented by the Jewish philosopher: his objective was not to give us information about the Greeks' matrimonial traditions but to contrast their endogamy with the biblical exogamy set down in chapter 18 of *Leviticus*.

In Hellenistic practice, a marriage between brother and sister with the same parents (*homognēsioi*) became possible. King Ptolemy II Philadelphus who married Arsinoe II, his full sister, provided an example in 278 B.C.E. This marriage gave rise to various reactions. Theocritus, more a courtier than a poet on this occasion, compared it to the divine marriage of Zeus and Hera (*Idyll* XVII: 121–34): the Alexandrians may not have found this comparison very tasteful. Some people expressed criticism more or less sharply, the most violent being from Sotades of Maronea, the pornographer; this earned him a particularly severe punishment (Athenaeus 14.620; Modrzejewski 1998a).

Should one see in such a union the adherence to an Egyptian model? This is what Philo's text may suggest, as before him already Diodorus of Sicily, according to whom the Egyptians, "against the general custom of mankind," instituted a law authorizing a man to marry his sisters (*Bibl. Hist.* 1.27.1). However, in the present state of our sources, Egyptology does not validate the idea that Ptolemy II and his sister had followed a Pharaonic example, unless one goes a thousand years back – to Amenophis III or Rameses II. The inevitable conclusion is that the children of the first Ptolemy pushed to its extreme limit a tendency conveyed by the Greek traditions favorable to endogamy.

Greek immigrants followed their example very quickly. As early as 267 B.C.E., at Tholthis, in the Oxyrhynchite nome, a certain Praxidamas had married a woman called Sosio, who almost certainly was also his sister (*PIena* inv. No. 904 = *SB* XX 11053). One hundred and thirty years later, Dionysios, another Greek, gave his banker in Tebtynis an order to pay a tax for his sister Euterpe, who was also his wife, as he specified (*PTebt.* III. 1, 766, about 136 B.C.E.). In the Roman period these practices were generalized; the numerous documents that attest them and the tolerant attitude of the Roman authorities, despite the regulations punishing endogamy according to Roman law, lead us to think that they were already more frequent in Ptolemaic Egypt than is indicated by the two documents we have just mentioned. Such marriages are more common among the descendants of the "Hellenes," in the *metropoleis*, than among village Egyptians; this is at variance with the opinion that derives marriage between brother and sister from an Egyptian tradition.

The Hellenistic era modified in various respects the status of Greek women. A woman was free to sell or buy or rent her property; she could join her husband when he gave their daughter in marriage, or she might do it herself when she was widowed or divorced. The power the head of the family had in classical Greece, as a *kyrios*, over the women under his control – wife, mistress, nonmarried daughters – was now limited to a sort of tutelage. To conclude a legal deed, the woman needed to be assisted by a *kyrios*, but the latter was no more a "master and lord": his intervention was just a formality, whose importance for the validity of the document is in practice not obvious.

Some of those phenomena may appear as signs of "progress" in the evolution of women's condition. Nonetheless, one should be careful of hasty generalizations. Thus, it is not certain that one can interpret as "progress" the alterations that we find in the clauses of the matrimonial agreements preserved by the papyri concerning divorce. This includes, first, the sanction of behavior forbidden by the contract, particularly conjugal unfaithfulness, which could result in the loss of the dowry for the wife and the husband's obligation to refund the dowry and an additional 50 percent penalty (*hēmiolion*). But since the beginning of the first century B.C.E., a new practice appeared, imposing on a husband who wanted to leave his wife the obligation of returning the simple amount of the dowry within a fixed time limit; the *hēmiolion* had to be given only when the time limit was not respected. For her part, the woman also obtained the right to take the initiative for her divorce, giving her husband a time limit for the return of the dowry. Eventually, divorce ceased to be a sanction and was supplanted by divorce by mutual consent.

This situation, which seems to establish the equality of husband and wife in the matter of divorce, is not necessarily more favorable to the wife than the initial system in which the threat of the *hēmiolion* toward the flighty husband effectively protected the wife who had done nothing deserving reproach. However, one can very well consider as "avant-garde" the women who themselves carry out the act of their *ekdosis*, that is to say who give themselves in marriage. In classical Greece, such "auto-*ekdosis*" was a sign of barbarism or of prostitution. But in the Hellenistic world the woman can indeed carry out her *ekdosis* with a legitimate union in mind. For Egypt this fact is attested by two documents, from the Ptolemaic and from the Roman periods (*PGiss*. I 2.173 B.C.E.; *POxy*. XLIX 3500, third century C.E.). A papyrus from Dura-Europos (*PDura* 30.232 C.E.) and the novel *Chaireas and Callirhoe* by Chariton of Aphrodisias attest its expansion beyond the Egyptian area (Karabélias 1990).

Succession

The data concerning the transmission of family property *mortis causa* can usefully complete those concerning marriage and the status of women. The testamentary restrictions, which in classical Greece protected the *oikos*, or family/household, by favoring the deceased's only male descendants, disappeared; daughters inherit in the same way as sons. Also disappearing was the epiclerate, an institution that made the deceased's only daughter, who was legally incapable of being his heir, hand down the property by forcing her to marry a close relative on her father's side so that the son descended from this union could perpetuate the *oikos* of his maternal grandfather (Karabélias 1982).

The compensation for the disappearance of institutions, which in the past served the needs of the classical *oikos*, was the emergence of new practices that benefited the nuclear family. For example, neither Greek nor Egyptian laws granted the surviving spouse intestate succession. In Hellenistic practice, this incapacity was alleviated by the husband's provisions by will in favor of his wife, notably the right of housing until her possible second marriage, and also, though more rarely, similar provisions on behalf of a woman in favor of her husband. Acts combining matrimonial agreements with the couple's provisions because of death (*syngraphodiathēkai*) helped to attain the same objective.

The interaction of two legal cultures lets a few Egyptian influences appear on Greek practice. This seems, as we already observed, to be the explanation for the eldest son's privileged situation in matters of succession, which one can detect in the Greek papyri of Ptolemaic and

Roman times (Seidl 1965), and also for dowry rights, such as the institution of *parapherna* derived from the demotic "Frauensachen" ("wife's property"; Häge 1968). Conversely, *PMoscow* dem. 123 (Malinine 1965), a will written in demotic in the first century B.C.E. following a Greek pattern, cannot serve as proof in support of the hypothesis of Greek influence on the Egyptian law: this is a document of Greek law written in Egyptian language and not a witness to the evolution of Egyptian law in contact with Greek law. We are possibly dealing with a similar situation in the Judean Desert material.

The most striking new legal development in the matter of successions was the "invention" of the rule that estates without heirs devolved to the state, that is, to the royal treasury. The succession law of Dura-Europos, preserved in a copy on parchment from the Roman era, but whose substance dates to the beginning of this city, which was built on the right bank of Euphrates in about 300 B.C.E., decrees that, if there are no regular heirs – legitimate and adopted children, a non-remarried father or mother, or collaterals up to the fourth degree (the circle of the grand-parents and of the cousins on the father's side) – the property of a settler who died intestate goes to the king (*PDura* 12, lines 14–16; Modrzejewski 1961). Paragraph 4 of the *Gnomon of the Idios Logos*, a collection of tax and legal provisions in force in Egypt under the Principate, suggests that the Roman system attributing the *bona vacantia* to the imperial treasury could have been inspired by such a rule of Hellenistic law (Modrzejewski 1971).

Thus, as we can see, the evolution of the Greek family law in the Hellenistic world acts according to its own dynamics, determined by political and social conditions and not by the influence of the local environment. The same conclusions should be drawn in other fields, the law of property and the law of contracts (see Rupprecht's chapter in this volume). Hellenistic law, by no means an "amalgam" or a "mixture," represents a stage in the evolution of ancient Greek law.

PART 5

OTHER APPROACHES TO GREEK LAW

19: LAW, ATTIC COMEDY, AND THE REGULATION OF COMIC SPEECH

Robert W. Wallace

Athens' Old and New Comedy illuminate that city's laws and legal practices in contrasting ways, reflecting political and social differences between the fifth and fourth centuries and shifting literary foci.[1]

Surviving chiefly in the plays of Aristophanes (active 427–388), Old Comedy pushed to its limits Athens' robust democracy, uncensored speech, and unrestrained freedom. These plays satirized many aspects of contemporary society, including politics and the democracy. Typically, their stance was that of conservative critic, in ambiguous tension with self-parody and comic release.[2] Old Comedy is important for the history of law in three ways. First (and often incidentally), many plays provide detailed evidence for various Athenian laws and legal procedures, such as the denunciations called "showing" (*phainein*), the litigation of market offenses, and credit regulations.[3] Although scattered and fragmentary, these testimonia can be of central importance in reconstructing Attic law during the fifth century, which is poorly known in contrast to "the age of the orators." Old Comedy's representations of that notorious figure the "sykophant," an abusive prosecutor, are fundamental to our understanding of that phenomenon.[4]

Second, Old Comedy staged a satiric response to the administration of justice by mass lawcourts. Adjudication by paid, representative

---

[1] Unless otherwise attributed, all translations are my own, sometimes adapted from standard versions.
[2] See Ste. Croix (1972: 355–71) (but Aristophanes also criticizes the upper classes); Ober (1998: 122–6), Goldhill (1991: 182–3 and *passim*).
[3] For these and other examples, see the indices to Aristophanes in Harrison (1968) and (1971).
[4] See esp. Christ (1998: e.g., 53–6, 61–2, 145–7).

groups of citizens was one of Athenian democracy's greatest innovations. Cases were heard by 200, 500, and sometimes more than 1000 popular judges, called dikasts and chosen from the people by lot. Old Comedy made merciless fun of this democratic innovation, causing long-lasting damage to the institutional reputations of democracy and popular juries (Roberts 1994: 159–60 and *passim*).

Finally, third, because of the power of comic satire, during one anxious period for their city the Athenians legislated to restrict comic license. In its robust traditions of free speech and the laws then enacted against them, Old Comedy contributes an important chapter to the history of freedom and democracy.

By contrast New Comedy was domestic, polite, and stereotyped. This genre is represented chiefly by the plays of Menander (342/1–ca. 292) and the Roman adaptations of Plautus and Terence. Old Comedy's public controversies and ribald sexuality now cede to family or neighborhood quarrels over marriage, money, and young love. These texts direct their humor not against Athens' public institutions or politicians, but against social types: the parasite, the clever slave, the braggart soldier, or stubborn father. They also end happily, in the reaffirmation of humane morality and civilized values. These plays needed no censor: they were self-censored. During the fourth century, Attic society itself became more regulated, restrained, and domesticated. Absorbing and reflecting this new world, comic drama no longer stood in opposition to Athens' government or legal system, but reinforced their order. Laws often provide the framework for dramatic action, now in the private rather than the public sphere. These comedies revolve around points of private law affecting relations between individuals. The polis and its institutions remain off stage.

Old Comedy, the Courts, and the Regulation of Comic Speech

Apotropaic and fecund, the obscene satirical license of *kōmōidia* – "song at a revel" – was born in the sixth century, in the topsy-turvy carnival of Dionysos's festival.[5] Athens' democracy also was born in the sixth century. During the decades before and after Ephialtes' democratic reforms (462/1), the demos grew increasingly conscious of its political

---

[5] Henderson (1990: 285–6), Goldhill (1990: 127–9 and 1991), Edwards (1993), Csapo and Slater (1995: 415–16) (with bibliographical survey).

power and of the freedom of each citizen to do and say what he wished, despite traditional hierarchies of birth and wealth. Free speech, denoted by the terms *isēgoria* ("equal speech," especially in the Assembly) and *parrhēsia* ("free and candid speech," in public and private), became a central element of democratic ideology and daily life.[6] In the aftermath of Ephialtes' reforms, comic poets merged Dionysos's festival license with democratic free speech. In 455 Kratinos's *Nemesis*, the first known political comedy, targeted Athens' entanglement in Egypt's revolt from Persia.

Politics now mixed with unchecked carnival speech to yield explosive social texts. Comic poets targeted whatever was conspicuous and controversial, including Athens' wars, the new intellectuals, the rising power of nonaristocratic − "demagogic" − politicians, and the city's ever more potent democracy. In front of the demos who bought tickets to watch, ordinary folk like *Acharnians'* Dikaiopolis ("Just City") or *Clouds'* Strepsiades ("Twister") berated any newfangled development that could be fit for ridicule. Coarse, vernacular bluntness attributed every lewd practice to those unlucky enough to attract comic ridicule (Henderson 1991: e.g., 58−9, 67−70).

In *Wasps* of 422, Aristophanes turned his sights on the popular lawcourts.[7] His enemy the "demagogue" Kleon had long used the demos's administration of justice for political and personal ends − or so the playwright alleges. In *Wasps*, large numbers of poor and elderly volunteer dikasts are said to take delight in stinging (wasps!) hapless defendants, when manipulated by evil demagogues attempting to retain power (see, e.g., lines 703−5, 1102−21). The character Philokleon ("Love-Kleon") is afflicted with jurophilia (line 88, cf. 87−96, 106−10). He comes to recognize that he has been tricked and attempts to give up judging, but he just cannot stay away. His son therefore arranges a private court for him at home. The play's famous "trial of the dog" for stealing cheese (835−1008), with speeches for and against its four-footed defendant, parodies some of the more notorious practices of Athens' popular courts, such as bringing in family members to elicit pity from the dikasts, adducing mitigating factors such as service to Athens, or struggling to keep the attention of impatient judges. *Wasps* found humor in the traditional Greek practice of adjudication by elders and the democratic use of large numbers of judges.

---

[6] See, e.g., Ps.-Xen. 1.6, Isokr. 12.248; Eur. *Hipp.* 421−3, *Ion* 670−5, *Phoen.* 391−3; Plat. *Republ.* 557b; Dem. 9.3.

[7] Cf. Dover (1972: 121−31), MacDowell (1994: 150−79).

Other Aristophanic comedies also ridiculed the Athenians' courts and legal practices, including litigiousness (*Ach.* 208, 494–6, *Knights* 1316–17, *Birds* 40–1, 108–11) and dikastic pay (Ste. Croix 1972: 362 with n. 10). In *Birds*, Euelpides and Peisthetairos have grown so tired of Athens' incessant litigation that they found a new city in Cloudcuckooland. Illegal conduct in Athens is fine (*kala*) in their new home (753–68).

As a social and cultural institution engaged with civic issues, Athens' comic performances had much in common with its Assembly and courts (Ober and Strauss 1990, Hall 1995). Assembly debates, courtroom speeches, and the plays were all elite verbal performances before popular judges who voted for winners and losers. Plato describes democratic courts as filled with shouts of praise or blame "just like the theaters" (*Laws* 876b). Many comedies and tragedies stage a verbal *agōn* (debate) between two characters, as in a lawcourt. These public texts all shared and reinforced common ideologies and values, such as putting the interests of the community ahead of personal advantage. Dispute settlements in the plays often reflect the provisions of Attic law, as in the trial of Orestes in Aeschylus's *Eumenides*, or the trial of the dog in *Wasps*.

Paradoxically, therefore, Old Comedies typically position themselves outside the world of law and order. Their heroes and heroines happily transgress both laws and social norms. In *Ekklesiazousai*, women dressed like men seize the Assembly; in *Lysistrata*, women seize the Akropolis; in *Acharnians*, Dikaiopolis strikes a personal peace treaty with Sparta; in *Birds*, Peisthetairos beats up Meton, a mathematician and astronomer; in *Clouds*, Strepsiades burns down Sokrates' "thinkery." Simultaneously ridiculing society and defying law and order, these comedies were provocations, sprung from the topsy-turvy license of Dionysos's festival and the defiant individualism that counterbalanced civic solidarity and loyalty.

Ancient writers recognized Old Comedy's extraordinary freedom of speech. In criticizing the demos Isokrates remarks, "I know that it is dangerous to oppose your views and that, although this is a democracy, there is no *parrhēsia* except what is enjoyed here in the Assembly by the most reckless orators... and in the theater by the comic poets" (8.14). Dio Chrysostom observed, "The Athenians were accustomed to hearing themselves abused and, by Zeus, they frequented the theater for the express purpose of hearing themselves abused, and established a contest with a prize for those who did this best" (*or.* 33.9). The Hellenistic scholar Platonios adds, "at the time of Aristophanes, Kratinos, and Eupolis, democracy ruled among the Athenians... Since *isēgoria* belonged to all, those who wrote comedies had no fear of mocking generals and dikasts who judged badly."[8] The plays confirm that the demos especially enjoyed attacks on its boldest democratic politicians. Aristophanes says that attacking politicians was good citizenship – to "dare to say what is just, and nobly step forth to confront the typhoon and the whirlwind [i.e., Kleon]" (*Knights* 510–11). Tolerance of gross public abuse is noteworthy in a society where social codes were dominated by honor and shame.

The conservative pamphleteer called the Old Oligarch (2.18), Isokrates (7.58), and other elite writers claim that the public loved to hear the comic poets attack those who did not support the democracy, but did not tolerate criticism of the demos or the democracy.[9] The Old Oligarch states that the Athenians "do not permit lampooning the demos in comedy or slandering them." Aristophanes and other comic poets bear out Dio and Platonios, however, that this complaint was false. In the playful, unstable shifting of perspectives that informs these dramas (Goldhill 1991: 167–222), poets often criticize the demos and the democracy. *Acharnians*' Dikaiopolis observes: "I know the ways of the farmers, who are overjoyed when some windbag praises them and the city, justly or unjustly. And then they cannot see that they're being sold out. And I know the hearts of the old men that look for nothing except stinging someone with voting pebbles" (370–6, trans. Sommerstein). In a *parabasis* speech worthy of the Old Oligarch (though playfully undercut immediately afterwards),[10] *Frogs* complains to the demos about its treatment of Athens' upper classes: "Those of the citizens who we know are well born and self-controlled, just, and upper class gentlemen (*kaloi kagathoi*), brought up on the wrestling ground and in choruses and in music: these we maltreat." Instead, the Athenians follow "base men, the sons of base men" (727–31). Dio illustrates his comments on Athens' comic criticism by quoting *Knights* 42–3: "We have a master who's rustic in his bad temper, a bean-chewer, quick to be irritated – Demos of the Pnyx, a peevish little hard-of-hearing old man" (trans. Sommerstein), and Eupolis fr. 234 K.-A.: "what deed is there that the Athenians would abjure?" As Moses Finley notes, Aristophanes and

---

[8] *Diff. Com.* 2 p. 3 Kost., K.-A. IV p. 116 fr. 18. See also Horace, *Sat.* 1.4.1–4.
[9] See Edwards (1993: 101–4), cf. Henderson (1998: 271).
[10] *Parabaseis* often directly addressed the audience on issues of the day.

other playwrights repeatedly criticized Athens' war against Sparta. Yet year after year their plays were performed for the demos at public expense. "The phenomenon has no parallel known to me" (1973: 83–4). Even after the disastrous oligarchic junta of 404 when public criticism of democracy became less acceptable, Aristophanes' *Ekklesiazousai* labels the Assembly "the shoemaking masses" (432, and also 385–7), echoing criticisms often made by Plato's antidemocratic Sokrates.[11] Therefore Gomme (1962: 44) rightly calls the Old Oligarch's claim "grotesque. Aristophanes' main task, not in the *Knights* only, but in the *Babylonians, Acharnians, Wasps, Peace, Birds, Lysistrata*, was precisely *kōmōidein ton dēmon*."

Under most circumstances extraordinarily tolerant, the Athenians legislated against free speech only when they judged that the city or innocent citizens were threatened with substantive, material harm (Wallace 1994a). Thus, for example, Athens' slander law forbade the abuse of a few specific words ("father beater," "mother beater," "murderer," "shield thrower") that could lead to a citizen's disfranchisement (Dem. 23.50, Lys. 10.2–11, 30). Some men implicated in the terror of Athens' 404 oligarchy were forbidden to speak in the Assembly or Council (Andok. 1.75–76). Comedy's potent ridicule of the democracy and its leaders explains why Athens' occasional limitations on comic speech are linked with danger to the city or to prominent citizens.[12] Three episodes are credibly attested.

First, when Aristophanes' *Acharnians* line 67 mentions the archonship (chief magistracy) of Euthymenes (437/6 B.C.), the scholiast (ancient commentator) notes:

> this is the archon in whose year of office the decree *mē kōmōidein*, passed in the archonship of Morychides [440/39], was abolished. It was in force for that year and the two next years, during the archonships of Glaukinos and Theodoros, following whom, in the archonship of Euthymenes, it was abolished.

The careful archon datings give this note some claim to credence. However, because comedies were staged in 440, 439, and 437 (*IG* XIV 1097),

---

[11] Demosthenes (20.106) observes that one main difference between Athens and Sparta is that the Athenians can praise Sparta and denigrate Athens, but Spartans can only praise Sparta. In the darkest days of the Peloponnesian War following Athens' major defeat in Sicily, *Lysistrata* ends with two long Spartan choruses, praising Athens' enemy.

[12] For a more detailed discussion of these issues, see Wallace forthcoming: Ch. 3.

mē kōmōidein should mean not "to forbid the production of comedies," but "to forbid lampooning" or "satirizing" in comedy. As lampooning seems essential to comedy, might this decree have prohibited lampooning something in particular – specific individuals or the city of Athens? Some years later, Aristophanes (*Ach.* 631) protests that he is not "lampooning the city," *kōmōidein tēn polin*. According to Platonios, the *Odysseuses* of Kratinos "censured no one but was a mockery of Homer's *Odyssey*" and lacked a *parabasis*.[13] Albeit exiguous, the fragments of this play (143–57 K.-A.) are consistent with Platonios's description. As we noted, Kratinos himself inaugurated political comedy in 455. Long ago, August Meineke suggested that his unusual *Odysseuses* might date from the years of our decree.[14]

Why should the Athenians have restricted public ridicule of individuals or the city? Between 441/0 and 440/439 Athens and Miletos were at war with Samos, which had revolted from the Athenian empire. The comic poets later made merciless fun of Athenian policy because of Perikles' liaison with the Milesian Aspasia (Plut. *Per.* 24–25.1, Ar. *Ach.* 527). Some of Athens' allies were in the theater audience. Did Perikles convince the Athenians to pass legislation limiting ridicule (*mē kōmōidein*) of city policy and its leaders – most conveniently, including himself – because ridicule encouraged allied disaffection? Perikles' political standing and Aristophanes' later harassment by Kleon for slandering Athens in front of foreigners (see below) have encouraged interpretation along these lines.[15]

From broader perspectives, the later 440s at Athens appear to have been clouded by an atmosphere of intellectual and political conservatism. Possibly in 444, Sophokles' *Ajax* presented arguments against personal freedom (1073–91), an important value of Athens' democracy, and against mass judgments (1247, cf. 440–9, 1135–7). In 442, his *Antigone* argued that elite families should sometimes prevail over the demos and the community, even when that meant honoring the traitor Polyneikes. Although in 443 Perikles overcame his conservative rival Thucydides son of Melesias, their struggle and the resulting fears that Perikles might become a tyrant (Plut. *Per.* 39; Knox 1957: 64) indicate widespread unease. Most likely the following year Perikles' friend and adviser the music theorist Damon was ostracised, as a "tyrant lover" and

---

[13] Platonios, *Diff. Com.* p. 4.29–30 Kost. = 5.56–57 Kaibel = p. 37 lines 63–65 Perusino (and p. 35 lines 36–38 [no *parabasis*]); trans. Csapo and Slater (1995: 172–4).
[14] Meineke (1839: 1 p. 43, 2.1 p. 93), see also Geissler (1969: 20–2), Bianchetti (1980: 13–15).
[15] Starkie (1909: 244), Bianchetti (1980: 11–16), Halliwell (1991: 58–9), Henderson (1998: 262).

"great meddler" (Plut. *Per.* 4), a "too clever intellectual" mixing music theory and politics (Plut. *Nik.* 6, *Arist.* 1). In 441 both Sophokles and the conservative Kimon's son Lakedaimonios were elected generals. For a shadowy half-decade this constellation of data seems impressive. The demos also shifted toward conservatism between 424 and 420, when Aristophanes' *Clouds* and other plays ridiculed Athens' "new intellectuals" (Wallace 1994b: 135), and again after 411.

In 440, the Athenians may have legislated to restrict comic ridicule in response to war and pressure from Perikles, in a conservative climate against intellectual and political freedoms. The demos was then prepared to curtail even its love of comic satire in defense of Athens. Three years later, comedy's freedoms were restored.

Following on this measure, in 426 Kleon and others attacked Aristophanes (or possibly his drama director Kallistratos) because Aristophanes' *Babylonians* had slandered Athens in the presence of foreigners. In *Acharnians* 377–82, Dikaiopolis describes, seemingly in the poet's voice, "what I suffered from Kleon because of last year's comedy. For he dragged me into the Council house, spoke badly of me, tongued out lies against me, brawled like a torrent, poured out abuse, so that I just about died all soiled from these quarrels." Aristophanes here nicely turns the tables, implying that Kleon had slandered him.

In *Acharnians* 502–6 Dikaiopolis returns to these events: "At least now Kleon will not speak badly of me, saying that I slander the city while foreigners are present. For we are by ourselves, at the Lenaia contest, and foreigners are not yet present." In the *parabasis* (628–33) the chorus comments: "Among the quick-deliberating (*tachybouloi*) Athenians our director is spoken badly of by his enemies, that he lampoons (*kōmōidein*) our city and outrages the demos. He needs to give an answer now to the quick-mind-changing (*metabouloi*) Athenians. The poet says that he is responsible for many good things for you" (which the *parabasis* now lists).

Acharnians can be taken to indicate that in 426 Kleon summoned Aristophanes before the Council and attacked him for having "spoken badly of" Athens in the presence of allies. Possibly Kallistratos came in for further censure. If so, the words compounded in *–bouloi* would suggest that Kallistratos also was denounced in the Council (*Boulē*).

Was Aristophanes or Kallistratos actually brought to trial? The *parabasis* ("he needs to give an answer now") would suggest that Kallistratos at least had not been tried, at any rate before the staging of

Acharnians. By contrast, the scholiast to *Acharnians* 378 says that in *Babylonians* Aristophanes had

> slandered many people, for he lampooned the public authorities (*archai*) chosen by lot and by election, and also Kleon, while there were foreigners present ... For this reason Kleon was angry and indicted (*egrapsato*) Aristophanes before the citizens for wrongdoing (*adikia*), claiming that Aristophanes had acted with intent to outrage the people and the Council. He also indicted him for being a foreigner, and brought him to trial.

Aristophanes himself does not mention a trial, and the scholiast's technical term *graphesthai* ("indict") is inconsistent with a trial before the Council.[16] On the other hand, the scholiast could not have inferred from *Acharnians* that *Babylonians* had "lampooned *archai* chosen by lot and by election," or that Kleon also indicted Aristophanes for being a foreigner. It is therefore possible that the scholiast knew something not otherwise recorded. Kleon may have denounced Aristophanes before the Council and later indicted him before the demos.

If Kleon did prosecute, the scholiast indicates that his principal charge was *adikia* for "insulting the demos and the Council in the presence of foreigners." (*Babylonians* represented Athens' allies as Babylonian slaves.) This charge would be consistent with Aristophanes' emphasis (*Ach*. 515–16) that he is attacking only individuals, not the polis. What law was Aristophanes accused of violating? Hartmut Wolff (1979: 284 n. 6) suggested the law of Kannonos, otherwise first attested in 406. This law specified that "if anyone wrongs (*adikein*) the Athenian demos, he shall be bound and plead his case before the people, and, if he is found guilty of wronging the demos, he shall be put to death" (Xen. *Hell*. 1.7.20). Wolff's suggestion is certainly possible, although if Aristophanes was actually bound in court he might have mentioned it!

Whether or not Kleon actually prosecuted the poet, as in 440/39 at issue was the damage Aristophanes was alleged to have done to Athens. Now, however, the demos showed its tolerance for free speech, even at its own expense. Aristophanes was not punished, and later plays continued to ridicule Kleon, the democracy, and the war effort. During

---

[16] *Eisangellein* would denote the correct procedure. Atkinson (1992: 56–64) and MacDowell (1994: 44) both doubt a trial.

the Peloponnesian War the Athenians did not reenact the restrictions on comedy of the Samian war years.

One final restriction on dramatic speech is linked with Aristophanes' *Birds* of 414. The scholiast on *Birds* 1297 quotes three lines from the comic poet Eupolis, that the politician Syrakosios resembled a little dog yapping on the walls. He adds:

> It seems that [Syrakosios] passed a decree against lampooning by name, as Phrynichos says in his *Hermit*: "Psoriasis on Syrakosios! May it make him a sight, big time, since he took away the people I wanted to lampoon." Therefore they [the comic poets] attack him rather bitterly.

The scholiast's guess ("it seems") that Syrakosios forbade lampooning by name cannot be right, because all comedies of this period lampoon by name – including Phrynichos's curse on Syrakosios that the scholiast quotes.[17] Phrynichos indicates that sometime before March 414, Syrakosios restricted comedy by "taking away the people whom" Phrynichos wanted to lampoon. Who are these people? An attractive answer, proposed long ago by Max Radin (1927), reflects a pattern of language in Aristophanes and other comic playwrights. As we have seen, Athens' slander law penalized false assertions that someone was a "father beater," "mother beater," "murderer," or that he had "thrown away his shield" (*tēn aspida apobalein*) in battle (Dem. 23.50, Lys. 10.2–11, 30 and *passim*). Was comedy bound by this law? Radin observed that before 420 Aristophanes does not hesitate to use language that if false would violate the slander law – most notably by saying that the politician Kleonymos had "thrown away his shield." In 422, *Wasps* lines 12–23 twice states that Kleonymos "threw away his shield" (*aspida apobalein*). *Wasps* line 592 coins for "Flatteronymos" the epithet *aspidapoblēs*, "shieldthroweraway." These expressions were certainly libellous, if (following Storey 1989) Kleonymos in fact did not drop his shield, and continued to be a politician, something forbidden those who had thrown away their shields. By contrast, in 414, in *Birds* 287–89 and 1473–81, Aristophanes ridicules Kleonymos for throwing away his shield, but avoids the forbidden words. Comparing various people to

---

[17] Contemporary plays also criticize people implicated in the recent scandals of the Mysteries and Herms: see Halliwell (1991: 59–63), Atkinson (1992), MacDowell (1994: 25 n. 57), and Dunbar (1995: 239). This will not support the interpretation of Syrakosios's decree proposed by Sommerstein (1986) and Henderson (1998: 262–3).

birds, Peisthetairos remarks, "How is it that being Kleonymos, he has not thrown away (*apobalein*) his – crest (*lophos*)?" (290, trans. Sommerstein). *Clouds* 353 calls Kleonymos a "shield-caster" (*rhipsaspis*), avoiding the verb *apoballō*.[18] Before 420 Aristophanes uses words forbidden by law. After 420 he does not. Radin notes, "no passage in our extant fragments [of comedies after 420] contains any of the epithets which, by the law we are considering, constituted actionable libel at Athens" (p. 229).

Although Radin concludes that Syrakosios introduced Athens' slander law, that law's archaic term for "murderer," *androphonos* (rather than *phoneus*), does not encourage a date for this measure as late as 420. MacDowell (1978: 128–9) therefore makes the excellent suggestion that Syrakosios's decree made comedy subject to the slander law. Kleonymos was not convicted or disfranchised, but before 420 he did receive constant abuse from Aristophanes. He and others might reasonably contend that such abuse unfairly jeopardized their status as city leaders. This interpretation is also consistent with Phrynichos's reference to Syrakosios, lamenting that he could no longer "lampoon [the father beaters, mother beaters, those who threw away their shields] whom [he] wanted to."

Syrakosios's measure may reflect Athens' conservative political and intellectual climate between 424 and 420 (see above). However, this measure scarcely affected either the poets' or the democracy's enjoyment of free speech. Even if Aristophanes avoided actionable language after 420, *Birds* continued to abuse Kleonymos for throwing away his shield and took further delight in mocking Athens' restrictions on comic license. The speaker of Lysias 10 (along with his audience) enjoyed this same pleasure. He dares not say that his opponent Theomnestos had thrown away his shield. Instead, he makes merry by indirect allusion. "I, who have seen him do that which you also know, but myself saved my own shield" (10.22, cf. also 23).

Comedy's relationship to Athens' other laws against abusive language is uncertain. Athens' occasional restrictions on comedy, and Aristophanes' troubles with Kleon in 426, are inconsistent with several late traditions that Attic law expressly granted free speech to the comic poets.[19] On the other hand, there is no sign that comedy paid any attention to laws against abuse other than the slander law. Aristophanes' attacks on Perikles in *Acharnians* and on Kleon in *Peace* would presumably

---

[18] Our *Clouds* is a revised text, produced between 420 and 417 (Dover 1968a: lxxx–lxxxii).
[19] Cicero *Republ.* 4.10, Horace *Ars poet.* 283, Themistius *Orat.* 8 p. 110 B. See Csapo and Slater (1995: 165–6).

have violated the law against insulting the dead (Dem. 20.104, 40.49, Plut. *Sol.* 21.1). However, politicians were a standard target of comedy and public criticism. Demosthenes (22.31) remarks, "of all types of government [a democracy] is most antagonistic to [leaders] of infamous habits, [because] every man is free to publish their shame." Comedy also ridiculed people's mothers for working, something outlawed at least in the fourth century. Most famously, Aristophanes mocked Euripides' mother as a "greengrocer" (e.g., *Ach.* 477–9). However, Aristophanes was joking. In Demosthenes 57.30–31, the primary source for this law, the defendant Euxitheos admitted that his mother sold ribbons in the Agora. By contrast, Euripides' mother did not sell vegetables!

Finally, according to Plutarch (*Sol.* 21.1), Athens' early lawgiver Solon outlawed "speaking ill of living persons" in temples, courts, official buildings, and "spectator competitions." Culprits were fined five drachmas – two for the polis, three for the victim. Whether or not Solonian, the five-drachma fine, insignificant by the fifth century, confirms that this measure was archaic. If "spectator competitions" included (or came to include) dramatic competitions, along with Radin (1927: 222) we can only assume that Athens' comic poets were happy to pay the five-drachma fine (the "franc ancien," as it were) to enjoy insulting fellow citizens. But no prosecutions are known (Bianchetti 1980: 4–8).

As Finley said, as a civic institution Old Comedy's license against the democracy and especially the war effort is unparalleled.[20] At the same time, comic license was entirely consistent with democratic *parrhēsia* and *isēgoria* – with the freedom of ordinary citizens like Dikaiopolis to speak their minds, to stand up and object to the demos or its leaders in any language. Comedy was restricted only in the war years between 440 and 437, in a conservative climate, when abuse of Athens and personal attacks against its leaders were judged dangerous to foreign affairs. In 426 Aristophanes was accused of harming Athens, but suffered no consequences. Sometime around 420, comedy was made subject to the slander law, to curtail the use of certain words that threatened individuals' civic standing. All three of these episodes were political, addressing substantive harm to the city or individuals. The Athenians' few restrictions on comedy are consistent with their limitations on speech in other contexts. Only materially harmful speech was, on occasion, subject to control. More often, robust criticism of the demos, the democracy, and its politicians was judged beneficial. The poets themselves saw their role as helping Athens.

---

[20] Or not quite: Middle Comedy took some of the same license (Nesselrath 1997).

Law's Dramatization in the Later Fourth Century

No laws restrained New Comedy, as there was no need. These plays avoid politics; they never criticize Athens, its politicians, the government, or the courts; they also lack *parabaseis*. According to Dionysios Thrax,[21] already Middle Comedy – almost entirely lost to us – had ceased to use names or open scoffing, alluding to well-known persons "in a riddling way and not clearly." Comic vulgarity was tamed. Aristotle remarks that *aischrologia*, "bad language," was now replaced by *hyponoia*, "suggestion" (*NE* 1128a 22–25). As Plutarch notes, themes of *eros* pervade Menander's comedies (fr. 134 Sandbach). These plays are delicate studies of love, marriage, money, and family relations.

What explains the changes between Old and New Comedy? For the apolitical qualities of New Comedy it is obviously important that in 322/1, when Menander staged his first play, Athens lost its freedom to Macedon and the democracy and popular courts were curtailed. Political adversity sometimes leads not to apolitical sitcoms but to protest drama, and many Athenians never acquiesced in Macedonian control. During these gloomy years, however, the theater was used for diversion not politics (Gomme and Sandbach 1973: 21–4). It is relevant to note that the festival plays were now paid for by the government rather than by wealthy citizens, and Menander was a friend of Athens' oligarchic governor Demetrios.

In addition, Greek literature had now become international, as Hellenic culture spread through much of the known world in the wake of Alexander's conquests. Distant audiences could not have understood any topical allusions to Athens' internal affairs. The dramatis personae of Middle and New Comedy were neighborhood stereotypes: the misanthrope, the cook, the clever slave. They were not contemporary counterparts of Perikles or Kleon (Halliwell 1991: 63–4, 66).

Finally, literary fashions had changed. Sparkling poetic fantasy and political satire had been done. Obscenity's shock value had been exploited. The best writers had to try something new. The immediate, then long-lived triumph of New Comedy, whose many heirs include Molière, Sheridan, *The Marriage of Figaro*, and television sitcoms, will sometimes validate these poets' artistic decisions.

It is therefore all the more remarkable how far these apolitical, deracinated sitcoms incorporate and dramatize Athens' laws and legal

---

[21] Schol. p. 15 Kaibel, cf. Andronicus, Bekker *Anec. Gr.* 749.3.

procedures. Plots unfold in accordance with forensic modes of conduct attested in the orators. Dialogue echoes Attic legal terminology. In her important study *The Forensic Stage* (1997), Adele Scafuro explores three areas where law and legal procedure shaped New Comedies, especially in the area of pretrial dispute settlement. First, threats of litigation, of legal summons, or of self-help often precede an invitation to private settlement. Scafuro (pp. 424–67) recovers some 85 instances of such threats in our meager remains of these plays. Family marriage dramas such as Menander's *Samia* ("And who will allow him [to go abroad] when he's a self-confessed seducer, caught in the act? I'll bind you right now!": lines 717–18) and the fragmentary *Misogynēs* ("I swear by the sun that I shall bring an indictment against you for maltreatment [*kakōsis*]": fr. 279 K-T.) reproduce the language of legal charges and often lead to settlements. Characters know the law and use it as a manipulative tool.

Second, extant plays include some thirty-two examples of private or official arbitration and reconciliation, often concerning money or property. In the most famous of these dramas, Menander's *Epitrepontes*, "Men Going to Arbitration," two slaves debate over trinkets (found with an abandoned child) in front of an arbitrator. Third, many plays present instances of framing or entrapment, where plotters entice their enemies to commit a criminal offense such as adultery or theft or to confess some crime. These offenses form the basis for negotiation or else can be penalized in court. So, for example, in Plautus's *Poenulus* (based on a Greek original), the pimp Lycus is tricked into harboring someone's slave bailiff, who is holding a large sum of money (Scafuro p. 337, with n. 10). Lycus is then subject to a charge of theft.

What explains the legal orientation of New Comedy – its absorption of Athens' laws and legal procedures – in contrast to the freewheeling violence of Old Comedy and its scorn for Athens' courts? Three historical factors helped effect this transformation.

First, whereas the conservative voice of Old Comedy ridiculed the democracy and its newfangled court system, these institutions now represented Athens' cherished old order, familiar to all and in danger of disappearing.

Second, as Scafuro points out, it is likely that the demos's long preoccupation with the adjudication of disputes came to affect other areas of life, including the contents of plays. For more than a century, thousands of citizens had served in the courts on a daily basis. The family dramas rehearsed in Athens' courts – problems over wills, adoptions, heiresses, or citizen birth – were transported onto its stage. Conversely, as Scafuro observes, a dramatic "staginess" came to color actual behavior both inside and outside the courtroom.

Finally, New Comedy's legalism reflects a broader social movement toward the ordering and regulation of daily life during the second half of the fourth century. Before 350, it was both the principle and the practice of Athens' democracy that people were free "to live as they liked." The Athenians enacted no laws regulating private conduct. Provided people avoided material damage to others or the polis, they might do or say what they liked. After 350, however, the Athenians moderated their earlier, sometimes quite remarkable tolerance of personal freedom. Law's spread into private life is especially visible in the Lykourgan period, between 336 and 324. Elected to a new and powerful four-year office "In Charge of Management," Lykourgos was vigilant in enforcing public morals. According to [Plutarch] (*X Orat.* 843d), he prosecuted a certain Lykophron for adultery and many citizens for religious offenses. "He was also charged with guarding the city and arresting evil-doers, whom he drove out altogether, so that some of the *sophistai* said that Lykourgos signed warrants against bad people with a pen dipped not in ink but in death." *Sōphronistai*, "Behavior Guardians," elected officials first attested in 335/4, now watched over groups of *ephēboi*, Athens' military trainees. An elected *kosmētēs*, "In Charge of Order," superintended the *ephēboi* generally. Sumptuary legislation was a new phenomenon of this period. A law of Lykourgos forbade women to travel in carriages to Eleusis during the Mysteries. According to Harpokration, a new law imposed 1000-drachma fines on "disorderly women in the streets."[22]

Legislation over private life was furthest developed under Demetrios of Phaleron in the decade after 317. As Duris notes, Demetrios "arranged the Athenians' lives." He regulated the costs and conduct of funerals. He introduced a board of "Supervisors of Women," *gynaikonomoi*. According to Philochoros, "the *gynaikonomoi* together with the Areopagites used to supervise gatherings in private homes, both in marriage feasts and in other religious celebrations." According to Pollux, the *gynaikonomoi* fined "disorderly women" and "published their offenses."[23] In other ways also, the Areopagos now became the guardian of public morals. According to [Plato] *Axiochos* 367a, it chose the ephebes'

---

[22] Carriage law: Aelian *VH* 13.24, [Plut.] *X Orat.* 842a; disorderly women: Harp. O 47 = 141.11 Bekker, see also Kroboulos fr. 11 K.–A.

[23] Duris: *FGrHist* 76 fr. 10 *ap.* Athen. 542d; funerals: Cic. *De leg.* 2.64–66; *gynaikonomoi*: Philoch. *FGrHist* 328 fr. 65; Athen. 245a–c, Poll. 8.112.

sōphronistai. We are told that it summoned the philosopher Stilpon (380–300) for saying that Athena was "not a god" (she was a goddess) and expelled him (Diog. Laert. 2.116). Also according to Diogenes (2.101), the philosopher Theodoros narrowly escaped being brought before the Areopagos on a charge of impiety, after Demetrios himself intervened. The Areopagos summoned Demetrios's grandson and ordered him "to live a better life" (Athen. 167e). The Areopagos was given the authority to investigate cases of "idleness" (*argia*). According to Athenaios (168a), Philochoros and Phanodemos said that the Areopagos "summoned spendthrifts and those not living from some property and punished them." It summoned two impoverished philosophers Menedemos and Asklepiades, who proved that they worked at night for a miller. A similar story is told of the penniless philosopher Kleanthes (Diog. Laert. 7.168–69).

Finally, the notion that laws were to make people morally better first occurs after 350, both in theoretical discussions and in the democracy. Plato's second version of a virtuous society, in *Laws*, is based on complex legislation; his *Republic* had rejected law in favor of the judgments of philosopher kings. Aristotle says that the purpose of law "is to make citizens good and just"; "self-control (*sōphrosunē*) is a virtue through which people behave as the law requires them to behave in respect to bodily pleasures" (*Rhet.* 1366b13–15, see also 1354a31–b1). In 345, Aeschines cites a series of laws regulating boys' attendance at school (1.14–19). These laws protected schoolboys from sexual assault by their schoolmasters by ensuring that they were never alone together in the dark early morning. Aeschines, however, interprets these measures as "governing the good conduct *of the boys*." The lawgivers "expressly prescribed what were to be the habits of the freeborn boy and how he was to be brought up; then they legislated for the young, and then for the other age groups." [Demosthenes] 25, possibly written between 338 and 324, states that laws are designed to keep men from doing what is not just, and by punishing those who transgress them, to make the other citizens better (25.17).

The Athenians now came to think it right that people's lives should be more carefully guided by legal regulation. That perspective was repeated and reenforced on the comic stage, as dramatic characters seek to resolve the difficulties they confront through recourse to laws and legal procedures. Laws no longer regulated comic speech; comic speech helped to regulate Athens. Aristophanes' rebellious and irreverent license has given way to a more structured and orderly world. Both phenomena were historically contingent. Military defeat, extended legal experience, and broader cultural shifts drew Athens away from the liberating freedoms of its young fifth-century democracy toward the greater regulation that characterized bourgeois fourth-century society and the years of Macedonian control. Situation comedy proved to be an ongoing success. Aristophanic license and the legalism of New Comedy were phenomena of their own periods.

20: Greek Tragedy and Law

Danielle Allen

Method

Greek tragedy abounds with political crises – struggles over wrongdoing and punishment, efforts to overturn or found regimes, contention about the rights of strangers and the weak. Clearly, punishment, constitutions, and asylum were all real legal issues in Athens, and the city had extensive institutions for dealing with them, some of which even work their ways into the plays as instruments available to the protagonists for resolving (or trying to resolve) their problems. Most famously in the *Oresteia* the Areopagus Court, with Athena's expert help, decides the fate of Orestes (*Eum.* 470–752) as does the Argive Assembly in Euripides' *Orestes* (866–956). Some form of conceptual continuum links tragedy and Athenian legal and political thought. But, because the political and legal crises of drama exist entirely in the realm of the imagination, what can be learned from them about the historical reality of law in Athens?

Scholars working on English-language literary texts have recently refined techniques for analyzing law and literature together.[1] Following the lead of eminent legal historian F. W. Maitland, who argued that "law and literature grew up together in the court of Henry II," scholars have been exploring how concepts that developed in the legal arena – e.g., contract, evidence, testimony, privacy – have affected literature and, inversely, how narrative techniques developed by writers have provided tools to lawyers and judges.[2] Classicists have made a similar

---

[1] James Boyd White's *The Legal Imagination* inaugurated the field but has since been superseded by W. Benn Michaels (1979), Stanley Fish (1989: Chs. 4–7, 13), Martha Nussbaum (1995), and Brook Thomas (1997). For the reaction against this scholarship, see Posner (1988).

[2] Id.

move with Euripides, pointing out how his characters, in contrast to their Aeschylean and Sohpoclean counterparts, employ the styles and tricks of courtroom argumentation.[3] But the typical treatment of the relationship between Euripides and the law casts the influence as going only in one direction, from the courts and rhetorical schools to Euripides. In the context of the English-language tradition, the bourgeoning law and literature scholarship depends on the simultaneity of the legal and literary archives under examination. One examines lyric poetry of the Cold War period — and its notions of intimacy, privacy, and confession — in respect to the growth in privacy law of exactly this same period.[4] Thanks to the simultaneity, one can actually make claims about how each discursive field (law on the one hand, literature on the other) influenced the other. In contrast, students of the Greek classical period do not, by and large, have the luxury of contemporaneous legal and literary archives because the bulk of tragedy originates in the fifth century, whereas the greatest part of the legal archive, oratory, derives from the fourth. How then are classicists to use tragedy to study law?

Several attempts have been made. In the middle of the twentieth century, old school historicists attempted to pin down each tragedy as a commentary on specific political and/or legal events. The *Eumenides* was (and still is) read as a commentary on reductions in the power of the Areopagus effected by Ephialtes and (maybe) Pericles around 462 B.C.E.[5] Aeschylus' *Suppliants* was interpreted as a comment on the exile of Themistocles and/or on Athens' relationship to Argos, with which Athens would soon conclude a treaty.[6] Indeed, this treaty with Argos of 462/1 was thought to lie behind the *Eumenides*, and another treaty with Argos in 420 is taken by scholars as the backdrop to Euripides' *Suppliants*.[7] And because so many of Euripides' plays were produced during the Peloponnesian War, it has been especially tempting to take them as commentary on the particular events of that conflict — for instance, as opinions on Alcibiades' behavior and the nature of the Spartans.[8]

---

[3] As examples, take Hecuba and Polymestor arguing before Agamemnon in *Hecuba*, Iolaus and Copreus before Theseus in *Children of Heracles*, Hecuba and Helen in the *Trojan Women*, and Lycus and Amphitryon in *Heracles*.

[4] E.g., Nelson (2002).

[5] Gagarin (1976: esp. 106, 115–17, 127) remains helpful here. See also Podlecki (1966).

[6] I owe research on this subject to Alex Gottesman. For the political issues in the play, see Garvie (1969) and also Forrest (1960) and Diamantopoulos (1957).

[7] Scholars (e.g., Decharme 1906: 139) point to parallels between the language of the treaty in the play in lines 1187–1995 and the language describing the treaty in Thucydides 5.47 and the fragment of the inscription found in Athens (*IG* I² 86).

[8] E.g., Decharme (1906).

Unfortunately, this method of connecting plays to specific events is not ultimately satisfactory. We know too little about the details (as opposed to the broad picture) of fifth-century law and politics, and the lack of specific references in the tragedies to personages and happenings has drawn scholars into speculation. Worse still, this approach misprises the project of tragedy. The Athenian reaction to Phrynichus' play on the Capture of Miletus – when the whole theater burst into tears at the portrayal of the recent catastrophe and the city subsequently fined Phrynichus 1000 drachmas and banned the play (Hdt. 6.21) – indicates that the Athenians did not want overly direct commentary on current events from their playwrights. This is not to say that the Athenians did not want responses from their tragedians to the hard issues of their day, but whatever of direct contemporary relevance they wanted from them, they preferred to get in an oblique fashion – addressing their own problems by "thinking through" the difficulties of mythic personages and other cities.[9] Regardless of whether tragedians alluded to particular political events, they certainly employed, manipulated, and refashioned the crucial concepts of the Athenian legal and political vocabulary, albeit vivifying those terms via the experiences of heroes, princesses, Thebans, and Danaids.[10]

To underscore this point about how the tragic discourse related to the conceptual universe underpinning Athenian law and politics, let me turn to one of the rare moments when a tragic playwright does directly discuss goings-on in Athens. Every year in late January the Athenians held a festival called Anthesteria, which was also known as the Older Dionysia. On the second day of this festival, the Athenians broke out the year's new wine. Named after the wine-pitchers, this day was called Choes. The Anthesteria was celebrated throughout Greece, but the Choes seems to have been an Athenian festival.[11] Known as one of the "most polluted days" of the Athenian year, it was said to be the day that Orestes had arrived in Athens, bearing blood-guilt from the murder of his mother and seeking purification.[12] On this festival day, the Athenians varnished their house doors with purifying pitch, and whole households retired behind the blackened fronts to drink

---

[9] For more elaborated accounts of the relationship between tragedy and the Athenian conceptual universe, see Zeitlin (1993), Goldhill (2000), and Allen (2000b: 73–6).

[10] On the subject of ancient practices of giving concepts embodied form through narrative and symbol, see Allen (2000a).

[11] Hamilton (1992: 32).

[12] Burkert (1985: 238–9); Padel (1992: 182). Callimachus fr. 178.2; Phot. *Lex. s.v. Choes.* Cf. Robertson (1993: 206–8). Athenians 10.49, 437c.

the new wine in one another's company.[13] Adults received individual jugs out of which to drink (although it is impossible to say whether women participated as well as men). Even slaves might receive their own individual pitchers.[14] Children, too, received jugs, although it is unlikely that they drank wine from them.[15] The ritual practice of the festival stood in strong contrast to the sympotic tradition of passing a shared cup. Also unlike sympotic drinkers, those who participated in the festival drank without exchanging a word, competing to see who could drink the fastest, while enveloped in a ritual silence.[16] The day was sufficiently important that the stages of an Athenian's initiation into the community could be listed as birth, *choes*, adolescence, and marriage.[17] On this day, all of the sanctuaries were closed except for one.[18]

In *Iphigeneia in Tauris*, Euripides gives an etiology of the festival that places its roots in Orestes' arrival in Athens and the response of the community to his guilt. Euripides puts the etiology in the mouth of Orestes who recounts that when he arrived in Athens:

> At first no host received me willingly. I was hated by the gods. Some had respect and pity, and set a table for me as their guest: a separate table, alone, under the same roof as them. By their silence they built up the feeling that I couldn't be spoken to (or that I might not speak) so I was apart from them in food and drink. Each enjoyed the pleasure of Bacchus, pouring an equal amount for all, but into private cups ... I was my mother's killer. I hurt in silence, pretending not to notice. I cried. *I hear my sufferings became a festival for the Athenians. And still the custom says: Athena's people honor a bowl made for the Choes.* (947–60; emphasis added)

According to Euripides' fictionalized etiology, Orestes' arrival forced the Athenians to confront the problem of how to deal with wrongdoing

[13] Hamilton (1992: 30–1) also emphasizes the private familial aspects of the festival.
[14] On equal measures and slave participation, *IG* II² 1672.204 (329 B.C.E.); Callimachus fr. 178.1–5ff, Schol. Hes. *Op.* 368; Athenaeus 10.50, 437E.
[15] Hamilton (1992: 114ff); Burkert (1985: 237).
[16] Burkert (1985: 237–38). For silence, see Athenaeus 7,276c; Pliny 4,613B, 643A. Callimachus, fr. 178; Suda *choes*; Ar. *Ach.* 1000ff. Hamilton (1992) rejects the claims of silence on the basis of the passage describing the Choes in Aristophanes' *Acharnians*. But the revelry displayed in that passage would by no means be incompatible with festival participants also having a ritual moment of silence around the time that they actually drank.
[17] *IG* II² 1368.10, 127–31 (178 B.C.E.). See Burkert (1985: 238–9); Padel (1992: 182); Hamilton (1992: 30). See also Phot. *Lex. sv Choes*, Th. 2.15.4; [Dem.] 59.73ff.
[18] Burkert (1985: 218 n. 11), and (1985: 238–9); Padel (1992: 182).

and pollution. This the Athenians did, in the etiology, by reorganizing fundamental social relationships. Their guest was polluted, and so Orestes could not be accorded the standard welcome given guests. Instead he was isolated. The situation was problematic enough that the Athenians could not continue in standard patterns of sympotic behavior with talking and singing. While Orestes was in their midst, they sat silent, repudiating one of the most important forms of social interaction. But the norms of guest/host relationships could not be broken entirely. Orestes was given food and drink. The festival commemorated the ways in which isolation and integration were brought to bear in an attempt to solve the problem of wrongdoing.

The festival not only ritualized the problem of the polluted wrongdoer in the community but also dramatized the various roles that the Athenians would have to play in dealing with that polluted wrongdoer. The citizenry had to confront the problem of Orestes not merely as a collective but also as individuals.[19] Most festivals took place in capacious public spaces. This one did not. The festival made the point that each Athenian had to face the problem of pollution as a member of an *oikos* or household. Each Athenian, however, also played another role as each sat drinking in silence. The drinkers were not only the citizens who had accepted Orestes into the city, not only members of households, but each was also Orestes, the lonely matricide. Callimachus described the day of the Choes as the day when festival drinkers drank from an Oresteian cup.[20]

The ritual signified to Athenians the lesson that dealing with the problem of the wrongdoer required keeping in mind the overlapping penal roles of each Athenian: each was at once an isolated and competitive individual, a member of an *oikos*, and a member of the *polis* understood as a set of isolated households. Athenian litigants and jurors entered the courtroom having participated in such communal explorations of the role of the citizen in punishment, and these gave them a shared vocabulary for analyzing legal and political problems. Lysias draws on this communal vocabulary in a speech written for the prosecution of Agoratus in 399:

> [Agoratus] had the nerve to go to Phyle [the democratic hold-out during the fight against the oligarchs] where some of those who had been banished [by the oligarchs] were. As

[19] Hamilton (1992: 31) also stress the emphasis on the individuation of citizens in the accounts of the festival.
[20] Call. fr. 178.2.

> soon as they saw him, they laid hold of him, and dragged him straightway to be killed where they execute whichever other people they capture as a pirate or wrongdoer. Anytus said that they ought not to do that on the ground that they were not yet in a position to punish certain of their enemies. At that moment they should have peace. But if they ever returned home, they would punish the guilty. So they did not kill him at Phyle, but no one would share table or tent with him, he received no tribal place, no one talked with him, considering him polluted. (Lys. 13.79)

When Agoratus, a man with ambiguous ties to the oligarchs whose behavior had brought about numerous Athenian deaths, went to join the democratic troops at Phyle, the prodemocracy forces treated him as Orestes was treated in the festival. Now we have a neat triangulation of an Athenian ritual and tragic commentary on that ritual with the oratorical deployment of that ritual's symbols to prosecute a treasonous citizen. Three different discursive forms (ritual, tragedy, and oratory) each address the same problem: pollution and its remedy. Each does so differently. What, then, is the precise contribution of tragedy to crafting the symbols, meanings, and aspirations used by citizens to fashion and analyze law in the courts and assembly?

The figure of Orestes in the Euripidean passage serves nicely as a figure of the tragic poet's relation to Athens. He says: "I hear my sufferings became a festival for the Athenians. And still the custom says: Athena's people honor a bowl made for the Choes." Like Orestes, the poet *hears* what goes on in Athens, in the sense that he notices what the city's central values and commitments are. Then he responds to these – sometimes to criticize, sometimes to explain, and sometimes simply to explore – with narratives, like Orestes' etiology, that highlight particular terms in the discourse above others and thereby rework the content of key terms available to the citizens for ethical and political evaluation. By turning to tragedy in our study of Athenian law, we can discover conceptual elaborations of and/or challenges to the key terms that guided Athenian legal thought.

In the second half of this chapter, I will therefore provide two brief examples of how tragedy can be mined to explicate the content of central terms in Athenian legal reasoning. For lack of space, I will not be able to address the particular arguments that any one of the tragedians develops through the dramatic movement of a single play but rather will analyze conceptual patterns that are repeated across the work of all three major tragedians. I will focus first on how the tragedians dealt with anger and second on how they dealt with law.

ANGER

The idea that anger was a key term for Athenian legal reasoning must be justified.[21] Although the city's penal laws allowed any citizen to prosecute on behalf of someone who had been the victim of a crime, or on behalf of the city in general, in roughly 96 percent of the cases for which we still have copies of the courtroom speeches, the prosecutor was in fact either himself the victim of the wrong done or else he was personally involved in some dispute with the wrongdoer. In court, one after another prosecutor would launch his case by invoking and explaining his personal animosity toward the defendant. This is what Aeschines is doing in 330 B.C.E. in the speech from his prosecution of Timarchus for speaking in the assembly despite having worked as a prostitute:

> When I saw that Timarchus was, though disqualified by law, speaking in your assembly, and when I myself was personally being slanderously accused [by him and his allies], I decided it would be most shameful not to help the whole city and the laws and you and myself. It would seem, O Athenians, that the usual saying about public trials is not false: i.e. the saying that private enmities do indeed correct many public matters. (1.1–2)

Aeschines does not here explicitly invoke the idea of anger in conjunction with the term enmity, but other orators do (e.g., Lys. 3.39, 12.2; Dem. 40.1–5). Usually, but not always, their term is *orgē*. Invocations of anger do not, however, stop here at the beginnings of a speech.

After the initial story of personal outrage, one after another prosecutor would move beyond that to argue that his jury should also adopt an anger equivalent to his own. Here is Demosthenes doing exactly this in the 360s:

> It's not right that Meidias' behavior should arouse my indignation alone and slip by, overlooked by the rest of you. Not at all. Really, it's necessary for everyone to be equally angry

---
[21] For a full justification, see Allen (2000b: esp. Chs. 3–8).

(*orgisteon*). (21.123; cf. Dem. 24.138; Lys. 14.39, 31.11, 32.19; Din. 2.4)

With rare exceptions, cases of punishment in Athens were directed at resolving a problem that had arisen between two people (and that might or might not have serious political consequences) and that was identified when someone said he was angry. Anger was so central to the Athenian experience of wrongdoing and punishment that courtroom litigants could describe laws as having been established for the purpose of establishing what levels of anger were appropriate for various acts of wrongdoing (e.g., Dem. 21.43; Aes. 1.176). Thus Demosthenes writes:

> Observe that the laws treat the wrongdoer who acts intentionally and with hubris as deserving greater anger and punishment; this is reasonable because while the injured party everywhere deserves support, the law does not ordain that the anger (*orgē*) against the wrongdoer should always be the same. (Dem. 21.42, 43; cf. Dem. 24.118, 138; Aes. 3.197; Lyc. 1.78)

The Athenians had no doubts about why they punished: it was simply because someone was *angry* at a wrong and wanted that anger dealt with. Specifically, the anger of the *victim* necessitated punishment, and the Athenians made this idea central to their penal practice. This does not mean that every punishment was meant to vent or express anger; there are myriad ways to respond to and resolve anger. But most importantly, anger was assumed to be not only the source of particular punishments but also, as in the Demosthenic passage just cited, at the root of law itself. The centrality of *orgē* to the debate between Cleon and Diodotus in Thucydides suggests that this term was important already in the fifth century.

All well and good, but this was by no means, in Athens, an end to the question of what role anger and other emotions might play in law and politics. As in oratory, in tragedy characters invoke anger (e.g., *thymos, kotos, orgē*) as the reason to punish but they also, in contrast to the orators, reiterate the idea that wrongdoing and its punishment involved the community in some sort of communal sickness.[22] This is especially evident in the tellings and retellings of the myth of the House of Atreus, the story of how King Agamemnon won the Trojan War and returned

---

[22] For a fuller argument, see Allen (2000b: Ch. 4).

to his hometown of Argos only to be killed by his wife Clytemnestra, who was in turn killed years later by their son Orestes. He then is driven out of the city by the Furies. All of the versions of this story use the metaphor of disease to describe the effect of wrongdoing on the diverse members of a community who participate in an event of wrongdoing and its punishment.

Euripides, for instance, describes the *victim*, that is, the murdered Agamemnon, as a festering wound within the household (*Electra*, 318). In another play, he makes the *wrongdoer*, Orestes, diseased and calls him a disease in the land (*Orestes* 395, 831). Aeschylus, in contrast, treats *would-be punishers*, namely the Furies, as bearers of illness to the land; he says that their disease drips from their eyes (*Eumenides*, 480). In the mythical tradition of the House of Atreus all the parties to wrongdoing and the responses to it – victim, wrongdoer, punisher, and the community or "land" – somehow share in a "disease," and this surely symbolizes the idea that no party to the experience of wrongdoing is exempt from the trouble it introduces to the community. But in exactly what sense is each of these parties diseased?

When Aeschylus describes the Furies' disease, the sickness of their anger, as dripping from their eyes, he employs the common Athenian habit of drawing connections among vision, anger, and the spread of the disease of social disruption.[23] Those who addressed or looked on a murderer were polluted by the sight; and a murderer's glance could flash poisonously like that of a snake.[24] In Greek conceptions of vision, sight involved the physical transfer of particles and properties from one person to another. Aristotle provides a graphic example of the idea that vision was a physical transfer of properties from seer to seen when he writes that whenever a woman who was menstruating looks into a mirror, the glass ends up covered with blood (*De insomnis* 495b.25–3). Vision was a two-way exchange between seer and seen and so an exchange of glances provided a figure for intersubjectivity in general. Wrongdoers and their acts of wrongdoing were poisonous and were like poisonous snakes, because they introduced anger to the community: glares, glances, and poisonous looks or, simply, negative forms of intersubjective exchange among citizens. They were "plagues" to the community as a whole precisely because sight of them made people angry. Whereas the victim and would-be punisher were diseased because they felt anger, the

---

[23] Id.
[24] For murderers as a cause of pollution, see Soph. *OT* 100, 241, 310; Eur. *IT* 202. For a murderer with a snaky glance, see Eur. *Or.* 479–80. See also Padel (1992: 123–4).

wrongdoer transmitted disease because, in angering people, he upset the harmony of social relations. Anger justified punishment because as a disease, it demanded a cure.

In Euripides' play *Orestes*, one of the characters gives his city the following advice on how to cure the city in respect to Orestes' pollution:

> If the wife who shares his bed kills a man and the son of this one kills the mother in turn, and afterwards the one born of this one does away with murder by means of murder, where will a limit of these evils be reached? The ancient fathers handled these matters nobly: whoever was stained with blood, they did not allow to come near to the sight of their eyes, nor to encounter them – but rather required such a person to make matters holy by exile and not to exchange blood for blood. (Eur. *Or.* 508)

Here the speaker recommends exile as a way to deal with wrongdoing and to avoid cycles of angry vendetta. Exile is useful precisely because it removes the wrongdoer from the *sight* of those who are angry. Tragedy thus reflects an awareness that the problem of anger can be addressed with words, and with attempts to restore friendship, as well as with exile.

Nonetheless the Athenians often used extremely violent methods of punishment in their attempts to cure the community and to restore its peacefulness. The word *pharmakon*, which means both remedy and poison and which is central to tragic analyses of anger and punishment, expresses particularly well the paradoxical idea that spectacular acts of violence could cure anger.[25] Creusa tries to punish her husband by using a *pharmakon* that is made out of the Gorgon's blood and of which it is said that one drop deals death, and the other heals disease (*noson*) (Eur. *Ion* 1005, 1221, 1225).[26] The *pharmakon* symbolizes the idea that destruction and healing can be two halves of one concept.[27]

The same idea appears when Cassandra predicts her death at the hands of Clytemnestra precisely by triggering the ambiguities lodged in the idea of curing anger. Before she enters the palace of Agamemnon, she describes Clytemnestra as not only preparing a penalty (*misthon*) for her in wrath (*kotōi*) but also as brewing a remedy (*pharmakon*) (*Ag.* 1261).

---

[25] Scarborough (1991: 139ff) elaborates on the meaning of *pharmaka*. See also Padel (1995: 134–5).

[26] On poison, passion, shame, and gender, see Segal (1981: 60–108).

[27] Girard ([1977] 1992: 38) also uses Creusa's poison for the sake of discussing the way violence and cleansing are interwoven.

Cassandra's death under Clytemnestra's axe is a poisonous penalty that cures Clytemnestra of her wrath although it cures no one else.

The Athenians employed a form of "remedy" that was meant to benefit the whole community: a scapegoat ritual where the scapegoats driven out of the city were called *pharmakoi*, human versions of remedies. In a ritual that resembled a stoning, the Athenians "cleansed" the city by driving out two of the city's least significant citizens who had been decked out with dried figs around their necks.[28] This event took place during a festival held on Thargelion, the last day of the Athenian year. In some sense, the ritual expulsion of the scapegoats rang in the new year. As myth had it, the festival had begun at a time when the city had killed a Cretan man named Androgeos and had repented of the deed. The *pharmakoi* were human remedies for the city's anger at itself. More importantly, the citizens' participation in the stoning reminded them, at the beginning and end of every year, that all the citizens were mutually implicated in the processes of violence that were involved in curing the problems of wrongdoing, passion, and punishment that arose in the community. The festival implied that the new year could not start until this act of cleansing and the communal admission of responsibility had taken place.

Endeavors to cure personal and social anger were not uniformly successful. The idea that the *pharmakon* was both poison and remedy signified not only the paradox that violence could cleanse but also warned the community about the dangers involved in trying to remedy anger. This warning is perhaps best encapsulated in Sophocles' depiction of how Deianira, the wife of Herakles, tries to deal with her anger at the fact that her husband is bringing a new wife home with him from his labors and journeys (after the manner of Agamemnon). As the story is told in the *Trachiniae*, Deianira decides that it is a mistake for her to be angry at Herakles because "It is not noble (*kalon*) for a woman who has any sense (*noun echousan*) to grow angry (*orgainein*)" (552–3). It occurs to her that she needs a better sort of remedy with which to ease her pain (*lutērion luphēma*).[29] She decides to use a love potion to win Herakles

---

[28] Farnell (1896–1909), Bremmer (1983: 299–320), Vernant and Vidal-Naquet (1988), Griffith (1993) (on scapegoating). See also Hipponax, fr. 4 et 5, Bergk; Ar. *Knights*. 1133, 1405; *Frogs* 730–4; Lyc. 1.98f; Men. *Sam.* 481; Plut. *Theseus* 15, 18, 22; Tzetzes Chiliades V, 729. It is interesting that Diogenes Laertius places Socrates' birthday on the day of the Thargelia (2.44).

[29] Easterling (1982) on lines 553–4 translates *lutērion luphēma* as "a pain which brings release." The reading of *luphēma* is contested. Campbell suggests *nosēma* and Jebb *lōphēma*. Stinton (1976) gives a persuasive defense of *lutērion luphēma*.

back (*philtrois kai thelktroisi* 584–7; *pharmakon* 685–6; cf. *pharmakeus*, 1140). The potion is made from the blood of the centaur Nessus, whom Herakles had killed, and the centaur has played a nasty trick on Deianira by telling her that the poison is an aphrodisiac. He sets her up to use a "remedy" that will transform the despairing but hopeful wife into an unwitting murderess. Deianira had wished to avoid acting on her anger in any way that would amount to punishment but her attempt to remedy her anger nonetheless led to violence. (It is worth noting here that the defendant in Antiphon's *Against the Stepmother* defends herself with a story that is a lot like Deianira's.) The ambiguous nature of the *pharmakon* available in situations of punishment indicates how easily the Athenians thought that an attempt to deal with it could go wrong.

Whereas the orators invoked anger, and expected to use it as a term with which to justify judicial and political choices, the tragedians did the hard work of analyzing the implications of constructing cultural and institutional forms around it. Orators could successfully use terms such as *orgē* in making their arguments only if they were sensitive to how tragedy, and the city's cultural activities more generally, had prepared the audience to receive the term. To the degree that particular laws and procedures evolved to permit the mediation of competitive contests among citizen men,[30] the city's conversations about the concepts that factored into competition, for instance, *orgē*, must have affected the direction of that evolution. Indeed, legal scholar Eugene Kontorovich has recently offered explanations both of *timēsis* and of Solon's law that all citizens must take sides in a *stasis* in terms of a culture that had decided to deal with anger by providing some institutional spaces for venting anger but also countervailing institutional mechanisms for moderating anger and converting it back to sociability.[31]

LAW

How, then, did the tragedians treat law itself? Again, I seek out not the particular arguments of one or another of the tragedians but rather the general conceptual fabric developed across their plays.

Let us return briefly to anger and punishment, for there is a relationship between them and law in tragedy. Anger in the community

---

[30] Cohen (1995).
[31] Kontorovich, forthcoming. Thus a reading of tragedy allows us to combine the positions of Cohen (1995) and Herman (1993, 1994, 1995, 1996). See also Allen (2000b: 126–8).

disturbed the peaceful relations among citizens. To cure anger was to restore and also order, and so punishment was used not only to cure anger but also to establish stable power structures. The queen Alcmene, for instance, is expected to want to witness the punishment of Eurystheus precisely so that she can see that he has been mastered by her hand (*sēi despotoumenon cheri*) (Eur. *Children of Herakles* 885). Punishment introduced to the community not only the problem of anger but also a struggle over the establishment of authoritative powers. *Prometheus Bound* is the best example of the relationship between punishment and power struggles. Importantly, whereas the spectacle of punishment satisfies the power hungry, like Alcmene, it could also pain others, in particular, those who suffer the punishment.

In Euripides' *Hippolytus* Aphrodite, goddess of love, punishes with death Hippolytus, who is the son of Theseus and an Amazon queen, because he has managed to resist the impulses of *eros* and remain a virgin. As he comes near death, Hippolytus expostulates against his punishment, and cries out in his agony: "Zeus, Zeus, do you see these things?... Some bloodstained family evil of ancient ancestors breaks the bounds (*exorizetai*) and does not rest but comes against me. Why, when I am in no way guilty of evils?" (1381). The treatment that he is receiving "breaks the bounds" insofar as it exceeds the norms of reciprocity. Choruses are the most common source of criticism, and they specify the nature of the "excessiveness" that often characterizes tragic punishment. In the *Oresteia* the chorus describes divine excess in punishment as arising from divine "unlawfulness." The chorus in the *Agamemnon* is tired of the cycle of murderous violence that the goddess Artemis has inspired and prays for a state of affairs free from excessive pain (*periōdynos*) (1448). Acknowledging the requirement that "to the doer something must be done" is a *thesmion* from Zeus (1560), the old men also wish that someone could end the curse and vengeful calamities (*ata*) inflicting the house of Atreus. They say: "If Agamemnon must pay for earlier murders and will in turn require further penalties and other deaths after he dies for the dead, what mortal could claim to have been born under a happy spirit once he has heard this?" (1335). The cause of their woes, they think, is Artemis' "unlawful" desire (*anomon*) to have Agamemnon sacrifice his daughter, a sacrifice that leads to Clytemnestra's murder of her husband (151). What is the nature of this unlawfulness?

Tragic characters who are said to punish excessively or lawlessly are often accused of three other violations: of impiety, of introducing novelty to the laws, and of treating law as a private possession.[32] Thus in Euripides' *Madness of Herakles* Herakles' enemy is the tyrant Lycus, who is a new ruler (*kainos anax*), has overturned the ancient line (*palaios*), and acts "in lawlessness (*anomia*) flouting the gods, and saying that the gods are not strong (*sthenousin*)" (755, 768). Similarly, the chorus of the *Prometheus* accuse Zeus of being a new ruler, but they also say that he rules with private laws: "new rulers (*neoi gar oiakonomoi*) rule in heaven and with new-fangled (*neochmois*) laws; Zeus rules arbitrarily and the things that were great before he makes nothing of.... (148–51)"; and "Zeus, ruling with private laws (*idiois nomois*), displays towards the earlier gods (*tois paros*) an over-weening (*hyperēphanon*) scepter (Aesch. *Prom.* 402–5)." Prometheus has introduced the theme of Zeus' possessiveness of law earlier in the play. He remarks that Zeus is harsh (*trachys*) and angry without limit (*atermanon... orgēn*) and possesses justice for himself (*kai par' heautōi / to dikaion echon Zeus*) (186–92). The injustice of Zeus' attempt to punish Prometheus somehow lies in the connections between his personal possession of law and his unlimited anger. Prometheus thus implies that what is just or lawful puts limits on anger. Zeus' attempt to punish Prometheus, however, is unjust not only because his anger is limitless but also because he has used private laws or a private justice to justify and explain the exercise of his anger.

But what exactly are private laws? And what is wrong with them? Euripides' *Suppliants* will be the most help here. Aethra, the mother of Theseus, wants her son to help a group of suppliant women who have come to Athens to seek support in reclaiming the bodies of relatives lost in a war. She bases her argument on the importance of preserving the laws of Greece (*nomima Hellados*):

> I would have held my peace, but now know that this duty falls on you, ... to stop the people who confound the laws of Greece (*nomima Hellados*); for the bond (*synechon*) of the cities of all men is this, when each preserves the law nobly (*nomous sōizei kalōs*) (300ff).

The chorus agree with Aethra but cast their arguments as having to do with not the laws of Greece but "the laws of mortals (*nomous brotōn*)."

---

[32] E.g., Medea equates new laws with an end of divine power (492–5). See Segal (1981: 168–70), on law in *Antigone*; Ostwald (1969). Cf. the arguments of the Erinyes in the *Eumenides* at lines 92, 695, 778.

These, they say, "must not be polluted (*miainein*)" (378). Theseus agrees both with his mother and with the chorus about the need to preserve law but he discusses the matter by referring to the need to preserve the laws of the community or publicly possessed laws:

> No worse foe has a city than a tyrant from whom there are first of all no common (*koinoi*) laws, but who rules (*kratei*) possessing (*kektēmenous*) the law (*nomon*). When this happens, equality (*ison*) is no more. From written laws the weak and wealthy have equal justice (*isēn dikēn*), ... thus freedom speaks (430).

On Theseus' account the tyrant's personal possession of the law violates equality and freedom. Such violations bring pollution to the city.[33] As we saw above, not only lawlessness but also excessive anger brought pollution to the city. And excessive anger played a role in Zeus' tyrannical behavior and in his use of private laws. The acceptable forms of law, then, which are common and not private, are also able to keep excessive anger under control. But what does it take for law to do this?

Later in the play Theseus amplifies what he says here by returning to his mother's topic – the laws of Greece. He says: "All Greece's law I preserve ... Never let it be said that when it came to me to uphold the ancient (*palaios*) law of the gods, it perished (*diephtharē*)" (526, 561–3). Aethra had begun the conversation by invoking the laws of Greece. Here Theseus treats the laws of Greece and the law of the gods as one and the same.[34] But the conversation has also established two other terms as synonymous to these. "The laws of Greece," "the laws of the gods," "the laws of mortals," and "the laws of the community" are all labels for the forms of law that uphold equality and freedom. But these four categories of law all share another feature too. If the tyrant's law is personally or privately possessed, then all four of the good types of law must somehow be a public possession. The word *koinos* was used by Theseus to describe the valid law that is set in opposition to the tyrant's law. That word denotes precisely that legitimate law is public or a communal or shared possession. The laws of Greece, the laws of

---

[33] As Theseus and Adrastus have an argument over what a good leader is, Theseus criticizes Adrastus for keeping the law to himself (431–2).

[34] Shaw (1982: 3–19) agrees that panhellenic law and divine law are equated in the play and discusses the relation of these to hubris and to memory and different forms of written law.

mortals, and the laws of the gods must all be different types of "common law" or "law of the community."[35] These types of law are publicly possessed insofar as none can be said to have a specific, named mortal author; they seem to come from the community as a whole. In a society whose religious laws were not based on a single divinely inspired text, even the laws of the gods took their authority from the community's valorization of religious beliefs. The tyrant's laws, in contrast, are issued by some specific, named person, who claims to be the author of the law and who claims authority on the basis of that authorship.

In *Oedipus Tyrannus*, the chorus draws a contrast between legitimate law – in this case divine law – and the tyrant's laws precisely in terms of authorship:

> May such destiny abide with me that I win praise for a reverent purity in all words and deeds sanctioned by the laws that stand high, generated in ethereal heaven, whose only father is Olympus. The mortal nature of men did not give birth to them, neither shall they be lulled to sleep by forgetfulness. Great in these laws is the god, nor does he ever grow old.
> Hubris gives birth to the tyrant (*hybris phyteuei tyrannon*)/ if it is sated with many things without reason (*ei pollōn hyperplēsthēi matan*) (863–873).

The chorus praise the divine laws because they have no anthropomorphic parent or author, whether divinity or mortal. Their only progenitor is Olympus, not even a specific god but only the "realm" or "place" of divinity.

The distinction between laws written by a single named person and laws written by the community or based on the consent of the community was crucial to the development of law in Greece. Ostwald and Shipp have independently shown that in the archaic period, *thesmos*, the standard term for law, denoted the decree or decision of a single, authoritative person. In contrast, the classical period used the word *nomos* for law, and this term signified rule that "was motivated less by the authority of the agent who imposed it than by the fact that it is regarded

---

[35] Burnett (1976: 5), writing on law in the *Children of Heracles*, argues that two legal distinctions matter in tragedy, the distinction between customary law and statute or decree law (although it does not matter whether or not either is written) and a difference between law that prosecutes and law that protects.

and accepted as valid by those who live under it" (Ostwald 1969, 55).[36] Athenian tragedy thus treats the archaic version of "lawfulness," rule by *thesmos*, as tyrannical and valorizes the idea that lawfulness arises from collective, not individual, opinion. In depicting tyrannies, the tragedians explored the myriad ways a strong communitarian approach to law might be undermined. The criticism of tyrants as "new men" or "new rulers" was thus a pointed statement about their disruption of communal norms.

Let us return for a moment to the *Oedipus Tyrannus* passage and the subject of new rulers. In that passage the chorus celebrates not merely laws that arise from no particular mortal author but also laws that never grow old. If the laws of the gods do not grow old, neither can they be said to be new. Like the gods they live forever and were simply ageless. They simply exist eternally. The famous dispute about law between Antigone and Creon in Sophocles' *Antigone* also invokes these distinctions between unnamed and named legislators and between old and new laws. According to the chorus Creon is a "new kind of man (*neochmos*) for new conditions" (155, cf. 735). And when Antigone gets caught burying her brother, their conversation takes up the subject of this novelty:

> Creon: You dared to step beyond the bounds of these laws?
>
> Antigone: Yes, for Zeus was not the herald of these, nor did Justice who is fellow administrator with the gods below draw up such laws, and I do not think that your proclamations, being mortal, are strong enough to overrule the unwritten and unfailing customs of the gods. For these live not just now and yesterday, but always and forever (*aei pote*) and no one knows when (*otou*) they appeared. (449–470)[37]

---

[36] Shipp (1978: 10) writes: "*Nomos* differs from *themis*, *rhetra*, *thesmos* in being secular and popular. If a community is governed by *nomoi* it cannot at the same time be ruled by other institutions." Scholars (e.g., Lanza and Vegetti 1977 and Steiner 1994) have usually approached the tensions about law attested in tragedy from the perspective that what is at issue is the distinction between written and unwritten laws. This is incorrect. *Either* written *or* unwritten law was *unproblematic* as long as it did not have a specific author. Written law is more frequently accused of being problematic in tragedy not because it is *per se* problematic but because written law can be made the property of a single author/authority more easily than oral law can be. Written law, if preserved as public property, was not problematic (e.g., Eur. *Supp.* 430). Even outside of tragedy, tyrants were criticized for treating law as their own possession. Anonymous Iamblichi 7.12–14; Solon Fragments 4, 9, 11 West; Heraclitus B33; Xen. *Mem.* 1.2.43.

[37] O'Brien (1978: 68) takes the *aei pote* as conveying infinity in both directions.

In tragedy, laws are called "old" or to be seen as displaying "longevity" only when they have no identifiable mortal author.[38] In contrast, laws with a named human author also have a birthdate (they can be dated in relation to the author's life), and insofar as they represent the will of one man and one lifetime, they cannot represent the cumulative opinion of a long-lived community. Laws that can be dated because they have authors with names fall short of legitimacy precisely because of their particularity to time, place, and person. This goes some way to explaining why students of Athenian law have such trouble finding dates for those laws. The very conceptual basis of legal legitimacy in Athens mitigated against a regularized dating system that would undermine the status of any given law as universally valid. That so many Athenian laws were wrongly attributed to Solon is the exception that proves the rule. The decision to identify laws with his name means that the Athenians wanted to periodize their history and to insist that a radical break with the past had occurred in his lifetime.

The problem at the heart of the *Antigone* is that both Antigone and her uncle want to act on the basis of laws that they have written for themselves in violation of communal norms. Creon violates religious prescriptions about the burial of relatives. Antigone violates political norms about the place of women in politics. The chorus knows this. They argue that Antigone is dying because she is the author of her own laws; she is autonomous or self-legislating (*autonomos*, 821). This is the earliest appearance of the word *autonomos* in extant Greek literature, and it is used not to praise but to condemn. In addition to calling Antigone autonomous, the chorus adds, fifty lines later, that she has destroyed herself with *autognōtos orga* or "self-chosen or independently chosen anger" (875). Antigone has refused to adhere to norms of justice generated by the consensual community of citizens and has claimed, in

---

[38] Indeed, in tragedy, when law is attributed a specific source *other than* the divine or the Hellenic, it is nearly always associated with the novel and tyrannical. The examples I've used thus far are but the beginning. Here are others: Soph. *OC* 905, 1382; *Ajax* 1129, 1343, 1349–50; *El.* 579–80, 1015, 1043; Eur. *Or.* 487, 527, 571, 941; *Med.* 238, 493, 811, 1000; *Ion* 20, 442, 1312; *Hipp.* 91; *IA* 1095; *Hec.* 800, 847, 864. Aesch. *Pers.* 585 (*personomountai = basileia ischys*); *Agam.* 140 (*oikonomos*); Eur. *Hipp.* 1046 (*ouk houtō thanēi/ su sautōi tonde prouthēkas nomon*) (Wheeler proposed deletion of this line); *Hel.* 1429 (Pelopid law). See also Xen. *Mem.* 4.4.17; 1.11.45–50. For a valorization of "Hellenic law," take Jason's comment to Medea (538): "By bringing you to Greece, I've given you an understanding of justice and the use of law for other than the sake of force (*ischyos*)." Burnett (1976: 5) notices that in Euripides' *Children of Herakles* (194), local Argive law (as opposed to general Hellenic custom) is problematic. Again law is problematic when it belongs to some specific author (or authors).

her own a name, a right to push off into new moral territory. Creon does the same. Legitimate law is thus set in contrast to individual wills. In the *Antigone* those wills are described in terms of anger and desire that lead to a violation of community norms.[39] Tragedy puts the case over and over again that punishment must work to control anger by allowing anger to be exercised only in accordance with norms that are based on consensual authority. Antigone and Creon ignore that argument, and the result is that instability and disorder spread through Thebes.

The remark that Antigone acts on *autognōtos orga* puns easily on the accusation that Antigone is *autonomos* but also on an important argument about human culture found earlier in the play in the famous Ode to Man. There the chorus praises the achievements of mortals and signs of how humankind tames the world and traps birds in the net of its mind, sails the seas, and plows the earth. Most important, people have learned how to build cities and practice politics. The chorus celebrates humankind for having been the architects of politics by teaching themselves voice (*phthegma*), wind-swift perception and/or thought (*anemoen phronēma*), and anger that is city-regulated and/or city-regulating (*astynomous orgas*) (354–5). In the Ode to Man Sophocles thus draws together the two themes under discussion in this chapter, anger and law, and makes the very arguments that I have been making: first, that in Athens a central task of law was to manage anger and, second, that the Athenians desired legal procedures and institutions that would shift attention from the choices of the individual to the choices of the city, thus emphasizing historical continuity above radical (and generational) transition. That is, the Athenians wanted a judicial system that was driven by the demands of anger (angers that regulate the city) but they also needed laws that could subdue the power of individual tempers and temperaments to communal norms (angers that are regulated by the community). Sophocles heard (I imagine) that these sorts of dealings with anger and law were going on in the Assembly and courtroom of Athens and responded with an extended meditation on the tension between individual tempers and communal norms.

Conclusion

Notably, many scholars have had difficulty understanding Sophocles' phrase *astynomous orgas*, and the line has been frequently atheticized.

---

[39] On the *orgai* of Creon, Antigone, and Haemon in Sophocles' *Antigone*, see Segal (1981: 152–4).

F. Storr's Loeb from 1912 emended the phrase to *astynomous agoras*.[40] Presumbly, the editor could easily understand how marketplaces are relevant to politics but had less straightforward a time parsing the relationship of anger to law. But Sophocles' remark makes perfect sense if one recognizes the centrality of *orgē* to Athenian legal and political reasoning. Here then is an instance where the study of Athenian law in fact enables our ability to read Greek tragedy, and not merely the other way around. This underscores the basic point about methodology that I have been making in this chapter. Tragedy becomes useful for studying Athenian law only after scholars have already taken the time to work out not merely the procedures of Athenian law but also its conceptual foundation and implications. The tragedians responded profoundly and robustly to the content of their contemporaries' political, legal, and ethical aspirations, that is, to their *ideas*, regardless of what they thought about current events.

[40] This emendation was based on Dindorff's edition of the text.

21: LAW AND POLITICAL THEORY

Josiah Ober

INTRODUCTION: LAW, THEORY, AND POLITICS

In the modern world law plays a major role in theoretical writing about politics. This is especially true in the United States, where prominent judges write political philosophy and political theorists actively seek to influence judicial interpretation of constitutional law. Although no formal body of expert writing about law comparable either to American constitutional jurisprudence or to the great corpora of the Roman Jurists developed in Greece, normative and evaluative reflections on lawmaking and judicial practice appear early in Greek literature. By the late classical period, jurisprudence, in the extended sense of "philosophical writing about law" was a feature of Athenian political theorizing and litigants in Athenian courts made jurisprudential arguments to mass juries. The practice of law and the development of political theory were closely intertwined within the Greek experience; showing how they became intertwined reveals distinctive features of Greek law and political theory alike.[1]

Greek theorizing about law was profoundly tied up with the question of justice: Answering the question "What is justice?" was among the driving concerns of Greek political philosophy. Although justice was ultimately associated with a divine order, the relationship between divinity, justice, and law was relatively weak in Greek thought. Although the gods were imagined as favoring justice, and sometimes as punishing injustice, the Greeks did not think of their gods as specifying a

---

[1] Judges who write political philosophy (e.g.): Scalia (1997), Posner (2000). Political theorists who seek to influence constitutional law (e.g.): Dworkin (1996), Macedo (1999). Roman jurists: Johnston (2000: 616–34). Definition of jurisprudence: *OED* s.v.

standard legal regime for Greek communities. Unlike other premodern legal-theoretical traditions (notably the medieval Catholic tradition associated with Thomas Aquinas) the classical Greeks did not develop a strong conception of "natural law": at least until the development of Stoic ethics, the Greeks do not argue that the laws of existing human societies (their own or other people's) were expressions of a universal set of core human values or a universal apprehension of the good that ought to be accepted as valid by all peoples.[2]

In the classical period, certain of the Sophists suggested that human nature (*physis*) and law (*nomos*) were in fact antithetical: Some of them (notably Antiphon, Plato's Thrasymachus, Plato's Callicles) argued that law was a ploy by the weak to restrain the "natural" impulse of the strong to oppress those weaker than themselves. Other Greek theorists (e.g., Protagoras [as depicted by Plato] and Aristotle) argued that the polis as a political community was natural, but their political naturalism was not driven by a belief in a universal natural law. Rather they believed that humans must cooperate to survive and flourish in a competitive natural environment. Along with a capacity for deliberation, an intrinsic ethical sense, namely a concern for justice and reverence (*dikē* and *aidōs*), was regarded by Plato's Protagoras as essential for the security and flourishing of communities. But deliberative capacity also implied the potential for disagreement about values.

Although committed to a conception of justice, Greek theorists were in some sense legal positivists who could sum up the separation between any given set of laws and objective morality with the phrase *nomos basileus* ("law/custom is king").[3] In the story that Herodotus (3.38) tells to illustrate this phrase, certain Indians and Greeks each express horror at the suggestion that they might accept money to adopt one another's burial practices. Herodotus does not suggest that either custom (burning of the dead or ritual eating of the dead) is either moral or immoral when measured against an objective standard. Similarly, and unlike medieval and modern "natural lawyers," Greek legal theorists paid relatively little attention to sexual morality as such. Greek lawmakers and theorists were indeed concerned with the regulation of burial practices and sexual conduct, but that concern was driven by ethical and especially by

---

[2] Rommen (1955), regards the "legal positivism" that he associates with Hobbes, Locke, and Rousseau as having displaced traditions of law he supposed were originally manifest in Greek and Roman life and thought, but his emphasis is on Cicero and Aquinas. Striker (1986) argues that the Stoics were committed to a version of natural law theory, but see Inwood (1987, 2003). See further Long in this volume.

[3] On modern legal positivism, see Hart (1958: 593–606).

political concerns rather than deriving from convictions about objective morality or natural law.

In Greek ethical thought, justice was understood as a virtue that ought to be manifest by the good man (along with, variously, courage, moderation, wisdom, and piety). In Greek political thought justice was associated with fairness in distribution, i.e., with the notion that each person or category of persons should receive that which was deserved ("to each according to his 'x' "). Yet there remained a great deal of debate about who deserved what, because the basis for distribution was open for discussion ("what is 'x' "?). Greek debates over distributive justice also revolved around the question of whether justice should be understood as the common good of a community and, if so, what the common good was. Some Greek legal theory (notably Plato's) was explicitly perfectionist, in that it sought to promote a unitary good. Another tradition of theorizing (notably the implicit theory of democratic Athenian law) tended toward the deontological in that it focused on guaranteeing individuals and groups the legal immunities that would protect them from suffering the constraints or indignities that would prevent each from pursuing his own conception of a potentially diverse range of human goods. These immunities (or "quasi-rights") were not, however, "natural human rights" – they were not regarded as universal or even panhellenic entitlements. Greek international law, insofar as it developed at all, remained grounded in considerations of property and contract.[4]

In Greek practice and theory alike, positive law (formal rules, written or traditional) was typically understood as a human artifact and as an expression of those values proper to a given political regime. By the classical period, when the canonical regime types had been specified, this general conception could be expressed in the form "democratic values are promoted by democratic laws in democratic regimes" – and likewise, *mutatis mutandis*, for oligarchies, aristocracies, and monarchies. But Greek law was explicitly political long before the classical period. The interplay between judicial practice and theorizing about the political order is already a prominent feature of the early poetic tradition, well before the elaboration of the first written codes of positive law. Hesiod is deeply concerned with the problem of fair decision making, even in the absence of a written "constitutional" frame guiding judicial decisions. The Greek political-theoretical enterprise takes a step forward as theorizing about law is conjoined with the act of formal lawmaking: the

---

[4] See, further, Ober (2000b).

early sixth-century Athenian poet and lawgiver Solon is the key figure. In the fifth century Thucydides brought the *nomos-physis* concerns of the Sophists to bear on the question of why "transnational" legal customs, based on traditional Greek conceptions of justice as fairness, failed to constrain the tendency of powerful states to do as they pleased. The interplay between law and theorizing about law can be traced in greatest detail in the fourth century, in the work of Athens-resident political philosophers, notably Plato and Aristotle. Fourth-century Athenian lawcourt speeches, written to gain a particular legal judgment, sometimes address general questions of political philosophy. Comparing the "practical" discourse of law with the "theoretical" discourse of political philosophy clarifies the historically distinctive ways in which Greek law and political thought were mutually implicated.

Greek political theory was concerned with power as well as with justice: with the structural organization of asymmetrical human relations into a system of legitimate authority capable of maintaining conditions of justice. From the perspective of Greek political theory, laws are rules for restraining and channeling the use of power, thus constituting the formal institutional conditions under which procedural justice is established. Procedural justice sets a baseline of fairness by ensuring that similar cases are judged according to similar procedural guidelines and by clarifying who has the right to judge and punish what category of delicts. Although procedural fairness cannot *gurantee* a substantively just outcome, the Greeks recognized that under procedurally fair conditions, authoritative judges were more likely to make decisions that were "right" – in that they conformed to the community's conception of just desert.

In the absence of well-developed conceptions of natural law or objective morality, the concern for achieving both procedural and substantive justice (fairness and rightness) means that creating and maintaining a legal regime entails thinking about how conditions of justice might be brought into being by political means, and what actions or behaviors threatened to disrupt regimes of justice. Thomas Hobbes argued in *Leviathan* that for a regime of justice to pertain, political power, in the form of legitimate authority, must be vested in an institutional entity (a sovereign) with the capacity to legislate (i.e., devise new rules as necessary), to adjudicate conflicts, and to punish those who break the rules. The Greeks did not develop a Hobbesian theory of sovereignty. But they recognized that if justice is to be impartial, and grounded in a general commitment to fairness, then new rules must be made for good reasons and should not be internally contradictory. They must be made according to accepted procedure by legitimate authorities. And they must be applied consistently. In sum, a legal regime requires that there be some agreement about the institutional conditions under which pronouncements that seek to create a new legal and political situation will be efficacious – that is, about whose "speech acts" will actually take effect. The issue of relating power to legitimate authority becomes explicit in decisions about how to punish those found guilty of disobeying the law. In Greece, the rules (*thesmoi, nomoi*) were understood to be part of the political regime (*politeia*) of a state (*polis*). Greek political theory attempted to answer the question, "what part?"

The "law and the political regime" concerns of Greek political theorists may be grouped around three primary topics:

Legislation and amendment. Who has authority to make legal rules and by what process of enactment? Once established, how is the law made known? Who has the authority to amend or revoke a law once it has been enacted and proclaimed? How do changes in the laws affect the regime and vice versa? How much legal change can a given regime tolerate? At what point do changed laws entail a "changed regime"?

Application and interpretation. Who has the authority to apply the established laws to specific cases? Who is subject to a legal regime? Who has access (and at what level) to the laws? How much interpretive leeway should judges have? What legal norms pertain between states? Under what circumstances and on what ethical basis is it right to disobey the law or to disregard a legal judgment?

Enforcement and penology. Who is responsible for legal enforcement? What is punishment of the lawbreaker meant to accomplish? Is it meant to reform the wrongdoer? Readdress a prior balance (sacred or profane) disturbed by transgression? Deter potential malefactors? Teach the members of the community something substantive about justice?

Archaic Theory and Practice: Hesiod and Solon

The conceptual links between legislation, application, and enforcement are prominent in the didactic poetry of Hesiod, although the lack of institutions capable of ensuring justice points to a gulf between normative ideals about justice and actual judicial practice. In the *Works and Days*

Hesiod is highly critical of the crooked legal judgments made by the "gift-swallowing" princely authorities (*basileis*: 38–39) of Boeotian Ascra. The problem is not only that the princes are arbitrary, arrogant, or careless (i.e., they are not simple analogues of Homer's Agamemnon in book 1 of the *Iliad*). Rather, Hesiod's charge of gift swallowing implies that they have deliberately chosen to deviate from known standards of fair and equitable judgment for one of two reasons: Either because of an illegitimate acceptance of gifts (*qua* bribes) from some interested party or because they accept the gifts traditionally offered to judges by disputants without rendering straight judgment in return. In any case, Hesiod's point is that all members of the Ascra community (princes and others) share an understanding of what *would* constitute an appropriate standard for fair judgment. The problem is not a lack of standards for judgment, but that standards are willfully ignored by those in power. Ascra's princes use their authority to seek selfish advantage (gifts) rather than to further the good of the community via "straight" judgments.

What is the standard of fairness that is being ignored by the gift-swallowing princes? Hesiod does not measure their corrupt decisions against an established "constitutional regime," but rather against "the justice of Zeus." Although Hesiod's Zeus does not mandate a code of law for the human community, the god is assumed to be concerned with justice and he is imagined as ultimately responsible for rectifying the judicial failures of powerful people in positions of authority. Zeus is called on in the poem's proem to "make judgments (*themistai*) straight with righteousness (*dikē*: 9)."[5]

The justice of Zeus might, initially, be imagined as something like natural law. But in a "riddle for rulers" (an *ainos* for *basileis*), Hesiod offers a parable about application and obedience that contrasts the behavior appropriate to weak and strong in a state of nature with the behavior appropriate for human communities: The powerful hawk, clutching the hapless nightingale in his claws, asserts the folly of the latter's protests, for "just as I please, I will eat you, or let you go" (203–10). Like the hawk, the princes of Ascra seem to hold power as a fact of nature. Yet Hesiod is not offering the hawk/nightingale story as a model of justice or a theory of ethical obedience. In the human realm, he imagines that righteousness (*dikē*) – a condition of fairness under which the weak receive decent treatment despite their relative powerlessness – will eventually win out against arrogant violence (*hybris*: 216–17). Yet that victory

---

[5] Cf. Lloyd-Jones (1971).

may not be either timely or tidy in human terms. The enforcement of fairness is ultimately left to divine providence. Powerful and potentially corrupt authorities are warned of Zeus' watchfulness and his harsh punishment, which will be delivered in retribution for their crooked legal judgments (*dikai*: 248–64). Yet, ominously, that punishment will not be limited to gift-swallowing judges: It will fall on the community as a whole. The justice of Zeus offers no quick and certain redress against the wrongdoing of corrupt judicial magistrates. Moreover, by visiting destruction on communities, it aggregates the innocent weak with the guilty princes in the category of those subject to punishment.

Hesiod's Ascra is an unhappy place at least in part because it lacks a reliable human mechanism for legislation, application, and enforcement of the rules. Hesiod offers no plan for implementing a just regime, for enacting fair new rules that could control the tendency of judicial authorities to act like predatory hawks, to prevent them from judging according to "bestial" self-interest rather than according to an equitable divine standard. Although the judicial authorities of Ascra choose to act in ways that are systematically unfair, Hesiod has no plan for political reform nor a theory of civil disobedience. Indeed, although Hesiod's poem is strongly ethical in content, much of his advice in the *Works and Days* is markedly apolitical or even antipolitical: he exhorts his readers to work hard, cultivate good relations with their neighbors, marry well, and stay away from the public realm of the agora.

Lacking any institutional framework for legal reform, fearing lest retribution aimed at the unjust fall on the entire community, and not trusting the didactic force of his own poetry to reform the wicked, Hesiod's political theory ends in a sort of ethical quietism: a personal moral autarky. Hesiodic quietism is a reasonable response to Ascra's legislative vacuum, its absence of human institutions capable of guiding the application and enforcement of law. Judicial authorities are assumed to know what constitutes fairness in respect to judgment, and they may be urged to judge fairly, but there is neither a secure body of "constitutional" rules against which corrupt judgments could in turn be judged, nor any institutional mechanism for such rules to be brought into being. Law itself, as a basis for right judgment, remains undefined, leaving the victim of unfair treatment no recourse other than withdrawing from active participation in the political community and appealing to divine justice.

Although sharing some of Hesiod's views about the relationship between individual human acts of injustice and generalized divine retribution, Solon of Athens transcended ethical quietism to forthrightly address the practical issues of legislation, application, and enforcement. In his own didactic poetry and in his actions as a lawgiver, Solon promoted a political regime predicated on a vision of social justice, and he grounded his political vision in a detailed code of law.[6] According to the account given in the Aristotelian *Athenaion Politeia*, in 594 B.C. Solon was appointed (through an unknown process) as archon (chief magistrate) with special powers of arbitration. It was in view of those evidently exceptional and ill-defined legislative powers that Solon successfully promulgated and published (i.e., made public on *axones*: wooden boards) a new code of laws for all Athenians; Solon's legal and political regime sought to create the institutions that would protect the weak from selfish and unfair behavior on the part of those holding social or political power. The legitimacy and applicability over time of Solon's legislation was confirmed through a public act that connected the authority of the divine realm (Hesiod's "justice of Zeus") to the willful choices of individual persons in a particular community: The Athenians took an oath promising to observe Solon's laws (*Ath Pol.* 7.1) and not to change them for a certain period of time.[7]

The fourth-century B.C. author of the Aristotelian *Ath. Pol.* wrote within a developed tradition of political theory that was explicitly concerned with the relationship between law and regime. He asserts that Solon's laws amounted to a new *politeia* for the Athenians (*Ath. Pol.* 7.1). He was, furthermore, very concerned to specify exactly how "democratic" this new Solonian regime actually was. His answer is more democratic than before, but still moderate. He staunchly rejects the notion that Solon's laws were *intentionally* drafted in obscure language. He thereby refutes the argument that Solon's laws were deliberately aimed at increasing the interpretive scope of democratic lawcourts and thus the practical legal authority of the jurors who would be responsible for interpreting intentionally vague statutes (9.2). The intellectual opponents that the Aristotelian *Ath. Pol.* sought to refute had evidently depicted Solon as a progressivist legislator who aimed at institutionalizing democratic judicial activism. That activism would, in their view, further the development of a radical form of democracy, a *politeia* only loosely tethered to the rule of law. The debate over Solon's intentions points to an ongoing Athenian theoretical debate on the relationship between the

---

[6] Contrast between Hesiod and Solon: Raaflaub (2000, 34–7, 39–42). On early lawgivers and law codes: Gagarin (1986).

[7] No change in the laws allowed for 100 years: *Ath Pol.* 7.2; for ten years (at which time Solon returned to Athens): Hdt. 1.29.

authority of fundamental legislation and its subsequent interpretation and the implications of that relationship for the nature of the political regime.

Solon himself theorized his act of lawmaking in poetry, apparently giving his new regime the name *Eunomia*: "Well governed."[8] After his act of lawmaking, Solon stated explicitly in his poems that his method in creating conditions of justice had conjoined force (*bia*) with justice (*dikē*) through the legislative authority of his office (*kratei nomou*). Thereby he established a code of laws (*thesmoi*) based on a standard of equitability: it was meant for the wretched (*kakos*) and distinguished (*agathos*) alike.[9] Solon asserted that his new regime distributed socio-political privileges fairly, despite complaints from selfish social factions – the *demos* on the one hand and the wealthy and powerful on the other.[10] In marked contrast to Hesiodic quietism, Solon's new regime demanded political activism from citizens to ensure the maintenance of the conditions of justice that his legislative act had brought into being: The enforcement of law was dependent on the voluntary choice of the individual Athenian (*ho boulomenos*) to serve as a prosecutor of the wrongdoer rather than being the responsibility of a particular magistrate or magisterial body. The preservation of justice was thus to be a mutual responsibility of the group, and the group encompassed by that mutuality was "all Athenians": A voluntary prosecutor could initiate proceedings against another for wrongs committed against any Athenian. The judging body to which the prosecutor would turn in exposing wrongdoing was the citizen body itself (or some very substantial fragment thereof), sitting in a judicial capacity.

Solon's new *politeia* answered the question of distributive justice by asserting that "to each according to his 'x' " meant to each citizen according to his citizenship – as well as according to his wealth. And this required greater clarity on the question of who was an Athenian citizen, as well as on the legal immunities enjoyed by each Athenian. Thus, Solon's legal reforms are conceptually consistent with his abolition of debt-slavery of Athenians by other Athenians, an act celebrated in Solon's own poetry (4W). Solon points out that among those he brought back from foreign places to the Athenian homeland, to be reintegrated into the citizen body, were men who had lost their Athenian "tongue." The point is that under the new regime, the previous markers of

---

[8] *Eunomia*: Solon 4W.30–39.
[9] Solon 36W 15–17. Cf. Raaflaub (2000: 41–2).
[10] Solon 5, 6, 34, 36, 37: *Ath. Pol.* 12.1–4.

"Athenianness" – residence in Attica and an Athenian accent – were no longer definitive: the citizen body was now to be defined by birthright, and to "be an Athenian" now meant to enjoy specific and clearly defined political rights (the right to engage in legislative activity according to one's wealth status) and specific legal immunities (security against the condition of being "owned" by any of one's fellow citizens). Again, we see a concern with interlocking legislation, application, and enforcement. Solon's reiterated claims that his reforms balanced the selfish demands of the powerful few and the ordinary many points to the centrality of a deep theoretical concern with the problem of fairness in respect to distribution as the foundation of his entire legislative program.[11]

THUCYDIDES AND INTERNATIONAL LAW

By the mid fifth century B.C. Greek interstate practice had become sufficiently complex and institutionalized to allow Greeks to conceive of something akin to "international law." The traditional rules that protected heralds, guaranteed safe passage to panhellenic festivals, allowed for interstate treaties, and regulated some aspects of interstate combat were sufficiently elaborate to enable people to speak of "Greek customary laws" (*hellenika nomima*) that were notionally binding on all Greeks. But international law remained an ill-defined body of practice. It lacked a written form, a legislative process, a "panhellenic court" competent to apply and interpret the rules and thereby arbitrate conflicts, and a mechanism for enforcement. The question of whether an inter-state legal regime did exist in some rudimentary form, or whether the play of power in the realm of international relations was defined entirely by state-actors acting in their own perceived best interests, engaged Greek political theorists, notably Thucydides.

Thucydides, as an analyst of interstate relations, has been characterized as a "moderate Realist." Given his apparent conviction that the Greek states operated in an essentially anarchic environment, this seems generally correct: Thucydides' narrative suggests that attempts to promulgate binding international legal norms foundered on the shoals of the national interests of the most powerful and aggressive state-actors. On the whole, Thucydides' history suggests that the traditional rules governing Greek interstate relations were maintained only because they suited the interests of powerful states. Public appeals to something like

---

[11] See Balot (2001).

international law were typically made either by people intent on advancing their state's interests under a spurious religious or moral cover or by people without other resources. In either case, the appeal had little practical effect.[12]

Thucydides (3.52) describes how Plataean survivors of a long Peloponnesian siege attempted to appeal to "Greek customary law" regarding fair treatment of prisoners of war. In the event, their Spartan captors held a kind of mock trial, whose trappings of legal judgment only served to underline the utter lack of standards of procedural fairness, such as might be expected to pertain within a Greek political community. The Spartan judges demanded that each of the Plataean prisoners answer a single question: What have you done in the current war to advance the cause of Sparta? There was no way for a surviving prisoner, who had been fighting hard and effectively against the Spartans for years on end, to sustain a claim that he had helped the Spartan cause. And so, as each Plataean failed to answer, he was taken away for summary execution.

Thucydides' description of the Plataeans' fate recalls Hesiod's state of nature in which the strong do as they will and unlucky weak are eaten. The Spartan judges who condemned the Plataeans were not greedy "bribe-swallowers," but, as in Hesiod's dystopic Ascra, the forms of legal judgment that might have been expected to produce justice were hostage to stark inequalities of power. In the Mytilenian Debate (Thuc. 3.37–49), the Athenian public speaker Diodotus lambastes his opponent, Cleon, for confusing the concerns of justice with those of foreign policy: Although Diodotus spoke in opposition to the man Thucydides (3.36.6) describes as the "most forcefully violent" of fifth-century politicians, and advocated leniency for a captive population, his stark rejection of the bearing of justice considerations on interstate affairs bespeaks a world in which the powerful do just as they please, unrestrained by anything like international law. The difference between the fifth-century international situation and Hesiod's Ascra was, as Thucydides makes clear in the Melian Dialogue (5.84–116), that "quietism" was not a viable option in the face of great interstate power inequalities. Thucydides narrates how residents of the island state Melos were not permitted by the vastly more powerful Athenians to appeal to their record of neutrality or to the possibility of divine justice; in the end, the Melians suffered a fate similar to the Plataeans, albeit without the added indignity of a mock trial.

---

[12] On Thucydides as Realist, see Crane (1998), with literature cited.

Plato and Aristotle on Law, Citizens, and Regimes

The relationship between law and the political regime was a central concern in the great fourth-century works of political philosophy, first by Plato and then by Aristotle (and his Lyceum students). According to the *Seventh Letter* (a product of Plato's Academy, if not his pen), Plato turned away from practical politics and toward philosophy as a vocation because of an encounter with Athenian law: the trial of Socrates in 399 B.C. and Socrates' subsequent acceptance of capital punishment. Several early dialogues, notably *Apology* and *Crito*, deal with the administration of justice and with the relationship between legal procedure and an ethical requirement to obey the law. In Plato's *Apology* Socrates draws attention to systematic problems with the democratic legal system. He notes that his "current accusers" (the prosecutor, Meletus, and his associates) were less dangerous than the "old accusers" – the longstanding rumors that falsely characterized Socrates as an atheistic natural scientist, a sophistical immoralist, and a teacher of dangerous verbal arts. Socrates notes that in the short time allowed to a defendant he was unlikely to undo years of prejudice and that the verdict would, therefore, be the product of prevalent false belief rather than demonstrated delicts.

The *Apology* leaves the impression that democratic legal procedure was systematically unjust, at least to defendants like Socrates. Yet in Plato's *Crito*, Socrates spurns the chance to escape from prison, and thus avoid execution, on the grounds that he had an unbreakable ethical obligation to obey the laws of Athens if he failed to "persuade" them. The apparent absence of grounds for ethical civil disobedience disturbs modern commentators. Yet the "persuade or obey" doctrine Socrates presents is consistent: Socrates quickly establishes the very strong ethical position that harm is impermissible and that disobedience would entail harm to the authority of the laws. Then, in an imagined conversation between Socrates and the "*nomoi* of Athens," an a fortiori argument is advanced: Because Socrates has received positive goods from the laws (his birth, upbringing, and education), it would clearly be unethical, even by the weaker conventional standard of "tit for tat" reciprocity, for him to return evil (harming the laws) for good. Moreover, Socrates could have chosen to leave Athens at any time if he believed the laws might require him to act wrongly; his voluntary presence in the city constituted acceptance of a contract with the laws: his obedience in exchange for goods received.[13]

The contradiction between this strict position on legal obedience and Socrates' statement in the *Apology* that piety would require him to disobey a law forbidding philosophizing is only apparent: Socrates must regard such a law as invalid without the prior (and politically inconceivable) legal annulment of the Athenian law forbidding impiety – the very law under which Socrates was, in fact, convicted. In the *Crito*, Socrates draws an analytically sharp distinction between the law itself and the jury's legal decision: The law forbade impiety, but left the definition of piety open to interpretation. Socrates was convicted because the jurors chose to accept Meletus' definition of piety. What must, to most modern readers, appear to be an inappropriately wide scope for judicial interpretation, was, for Plato's Socrates, an institutional virtue: Because Socrates regarded it as likely that a legislative assembly would produce bad definitions of moral abstractions (e.g., impiety or outrage) it was better to leave them undefined. Socrates could readily agree that "impiety is worthy of legal punishment," so long as he was not asked to subscribe to a legislative body's definition of piety. Extrapolating from the arguments of the *Crito*, we can say that Socrates chose to live in Athens, despite democracy's "lack of excellence," because the proceduralist focus of Athenian law allowed him to be at once philosophically adventurous and law-abiding and that he regarded his eventual conviction as procedurally correct, although substantively unjust.[14] Athens' "legal positivism" is, for Socrates, preferable to any system of law based on – and thus committed to enforcing – false ideas about morality.

Plato's early dialogues showed that Athenian "positivistic" legal practice allowed substantive injustice; in his later political dialogues Plato attempted to show that superior alternatives to procedural justice were possible. The ideal society of the *Republic* is ultimately predicated not on established law but on fundamental moral principles on the one hand and the enlightened leadership of philosopher-kings on the other. Yet the *Republic*'s small band of interlocutors, who devise the "city constructed by arguments" call themselves "legislators" (*nomothetai:* 530c). The relationship between justice and fundamental legislation is more explicit in the *Laws* – a monumental dialogue defining the legal regime for Magnesia, a hypothetical new city on Crete. There will be no

---

[13] On Plato's *Crito*, see R. Kraut (1984); Weiss (1998).
[14] See, further, Ober (2000a: 541–52).

philosopher-kings in Magnesia: their regulating role will be fulfilled by the laws themselves. Plato's *Laws* thus makes a strong claim for the rule of law itself.

The laws of Magnesia were meant to be relatively stable, although provision was made for amendment. Moreover, the citizens of Magnesia would not obey the laws blindly: each of the laws was to be provided with a preface, which would allow each citizen to correctly interpret the reasoning behind the act of legislation and thereby willingly and reasonably to accept the law's application to himself. Obedience was thus predicated on assent rather than coercion: the persuasive power of reason allowed Plato's legislators to avoid Solon's embrace of coercive force. Perhaps the most striking legal innovation of Magnesia comes in the area of penology: Plato broke new ground by predicating punishment directly on correction: Punishment in Magnesia was meant to cure the criminal of his erroneous beliefs – and ergo of criminal behaviors, because Plato supposed that right belief entailed correct behavior. Correction might require inflicting suffering, but punishment was now to be analogized to medical procedure. It was intended to cure the criminal-patient rather than to extract suffering from him in reciprocal exchange for the suffering of those he had offended against.[15]

Whereas Plato's political dialogues focused on the ethical relationship between law and the individual, in his *Politics* Aristotle dealt explicitly with the relationship between law and regime. He gave precise and explicit formulation to the conception that a state's laws are a reflection of the values peculiar to a specific regime and that a substantial change in the law could imply regime change. Each regime's laws supported its particular values: democratic law was good for promoting freedom and equality – the fundamental values of democracy. Some regimes (monarchy, aristocracy, polity) were qualitatively superior to others (democracy, oligarchy, tyranny). But with regard to the most common forms of potentially law-abiding regime, democracy and oligarchy, Aristotle makes it clear that an established rule of fundamental law, capable of overriding and thereby restraining the momentary legislative impulses of political bodies, was a key differentiator between better (more moderate) and vicious varieties: "Extreme" regimes were those in which the laws had no real purchase and the ruling body did whatever it pleased. Xenophon, among other aristocratic theorists, had unambiguously

---

[15] On Plato's *Laws*, see Morrow (1960), Bobonich (2002). Plato on punishment: Saunders (1991), Allen (2000b).

portrayed late-fifth-century democratic Athens as a society in which the law had no purchase on the will of the people. Whether Aristotle likewise regarded fourth-century Athens as an "extreme" democracy is debatable.[16]

DEMOSTHENES AND THE RECURSIVITY OF LAW AND THEORY

The emerging Athenian tradition of theorizing about law and judicial processes was developed through an ongoing interchange among the ideas developed by philosophers and the legal practice of dicanic orators such as Demosthenes. By the mid fourth century, practitioners of Athenian law had become used to the interweaving of legal and political-theoretical arguments; jurisprudence had become an integral part of the public discourse of law. The following passage from Demosthenes' courtroom speech *Against Timocrates* (353 B.C.) assumes an audience of jurors capable of drawing on a tradition of political theorizing about law:

> I should like, gentlemen of the jury, to give you a description of the method of legislation among the Locrians. It will do you no harm to hear an example, especially one set by a well-governed community. In that country the people are so strongly of the opinion that it is right to observe old-established laws, to preserve the institutions of their forefathers, and never to legislate for the gratification of whims or for a compromise with transgression, that if a man wishes to propose a new law, he legislates with a noose round his neck. If the law is accepted as good and beneficial, the proposer departs with his life, but, if not, the noose is drawn tight, and he is a dead man. In very truth [the Locrians] are not bold enough to propose new laws, but punctually obey the old ones. And ... we are told, gentlemen of the jury, that they have enacted only one new statute [mandating that he who puts out a one-eyed man's eye be blinded in both eyes] ... for more than two hundred years. But in [Athens], gentlemen

[16] See discussion in Strauss (1991). My thanks to Danielle Allen, Ryan Balot, Chris Eisgruber, Amy Gutmann, Susan Lape, and Stephen Macedo for discussions, over the years, which have helped me to better understand the complex relationship between law and Greek political theory.

of the jury, our politicians rarely let a month go by without legislating to suit their private ends. When in office they are always hauling private citizens to jail; but they disapprove of the application of the same measure of justice to themselves. They arbitrarily repeal those well-tried laws of Solon, enacted by their forefathers, and expect you to obey laws of their own, proposed to the detriment of the community. If, then, you decline to punish the men before you, in a very little time the *demos* will be in slavery to those beasts of prey. (Demosthenes 24.139–43)

Like Herodotus, Demosthenes invites his audience to "think with" foreign practices and attitudes toward law. Among the Locrians (as among the Athenians) anyone may seek to serve as a "lawmaker" by proposing new legislation. As in Athens, where a legislator could be subjected to prosecution for passing bad legislation (decree or law), there is personal risk involved in the procedure of lawmaking. The Locrian noose renders the risk visible and immediate. The Locrians' fundamental law establishing an extraordinarily high-risk procedure for subsequent lawmaking meant that in the past 200 years only one individual (a one-eyed man whose enemy threatened to blind him) had elected to put himself forward as legislator. The theoretical premise behind Locrian lawmaking procedure is a settled preference for established law and a suspicion that, absent grave risk, would-be lawmakers will seek to benefit themselves rather than the community at large.

Demosthenes does not say who among the Locrians has authority to judge whether the proposed law is excellent and useful (*kalos* and *chrēsimos*) or who is responsible for enforcing the law by tightening the noose if the proposed law fails. But the ultimate agent of judgment and enforcement is evidently a *demos*, because the story is meant to teach the Athenian *demos* how to treat their own "beastly" (*thērion*) politicians/lawmakers. The latter, in Demosthenes' scenario, wantonly create bad new laws and casually repeal good established laws (those of Solon) to further their own selfish interests. The politicians regard themselves as outside the law, although they expect their harmful new laws to command general obedience. Demosthenes warns that if the Athenians continue to obey these miscreants rather than punishing them, the result will be the *demos*' enslavement to the "beasts" – that is, the Athenians will descend to the remediless, natural and prepolitical, condition of Hesiod's nightingale. The force of Demosthenes' Locrian digression is explicitly critical. In comparison to the conservative and upright Locrians, the Athenian democratic regime is asserted to be at risk due to promiscuous legal amendment because bad new laws will lead to regime change: The rule of the *demos* risks being replaced by the tyrannical authority of beastly politicians. But Demosthenes concludes this section (24.143) on an optimistic note: Proper expressions of anger toward politicians will quickly reign them in. The optimism points to Athenian faith in the resilience of their own legal process and in the capacity of popular juries to judge sophisticated arguments rightly: In stark contrast to Hesiod's cryptic "riddle for princes," Demosthenes' theorizing offers a clear and practical lesson for the many.

In his speech *Against Meidias* (346 B.C.), Demosthenes inverts the "view from outside" offered in his earlier account of the Locrian noose. After citing the Athenian law against *hybris*, which explicitly forbade committing outrage against slaves, Demosthenes asks his audience to imagine that someone were to transport this law to "the barbarians from whom slaves are imported into Greece." Demosthenes suggests that upon being apprised of the Athenian law, the barbarians, duly impressed, would immediately appoint "all of you" to the honorific position of *proxenoi*: "local consuls" who look after the interests of persons from a foreign locale (21.48–50). Here, Demosthenes highlights a peculiarity of Athenian law (its refusal to condone arbitrary insolence toward foreign slaves) by imagining the startled and grateful "external" reaction of non-Greeks.

The argument of *Against Meidias* revolves around the relationship between political and legal regimes: In another thought experiment, Demosthenes asks the jurors to imagine that the wealthy cronies of his opponent were the city's rulers and that "one of you, the many and demotic" were to be hauled up before a jury of rich men. In this case, Demosthenes predicts, the poor man would have no chance of just treatment (21.209–10). Demosthenes' point is that the democratic legal regime protects the poor and weak citizens from the predations of the rich and powerful. Yet, in a remarkable jurisprudential passage, Demosthenes refutes the idea that a "rule of law" could operate automatically in the face of citizen apathy. He reemphasizes the recursive relationship between the actions taken by participatory citizens and a legal order sufficiently robust to defend the weak. After stating that the *demos* is powerful through the maintenance of the democratic legal regime, Demosthenes asks, "And what is the power of the laws?" He notes that if someone is attacked and shouts out for help, the laws themselves will not come running to that person's rescue. "No, they are just inscribed letters and have no ability to do that. What then is their motive power?

You are, if you secure them and make them authoritative whenever anyone asks for aid. So the laws are powerful through you [the people], and you through the laws" (21.224–25).

Athenians were not unique among Greeks in their conjoined concern for law and political theory. But democracy in the distinctive Athenian style provided an especially fertile ground for that conjunction. In his career as democratic politician, Demosthenes served as legislator (proposing important new laws) and as a "consumer" of law (frequent legal prosecutor and defendant). But he also served as a "public political theorist of law," concerned with law's operative authority, the relationship between amendment procedure and legal substance, and the relationship between the regime and the effects of legal judgment. Demosthenes' roles as legislator, litigant, and theorist were intertwined and, in the eyes of his fellow citizens, appropriately so. Although all Greek states had laws of one sort or another, and we find political theorizing in the earliest works of Greek literature, it was in classical Athens that the recursive relationship between self-conscious political theorizing and current legal practice was most fully realized.

22: LAW AND NATURE IN GREEK THOUGHT

A. A. Long

I

Nomos and *physis*, the Greek words for law and nature, were adaptable to a remarkably wide range of theoretical presuppositions. Philosophers could conjoin them, exploiting their inherent semantic similarities, or they could contrast them, dwelling on salient differences between them that usage and ideology had conferred. There are contexts where either word might be translated by norm ("according to" *nomos* or "according to" *physis*) or even by constitution or arrangement; for the *physis* of something is its basic structure or essence, and *nomos* identifies such items as musical modes, social customs, divine rules, or codified laws, all of which designate systematic procedures applicable to all members of the class of things to which they pertain. This is not to say that the terms are ever synonymous. A *nomos* is almost always prescriptive and normative, tinged with the idea of being sanctioned, required, and entailing retributive or harmful consequences if it is ignored. The domain of *physis* is primarily factual and descriptive. Yet, like "natural" in English, *physis* could also acquire strongly prescriptive and normative connotations, as in the Hellenistic ethical formula that the best human life needs to be "in agreement with nature" or the Hippocratic physicians' proposals concerning the body's "natural" requirements for health.

The semantic overlap and the fuzzy differences between *nomos* and *physis* are greatly complicated by the history of how the words were used and by the different connotations they respectively acquired. In fifth-century Greece, which offers us very rich discussions of both law and nature, we occasionally read about nature's law(s). Yet, far more often the terms are set in a strong antithesis to one another, especially in ethical and political contexts where custom or law is contrasted, often disparagingly, with supposedly natural values and conditions. Why that occurred, and why it is largely later that we find nature and law positively conjoined, are the principal questions I want to address in this chapter.

In modern thought the connection between nature and law pertains to two quite distinct domains. On the one hand, there is the idea of a moral code, authorized by God or at least no identifiable human legislator, that is invariant and universally authoritative in space and time. On the other hand, there is the idea of physical regularities or forces (laws of motion, for instance) that all natural phenomena "obey." It is possible to connect the two ideas, as some medieval thinkers did, by supposing that God underwrites both kinds of laws; but conceptually speaking, a universal moral code is a quite different notion from that of the basic principles governing physical reality. Much of the modern literature on this topic overlooks that basic distinction; and so, for the sake of clarity, I shall refer to the former as the idea of natural law and to the latter as the idea of laws of nature.[1] What the two ideas have in common is their positing a type of law that, in contrast with human contrivance or custom, is absolutely objective, authoritative, and binding on everything that falls within its compass. Yet, they also differ importantly because the conduct prescribed by natural law can be infringed, whereas laws of nature are completely predictive with respect to compliance.

We shall find that an ethical and theological concept of natural law was explicitly established in Stoicism and in the Stoically influenced work of the Roman jurist and philosopher Cicero. Yet, it appears only spasmodically and sketchily in earlier thinkers; so the question arises of why it fully emerged so late in ancient thought. As to exceptionless laws of nature, the scientific concept, a similar question arises. Plato and Aristotle have no such expression or exactly corresponding thought, but it is an important component of the Epicurean poem of Lucretius and it is also found in the scientific writings of the Stoic Seneca. The presence of natural law and laws of nature in these Roman thinkers does not imply that they anticipated the essentially Christian background of the former or the mathematical presuppositions of the latter. Nonetheless, some continuity, whether by accident or design, is unmistakable.

Plato and Aristotle, of course, say a great deal about law in their ethical and political writings. That, however, is not my main topic in

---

[1] On the former see Finnis (1980), and on both kinds of law, see Wollheim (1967) and Funkenstein (1986).

this chapter. What concerns me here is fully articulated linkage between law and nature, with law construed as a term that signifies the scientific and/or moral fabric of the universe and its essential rationale. When the earliest Greek cosmologists began to develop the idea of objective "nature" (*physis*), they drew on social and ethical concepts such as justice and harmony as metaphors for their models of cosmic order. Yet, with the partial exception of Heraclitus, they did not have recourse to law (*nomos*) as such. What accounts for this early Greek reticence about law as a *positive* ingredient of scientific discourse?

II

To approach this question, we need to begin by noting the variety of uses the term *nomos* acquired during the period from Hesiod to Plato. In Hesiod (see below) *nomos* signifies god-given practices or norms, and fifth-century authors, most famously Sophocles in *Antigone*, may contrast "divine" or "unwritten" laws with merely human enactments.[2] Because the point of this contrast is to criticize local prescriptions by recourse to a universal standard, we seem to be close to the idea of natural, because divinely sactioned, law. Yet authors who speak this way do not call such higher laws "natural." Rather, in the later years of fifth-century Greece *nomos* (in the singular) is frequently contrasted with *physis*, to oppose what is merely customary, conventional, or arbitrary to objective, ultimately real, and necessary states of affairs. However, with the institution of codified laws, starting more than a century earlier, *nomoi* (in the plural) have acquired identifiable origins (actual or supposed legislators such as Draco or Lycurgus). Still more importantly, they have acquired immense local authority and prestige as the laws of Athens, Sparta, and so forth. As such, they are taken to be the essential fabric of a community's life and are typically contrasted with the savage condition or nature of precivilized humans.

The connotations and evaluations of *nomos* are correspondingly various and may be as antithetical as the contrast with *physis* itself. The customs, laws, and practices brought under the term may be judged socially beneficial or coercive, usefully regulative or constrictive, universally valid or merely relatively so, an improvement on the state of nature or an unwarranted imposition. What links all of the usages – divine,

---

[2] *Antigone*, lines 450–57, who calls them *nomima* by way of contrast to King Creon's secular *nomoi*; see Ostwald (1986: 101–2) and his further references to unwritten laws, 130 n. 133.

customary or conventional, and legislative – is the thought that any *nomos* owes its existence to some kind of intentional assignation or deliberate practice, though not necessarily one that can be ascribed to specific acts and specific originators.

In the case of *physis*, we have a term that the pioneering cosmologists and physicians of the fifth century B.C.E chose to signify both the world as a whole and also all phenomena and processes that happen by virtue of the irreducible way things are, independent of human intention or intervention.[3] Hence the early Greek inquiry into "nature" was an investigation of how and why the physical world is regular and systematic in its general workings. Because human beings are a part of the "natural" world, some of the earliest thinkers included human physiology among their inquiries. Although they were chiefly interested in the normal or invariant features of our human makeup, they were also acutely aware of *cultural* differences between human groups, mediated by their local traditions, environments, and lifestyles. This pioneering study of *physis* was the catalyst for the so-called *nomos/physis* antithesis, according to which human institutions and values are strictly relative and changeable in contrast with the necessary and constant properties of the physical world.

Should we, then, conclude that *nomos* was too closely invested with mental connotations to become an appropriate metaphor for "natural" regularities and values in early Greek philosophy? That cannot be quite right without qualification, for, although the atomist Democritus took the domain of *physis* to be strictly mechanical and mindless, he was exceptional among the early cosmologists. Most of them retained a concept of divine agency and intelligence, albeit a very different kind of divinity from the traditional anthropomorphic pantheon. Yet we scarcely find in philosophy before Plato any elaborated concept of divine teleology or cosmic purposiveness. The divine air of Anaximenes, Empedocles' antithetical principles Love and Strife, and the *Nous* of Anaxagoras are all endowed with mind. But their cosmic agency is a far cry from anything directly analogous to human legislation with its civic and civilizing goals.

The principal reason, I suggest, for early Greek philosophy's reticence about associating law with nature was not an inherent disparity between the terms, *nomos* having normative and strictly human connotations and *physis* construed as value-neutral and purely mechanical; if that had been so, we would never hear, as we do, of natural law or

---

[3] Guthrie (1962: 82–3) and Lloyd (1987: 13–14).

laws of nature or divine law or personification of nature. The deeper explanation must be the strongly human and specifically legislative and local connotations that *nomos* acquired in fifth-century political life.

In favor of this historicizing explanation is the fact that as early as Hesiod we find an implicit adumbration of natural law *and* laws of nature or, rather, an application of the term *nomos* to domains that we ourselves might gloss in that way:

> The son of Kronos [Zeus] has appointed the following *nomos* for humans: that fish and beasts and winged birds should devour one another, because they have no share in justice. But to human beings he gave justice, which is far the best. (*Works and Days* 276–80)

The interest of this text consists in the fact that Hesiod probably knew nothing of codified laws. For him, human and nonhuman behavior are differentiated by a divine *nomos*. Yet, the universality and divinity (or naturalness) of that *nomos* shifts in its sense as we move from the other animals to human beings. They (we would say) have a mutually predatory endowment, which inevitably controls them; it is the law of their nature. The normativity of justice to humans is equally universal, but unlike the beasts we can spurn that gift. Animal behavior is predictably predatory; human action is not predictably just.

Hesiod's slide from a descriptive to a prescriptive law is a tendency that seems to be endemic to the very concept of natural law. However, Hesiodic justice is construed as inevitable in the long run, even if it appears to be late in coming. Unlike human laws, which persons may succeed in flouting with impunity, divine justice incorporates the necessity of requital and retribution.

Notwithstanding Hesiod and sporadic statements elsewhere about the universal power of *nomos*, it was justice rather than law that established itself as a powerful metaphor in early Greek science.[4] The Milesian cosmologist Anaximander set the stage for this usage when he said that the basic features of the cosmos (probably identifying them with such opposites as hot and cold) "pay penalty and retribution to one another for their injustice, according to the assessment of time" (DK 12 B1). According to this statement, natural change is inherently regulated, with the cosmic agents construed as if they were competitive citizens whose mutual encroachments on one another are *judicially* rectified by

---

[4] See Vlastos (1947).

reciprocal reparations. Heraclitus says: "The sun will not transgress his measures. If he does, the Furies, ministers of Justice, will find him out" (DK 22 B94). In Empedocles' cosmology the equal and alternate waxing and waning of the antithetical powers Love and Strife is construed on the model of a constitutional, time-governed rotation of offices (DK 31 B 26 and 30). Parmenides invokes Justice as the power ensuring that true reality, as distinct from the way things seem, is constrained to remain constant in time and space and impervious to all change (DK28 B 8.14–15).

In all these thinkers the order of nature is represented on the model of a social system writ large. Given the emphatic role assigned to justice, we seem to have the makings, if not the exact expression, of the idea of invariant laws of nature. Yet, the authors' collective preference for using justice rather than law is hardly accidental. What they were seeking to articulate is the idea of a necessary order and system to physical reality. Justice was available to them, not simply as a human institution, but as a concept hallowed by religious authority, and already applied metaphorically to natural processes, as in Solon's description of an undisturbed sea as "most just" (fr. 12 W). One cannot imagine the use of "most law-abiding" for such a context. Anaximander and the subsequent early cosmologists were working in an environment where *nomoi*, whether customs or codified laws, were too varied, changeable, and civically colored to establish themselves as an appropriate model for the suprapersonal system of cosmic order. In fact, both Empedocles and Democritus use the term *nomos* with the sense "mere convention" to contrast unscientific beliefs and terminology with the "reality" of things.[5]

No early Greek cosmologist speaks explicitly of laws of nature or natural law. Yet, one text of Heraclitus is exceptional to the general preference, including his own practice, for invoking cosmic justice rather than cosmic law.

> Speaking with intelligence they must resolutely adhere to what is common to all things, as a city adheres to its law, and even more resolutely; for all human laws are nourished by one law, the divine one; for it has all the power that it wishes, and suffices and more than suffices for all. (DK 22 B114)

---

[5] Empedocles DK 31 B 9, Democritus DK 68 B 9. Empedocles DK 31 B 8 also identifies as false a conventional understanding of *physis* meaning "birth" as distinct from real nature.

Like all Heraclitus' cryptic sayings this passage lacks an explanatory context by the author. However, its injunction to focus intelligence on "what is common" fits his general insistence on the need for human beings to open their minds to the public truths of nature and forego a purely private and local orientation. These natural truths (which he generally calls *logos* or "rationale") are "common" in the sense that they are accessible to all and also explanatory of all things. We need not explore the precise content and import of the Heraclitean *logos* for the purposes of this study.[6] Suffice it to say that this concept includes the uniformity of natural processes and the idea that conventional opposites such as life and death, and war and peace, are mutually implicated in one another.

Here Heraclitus starts with an analogy between the strength a city derives from its law and the appropriate mentality generated by adherence to his objective and common principle. He then asserts a still closer relation between civic law and "divine law," a relation we should take to be implicit in his earlier reference to "the common" thing. The divine law, which is universal and omnipotent, is the "nutriment" of human laws. This metaphor suggests that civic statutes are effective to the extent that they incorporate the common law as distinct from being merely local and contingent prescriptions.

Heraclitus does not explain what this incorporation requires specifically and practically. One wants to know how it relates to the radical statements he makes elsewhere, including "Justice is strife" and "War is father and king of all."[7] Is he proposing that human legislation is (or at least should be) grounded in his general principle of the harmony of opposites, such that infraction and retribution are balanced and inevitably correlated, with the punishment fitting the crime? If so, he would be giving Anaximander's cosmic justice a civic correlate, which could explain why he speaks here of law. We can only speculate. But for our conceptual inquiry, the interpretive uncertainty hardly matters. His divine law *is* a law of nature, manifesting itself in cosmic regularities and reciprocities, the sun's diurnal rotation, seasonal changes, and the cycle of life and death. It also appears to be natural, as distinct from human, law, with a universal, authoritative, and objective scope that civic laws can at best seek to approximate.

On the evidence of this passage, Heraclitus did not endorse the polarization of *nomos* and *physis* that became so fashionable soon after

---

[6] The best modern treatment of Heraclitus is Kahn (1979).
[7] DK 22 B 80 and 53.

his time. Although he was highly sensitive to the relativity of the value judgments people conventionally make, the overall thrust of his thought is on the world's underlying, though obscure, unity. Law or lawlike processes are constitutive of that, and seemingly embodied in or equivalent to the governing and divine *logos*. He did not elaborate on these big ideas, but reflection on his cryptic statements would help to inspire the Stoics in their fully articulated conception of natural law.

Important though Heraclitus is for the prehistory of our subject, even he does not explicitly conjoin the terms *nomos* and *physis*. That collocation first occurs in the ruthless speech that Thucydides (5.105), writing toward the end of the fifth century, assigns to the Athenian envoys in their confrontation with the people of Melos, a rebellious member of the Athenian empire:

> Nature always compels gods (we believe) and men (we are certain) to rule over anyone they can control. We did not make this law, and we were not the first to follow it; but we shall take it as we found it and leave it to posterity for ever, because we know that you would do the same if you had our power, and so would anyone else. (transl. Gagarin and Woodruff 1995)

Here we have a deliberately shocking inversion of the civic associations of *nomos* with normative justice. The Athenians are not invoking natural law to signify the universally right moral norm; they are not saying that they ought to subjugate the Melians. They appeal, rather, to a law of nature, mooted as being exceptionless and predictive not only for human behavior but even for gods as well. The reference to law is justificatory in a quasi-scientific, nonmoral sense. It appeals to "the facts," as it were, but its descriptive and dispassionate tenor carries a clearly prescriptive message: resistance to our power is useless; therefore submit. Stated as an algorithm, we get the following principle: If agent A is more powerful than agent B, agent A will necessarily seek to control agent B. Notwithstanding the human context, this is the idea of an irrefrangible law of nature.

The Athenians' link between nature and law needs to be distinguished from the superficially similar conjunction of the terms assigned by Plato to the hyperambitious politician Callicles in his dialogue *Gorgias* (483c-e). There Callicles distinguishes justice "according to law" (JL) from justice "according to nature" (JN). JL is the purely conventional principle that doing wrong to others is shameful and unjust. As such, it is adopted by the weak to protect themselves against the strong. As for JN:

> I think nature itself shows that it is just for the superior man to have more than the inferior, and the more powerful than the less powerful. Nature shows that this is so... both among other animals and in whole communities and races of human beings, that justice is so determined for the superior to rule over the inferior and to have more. What sort of justice did Xerxes employ when he marched against Greece or his father against the Scythians?... I think these men acted according to the nature of justice – indeed *according to the very law of nature*, though doubtless not according to the law we ourselves posit.

Like the Athenians, Callicles justifies aggressive behavior by reference to nature. Unlike the Athenians, however, he advances JN as a moral principle, associating nature not only with law but also with justice. He is not saying, as the Athenians do, that the strong are bound to subjugate the weak, but rather that it is naturally right for them to do so, and if they choose to do so (which they may decline to do) they are not really culpable but only conventionally so.

Scholars regularly characterize Callicles' appeal to natural law as an intentional paradox or virtual contradiction on Plato's part. What motivates these assessments is presumably the thought that Callicles' natural law, because it sanctions aggression, negates such standard connotations of law as equitable, socially beneficial, and civically sacrosanct. Certainly Callicles' proposal moves in the opposite direction from Heraclitus's derivation of community laws from a divine and universal norm. Callicles intends to shock. However, although his natural law is the reverse of a universal moral standard (as in the Stoic and Christian tradition), it anticipates the rhetorical appeal of that notion by suggesting that particular law codes can be challenged as to their conformity with an invariant and independently valid criterion of justice.

The contexts of Thucydides and Plato are redolent of the *nomos/physis* controversy, which generated lively debate over such topics as the foundations of language as well as the grounding of ethical principles.[8] If languages, though rule-governed, were merely human conventions, did social tradition and laws themselves have any authority other

---

[8] This controversy is fully explored in Guthrie (1969); see also Gagarin and Woodruff (1995).

than custom? Nature, with its connotations of necessity, became a catchword for characterizing the arbitrariness of *nomos*, as in Aristophanes' comic travesty of fashionable intellectualism where the character Unjust Argument advocates complete licence to "make use of one's nature" and "think (*nomize*, playing on the word *nomos*) nothing to be immoral" (*Clouds* 1077–8). Upholding *physis* against *nomos* could be, or could be perceived to be, the position that anything goes, a rejection of all cultural norms.

Yet, it could also be a positive recommendation to criticize conventional customs and laws, with the promise that a correct understanding of one's human nature could free one up to live a more authentic life, based on the norms of nature as distinct from those of culture. That was the route influentially taken by the Cynic Diogenes in the middle years of the fourth century. In flouting conventional standards of decency – even by masturbating in public – Diogenes claimed that he was "defacing the currency": that is to say, scorning *nomoi* that lacked any grounding in nature, as he liked to demonstrate by comparison with animal behavior. This Cynic appeal to nature's norms, though extreme in its manifestations, would resonate powerfully with the Hellenistic schools of philosophy.[9]

III

Before turning to them, we should ask where Plato and Aristotle placed themselves in the debate over *nomos* and *physis*. They each took human nature to be naturally social; they were ethical objectivists, opposed to relativism, with theories of natural justice; and they had powerful ideas about the rationality and order of the physical world. Could they not, indeed should they not, have endorsed the ideas of natural law and laws of nature? These are big questions, to which my responses will have to be brief and partial.[10]

As regards laws of nature, Aristotle's reticence seems fairly easy to explain. His ultimate principle, the prime unmoved mover, is completely detached from the physical world. This unembodied and super

---

[9] See Long (1996).
[10] For Platonic and Aristotelian conceptions of law see Rowe and Schofield (2000). Finnis (1980) cites both ancient philosophers frequently in support of his own theory of natural law, which, however, differs significantly from that of Stoicism and Aquinas. I know of no study that considers Plato and Aristotle in relation to laws of nature in my use of that expression.

mind does not function as a providential creator; beyond nature as such, the Aristotelian divinity is simply a perfect intellect whose eternal and changeless activity causes everything in nature to have its appropriate place and role in the great chain of being. Aristotle's god has nothing in common with a legislator. In addition, the physical world of which this god is the ultimate cause, has a variability and contingency quite foreign to the divine nature itself and the motions of the heavens that it directly causes. Aristotelian *physis* is a systematic and goal-directed structure; as he likes to say, "Nature does nothing in vain," but natural processes, though they are not chance events, happen "always or for the most part" (*Physics* 2. 198b35). The second disjunct "for the most part" in this formula distances Aristotle from the idea of absolutely predictable and exceptionless forces or laws of nature in reference to the sublunary world.

Plato, unlike Aristotle, does envision a providential mind as the ultimate cause of the physical world. That mind in its rationality and benevolence causes the world to be the best possible. Plato strenuously resists the mechanistic model of cosmology, which would have it that mindless nature or strictly physical states and events are prior to mental activity and mental impositions, including craft and law (*Laws* 10.889c). His mentalist model of causality seems to make room for physical laws or at least a cosmic legislator for the world. And Plato does use the Greek expression for "laws of nature" (*Timaeus* 83e4–5). Yet, strikingly, his context is a physiological one concerning "morbid secretions" that occur "contrary to nature's *nomoi*," i.e., normative outcomes. He does not invoke exceptionless laws of nature. The reason almost certainly is his view that bodily stuff or the world's basic matter is a necessary given, not something created; though amenable to divine craftsmanship, Platonic nature is too intractable to generate a world where events take place in accordance with absolutely exceptionless laws.

When we ask whether Plato and Aristotle have a theory of natural law in the moral domain, we are confronted by difficult questions of definition. It is generally agreed that neither philosopher fully anticipated the Stoic conception of morality as obedience to a divinely legislated code of conduct, whose universal validity is grounded in the same divine rationality that determines everything in empirical nature. Both thinkers tend to treat law as a specifically social institution, too general in its prescriptions to serve as an appropriate concept for identifying the circumstantial reflectiveness and decisions of a virtuous character. Hence they primarily treat law in political contexts rather than in their analyses of human excellence as such.

Yet, although well aware that some laws are mere customs, with no necessary basis in objective justice, Plato and Aristotle sometimes invoke nature as a criterion for good law; and they also think that it is humanly natural (i.e., beneficial and appropriate) for citizens to submit themselves to the rule of law.

Aristotle comes closest to Stoic formulations at a point in his *Rhetoric* (1.13) where he distinguishes between "particular" and "common" law. Calling the latter "natural," he characterizes it "as everyone's virtual intuition that there is a naturally common justice and injustice, which is independent of any mutual association or agreement"; and he illustrates it by citing Antigone's declaration that it was right for her to bury her brother despite the particular law forbidding that. As we have seen, Aristotle's criterion for naturalness is what holds always or for the most part. He clearly had the conceptual tools to come up with a full-fledged theory of natural law, but he did not do so. For the most part, he treats laws as particular to their political constitutions, viewing them not as moral prescripts but as the "legal" and nonnatural element in political justice. Their only authority, he says in the *Politics* (2.1269a20), is custom, which in turn depends on its longevity.

One could probably categorize Aristotle's overall theory of law as one that steers a middle course between nature and convention. Law is natural in virtue of the fact that human beings are naturally sociable and rational, but that general fact does not imply that any law as such could be the appropriate criterion or repository of moral goodness for humanity as a whole.

Plato's closest approach to Stoicism occurs towards the end of his great work *Laws*. Having been told that atheism is pernicious, especially the atheism encouraged by purely mechanistic accounts of nature, one of Plato's spokesmen says (10. 890d):

> A proper legislator should defend law itself and art as either natural or not inferior to nature, since they are actually products of intelligence when correctly described.

This alignment of law and nature is offered as a retort to the atheistic proposal that legislation is merely a product of art (*technē*), and therefore, because its ordinances are not grounded in "nature," they lack truth. Plato recalls and seeks to dissolve the old *nomos/physis* controversy by claiming that nature itself includes intelligent design at its heart. That thesis will be cardinal to the Stoic theory of natural law and very likely influenced it directly. But for all that, Plato does not suggest, as the Stoics will maintain, that reflection on the rational order of nature can actually deliver lawlike norms for invariably just and virtuous action.

IV

The context of Platonic and Aristotelian thinking about law was the Greek city-state. Its smallness and its diverse forms are evident throughout their political theory. Moreover, substantive features of their ethics, especially in the case of Aristotle, strongly reflect contemporary Hellenic values. The Hellenistic world, ushered in by Alexander the Great's conquests of Egypt and the Middle East, provided larger vistas and a stronger sense of a common human nature. This wider vision with diminished emphasis on ethnicity and local Greek practices is a distinguishing mark of the new Hellenistic schools of philosophy, the Epicurean Garden and the Stoa. Each of these began its life at Athens, but their mission and their influence were ecumenical.

Both schools sought to establish an ethical theory that conformed with human nature. They agreed with the Cynics that much of what was conventionally deemed necessary to happiness was merely a conventional estimate, unjustified by a proper understanding of human needs and satisfactions. They disagreed with one another over their doctrinal specifications of the natural goal. For the Epicureans, who identified the only intrinsic good with pleasure and absence of pain, civic life and justice were only instrumentally valuable as a source of mutual protection. However, Epicurus calls social contracts to refrain from mutual aggression "natural justice" while also denying that justice is anything *per se*.[11] In Stoicism, by contrast, where happiness is grounded purely in excellence of character, the world as a whole was characterized as the community of gods and human beings. This extraordinary conception of the cosmos as a quasi-civic and political entity is the best context for understanding the Stoic idea of natural law in its mature formulation.

Much has been written lately about what Zeno of Citium, the founder of Stoicism, intended by promoting an idea of natural law.[12] Our sources for this earliest phase of the Stoa are very fragmentary,

---

[11] Epicurus *Key doctrines* 31 and 37. See Long and Sedley (1987) – henceforth LS – 22A and 22B.

[12] See Watson (1971), Striker (1987), Inwood (1987), Vander Waerdt (1994b), and De Philippo and Mitsis (1994).

but we know enough about Zeno's most famous work (*Republic*) to see that it presented a utopian community whose citizens governed themselves without any judicial institutions or codified laws. They were "nurtured by a common law" (LS 67A, echoing Heraclitus, discussed above), which Zeno identified with "correct reason" (*orthos logos*). The notion that good law is well-reasoned was no novelty. Zeno's new and radical step, partly anticipated by his Cynic predecessors, was to propose that a community of the wise could and should dispense with all conventional civic institutions. Human nature is essentially rational, and when perfected, reason provides persons with an infallible guide to conduct. Correct reason is inherently prescriptive and prohibitive, sufficient by itself to fulfill the function of law. Because it is the function of normative human nature, its scope is universal or common. Hence natural law simply is the correctness of reason that any human being, in principle, can achieve and act on.

If Zeno had left things there, his idea of natural law would appear to be a pious hope at best. His *Republic* is described as being "a dream or image of a philosopher's well-governed society" (LS 67A) and thus quite remote from practicality. What gives natural law in Stoicism its powerful charge is its foundation not simply in the perfection of human nature but in nature as such, with nature identified as God, the perfectly rational and all-pervasive cause of the universe. Even if no human being has ever achieved perfect rationality, that condition is an objective feature of the world, instantiated in the mind of God and accessible to human minds through their own rational endowment. The Stoics take the world as a whole, both physical processes and the human organism in particular, to be divinely and rationally administered. By properly reflecting on that natural order, they argued, we shall recognize that goodness and authentic lawfulness consist in conformity to correct reason. The idea is not that we can simply read the book of nature and infer rules of conduct therefrom. Rather, the rational structure of nature as a whole, and the benevolence and wisdom of its author, are taken to authorize the principle that, by cultivating our own rational nature and conforming to its dictates, we shall be in tune with natural law or divine authority.

The Stoic Cleanthes wrote a hymn (LS 54I) in which he praises Zeus (the name Stoics gave to their cosmic divinity) for steering everything with his law. "All this cosmos," he says, "obeys you, whichever way you lead, and willingly submits to your sway." He repeatedly emphasizes the "common law" or "*logos*" (again echoing Heraclitus). The only exception to this conformity to law is human wrongdoing; for human beings in their folly err in their pursuit of things that are not authentically in their interests. However, Zeus sees to it in the end that "everything, good and bad, shares in a single everlasting rationale." Cleanthes ends his hymn by praying for trust in the just dispensations that God's common law dispenses.

Here, it appears, we find reference not only to natural law, the universal moral principle, but also to laws of nature; for the unqualified obedience of the cosmos fits the latter idea, whereas the disobedience of foolish persons pertains to the former. As I said at the beginning of this study, natural law in the moral sense can be infringed, whereas laws of nature should be inviolate. Yet, according to Cleanthes the violation of natural law by the foolish does not in the end undermine the overall rationality of the divine dispensation.

This is a complicated story, and it is further complicated when we register the fact that the Stoics were strict determinists, holding that everything that happens, including human actions, is preordained by the divine plan. This is not the appropriate place for an interpretation of the complexity.[13] I mention it because it underlines both the attractions and the problems of associating the ideas of law and nature. Unlike human law, natural law should be uniquely authoritative and universal, prescribing unequivocally objective values. Focus on the regularity of physical events promotes the idea that they are lawlike in their systematicity and that thought in turn may promote the further idea that there is an analogously systematic and universal code of conduct. Yet, as Cleanthes himself recognizes, natural law is not directly enforceable. I do not want to assert that he has simply conflated natural law and laws of nature; but it does seem as if he draws support for the former from the latter, and that is highly problematic.

Actually, the Greek Stoics do not generally invoke law when speaking about strictly physical events and processes. However, the Roman Stoic Seneca frequently does so. The motions of the heavenly bodies, tides, biological phenomena, death, and the fated sequence of events – all of these are said to occur by fixed laws or *laws of nature*, signifying their regularity and inevitability.[14] But not only that. For Seneca, as for all Stoics, what nature in its rationality determines is also right, and the regularity of nature is a sign of this prescriptiveness. For law in the formula "natural law" to do its work as a moral principle, the Stoics need a clear distinction between ethics, telling us what it is rational to

---

[13] It is studied with great skill by Bobzien (1998).
[14] See, for instance, *Natural Questions* 2.35.2, 3.29.3, 3.29.7, 6.32.12, 7.12.4 and further passages studied by Inwood (2003).

do and to refrain from doing, and the brute facts of nature that fall outside our own concerns and responsibilities. Once those facts are also taken to fall under a law, we need more care than Seneca displays in distinguishing the natural law that bears on human behavior from the laws that govern physical nature in general.

V

Seneca's readiness to picture physical events as governed by laws of nature raises the final questions I want to address. We have found partial antecedents to the Stoic conception of natural law in earlier Greek material, but laws of nature, in Seneca's ubiquitous use of that expression, have no clear precedent in our Greek sources, even including the Stoics. Did Roman culture, with its enormous investment in civic law and its imperial extension, facilitate a readier application of law as a philosophical metaphor than we find in the Greek world? Also, did the Stoic conception of natural law acquire fresh resonance when it was imported to Rome? For responding to the first question, I turn to Lucretius and for the second to Cicero.

The *De rerum natura*, Lucretius's great didactic poem, is an extraordinarily detailed and accurate rendition of the philosophy of Epicurus. Cardinal to its message is the doctrine that the foundations of reality are atomic particles whose fortuitous aggregations constitute the building blocks of the universe. Thus the Epicurean world, in sharp contrast with the Stoic cosmos, has no divine agent and plan as its cause. It is a strictly mechanistic system, mindless and purposeless in its essence. The Epicureans faced the same kind of challenges as are offered today against a godless world by proponents of Intelligent Design. How could the wondrous order of nature and the complex structures of living things be merely outcomes of the way matter has organized itself without any built-in purpose or goal?

Epicurus, whose surviving work is quite fragmentary, hardly faces this challenge head on. But Lucretius, writing in Latin some 250 years later, does so. The basic elements that the innumerable atoms form, in consequence of their interactions, are strictly limited in their structure and type because only atoms of appropriate shape and size can generate durable elements. These elements in their turn have a determinate structure, which, together with the sheer supply of material, is sufficient to explain both the variety and the specific character of things, including living beings.

Lucretius registers these claims by repeatedly invoking what he calls nature's laws, sometimes using the word *leges*, but more often the word *foedera*, which is used in ordinary Latin to signify treaties between states, compacts between persons, or ties of friendship.[15] The unwary reader could suppose that he takes nature to be an independently existing agent, a cosmic organizer like the Stoic divinity; for Lucretius loves to personify the word *natura*. Yet in fact this is figurative language, chosen to underscore the absolute regularity of the physical processes that constitute the observable world, as in the following lines:

> Since things have a limit placed on their growth and lifespan according to their species, and since what each can and cannot do is *decreed through the laws of nature*, and nothing changes but everything is so constant that all the varieties of birds display from generation to generation on their bodies the markings of their own species, they naturally must have a body of unalterable matter. (1.584–92)

Faithful though Lucretius was to Epicurus, his expressions for the laws of nature have no obvious antecedent in the surviving words of his master. It is a fair guess, I think, that this language is his own, indicating a distinctly Roman tendency to represent order and regularity by reference to law. Two later poets, Virgil and Manilius, who were strongly influenced by Lucretius, repeat his favorite word for the laws of nature, *foedus*.[16]

Cicero, Lucretius's contemporary, makes an appropriate end for this chapter because it was primarily through his works on political theory that the Stoic idea of natural law gained currency in the subsequently Christian era.[17] Cicero, who was consistently hostile to the apolitical stance of Epicureanism, did not espouse Stoicism as his philosophical school. He called himself an Academic, i.e., a follower of Plato, and in writing works entitled *Republic* and *Laws* he registered his allegiance to Plato with characteristic immodesty. Yet Cicero's Platonism is consistently tinged with Stoic ideas when he writes about ethics and politics.

---

[15] See Lucretius 1.586; 2.302, 719; 3.416; 5.57–8, 310, 924; 6.906 with discussion by Long (1977).

[16] Virgil, *Georgics* 1.60, Manilius 1.252, 2.62, 3.55; and note Manilius' focus on the "laws" (*leges*) of fate, 1.56–65. For an instance of how easily legal metaphors came to the Roman mind, note how Horace in his *Art of Poetry* 72, 464, speaks of "a right" (*ius*) and "norm" (*norma*) of speech.

[17] See Watson (1971).

It is also strongly marked by his own political commitments and his reverence for the Roman tradition of constitutional government, which had come under enormous strain from competing warlords during his mature years.

In his *Republic* Cicero imagines a conversation between opponents and proponents of the idea of natural law. The arguments of the opponents are missing from the text in its transmitted form, but Lactantius, the source of the following citation, says that they focused on the notion that justice, as conventionally understood, is merely the utilitarian and mutually protective policy of the weak, with no basis in nature. In response, Cicero's proponent of natural law says the following (3.33 = LS 67S):

> True law is right reason, in agreement with nature, diffused over everyone, consistent, everlasting, whose nature is to advocate duty by prescription and to deter wrongdoing by prohibition ... It is wrong to alter this law, nor is it permissible to repeal any part of it, and it is impossible to abolish it completely. We cannot be absolved from this law by senate or people, nor need we look for any outside interpreter of it or commentator. There will not be a different law at Rome and at Athens, or a different law now and in the future, but one law, everlasting and immutable, will hold good for all peoples and at all times. And there will be one master and ruler for us all in common, God, who is the founder of this law, its promulgator and its judge.

This is probably the classic statement of the idea of natural law. The basic ideas are clearly Stoic, but from Cicero we hear nothing about an ideal polity of the perfectly wise. So far as we can tell, he has injected his own sense of internationalism, registering that by the natural law's complete indifference to time and place.

According to Heraclitus, four and a half centuries earlier, civic laws, as we saw, are said to be "nurtured" by the common divine law. Our citation from Cicero does not consider the actual relation between the two kinds of law; but it is clear, from his work *On Laws* 1.19 that Cicero thought that natural law ("the mind and reason of the wise person"), and not particular law, is the proper place to look for "the standard regulating justice and injustice." In the same context he characterizes "that supreme law" as originating prior to any written law or civil society.

What he could also have referred to, as he does elsewhere, is the Roman institution of *ius gentium*, the law pertaining to relations between states and covering aliens as well as Roman citizens. To the best of my knowledge he nowhere explicitly tests principles of international law against the standard of natural law, but I think we see an instance of that where he says in *On duties* 1.34 that war is only justified, as the way of settling disputes, after discussion has been exhausted, and then only in self-defence. His own endorsement of natural law was surely encouraged by the Roman ideal that the rule of law should know no civic boundaries.

Greek reflections on the connection or lack of connection between law and nature took many forms. As we survey the period from Hesiod to Aristotle, we sometimes glimpse the ingredients of the two ideas, natural law and laws of nature, but they are scarcely worked out into anything that could be called theory. The principal reasons I have suggested for this reticence are twofold: first, the contested connotations of the terms *nomos* and *physis* and, second, the pressure of civic custom and codified law on the term *nomos*. With the extension of Hellenism, accompanied by the decline in autonomy of the numerous city-states, the idea of law fully transcended local boundaries, as we observe in the early Stoic concept of natural law. When Greek philosophy infiltrated Rome, it encountered a tradition of law that was far more systematic and articulated than local Greek experience had at hand. Untrammelled by the *nomos/physis* controversy, Roman thinkers found it easier than their Greek forbears to construe nature in terms of law and quasi-legal regulation.

Bibliography

Adkins, A. 1961. *Merit and Responsibility*. Oxford.
Alessandri, S. 1984. "Il significato storico della legge di Nicofonte sul dokimastes monetario." In *Annali della Scuola Normale Superiore di Pisa* (3rd Ser. 14): 369–93.
Allen, Danielle S. 1997. "Imprisonment in Classical Athens." *Classical Quarterly* 47: 121–35.
Allen, Danielle S. 2000a. "Envisaging the Body of the Condemned: The Power of Platonic Symbols." *Classical Philology* 95: 133–50.
Allen, Danielle S. 2000b. *The World of Prometheus: The Politics of Punishing in Democratic Athens*. Princeton.
Arnaoutoglou, Ilias. 1998. *Ancient Greek Laws*. London/New York.
Atiyah, P. 1986. *Essays on Contract*. Oxford.
Atkinson, J. E. 1992. "Curbing the Comedians: Cleon versus Aristophanes and Syracosius' Decree." *Classical Quarterly* 42: 56–64.
Avramovic, Sima. 1990. "Die epiballontes als Erben im Gesetz von Gortyn." *Zeitschrift der Savigny-Stiftung* 107: 363–70.
Avramovic, Sima. 1991. "Response to Alberto Maffi." *Symposion* 1990: 233–7.
Avramovic, Sima. 1994. "Response to Monique Bile." *Symposion* 1993: 53–60.
Avramovic, Sima. 1997. *Iseo e il diritto attico*. Naples.
Balot, R. K. 2001. *Greed and Injustice in Classical Athens*. Princeton.
Barkan, I. 1935. *Capital Punishment in Ancient Athens*. Chicago.
Beauchet, L. [1897] 1969. *Histoire du droit privé de la république athénienne*. 4 Vols. Amsterdam.
Behrend, D. 1970. *Attische Pachturkunden – Ein Beitrag zur Beschreibung der μίσθωσις nach den griechischen Inschriften*. München.
Behrend, D. 1975. "Die *anadikos dike* und das Scholion zu Plato Nomoi 937d." *Symposion* 1971: 131–56.
Bennett, W. L., and M. S. Feldman. 1981. *Reconstructing Reality in the Courtroom*. New York.
Berneker, E. 1959. "Pseudomartyrion Dike." *Real-Encyclopädie* 23/2: 1364–75.
Bers, V. 1985. "Dikastic *thorubos*." In *Crux: Essays Presented to G. E. M. de Ste. Croix on his 75th birthday*, eds. P. A. Cartledge and F. D. Harvey. Exeter: 1–15.
Bertrand, J.-M. 1997. "De l'usage de l'epigraphie dans la cité des Magnètes platoniciens." *Symposion* 1995: 27–47.
Bertrand, J.-M. 1999. *De L'écriture à l'oralité. Lectures des lois de Platon*. Paris.
Bianchetti, S. 1980. "La commedia antica e la libertà di parola." *Atti e mem. dell'Accadem. Tosc. di Sci. e Lett. La Colombaria* [Florence] n.s. 31: 1–40.

Bile, Monique. 1980. "Système de parenté et systèmes matrimoniaux à Gortyne." *Verbum* 3: 1–21.
Bile, Monique. 1981. "Le vocabulaire des structures socials dans les Lois de Gortyne." *Verbum* 4: 11–45.
Bile, Monique. 1988. *Le dialecte crétois ancien. Étude de la langue des inscriptions. Recueil des inscriptions postérieures aux IC. Études crétoises, 27*. Paris.
Bile, Monique. 1994a. "L'organisation matérielle du texte des lois de Gortyne." *Verbum* 17: 203–17.
Bile, Monique. 1994b. "La *patrioikos* des lois de Gortyne: Etude linguistique." *Symposion 1993*: 45–51.
Biscardi, Arnaldo. 1970. "La 'gnome dikaotate' et l'interprétation des lois dans la Grèce ancienne." *Revue internationale des droits de l'antiquité* 17: 219–32.
Biscardi, Arnaldo. 1982a. *Diritto greco antico*. Milano.
Biscardi, Arnaldo. 1982b. "Introduction à l'étude des pratiques commerciales dans l'histoire des droits de l'Antiquité." *Revue internationale des droits de l'antiquité* 29: 21–44.
Biscardi, Arnaldo. 1991. *Αρχαίο Ελληνικό Δίκαιο*. Athens. (Translation of *Diritto greco antico*, Milan 1982.)
Bleicken, J. 1985. *Die athenische Demokratie*. Paderborn.
Bleicken, J. 1994. *Die athenische Demokratie*, 2nd ed. Paderborn.
Blundell, S. 1995. *Women in Ancient Greece*. Cambridge, MA.
Bobonich, C. 2002. *Plato's Utopia Recast: His Later Ethics and Politics*. Oxford.
Bobzien, S. 1998. *Determinism and Freedom in Stoic Philosophy*. Oxford.
Boedeker, D., and K. Raaflaub, eds. 1998. *Democracy, Empire and the Arts in Fifth-Century Athens*. Cambridge, MA.
Boegehold, Alan L., and Adele Scafuro, eds. 1994. *Athenian Identity and Civic Ideology*. Baltimore.
Boegehold, Alan L. 1995. *The Law-Courts at Athens. Sites, Buildings, Equipment, Procedure, and Testimonia (The Athenian Agora XXVIII)*. Princeton.
Boersma, J. S. 1970. *Athenian Building Policy from 561/0 to 405/4*. Groningen.
Bogaert, R. 1968. *Banques et banquiers dans les cités grecques*. Leyden.
Bohannan, Paul. 1957. *Justice and Judgment among the Tiv*. London.
Bongenaar, J. 1933. *Isocrates' trapeziticus vertaald en toegelicht*. Utrecht.
Bonner, R. J. 1905. *Evidence in Athenian Courts*. Chicago.
Bonner, R. J., and G. Smith. 1938. *The Administration of Justice from Homer to Aristotle*, vol. II. Chicago.
Branham. R. B., and M.-O. Goulet-Cazé, eds. 1996. *The Cynics. The Cynic Movement in Antiquity and its Legacy*. Berkeley/Los Angeles/London.
Bremmer, J. 1983. "Scapegoat Rituals in Ancient Greece." *Harvard Studies in Classical Philology* 87: 299–320.
Bresson, A. 1994. "L'attentat d'Hiéron et le commerce grec." In *Économie antique. Les échanges dans l'Antiquité: le rôle de l'État*, eds. J. Andreau, P. Briant, and R. Descat. Saint-Bertrand-de-Comminges: 47–68. (Reprinted in, and quoted from, Bresson, *La cité marchande*, Bordeaux 2000: 131–49.)
Bresson, A. 2000. "Prix officiels et commerce de gros à Athènes." In Bresson, *La cité marchande*, Bordeaux: 183–210.
Brixhe, Claude, and Monique Bile. 1999. "La circulation des biens dans les lois de Gortyne." In Dobias-Lalou 1999: 75–116.

Brown, Peter. 1982. "Society and the Supernatural: A Medieval Change." In Brown, *Society and the Holy in Late Antiquity*. Berkeley: 302–32.
Brulé, P., and J. Oulhen, eds. 1997. *Esclavage, guerre, économie en Grèce ancienne: Hommages à Yvon Garlan*. Rennes.
Buck, C. D. 1955. *The Greek Dialects*, 3rd ed. Chicago.
Burkert, W. 1985. *Greek Religion*. Cambridge, MA. (Translated by J. Raffan from 1977 *Griechische Religion der archaischen und klassischen Epoche*).
Burnett, A. 1976. "Tribe and City, Custom and Decree in *Children of Heracles*." *Classical Philology* 71: 4–26.
Calero Secall, I. 1997. *Leyes de Gortina*. Madrid.
Calhoun, G. 1927. *The Growth of Criminal Law in Ancient Greece*. Berkeley.
Camassa, G. 1988. "Aux origines de la codification écrite des lois en Grèce." In *Les Savoirs de l'écriture en Grèce ancienne*, ed. M. Detienne. Lille: 130–55.
Cane, P. 1991. *Essays for Patrick Atiyah*. Oxford.
Cantarella, Eva. 1976. *Studi sull' omicidio in diritto greco e romano*. Milan.
Cantarella, Eva. 1979. *Norma e Sanzione in Omero*. Milan.
Cantarella, Eva. 1987. *Pandora's Daughters: The Role and Status of Women in Greek and Roman Antiquity*. Baltimore/London.
Cantarella, Eva. 1991a. "Moicheia, Reconsidering a Problem." *Symposion 1990*: 289–96.
Cantarella, Eva. 1991b. *I Supplizzi Capitali*. Milan.
Cantarella, Eva. 1997. "Filiazione e cittadinanza ad Atene." *Symposion 1995*: 97–111.
Cantarella, Eva. 2002a. *Bisexuality in the Ancient World*, 2nd ed. New Haven/London.
Cantarella, Eva. 2002b. "Dispute Settlement in Homer: Once Again on the Shield of Achilles. In *Mélanges en l'honneur Panayotis Dimakis: Droits antiques et société*. Athens: 147–65.
Cantarella, Eva. 2002c. *Itaca. Eroi, donne, potere tra vendetta e diritto*. Milan.
Capdeville, G. 1997. "Le droit international dans la Crète antique." *Comptes rendus de l'Académie des Inscrptions et Belles-Lettres*, 273–307.
Carawan, Edwin. 1998. *Rhetoric and the Law of Draco*. Oxford.
Carawan, Edwin. 2002. "The Athenian Amnesty and the 'Scrutiny of the Laws'." *Journal of Hellenic Studies* 122: 1–23.
Carey, Christopher. 1992. *Apollodoros Against Neaira*. Warminster, England.
Carey, Christopher. 1993. "Return of the Radish, or Just When You Thought It Was Safe to Go Back into the Kitchen." *Liverpool Classical Monthly* 18: 53–55.
Carey, Christopher. 1994. "'Artless' Proofs in Aristotle and the Orators." *Bulletin of the Institute of Classical Studies* 39: 95–106.
Carey, Christopher. 1995a. "Rape and Adultery in Athenian Law." *Classical Quarterly* 45, 2: 407–17.
Carey, Christopher. 1995b. "The Witness's *exomosia* in the Athenian Courts." *Classical Quarterly* 45: 114–19.
Carey, Christopher. 1996. "Nomos in Attic Rhetoric and Oratory." *Journal of Hellenic Studies* 116: 33–46.
Carey, Christopher. 2000. *Aeschines*. Translation with introductions and notes. Austin.
Carey, Christopher, and R. Reid. 1985. *Demosthenes: Selected Private Speeches*. Cambridge.
Cartledge, Paul, Paul Millett, and S. C. Todd, eds. 1990. *Nomos: Essays in Athenian Law, Politics and Society*. Cambridge.
Casabona, J. 1966. *Recherches sur le vocabulaire des sacrifices en grec*. Aix-en-Provence.

Cawkwell, G. L. 1969. "The Crowning of Demosthenes." *Classical Quarterly* 19: 163–80.
Chaniotis, Angelos. 1995. "Problems of 'Pastoralism' and 'Transhumance' in Classical and Hellenistic Crete." *Orbis Terrarum* 1: 39–89.
Chaniotis, Angelos. 1996. *Die Verträge zwischen kretischen Poleis in der hellenistischen Zeit*. Stuttgart.
Chaniotis, Angelos. 1997. "'Tempeljustiz' im kaiserzeitlichen Kleinasien." *Symposion 1995*: 353–384.
Chaniotis, Angelos. 1999a. *From Minoan Farmers to Roman Traders. Sidelights on the Economy of Ancient Crete*. Stuttgart.
Chaniotis, Angelos. 1999b. "Milking the Mountains. Economic Activities on the Cretan Uplands in the Classical and Hellenistic Period." In Chaniotis 1999a: 181–220.
Christ, Matthew R. 1998. *The Litigious Athenian*. Baltimore.
Clanchy, Michael T. 1993. *From Memory to Written Record: England 1066–1307*. 2nd ed. Oxford.
Clarysse, Willy. 1985. "Greeks and Egyptians in the Ptolemaic Army and Administration. *Aegyptus* 65: 57–66.
Clarysse, Willy. 1988. "Une famille alexandrine dans la chora." *Chronique d'Égypte* 63: 137–140.
Clinton, K. 1982. "The Late Fifth-Century Revision of the Athenian Law-Code." *Hesperia Suppl.* XIX: 27–37.
Cohen, David. 1983. *Theft in Athenian Law*. Munich.
Cohen, David. 1984. "The Athenian Law of Adultery." *Revue internationale des droits de l'antiquité* 31: 147–65.
Cohen, David. 1985. "A Note on Aristophanes and the Punishment of Adultery in Athenian Law." *Zeitschrift der Savigny-Stiftung* 102: 385–7.
Cohen, David. 1989. "Problems, Methods, and Models in the Study of Greek Law." *Zeitschrift der Savigny-Stiftung* 106: 81–105.
Cohen, David. 1991. *Law, Sexuality and Society: The Enforcement of Morals in Classical Athens*. Cambridge.
Cohen, David. 1993. "Law, Autonomy, and Political Community in Plato's *Laws*." *Classical Philology* 88: 301–17.
Cohen, David. 1995. *Law, Violence, and Community in Ancient Athens*. Cambridge.
Cohen, David. 1996. "Seclusion, Separation and the Status of Women in Classical Athens." In *Women in Antiquity*, eds. I. McAuslan and P. Walcot. Oxford. 135–45.
Cohen, David. 2003. "Writing, Law, and Legal Practice in the Athenian Courts." In *Written Texts and the Rise of Literate Culture in Ancient Greece*, ed. H. Yunis. Cambridge: 78–96.
Cohen, Edward E. 1973. *Ancient Athenian Maritime Courts*. Princeton.
Cohen, Edward E. 1990. "Commercial Lending by Athenian Banks: Cliometric Fallacies and Forensic Methodology." *Classical Philology* 85: 177–90.
Cohen, Edward E. 1992. *Athenian Economy and Society: A Banking Perspective*. Princeton.
Cohen, Edward E. 2000a. *The Athenian Nation*. Princeton.
Cohen, Edward E. 2000b. "Whoring under Contract": The Legal Context of Prostitution in Fourth-Century Athens." In *Law and Social Status in Classical Athens*, eds. V. Hunter and J. Edmondson. Oxford. 113–47.
Cole, David. 1976. *Asty and Polis: "City" in Early Greek*. Ph.D. dissertation, Stanford University.

Cole, Susan G. 1984. "Greek Sanctions against Sexual Assault." *Classical Philology* 79: 97–113.

Cole, T. 1991. *The Origins of Rhetoric in Ancient Greece*. Baltimore.

Collins, D. 2001. "Theoris of Lemnos and the Criminalization of Magic in 4th c. Athens." *Classical Quarterly* 51: 477–93.

Connor, W. R. 1985. "The Razing of the House in Greek Society." *Transactions of the American Philological Association* 115: 79–102.

Coquillette, D. R. 1999. *The Anglo-American Legal Heritage: Introductory Materials*. Durham.

Cowey, M. S., and K. Maresch. 2001. *Urkunden des Politeuma der Juden von Herakleopolis (144/3-133/2 v. Chr.)* (P. Polit. Iud.) (Pap. Col. XXIX). Wiesbaden.

Crane, G. 1998. *Thucydides and the Ancient Simplicity: The Limits of Political Realism*. Berkeley.

Csapo, E., and W. J. Slater. 1995. *The Context of Ancient Drama*. Ann Arbor.

Darmezin, L. 1999. *Les affranchissements par consécration en Béotie et dans le monde grec hellénistique*. Nancy/Paris.

Daube, B. 1939. *Zu den Rechtsproblemen in Aischylos' Agamemnon*. Basel.

Daube, D. 1947. *Studies in Biblical Law*. Cambridge.

Daube, D. 1973. "The Self Understood in Legal History." *The Juridical Review* 85: 126–34.

Davidson, J. 1997. *Courtesans and Fishcakes: The Consuming Passions of Classical Athens*. London.

Davies, John K. 1977–1978. "Athenian Citizenship: The Descent Group and the Alternatives." *Classical Journal* 73: 105–21.

Davies, John K. 1984. "Cultural, Social and Economic Features of the Hellenistic World." In *Cambridge Ancient History*, 2nd ed., 7.1: 257–320.

Davies, John K. 1996. "Deconstructing Gortyn: When is a Code a Code?" In Foxhall and Lewis 1996b: 33–56.

De Brauw, Michael. 2001. " 'Listen to the Laws Themselves': Citations of Laws and Portrayal of Character in Attic Oratory." *Classical Journal* 97: 161–76.

De Philippo, G., and P. Mitsis. 1994. "Socrates and Stoic Natural Law." In Van der Waerdt 1994a: 252–71.

Deacy, Susan, and Karen F. Pierce. 1997. *Rape in Antiquity*. London.

Decharme, P. 1906. *Euripides and the Spirit of His Dramas*, trans. by J. Loeb. New York.

Demeyere, J. 1952. "La formation de la vente et le transfert de la propriété en droit grec classique." *Revue internationale des droits de l'antiquité*. 3rd Ser. 1: 215–66.

Demeyere, J. 1953. "Le contrat de vente en droit grec classique: les obligations des parties." *Revue internationale des droits de l'antiquité*. 3rd Ser. 2: 197–228.

Diamantopoulos, A. 1957. "The Danaid Tetralogy of Aeschylus." *Journal of Hellenic Studies* 77: 220–29.

Diamond, A. S. 1935. *Primitive Law*. London.

Dickie, M. W. 2001. *Magic and Magicians in the Greco-Roman World*. London.

Di Lello-Finuoli, A. L. 1991. "Trasmissione della proprietà per successione ereditaria femminile e sistema di parentela nel Codice di Gortina." In Musti et al. 1991: 215–30.

DK = Diels, H., and W. Kranz. 1951–1952. *Die Fragmente der Vorsokratiker*. Berlin.

Dobias-Lalou, C. ed. 1999. *Des dialectes grecs aux lois de Gortyne*. Nancy: ADRA and Paris: De Boccard.

Dobrov, Gregory, ed. 1997. *The City as Comedy. Society and Representation in Athenian Drama*. Chapel Hill.
Donker van Heel, K. 1990. *The Legal Manual of Hermopolis [P. Mattha]. Text and Translation*. Leiden.
Dorjahn, A. P. 1930. "Extenuating Circumstances in Athenian Courts." *Classical Philology* 25: 162–72.
Dover, Kenneth J. 1968a. *Aristophanes Clouds*. Oxford.
Dover, Kenneth J. 1968b. *Lysias and the Corpus Lysiacum*. Berkeley/Los Angeles.
Dover, Kenneth J. 1972. *Aristophanic Comedy*. Berkeley/Los Angeles.
Dover, Kenneth J. 1974. *Greek Popular Morality in the Time of Plato and Aristotle*. Berkeley.
Dover, Kenneth J. 1978. *Greek Homosexuality*. New York.
Dover, Kenneth J. 1988. "The Freedom of the Intellectual in Greek Society." In Dover, *The Greeks and Their Legacy*. Oxford: 135–58. (First in *Talanta* 7, 1976.)
Drew, Katherine Fischer. 1973. *The Lombard Laws*. Philadelphia.
Drew, Katherine Fischer. 1991. *The Laws of the Salian Franks*. Philadelphia.
Dunbar, N. 1995. *Aristophanes Birds*. Oxford.
Dworkin, R. M. 1996. *Freedom's Law: The Moral Reading of the American Constitution*. Cambridge, MA.
Easterling, Pat, ed. 1982. *Sophocles' Trachinae*. Cambridge.
Eder, W. 1986. "The Political Significance of the Codification of Law in Archaic Societies: An Unconventional Hypothesis." In *Social Struggles in Archaic Rome*, ed. K. Raaflaub. Berkeley/Los Angeles: 262–300.
Edwards, A. T. 1993. "Historicizing the Popular Grotesque: Bakhtin's *Rabelais* and Attic Old Comedy." In Scodel 1993: 89–117.
Edwards, P., ed. 1967. *The Encyclopaedia of Philosophy*. New York/London.
Engels, J. 2001. "Das athenische Getreidesteuer-Gesetz des Agyrrhios." *Zeitschrift für Papyrologie und Epigraphik* 134: 97–124.
Erxleben, E. 1974. "Die Rolle der Bevölkerungsklassen im Aussenhandel Athens im 4. Jahrhundert v.u.Z." In *Hellenische Poleis*, ed. E. C. Welskopf. Vol. I. Berlin: 460–520.
Faraguna, M. 1999. "Intorno alla nuova legge ateniese sulla tassazione del grano." *Dike* 2: 63–97.
Faraguna, M. 2003. "Vendite di immobili e registrazione pubblica nelle città greche." *Symposion* 1999: 97–122.
Farnell, L. R. 1896–1909. *The Cults of the Greek States*. Oxford.
Feinberg, J. 1970. *Doing and Deserving*. Princeton.
Feinberg, J. 1984. *The Moral Limits of the Criminal Law*, vols. 1–2. Oxford.
Figueira, T. 1986. "*Sitopolai* and *Sitophylakes* in Lysias' 'Against the Graindealers': Governmental Intervention in the Athenian Economy." *Phoenix* 40: 149–71.
Fine, John V. A. 1951. *Horoi: Studies in Mortgage, Real Security and Land Tenure in Ancient Athens*. Baltimore.
Finkelstein, J. J. 1961. "Ammisaduqa's edict and the Babylonian 'Law Codes.'" *Journal of Cuneiform Studies* 15: 91–104.
Finley, Moses I. (Finkelstein). 1935. "'Έμπορος, ναύκληρος and κάπηλος." *Classical Philology* 30: 320–36.
Finley, Moses I. 1951. "Some Problems of Greek Law (review of Pringsheim 1950)." *Seminar* 9: 72–91.
Finley, Moses I. 1966. "The Problem of the Unity of Greek Law." In *La storia del diritto nel quadro delle scienze storiche (Atti del primo Congresso Internazionale della Società*

Italiana di Storia del Diritto). Florence: 129–42. (Reprinted in *The Use and Abuse of History.* London, 1975, 134–52, 236–37.)
Finley, Moses I. 1973. *Democracy Ancient and Modern.* New Brunswick, NJ.
Finley, Moses I. 1983. *Politics in the Ancient World.* Cambridge.
Finley, Moses I. [1951]1985. *Studies in Land and Credit in Ancient Athens* (with a new introduction by P. Millett). New Brunswick, NJ.
Finley, Moses I. [1973]1999. *The Ancient Economy* (with a new foreword by I. Morris). Berkeley.
Finnis, J. 1980. *Natural Law and Natural Rights.* Oxford.
Fish, S. 1989. *Doing What Comes Naturally: Change, Rhetoric, and the Practice of Theory in Literary and Legal Studies.* Durham, NC.
Fisher, N. R. E. 1976. "*Hybris* and Dishonour I." *Greece and Rome* 23: 177–193.
Fisher, N. R. E. 1979. "*Hybris* and Dishonour II." *Greece and Rome* 26: 32–47.
Fisher, N. R. E. 1990. "The Law of *Hybris* in Athens." In Cartledge, Millett, and Todd 1990: 123–38.
Fisher, N. R. E. 1992. *Hybris: A Study of the Values of Honour and Shame in Ancient Greece.* Warminster.
Fisher, N. R. E. 1995. "*Hybris*, Status and Slavery." In *The Greek World*, ed. A. Powell. London/New York: 44–84.
Flensted-Jensen, P., T. H. Nielsen, and L. Rubinstein, eds. 2000. *Polis and Politics: Studies in Ancient Greek History Presented to Mogens Herman Hansen.* Copenhagen.
Fletcher, G. 1998. *Basic Concepts of Criminal Law.* Oxford.
Forrest, W. G. 1960. "Themistocles and Argos." *Classical Quarterly* 10: 221–41.
Foucault, M. 1977. *Discipline and Punish.* New York.
Foxhall, Lin. 1989. "Household, Gender and Property in Classical Athens." *Classical Quarterly* 39: 22–44.
Foxhall, Lin, and Andrew D. E. Lewis. 1996a. "Introduction." In Foxhall and Lewis 1996b: 1–8.
Foxhall, Lin, and Andrew D. E. Lewis, eds. 1996b. *Greek Law in Its Political Setting: Justifications Not Justice.* Oxford.
Funkenstein, A. 1986. *Theology and the Scientific Imagination.* Princeton.
Gabrielsen, V. 1986. "φανερά and ἀφανὴς οὐσία in Classical Athens." *Classica et Mediaevalia* 37: 99–114.
Gabrielsen, V. 1987. "The Antidosis Procedure in Classical Athens." *Classica et Mediaevalia* 38: 8–38.
Gabrielsen, V. 1994. *Financing the Athenian Fleet: Public Taxation and Social Relations.* Baltimore.
Gagarin, Michael. 1976. *Aeschylean Drama.* Berkeley.
Gagarin, Michael. 1979. "The Athenian Law against Hybris." In *Arktouros: Hellenic Studies Presented to Bernard M. W. Knox*, ed. G. W. Bowersock et al. Berlin: 229–36.
Gagarin, Michael. 1981. *Drakon and Early Athenian Homicide Law.* New Haven.
Gagarin, Michael. 1982. "The Organisation of the Gortyn Law Code." *Greek, Roman and Byzantine Studies* 23: 129–46.
Gagarin, Michael. 1984. "The Testimony of Witnesses in the Gortyn Laws." *Greek, Roman and Byzantine Studies* 25: 345–9.
Gagarin, Michael. 1986. *Early Greek Law.* Berkeley.
Gagarin, Michael. 1988. "The First Law of the Gortyn Code." *Greek, Roman and Byzantine Studies* 29: 335–43.

Gagarin, Michael. 1989. "The Function of Witnesses at Gortyn." *Symposion* 1985: 29–54.
Gagarin, Michael. 1990. "The Nature of Proofs in Antiphon." *Classical Philology* 85: 22–32.
Gagarin, Michael. 1991. "Response to Henri van Effenterre." *Symposion* 1990: 87–91.
Gagarin, Michael. 1994. "The Economic Status of Women in the Gortyn Code: Retroactivity and Change." *Symposion* 1993: 61–71.
Gagarin, Michael. 1995. "The First Law of the Gortyn Code Revisited." *Greek, Roman and Byzantine Studies* 36: 7–15.
Gagarin, Michael. 1996. "Review of Sealey 1994." *Classical Philology* 91: 276–81.
Gagarin, Michael. 1997. "Oaths and Oath-Challenges in Greek Law." *Symposion* 1995: 125–34.
Gagarin, Michael. 2001. "The Gortyn Code and Greek Legal Procedure." *Symposion* 1997: 41–51.
Gagarin, Michael. 2002. *Antiphon the Athenian. Oratory, Law, and Justice in the Age of the Sophists*. Austin.
Gagarin, Michael. 2003. "Letters of the Law. Written Texts in Archaic Greek Law." In *Written Texts and the Rise of Literate Culture in Ancient Greece*, ed. H. Yunis. Cambridge: 59–77.
Gagarin, Michael. 2004. "Writing Athenian Law." In *Law, Rhetoric, and Comedy in Classical Athens: Essays in Honour of Douglas M. MacDowell*, ed. D. L. Cairns and R. A. Knox. London: 15–31.
Gagarin, Michael. forthcoming. "Inscribing Laws in Greece and the Near East." *Symposion* 2003.
Gagarin, Michael, and Paul Woodruff. 1995. *Early Greek Political Thought From Homer to the Sophists*. Cambridge.
Garland, D. 1985. *Punishment and Welfare*. London.
Garland, Robert. 1984. "Religious Authority in Archaic and Classical Athens." *Annual of the British School at Athens* 79: 75–123.
Garland, Robert. 1987. *The Piraeus*. Ithaca, NY.
Garner, Richard. 1987. *Law and Society in Classical Athens*. London.
Garnsey, Peter. 1970. *Social Status and Legal Privilege in the Roman Republic*. Oxford.
Garvie, A. F. 1969. *Aeschylus' Supplices: Play and Trilogy*. Cambridge.
Gauthier, P. 1972. *Symbola. Les étrangers et la justice dans les cités grecques*. Nancy.
Gauthier, P. 1974. "Review of E. Cohen 1973." *Revue des Etudes Grecques* 87: 424–25.
Gauthier, P. 1981. "De Lysias à Aristote (Ath. Pol. 51, 4): Le commerce du grain à Athènes et les fonctions des sitophylaques." *Revue historique de droit français et étranger* 59: 5–28.
Gehrke, H.-J. 1985. *Stasis*. Munich.
Gehrke, H.-J., ed. 1994. *Rechtskodifizierung und soziale Normen im interkulturellen Vergleich*. Tübingen.
Gehrke, H.-J. 1997. "Gewalt und Gesetz. Die soziale und politische Ordnung Kretas in der archaïschen und klassischen Zeit." *Klio* 79: 23–68.
Geissler, P. 1969. *Chronologie der altattischen Komödie*. Dublin/Zurich.
Gernet, Louis. 1938a. "Introduction à l'étude du droit grec ancien." *Archives d'Histoire du Droit Oriental* 2: 261–92.
Gernet, Louis. 1938b. "Sur les actions commerciales en droit athénien." *Revue des Études Grecques* 51: 1–44.

Bibliography

Gernet, Louis. 1951. "Droit et prédroit en Grèce ancienne," *L'Année Sociologique* 3e série (1948–1949): 175–260. (Reprinted in Gernet, *Anthropologie de la Grèce antique*, Paris 1968; Eng. tr. Baltimore 1981.)

Gernet, Louis. 1953. "Sur l'obligation contractuelle dans la vente hellénique." *Revue internationale des droits de l'antiquité*. 3rd Ser. 2: 229–47. (Reprinted in Gernet 1955b.)

Gernet, Louis, ed. 1954–1960. *Démosthène, Plaidoyers Civils*. 4 Vols. Paris.

Gernet, Louis. 1955a. "Sur la notion du jugement en droit grec." In Gernet 1955b: 61–81.

Gernet, Louis. 1955b. *Droit et société dans la Grèce ancienne*. Paris.

Girard, R. 1992 [1977]. *Violence and the Sacred*. Trans. by P. Gregory. Baltimore.

Gofas, D. 1978. "Les 'emmenoi dikai' à Thasos." *Symposion 1974*: 175–86.

Gofas, D. 1989a. "La vente sur échantillon à Athènes d'apres un texte d'Hypéride." *Symposion 1982*: 121–29.

Gofas, D. 1989b. "Epiplous: une institution du droit maritime grec." *Symposion 1985*: 425–44.

Gofas, D. 1993. Μελέτες ἱστορίας τοῦ ἑλληνικοῦ Δικαίου τῶν συναλλαγῶν. Athens.

Goldhill, Simon. 1990. "The Great Dionysia and Civic Ideology." In Winkler and Zeitlin 1990: 97–129.

Goldhill, Simon. 1991. *The Poet's Voice*. Cambridge.

Goldhill, Simon. 1994. "Representing Democracy: Women at the Great Dionysia." In *Ritual, Finance, Politics: Athenian Democratic Accounts Presented to David Lewis*, eds. Robin Osborne and Simon Hornblower. Oxford: 347–69.

Goldhill, Simon. 2000. "Greek Drama and Political Theory." In Rowe and Schofield 2000: 60–88.

Gomme, A. W. 1962. *More Essays in Greek History and Literature*. Oxford.

Gomme, A. W., and F. H. Sandbach. 1973. *Menander: A Commentary*. Oxford.

Green, T. A. 1985. *Verdict According to Conscience: Perspectives on the English Criminal Trial Jury, 1200–1800*. Chicago.

Grenier, J.-Y. 1997. "Économie de surplus, économie du circuit. Les prix and les échanges dans l'antiquité gréco-romaine et dans l'ancien régime." In *Prix et formation des prix dans les économies antiques*, eds. J. Andreau, P. Briant, and R. Descat, *Entretiens d'archéologie et d'histoire*. Saint-Bertrand-de-Comminges: 385–404.

Griffith, R. D. 1993. "Oedipus Pharmakos? Alleged Scapegoating in Sophocles' *Oedipus the King*." *Phoenix* 47: 95–114.

Guarducci, Margherita. 1946. "Tripodi, lebeti, oboli." *Rivista di filologia e di istruzione classica* 72–73: 171–80.

Guarducci, Margherita, ed. 1950. *Inscriptiones Creticae*, IV. Rome.

Guizzi, F. 1997. "Terra commune, pascolo e contributi al 'sussitia' in Creta arcaica e classica." *Aion Arch.²* 4: 45–51.

Guthrie, W. K. C. 1962. *A History of Greek Philosophy, Vol. 1. The Earlier Presocratics and Pythagoreans*. Cambridge.

Guthrie, W. K. C. 1969. *A History of Greek Philosophy. Vol. 3. The Fifth-Century Enlightenment*. Cambridge.

Habermann, W. 1998. "Zur chronologischen Verteilung der papyrologischen Zeugnisse." *Zeitschrift für Papyrologie und Epigraphik* 122: 144–60.

Häge, Günther. 1968. *Ehegüterrechtliche Verhältnisse in den griechischen Papyri Aegyptens bis Diokletian*. Köln/Graz.

Hall, Edith. 1995. "Lawcourt Dramas: The Power of Performance in Greek Forensic Oratory." *Bulletin of the Institute of Classical Studies* 40: 39–58.

Halliwell, S. 1991. "Comic Satire and Freedom of Speech in Classical Athens." *Journal of Hellenic Studies* 111: 48–70.

Hamel, Debra. 2003. *Trying Neaira: The True Story of a Courtesan's Scandalous Life in Ancient Greece*. New Haven.

Hamilton, R. 1992. *Choes and Anthesteria: Iconography and Ritual*. Ann Arbor.

Hansen, Mogens H. 1975. *Eisangelia: The Sovereignty of the People's Court in Athens in the Fourth Century B. C. and the Impeachment of Generals and Politicians*. Odense.

Hansen, Mogens H. 1976. *Apagoge, Endeixis and Ephegesis against Kakourgoi, Atimoi and Pheugontes: A Study in the Athenian Administration of Justice in the Fourth Century BC*. Odense.

Hansen, Mogens H. 1983. "Two Notes on the Athenian *dikai emporikai*." *Symposion 1979*: 167–75.

Hansen, Mogens H. 1989. "Solonian Democracy in Fourth-Century Athens." *Classica et Mediaevalia* 40: 71–99.

Hansen, Mogens H. 1990a. "Diokles' law (Dem. 24.42) and the Revision of the Athenian Corpus of Laws in the Archonship of Eukleides." *Classica et Mediaevalia* 41: 63–71.

Hansen, Mogens H. 1990b. "The Political Powers of the People's Court in Fourth-Century Athens." In *The Greek City from Homer to Alexander*, eds. O. Murray and S. Price. Oxford: 207–26.

Hansen, Mogens H. 1991. *The Athenian Democracy in the Age of Demosthenes*. Oxford.

Hansen, Mogens H. 1994. "*Poleis* and City-States, 600–323 B.C.: A Comprehensive Research Programme." In *From Political Architecture to Stephanus Byzantius*, ed. D. Whitehead. Historia Einzelschriften, 87. Stuttgart: 9–17.

Hansen, Mogens H. ed. 1996. *Introduction to an Inventory of Poleis. Symposium August 23–26 1995*. CPCActs 3. Copenhagen.

Hansen, M. V. 1984. "Athenian Maritime Trade in the 4th Century B.C.: Operation and Finance." *Classica et Mediaevalia* 35: 71–92.

Hardcastle, M. 1980. "Some Non-legal Arguments in Athenian Inheritance Cases." *Prudentia* 12: 11–22.

Harris, Edward M. 1988. "When Is a Sale Not a Sale? The Riddle of Athenian Terminology for Real Security Revisited." *Classical Quarterly* 38: 351–81.

Harris, Edward M. 1990. "Did the Athenians Regard Seduction as a Worse Crime Than Rape?" *Classical Quarterly* 40: 370–7.

Harris, Edward M. 1994. "Law and Oratory." In *Persuasion: Greek Rhetoric in Action*, ed. I. Worthington. London: 130–50.

Harris, Edward M. 1995. *Aeschines and Athenian Politics*. Oxford.

Harris, Edward M. 1999a. "Notes on the New Grain-Tax Law." *Zeitschrift für Papyrologie und Epigraphik* 128: 269–72.

Harris, Edward M. 1999b. "The Penalty for Frivolous Prosecutions in Athenian Law." *Dike* 2: 123–42.

Harris, Edward M. 2000. "Open Texture in Athenian Law." *Dike* 3: 27–79.

Harris, William V. 1989. *Ancient Literacy*. Cambridge, MA.

Harris, William V. 2001. *Restraining Rage*. Cambridge, MA.

Harrison, A. R. W. 1968. *The Law of Athens, I, The Family and Property*. Oxford.

Harrison, A. R. W. 1971. *The Law of Athens, II, Procedure*. Oxford.

Hart, H. L. A. 1958. "Positivism and the Separation of Law and Morals." *Harvard Law Review* 71: 593–606.
Hart, H. L. A. 1968. *Punishment and Responsibility*. Oxford.
Harvey, F. 1966. "Literacy in the Athenian Democracy." *Revue des études grecques* 79: 585–635.
Hastie, R., S. D. Penrod, and N. Pennington, eds. 1983. *Inside the Jury*. Cambridge.
Hatzopoulos, M. B. 1994. *Cultes et rites de passage en Macédoine*. Athens.
Headlam, J. W. 1892–1893. "The Procedure of the Gortynian Inscription." *Journal of Hellenic Studies* 13: 48–69.
Henderson, J. 1990. "The *dēmos* and the Comic Competition." In Winkler and Zeitlin 1990: 271–313.
Henderson, J. 1991. *The Maculate Muse: Obscene Language in Attic Comedy*. Oxford.
Henderson, J. 1998. "Attic Old Comedy, Frank Speech, and Democracy." In Boedeker and Raaflaub 1998: 255–73.
Herman, Gabriel. 1993. "Tribal and Civic Codes of Behaviour in Lysias 1." *Classical Quarterly* 43: 406–19.
Herman, Gabriel. 1994. "How Violent was Athenian Society?" In *Ritual, Finance, Politics: Athenian Democratic Accounts Presented to David Lewis*, eds. R. Osborne and S. Hornblower. Oxford: 99–117.
Herman, Gabriel. 1995. "Honour, Revenge, and the State in Fourth-Century Athens." In *Die athenische Demokratie im 4. Jahrhundert v. Chr*, ed. Walter Eder. Stuttgart, 43–66.
Herman, Gabriel. 1996. "Ancient Athens and the Values of Mediterranean Society." *Mediterranean Historical Review* 11: 5–36.
Herrmann, P. 1981. "Teos und Abdera im 5. Jahrhundert v. Chr." *Chiron* 11: 1–30.
Hillgruber, Michael. 1988. *Die zehnte Rede des Lysias. Einleitung, Text und Kommentar mit einem Anhang über die Gesetzesinterpretationen bei den attischen Rednern*. Berlin.
Hoebel, E. A. 1954. *The Law of Primitive Man*. Cambridge, MA.
Hoffmann, G. 1990. *Le châtiment des amants dans la Grèce classique*. Paris.
Hölkeskamp, Karl-Joachim. 1992. "Written Law in Archaic Greece." *Proceedings of the Cambridge Philological Society* 38: 87–117.
Hölkeskamp, Karl-Joachim. 1994. "Tempel, Agora und Alphabet. Die Entstehungsbedingungen von Gesetzgebung in der archaischen polis." In Gehrke 1994: 135–64.
Hölkeskamp, Karl-Joachim. 1999. *Schiedsrichter, Gesetzgeber und Gesetzgebung im archaischen Griechenland. Historia Einzelschrift* 131. Stuttgart.
Hölkeskamp, Karl-Joachim. 2000. "(In-)Schrift und Monument. Zum Begriff des Gesetzes im archaischen und klassischen Griechenland." *Zeitschrift für Papyrologie und Epigraphik* 132: 73–96.
Hopkins, K., and P. J. Roscoe. 1978. "Between Slavery and Freedom: On Freeing Slaves at Delphi." In *Conquerors and Slaves*, ed. K. Hopkins. Cambridge: 133–71.
Hopper, R. 1979. *Trade and Industry in Classical Greece*. London.
Horwitz, Morton J. 1977. *The Transformation of American Law 1780–1860*. Cambridge, MA.
Humphreys, S. C. 1974. "The Nothoi of Kynosarges." *Journal of Hellenic Studies* 94: 88–95.
Humphreys, S. C. 1983. "The Evolution of Legal Process in Ancient Attica." In *Tria Corda. Studi in onore di Arnaldo Momigliano*, ed. E. Gabba. Como: 229–56.

Humphreys, S. C. 1985. "Social Relations on Stage: Witnesses in Classical Athens." In *The Discourse of Law*, ed. S. Humphreys. (= *History and Anthoropology* 1.2): 313–69.

Humphreys, S. C. 1988. "The Discourse of Law in Archaic and Classical Greece." *Law and History Review* 6: 465–93.

Hunter, Virginia J. 1994. *Policing Athens: Social Control in the Attic Lawsuits, 420–320 B.C.* Princeton.

Hunter, Virginia J. 1997. "The Prison of Athens: A Comparative Perspective." *Phoenix* 51: 296–326.

Inwood, B. 1987. "Commentary on Striker." *Proceedings of the Boston Area Colloquium in Ancient Philosophy* 2: 95–102.

Inwood, B. 2003. "Natural Law in Seneca." *Studia Philonica* 15: 81–99.

IPArk = G. Thür/H. Taeuber. 1994. *Prozeßrechtliche Inschriften der griechischen Poleis: Arkadien*. Vienna.

Isager, S., and M. Hansen. 1975. *Aspects of Athenian Society in the Fourth Century B.C.* Odense.

IvKnidos I = W. Blümel. 1992. *Die Inschriften von Knidos* I (= Inschriften griechischer Städte aus Kleinasien 41). Bonn.

Jacoby, F. 1949. *Atthis*. Oxford.

Jakab, Eva. 1989. "Zwei Kaufvorschriften im Recht von Gortyn." *Zeitschrift der Savigny-Stiftung* 106: 535–44.

Jameson, M. 1997. "Women and Democracy in Fourth-Century Athens." In Brulé and Ouhlen 1997: 95–107.

Janko, R. 2001. "The Derveni Papyrus (Diagoras of Melos, *Apopyrgizontes Logoi?*): A New Translation." *Classical Philology* 96: 1–32.

Jebb, R. C. 1893. *The Attic Orators from Antiphon to Isaeus*, 2nd ed. London.

Jeffery, L. H. 1990. *The Local Scripts of Archaic Greece*, revised ed. by A. Johnston. Oxford.

Jeffery, L. H., and A. Morpurgo-Davies. 1970. "Poinikastas and poinikazein: BM 1969. 4–2.1, A New Archaic Inscription from Crete." *Kadmos* 9: 118–54.

Johnston D. 2000. "The Jurists." In Rowe and Schofield 2000: 616–34.

Johnstone, S. 1999. *Disputes and Democracy: The Consequences of Litigation in Ancient Athens*. Austin.

Jones, J. Walter. 1956. *The Law and Legal Theory of the Greeks*. Oxford.

Just, R. 1989. *Women in Athenian Law and Life*. London.

Kahn, C. H. 1979. *The Art and Thought of Heraclitus*. Cambridge.

Kahn, C. H. 1993. "Foreword." In Morrow 1993: xvii–xxxi.

Kapparis, K. 1999. *Apollodoros "Against Neaira."* Berlin.

Karabélias, Evanghélos. 1982. "La situation successorale de la fille unique dans la koinè juridique hellénistique." *Symposion 1977*: 223–34.

Karabélias, Evanghélos. 1990. "Le roman de Chariton d'Aphrodisias et le droit. Renversements de situations et exploitation des ambiguïtés juridiques." *Symposion 1988*: 369–96.

Kaser, M. 1944. "Der altgriechische Eigentumsschutz." *Zeitschrift der Savigny-Stiftung* 64: 134–205.

Kennedy, George. 1963. *The Art of Persuasion in Greece*. Princeton.

Kerferd, G. B. 1981. *The Sophistic Movement*. Cambridge.

Knorringa, H. [1926.] 1987. *Emporos: Data on Trade and Trader in Greek Literature from Homer to Aristotle*. Amsterdam.

Knox, B. M. W. 1957. *Oedipus at Thebes*. New York.
Koerner, Reinhard. 1993. *Inschriftliche Gesetzestexte der frühen griechischen Polis*. Cologne.
Kohler, J. and E. Ziebarth. 1912. *Das Stadtrecht von Gortyn und seine Beziehungen zum gemeingriechischen Rechte*. Göttingen.
Konstan, David. 2000. "Pity and the Law in Greek Theory and Practice." *Dike* 3: 125–45.
Kontorovich, E. forthcoming. "Law and Social Cohesion in Democratic Athens."
Korver, J. 1934. *De Terminologie van het Crediet-wezen in het Grieksch*. Amsterdam.
de Koutorga, M. 1859. *Essai sur les trapezites ou banquiers d'Athènes*. Paris.
Kränzlein, A. 1963. *Eigentum und Besitz im griechischen Recht des fünften und vierten Jahrhunderts v. Chr*. Berlin.
Kraut, R. 1984. *Socrates and the State*. Princeton.
Kristensen, K. R. 1994. "Men, Women, and Property in Gortyn: The *karteros* of the Law Code." *Classica et Mediaevalia* 45: 5–26.
Lafont, Sophie. 2000. "Codification et subsidiarité dans les droits du Proche-Orient ancien." In Lévy. 2000a: 49–64.
Lambert, S. D. 2002. "Review of I. Worthington, C. Cooper and E. M. Harris, *Dinarchus, Hyperides and Lycurgus*: Translation with Introductions and Notes." *Bryn Mawr Classical Review* 2002.05.24. (http://ccat.sas.upenn.edu/bmcr/2002/2002-05-24.html)
Lämmli, F. 1938. *Das attische Prozeßverfahren in seiner Wirkung auf die Gerichtsrede*. Paderborn.
Langdon, Merle K. 1991. "Poletai Records." In *The Athenian Agora* XIX. Princeton.
Lanni, A. M. 1997. "Spectator Sport or Serious Politics? οἱ περιεστηκότες and the Athenian Lawcourts." *Journal of Hellenic Studies* 117: 183–9.
Lanza, D., and M. Vegetti. 1977. "L'ideologia della città." In *L'ideologia della città*, eds. D. Lanza, M. Vegetti, G. Caiani, and F. Sircana. Naples: 13–28.
Larsen, J. A. O. 1947. "The Origin and Significance of the Counting of Votes." *Classical Philology* 44: 164–81.
Latte, Kurt. 1920. *Heiliges Recht: Untersuchungen zur Geschichte der sakralen Rechtsformen in Griechenland*. Tübingen.
Latte, Kurt. 1930. "Martyria," *Real-Encyclopädie* 14.2: 2032–9.
Latte, Kurt. 1948. "Kollektivbesitz und Staatsschatz in Griechenland." *Nachricht. Ak. Wiss. Göttingen* 1945/1948, phil.-hist. Klasse 1946/47, 64–75; reprinted in *Kleine Schriften*: 294–312.
Lavency, M. 1964. *Aspects de la logographie judiciare attique*. Louvain.
Lavrencic, M. 1988. "Andreion." *Tyche* 3: 147–61.
Lawless, J. M. 1991. *Law, Argument, and Equity in the Speeches of Isaeus*. Ph.D. dissertation, Brown University.
Leduc, C. 1991. "Comment la donner en marriage?" In *Histoire des femmes en Occident I: L' antiquité*, ed. P. Schmitt-Pantel. Paris: 259–316 and 535–9.
Leisi, E. 1908. *Der Zeuge im attischen Recht*. Frauenfeld.
Lemosse, M. 1957. "Les lois de Gortyne et la notion de codification." *Revue internationale des droits de l'antiquité* 4: 131–7.
Lempert, R. 1991. "Telling Tales in Court: Trial Procedure and the Story Model." *Cardozo Law Review* 13: 559–73.
Lévy, Edmond. 1997. "Libres et non-libres dans le Code de Gortyne." In Brulé and Oulhen 1997: 25–41.

Lévy, Edmond, ed. 2000a. *La codification des lois dans l'antiquité. Actes du colloque de Strasbourg, 27–29 Novembre 1997*. Strasbourg.
Lévy, Edmond. 2000b. "La cohérence du code de Gortyne." In Lévy 2000a: 185–214.
Lewis, D. M. 1959. "Attic Manumissions." *Hesperia* 28: 208–38.
Lewis, N. 1982. "Aphairesis in Athenian Law and Custom." *Symposion* 1977: 161–78.
Link, Stefan. 1991. *Landverteilung und sozialer Frieden im archaischen Griechenland*. Stuttgart.
Link, Stefan. 1994a. "Die Ehefrau als Erbtochter im Recht von Gortyn." *Zeitschrift der Savigny-Stiftung* 111: 414–20.
Link, Stefan. 1994b. *Das griechische Kreta. Untersuchungen zu seiner staatlichen und gesellschaftlichen Entwicklung vom 6. bis zum 4. Jahrhundert v. Chr*. Stuttgart.
Link, Stefan. 1997. "Versprochene Töchter? Noch einmal zur Ehefrau als Erbtochter im Gesetz von Gortyn." *Zeitschrift der Savigny-Stiftung* 114: 378–91.
Link, Stefan. 1998. "Die vermögensrechtliche Stellung der Frau nach dem grossen Gesetz von Gortyn." *Zeitschrift der Savigny-Stiftung* 115: 214–34.
Link, Stefan. 2001. "'Dolos' und 'Woikeus' im Recht von Gortyn." *In Dike* 4: 87–112.
Lipsius, J. H. 1905–1915. *Das attische Recht und Rechtsverfahren*. Leipzig.
Lloyd, Geoffrey E. R. 1966. *Polarity and Analogy: Two Types of Argumentation in Early Greek Thought*. Cambridge.
Lloyd, Geoffrey E. R. 1979. *Magic, Reason and Experience: Studies in the Origin and Development of Greek Science*. Cambridge.
Lloyd, Geoffrey E. R. 1987. *The Revolutions of Wisdom: Studies in the Claims and Practice of Ancient Greek Science*. Berkeley/Los Angeles/London.
Lloyd-Jones, H. 1971. *The Justice of Zeus*. Berkeley.
Long, A. A., ed. 1971. *Problems in Stoicism*. London.
Long, A. A. 1977. "Chance and Natural Law in Epicureanism." *Phronesis* 22: 63–88.
Long, A. A. 1996. "The Socratic Tradition: Diogenes, Crates, and Hellenistic Ethics." In Branham and Goulet-Cazé 1996: 28–46.
Long, A. A., and D. N. Sedley. 1987. *The Hellenistic Philosophers*. Cambridge.
Lopez, G. P. 1984. "Lay Lawyering," *U.C.L.A. Law Review* 32: 1–60.
Lotze, D. 1959. Μεταξὺ ἐλευθέρων καὶ δούλων. *Studien zur Rechtsstellung unfreier Landbevölkerungen in Griechenland bis zum 4. Jahrhundert v. Chr*. Berlin.
LS = Long and Sedley 1987.
MacDowell, D. M. 1963. *Athenian Homicide Law in the Age of the Orators*. Manchester.
MacDowell, D. M. 1976a. "Hybris in Athens." *Greece and Rome* 23: 14–31.
MacDowell, D. M. 1976b. "Review of E. Cohen 1973." *Classical Review* 26: 84–5.
MacDowell, D. M. 1978. *The Law in Classical Athens*. London.
MacDowell, D. M. 1986. *Spartan Law*. Edinburgh.
MacDowell, D. M., ed. 1990. *Demosthenes Against Meidias*. Oxford.
MacDowell, D. M. 1994. *Aristophanes and Athens*. Oxford.
MacDowell, D. M., ed. 2000a. *Demosthenes, On the False Embassy (Oration 19)*. Oxford.
MacDowell, D. M. 2000b. "The Length of Trials for Public Offences in Athens." In Flensted-Jensen et al. 2000: 563–8.
Macedo, S. 1999. *Deliberative Politics: Essays on Democracy and Disagreement*. New York/Oxford.
Mackenzie, M. M. 1981. *Plato on Punishment*. Berkeley.
Maffi, Alberto. 1983. *Studi di epigrafia giuridica greca*. Milan.

Maffi, Alberto. 1987. "Le marriage de la patrôoque 'donnée' dans le Code de Gortyne." *Revue historique de droit français et étranger* 65: 507–25.
Maffi, Alberto. 1991. "Adozione e strategie successorie a Gortina e ad Atene." *Symposion* 1990: 205–32.
Maffi, Alberto. 1995. "Encore une fois le marriage de la patrôoque 'donnée' dans le Code de Gortyne." *Revue historique de droit français et étranger* 73: 221–6.
Maffi, Alberto. 1997a. *Il diritto di famiglia nel Codice di Gortina*. Milan.
Maffi, Alberto. 1997b. "Nomima: droit et épigraphie dans la Grèce archaïque (à propos d'un ouvrage récent)". *Revue historique de droit français et étranger* 75: 435–46.
Maffi, Alberto. 2003. "Giudice e mezzi di prova nel diritto di Gortina." Web publication: http://www.ledonline.it/rivistadirittoromano/attipontignano.html.
Maine, H. S. 1861. *Ancient Law*. London.
Maine, H. S. 1883. *Dissertation on Early Law and Customs*. London.
Malinine, Michel. 1965. "Partage testamentaire d'une propriété familiale." In *Nachrichten d. Akad. d. Wiss. Göttingen, philol.-hist. Klasse*, no. 4, 97–101.
Mandalaki, A. 2000. "O 'klaros' sti megali dodekadelto epigrafi tis Gortynos." *Tekmeria* 5: 71–85.
Manning, J. G. 2003. "Demotic Law." In Westbrook 2003: 2.819–62.
Manville, Brook. 1990. *The Origins of Citizenship in Ancient Athens*. Princeton.
Martini, R. 1998. "La terra a Gortina." *Dike* 1: 87–94.
Marzi, M. 1977. "Iperide." In *Oratori Attici Minori I: Iperide, Eschine, Licurgo*, eds. M. Marzi, P. Leone, and E. Malcovati. Turin: 7–328.
Mattha-Hughes, P. 1975. *The Demotic Legal Code of Hermopolis*. Inst. Franc. d'Archeol. Orientale du Caire, Bibl. d'Etudes XLV, Cairo. (New, more clearly arranged edition: Donker van Heel 1990.)
Meier, C. 1988. *Die politische Kunst der griechischen Tragoedie*. Munich.
Meier, C. 1990. *The Greek Discovery of Politics*. Cambridge, MA.
Meiggs, Russell, and David Lewis. 1969. *A Selection of Greek Historical Inscriptions*. Oxford.
Meinecke, J. 1971. "Gesetzesinterpretation und Gesetzesanwendung im Attischen Zivilprozess." *Revue internationale des droits de l'antiquité* 18: 275–360.
Meineke, A. 1839. *Fragmenta Comicorum Atticorum*. Berlin.
Meister, R. M. E. 1908. "Eideshelfer im griechischen Rechte." *Rheinisches Museum*. 63: 559–86.
Metzger, R. R. 1973. *Untersuchungen zum Haftungs- und Vermögensrecht von Gortyn*. Schweizerische Beiträge zur Altertumswissenschaft, Vol. 13. Basel.
Meyer-Laurin, H. 1965. *Gesetz und Billigkeit im attischen Prozeß*. Gräzistische Abhandlungen, vol. 1. Weimar.
Meyer-Laurin, H. 1969. "Review of Willetts 1967." *Gnomon* 41: 160–9.
Michaels, W. B. 1979. "Against Formalism: The Autonomous Text in Legal and Literary Interpretation." *Poetics Today* 1: 23–34.
Migeotte, L. 2002. *L'économie des cités grecques*. Paris.
Millett, Paul C. 1990. "Sale, Credit and Exchange in Athenian Law and Society." In Cartledge, Millett, and Todd 1990: 167–94.
Millett, Paul C. 1991. *Lending and Borrowing in Ancient Athens*. Cambridge.
Millett, Paul C. 2000. "Mogens Hansen and the Labelling of Athenian Democracy." In Flensted-Jensen et al. 2000: 337–62.

Mirhady, David C. 1990. "Aristotle on the Rhetoric of the Law." *Greek, Roman and Byzantine Studies* 31: 393–410.
Mirhady, David C. 1991a. "Non-technical *Pisteis* in Aristotle and Anaximenes." *American Journal of Philology* 112: 5–28.
Mirhady, David C. 1991b. "The Oath-Challenge in Athens." *Classical Quarterly* 41: 78–83.
Mirhady, David C. 1996. "Torture and Rhetoric in Athens." *Journal of Hellenic Studies* 116: 119–31.
Mirhady, David C. 2002. "Athens' Democratic Witnesses." *Phoenix* 56: 255–74.
Mitteis, Ludwig. 1891. *Reichsrecht und Volksrecht in den östlichen Provinzen des römischen Kaiserreichs: Mit Beitragen zur Kenntniss des griechischen Rechts und der spätrömischen Rechtsentwicklung.* Leipzig.
Modrzejewski, Joseph Mélèze. 1961. "La dévolution à l'État des successions en déshérence dans le droit hellénistique." In *Revue internationale des droits de l'antiquité* 8: 79–113. = *Statut personnel et liens de famille*, Aldershot, 1993, n° IX.
Modrzejewski, Joseph Mélèze. 1971. "La dévolution à l'État des biens vacants d'après le Gnomon de l'Idiologue (BGU 1210 § 4)." In *Studi in onore di E. Volterra* VI, Milan: 91–125 = *Droit impérial et traditions locales*, Aldershot, 1990, n° IV.
Modrzejewski, Joseph Mélèze. 1983. "La structure juridique du mariage grec." *Symposion 1979*: 37–71.
Modrzejewski, Joseph Mélèze. 1984. "Dryton le Crétois et sa famille ou les mariages mixtes dans l'Égypte hellénistique." In *Aux origines de l'hellénisme, la Crète et la Grèce. Mélanges Henri van Effenterre*, Paris: 353–77 = *Statut personnel et liens de famille*, Aldershot, 1993, n° VIII.
Modrzejewski, Joseph Mélèze. 1988. " 'La loi des Égyptiens': le droit grec dans l'Égypte romaine." In *Proceedings of the XVIII International Congress of Papyrology (Athens, 25–31 May 1986)*, Athens: 383–99 and *"Historia Testis." Mélanges T. Zawadzki*, Fribourg, 1989: 97–115 = *Droit impérial et traditions locales*, Aldershot, 1990, n° IX.
Modrzejewski, Joseph Mélèze. 1993. "Diritto romano e diritti locali." In *Storia di Roma* dir. A. Schiavone, III/2, Torino: 985–1009.
Modrzejewski, Joseph Mélèze. 1995. "Law and Justice in Ptolemaic Egypt." In *Legal Documents of the Hellenistic World: Papers from a Seminar*, eds. M. J. Geller, H. Maehler, and A. D. E. Lewis. London: 1–11.
Modrzejewski, Joseph Mélèze. 1996. "Jewish Law and Hellenistic Legal Practice in the Light of Greek Papyri from Egypt." In *An Introduction to the History and Sources of Jewish Law*. Oxford: 75–99.
Modrzejewski, Joseph Mélèze. 1997. "La Septante comme nomos. Comment la Tora est devenue une "loi civique" pour les Juifs d'Égypte." In *Annali di scienze religiose* 2: 143–58; English version: "The Septuagint as Nomos: How the Torah Became a "Civic Law" for the Jews of Egypt." In *Critical Studies in Ancient Law, Comparative Law and Legal History. Essays in Honour of Alan Watson*, eds. John Cairns and Olivia Robinson. Oxford: 183–99.
Modrzejewski, Joseph Mélèze. 1998a. " 'Paroles néfastes' et 'vers obscènes.' À propos de l'injure verbale en droit grec et hellénistique." In *Anthropologies juridiques. Mélanges Pierre Braun*, eds. J. Hoareau-Dodinau and P. Texier. Limoges: 569–85 and *Dike* 1: 151–69.

Modrzejewski, Joseph Mélèze. 1998b. "Le forme del diritto ellenistico." In *I Greci. Storia, cultura, arte, società* 2.III: *Una storia greca, Trasformazioni*, ed. Salvatore Settis. Torino: 636–64.
Modrzejewski, Joseph Mélèze. 1999. "Le droit hellénistique et la famille grecque." In *Nonagesimo anno. Mélanges en hommage à Jean Gaudemet*, ed. Claude Bontems. Paris: 261–80.
Modrzejewski, Joseph Mélèze. 2000. "What is Hellenistic Law? The Documents of the Judean Desert in the Light of the Papyri from Egypt." *The Qumran Chronicle* 9.1. Cracow: 1–16.
Montevecchi, O. 1982. *La papirologia*, 2nd ed. Milano.
Moore, M. 1997. *Placing Blame: A General Theory of the Criminal Law*. Oxford.
Morris, Herbert. 1968. "Persons and Punishment." *The Monist* 52: 475–501.
Morris, Herbert. 1981. "A Paternalistic Theory of Punishment." *American Philosophical Quarterly* 18: 263–71.
Morris, Ian. 1987. *Burial and Ancient Society: The Rise of the Greek City-State*. Cambridge.
Morris, Ian. 1990. "The Gortyn Code and Greek Kinship." *Greek, Roman and Byzantine Studies* 31: 233–54.
Morris, Ian. 1999. "Gender Relations in the Classical Greek Household: The Archaeological Evidence." *Annual of the British School at Athens* 90: 363–81.
Morrow, G. R. 1960. *Plato's Cretan City: A Historical Interpretation of the Laws*. Princeton.
Morrow, G. R. 1993. *Plato's Cretan City: A Historical Interpretation of the Laws*, 2nd ed. Princeton.
Mossé, C. 1996. *Les institutions grecques*. Paris.
Murray, A. 1978. *Reason and Society in the Middle Ages*. Oxford.
Musti, D. et al., eds. 1991. *La transizione dal miceneo all'alto arcaismo. Dal palazzo alla città. Atti del convegno internazionale, Roma 14–19 Marzo 1988*. Roma.
Nelson, D. 2002. *Pursuing Privacy in Cold War America*. New York.
Nesselrath, H.-G. 1997. "The Polis of Athens in Middle Comedy." In Dobrov 1997: 271–88.
Nevett, L. 1994. "Separation or Seclusion? Toward an Archaeological Approach to Investigating Women in the Greek Household in the Fifth to Third Century B.C.E." In *Architecture and Order: Approaches to Social Spaces*, eds. M. Parker Pearson and C. Richards. London: 98–112.
Nevett, L. 1999. *House and Society in the Ancient Greek World*. Cambridge.
Nielsen, T. H., ed. 2002. *Even More Studies in the Ancient Greek Polis: CPC Papers 6*. Stuttgart.
Nightingale, A. 1999. "Plato's Lawcode in Context: Rule by Written Law in Athens and Magnesia." *Classical Quarterly* 49: 100–22.
Nomima. See van Effenterre and Ruzé 1994.
Nussbaum, M. 1995. *Poetic Justice: The Literary Imagination and Public Life*. Boston.
Oates, J. F. et al. 2001. *Checklist of Editions of Greek, Latin, Demotic, and Coptic Papyri, Ostraca, and Tablets*, 5th ed. Oakville, CT.
O'Barr, W. M., and J. M. Conley. 1985. "Litigant Satisfaction vs. Legal Adequacy in Small Claims Court Narratives." *Law and Society Review* 19: 661–701.
Ober, J. 1989. *Mass and Elite in Democratic Athens: Rhetoric, Ideology, and the Power of the People*. Princeton.
Ober, J. 1998. *Political Dissent in Democratic Athens: Intellectual Critics of Popular Rule*. Princeton.

Ober, J. 2000a. "Living Freely as a Slave of the Law: Notes on Why Socrates Lives in Athens." In Flensted-Jensen et al. 2000: 541–52.
Ober, J. 2000b. "Quasi-Rights: Political Boundaries and Social Diversity in Democratic Athens." *Social Philosophy and Policy* 17: 27–61.
Ober, J., and B. Strauss. 1990. "Drama, Political Rhetoric, and the Discourse of Athenian Democracy." In Winkler and Zeitlin 1990: 237–70.
O'Brien, J. V. 1978. *Guide to Sophocles' Antigone*. Carbondale, IL.
Oelsner, J. 1995. "Recht im hellenistischen Babylonien: Tempel – Sklaven – Schuldrecht – allgemeine Charakterisierung." In *Legal Documents of the Hellenistic World*, ed. M.J. Geller, H. Maehler, and A. D. E. Lewis. London: 106–27.
Ogden, D. 1996. *Greek Bastardy in the Classical and Hellenistic Periods*.
Ogden, D. 1997. "Rape, Adultery and the Protection of Bloodlines in Classical Athens." In Deacy and Pierce 1997: 25–41.
Ogden, D. 1999. "Binding Spells: Curse Tablets and Voodoo Dolls in the Greek and Roman World." In *The Athlone History of Witchcraft and Magic in Europe. Vol. ii. Ancient Greece and Rome*. London: 1–90.
Omitowoju, R. 1997. "Regulating Rape: Soap Operas and Self-Interest in the Athenian Courts." In Deacy and Pierce 1997: 1–24.
Omitowoju, R. 2002. *Rape and the Politics of Consent in Classical Athens*. Cambridge.
Osborne, M. J. 1981–1983. *Naturalization in Athens*. Brussels.
Osborne, R. 1985. "Law in Action in Classical Athens." *Journal of Hellenic Studies* 105: 40–58.
Osborne, R. 1988. "Social and Economic Implications of the Leasing of Land and Property in Classical and Hellenistic Greece." *Chiron* 18: 279–323.
Osborne, R. 1990. "Vexatious Litigation in Classical Athens." In Cartledge, Millett and Todd 1990: 83–102.
Osborne, R. 1997. "Law and Laws: How Do We Join up the Dots?" In *The Development of the Polis in Archaic Greece*, eds. L. Mitchell and P. Rhodes. London: 74–82.
Osborne, R. 2000a. "Religion, Imperial Politics and the Offering of Freedom to Slaves." In *Law and Social Status in Classical Athens*, eds. V. Hunter and J. Edmondson. Oxford: 76–92.
Osborne, R. 2000b. "Review of Stroud 1998." *Classical Review* 50: 172–3.
Ostwald, Martin. 1969. *Nomos and the Beginnings of Athenian Democracy*. Oxford.
Ostwald, Martin. 1973. "Was There a Concept ἄγραφος νόμος in Classical Greece?" In *Exegesis and Argument: Studies in Greek Philosophy Presented to G. Vlastos*, eds. E. N. Lee, A. P. D. Mourelatos, and R. M. Rorty. *Phronesis* Suppl. 1: 70–104.
Ostwald, Martin. 1986. *From Popular Sovereignty to the Sovereignty of Law: Law, Society, and Politics in Fifth-Century Athens*. Berkeley.
Ostwald, Martin. 1996. "Shares and Rights: 'Citizenship' Greek Style and American Style." In *Demokratia*, eds. J. Ober and C. Hedrick. Princeton: 49–61.
Padel, R. 1992. *In and Out of the Mind: Greek Images of the Tragic Self*. Princeton.
Padel, R. 1995. *Whom Gods Destroy*. Princeton.
Panagos, C. 1968. *Le Pirée*. Athens.
Paoli, U. E. [1930]1974. *Studi di diritto attico*. Milan.
Paoli, U. E. 1935. "Sull' inscindibilità di processo nel diritto attico." *Rivista di diritto processuale civile* 12: 253 ff.
Parker, R. 1983. *Miasma. Pollution and Purification in Early Greek Religion*. Oxford.
Parker, R. 1996. *Athenian Religion: A History*. Oxford.

Parker, R. 2004. "What Are Sacred Laws?" In *The Law and the Courts in Ancient Greece*, eds. E. Harris and L. Rubinstein. London: 57–70.
Partsch, J. 1909. *Griechisches Bürgschaftsrecht I: Das Recht des altgriechischen Gemeindestaats.* Leipzig.
Patterson, C. 1981. *Pericles' Citizenship Law of 451/0 B.C.* New York.
Patterson, C. 1986. "*Hai Attikai*: The Other Athenians." *Helios* 13: 49–67.
Patterson, C. 1990. "Those Athenian Bastards." *Classical Antiquity* 9: 40–73.
Patterson, C. 1991. "Marriage and the Married Woman in Athenian Law." In Pomeroy 1991: 48–72.
Patterson, C. 1994. "The Case against Neaira and the Public Ideology of the Athenian Family." In Boegehold and Scafuro 1994: 199–216.
Perlman, Paula. 1992. "One-Hundred-Citied Crete and the Cretan Politeia." *Classical Philology* 87: 193–205.
Perlman, Paula. 1996. "Πόλις Ὑπήκοος: The Dependent *Polis* and Crete." In Hansen 1996: 233–87.
Perlman, Paula. 2000. "Gortyn: The First Seven Hundred Years. Part I." In Flensted-Jensen et al. 2000: 59–89.
Perlman, Paula. 2002. "Gortyn. The First Seven Hundred Years, Part II. The Laws from the Temple of Apollo Pythios." In Nielsen 2002: 187–227.
Pestman, Pieter W. 1974. "Hellenistic Law." In *Encyclopaedia Britannica*, 15th ed.: 746–8.
Pestman, Pieter W. 1985a. "Registration of Demotic Contracts in Egypt." In *Satura Roberto Feenstra*, ed. J. A. Ankum, J. E. Spruit, and F. B. J. Wibbe. Fribourg: 17–25.
Pestman, Pieter W. 1985b. "Ventes provisoires de biens pour sûreté de dettes: *onai en pistei* à Pathyris et à Krokodilopolis." *Papyrologica Lugduno–Batava* 23: 45–59.
Pestman, Pieter W. 1990. *The New Papyrological Primer*, 5th ed. Leiden.
Petsas, P. M., M. B. Hatzopoulos, L. Gounaropoulou, and P. Paschidis, eds. 2000. *Inscriptions du sanctuaire de la Mère des Dieux Autochthone de Leukopétra (Macédoine)*. Athens.
Petzl. G. 1994. *Die Beichtinschriften Westkleinasiens* (*Epigraphica Anatolica* 22).
Piccirilli, L. 1981. "'Nomoi' cantati e 'nomoi' scritti." *Civiltà classica e cristiana* 2: 7–14.
Podlecki, A. 1966. *The Political Background of Aeschylean Tragedy*. Ann Arbor.
Pomeroy, Sarah B., ed. 1991. *Women's History and Ancient History*. Chapel Hill.
Pomeroy, Sarah B. 2002. *Spartan Women*. New York.
Popper, K. 1966. *The Open Society and Its Enemies*. Princeton.
Posner, E. A. 2000. *Law and Social Norms*. Cambridge, MA.
Posner, R. 1988. *Law and Literature: A Misunderstood Relation*. Cambridge, MA.
Pringsheim, F. 1950. *The Greek Law of Sale*. Weimar.
Pringsheim, F. 1953. "Griechische Kauf-horoi." In *Festschrift Hans Lewald*. Basel: 143–60. (Reprinted in Pringsheim 1961, II: 382–400.)
Pringsheim, F. 1955. "The Transition from Witnessed to Written Transactions in Athens." In *Aequitas und Bona Fides: Festgabe für A. Simonius*. Basel: 287–97.
Pringsheim, F. 1961. *Gesammelte Abhandlungen*, 2 vols. Heidelberg.
Purpura, G. 1987. "Ricerche in tema di prestito marittimo." *Annali del Seminario Giuridico dell' Università di Palermo* 39: 189–337.
Quass, F. 1971. *Nomos und Psephisma*. Munich.
Raaflaub, Kurt. 2000. "Poets, Lawgivers, and the Beginnings of Political Reflection in Archaic Greece." In Rowe and Schofield 2000: 34–7, 39–42.

Radin, M. 1927. "Freedom of Speech in Ancient Athens." *American Journal of Philology* 48: 215–30.
Rhodes, P. J. 1981. *A Commentary on the Aristotelian Athenaion Politeia.* Oxford.
Rhodes, P. J. 2004. "Keeping to the Point." In *The Law and the Courts in Ancient Greece*, eds. E. M. Harris and L. Rubinstein. London: 137–59.
Ricl, M. 1995. "Les ΚΑΤΑΓΡΑΦΑΙ du sanctuaire d'Apollon Lairbenos." *Arkeoloji Dergisi* 3: 167–95.
Roberts, J. T. 1994. *Athens on Trial. The Anti-Democratic Tradition in Western Thought.* Princeton.
Robertson, N. 1990. "The Laws of Athens, 410–399 B.C.: The Evidence for Review and Publication." *Journal of Hellenic Studies* 110: 43–75.
Robertson, N. 1993. "Athens' Festival of the New Wine." *Harvard Studies in Classical Philology* 95: 197–250.
Robinson, E. W. 1997. *The First Democracies: Early Popular Government Outside Athens. Historia Einzelschriften,* 107. Stuttgart.
Robinson, E. W. 2003. "Review of Hölkeskamp (1999)." *Bryn Mawr Classical Review* 2003.04.16. (http://ccat.sas.upenn.edu/bmcr/2003/2003-04-16.html)
de Romilly, J. 1971. *La loi dans la pensée grecque, des origines à Aristote.* Paris.
Rommen, H. A. 1955. *The Natural Law: A Study in Legal and Social History and Philosophy.* St. Louis.
Rosén, Haiim B. 1982. "Questions d'interpretation de textes juridiques grecs de la plus ancienne époque." *Symposion 1977:* 9–32.
Roth, Martha T. 1995. *Law Collections from Mesopotamia and Asia Minor.* Atlanta.
Roth, Martha T. 2000. "The Law Collection of King Hammurabi: Toward an Understanding of Codification and Text." In Lévy 2000: 9–31.
Rowe, C., and M. Schofield, eds. 2000. *The Cambridge History of Greek and Roman Political Thought.* Cambridge.
Roy, J. 1991. "Traditional Jokes about the Punishment of Adulterers in Ancient Greek Literature." *Liverpool Classical Monthly* 16: 73–6.
Rubinstein, Lene. 2000. *Litigation and Cooperation: Supporting Speakers in the Courts of Classical Athens.* Stuttgart.
Rubinstein, Lene. 2005. "Main Litigants and Witnesses in the Athenian Courts: Procedural Variations." *Symposion* 2001: 99–120.
Rupprecht, H.-A. 1984. "Vertragliche Mischtypen in den Papyri." *Mneme Petropoulos II.* Athens: 271–83.
Rupprecht, H.-A. 1994. *Kleine Einführung in die Papyruskunde.* Darmstadt. (Italian trans.: *Introduzione alla Papirologia*, a cura di Livia Migliardi Zingale. Turin 2000.)
Rupprecht, H.-A. 1995. "Sechs-Zeugenurkunde und Registrierung." *Aegyptus* 75: 37–53.
Rupprecht, H.-A. 1997a. "Veräußerungsverbot und Gewährleistung in pfandrechtlichen Geschäften." *Akten XXI. Intern. Papyrologenkongreß,* Stuttgart/Leipzig II: 870–80.
Rupprecht, H.-A. 1997b. "Zwangsvollstreckung und dingliche Sicherung in den Papyri der ptolemäischen und römischen Zeit." *Symposion 1995:* 291–302.
Ruschenbusch, Eberhard. 1966. *Solonos Nomoi. Historia Einzelschriften* 9. Wiesbaden.
Ruschenbusch, Eberhard. 1978. *Untersuchungen zu Staat und Politik in Griechenland vom 7.-4. Jh. v. Chr.* Bamberg.
Ruschenbusch, Eberhard. 1983. "Die Polis und das Recht." *Symposion 1979:* 303–26.

Ruschenbusch, Eberhard. 1984. "Die Bevölkerungszahl Griechenlands im 5. und 4. Jh. v. Chr." *Zeitschrift für Papyrologie und Epigraphik* 56: 55–7.
Ruschenbusch, Eberhard. 1985. "Die Zahl der griechischen Staaten und Arealgrösse und Bürgerzahl der 'Normalpolis'." *Zeitschrift für Papyrologie und Epigraphik* 59: 253–63.
Ruzé, Françoise. 1988. "Aux débuts de l'écriture politique: le pouvoir de l'écrit dans la cité." In *Les savoirs de l'écriture en Grèce ancienne*, ed. M. Detienne. Lille: 82–94.
Ruzé, Françoise. 1997. *Délibération et pouvoir dans la cité grecque de Nestor à Socrate*. Paris.
Saunders, T., trans. 1951. *Plato: The Laws*. Middlesex: Penguin.
Saunders, T. 1991. *Plato's Penal Code: Tradition, Controversy, and Reform in Greek Penology*. Oxford.
Scafuro, Adele C. 1994. "Witnessing and False Witnessing: Proving Citizenship and Kin Identity in Fourth-Century Athens." In Boegehold and Scafuro 1994: 156–98.
Scafuro, Adele C. 1997. *The Forensic Stage: Settling Disputes in Graeco-Roman New Comedy*. Cambridge.
Scalia, Antonin. 1997. *A Matter of Interpretation: Federal Courts and the Law, An Essay*. Princeton.
Scarborough, J. 1991. "The Pharmacology of Sacred Plants, Herbs, and Roots." In *Magika Hiera*, eds. C. A. Faraone and D. Obbink. New York: 138–74.
Schaps, D. M. 1979. *Economic Rights of Women in Ancient Greece*. Edinburgh.
Scheyhing, R. 1971. "Eideshelfer." In *Handwörterbuch zur deutschen Rechtsgeschichte*, Vol. I. Berlin: 870–72.
Schodorf, K. 1904. *Beiträge zur genaueren Kentnis der attischen Gerichtssprache aus den Zehn Rednern*. Beiträge zur historischen Syntax der griechischen Sprache, vol. 17. Würzburg.
Schuhl, P. 1953. "Adêla." *Annales publiées par la Faculté des Lettres de Toulouse, Homo: Études philosophiques*, I (May): 86–93.
Scodel, Ruth, ed. 1993. *Theater and Society in the Classical World*. Ann Arbor.
Seager, R. 1966. "Lysias and the Corn-dealers." *Historia* 15: 172–84.
Sealey, Raphael. 1987. *The Athenian Republic: Democracy or the Rule of Law?* London.
Sealey, Raphael. 1990. *Women and Law in Classical Greece*. Chapel Hill.
Sealey, Raphael. 1994. *The Justice of the Greeks*. Ann Arbor.
Segal, C. 1981. *Tragedy and Civilization: An Interpretation of Sophocles*. Cambridge MA.
Seidl, Erwin. 1965. "La preminènte posizione successoria del figlio maggiore nel diritto dei papyri." *Rendiconti dell'Istituto Lombardo, Classe di Lettere* 99: 185–92.
Seidl, Erwin. 1969. *Der Eid im ptolemäischen Recht*. Munich.
Shaw, M. H. 1982. "The ἦθος of Theseus in 'The Suppliant Women.'" *Hermes* 110: 3–19.
Shipp, G. 1978. *Nomos "Law."* Sydney.
Sickinger, J. P. 1999. *Public Records and Archives in Classical Athens*. Chapel Hill.
Smith, R. M. 1995. "A New Look at the Canon of the Ten Attic Orators." *Mnemosyne* 48: 66–79.
Sokolowski, F. 1955. *Lois sacrées de l'Asie Mineure*. Paris.
Sokolowski, F. 1962. *Lois sacrées des cités grecques, supplément*. Paris.
Sokolowski, F. 1969. *Lois sacrées des cités grecques*. Paris.
Sommerstein, A. 1986. "The Decree of Syracosios." *Classical Quarterly* 36: 101–8.
Sourvinou-Inwood, C. 1990. "What Is Polis Religion?" In *The Greek City*, eds. O. Murray and S. Price. Oxford: 295–322. (Reprinted in *Oxford Readings in Greek Religion*, ed. R. Buxton, Oxford, 2000, 13–37).

Starkie, W. J. M. 1909. *The Acharnians of Aristophanes.* London.
de Ste. Croix, G. E. M. 1972. *Origins of the Peloponnesian War.* London.
de Ste. Croix, G. E. M. 1974. "Ancient Greek and Roman Maritime Loans." In *Debits, Credits, Finance and Profits: Essays in Honour of W. T. Baxter*, eds. H. Edey and B. Yamey. London: 41–59.
Steiner, D. T. 1994. *The Tyrant's Writ: Myths and Images of Writing in Ancient Greece.* Princeton.
Steinwenter, A. 1925. *Die Streitbeendigung durch Urteil, Schiedsspruch und Vergleich nach griechischem Rechte.* Munich.
Stinton, D. 1976. "Notes on Greek Tragedy." *Journal of Hellenic Studies* 96: 121–45.
Stoddart, Robert. 1990. *Pindar and Greek Family Law.* New York.
Storey, I. C. 1989. "The 'Blameless Shield' of Kleonymos." *Rheinisches Museum* 132: 247–61.
Strauss, B. S. 1991. "On Aristotle's Critique of Athenian Democracy." In *Essays on the Foundations of Aristotelian Political Science*, eds. C. Lord and D. K. O'Connor. Berkeley: 212–33.
Striker, G. 1986. "Origins of the Concept of Natural Law." *Proceedings of the Boston Area Colloquium in Ancient Philosophy* 2: 79–94. (Reprinted in Striker 1996, 209–20).
Striker, G. 1996. *Essays on Hellenistic Epistemology and Ethics.* Cambridge.
Stroud, R. 1968. *Drakon's Law on Homicide.* Berkeley/Los Angeles.
Stroud, R. 1974. "An Athenian Law on Silver Coinage." *Hesperia* 43: 157–88.
Stroud, R. 1979. *The Axones and Kyrbeis of Drakon and Solon.* Berkeley/Los Angeles.
Stroud, R. 1998. *The Athenian Grain-Tax Law of 374/3 B.C. Hesperia*, Supplement 29. Princeton.
Strubbe, J. H. M. 1991. "Cursed Be He That Moves My Bones." In *Magika Hiera*, eds. C. A. Faraone and D. Obbink. New York/Oxford: 33–59.
Stumpf, G. 1986. "Ein athenisches Münzgesetz des 4. Jh. v. Chr." *Jahrbuch für Numismatik und Geldgeschichte* 36: 23–40.
Symposion 1971. Vorträge zur griechischen und hellenistischen Rechtsgeschichte. Ed. Hans Julius Wolff. Köln/Wien: 1975.
Symposion 1974. Vorträge zur griechischen und hellenistischen Rechtsgeschichte (Gargnano am Gardasee, 5–8 Juni 1974). Ed. A. Biscardi. Köln/Wien: 1979.
Symposion 1977. Vorträge zur griechischen und hellenistischen Rechtsgeschichte (Chantilly, 1–4 Juni 1977). Eds. J. Modrzejewski and D. Liebs. Köln/Wien: 1982.
Symposion 1979. Vorträge zur griechischen und hellenistischen Rechtsgeschichte (Ägina, 3–7 September 1979). Ed. P. Dimakis. Köln/Wien: 1983.
Symposion 1982. Vorträge zur griechischen und hellenistischen Rechtsgeschichte (Santander, 1–4 Sept 1982). Ed. F. J. Fernández Nieto. Köln/Wien: 1989.
Symposion 1985. Vorträge zur griechischen und hellenistischen Rechtsgeschichte (Ringberg, 24–26 Juli 1985). Ed. G. Thür. Köln-Wien: 1989.
Symposion 1988. Vorträge zur griechischen und hellenistischen Rechtsgeschichte (Siena-Pisa, 6–8 Juni 1988). Eds. G. Nenci and G. Thür. Köln/Wien: 1989.
Symposion 1990. Vorträge zur griechischen und hellenistischen Rechtsgeschichte (Pacific Grove CA, 24–26 Sept 1990). Ed. M. Gagarin. Köln/Weimar/Wien: 1991.
Symposion 1993. Vorträge zur griechischen und hellenistischen Rechtsgeschichte (Graz-Andritz, 12–16 Sept. 1993). Ed. G. Thür. Köln/Weimar/Wien: 1994.

Symposion 1995. Vorträge zur griechischen und hellenistischen Rechtsgeschichte (Korfu, 1–5 September 1995). Eds. G. Thür and J. Vélissaropoulos-Karakostas. Köln/Weimar/Wien: 1997.
Symposion 1997. Vorträge zur griechischen und hellenistischen Rechtsgeschichte (Altafiumara, 8–14 Sept. 1997). Eds. E. Cantarella and G. Thür. Köln/Weimar/Wien: 2001.
Symposion 1999. Vorträge zur griechischen und hellenistischen Rechtsgeschichte (Pazo de Mariñán, La Coruña, 6–9 Sept. 1999). Eds. G. Thür and F. J. Fernández Nieto. Köln/Weimar/Wien: 2003.
Symposion 2001. Vorträge zur griechischen und hellenistischen Rechtsgeschichte (Evanston, Illinois 5.–8. September 2001). Eds. Robert W. Wallace and Michael Gagarin. Vienna: 2005.
Szegedy-Maszak, Andrew. 1978. "Legends of the Greek Lawgivers." *Greek, Roman and Byzantion Studies* 19: 199–209.
Szegedy-Maszak, Andrew. 1981. *The Nomoi of Theophrastus.* New York.
Talamanca, Mario. 1953. *L'arra della compravendita in diritto greco e in diritto romano.* Milan.
Talamanca, Mario. 1979. "Dikazein e krinein nelle testimonanze greche piu antiche." *Symposion 1974*: 103–35.
Taubenschlag, R. 1955. *The Law of Greco-Roman Egypt in the Light of the Papyri, 332 BC–640 AD*, 2nd ed. Warsaw.
Thomas, B. 1997. *American Literary Realism and the Failed Promise of Contract.* Berkeley.
Thomas, Rosalind. 1989. *Oral Tradition and Written Record in Classical Athens.* Cambridge.
Thomas, Rosalind. 1994. "Law and the Lawgiver in the Athenian Democracy." In *Ritual, Finance, Politics: Athenian Democratic Accounts Presented to David Lewis*, eds. R. Osborne and S. Hornblower. Oxford: 119–33.
Thomas, Rosalind. 1995. "Written in Stone? Liberty, Equality, Orality and the Codification of Law." *Bulletin of the Institute of Classical Studies* 40: 59–74.
Thomas, Rosalind. 2000. *Herodotus in Context: Ethnography, Science and the Art of Persuasion.* Cambridge.
Thür, Gerhard. 1970. "Zum *dikazein* bei Homer." *Zeitschrift der Savigny-Stiftung* 87: 426–44.
Thür, Gerhard. 1977. *Beweisführung vor den Schwurgerichtshöfen Athens: Die Proklesis zur Basanos.* Wien.
Thür, Gerhard. 1987. "Der Streit über den Status des Werkstättenleiters Milyas." In *Demosthenes*, ed. U. Schindel, Darmstadt, 403–430.
Thür, Gerhard 1989. "Zum *dikazein* im Urteil aus Mantineia (*IG* V 2, 262)." *Symposion 1985*: 55–69.
Thür, Gerhard. 1995. "Die athenischen Geschworenengerichte – eine Sackgasse?" In *Die athenische Demokratie im 4. Jh. v. Chr.*, ed. W. Eder. Stuttgart: 321–34.
Thür, Gerhard. 1996a. "Oaths and Dispute Settlement in Ancient Greek Law." In Foxhall and Lewis 1996b: 57–72.
Thür, Gerhard. 1996b. "Reply to D. C. Mirhady, Torture and Rhetoric in Athens." *Journal of Hellenic Studies* 116: 132–34.
Thür, Gerhard. 2000. "Das Gerichtswesen Athens im 4. Jahrhundert v. Chr." In *Große Prozesse im antiken Athen*, eds. L. Burckhardt and J. von Ungern-Sternberg. München: 30–49.
Thür, Gerhard. 2002. "Review of Scafuro 1997." *Zeitschrift der Savigny-Stiftung* 119: 403–10.

Thür, Gerhard. 2003. "Sachverfolgung und Diebstahl in den griechischen Poleis (Dem. 32, Lys. 23, IC IV 72 I, IPArk 32 u. 17)." *Symposion* 1999: 57–96.

Thür, Gerhard, and H. Taeuber. 1994. See *IPArk*.

Todd, S. C. 1990. "The Purpose of Evidence in Athenian Courts." In Cartledge, Millett, and Todd, 1990: 19–39.

Todd, S. C. 1993. *The Shape of Athenian Law*. Oxford.

Todd, S. C. 1996. "Lysias against Nikomakhos: The Fate of the Expert in Athenian Law." In Foxhall and Lewis 1996b: 101–31.

Todd, S. C. 2002. "Advocacy, Logography and *erōtēsis* in Athenian Lawcourts." In *Thinking Like a Lawyer: Essays on Legal History and General History for John Crook on his Eightieth Birthday* (= *Mnemosyne* suppl. 231), ed. P. McKechnie. Leiden: 151–65.

Todd, S. C., and P. Millett. 1990. "Law, Society and Athens." In Cartledge, Millett, and Todd 1990: 1–18.

Trevett, J. 1992. *Apollodoros, the Son of Pasion*. Oxford.

Usher, S. 1976. "Lysias and His Clients." *Greek, Roman and Byzantine Studies* 17: 31–40.

Usher, S. 1999. *Greek Oratory: Tradition and Originality*. Oxford.

Van Caenegem, R. C. 1991. *Legal History: A European Perspective*. London.

Vander Waerdt, P., ed. 1994a. *The Socratic Movement*. Ithaca/London.

Vander Waerdt, P. 1994b. "Zeno's *Republic* and the Origins of Natural Law." In Vander Waerdt 1994a: 272–308.

Van Effenterre, Henri. 1982. "Les epiballontes." In *Studi in onore di A. Biscardi* III. Milano: 459–62.

Van Effenterre, Henri. 1991. "Criminal Law in Archaic Crete." *Symposion* 1990: 83–6.

Van Effenterre, Henri, and Micheline. 1994. "Ecrire sur les murs." In Gehrke 1994: 87–96.

Van Effenterre, Henri, and Micheline. 1997. "Du nouveau sur le Code de Gortyne." *Symposion* 1995: 11–15.

Van Effenterre, Henri, and Micheline. 2000. "La codification gortynienne, mythe ou realité?" In Lévy 2000a: 175–84.

Van Effenterre, Henri, and Françoise Ruzé, eds. 1994–1995. *Nomima. Recueil d'inscriptions politiques et juridiques de l'archaïsme grec*. École française de Rome.

Vélissaropoulos, J. 1977. "Le monde de l'*emporion*." *Dialogues d'histoire ancienne*: 61–85.

Vélissaropoulos, J. 1980. *Les nauclères grecs: Recherches sur les institutions maritimes en Grèce et dans l'Orient hellénisé*. Geneva.

Vélissaropoulos, J. 1993. Λόγοι Εὐθυνης. Athens.

Vernant, J.-P., and P. Vidal-Naquet. 1988. *Oedipe et ses mythes*. Brussels.

Vlastos, G. 1947. "Equality and Justice in Early Greek Cosmologies." *Classical Philology* 42: 156–78. (Reprinted in Vlastos, *Studies in Greek Philosophy* 1995, 1.57–88.)

Von Reden, S. 2001. "The Politics of Monetization in Third-Century BC Egypt." In *Money and Its Uses in the Ancient Greek World*, eds. A. Meadows and K. Shipton. Oxford: 65–76.

Wallace, Robert W. 1989. *The Areopagos Council to 307 B.C.* Baltimore.

Wallace, Robert W. 1994a. "The Athenian Laws against Slander." *Symposion* 1993: 109–24.

Wallace, Robert W. 1994b. "Private Lives and Public Enemies: Freedom of Thought in Classical Athens." In Boegehold and Scafuro 1994: 127–55.

Wallace, Robert W. 2001. "*Diamarturia* in Late Fourth-Century Athens." *Symposion* 1997: 89–101.

Wallace, Robert W. forthcoming. *Freedom and Democracy: "Living as You Like" in Ancient Athens.*
Watson, G. 1971. "The Natural Law and Stoicism." In Long (1971), 216–38.
Weiss, E. 1923. *Griechisches Privatrecht auf rechtsvergleichender Grundlage.* Leipzig.
Weiss, R. 1998. *Socrates Dissatisfied: An Analysis of Plato's Crito.* New York/Oxford.
Westbrook, Raymond. 1989. "Cuneiform Law Codes and the Origins of Legislation." *Zeitschrift für Assyriologie und vorderasiatische Archäologie* 79: 201–22.
Westbrook, Raymond, ed. 2003. *A History of Ancient Near Eastern Law.* Leiden.
Whitby, M. 1998. "Athenian Grain Trade in the Fourth Century B.C." In *Trade, Traders and the Ancient City*, eds. H. Parkins and C. Smith. London: 102–28.
White, J. B. 1988. *The Legal Imagination*, abridged ed. Chicago.
Whitehead, David. 1977. *The Ideology of the Athenian Metic.* Cambridge.
Whitehead, David 2000. *Hypereides: The Forensic Speeches.* Oxford.
Whitley, James. 1997. "Cretan Laws and Cretan Literacy." *American Journal of Archaeology* 101: 635–61.
Wickersham, John, and Gerald Verbrugghe. 1973. *The Fourth Century B.C.* Toronto.
Willetts, R. F. 1955. *Aristocratic Society in Ancient Crete.* London.
Willetts, R. F. 1961. "Leg. Gort. 35–55." *Classical Quarterly* 11: 55–60.
Willetts, R. F. 1967. *The Law Code of Gortyn.* Kadmos Supplement 1. Berlin.
Williams, B. 1993. *Shame and Necessity.* Berkeley.
Wilson, P. 1992. "Demosthenes 21 (Against Meidias): Democratic Abuse." *Proceedings of the Cambridge Philological Society* 37: 164–95.
Winand, Jean. 1985. "Le rôle des hiérothytes en Égypte." *Chronique d'Égypte* 60: 398–411.
Winkler, J., and F. Zeitlin, eds. 1990. *Nothing to Do with Dionysos? Athenian Drama in Its Social Context.* Princeton.
Wolf, E. 1952. *Griechisches Rechtsdenken*, vol. 1. Frankfurt.
Wolff, Hans Julius. 1946. "The Origin of Judicial Litigation among the Greeks." *Traditio* 4: 31–87.
Wolff, Hans Julius. 1957. "Die Grundlagen des griechischen Vertragsrechts." *Zeitschrift der Savigny-Stiftung* 74: 26–72 = *Zur griechischen Rechtsgeschichte*, ed. E. Berneker. Darmstadt 1968: 483–533.
Wolff, Hans Julius. 1962. "Gewohnheitsrecht und Gesetzesrecht in der griechischen Rechtsauffassung." *Deutsche Landesreferate zum 6. internationalen Kongreß für Rechtsvergleichung in Hamburg:* 3–18.
Wolff, Hans Julius. 1965. "Griechisches Recht" and "Ptolemäisches Recht." In *Lexicon der Alten Welt.* Zurich: 2516–30, 2530–32.
Wolff, Hans Julius. 1966. *Die attische Paragraphe.* Weimar.
Wolff, Hans Julius. 1968a. *Demosthenes als Advokat. Funktionen und Methoden des Prozeßpraktikers im klassischen Athen.* Berlin.
Wolff, Hans Julius. 1968b. "Review of Willetts, 1967." *Zeitschrift der Savigny-Stiftung* 85: 418–28.
Wolff Hans Julius. 1970a. *Das Justizwesen der Ptolemäer*, 2nd ed. München.
Wolff, Hans Julius. 1970b. *"Normenkontrolle" und Gesetzesbegriff in der attischen Demokratie.* Heidelberg.
Wolff, Hans Julius. 1973. "Hellenistisches Privatrecht." In *Zeitschrift der Savigny-Stiftung* 90: 63–90. (English version, "Hellenistic Private Law." In *Compendia rerum Iudaicarum ad Novum Testamentum*, vol. 1, Assen 1974: 534–60.)

Wolff, Hans Julius. 1975. "Juristische Gräzistik – Aufgaben, Probleme, Möglichkeiten." *Symposion* 1971: 1–22.
Wolff, Hans Julius. 1978. *Das Recht der griechischen Papyri Ägyptens in der Zeit der Ptolemäer und des Prinzipats. Organisation und Kontrolle des privaten Rechtsverkehrs*. München. (Rechtsgeschichte des Altertums im Rahmen des Handbuchs der Altertumswissenschaft 5.2.)
Wolff, Hans Julius. 1983. "Neue juristische Urkunden VII, Neues Material zum Zwangsvollstreckungsrecht der Papyri." *Zeitschrift der Savigny-Stiftung* 100: 444–53.
Wolff, Hans Julius. 1998. *Vorlesungen über juristische Papyruskunde*. Berlin.
Wolff, Hans Julius. 2002. *Das Recht der griechischen Papyri Ägyptens in der Zeit der Ptolemäer und des Prinzipats. Bedingungen und Triebkräfte der Rechtsentwicklung*, ed. Hans-Albert Rupprecht, München. (Rechtsgeschichte des Altertums im Rahmen des Handbuchs der Altertumswissenschaft 5.1.)
Wolff, Hartmut. 1979. "Die Opposition gegen die Radikale Demokratie in Athen bis zum Jahre 411 v. Chr." *Zeitschrift für Papyrologie und Epigraphik* 36: 279–302.
Wollheim, R. 1967. "Natural Law." In Edwards 1967, vol. 5: 450–54.
Wolpert, A. 2002. *Remembering Defeat: Civil War and Civic Memory in Ancient Athens*. Baltimore.
Wormald, Patrick. 1999. *The Making of English Law: King Alfred to the Twelfth Century. Vol. I. Legislation and its Limits*. Oxford.
Worthington, Ian. 1989. "The Duration of an Athenian Political Trial." *Journal of Hellenic Studies* 109: 204–7.
Worthington, Ian. 1994. "The Canon of the Ten Attic Orators." In *Persuasion: Greek Rhetoric in Action*, ed. I. Worthington. London/New York: 244–63.
Yiftach, Uri. 1997. "The Role of the *Syngraphe* 'Compiled through the *Hierothytai*.' A Reconsideration of W. Schubart's Theory in Light of a Recently Published Alexandrian Marriage Contract (P. Berol. 25423)." *Zeitschrift für Papyrologie und Epigraphik* 115: 178–82.
Yiftach-Firanko, Uri. 2003. *Marriage and Marital Agreements. A History of the Greek Marriage Document in Egypt. 4th century BCE – 4th century CE*. München: Münchener Beiträge zur Papyrusforschung und antiken Rechtsgeschichte 93.
Youni, M. 2000. *Provincia Macedonia*. Θεσμοὶ ἰδιωτικοῦ δικαίου στὴ Μακεδονία ἐπὶ Ρωμαιοκρατίας. Athens/Komotini.
Youni, M. 2001. "The Different Categories of Unpunished Killing and the Term ΑΤΙΜΟΣ in Ancient Greek Law." *Symposion* 1997: 117–37.
Yunis, Harvey. 1988. "Law, Politics, and the *Graphe Paranomon* in Fourth-Century Athens." *Greek, Roman and Byzantine Studies* 29: 361–82.
Yunis, Harvey. 1996. *Taming Democracy: Models of Political Rhetoric in Classical Athens*. Ithaca.
Yunis, Harvey. 1998. "The Constraints of Democracy and the Rise of the Art of Rhetoric." In Boedeker and Raaflaub 1998: 223–40.
Yunis, Harvey. 2000. "Politics as Literature: Demosthenes and the Burden of the Athenian Past." *Arion* 8: 96–117.
Zeitlin, Froma. 1993. "Staging Dionysos between Thebes and Athens." In *Masks of Dionysos*, eds. T. Carpenter and C. Faraone. Ithaca: 147–82.

Index Locorum

Ancient Authors

Aelian
Var. Hist. 13.24, ... 244–245, 371

Aeschines
1.1 223
1.1–2 .... 223, 380
1.5 223
1.6 224
1.14–19 372
1.15–17 243
1.36 224
1.44–50 168
1.46 160
1.46f 168
1.47 .... 166, 168
1.50 169
1.90–91 .... 138, 226
1.92 124
1.94 102
1.119 252
1.176 381
1.176–7 138
1.192–3 138
2.68 .... 160, 168
2.87 75
2.124 109
2.156 109
2.170 152
2.180 102
2.184 152
3.6–7 224
3.8 234
3.14 203
3.16 .... 198, 204
3.37 201
3.137 198
3.173 102
3.197 381
3.198 116
3.200 198
3.219 301
3.246 138
3.254 301
3.245–7 141

Aeschylus
Agamemnon
140 391
151 386
1261 383
1335 386
1448 386
1560 386
1564–66 174
Eumenides 278
92 387
235–43 84
429–32 89
431–35 84
467–69 84
470–752 374
480 382
583 84
695 387
778 387
Persians
585 391
Prometheus Bound
148–151 387
186–192 387
400 387

457

Index Locorum

Aesop
56 (Housrath) 67

Anaximander
Fr. 1 416

Anaximenes
Rhetorica ad Alexandrum
7.2 148
14–17 107

Andocides
1 65
1.14 159
1.47 155
1.68 155
1.69 154
1.70 155
1.71–91 204
1.75–76 362
1.85 51
1.87 51
1.91 204
1.111–2 64
1.113–116 65
1.117ff 115

Anecdota Graeca
242.20–22 . . . . 73, 90
749.3 369

Anonymous Iamblichi
7.12–14 390

Antiphon
1 385
1.3 125
1.8 . . . . 74, 155, 165
1.21 125
1.25 125
1.28 . . . . 74, 155, 165
2.1.6 64
5.9–10 129
5.11 . . . . 113, 124
5.12 165
6.9 . . . . 113, 124
6.16 74
Fr. 1 102

Apollodorus
3.14.2 240

Aristophanes
Acharnians
67 362
208 360
370–6 361
377–82 364
378 365
477–79 368
494–96 360
502–06 364
515–16 365
527 363
532 52
628–33 364
631 363
1000 ff 377
Babylonians 364
Birds
40–41 360
108–111 360
287–89 366
290 367
753–68 360
1071–3 66
1297 366
1473–81 366
Clouds
353 367
1077–8 421
Ekklesiazousai
432 362
385–387 362
1024–25 248
Frogs
727–31 361
730–4 384
Knights
42–3 361
510–511 361
1133 384
1316–17 360
1405 384
Lysistrata
591–93 284

Wasps

12–23	366
87–96	359
88	359
106–10	359
592	366
703–5	359
835–1008	359
897	119
1102–21	359

Aristotle

Athenaiōn Politeia (Ath. Pol.)

5.1	271
6	272
6.3	215
7.1	157, 401
7.2	401
8.4	215
8.5	273
9	272
9.1	272
9.1–2	232
9.2	36, 41, 42, 401
12.1–4	402
12.3	273
12.4	272, 273
16.8	274
16.10	274
19.4	275
20	276
21	276
26.4	268, 278
27.4–5	232
29.5	284
35.2	41, 232
40	285
41.2	232
42.1	240, 245, 286
43.4	134, 299
44.1	229
50.2	252
51.1	292
51.3	299
51.4	299, 300
52.1	226
53.1–3	156
53.2	148, 150, 154
53.3	148, 156, 159
55.3	256
55.5	157, 168
56.2	260
56.6	255
57.2	258
59.1	159
59.3	244
60.2	64
63–69	147
67.1	113, 136
67.1–2	110
67.2	132
67.2–5	147
67.3	133, 148
68.4	159
69.1	160

De Insomniis

495b25–30	382

De Gen. An.

728a	252

Nicomachean Ethics

1095a28	116
1128a22–25	369
1137b	41, 59
1160a3ff	116

Physics

198b35	422

Politics

1253b	254
1254b	253
1257a	260
1260a	253
1267a–b	256
1268b39	59
1269a1–3	35, 74
1269a8ff	59
1269a20	423
1269a38–40	315
1271b20–72b23	305
1271b30–40	309
1272a36–39	46–49, 311
1272b16–19	315
1274a–b	256
1274b40–2	267
1275a	300
1275b19–21	267
1275b21–22	350

1275b23–33	267
1275b34–39	277
1280b10–12	327
1282b2	42, 59
1286a10	59
1287b	42, 53, 59
Rhetoric	199
1.1.3–5	199
1.1.5	200
1.1.6	200
1.1.7	59
1.2.2–5	200
1.13	423
1.13.13	59
1.15	150
1.15.1–2	107, 200
1354a	59, 124
1354a31–b1	372
1355b36	148
1361a	260
1361a21–22	293
1366b13–15	372
1370b–1371a	171
1373–1374	59
1374a13–15	216
1375a 22–25	107
1375a24	146, 148
1375b9–10	296
1377a18–21	69
1378a–b	171, 174
1378b23–5	216

Athenaeus
167e	372
168a	372
245a–c	371
276c	377
437c	376
437e	377
542d	371
619b	45
620	351

Babrius
Fable 2	74

Callimachus
Fr. 178	377

Chariton
Chair. and Call.	353

Cicero
De Legibus
1.19	429
2.64–66	371

De Officiis
1.34	430

De Republica
3.33	429
4.10	367

Cleanthes
LS 54I	425

Cratinus
Nemesis Fr.18 K-A	361
Odyssey 143–57 K-A	363

Democritus
Fr. 9	417

Demosthenes
5.8	290
9.3	359
18.2	201
18.123	224
19.232	138
19.246–250	102
19.284	106
19.293	64
20	138
20.9	292
20.92	45, 59
20.104	368
20.106	362
20.141–142	122
21.7–8	217
21.8–12	206
21.19	218
21.20–21	217, 219
21.25–26	129
21.37	175
21.42	381
21.42–61	206

Index Locorum

21.43	381	23.94	138
21.44–45	218	24.8	138
21.45–46	206	24.19	119
21.47	160	24.101	138
21.48–50	410	24.113	222
21.54–55	207	24.115	222
21.74–76	220	24.118	381
21.78ff	115	24.138	381
21.98	138	24.139ff	46, 60
21.112	233	24.139–43	409
21.123	381	24.143	410
21.123–25	233	24.148–52	197
21.126	64	24.154	233
21.169–70	233	24.218	138
21.175–80	64	25.10	138
21.176	300	25.15	122
21.183	138	25.15–17	181
21.188	201	25.25–27	181
21.207	138	25.53	138
21.209–10	410	25.60	301
21.218	64	25.79	65
21.219–22	207	26.1–2	138
21.219–25	219	26.24	107
21.220–225	138	27	115
21.223–24	207	27.1	115
21.224–25	219, 411	27.4ff	246
21.227	138, 175, 219	27.9	294
22.2	65	27.63	138
22.7	138	27.67	140
22.25–28	129	27.66–69	118
22.27	65	28.1	138
22.29	138	28.18–19	119
22.31	368	28.19	120
22.55–6	170	28.24	123
22.68	138, 175	29.9	115
22.88	175	29.27	115
23	105, 228–229	29.33	151
23.25–26	228	29.50	140
23.31–32	228	29.58	115
23.38	228	30.2	115
23.39	228	30.15	247
23.50	362, 366	30.17	247
23.53	202, 239	30.26	247
23.66	227	30.31	247
23.67	74	30.35	153
23.69	228, 229	32.1	300
23.72	68	32.5–8	297
23.75–76	220	32.14	297, 298

32.16	298
32.18	300
32.29	301
32.30	161
33.1	302
34.37	299
34.51	127, 297
35	298
35.3	291
35.10–13	330
35.11	298
35.20	162, 298
35.29	291
35.31–2	297
35.32–3	298
35.33	298
35.34	162, 298
35.39	299
35.50–1	299
35.51	299, 300
35.54	127
35.47	140
36	109
36.1	101
36.7	149
36.42	127
36.45	127
36.52	127
36.55	114, 122
36.55–56	127
36.55–57	127
36.58	138
36.59	127
37	295
37.33–38	129
37.48	127
37.52	127
37.54	127
40.1–5	380
40.49	368
40.52	295
40.56	140
41.1–2	115
41.8	295
42.11–12	115
43.1–2	115
43.31	153
43.35	153
43.35–46	153
43.36	153
43.42	153
43.51	248
44.31–2	115
44.42	151
45.1–2	115
45.6	109
45.7	138
45.46	119
45.57–62	167
45.58	157, 167
45.60	166, 167, 169
45.61	167
45.63ff	123
45.64	300
45.85	118
45.87	138
46.6–7	153
46.7	161
46.8	149
46.10	152
46.22	134, 301
47	164
47.11	153
47.42–43	119
47.46	115
47.77	296
47.81	115
48.2	115
48.40	115
49.19	158
49.19–21	157
49.20	158, 161
49.35–36	295
50.24	291
50.28	295
50.65	138
50.66	138
51.111–12	233
52.1–2	114, 121
53.1–2	138
53.14–15	115
53.29	138
54	127, 220–221
54.1	221
54.15	138
54.21–22	116

54.42	138	**Dinarchus**	
54.42–43	179, 221	1.26–7	170
54.43	138	1.27	138
55.27	151	1.46	138
55.35	118	1.67	138
56.2	296, 298	1.88	138
56.4	140, 302	1.89	240
56.6	298	1.107	138
56.11	299	1.113	138, 225
56.24	297	2	179
56.26	299	2.4	381
56.43–4	119	2.8–13	122
56.47	300	2.11	123
56.48	127	2.21–23	138
56.48–50	138	3.4	296
57	286–287	3.5	123
57.25	287	3.8	179, 225
57.30	287	3.19	138, 180, 225
57.30–31	368		
57.31	287	**Dio Chrysostom**	
57.46	287	Or. 33.9	360
57.49	287		
57.59	113	**Diodorus Siculus**	
57.63	121	1.27.1	351
57.67	151	1.79.1	71
57.70	118	5.64–80	305
58.1	138	11.89.5–6	74
58.8	300		
58.9	300	**Diogenes Laertius**	
58.19	119	2.26	284
58.28	122	2.44	384
58.58	138	2.101	372
59	287–288	2.116	372
59.1	138	7.168–9	372
59.12	138		
59.14–15	101	**Dionysius of Halicarnassus**	
59.15	138	*Anc. Orat.*	
59.16	288	4	99
59.23	153	*Dinarchus*	
59.28	168	3	119
59.59	113	*Isaeus*	
59.73ff	377	19–20	99
59.104–106	283	*Isocrates*	
59.111–113	138	1	102
59.115	201	18	102
59.116	65		
58.122	250	**Dosiadas**	
59.126	138	FGH 458 F 2	305

Empedocles
Fr. 8 417
Fr. 9 417
Fr. 26 417
Fr. 30 417

Ephorus
FGH 70 F 149 305

Epicurus
LS 22A 424
LS 22B 424

Eumelus
Fr. 2 285

Eupolis
Fr. 234 K-A 361

Euripides
Children of Heracles
194 391
885 386
Electra
318 382
579–80 391
1015 391
1043 391
Hecuba
800 391
847 391
864 391
Helen
1429 391
Heracles
755 387
768 387
Hippolytus
91 391
421–23 359
1046 391
1381 386
Ion 278
20 391
442 391
670–75 359
1005 383

1221 383
1225 383
1312 391
Iphigenia at Aulis
1095 391
Iphigenia at Taurus
947–60 377
Medea
226ff 247
238 391
492–5 387
493 391
538 391
811 391
1000 391
Orestes
395 382
479–80 382
487 391
508 383
527 391
571 391
831 382
866–956 374
941 391
Phoenissae
391–93 359
Suppliants
300ff 387
378 388
429–434 .... 42, 52, 98
430 .... 388, 390
431–32 388
526 388
561–3 388
1187–1995 375

Eustathius
ad Od. 16.118 238

Gorgias
Palamedes 30 .... 42, 59

Harpocration
s.v. ἀφανὴς οὐσία 290
s.v. ἐπιμεληταὶ ἐμπορίου 299
s.v. κατὰ τὴν ἀγορὰν ἀψεύδειν ... 292
O 47 371

Hellanicus
FGH 323a F22 240

Heracleides Ponticus
FHG 2, p.217ff 244

Heraclitus
Fr. 33 390
Fr. 53 418
Fr. 80 418
Fr. 94 417
Fr. 114 417–9

Hermippus
88 45

Hermogenes
Peri Ideōn 2.11 104

Herodotus
1.29 401
1.59.6 274
1.65.4 49
1.65.4 49
1.96–100 85
3.38 395
4.161–2 56
2.177.2 51
5.63 275
5.66 275
5.78 277
6.21 376
6.86.5 74
6.123 275
7.104.4 51
7.169–171 305

Hesiod
Works and Days
9 399
38–39 399
203–10 399
216–217 399
248–64 400
276–80 416
320 91
368 377

Theogony
3 238
80–92 84
94–103 85

Hesychius
s.v. ἀστικοὶ νόμοι 291

Hipponax
Fr. 4 384
Fr. 5 384

Homer
Iliad
1.245–84 86
1.542 89
3.162–65 238
8.431 89
9.632–36 91
16.542 83
18.109 174
18.478–616 270
18.497–508 . . . . 57, 83–84, 98
23.573–74 88
23.579–80 88
23.585 88
23.586–95 88
Odyssey
1.56 238
3.266–72 238
11.547 89
11.568–71 86
12.444 83
19.395ff 66

Homeric Hymns
To Hermes 274–5 89

Horace
Ars Poetica
72 428
283 367
464 428
Satires
1.4.1–4 361

Hyperides

1 (*Lyc.*) 8–9	121
1 (*Lyc.*) 12	129
1 (*Lyc.*) 14	122
1 (*Lyc.*) 18	122
1 (*Lyc.*) 19–20	118
2 (*Phil.*) 12	158
3 (*Ath.*) 5–9	295
3 (*Ath.*) 13	296
3 (*Ath.*) 14	292
3 (*Ath.*) 15	292
4 (*Eux.*) 3	252
4 (*Eux.*) 5–6	129
4 (*Eux.*) 32	114, 121

Isaeus

1.4	117
1.17	117
1.19	117
1.20	117
1.30	117
1.33	117
1.37	117
1.42	117
2.9	248
2.27–37	115
3.2–4	139
3.8	247
3.30	138
3.78	247
4.19	117
4.27–29	135
5.5ff	115
5.7–9	248
5.12	121
5.18	119
5.28–30	115
6.14	249
6.51	117
6.56	138
6.61	123
7.3	151
7.8	117
7.11	117
7.12	117
7.20–22	248
7.33–37	117
7.38–42	123
8.8	248
8.23	295
8.40	122
9.4	117
9.18	166
9.18–19	167
9.27–32	117
9.35	198
10.1	198
11.1–3	248
11.32–35	129
12.1	152
12.4	152
12.5	151

Isocrates

7.37	184
7.39	184
7.40	184
7.40–41	183–184
7.43	184
7.44–45	184
7.46	184
7.46–47	231
7.47	184
7.47–8	185
7.58	361
8.14	360
8.40	122
12.248	359
15	102
15.22	229
16.45–46	120
16.47	118, 120
17.12	301
17.20	297, 298
17.35–37	295
18.21	198
18.27–32	137
18.33–34	137
18.34–5	114
18.47	123
18.54–56	162
19.50	117–120
20.1	216
20.2	129, 216
20.5	216
20.12–14	138

20.13	123
20.15–18	217
20.19	119
21.18	138, 141–143

Justinian
Digest 48.5.24(23).4 241

Longinus
On the Sublime
34.1–2 104

Lucian
Anacharsis 19 124
Eunuchus 19 241

Lucretius
1.584–92	428
1.586	428
2.302	428
2.719	428
3.416	428
5.57–8	428
5.310	428
5.924	428
6.906	428

Lycurgus
1	224–226
1.3–5	224
1.3–6	201
1.5–6	225
1.9–10	185
1.11–13	124
1.12–13	200
1.14–15	185
1.20	157, 160, 168
1.23	295
1.27	299
1.78	381
1.98	384
1.100	114
1.103	114
1.107	114
1.124–27	231
1.138	225
1.141–46	225

Lysias
1	105, 204, 226–227
1.23–24	72
1.23–28	227
1.26	202, 227
1.28–30	202
1.29	203, 227
1.29–30	204
1.30	202
1.31–33	204
1.32	242, 243
1.32–33	242
1.34	202, 227
1.34–36	204
1.37	227
1.47	227
1.47–49	205
3.39	380
3.44–46	125
3.46	113, 124, 200
3.48	125
4.20	125
6.17–18	66
6.54	138
7	64
7.31	125
7.41	125
7.41–42	125
9.1	113
9.3	121
9.21	120
9.22	118
10.2–11	362, 366
10.3	138
10.6–8	136
10.17	90
10.22	162, 367
10.23	367
10.28	138
10.30	362, 366
12.2	380
12.35	138
12.85	138
13.1	138
13.3	138, 171, 172
13.23	301
13.41	138
13.42	138, 172

13.48–9 . . . . 171, 172	Fr. CXII 105
13.79 379	Fr. CXXXIV 290
13.83–4 138	
13.92 172	**Manilius**
13.97 172	1.56–65 428
14.1 138	1.252 428
14.3 175	2.62 428
14.4 . . . . 138, 206	3.55 428
14.12 138	
14.12–13 175	**Menander**
14.39 381	*Misogynes*
14.45 . . . . 138, 175	Fr. 279 K-T 370
15.9 . . . . 117–120, 138	*Samia*
15.12 138	481 384
16 105	717–18 370
17.2 . . . . 154, 155	Fr. 459 295
17.5 301	Fr. 134 369
18.1 120	
18.20–21 123	**Old Testament**
18.27 118	*Leviticus* 18 351
19.33 . . . . 118, 120	
19.45 119	**Parmenides**
19.53 118	Fr. 8.14–15 417
19.61 123	
20.34 . . . . 120, 123	**Pausanias**
20.34–35 118	1.21.1 240
21.24–25 120	
21.25 . . . . 118, 123	**Philo of Alexandria**
22.2–4 230	*De spec. leg.* 3:22–24 351
22.8 299	
22.17–20 138	**Philochorus**
22.21 138	*FGrH* 328 Fr. 65 371
25–26 105	
27.6–7 138	**Photius**
29.13 138	*s.v. Choes* 376, 377
30 58–60	
30.6 123	**Plato**
30.15 121	*Apology*
30.23 138	17a–18a 199
30.23–4 175	*Axiochos*
31 105	367a 371
31.11 381	*Gorgias*
32.12 . . . . 70, 138	470–81 187
32.19 381	472–73 186
34.3 283	478–9 187
Fr. I (Carey) 295	481 187
Fr. L 105	483c–e 419
Fr. LXX 100	

521c–522e	198
525	187
Laws	199
713–15	232
849e	294
853	189
862	189
862–3	175
876b	360
889c	422
890d	423
908–09	190
910b1–6	68
914c–d	265
915d6–e2	294
937d–938c	199
948d	74

Protagoras
323d	177
324a–b	173–174
325a–b	177
347c	294

Republic
530c	406
371c	294
427b–c	62
557b	359

Statesman
289e	294

Symposium
196c	296

Timaeus
83e4–5	422

Platonius
Differentiae Comediae
p.3 Kost	361
p.4 Kost	363

Plautus
Mostellaria
637–48	295
Poenulus	370

Pseudolus
342–6	295
373–4	295

Rudens
45–6	295

860–2	295
1281–3	295

Pliny the Elder
613b	377
643a	377

Plutarch
Aristeides
1	364

Demosthenes
15.3	106
24.2	106

Lycurgus
6	53–54
13.3	44

Nikias
6	364

Pericles
4	364
24–25.1	363
32.2	66
37	278
37.3	268
39	363

Quaest. Gr.
2	244

Solon
5	272
8.2	271
14	271
15	272
15.2–3	302
18	41, 59
20	273
21.1	368
23	242, 243, 260
24.4	273

Theseus
15	384
18	384
22	384
Vitae X Orat.	99
837a5–10	102
840cd	106
842a	371
843d	371

Pollux
8.37 157
8.55 74
8.112 371
8.117 124
9.34 . . . . 291, 295

Polybius
12.16 . . . . 47, 60

Rhetores Graeci
1.455.8–11 67

Seneca
Natural Questions
2.35.2 426
3.29.3 426
3.29.7 426
6.32.12 426
7.12.4 426

Solon (West)
4 . . . . 390, 402
4.30–39 402
5 402
6 402
9 390
11 390
12 417
34 402
36 . . . . 46, 51, 52, 402
36.15–17 402
37 402

Sophocles
Ajax
440–9 363
1073–91 363
1129 391
1135–37 363
1247 363
1343 391
1349–50 391
Antigone
155 390
264–67 90
354–55 392

449–470 390
450–57 414
454–5 52
735 390
821 391
875 391
OC
905 391
1382 391
OT
100 382
241 382
310 382
863–873 389
Trachiniae
552–3 384
584–7 385
685–86 385
1140 385

Stobaeus
4.2.24 . . . . 45, 59

Strabo
10.3.1 305

Suda
choes 377
deigma 291
epimelētai emporiou 291

Themistus
Orat. 8 367

Theocritus
Idylls 17: 121–34 351

Theophrastus
Laws
Fr. 5–6 295
Fr. 20 293
Fr. 21.4 293

Thucydides
2.15.4 377
2.37 52
2.85.5–6 305
3.36 178

3.36.6	404
3.37–49	404
3.38	179
3.39	178
3.39–40	178
3.40	179
3.44	180
3.45	181
3.46	182
3.52	404
5.47	375
5.84–116	404
5.105	419
6.27–9	65
6.54.5–6	274
6.60–61	65
8.68.1–2	102

Tzetzes Chiliades
V, 729	384

Virgil
Georgics
1.60	428

Xenophon
Anabasis
7.5.14	298

Constitution of the Athenians
1.6	359
2.18	361

Hellenica
1.7.20	365
1.7.22	65
4.2.16	305
4.8.6	305
5.1.21	291
7.5.10	305

Memorabilia
1.2.43	390
1.11.45–50	391
2.7	295
4.4.13ff	51
4.4.17	391

Poroi
3.13	291

Zeno
LS 67A	425

Epigraphical Sources

GDI
5635, C.5–10	56

IC 4
1	326
3	326
4	312, 323, 327
8	325
9	325
13	317, 326
14	310, 311
15	311
18	318
19	310
20	318
21	318
22	312
27	326
28	313
29	310
30	310, 320, 326
41	306, 307, 310, 312, 313, 316, 323, 324–5, 326
42	306, 310, 311, 312
43	309, 310, 319, 320, 323, 324
45	310, 313
46	310, 319
47	71, 325, 326
51	74, 312
52	326
53	326
62	310
63	313, 326
64	309, 310
65	309, 315, 326
66	326
68	310
72	306, 307, 311
l.2–7	87
l.2–24	313

Index Locorum

I.16–18	313	VIII.32	310
I.18–24	71, 312	VIII.35–40	322
I.42–3	326	VIII.42–53	322
I.51 ff	310	VIII.53–IX.1	322
I.56–II.2	324	IX.1–24	322
II	314	IX.23–4	311
II.2–10	314	IX.24–40	48, 313
II.5–20	325	IX.32–3	49, 311, 314
II.11–13	316	IX.36–40	72
II.15–16	72, 313, 316	X.14–20	320
II.16–20	313	X.25–32	323
II.20–45	245, 315, 318	X.33–XI.23	318–19
II.28–33	313	X.35–36	314
II.36–45	72	X.37–9	327
II.45–III.16	317	XI.13–14	314
III.5–9	71, 88, 312, 313, 326	XI.16–17	310, 311
III.12–16	73	XI.19–23	48, 50
III.17–31	317, 318	XI.26–31	35, 48, 70, 89, 311
III.22–23	320	XI.46–55	313, 314, 317
III.24–31	320	XI.48	71
III.31–37	317	XII.1–5	93, 320
III.37–44	317	XII.6–19	321, 322
III.40–44	316, 320	XII.7	311, 318
III.44–52	318	XII.11–12	311, 318
III.49–52	71, 72, 313	XII.13–14	322
III.52–IV.8	318	XII.16–19	314, 317
IV.6–8	71, 72, 313	73	326
IV.8–17	318	75	311, 312, 323, 327
IV.13–14	316	76	319, 326
IV.18–23	318	77	311, 326
IV.23–48	320	78	309, 310, 311, 317
IV.23–VI.46	320	79	310, 311, 317
IV.31–37	316	80	310, 311, 317, 326
IV.48–51	320	81	312, 320, 326
V.1–9	321	82	312
V.5–6	306, 310	84	310, 311, 314
V.9–28	320	87	311
V.28 ff	320	91	311
V.39–41	319	102	311
VI.2–46	322–3	104	310
VI.25–31	311	107	311
VI.56–VII.10	317, 318	142	326
VII.10–15	316, 323	143	326
VII.15–IX.24	314, 321	144	310, 317
VII.15–VIII.30	321–2	145	326
VII.35–6	314	146	326
VII.51	310	147	326
VIII.30–35	322	160	311, 327

165 311	
184 327	

I. Fayoum
I 2 . . . .

IG I²
86 375

IG I³
136 62
104.13 165

IG II²
1258 162
1368.10, 127–131 377
1635 65
1672.204 377
2762 295

IG VII
3083 78

IG XII
7.27 299
7.67 299
7.76 299
Supp. 347 298

IG XIV
1097 362

IPArk
8 75
17.10–14 158
17.42–46 148
17.43–46 157

IvO
2 . . . . 45, 50
7 50

IvKnidos
I 221 . . . . 148, 161

LSAM
30 44

Meiggs-Lewis
2 . . . . 46, 54, 60
10 55
13 . . . . 51, 55
20 . . . . 51, 76
32 90
44 61
30 . . . . 47, 55, 76
86 53–54

SEG
23.585 . . . . 306, 311
26.72 291
27.631 311
31.985 . . . . 47, 56, 60
33.679 335
33.1177 335
34.167 295
40.956 62
45.1276 312
45.1279 312
46.1217 317
49.1221–3 306

Syll.³
364.30–32 77
953.43–45 148

Van Effenterre/Ruzé = *Nomima*
1.7 . . . . 317, 326
1.19 90
1.21 75
1.22 311
1.23 . . . . 45, 75
1.30 317
1.43 76
1.44 76
1.47 323
1.49 326
1.51 75
1.59 326
1.78 53
1.104 76
1.105 76
2.8 312
2.12 313
2.13 74
2.45 72

2.61 323
2.65 . . . . 307, 323, 326
2.70 324
2.73A 319
2.84 312
2.90 319

Papyrological Sources
BGU
I 189 331
VI 1258 334
VI 1273 331
CPR
XVIII 334
Gnomon of the Idios Logos
4 354
MChr
216 331
P.Dura
12 354
30 353
P.Eleph.
1 349
P.Giss.
I 2 . . . . 350, 353
P.Hal.
1.70–73 161
P.Hamb.
II 188 340–342
P.Iena
904 351
P. Lond.
II 262 p.176 333
P.Mich.
V 340 333
V 341 333
P.Moscow dem.
123 354
P.Oxy.
2385 333
2537 104
3285 345–350
3500 353
P.Par.
5 335
P.Ryl.
II 160d 334
P.Sphinx
1914 333
P.Tebt.
I 5.l.207–220 334
III 1 334
III 1.776 352
III 815 334
P.Vind.Sal.
4 333
SB
4638.16 69
XX 11053 351
SP
I 65 331
II 210 334
II 410 335
V 7532 . . . . 336, 338–340
XII 11061 . . . . 337, 340–342
UPZ
I p.596f 335

General Index

Administrative law 310–311
Adoption 257–258, 318–319
Adultery 240–241, 245, 315, 318
Advocate . . . . 110; see also *Synegoros*
Aeschines 101, 102
Aeschylus 382
    Eumenides 375
    Oresteia 386
    Prometheus Bound 386, 387, 388
    Suppliants 375
Agora (landed market) 290–296
Aliens 317
Amasis 51
Amnesty of 403 105
Anakrisis . . . . see Pretrial proceedings
Anaxagoras 66
Anaximander 416–417
Anchisteia 282
Andocides 101
Anger 380–385, 387, 388, 393
Anthesteria 376
Antichrēsis 331
Antigone . . . . see Sophocles, *Antigone*
Antilochus 87–88, 89
Antiphon 101, 104
Apollodorus 103, 106
Arbitration . . 108, 154, 156–158, 163, 370
Areopagus 124, 184–185, 200, 215, 371–372
Arginusae, trial of generals after 230
Argument, strategies of 129–145
Aristophanes 357, 364–366
    Clouds 198, 421
    Wasps 359

Aristotle 66, 185, 199–200, 214–215, 229–231, 232, 252–253, 254, 267–268, 421–423
Aristotle, *Politics* 305, 407–408
Aspasia 66
Assault 215–217, 220
Astos . . . . 269; see also Pericles' "citizenship law"
Athēnaios 269–270
Atimia 280
Attikos 269–270

Background information, in litigation . . . 115–118
Boulomenos, ho . . see Volunteer prosecuter

Caecilius of Calacte 99, 102–103
Callicles 419–420
Callistratus 364–365
Calypso 238
Cassandra 383–384
Challenge (*proklēsis*) 149–150
Character . . . 121–123, 124–125, 126, 127
Charondas 44, 45
Children 254–258, 317–318
Chios 46, 53–54
Choes 376–379
Cicero 428–430
Circe 238
Citizenship . . 267–289, 314–315, 402–403
Cleanthes 425–426
Cleisthenes 274–278
Cleon 178–180, 364–366
Clytemnestra 238
Codification 309, 345, 401, 416
Comedy, and law 357–373

475

Comedy, New 358, 369–373
   Old .... 357–368; *see also* Aristophanes
Commerce, commercial law 106,
   290–302
Commerce, maritime and landed 290–292
Comparative method 89–90
Consent, by women 240–241, 245
Constitutional law 310–311
Contracts 126, 298–299, 322–325,
   335–337, 338–342; *see also* Marriage contract, *Syngraphē*
Courts, Athenian 112–128, 214–215,
   97–302 *passim*
   Egyptian 334
   Greek, in Egypt 334
   homicide 124–126, 127
   maritime 126–127, 300–302
   popular 113–123
Cratinus 359
Credit .. 294–295, 331; *see also* Financing
Crete 47, 305–306
Crime 211–235, 325–326
Critical legal studies 194
Curse .... 76–77; *see also* Tean curses
Cynics ... 424, 425; *see also* Diogenes the Cynic

Damon 363
Deianira 384–385
Deioces 85
Delos 65
Delphi 73, 79
Deme 276, 277, 286–287
Demetrius of Phalerum 371–372
Democracy, and law . 191–193, 201–208,
   218–219, 223–226, 276–278,
   401–402, 407–408, 410, 411
Democritus 415, 417
Demosthenes 101, 102, 103, 108,
   408–411
   Against Meidias 410–411
Diadikasia 134–135, 264–265
Dikastai 100, 194–195, 197–199,
   203–208
Dikē 212, 215–216
Dikē pseudomartyriōn 162, 166

Diodotus 180–181, 183
Diogenes of Apollonia 66
Diogenes the Cynic 421
Dionysius of Halicarnassus . . 99, 102–103
Diopeithes, decree of 66
Divorce 246–247, 255, 317, 352
Documents 108, 147–148, 149,
   330, 332–334, 335–336, 345–346
   bilingual 347
   double (Doppelurkunde) 346
Dokimasia 105
Dowry 246, 247, 254, 330, 349, 352
Draco 44, 53–54, 90, 239–240, 242,
   243, 271
Dreros 43, 46, 53–54, 55, 56, 91
Dura-Europus 354

Easements 319
Echinos 148, 154, 156–157
Eikos 122
Eleven, The 226
Elis 75
Empedocles 417
Emporion (maritime market) ... 291–292,
   297–302
Entrapment 370
Ephialtes 358
Epicureans 424, 427–428
Epieikeia 59
Epigamia 283, 330, 350
Epiklerate 353
Epiklēros .... *see* Heiress
Euripides 375, 382
   Heracles Furiens 387, 388
   Hippolytus 386
   Iphigeneia in Tauris 377–378
   Orestes 383
   Suppliants 387–389
Evidence ...... 146, 150, 311–313; *see also* Proofs
Exōmosia ... 157, 160, 161, 163–164, 166,
   167–169
Exposure 318

Family 254–256, 317–319, 351–353
Festival, laws concerning 63–64, 206;
   see also Choes

General Index

Financing, maritime 297–298
Fines, sacred 76
Foreigners 301–302, 326
Formalism 35, 68–75
Free speech 359, 360–368
Friendship 116

Gaps in legislation 35–36
Gender, and law 236–253
Gortyn 31, 32, 35–36, 37, 47–49, 87, 89, 245, 305–327
    Great Code 44, 70–73, 88–89, 92, 307–308
    Little Code 307
Grain trade 299–300
Graphē 212
Graphos 50, 93
Guardianship . . . . 258; *see also* Kyrios

Halicarnassus 90
Hammurabi 37
Harpocration 99
Heiress . . . . . . 54, 248–249, 254, 256–257, 314, 321–322; *see also* Epiklerate
Helen 238
Heraclitus 417–419
Hermopolis Legal Code 345
Hesiod . . . 84–85, 395, 396, 398–400, 416
Hetairai 250–251
Hippias 51
Historiography 236–237
Hobbes 397
Homer 82–84, 238–239
Homicide 53–54, 56, 74, 104–105, 228–229, 239, 325
Horos 262
Human nature 178–182
Hybris 206, 216, 217, 218, 219, 220, 410
Hyperides 101, 103

Impiety 63–68
Incest . . . . *see* Marriage, brother-sister
Inheritance 104, 247–249, 256–258, 320–322, 353–354
Isaeus 104
Isocrates 102, 183–186

Judge 72–73, 311, 312
Judicial decision 86–90, 98, 312
Jurisprudence 194, 394, 410
Jurors . . . . *see* Dikastai
Jury nullification 120
Jury selection 147
Justice 394–395, 396, 397–404, 414, 416–420

Keos 53–54, 63
King (*basileus*) . . . 83, 84–85, 94, 332–340, 342
Klepsydra . . . . *see* Water clock
Kosmos 53–54, 310–311
Kyme 74
Kyrios 245–249, 330, 352

Law and literature 374–375
Law, American 33
    Athenian . . . . 97–302 *passim*
    Egyptian 332–334, 345–348, 354
    English 37, 107, 213
    Germanic, Nazi 212
    Germanic, early 89
    Greek, early (archaic) 43, 82–94
    Greek, in Egypt 38–39, 40, 69, 328–342, 344–348
    Greek, unity of 29–40, 329, 338, 344–345
    Hellenistic . . . . . . 343–354; *see also* Law, Greek, in Egypt
    international 403–404
    Jewish 345, 346, 347
    Medieval 36, 41–60, 90
    natural . . . . *see* Natural law
    Near-Eastern . . . 36–37, 89, 90; *see also* Hammurabi
    Roman 29, 36, 93, 352
    and nature . . . . . . *see Nomos* and *Physis*
Lawgiver 82, 91, 201–202, 204–208, 217–218, 309
Laws of Greece . . . . *see Nomoi koinoi*
Laws of nature 413, 421–422
Lease 332–340, 342
Lebadeia 78
Legal positivism 395, 406

477

Legal profession 38, 100, 102
Legal training 195–196
Legitimacy, of children 255, 278, 280–281
Literature, and law see Law and literature
Loan 338–340
Logography, logographer . . . 99–102, 193
Lucretius 427–428
Lycurgus (Attic orator) 101, 113, 371
Lycurgus (Spartan lawgiver) 44, 49
Lysias 103, 104

Mantinea 75
Manumission 77–79
Marriage . . . . 30, 31–32, 34, 246–247, 254–256, 316, 317–318, 321–322, 333, 348–350; see also *Epigamia*
Marriage contract 349–350
Marriage, brother-sister 351–352
Meidias 206–208, 217
Melian dialogue 404, 419
Menelaus 87–88, 89
Metics 99–100
Mines 259
Minos 49
Misthōsis 330, 331
Mnemon (*mnamon*) 48, 310
Moicheia . . . . 241; see also Adultery
Monarchy 344, 348
Monument, monumental law 55–56
Morals, and law 372, 395–396
Mytilenean debate 178–182, 404

Narrative 110–111
Natural law . 395, 413, 422–424, 428–430
Nature . . . . see *Physis*
Neaira 287–289
Nomoi koinoi 52, 388–389
Nomos (pl. *nomoi*) . 51, 218–219, 229, 389, 414–416; see also Statutes
and *Physis* 395, 397, 412–430
Nothos 278, 280–282

Oath . . . . . . 69–70, 71–72, 73–75, 86–90, 113, 149, 312–313; see also *Exōmosia*
Oath, jurors' 35, 197, 231
Oath-helpers 164, 165
Olive trees, sacred 64

Oral law . . . . see Unwritten law
Orators, Attic 99, 101–103
Oratory 97–111
Ordeal 69, 90
Orestes 377–378, 379
Ostracism 276
Ownership 259–266, 319

Papyri 329
Parmenides 417
Peisistratus 273–274
Penalties . . . . 75–77, 119–121; see also Punishment
Pericles 363
Pericles' "citizenship law" 268, 270, 278–283
Perjury . . . . see Oath
Pharmakon 383–385
Philolaus (of Corinth) 44
Phryne 67
Phrynichus (tragedian) 376
Physis . . . . . 415; see also *Nomos* and *Physis*
Piraeus 291–292, 301
Pisteis . . . . see Proofs
Pity, appeal to 118–121, 125–126, 127
Plataea, and Athenian citizenship 283
Plato 186–190, 198–199, 232, 405–407, 422–424
 Apology 405
 Crito 405–406
 Gorgias 419–420
 Laws 406–407
 Republic 406
Polis 58, 344–345, 348, 424
Politēs 269
Political theory, and law 394–411
Politics, and law 196
Pollution 68, 388
Pornai 250–252
Pretrial proceedings . . . 108, 152, 156–159, 163, 370
Private laws 387, 388
Private life, regulation of 371–373
Private litigation . . see Public and private litigation

General Index

Probability argument.......... see Eikos
Procedural law .... 34–38, 40, 53, 82–90, 129–145, 311–313; see also Sacred Law (*Heiliges Recht*)
Prodicus............................66
Proofs...... 146, 147–150, 163, 199–200
Property..... 259–266, 319–322, 337–338
    movable 263–264, 265–266
    protection of............... 262–266
    real....................... 259–266
    visible and invisible.............. 290
Prostitution .... see Hetairai, Pornai
Protagoras........ 66, 173–178, 395, 396
Public and private litigation.... 129–145, 212, 214–235
Punishment......... 170–190, 211–235, 244–245, 385–387
    as cure..................... 187–190
    as deterrence.. 176, 177, 178, 180–181, 183, 184
    as rehabilitation............. 176–178
    as retribution...... 172–173, 174, 175, 178, 179, 180

Rape....... 240–241, 242–245, 314, 325
Relevance, in legal argument ... 112–128
Religion, and law 61–80
Retroactivity.......................37
Revenge ... 171–172, 173, 174, 175, 179, 183, 219, 220, 226–229
Revision of laws 58–59
Rhetoric ... 129–145, 191–208, 221, 222
Rhētra........................ 50, 93
Rhetra, Great................... 51, 53
Rule of law............... 112, 211–235

Sacred Law (*Heiliges Recht*) 68–79
Sacred laws 57, 61–63, 326
Sale.... 260–261, 293–295, 323, 330, 331
Sanctuary..........................326
Seclusion, of women 249–250
Security, for debt 261–262, 323–325, 331–332
Self-help.................. 226–229, 370
Seneca...................... 426–427
Serf........................ 316–317
Sexual crimes................. 240–245
Sexuality, and law 236–253

Shield of Achilles......... 83–84, 87, 98
Slander 362, 366–367
Slaves 170, 258–259, 315–317, 326
    see also Torture of slaves
    testimony of.....................65
Socrates...... 66–67, 199–200, 405–406
Solon 41, 43, 44, 46, 51, 90, 260, 270–273, 368, 397, 400–403, 417
Sophocles, *Antigone*............ 390–392
    Oedipus Tyrannus............ 389, 390
    Trachiniae.................... 384–385
Speech writer .... see Logography
Speeches, revision of 108–109
    survival of 102–106
Spensithios decree.............. 48, 311
Statutes.................... 200, 201–205
Stoics............ 424–427, 428–430
Substantive law 34, 39, 91
Summary procedures.......... 226, 230
Summons 160–161, 168–169, 370
Synēgoros 101, 152
Syngraphē..........................330
Syracosius................... 366–367
Syssitia 327

Tean curses.............. 47, 54, 76–77
Temple robbery.................. 64–65
Thaletas......................... 309
Theft 222, 325
    of sacred money 64
Theophrastus 66
Thersites 39
Thesmos............ 46, 51, 93, 389–390
Thucydides..... 178–182, 397, 403–404, 419
Tiv.............................. 87
Torah 345, 347
Torture of slaves................... 149
Tragedy, and law 111, 374–393
Trial, Athenian 74–75, 109–110, 159, 163–164, 193–200
    by combat...................... 90
Tribe....................... 276, 277
Trittyes......................... 276
Tyrant's law 388–389

Unwritten law 52–53, 57, 390

Volunteer prosecuter (*ho boulomenos*) 130–131, 402

Water clock 109, 133, 147

Wills 126, 257

Witnesses 70–71, 72, 73, 107, 110, 146–169, 312–313

Woikeus 315–317, 326

Women, and law ..... 238–253, 320–321, 352–353, 371; *see also* Heiress

Writing, written law. 37–38, 41–60, 91–93, 98, 126, 147, 154, 163, 195, 297, 298, 300–301, 306, 317, 330, 349, 390

Xenophanes 69
Xenophon......................... 407

Zaleucus...................... 44, 244
Zeno, the Stoic 424, 425
Zeus, and justice 399–400

Lightning Source UK Ltd.
Milton Keynes UK
UKOW02f1047070916

282405UK00001B/209/P